ARCANA CŒLESTIA.

NOTE.

In this Volume, the numbers referring to passages have been revised and corrected; but where the correct number could not be discovered the erroneous one is retained, and distinguished by an asterisk.

ARCANA CŒLESTIA.

THE

HEAVENLY ARCANA

CONTAINED IN

THE HOLY SCRIPTURES OR WORD OF THE LORD

UNFOLDED,

BEGINNING WITH THE BOOK OF GENESIS:

TOGETHER WITH

WONDERFUL THINGS SEEN IN THE WORLD OF SPIRITS
AND IN THE HEAVEN OF ANGELS.

Translated from the Latin of
EMANUEL SWEDENBORG,
Servant of the Lord Jesus Christ.

VOL. X.

NEW YORK:
AMERICAN SWEDENBORG PRINTING AND PUBLISHING SOCIETY.

1870.

Published by The American Swedenborg Printing and Publishing Society, *organized for the purpose of Stereotyping, Printing, and Publishing Uniform Editions of the Theological Writings of* Emanuel Swedenborg, *and incorporated in the State of New York*, A. D. 1850.

EXODUS.

CHAPTER THE TWENTY-NINTH.

THE DOCTRINE OF CHARITY AND OF FAITH.

9974. THOSE who believe, that by the goods which they do they merit heaven, do good from themselves, and not from the Lord.

9975. The goods which men do from themselves, are all of them not good, because they are done for the sake of self, since for the sake of reward, thus in them they primarily respect themselves; but the goods which men do from the Lord are all of them good, since they are done for the sake of the Lord and for the sake of the neighbor; thus in them the doers primarily respect the Lord and the neighbor.

9976. Wherefore those who place merit in works, love themselves, and those who love themselves despise the neighbor, yea they are angry with God Himself, if they do not receive the hoped-for recompense, for what they do is for the sake of the recompense.

9977. Hence it is evident, that their works are not from celestial love, thus neither from a true faith, for the faith which regards good as derived from self, and not from God, is not true faith. Such persons cannot receive heaven in themselves, for heaven with man is from celestial love and from true faith.

9978. Those who place merit in works, cannot fight against the evils which are from the hells, for no one can do this from himself; but in the case of those who do not place merit in works, the Lord fights for them and conquers.

9979. The Lord alone has merit, because He alone from Himself conquered the hells, and subdued them; hence the Lord alone is merit and justice.

9980. Moreover man of himself is nothing but evil, therefore to do good from himself is to do it from evil.

9981. That good ought not to be done for the sake of recompense, the Lord Himself teaches in Luke," *If ye love those who love you, what favor have ye? if ye do good to those who do good to you, what favor have ye? for sinners do the same: rather love your enemies, and do good, and lend hoping for nothing, then shall your recompense be great, and ye shall be the sons of the Highest*," vi. 32—35. That neither can man do good from himself which is real good, but from the Lord, the Lord also teaches in John, "*A man cannot take any thing unless it be given him from heaven*," iii. 27: and in another place, "*Jesus said, I am the vine, ye are the branches; he who abideth in Me, and I in him, the same beareth much fruit; for without Me ye can do nothing*," xv. 5.

9982. To believe that they are rewarded if they do good, is not hurtful with those who are in innocence—as with infants and with the simple; but to confirm themselves therein when they become adults, is hurtful; for man is initiated into good by respecting reward, and he is deterred from evil by respecting punishment; but so far as he comes into the good of love and of faith, so far he is removed from respecting merit in the goods which he does.

9983. To do good, which is good, must be from the love of good, thus for the sake of good; those who are in that love abhor merit, for they love to do, and hence they perceive satisfaction; and *vice versa*, they are sorrowful, if it be believed that what they do is for the sake of any thing of themselves. The case herein is nearly as with those who do good to friends for the sake of friendship, to a brother for the sake of brotherhood, to a wife and children for the sake of the wife and children, to their country for the sake of their country,—thus from friendship and from love; those who think well, also say and insist, that they do no good for the sake of themselves, but for the sake of others.

9984. The delight itself, which is in the love of doing good without reward as an end, is the recompense which remains to eternity, for every affection of love is permanent, being inscribed on the life;—into that love is insinuated heaven and eternal happiness from the Lord.

CHAPTER XXIX.

1. AND this is the word which thou shalt do to them, to sanctify them, to perform the office of the priesthood to Me; take one bullock, a son of the herd, and two rams entire.

2. And bread of what is unleavened, and cakes of what is unleavened, mixed with oil, and wafers of what is unleavened anointed with oil; with fine flour of wheat thou shalt make them.

3. And thou shalt give them upon one basket, and thou shalt cause them to approach in the basket; and the bullock and the two rams.

4. And Aaron and his sons thou shalt cause to approach to the door of the tent of the congregation, and thou shalt wash them with waters.

5. And thou shalt take garments, and shalt clothe Aaron with the tunic, and with the robe of the ephod, and with the ephod, and with the breast-plate, and thou shalt gird him with the girdle of the ephod.

6. And thou shalt set the mitre on his head, and thou shalt give the coronet of holiness upon the mitre.

7. And thou shalt take the oil of anointing, and shalt pour it upon his head, and shalt anoint him.

8. And thou shalt cause his sons to approach, and shalt clothe them with tunics.

9. And thou shalt gird them with a belt, Aaron and his sons, and shalt tie turbans to them, and the priesthood shall be to them for the statute of an age; and thou shalt fill the hand of Aaron, and the hand of his sons.

10. And thou shalt cause the bullock to approach before the tent of the congregation, and Aaron and his sons shall put their hands upon the head of the bullock.

11. And thou shalt slay the bullock before JEHOVAH at the door of the tent of the congregation.

12. And thou shalt take of the blood of the bullock, and shalt give it upon the horns of the altar with thy finger; and all the blood thou shalt pour forth at the foundation of the altar.

13. And thou shalt take all the fat covering the intestines, and the caul upon the liver, and the two kidneys, and the fat which is upon them, and thou shalt make the altar to burn.

14. And the flesh of the bullock, and his skin, and his dung, thou shalt burn with fire out of the camp; this is sin.

15. And thou shalt take one ram, and Aaron and his sons shall put their hands upon the head of the ram.

16. And thou shalt slay the ram, and shalt take his blood, and shalt sprinkle [it] upon the altar round about.

17. And thou shalt cut the ram into his segments, and shalt wash his intestines, and his legs, and shalt give [them] upon his segments, and upon his head.

18. And thou shalt make the altar to burn with the whole ram, this is a burnt-offering to JEHOVAH, an odor of rest, this is an offering made by fire to JEHOVAH.

19. And thou shalt take the second ram, and Aaron and his sons shall put their hands upon the head of the ram.

20. And thou shalt slay the ram, and shalt take of his blood, and shalt give [it] upon the auricle* of the ear of Aaron, and

* The *auricle* of the ear is that part of the *external ear* which is on the outside of the head, thus all that is *commonly* understood by the term *ear*. Anatomists use the word *ear* to denote the whole of the organ of hearing, and divide the whole into the *external ear*, the *middle ear*, and the *internal ear*. The *external*

upon the auricle of the right ear of his sons, and upon the thumb of their right hand, and upon the great toe of their right foot; and thou shalt sprinkle the blood upon the altar round about.

21. And thou shalt take of the blood which is upon the altar, and of the oil of anointing, and shalt sprinkle [it] upon Aaron, and upon his garments, and upon his sons, and upon the garments of his sons with him, and he [shall be] holy, and his garments, and his sons, and the garments of his sons with him.

22. And thou shalt take the fat of the ram, and the tail, and the fat covering the intestines, and the caul of the liver, and the two kidneys, and the fat which is upon them, and the right flank, because it is the ram of fillings.

23. And one piece of bread, and one cake of bread of oil, and one wafer, out of the basket of the unleavened things which are before JEHOVAH.

24. And thou shalt put all the things upon the palms of the hands of Aaron, and upon the palms of the hands of his sons and shalt shake them a shaking before JEHOVAH.

25. And thou shalt receive them out of their hand, and shalt cause the altar to burn on the burnt-offering, for an odor of rest before JEHOVAH, this is an offering made by fire to JEHOVAH.

26. And thou shalt take the breast of the ram of fillings, which is for Aaron, and thou shalt shake it a shaking before JEHOVAH, and it shall be to thee for a portion.

27. And thou shalt sanctify the breast of shaking, and the flank of up-lifting, which is shaken, and which is up-lifted of the ram of fillings, of that which is for Aaron, and of that which is for his sons.

28. And it shall be for Aaron and for his sons for the statute of an age from with the sons of Israel, because this is the up-lifting, and the uplifting shall be from with the sons of Israel of their peace-making sacrifices, their up-lifting to JEHOVAH.

29. And the garments of holiness which are for Aaron shall be for his sons after him, to anointing in them, and to filling in them their hand.

30. Seven days shall the priest after him of his sons put them on, who shall enter into the tent of the congregation, to minister in the holy [place].

31. And thou shalt take the ram of fillings, and shalt boil his flesh in the holy place.

32. And Aaron and his sons shall eat the flesh of the ram, and the bread which is in the basket, at the door of the tent of the congregation.

ear consists of the *auricle* and the *meatus auditorius*, or the passage which leads from the auricle to the membrane of the tympanum or drum of the ear.

33. And they shall eat those things wherein is what is expiated, to fill their hand, to sanctify them; and a stranger shall not eat, because they are holy.

34. And if there should have been left of the flesh of fillings, and of the bread until the morning, then thou shalt burn what is left with fire, it shall not be eaten, because it is holy.

35. And thus thou shalt do to Aaron and to his sons, according to all which I have commanded thee: seven days thou shalt fill their hand.

36. And a bullock of sin thou shalt offer every day on the propitiations, and thou shalt cleanse from sin upon the altar in propitiating thyself upon it, and thou shalt anoint to sanctify it.

37. Seven days thou shalt propitiate upon the altar, and shalt sanctify it, and the altar shall be the holy of holies; every one touching the altar shall be sanctified.

38. And this is what thou shalt do: offer upon the altar two lambs the sons of a year every day, continually.

39. One lamb thou shalt offer in the morning, and the other lamb thou shalt offer between the evenings.

40. And a tenth of fine flour mixed with bruised oil, the fourth of a hin, and a libation of the fourth of a hin of wine with the first lamb.

41. And the second lamb thou shalt offer between the evenings, according to the morning meat-offering, and according to the libation thereof, thou shalt offer it, for an odor of rest, an offering made by fire unto JEHOVAH.

42. And a burnt-offering continually throughout your generations at the door of the tent of the congregation before JEHOVAH, where I will meet you to speak there unto thee.

43. And there I will meet the sons of Israel, and he shall be sanctified with My glory.

44. And I will sanctify the tent of the congregation, and the altar, and Aaron, and his sons I will sanctify to perform the office of the priesthood to Me.

45. And I will dwell in the midst of the sons of Israel, and I will be to them for a GOD.

46. And they shall know that I am JEHOVAH their GOD, who brought them forth out of the land of Egypt, to dwell Myself in the midst of them; I am JEHOVAH their GOD.

THE CONTENTS.

9985. THE subject treated of, in the internal sense, in this chapter, is the glorification of the Lord as to the Human [principle], which is signified by the inauguration of Aaron and his sons into the priesthood.

THE INTERNAL SENSE.

9986. VERSES 1, 2, 3. *And this is the word which thou shalt do to them, to sanctify them, to perform the office of the priesthood to Me: take one bullock, a son of the herd, and two rams entire. And bread of what is unleavened, and cakes of what is unleavened mixed with oil, and wafers of what is unleavened anointed with oil, with fine flour of wheat thou shalt make them. And thou shalt give them upon one basket, and thou shalt cause them to approach in the basket; and the bullock and the two rams.* And this is the word which thou shalt do to them, signifies the law of order. To sanctify them, signifies a representation of the Lord as to the Divine Human [principle]. To perform the office of the priesthood to Me, signifies to represent all the work of salvation by Him. Take one bullock, a son of the herd, signifies the purification of the natural or external man. And two rams entire, signifies the purification of the spiritual or internal man. And bread of what is unleavened, signifies the purification of the celestial principle in the inmost of man; and cakes of what is unleavened mixed with oil, signifies the purification of the middle celestial principle. And wafers of what is unleavened anointed with oil, signifies the celestial principle in the external man. With fine flour of wheat thou shalt make them, signifies truth which is from Divine Good; and thou shalt give them upon one basket, signifies the sensual principle in which they are. And thou shalt cause them to approach in the basket, signifies thereby the presence of all things. And the bullock and the two rams, signifies the natural or external principle of man, and his spiritual or internal principle, which were to be purified.

9987. "And this is the word which thou shalt do to them"—that hereby is signified the law of order, appears from the signification of the Word, as denoting the Divine Truth, and hence the law of order, of which we shall speak presently. Word in the general sense signifies what is uttered by the mouth or discourse; and since discourse is the thought of the mind uttered by expressions, therefore word signifies the thing thought of, hence every thing which really exists, and is any thing, in the original tongue is called the word. But in an eminent sense the Word is the Divine Truth, by reason that every thing which really exists, and which is any thing, is from the Divine Truth, therefore it is said in David, "*By the Word of Jehovah the heavens were made, and by the breath of His mouth all the host of them,*" Psalm xxxiii. 6; where the Word of Jehovah is the Divine Truth proceeding from the Lord; the breath of the mouth of Jehovah is life thence derived; the heavens thence made, and all the host of them, are the angels so far as they are receptions of the Divine

Truth. The reason why the heavens denote angels is, because angels constitute heaven; and since angels are receptions of Divine Truth, therefore by angels in the abstract sense are signified the Divine Truths which are from the Lord, see n. 8192; and that the host of heaven in the same sense denotes Divine Truths, see n. 3448, 7236, 7988. Hence it may be manifest what is signified by the Word in John, "*In the beginning was the Word, and the Word was with God, and God was the Word. All things were made by Him, and without Him was nothing made, which was made. And the Word was made flesh, and dwelt in us, and we beheld His glory*," i. 1, 3, 14. That the Lord is here meant by the Word, is evident, for it is said that the Word was made flesh. The reason why the Lord is the Word is, because the Lord, when He was in the world, was the Divine Truth itself, and when He departed out of the world the Divine Truth proceeded from Him. See the passages cited, n. 9199, 9315. That the Word in the supreme sense is the Lord as to Divine Truth, or, what is the same thing, that the Word is the Divine Truth proceeding from the Lord, is manifest from numerous passages, as from David, "They cried to Jehovah, and *He sent His Word, and healed them*," Psalm cvii. 19, 20. And from John, "*Ye have not the Word of the Father abiding in you*, because whom He hath sent, Him ye do not believe: nor are willing to come to Me, that ye may have life," v. 38, 40. Again, "*I have given to them Thy Word*, therefore the world hateth them; *sanctify them in Thy Truth, Thy Word is Truth*," xvii. 14, 17. And in the Apocalypse, "He that sat on the white horse was clothed with a vesture tinged with blood, *and His name is called the Word of God;* and He had upon His vesture, and upon His thigh, a name written, King of kings and Lord of lords," xix. 13, 16. From these and from other passages it is manifest, that the Divine Truth proceeding from the Lord is the Word, and in the supreme sense the Lord as to Divine Truth, for it is said that the name of Him who sat on the white horse is the Word of God, and that He is King of kings and Lord of lords; and whereas the Word is Divine Truth, therefore it is said, that He was clothed with a vesture tinged with blood, for by vesture is signified truth, n. 9952, and by blood truth derived from good; see these things more fully explained, n. 2760, 2761, 2762. Hence it is that all truth, which is from the Divine, is called the Word, as in Joel, "Jehovah uttered His voice before His army, His camp is exceedingly great, because [His army] *is innumerable which doeth His Word*," ii. 11; where the voice which Jehovah utters is truth from the Divine, n. 9926. The camp of Jehovah is heaven, n. 4236, 8193, 8196; hence it is evident that [the army] being innumerable which does His Word, denotes which does Divine Truth; and in Matthew, "*If any one heareth the Word of the kingdom*, and does not attend, the evil one cometh, and snatcheth away what was sown in his heart: he that received the seed upon stony places, is he *who heareth the Word*, and immediately with joy receiveth it, but hath not root: he that receiveth seed among thorns, is he *who heareth the Word*, but the care of the age and the deceitfulness of riches *choketh the Word:* he that receiveth seed into good ground, is he *who heareth the Word and attendeth*, and thence bringeth forth fruit," xiii. 19 to 23. That the Word in this passage is Divine Truth, is evident without explication; it is called the Word of the kingdom, because it is the truth of heaven and the church, for the kingdom denotes heaven and the church. Hence it may be manifest, that words denote Divine Truths which are from the Lord, as in John, "*The words which I speak to you*, are spirit and are life," vi. 63; therefore also the precepts of the decalogue are called the "*ten words*," Exod. xxxiv. 28. The reason why the Word denotes the law of order is, because the Divine Truth proceeding from the Lord makes order in the heavens, insomuch that it is order there, hence the laws of heavenly order are Divine Truths, see n. 1728, 1919, 2247, 2258, 4839, 5703, 7995, 8513, 8700, 8988. The law of order, which is signified by the Word in this chapter, is how the Lord glorified His Human, that is, made it Divine, for this is the subject here treated of in the internal sense; and hence, in the respective sense, the regeneration of man is treated of, for the regeneration of man is an image of the glorification of the Lord, n. 3130, 3212, 3296, 4402, 5688, 9145, 9146. The reason why this principally is the law of order is, because the Lord, as to the Divine Human, is order in the heavens; and because every one who is regenerated is reduced to that order; wherefore those who are in that order, are in the Lord.

9988. "To sanctify them"—that hereby is signified to represent the Lord as to the Divine Human, appears from the signification of sanctifying, as denoting to represent the Lord as to the Divine Human, see n. 9958. The reason why this is meant by sanctifying is, because the Lord alone is holy [*sanctus*], and because every thing that is holy proceeds from Him, and all sanctification represents Him, n. 9479, 9680, 9820.

9989. "To perform the office of the priesthood to Me"—that hereby is signified all the work of salvation by Him, appears from the signification of the priesthood, as being representative of the Lord as to the work of salvation, see n. 9809.

9990. "Take one bullock, a son of the herd"—that hereby is signified the purification of the natural or external man, appears from the signification of a bullock, as denoting the good of innocence and of charity in the natural or external man, see n. 9391 and because it is said a son of the herd, it signifies also the truth of that good, for a son denotes truth, and a herd denotes the natural principle. That a son denotes truth, see n. 489, 491, 533, 2623, 3373, 9807; and that the herd denotes the natural principle, see n. 2566, 5913, 8937. The reason why by a bullock the son of the herd is here signified the purification of the natural or external man is, because he was sacrificed, and by sacrifices were signified purification from evils and falses, or expiation, in this case purification from the evils and falses which are in the natural or external man; but purification in the spiritual or internal man, is signified by the burnt-offering of the ram. That it may be known what the burnt-offerings and sacrifices specially represented, it is to be noted, that in man there is an external and an internal principle, and that in each there is what has relation to truth, and what has relation to good; wherefore when man is to be regenerated, he must be regenerated as to the external principle and as to the internal, and in each as to truth and as to good; but before man can be regenerated, he must be purified from evils and from falses, for these are opposed [to it]. The purifications of the external man were represented by burnt-offerings and sacrifices of oxen, of bullocks, and of he-goats; and the purifications of the internal man by burnt-offerings, and sacrifices of rams, of kids, and of she-goats; but the purification of the internal principle itself, which is inmost, by burnt-offerings and sacrifices of lambs; wherefore from the animals themselves, which were sacrificed, it may be manifest what purification or expiation was represented. It is said what purification or expiation was represented, because burnt-offerings and sacrifices did not purify or expiate man, but only represented purification or expiation; for who cannot know that such things do not take away any thing of evil and of the false appertaining to man, see passages from the Word, n. 2180. The reason why they did not take away, but only represented, was, because with the Israelitish and Judaic nation was instituted the representative of a church, by which conjunction was effected with the heavens, and by the heavens with the Lord, on which subject see what was shown in the passages cited, n. 9320, 9380, but what was specifically represented by the burnt-offerings and sacrifices of bullocks, and of rams, and of lambs, will be seen in what follows in this chapter, for it there treats concerning them.

9991. "And two rams entire"—that hereby is signified the purification of the spiritual or internal man, appears from the signification of a ram, as denoting the internal principle of man, thus his spiritual principle, see n. 2830; for the internal principle with man is called spiritual, and the external natural. The reason why purification is signified is, because burnt-offerings were made of rams, and by burnt-offerings and sacrifices in general were represented purifications from evils and falses, or expiations, and by burnt-offerings and sacrifices of rams the purifications or expiations of the internal or spiritual man, mentioned subsequently in this chapter, where they are treated of.

9992. "And bread of what is unleavened"—that hereby is signified the purification of the celestial principle in the inmost man, appears from the signification of bread, as denoting the celestial principle, see n. 2165, 2177, 3478, 9545; and from the signification of what is unleavened, as denoting what is purified, of which we shall speak presently. The reason why it denotes the inmost of man is, because the celestial principle is the good of love, and the good of love is inmost. There are three [things or principles] appertaining to man, which follow in successive order; those three are called celestial, spiritual, and natural. The celestial is the good of love to the Lord, the spiritual the good of charity towards the neighbor, and the natural thence derived the good of faith, which being grounded in what is spiritual, is called spiritual-natural. For the case with man is similar to what exists in the heavens; in the inmost heaven, which is also called the third heaven, is the celestial principle; in the second or middle heaven, is the spiritual principle; and in the first or ultimate heaven, is the natural principle thence derived, or the spiritual-natural. The cause of its being with man similarly to what it is in the heavens is, because man, who is in good, is a heaven in the least form,—see what is cited, n. 9279. Concerning the tri-partition also of heaven, or of the heavenly kingdom, we shall speak presently, when we come to treat of the cakes, and wafers of fine flour of wheat. The reason why what is unleavened signifies what is purified is, because leaven signifies what is false derived from evil, n. 2342, 7906; hence what is unleavened signifies what is pure, or without that false principle. The reason why leaven signifies what is false derived from evil is, because this false principle defiles good and also truth, likewise because it excites combat, for on the approach of that false principle to good, heat is produced, and as it approaches to truth it excites collision. Hence it is, that a meat-offering of unleavened bread was employed in the burnt-offerings and in the sacrifices. Therefore it was ordained that "*every meat-offering, which they should bring to Jehovah, should be prepared without leaven*," Levit. ii. 11. "*That they should not sacrifice upon what is leavened the blood of the sacrifices*," Exod. xxiii. 18. "And that on the feast of the passover, *they should not eat at all what was leavened, and that he who did eat should be cut off from Israel*," Exod. xii. 15, 18, 19, 20. The reason why he was to be cut off from Israel, who ate what was leavened on the feast of the passover, was, because the feast of the passover signified liberation from damnation, and specifically liberation from falses derived from evil, with those who suffer themselves to be regenerated by the Lord, see n. 7093, 9286 to

9292. Hence also, that festival was called the feast of unleavened things.

9993. "And cakes of what is unleavened mixed with oil"—that hereby is signified the purification of the middle celestial principle, appears from the signification of cakes, as denoting the middle celestial principle, of which we shall speak presently; and from the signification of oil, as denoting the good of love, see n. 886, 4582, 4638. Hence it is evident, that by cakes mixed with oil is signified the celestial principle which is from the inmost, for oil is the good of love, which is inmost. The case herein is this; the heavens are distinguished into two kingdoms, one of which is called spiritual, the other celestial; to the spiritual kingdom in the heavens, corresponds the intellectual principle appertaining to man, and to the celestial kingdom there corresponds his will principle, n. 9835. In each kingdom there is an internal and an external, as also is the case with man as to the intellectual principle, for the intellectual principle appertaining to man is internal and external, and the will principle is internal and external. The internal intellectual principle makes the spiritual life of the internal man, and the external intellectual principle makes the spiritual life of the external man; but the internal will principle makes the celestial life of the internal man, and the external will principle makes the celestial life of the external man. That there is an internal and an external appertaining to man, may be manifest to every one who reflects, especially from the case of hypocrites, of the deceitful, of the cunning, and of the malicious, in that they interiorly with themselves think against the truths of faith, and also will against the goods of celestial love, but exteriorly think and will with them, whence also they speak and act, that they may appear before the world. It is moreover to be noted, that each kingdom, namely, the spiritual and celestial, in the heavens is tripartite, having an inmost, a middle, and an external, see n. 9873. The inmost of the celestial kingdom is the good of love to the Lord, the middle there is the good of mutual love, which is the good thence proceeding, and the external is the delight proceeding from that good; the two former are in the internal man with those who are in the Lord's celestial kingdom, but the third is in the external man with the same. These three were represented by bread of what is unleavened, by cakes of what is unleavened mixed with oil, and by wafers of what is unleavened anointed with oil; and their purification is represented by the offering of those three upon the altar together with the burnt-offering or sacrifice. That such things in order are signified, may be evident solely from this consideration, that those three things were commanded, and also their preparation described in the books of Moses, which would not have occurred, unless they had involved arcana of heaven and of the church, for on any other idea, to what purpose could such things have been required? But I am aware, that those arcana can be apprehended scarcely by any one at this day, by reason that a worldly principle is now every thing in the understanding and the will, and those who think about heaven and will it, have, and are willing to have no other idea concerning it, than a natural and terrestrial idea, and where there is such an idea, and such a will, thus where there is such a love, there the arcana of heaven have no place. It would be altogether otherwise if the mind were delighted with heavenly rather than with worldly things, for those things with which man is delighted, are apprehended, as when he is delighted with the arcana of the civil state of kingdoms, and with the arcana of the moral state appertaining to man; by the moral state is meant the state of the loves and affections, and thence of the thoughts, the arcana of which a cunning man easily perceives; the reason is, because he delights to lead others by such things, in order to secure honors, or gains, or reputation on their account. That cakes signify the celestial principle in the internal man, is because they are in the second order, for in the first order is bread of what is unleavened, in the second are cakes mixed with oil, and in the third are wafers anointed with oil; those three were called meat-offerings, and were offered on the altar together with burnt-offerings and sacrifices. The mode in which they were to be prepared is described in Leviticus, chap. ii. and how they were to be offered is described in various passages, as how by Aaron on the day of his anointing, Levit. vi. 13 to 16. By cakes also in the Word the good of love in general is meant; hence it is, that the breads of faces or of proposition are called cakes in Moses. "Thou shalt take fine flour *and bake twelve cakes thereof*, *one cake* shall be of two-tenths; and thou shalt set them on the table before Jehovah, and shalt give upon the order pure frankincense," Levit. xxiv. 5 to 9, where the pure frankincense, which was given upon the cakes, signified truth from celestial good, which is the ultimate or extreme of the celestial kingdom. By cakes also the good of love in general is signified in Jeremiah. "The sons gather wood, and the fathers kindle a fire, the women knead dough, *to make cakes to the queen [Melecheth] of the heavens*, and to offer libations to other gods," vii. 18; chap. xliv. 19, where to make cakes to the Melecheth of the heavens denotes to worship the devil from the good of celestial love, and to offer libations to other gods, denotes to worship Satan from the truths of faith, for by the Melecheth of the heavens those are signified who are in the hell of genii, and by other gods, those who are in the hell of evil spirits, concerning whom see n. 5977, 8593, 8622, 8625. Those who are in the hell of genii, taken together, are called the devil, but those who are in the hell of evil spirits are called Satan. But the good of spiritual love is signified by cakes in Hosea, "*Ephraim is become a cake not turned*," vii. 8; but cake is here expressed by another name in the original tongue, which signifies the good of spiritual love. A cake not turned is, when the external man rules over the internal; when this is the case with man, order is inverted, for then the external rules, and the internal serves; Ephraim is the intellectual principle of the church, which is illustrated and affected, when the goods and truths of faith are received.

9994. "And wafers of what is unleavened anointed with oil"—that hereby is signified the celestial principle in the external man, appears from the signification of wafers, as denoting the celestial principle in the external man, of which we shall speak presently; and from the signification of what is unleavened, as denoting what is purified, see above, n. 9992; and from the signification of oil, as denoting the good of love, see n. 886, 4582, 4638; hence it is evident that by wafers of what is unleavened anointed with oil, the celestial principle in the external man is signified, which proceeds in order from the foregoing. The wafers are said to be anointed with oil, but the cakes mixed with oil, by reason that wafers are in the third order, and cakes in the second, as was said just above, n. 9993; and what is in the second order proceeds from the inmost immediately, and hence has in it the inmost celestial principle, which is signified by oil; and what is in the third order proceeds from the inmost mediately, namely, by that which is in the second order, and hence has the inmost principle not so in itself as that which is in the second order; on this account the cakes, because they signify the celestial principle of the second order, are said to be mixed with oil, and the wafers, because they signify the celestial principle of the third order, are said to be anointed with oil. But these things are of difficult apprehension, unless it be known how the case is with the existence of things in successive order, which is as end, cause and effect; the inmost is the end, the middle is the cause, and the ultimate is the effect; the end must be in the cause to make it a cause of that end, and the cause must be in the effect to make it an effect of that cause; the end does not appear in the effect as in the cause, because the effect is further removed from the end than the cause. From these considerations the mind may be illustrated [so as to see] how the case is with what is inmost, middle, and external in successive order.

9995. "With fine flour of wheat thou shalt make them"—that hereby is signified truth which is from Divine Good, from which those things are, appears from the signification of fine flour, as denoting truth, of which we shall speak presently; and from the signification of wheat, as denoting the good of love, see n. 3941, thus in the supreme sense the Divine Good; and from the signification of making them, as denoting that those celestial goods, which are signified by bread, cakes and wafers of what is unleavened, are from that truth. The case herein is this; all the truths and goods, which are in the heavens, are from the Divine Truth proceeding from the Divine Good of the Lord; this Divine Truth received by the angels in the celestial kingdom is called celestial good, but in the spiritual kingdom, received by the angels there, it is called spiritual good; for although the Divine Truth proceeding from the Divine Good of the Lord is called truth, it is still good. The reason why it is called truth is, because it appears in the heavens, before the external sight of the angels there, as light, for light in the heavens is the Divine Truth; but the heat in that light, which is the good of love, makes it to be good. It is similarly with man, the truth of faith, when it proceeds from the good of charity, as occurs when man is regenerated, then appears as good, which is also thence called spiritual good, for the esse of truth is good, and truth is the form of good. Hence it may be manifest, why man can with difficulty distinguish between thinking and willing, for he says, when he wills anything, that he thinks it, and frequently when he thinks anything, that he wills it, when yet they are distinct as truth and good, for the esse of thought is will, and the form of will is thought, as the esse of truth is good, and the form of good is truth, as was just now stated. Since man with so much difficulty distinguishes between those two principles, therefore neither does he know what is the esse of his life, and that this esse is good, and not truth, only so far as it exists from good: good appertains to the will, and the will is that which a man loves, wherefore truth does not become the esse of man's life until he loves it, and when he loves it he does it; but truth appertains to the understanding, the province of which is to think, and when man thinks it, he can discourse concerning it; moreover it is given to understand and think truth without willing and doing it, but when it is not willed, it is not appropriated to the life of man, because it has not in it the esse of his life: it is in consequence of man's ignorance of this, that he attributes to faith the all of salvation, and scarcely anything to charity, when yet faith derives its esse of life from charity, as truth from good. Moreover a'l good appertaining to man is formed by truth, for good flows in by an internal way from the Lord, and truth enters by an external way; and they unite in marriage in the internal man, but in one manner with the spiritual man and angel, and in another with the celestial man and angel. With the spiritual man and angel the marriage is effected in the intellectual part, but in the celestial man and angel in the will part. The external way, by which truth enters is by the hearing and sight into the understanding; but the internal way, by which good flows in from the Lord, is through his inmost principle into the will, on which subject see what was shown in the passages cited, n. 9596. From these considerations it is evident that the celestial goods, which are signified by bread, by cakes, and by wafers of what is unleavened, exist by the Divine Truth proceeding from the Divine Good of the Lord, and that this is meant by what is said, "With fine flour of wheat thou shalt make them." Since this is the case, all the meat-offerings, which were prepared by various methods, were made of fine flour mingled with oil, see Levit. ii. 1 to the end; chap. vi. 13 to 16; Numb. vii. 19 and the following verses; chap. xv. 2 to 15; chap. xxviii. 11 to 15. That fine flour, and also meal, denotes truth which is from good, is manifest from the following passages, "*Thou didst eat fine flour, honey and oil*, whence thou becamest exceedingly beautiful," Ezek. xvi. 13; these things are said of Jerusalem, by which is there meant the Ancient Church; fine flour denotes the truth derived from the good of that church, honey its delight, oil the good of love, and to eat is to appropriate; wherefore it is said thou becamest beautiful, for spiritual beauty is from truths and goods. And in Hosea, "It hath no standing corn, *the germ shall not yield meal*, if so be it yield, strangers shall devour it," viii. 7; where standing corn denotes the truth of faith derived from good in conception, n. 9146; the germ shall not yield meal denotes barrenness, because truth is not derived from good; the strangers who shall devour denote falses derived from evil which will consume. And in the 1st book of Kings, "A woman of Zidon in Zarephtha said to Elias, that she had nothing of which to make a cake, *but a handful of meal in a cask*, and a little oil in a cruse: Elias said, that she should make for him a cake in the first place, and *the cask of meal would not be consumed*, and the cruse of oil would not fail: which also came to pass," xvii. 12 to 15. By meal is here signified the truth of the church, and by oil its good, for by the woman of Zidon is represented the church which is in the knowledges of truth and good, and by Elias the prophet, the Lord as to the Word; hence it is evident what this miracle involves, for all the miracles recorded in the Word involve such things as relate to the church, n. 7337, 8364, 9086; hence it is manifest what is signified by the cask of meal not being consumed, and the cruse of oil not failing, if the woman made a cake of what few things she had for Elias in the former place, and for her son in the latter. That woman denotes the church, see n. 252, 253; that Zidon denotes the knowledges of truth and good, n. 1201; and that Elias denotes the Lord as to the Word, n. 2762, 5247. And in Isaiah, "O daughter of Babel, *take a millstone, and grind meal*," xlvii. 2; where the daughter of Babel denotes those in the church who are in a holy external, but in a profane internal; to grind meal denotes to select such things from the sense of the letter of the Word, as serve to confirm the evil of self-love and the love of the world, which evil is profane; to grind denotes to select, and also to explain in favor of those loves; and meal denotes truth that is serviceable, see n. 4335; hence it is evident what is meant by grinding, and consequently by what is ground, as in Jeremiah, "Princes are hanged up by their hand, the faces of the old were not honored, *they brought the young men to grind*," Lam. v. 12, 13. And in Moses, "Moses took the calf which they had made, and burned it with fire, and *ground it* until it became most minute, then he sprinkled the surface of the waters, and made the sons of Israel to drink," Exod. xxxii. 20; Deut. ix. 21. And in Matthew, "Then two shall be in the field, one shall be taken, the other shall be left; [*two women*] *shall be grinding*, one shall be taken, the other shall be left," xxiv. 40, 41. Hence it is evident what is denoted by grinding, that in a good sense it denotes to select truths from the Word and explain them to the service of what is good, and in a bad sense to the service of what is evil, see n. 7780; whence also it is manifest what is signified by what is ground, consequently what by meal and fine flour.

9996. "And thou shalt give them upon one basket"—that hereby is signified the sensual principle in which those things are, appears from the signification of basket, as denoting the sensual principle. The reason why basket denotes the sensual principle is, because the sensual principle is the ultimate of the life of man, and in the ultimate are stored up all interior things in order, see n. 9828, 9836; and by vessels of every kind in the Word are signified external things, wherein are things interior, n. 3079. Hence now it is that it is said, that the bread, the cakes, and the wafers of what is unleavened should be given into a basket, and should be brought in a basket; that the sensual principle appertaining to man is the ultimate of his life, see n. 9212, 9216. But the case herein is this; there are two principles appertaining to man which constitute his life, the intellectual principle and the will principle; the ultimate of the intellectual principle is called the sensual scientific, and the ultimate of the will principle is called sensual delight; the sensual scientific, which is the ultimate of the intellectual principle, is imbibed through two senses, which are hearing and seeing, and the sensual delight, which is the ultimate of the will principle, is imbibed also through two senses, which are tasting and touching; the ultimate of the perception of each is smelling. The sensual scientific, which is the ultimate of the intellectual principle, is meant in the Word by a cup, for the wine which is therein, or the water, denotes the truths which are of the intellectual part; but the sensual delight, which is the ultimate of the will principle, is meant in the Word by a basket; and whereas the ultimate is the continent of all interior things, therefore also interior things are meant by those vessels,—by a cup intellectual truths, and in the opposite sense falses, and by a basket goods of the will, and in the opposite sense evils; for goods appertain to the will, and truths to the understanding; that cups denote intellectual truths in the complex, see n. 5120, 9557; and that baskets denote goods of the will in the complex, n. 5144. Whether we speak of goods of the will, or of celestial goods, it is the same thing, in like manner whether we speak of intellectual truths or of spiritual truths; that those things which were placed in the basket signify celestial goods, see just above, n. 9992, 9993, 9994, and whereas the sensual principle is their ultimate, and thereby the continent of all, therefore it is said that all those should be given upon a basket.

9997. "And thou shalt cause them to approach in the basket"—that hereby is signified thus the presence of all things appears from the signification of causing to approach, as denoting conjunction and presence, see n. 9378; and from the signification of a basket, as denoting the sensual principle, containing all things, see just above, n. 9996.

9998. "And the bullock, and the two rams"—that hereby is signified the natural or external principle of man, and his spiritual and internal principle, which were to be purified, appears from the signification of the bullock, as denoting the natural or external principle of man, which is to be purified, see above, n. 9990; and from the signification of the rams, as denoting the spiritual or internal principle of man which is to be purified, see also above, n. 9991.

9999. Verses 4 to 9. *And Aaron and his sons thou shalt cause to approach to the door of the tent of the congregation, and thou shalt wash them with waters. And thou shalt take garments, and shalt clothe Aaron with the tunic, and with the robe of the ephod, and with the ephod, and with the breast-plate; and thou shalt gird him with the girdle of the ephod. And thou shalt set the mitre upon his head, and thou shalt give the coronet of holiness upon the mitre. And thou shalt take the oil of anointing, and shalt pour it upon his head, and shalt anoint him. And thou shalt cause his sons to approach, and shalt clothe them with tunics. And thou shalt gird them with a belt, Aaron and his sons, and shalt tie turbans to them, and the priesthood shall be to them for the statute of an age; and thou shalt fill the hand of Aaron and the hand of his sons.* And Aaron and his sons, signifies the Lord as to the Divine Good, and as to the Divine Truth thence derived. Thou shalt cause to approach to the door of the tent of the congregation, signifies the conjunction of each in heaven. And thou shalt wash them with waters, signifies purification by the truths of faith. And thou shalt take garments, and clothe Aaron, signifies a representative of the Lord's spiritual kingdom. With the tunic,* signifies the inmost of that kingdom. And with the robe of the ephod, signifies the middle of that kingdom. And with the ephod, signifies its ultimate. And with the breast-plate, signifies Divine Truth shining forth from the Divine Good of the Lord. And thou shalt set the mitre upon his head, signifies the Divine Wisdom. And thou shalt give the coronet of holiness upon the mitre, signifies the Divine Human of the Lord. And thou shalt take the oil of anointing, signifies a representative of inauguration into the Divine Good. And shalt pour it upon his head and anoint him, signifies a representative of the Divine Good in the Lord as to the whole Human [principle]. And thou shalt cause his sons to approach, signifies the conjunction of the Divine Truth proceeding from the Divine Good of the Lord. And thou shalt clothe them with tunics, signifies a representative of the Divine Spiritual [principle] proceeding. And thou shalt gird them with a belt, signifies a bond of conjunction that all things may be kept in connexion, and hence in a heavenly form. Aaron and his sons, signifies the Lord as to Divine Good and the Divine Truth thence proceeding. And shalt tie turbans to them, signifies intelligence from wisdom. And the priesthood shall be to them, signifies the Lord as to the work of salvation in successive order. For the statute of an age, signifies according to the eternal laws of order. And thou shalt fill the hand of Aaron, and the hand of his sons, signifies a representative of the Divine Power of the Lord by Divine Truth derived from Divine Good.

10,000. "And Aaron and his sons"—that hereby is signified the Lord as to Divine Good, and as to the Divine Truth thence derived, appears from the representation of Aaron, as denoting the Lord as to Divine Good, see n. 9806; and from the representation of his sons, as denoting the Lord as to the Divine Truth thence derived, see n. 9807.

10,001. "Thou shalt cause to approach to the door of the tent of the congregation"—that hereby is signified the conjunction of each in heaven, appears from the signification of causing to approach, as denoting presence and conjunction, as above, n. 9997, here the conjunction of Divine Good and Divine Truth in heaven; and from the signification of the door, as denoting introduction, see n. 8989; and from the representation of the tent of the congregation, as denoting heaven, see n. 9457, 9481, 9485, 9963. The reason why the bullock, the rams, the bread, the cakes, and the wafers of what was unleavened in the basket, and Aaron with his sons, were to be presented at the door of the tent of the congregation, and that these latter

*The tunic was a garment immediately investing the body.

should be there clothed with garments, and anointed, and the former should be there offered upon the altar, was, because the place where the door of the tent of the congregation was, represented the marriage of Divine Good with Divine Truth; for by the altar, which also was set at the door of the tent, was represented the Lord as to Divine Good, and by the tent of the congregation was represented the Lord as to Divine Truth; hence by the place at the door of the tent was represented the conjunction of good and of truth, which conjunction is called the heavenly marriage. That by the altar of burnt-offering was represented the Lord as to Divine Good, see n. 9964; and that by the tent of the congregation was represented the Lord as to Divine Truth, n. 9963. That the altar was there placed is manifest from Moses, "And *Moses set the altar of burnt-offering at the door of the tent*," Exod. xl. 29. That the conjunction of good and of truth is the heavenly marriage, and that it is heaven, see n. 2173, 2508, 2618, 2803, 3204, 3132, 3952, 4434, 6179. From these considerations it is now evident, that by causing Aaron and his sons to approach to the door of the tent of the congregation, is signified the conjunction of each, namely of Divine Good and Divine Truth from the Lord in heaven.

10,002. "And thou shalt wash them with waters"—that hereby is signified purification by the truths of faith, appears from the signification of washing with waters, as denoting purification by the truths of faith, see n. 3147, 5954, 9089. That all purification and regeneration is effected by the truths of faith, see n. 2769, 7044, 8625 to 8640, 8772; and that waters denote the truths of faith, n. 739, 2702, 3058, 3424, 4976, 7037, 8568.

10,003. "And thou shalt take garments, and shalt clothe Aaron"—that hereby is signified a representative of the Lord's spiritual kingdom, appears from the signification of the garments of Aaron, as being a representative of the Lord's spiritual kingdom, see n. 9814.

10,004. "With the tunic"—that hereby is signified the inmost of that kingdom, appears from the signification of the tunic with which Aaron was clothed, as denoting the Divine Spiritual immediately proceeding from the Divine Celestial, thus the inmost of the spiritual kingdom, see n. 9826, 9942.

10,005. "And with the robe of the ephod"—that hereby is signified the middle of that kingdom, appears from the signification of the robe, as denoting the Divine Spiritual mediately proceeding from the Divine Celestial, thus the middle of the spiritual kingdom, see n. 9825. The reason why it is called the robe of the ephod is, because the robe belonged to the ephod; it was also divided from the tunic by the girdle; for there were two girdles, one common to the ephod and the robe together.

the other for the tunic only, which signified that those things of the spiritual kingdom, which were represented by the tunic, were distinct from those which were represented by the robe and the ephod together; the girdle or belt signifies a common bond, by which interior things are held in connexion, n. 9828, and also by which one is separated from the other, n. 9943. The case herein is this; there are three things which follow or succeed in order; those three in the heavens are denominated the celestial, the spiritual, and the natural thence derived. The celestial [principle] is the good of love to the Lord, the spiritual is the good of charity towards the neighbor, and the natural thence derived is the good of faith. The celestial, which is the good of love to the Lord, constitutes the inmost or third heaven; the spiritual, which is the good of charity towards the neighbor, constitutes the middle or second heaven; and the natural thence derived, which is the good of faith, constitutes the ultimate or first heaven. Inasmuch as the garments of Aaron represented the spiritual kingdom of the Lord, n. 9814, it is evident from what has been said what the tunic represented, and what the robe, and what the ephod, namely, that the tunic represented the uniting medium of the spiritual kingdom with the celestial kingdom, wherefore also it was divided by the girdle from the robe and the ephod, which represented the internal and external spiritual kingdom. Concerning the tunic, see n. 9826, 9942; of the robe, n. 9825; and of the ephod, n. 9822. An idea of this subject may also be obtained from what has been before stated concerning the tent of the congregation, by which was represented heaven wherein the Lord is; by its inmost, where the ark of the testimony was, was represented the inmost or third heaven; by the habitation, which was without the vail, was represented the middle or second heaven; and by the court, the first or ultimate heaven; thus also the celestial, the spiritual, and the natural thence derived. But the uniting medium of the inmost and middle heaven was represented by the vail between the holy and the holy of holies, the like as by the tunic upon Aaron. Concerning the inmost of the tent where the ark was, see n. 9485; of the habitation which was without the vail, n. 2594, 9632; of the court, n. 9741; and of the vail, as being the uniting medium of the inmost and middle heaven, n. 9670, 9671. A still better idea may be conceived of this subject from the correspondence of man with the heavens, in that there is a correspondence of all things appertaining to man with all things in the heavens; see what has been above shown at the close of several chapters. The head with man corresponds to the inmost or third heaven, where celestial good is; the breast even to the loins corresponds to the middle or second heaven, where spiritual good is; and the feet correspond to the ultimate or first heaven, where natural good is; but the neck from correspondence denotes the uniting medium of the inmost heaven and the middle, n. 9913, 9914; in like manner as the vail in the tent; for all representatives in nature have reference to the human form, and have a signification according to their relation to it, see n. 9496. From these considerations it may now be manifest, why the tunic was divided by the girdle from the robe and the ephod, and also why the robe is called the robe of the ephod.

10,006. "And with the ephod"—that hereby is signified the ultimate thereof, namely, of the spiritual kingdom, appears from the signification of the ephod, as denoting the ultimate of the spiritual kingdom, see n. 9824.

10,007. "And with the breast-plate"—that hereby is signified Divine Truth shining forth from the Divine Good of the Lord, appears from what was shown concerning the breast-plate, n. 9823, 9863 to 9873, 9905.

10,008. "And thou shalt set the mitre upon his head"—that hereby is signified the Divine Wisdom, appears from the signification of a mitre, as denoting intelligence, and when concerning the Lord, who is represented by Aaron, as denoting the Divine Wisdom, see n. 9827.

10,009. "And thou shalt give the coronet of holiness upon the mitre"—that hereby is signified the Divine Human of the Lord, appears from what was said above, n. 9930, 9931, concerning the plate of gold, in which was engraven Holiness to Jehovah, which is here called the coronet of holiness.

10,010. "And thou shalt take the oil of anointing"—that hereby is signified a representative of Divine Good in the Lord, appears from the signification of oil, as denoting good, and in the supreme sense the Divine Good of the Divine Love in the Lord; and from the signification of anointing, as denoting inauguration to represent that good, see n. 9474, 9954.

10,011. "And shalt pour it upon his head, and shalt anoint him"—that hereby is signified a representative of the Divine Good in the Lord as to the whole Human [principle], appears from the signification of pouring oil upon Aaron's head, as denoting the Divine Good upon the whole Human of the Lord, for by oil is signified Divine Good, n. 4582, 9474, by Aaron the Lord as to the Divine Good, n. 9806, and by the head the whole Human [principle]; and from the signification of anointing, as being a representative of this, see n. 9474, 9954. The reason why the head denotes the whole Human [principle], or the whole man is, because from the head descends the all of the man, for the body is a derivation thence, wherefore also what man thinks and wills, which is done in the head, this is presented in effect in the body. The head is as the supreme or inmost principle in the heavens, which descends and flows-in into the heavens which are beneath, and produces and is derived into them, wherefore also the head with man corresponds to the inmost heaven, the body even to the loins to the middle heaven, and the feet to the ultimate heaven. In fine, what is inmost, this in the derivatives is the only principle which essentially lives. Hence it is evident that the Divine, since it is the inmost of all, or what is the same thing, the highest of all, is the only principle from which is the life of all, wherefore so far as man receives from the Divine, so far he lives. Moreover the oil, with which the priest was anointed, flowed down from the crown of the head even to the body, as is manifest from David, "*As the good oil upon the head descending to the beard of Aaron, which descends upon the border of his garment*," Psalm cxxxiii. 2. And in Matthew, "*A woman poured an alabaster box of balsam upon the head of Jesus*, as he lay down; Jesus said, she hath poured the balsam *upon my body* for the sepulchre," xxvi. 7, 12. And in Mark, "There came a *woman having an alabaster box of ointment of spikenard* very precious, *and breaking the alabaster box, she poured it upon the head of Jesus;* and Jesus said, she is come beforehand *to anoint my body* for the burial," xiv. 3, 8. Hence also it is evident, that anointing the head is anointing the whole body. That by the head is meant the whole man, is also manifest from several passages in the Word, as in Isaiah, "The redeemed of Jehovah shall return, and shall come to Zion with singing, and *the joy of eternity shall be on their head*," xxxv. 10. And in Moses, "The precious things of the products of the sun, the first fruits of the mountains of the east, and *the precious things of the earth for the head of Joseph*, and for the crown of the head of the Nazarite of his brethren," Deut. xxxiii. 14, 15, 16. And in Jeremiah, "The storm of Jehovah *shall dash upon the head of the wicked*," xxx. 23. And in Ezekiel, "Their way I will give *upon their head*," xi. 21; chap. xvi. 43; chap. xxii. 31; Joel iii. 4; Obad. verse 15. Again, in Ezekiel, "Woe to them that make kerchiefs *upon the head of every statue* to hunt souls," xiii. 18. And in David, "*God shall bruise the head*, the scalp of the hair," Psalm lxviii. 21. From these considerations it is now evident, that by the head is signified the whole man, and thus that by pouring oil upon the head of Aaron, is signified the Divine Good in the Lord upon the whole Human [principle]. That the Lord, when He was in the world, made Himself Divine Truth, and when He departed out of the world, made Himself Divine Good, see what is cited, n. 9315, 9199.

10,012. "And thou shalt cause his sons to approach"—that hereby is signified the conjunction of the Divine Truth proceeding from the Divine Good of the Lord, appears from the representation of the sons of Aaron, as denoting the Divine

Truth proceeding from the Divine Good of the Lord, see n. 9807; and from the signification of causing to approach, as denoting conjunction, see n. 3806, 10,001.

10,013. "And shalt clothe them with tunics"—that hereby is signified a representative of the Divine Spiritual proceeding, appears from the signification of the tunics which were for the sons of Aaron, as denoting the Divine Truth proceeding from the Divine Spiritual, which is represented by the tunics of Aaron, see n. 9947.

10,014. "And thou shalt gird them with a belt"—that hereby is signified a bond of conjunction that all things may be kept in connexion, and thence in a heavenly form, appears from the signification of the belt, as denoting an external bond keeping together all the truths and goods of faith in connexion and in form, see n. 3341, 9828, 9837, 9944.

10,015. "Aaron and his sons"—that hereby is signified the Lord as to the Divine Good, and the Divine Truth thence proceeding, appears from the representation of Aaron, as denoting the Lord as to the Divine Good, see n. 9806; and from the representation of the sons of Aaron, as denoting the Lord as to the Divine Truth thence proceeding, see n. 9807.

10,016. "And shalt tie turbans [tiara] to them"—that hereby is signified intelligence grounded in wisdom, appears from the signification of turbans, as denoting intelligence grounded in wisdom, see n. 9949.

10,017. "And the priesthood shall be to them"—that hereby is signified the Lord as to the work of salvation in successive order, appears from the signification of the priesthood, as being a representative of the Lord, as to all the work of salvation, see n. 9809. The reason why it is in successive order is, because the priesthood of the sons of Aaron is here treated of, and by his sons are represented those things which proceed, thus things which succeed in order, n. 9807. The case herein is this; the priesthood, which is represented by Aaron, is the work of the salvation of those who are in the Lord's celestial kingdom, which kingdom is properly meant in the Word by a kingdom of priests; but the priesthood, which is represented by the sons of Aaron, is the work of the salvation of those who are in the Lord's spiritual kingdom proximately proceeding from His celestial kingdom. Hence it is, that by the priesthood is here meant the Lord's work of salvation in successive order; but the priesthood, which is represented by the Levites, denotes the Lord's work of salvation again proceeding from the former. There are three [principles] which succeed in order; there is the celestial, which is the good of love to the Lord; there is the spiritual, which is the good of charity towards the neighbor; and there is the natural, thence derived, which is the good of faith. Inasmuch as there are those three which succeed in order, there are also three heavens, and in them goods in that order; the work of the salvation of those who are in celestial good, is represented by the priesthood of Aaron; but the work of the salvation of those who are in spiritual good, is represented by the priesthood of the sons of Aaron; and the work of the salvation of those who are thence in natural good, is represented by the priesthood of the Levites; and since those things, which succeed in order, proceed from the good of love to the Lord, which is represented by Aaron and his priesthood, therefore it is said of the Levites, that they should be given to Aaron, for those things which proceed are of that from which they proceed, for the things proceeding or succeeding, thence derive their esse; according to what was said just above, n. 10,001. That the Levites were given to Aaron and his sons that they might perform the ministry of the priesthood under them, see Numb. iii. 1 to the end.

10,018. "For the statute of an age"—that hereby is signified according to the eternal laws of order, appears from the signification of a statute, as denoting a law of order, see n. 7884, 7995, 8357; and from the signification of an age, as denoting what is eternal.

10,019. "And thou shalt fill the hand of Aaron, and the hand of his sons"—that hereby is signified inauguration to represent the Divine Power of the Lord by Divine Truth derived from Divine Good, is evident from the signification of filling the hand, which is to inaugurate to represent the Lord as to Divine Truth derived from Divine Good, and the power thence resulting. There were two things by which inauguration into the priesthood was effected, anointing and filling of the hand; by anointing was effected inauguration to represent the Lord as to Divine Good, for the oil, by which anointing was effected, signifies the good of love, n. 10,011, and by filling of the hand was effected inauguration to represent the Lord as to Divine Truth derived from Divine Good, and thereby as to power; for by the hand is signified power, n. 878, 4931 to 4937, 5327, 5328, 6947, 7011, 7188, 7189, 7518, 7673, 8050, 8069, 8153; and the hand is predicated of the truth which is from good, n. 3091, 3563, 4931, 8281, 9025. Since all power is of truth derived from good, n. 5623, 6344, 6413, 6948, 8200, 8304, 9327, 9410, 9639, 9643; and whereas the head and the whole body exercise their power by the hands, and power is the activity of the life appertaining to man, therefore by the hand is also signified whatsoever appertains to man, thus the man himself so far as he is an agent, n. 9133; from which considerations it may be manifest what is signified by filling the hand. That the Lord alone has all power, and that no angel, spirit, nor man has any, unless what is thence derived, see n. 8200, 8281, 9327, 9410, 9639. The reason why by those two things, namely, by anointing and filling the hand, inauguration into the priesthood was effected, was, because all things whatsoever which are and exist, in the heavens and in the earths, have reference to goodness and to truth. But in what manner the filling of the hand was effected, is described in this chapter from verse 9 to 36; and also in Levit. chap. viii. 22 to the end; it was effected by the second ram, which is therefore called the ram of fillings. The process of filling was, that the ram should be slain; that of his blood [a part] should be given upon the auricle of the right ear, the thumb of the right hand, and the great toe of the right foot, of Aaron and of his sons; that some of the blood from the altar, and of the oil of anointing, should be sprinkled upon Aaron and upon his sons, and upon their garments; that the fat, the tail, the fat on the intestines, the caul of the liver, the kidneys and their fat, and the right shoulder, of that ram, also the bread, the cakes and the wafers of what is unleavened from the basket, should be set upon the palms of the hands of Aaron and of his sons, and should be shaken; and afterwards they were to be burnt upon the burnt-offering of the first ram, that the breast, after it was shaken, and the left shoulder, should be for Aaron and his sons, and the flesh baked in the holy place, and the bread remaining in the basket, should be eaten by them, at the door of the tent of the congregation; this was the process of the fillings of the hands; but what each of these rites signified, will be shown, by the Divine Mercy of the Lord, in the following pages. The Divine Power of the Lord, which was represented by the filling of the hand of Aaron and of his sons, is the Divine Power of saving the human race; and the power of saving the human race is power over the heavens and over the hells; for by that power of the Lord, and by no other, man is saved; for all the good which is of love, and all the truth which is of faith, flow in through the heavens from the Lord, which cannot flow in unless the hells are removed, for from the hells are all evils, and thence every thing that is false; by the removal of evils and the falses thence derived which enter in from the hells, and then by the influx of the good of love and of the truth of faith through heaven from the Lord, man is saved. That the Lord, when He was in the world, subdued the hells, and reduced the heavens into order, and acquired to Himself Divine Power over them, see n. 9486, 9715, 9809, 9937, and what is cited n. 9528 at the end. This power of the Lord is what was represented by the filling of the hand of the priests; for by the priesthood was signified the whole work of the Lord's salvation, n. 9809. That the Lord has that power, He Himself teaches in express words in Matthew, "*All power is given unto Me in the heavens and in the earths,*" xxviii. 18. And in Luke, "Jesus said to the seventy, who said *that the demons were obedient to them*, *Behold, I give you power to tread upon serpents, and upon scorpions, and upon all the power of the enemy*, and nothing shall in any wise hurt you. *All things are delivered to Me of My Father*," x. 19, 22. By these words is described the power of the Lord over the hells; demons are those who are in the hells; serpents and scorpions denote evils and the falses of evil; to tread upon them is to destroy them; the hells are also meant by the enemy, over whom they were to have power. That the Lord acquired to Himself that power when He was in the world, is manifest from Isaiah, "*Who is this that cometh from Edom, walking in the multitude of His strength, mighty to save; my own arm brought salvation to me; therefore He was made a Saviour to them*," lxiii. 1 to 10; that those things are said of the Lord, is known in the church. In like manner what is said elsewhere in the same prophet, "*His own arm brought salvation to Him, and His justice stirred Him up, therefore He put on justice as a coat of mail, and a helmet of salvation upon His head, and the Redeemer came to Zion*," lix. 16 to 21. And in David, "*The saying of Jehovah to My Lord, Sit thou at My right hand, until I place thy foes thy footstool; Jehovah shall send the sceptre of thy strength out of Zion; have thou dominion in the midst of enemies; the Lord is at thy right hand*," Psalm cx. 1 and following verses. That these things were said of the Lord, the Lord Himself teaches in Matthew, chap. xxii. 42; in this passage is described His dominion over the hells by sitting at the right hand, for by the right hand is signified the power which Divine Truth has from Divine Good; the hells and the evils and falses thence derived are the foes, who were to be placed for His footstool, and also the enemies in the midst of whom he was to have dominion. That the right hand of Jehovah is Divine Power, is evident from numerous passages in the Word, as in Moses, "*Thy right hand, O Jehovah, is magnificent in strength, thy right hand, O Jehovah, hath broken in pieces the enemy*," Exod. xv. 6. And in David, "O God, thou givest me the shield of salvation, and *thy right hand sustaineth me*," Psalm xviii. 35. Again, "Their arm did not preserve them, but *thy right hand, and thine arm, and the light of thy faces*," Psalm xliv. 3; it is said, thy right hand, and thine arm, and the light of thy faces, because the right hand denotes power, the arm denotes strength, and the light of faces Divine Truth from the Divine Good; that arm denotes strength, see n. 4932, 4934, 4935, 7205; that light is the Divine Truth, n. 9548, 9684; and that the face of Jehovah is the Divine Good, n. 222, 5585, 9306. Again, "O God, *Thy right hand sustaineth me*," Psalm lxiii. 8. Again, "O Jehovah, thou hast an arm with virtue, strong is Thy hand, *Thy right hand shall be exalted*," Psalm lxxxix. 13. And in Isaiah, "*Jehovah hath sworn by His right hand*, by the arm of His strength," lxii. 8.

And in David, "*O Jehovah, let Thy hand be for the man of Thy right hand;* for *the Son of Man,* [whom] Thou hast strengthened for Thyself; then will we not recede from Thee," Psalm lxxx. 17, 18. From these passages it may now be manifest what is meant by the Lord's words in Matthew, "Jesus said, *henceforth ye shall see the Son of Man, sitting on the right hand of power,*" xxvi. 64; and in Luke, "*Henceforth shall the Son of Man sit on the right hand of the virtue of God,*" xxii. 69; that the Son of Man denotes the Lord as to Divine Truth, see n. 9807; but that the right hand denotes Divine Power, is manifest from what has been now shown, therefore also it is called the right hand of power and the right hand of virtue. From these considerations it is now evident what was represented by the anointing of Aaron and of his sons, and what by the filling of their hand, namely, by anointing, the Divine Good of the Divine Love in the Lord, n. 9954 at the end, and by the filling of the hand, Divine Truth and the Divine Power thence derived. That Divine Good has all power by Divine Truth, and that the Lord alone has that power, see the passages cited above. On this account also, in the Word of the Old Testament the Lord is called hero, a man of war, and also Jehovah Sabaoth, or of armies.

10,020. Verses 10, 11, 12, 13, 14. *And thou shalt cause the bullock to approach before the tent of the congregation, and Aaron and his sons shall put their hands upon the head of the bullock. And thou shalt slay the bullock before Jehovah at the door of the tent of the congregation. And thou shalt take of the blood of the bullock, and shalt give it upon the horns of the altar with thy finger; and all the blood thou shalt pour forth at the foundation of the altar. And thou shalt take all the fat covering the intestines, and the caul upon the liver, and the two kidneys, and the fat which is upon them, and thou shalt make the altar to burn. And the flesh of the bullock, and his skin, and his dung, thou shalt burn with fire out of the camp; this is sin.* And thou shalt cause the bullock to approach, signifies the state of the application of the natural or external man, such as it is in its infancy. Before the tent of the congregation, signifies for purification, the reception of truth from heaven, and the conjunction thereof with good. And Aaron and his sons shall put their hands on the head of the bullock, signifies a representative of the reception of good and of truth in the natural or external man. And thou shalt slay the bullock before Jehovah, signifies preparation for the purification of good and of truth from the Divine in the external or natural man. At the door of the tent of the congregation, signifies that there may be conjunction of those principles. And thou shalt take of the blood of the bullock, signifies Divine Truth accommodated in the natural or external man. And shalt give it upon the horns of the altar with thy finger, signifies the Divine Power of the Lord from the proprium. And all the blood thou shalt pour forth at the foundation of the altar, signifies Divine Truth, the whole of it in the sensual principle, which is the ultimate of the life of man. And thou shalt take all the fat, signifies good accommodated. That covers the intestines, signifies which appertains to ultimates or lowest principles. And the caul upon the liver, signifies interior good of the external or natural man. And the two kidneys, and the fat upon them, signifies interior truth of the external or natural man and its good. And thou shalt make the altar to burn, signifies from the Divine Love of the Lord. And the flesh of the bullock, signifies the evil of the former loves there. And his skin, signifies the false in ultimates. And his dung, signifies the rest of the unclean things. Thou shalt burn with fire out of the camp, signifies that they are to be committed to hell, and to be consumed with the evils of self-love. This is sin, signifies that it is purified from evils.

10,021. " And thou shalt cause the bullock to approach "—that hereby is signified the state of the application of the natural or external man such as it is in its infancy, appears from the signification of causing to approach, as denoting presence and conjunction, see n. 9378, 9997, 10,001, and also application, n. 8439, in this case application for purification and for the reception of good and of truth from the Divine, for by this sacrifice, and by sacrifices in general, this is signified; and from the signification of the bullock, as denoting the good of charity and of innocence in the natural or external man, see n. 9391, thus the external or natural man, such as he is in his infancy, for then he is in the good of innocence; whilst he is in that state, he is also in a state of application for purification and for reception of good and truth from the Divine. Since those things are now treated of in the internal sense, it may be expedient to say how the case herein is. When man is regenerated, which occurs when he is of adolescent years, then he is first let into a state of innocence, but into a state of external innocence, almost like that of infants, the innocence of these latter being external innocence, which dwells in ignorance; this state is the plane of the new life when man is regenerating; the man is also on this occasion as an infant, for during regeneration he is conceived anew, is born, becomes an infant, and grows up to maturity, which is effected by truth implanted in good; and so far as he then comes into genuine good, so far he comes into the good of internal innocence, which innocence dwells in wisdom. And whereas the regeneration of man is an image of the glorification of the Lord, it is evident that the Lord so glorified Himself, that is, made His Human [principle] Divine; for the subject treated of, in the internal sense, in this chapter, is concerning the glorification of the Lord, n. 9985; but since the glorification of the Lord as to His Human [principle] transcends the understanding, therefore, that it may in some measure be apprehended, it is explained by its resemblance or image. These statements are premised, to the intent that it may be known what is meant by purification and by the reception of good and of truth, and their conjunction, which are signified by sacrifices in general, and here specifically by the sacrifices of the inauguration of Aaron and of his sons into the priesthood. That the regeneration of man is an image of the glorification of the Lord, see n. 3130, 3212, 3296, 3490, 4402, 5688. That the innocence of infants is external innocence, and dwells in ignorance, n. 2306, 3474, 3504, 4563, 4797, 5608, 7305, 9301. That man, who is regenerating, is conceived anew, is born, becomes an infant and a boy, and grows up to adolescence, n. 3203. That the innocence of infancy is a plane, n. 2780, 3183, 3994, 4797, 5608, 7840. That the knowledges of truth and of good are implanted in the innocence of infancy as their plane, n. 1616, 2299, 3504, 4797. That the innocence of the regenerate is internal innocence, and dwells in wisdom, n. 1616, 3495 3994, 4797, 5608, 9301, 9939. The difference of the external innocence which is of infants, and of the internal innocence which is of the wise, n. 2280, 4563, 9301. That this difference exists, is manifest from the education and regeneration of infants in the other life, see n. 2289 to 2309. That every good of the church and of heaven, has in it innocence, and that without innocence good is not good, n. 2736, 2780, 6013, 7840, 7887, 9262. What innocence is, see n. 3994, 4001, 4797, 5236, 6107, 6765, 7902, 9262, 9936.

10,022. "Before the tent of the congregation"—that hereby is signified for purification, the reception of truth from heaven, and the conjunction thereof with good, appears from the representation of the tent of the congregation, as denoting heaven where the Lord is, see n. 9457, 9481, 9485. The reason why purification, the implantation of truth, and the conjunction thereof with good, is here also signified, is, because the bullock was brought thither to be sacrificed, and by sacrifices are signified both purification, and the implantation of truth and of good, and their conjunction. That by sacrifices were represented purifications from evils and falses, and also expiations, see n. 9990, 9991; and that by the place before the tent, which is called the door thereof, is represented the marriage of truth and of good, which is called the heavenly marriage, see n. 10,001. Hence now it is, that by causing the bullock to approach before the tent of the congregation, is signified the application of the external or natural man, such as he is in his infancy, to his purification from evils and falses, and thus to the reception of truth from heaven, and the conjunction thereof with good.

Inasmuch as the subject treated of in what now follows in this chapter is concerning sacrifices and burnt-offerings, it may be expedient to say what was in general represented by them. By burnt offerings and sacrifices in general purification from evils and falses was represented, and since purification was represented, the implantation of good and of truth from the Lord, and likewise their conjunction, was also represented. For when man is purified from evils and falses, which is effected by their removal, then good and truth from the Lord flow in, and so far as good and truth in that state flow in, so far they are implanted, and so far conjoined; for the Lord is continually present with good and truth with every man, but He is not received, only so far as evils and falses are removed, thus so far as man is purified from them; the conjunction of truth and of good is regeneration. Hence it may be manifest what was represented by burnt-offerings and by sacrifices in general; but what was specifically represented, is manifest from the animals of divers species which were sacrificed. Inasmuch as those three things, namely, purification from evils and falses, the implantation of truth and of good, and their conjunction, were represented by sacrifices and burnt-offerings, therefore all worship grounded in the truth of faith and in the good of love is also signified by them, n. 6905, 8680, 8936. For all worship has for its end, that man may be purified from evils and falses, consequently that goods and truths from the Lord may be implanted in him, and that thus he may be regenerated, which is effected by the conjunction of those principles. Their conjunction is heaven, or the Lord's kingdom with man.

10,023. "And Aaron and his sons shall put their hands upon the head of the bullock"—that hereby is signified a representative of the reception of good and of truth in the natural or external man, appears from the signification of the laying on of hands, as denoting to communicate that which is his own with another. The reason why it also denotes reception is, because that which is communicated is received by another; and from the signification of the head, as denoting the whole, see n. 10,011; and from that of the bullock, as denoting the good of innocence and of charity in the external or natural man, see n. 9391, 10,021. The reason why the laying on of hands signifies communication and reception is, because by the hands power is signified, and since this is the active principle of life, by hands is also signified whatsoever appertains to the man, thus the whole man, so far as he is an agent, see what was cited, n. 10,019; and by laying on is signified communication in reference to him who lays on, and reception in respect to him or to it on which it is laid. Hence it is evident, what was signified by the imposition of the hand amongst the ancients, namely, the communication and transference of that which is treated of, and also its reception by another, whether that be power, or obedience, or benediction, or testification. That by the imposition of the hand is signified power, is manifest from the following passages in Moses, "Jehovah said to Moses, that he should *lay the hand upon Joshua*, and should set him in the presence of Eleazar the priest, before the whole congregation, and *thus should give of his glory upon him*, and all the congregation *should obey him*," Numb. xxvii. 18, 20. That by the laying on of the hand is here signified the communication and transferring of the power which Moses had, and its reception by Joshua, is evident; hence it is said, *that thus he should give of his glory upon him*. Again, "When the Levites were purified, and the ministry of the priesthood under Aaron was ascribed to them, it was commanded, that two bullocks should be brought with a meat-offering, and that Aaron should bring the Levites before Jehovah, and the *sons of Israel should lay their hands upon the Levites; and the Levites should lay their hands upon the head of the bullocks*, one of which was to be offered for a sacrifice, the other for a burnt-offering; and thus they were to separate the Levites from the midst of the sons of Israel, and they were to be Jehovah's," Numb. viii. 7 to 14. By the sons of Israel laying their hands upon the Levites was signified the transference of the power of ministering for them, and reception of it by the Levites, thus separation. And by the Levites laying their hands upon the head of the bullocks, was signified a transferring of that power to Jehovah, that is, the Lord; therefore it is said that thus they should be separated from the midst of the sons of Israel, and should be Jehovah's. Again, "After that the sons of Israel confessed their sins, *then Aaron was to lay both his hands upon the head of the living goat Asasel*, and was to confess over him all the iniquities of the sons of Israel, and all their sins, and was to give them upon the head of the goat, and send him into the wilderness," Levit. xvi. 21. That the laying on of hands upon the goat signified the communication and translation of all the iniquities and sins of the sons of Israel, and their reception by the goat, is evident. The wilderness, whither the goat was to be sent, denotes hell. "*That the witnesses and all who heard, were to lay their hands upon him who was to be stoned*," Levit. xxiv. 14; signified testification thereby communicated and transferred, which being received he was adjudged to death. Again, "The man who bringeth from the herd or from the flock a burnt-offering for a present to Jehovah, *shall lay his hand on the head of the burnt-offering*, in which case it shall be received from him with good pleasure, to expiate him," Levit. i. 2, 3, 4. In like manner, "*upon the head of the present which was for sacrifice*," Levit. iii. 1, 2, 8, 13. And so also *the priest* was to do, if he sinned; in like manner *the elders;* likewise *the whole congregation;* also *the prince*, if he sinned; and in like manner, *every soul whatsoever*, if they sinned, Levit. iv. 4, 15, 24, 29. By the laying of their hand upon the burnt-offering and upon the sacrifice, was signified the all of the worship of him who offered, namely, the acknowledgment of sins, confession, thence purification, the implantation of good and of truth, thus conjunction with the Lord, all which were effected by communication, translation, and reception; by translation and reception is meant that which is signified by the carrying of iniquities, see n. 9937, 9938. Inasmuch as communications, translations, and receptions, were signified by the imposition of hands, it may be known what is signified by the imposition of hands in Matthew, "The ruler came to Jesus, and said, my daughter is just now dead, *but coming lay thy hand upon her*, then she shall live. Jesus entering in *took hold of her hand*, and the damsel arose," ix. 18, 19, 25. And in Mark, "*Jesus laid His hands upon the eyes of the blind man*, and he was restored," viii. 25. Again, "They bring one that was deaf to Jesus, *that he should lay the hand upon him;* He taking him from the people put His finger into his ears, and *touched his tongue*, and his ears were opened," vii. 32, 33, 35. And in Luke, "A woman was bowed down by the spirit of infirmity, *Jesus laid hands upon her, and healed her*," xiii. 11, 13. Also in Mark, "*Jesus laid hands on the infirm, and healed them*," vi. 5. In these passages by the laying on of the Lord's hands, and also by His touch, is signified the communication and reception of Divine Virtue, as is manifest in Mark, "A certain woman came from behind, *and touched the garment of Jesus*, saying, if *I shall touch even His garment*, I shall be healed, and immediately she was healed of the plague: *Jesus knew in Himself that virtue was gone forth from Him*," v. 27 to 30. And in Luke, "*A woman touching the garment of Jesus* was healed; Jesus said, *some one hath touched me; for I know that virtue is gone forth from me*," viii. 44, 46. And again, "*The whole crowd sought to touch Jesus, because virtue went forth from Him, and healed all*," vi. 19. Hence it is evident what is signified by touching with the hand or finger. And also by what is said elsewhere in the same evangelist, "*Jesus coming near touched the bier*, in which the dead man was, and they that bare it stood still; then He said, young man, I say unto thee, arise, and he that was dead sat up, and began to speak," vii. 14, 15. Also what by the imposition of hands upon boys and infants; upon boys in Matthew, "Boys were brought to Jesus, *that He should lay hands upon them;* Jesus said, suffer the boys, and forbid them not, to come unto me, of such is the kingdom of the heavens, *and He laid hands on them*," xix. 13, 15; and upon infants, in Mark, "Jesus took infants up in His arms, and *put His hands* upon them, and blessed them," x. 16. By the laying on of the hand upon the boys and upon infants is here also signified the communication and reception of Divine Virtue, whereby was effected the healing of the interiors, which is salvation. This signification of touching, which is effected by the hands, originates in representatives in the other life, where those who are in a dissimilar state of life, appear removed at a distance, but those who are in a similar state, appear consociated, and those in that life, who mutually touch each other, communicate the state of their life with each other; if this is done by the hands, the all of the life is communicated, because by the hands, as was said above, from correspondence is signified power, which is the active principle of life, thus whatsoever appertains to any one; such representatives exist in the world of spirits, but they are effected by influx from heaven, where alone are perceived consociations as to the affections of goodness and of truth.

10,024. "And thou shalt slay the bullock before Jehovah"—that hereby is signified preparation for the purification of good and truth from the Lord in the external or natural man, appears from the signification of slaying, when concerning the animals which were offered for a burnt-offering or for sacrifices, as denoting preparation for those things which are represented by burnt-offerings and sacrifices;—that those were purifications from evils and falses, the implantation of good and of truth, and their conjunction, see above, n. 10,022; and because those are from the Divine, therefore it is said, before Jehovah; and from the signification of the bullock, as denoting the purification of the external or natural man, see above, n. 9990. Hence it is, that by slaying, when concerning the burnt-offerings and sacrifices, in the Word is signified all that which is represented by the burnt-offering and sacrifice itself, since all that is then understood.

10,025. "At the door of the tent of the congregation"—that hereby is signified that there may be conjunction of those principles, appears from the signification of the door of the tent of the congregation, as denoting the conjunction of truth and of good, which is called the heavenly marriage, see above, n. 10,001. Inasmuch as this is signified by the door of the tent of the congregation, therefore it was ordained, "That if [the animal offered in sacrifice was slain] elsewhere, blood should be imputed, and that soul should be cut off from the people," Levit. xvii. 3, 4, 8, 9; the reason was, because in such case the conjunction of good and of truth was not represented, thus not the heavenly marriage, but the infernal marriage, which is the conjunction of evil and of the false.

10,026. "And thou shalt take of the blood of the bullock"—that hereby is signified Divine Truth accommodated to the natural or external man, appears from the signification of blood, as denoting the Divine Truth proceeding from the Divine Good of the Lord, of which we shall speak presently; and from the signification of the bullock, as denoting the natural principle of man, which was to be purified, and in which truth and good were to be implanted, see n. 9990. The reason why mention is here first made of blood, and that it was to be given on the horns of the altar, and the remainder of it to be poured out at its foundation, is, because by blood in the Word is signified the Divine Truth proceeding from the Divine Good of the Lord, and by this truth all purification is effected, for truth teaches man what is good, and how he ought to live, and when man knows this, then the affection of love of good may first be implanted, and thus he may be regenerated; for knowledge must precede, before man can have faith, and live the life of faith, which is the life of good;—that all purification from evils and falses is effected by the truths of faith, consequently all regeneration, see what is cited, n. 9959. Those who do not know the internal sense of the Word,—thus who do not know that by blood is signified Divine Truth, and that by this from the Lord is effected purification,—believe that man is purified by the blood of the Lord, by which they mean the passion of His cross; but let them know, that by the passion of the Lord's cross, thus by His blood, no one is purified, but by a life according to His precepts, as He Himself teaches in many places. The passion of the cross was the ultimate of the Lord's temptation, by which He fully glorified His Human, as He Himself also says in Luke, "*Ought not Christ to suffer these things, and to enter into His glory?*" xxiv. 26; for the Lord came into the world that He might subdue the hells, and reduce all things into order, even in the heavens, which was effected by temptations admitted into Himself. And the passion of the cross was the ultimate of His temptation, by which He fully conquered the hells, and arranged the heavens into order, and at the same time glorified His Human; and unless He had done so, no man could have been saved; but see what has been copiously shown before on these subjects in the passages cited, n. 9528, 9715, 9937, 10,019, also that by the blood of the Lord is signified the Divine Truth proceeding from His Divine Good, n. 4735, 4978, 6378, 7317, 7326, 7850, 9127, 9393.

10,027. "And thou shalt give [it] upon the horns of the altar with thy finger"—that hereby is signified the Divine Power of the Lord from the proprium, appears from the signification of the horns of the altar, as denoting the power of truth from good. That horns denote power, see n. 9081, 9719, 9720, 9721, and that the altar is representative of the Lord as to Divine Good, or representative of Divine Good in the Lord, n. 9388, 9389, 9714, 9964: and from the signification of finger, as denoting power, see n. 7430. The reason why it denotes from proper power, or from the proprium, is because this was done by Moses, and by Moses is represented the Lord, as to Divine Truth, n. 9372, 9806, wherefore it is said with thy finger. The reason why the blood was first to be given upon the horns of the altar was, that the power itself of the Divine Truth from the Divine Good might be represented; for by the power of Divine Truth from Divine Good all things are made [or done], and without it nothing, see what is cited above, n. 10,019.

10,028. "And all the blood thou shalt pour forth at the foundation of the altar"—that hereby is signified the whole Divine Truth in the sensual principle which is the ultimate of the life of man, appears from the signification of blood, as denoting the Divine Truth from the Divine Good of the Lord, see just above, n. 10,026; and from the signification of the foundation of the altar, as denoting the sensual principle, which is the ultimate of the life of man. The reason why the foundation of the altar has this signification is, because the altar was representative of the Lord's Divine Human, wherefore its foundation signifies that which is the ultimate of life in the human principle, and the ultimate of life in the human principle, is that which is called the external sensual principle, which is here meant. That the altar was the chief representative of the Lord's Divine Human, see n. 9388, 9389, 9714, 9764; that the foundation is its ultimate, is evident;—that this with man is the external sensual principle, and what its quality is, see n. 9212, 9216, 9996. How the case herein is, it may be expedient briefly to say: when man is purifying, then first of all are learnt such truths as can be apprehended by the sensual man, such as are the truths in the literal sense of the Word. Afterwards interior truths are learnt, such as are collected from the Word by those who are in illustration, for these persons collect its interior sense from various passages, where the sense of the letter is there explained; from these when known, truths still more interior are afterwards drawn forth by those who are enlightened, which truths with the former serve the church for doctrine, these latter for doctrine to those who are men of the internal church, the former for doctrine to those who are men of the external church. Both the former and the latter men, if they have lived acccording to those truths, are elevated into heaven amongst the angels, and are there imbued with angelic wisdom, which is derived from truths still interior, and at length from inmost truths in the third heaven. These truths with the former in their order, close into ultimates, which are those of the external sensual principle, and are together there; hence it is evident, that all interior truths are together in the truths of the literal sense of the Word, for these truths, as was said above, are the ultimates,—that all interior things in order are stored up in ultimates, and are there together, may be seen, n. 9825, 9826. From these considerations it is evident, what is meant by Divine Truth being wholly in the sensual principle, which is signified by all the blood being poured out at the foundation of the altar.

10,029. "And thou shalt take all the fat"—that hereby is signified good accommodated, appears from the signification of fat, as denoting good, see n. 5943. It is called good accommodated, because the subject here treated of is the purification of the external or natural man, and the implantation of truth and of good, and thus the conjunction of both there, for these are what are signified by sacrifices and burnt-offerings; therefore by the fat from the bullock is here meant good accommodated to the natural or external man, such as can be conjoined with truth there, for truth must be accommodated to its own good, and good to its own truth, by reason that they are to be a one. It is also to be observed, that truth and good in the natural or external man differ from truth and good in the internal man, as what is exterior and interior differ, or as what is inferior and superior, or, what is the same thing, as that which is posterior, and prior. Truth in the natural man is scientific, and good there is the delight thereof, each perceptible to the man whilst he is in the world, for it then appears when it becomes an object of the thought; truth however in the internal man is not apparent scientific truth, but is truth implanted in his intellectual part; good also in him is not perceptible, because it is implanted in his will, each in the interior life of the man, in which truth is of faith and good is of love. Such is the difference between truth and good in the internal or spiritual man, and truth and good in the external or natural man; the implantation and conjunction of the latter is signified by the sacrifice from the bullock, but the implantation and conjunction of the former by the burnt-offering from the ram are treated of in what follows in this chapter. From these considerations it is evident what is meant by the accommodated good which is signified by the fat from the bullock.

10,030. "Covering the intestines"—that hereby is signified what belongs to ultimates or lowest principles, appears from the signification of the intestines, as denoting ultimate or lowest principles. The reason why the intestines denote ultimate or lowest principles is, because they are the ultimate and lowest of the interior viscera of man, not only as to situation, but also as to use;—as to situation, they are below the stomach, to which they are appended;—and as to use, they ultimately receive those things which are digested with man. Above them, as it is known, are situated the stomach, the liver, the pancreas, the spleen, and still higher, the heart and lungs, and higher still, the head. It is also well known, that these superior organs, cast their filth and refuse into the intestines, and thereby remove them, partly by the stomach, partly by the ducts from the liver, which are denominated the hepatic ducts, and also the cystic or biliary ducts, partly through the ducts from the pancreas, which ducts with the rest have their termination in the intestine, called the duodenum. Hence it is now evident why ultimate or lowest principles are signified by the intestines. That by the viscera, which appertain to man, are signified such things as are of the spiritual world, may be manifest from what has been copiously shown at the close of several chapters, where the correspondence of the GRAND MAN, which is heaven, with all things appertaining to man, was treated of,—what specifically corresponds to the intestines, may be seen n. 5392; and that the hells correspond to the fæces and excrements thence ejected, n. 5393 to 5396. Inasmuch as in what now follows mention is made of some of the viscera of the body, as of the caul or omentum, the liver, the kidneys, the legs, the breast, the shoulder, the head, and as their ordination in the sacrifices is treated of, therefore it may be here first expedient to show that by man's members in general are signified such things as are in the GRAND MAN, that is, in heaven. At present we shall confine ourselves to the consideration of those members, by which the statue of Nebuchadnezzar is described in Daniel, where it is said, "That its *head* was pure gold, the *breast and arms* silver, *the belly and side* brass, the *legs* iron, and the *feet* partly iron and partly clay," ii. 32, 33. He who does not know that the Word of the Lord is spiritual, believes that these things were said concerning the kingdoms of the earth, but in the Word the kingdoms of the earth are not treated of, but the kingdom of God is, thus heaven and the church. The reason why these are described by such things as are in the earths, and in the kingdoms of the earths, is, because worldly and terrestrial things correspond to such as are in heaven; for universal nature, and the universal world, is a theatre representative of the Lord's kingdom, (see what is cited, n. 9280,) and terrestrial and worldly things are what man first apprehends. Hence it may be manifest, that by the statue seen by Nebuchadnezzar in a dream, are not signified wordly things, but heavenly things. What, however, is specifically signified by the head, by the breast, by the belly and side, by the legs and by the feet, may be known from their correspondence—thus from the internal sense of the Word. From correspondence it is known, that by the head is signified the first state of the church, by the breast and arms the second, by the belly and side the third, by the legs the fourth, and by the feet the last. Now, as the first state of the church was a state of the good of love to the Lord, it is said that the head was of gold; and since the second state was a state of truth from that good, it is said that the breast and arms were of silver; and whereas the third state was the good of love and its truth in the external or natural man, it is said that the belly and side were of brass; and as the fourth state was the truth of faith, it is said that the legs were of iron; and since the last state was the truth which is called [the truth] of faith without good, it is said that the feet were partly of iron, and partly of clay; and whereas such a state of the church was its ultimate state, it is said *that out of a rock was cut a stone, which brake in pieces and dispersed all things, insomuch that the wind carried them away, and no place was found for them*, verses 34, 35, by which is signified, that the good of love to the Lord, the good of charity towards the neighbor, and the good of faith, were utterly dispersed, insomuch that it was not known what they are, but only something about the truths of faith without good, or with a good which is not good, thus which does not cohere with the truths of faith. This good is external without internal good—such as is the good of merit—good for the sake of self and for the sake of the world—thus for the sake of gain, of honor, and of reputation, for the sake of friendship on account of those things, or for the sake of favor, and also for the sake of the fear of the law alone, and not for the sake of the good of charity, which is the good of a fellow citizen, the good of human society, the good of a man's country, and the good of the church. Such goods as are mentioned above are signified by clay, and the truth, with which that good does not cohere, is the iron; therefore it is said, "*The iron, which thou sawest mixed with clay of mud, shalt mix themselves together by the seed of man, but they shall not cohere the one with the other, as iron is not mixed together with clay*," verse 43. The seed of man is the truth of faith derived from the proprium—thus truth falsified and adulterated by application to the evils resulting from a regard to self and the world. From these considerations it is evident, that by the members of man from his head even to the sole of the foot are signified such things as relate to the church. That in general the head signifies celestial good, which is the good of love to the Lord; the breast spiritual good, which is the good of charity towards the neighbor; and the feet natural good, which is the good and truth of faith, may be seen, n. 9913, 9914. That similar things are also signified by gold, silver, brass and iron, n. 5658; but what is specifically signified by the head may be seen, n. 4938, 4939, 5328, 9913, 9914; what by gold, n. 113, 1551, 1552, 5658, 9510, 9881; what by the breast, n. 4938, 4939, 5328, 6436, 9913, 9914; what by silver, n. 1551, 5658, 6914, 6917: hence it is evident what is signified by the belly and by the side, which are below the breast. Moreover, what is denoted by brass, may be seen n. 425, 1551; what by the feet, n. 2162, 3147, 3761, 4938 to 4952; what by iron, n. 425, 426; and what by clay or mud,

n. 1300, 6669. From these considerations it may now be known, that by the members or viscera of man are signified such things as correspond to those in the GRAND MAN, or in heaven, which have reference to the good of love and to the truth of faith, and what correspond to these, correspond also to the same things in the church—for the Lord's heaven in the earths is the church. That there is a correspondence of man and of all things appertaining to man with the GRAND MAN, which is heaven, may be seen in what has been shown from experience itself at the end of several chapters, in the following places, n. 3624 to 3649, 3741 to 3751, 3883, 3896, 4039 to 4051, 4218 to 4228, 4318 to 4331, 4403 to 4421, 4527 to 4533, 4622 to 4633, 4652 to 4660, 4791 to 4805, 4931 to 4953, 5050 to 5061, 5171 to 5189, 5377 to 5396, 5552 to 5573, 5711 to 5727, 5846, 5866, 5976 to 5993, 6053 to 6058, 6189 to 6215, 6307 to 6326, 6466 to 6495. And what correspondence is, n. 2987 to 3003, 3213 to 3227, 3337 to 3352, 3472 to 3485.

10,031. "And the caul upon the liver"—that hereby is signified the interior good of the external or natural man, appears from the signification of the caul which is upon the liver, as denoting the interior good of the external or natural man. The reason why the caul denotes this good is, because the whole is fat, and by fat is signified good, see above, n. 10,028; that it denotes interior good is, because that fat is higher or more interior in the body than the fat covering the intestines, spoken of just above; by the liver also is signified interior purification, for the liver purifies the blood, but the intestines those things from which the blood is formed. The reason why it denotes the good of the external or natural man is, because by the bullock, in which that caul is, is signified the good of innocence and of charity in the external or natural man, n. 9990. In other cases by the liver is signified the external good of innocence, such as appertains to infants, because infants, before the rest of the viscera are fully formed to their use, as is the case when they are embryos, receive their nourishment through the liver, for every nutritious juice is brought thither through the placenta and the navel from the womb of the mother—this juice corresponds to the good of innocence. That this good is signified by the liver, is manifest from Jeremiah, "Mine eyes are consumed by tears, my bowels are disturbed, *my liver is poured forth into the earth*, upon the breach of the daughter of my people: *the infant and the suckling* faint in the streets, they say to their mothers, where is the corn and the wine," Lam. ii. 11, 12. In this passage is described the grief of the vastated church; grief on account of truth destroyed is signified by the eyes being consumed by tears; grief on account of the truth of innocence being destroyed by the bowels being disturbed; and grief on account of the good of innocence being destroyed by the liver being poured forth into the earth; wherefore it is said, the infant and the suckling faint in the streets, and they say to their mothers, where is the corn and wine. The daughter of the people, on account of whose breach is this grief, denotes the church, n. 2362, 3963, 6729; eyes denote the things which are of the internal sight, thus the truths of faith, n. 4526, 4528, 9051; bowels [viscera] denote the truths of innocence, n. 3294; the liver denotes the good of innocence, for the infants and sucklings, who faint in the streets, denote those who are in the good of innocence, n. 430, 3183, 4563, 5608; the corn and the wine, concerning which they say to their mothers where are they, denote the good of truth and the truth of good—corn the good of truth, n. 5959—wine the truth of good, n. 1071, 1798.

10,032. "And the two kidneys, and the fat which is upon them"—that hereby is signified the interior truth of the external or natural man and its good, appears from the signification of the kidneys, as denoting interior truths, of which we shall speak presently; and from the signification of fat, as denoting good, see above, n. 10,028. The reason why it denotes the good of that truth is, because it was the fat upon the kidneys. It is said the good of that truth, since every good has its truth, and every truth has its good. There are innumerable genera of good, and every genus of good has truth which is of the same genus; for in the universal heaven goods and truths are what constitute the life there, and they are every where various. What is the quality of the good which is signified by the fat upon the kidneys, is manifest from the truths which are signified by the kidneys; by the kidneys are signified truths exploring, purifying, and chastising;—this signification is grounded in their function. Hence it is evident what is signified by kidneys in the following passages, "*Jehovah that proveth the kidneys and the heart,*" Jer. xi. 20. And in David, "*Thou provest the heart and the kidneys, O just God,*" Psalm vii. 9. Again, "*O Jehovah, explore my kidneys and my heart,*" Psalm xxvi. 2. Again, "O *Jehovah, thou possessest my kidneys,*" Psalm cxxxix. 13. And in the Revelations, "*I am, who search the kidneys and the heart,*" ii. 23. To search and to prove the kidneys denotes to explore the truths of faith; and to search and prove the heart denotes to explore the goods of love—for the heart denotes the good of love, n. 3883 to 3896, 7542, 9050. That the truths of faith are signified by the kidneys, evidently appears in David, "*O Jehovah, behold thou desirest truth in the kidneys,*" Psalm li. 6. The reason why by the kidneys is signified interior truth, and its exploration, is, because by the ureters and the bladder, which go forth from the kidneys, is signified exterior truth, and its exploration, and also chastisement, n. 5381, 5382, 5383, 5384.

10,033. Inasmuch as this chapter treats of the sacrifice and the burnt-offering, by which Aaron and his sons were to be inaugurated into the priesthood, it may be expedient to make a few more observations concerning the blood and the fat. That all the blood of the sacrifice and of the burnt-offering was to be poured forth at the altar, and that all the fat was to be burnt upon the altar, is manifest from the statutes and the laws con cerning the burnt-offerings and the sacrifices in Leviticus. The reason why it was so ordained was, because the blood signified the Divine Truth, and the fat the Divine Good; that blood has this signification, is manifest from what was shown concerning blood, n. 4735, 4978, 6378, 7317, 7326, 7850, 9127, 9393; and that fat signified Divine Good, from what was shown, n. 5943. That by blood is signified Divine Truth, is manifest from Ezekiel, "Gather ye together from the circuit upon My sacrifice, which I sacrifice for you, a great sacrifice upon the mountains of Israel, that ye may eat flesh, and *drink blood*, ye shall eat the flesh of the mighty, and *shall drink the blood of the princes of the earth:* ye shall eat *fat* to satiety, and *shall drink blood even to drunkenness*, of my sacrifice which I will sacrifice for you; ye shall be satisfied at My table with the horse, with the chariot, with the mighty one and every man of war; thus will I give My glory amongst the nations," xxxix. 17 to 22. That by blood is not here meant blood, every one may see, for it is said that they should drink the blood of the princes of the earth, and even to drunkenness; and also that they should eat fat even to satiety; and then that they should be satisfied with the horse and with the chariot; hence it is evident that something else besides blood is signified by the blood, and something else besides the princes of the earth by the princes of the earth, also something else by the fat, likewise by the horse and by the chariot, besides the fat, horse, and chariot. What is signified, however, cannot be known, except from the internal sense, which teaches, that blood denotes the Divine Truth, the princes of the earth the primary truths of the church, that fat is the Divine Good, that horse is the internal sense of the Word, and that chariot is the doctrine itself thence derived. That blood is the Divine Truth is manifest from the passages above cited; that the princes of the earth are primary truths, see n. 5044; that the earth is the church, n, 9325; that the horse denotes the internal sense of the Word, n. 2760, 2761, 2762; and that chariot denotes doctrine, n. 5321, 8218. From these considerations it is now evident what is signified by the Lord's words in John, "Jesus said, unless ye *eat the flesh of the Son of Man and drink His blood*, ye have no life in you; he that eateth My *flesh*, and *drinketh My blood*, hath eternal life, and I will raise him up at the last day: *for My flesh is truly meat, and My blood is truly drink:* he that *eateth My flesh, and drinketh My blood*, abideth in Me, and I in him," vi. 53—56. That flesh is the Divine Good, see n. 3813, 7850, 9127; and that the Son of Man, whose flesh they were to eat, and whose blood they were to drink, is the Lord as to the Divine Truth from the Divine Good, n. 9807. That fat denotes the Divine Good, is moreover demonstrable from Isaiah, " Jehovah shall make for all people in this mountain a *feast of fat things*," xxv. 6. Again in the same prophet, " Attend to Me, *and eat good, and your soul shall be delighted in fatness*," lv. 2 ; and in Jeremiah, " I will fill the soul of the priests *with fatness:* and My people *shall be satiated with My good*," xxxi. 14. From these considerations it may be manifest why all the fat of the sacrifice was to be burnt upon the altar, and why all the blood was to be poured forth at its side. Inasmuch as blood and fat signify those Divine things, therefore the Israelitish people were altogether forbidden to eat fat and blood, as is manifest from Moses, " A statute of eternity to your generations, *ye shall eat no fat and no blood*," Levit. iii. 17. Again, " *Ye shall eat no fat, whether of an ox, or of a bird, or of a she-goat ; every one who shall eat the fat of a beast whereof an offering is made by fire to Jehovah*, the soul that eateth shall be cut off from his people," Levit. vii. 23, 25. And again, " *Whosoever shall eat any blood*, I will give My faces against the soul *that eateth blood*, and I will cut it off from the midst of his people," Levit. xvii. 10 to 14; also Deut. xii. 23, 24, 25. The reason why it was so severely prohibited to eat the blood and the fat was, because by it was represented the profanation of Divine Truth and Divine Good ; for the Israelitish and Judaic nation was in externals separate from internals thus in no Divine Truth and in no Divine Good as to faith and love, but in external worship without them ; for they were principled in the love of self and of the world more than other nations, consequently in the evils therein originating, which are contempt of others, enmity, hatred, revenge, barbarity and cruelty ; hence also it was, that internal truths were not revealed to them, for if they had been revealed, they could not but profane them. That that nation was of such a quality, may be seen in what is cited, n. 9320, 9380 ; wherefore they would have represented profanation, if they had eaten blood and fat, for whatsoever was instituted amongst them, was representative of the interior things of the church and of heaven. From these considerations it is further evident, what is signified by eating fat to satiety, and by drinking blood, the blood of the princes of the earth, even to drunkenness, in Ezekiel, chap. xxxix. 17 to 22, spoken of above, namely, that when interior things were opened, then to those who were in interior things, that is, in faith and in love to the Lord, would be appropriated Divine Truth and Divine Good, which was effected amongst the nations when the Lord came into the world, wherefore also it is there said, *thus will I give my glory among the nations*—by glory is signified the Divine Truth proceeding from the Lord, such as it is in heaven, n. 9429 ; and by nations are signified all who are in good, n. 1259, 1260, 1416, 1849, 4574, 6005, 8771, 9256. These things the Lord Himself confirms, when He says, that *His flesh was truly meat, and His blood was truly drink*, and that whosoever *eateth His flesh, and drinketh His blood*, abideth in Him, and He in him," John vi. 55, 56; and also when He instituted the Holy Supper, in which *they were to eat His flesh, and to drink His blood*, Matt. xxvi. 27, 28, by which is signified the appropriation of Divine Good and Divine Truth from Him; and the appropriation of Divine Good and Divine Truth from the Lord cannot be given except with those who acknowledge the Divine [principle] of the Lord, for this is the first and the very essential of all things which are of faith in the church; for heaven cannot be unclosed to others, since the whole heaven is in that faith, thus the Divine Truth proceeding from the Divine Good of the Lord, which is there meant by blood, cannot be communicated to others. Let every one therefore who is within the church, take heed to himself, lest he deny the Lord, and also lest he deny His Divine [principle], for to that denial heaven is closed and hell is opened; for all such are separated from heaven where the Divine of the Lord is the all in all, for this makes heaven; and when heaven is closed, the science of the truths of faith derived from the Word, and the doctrine of the church is indeed given, but in no case faith which is faith, for the faith which is faith comes from above, that is through heaven from the Lord. The reason why the Lord so spake, namely, why He called the Divine Good proceeding from Himself His flesh, and the Divine Truth proceeding from His Divine Good, His blood, was, because the Word, which was from Him, was the Divine filling the universal heaven; such Word must be [written] by correspondences, consequently must be representative and significative in all and every expression, for thus and no otherwise it conjoins the men of the church with the angels in the heavens; for when men perceive the Word according to the letter, the angels perceive it according to the internal sense, thus instead of the flesh of the Lord they perceive the Divine Good, and instead of His blood the Divine Truth, each from the Lord:—hence what is holy flows in through the Word.

10,034. "And thou shalt make the altar to burn"—that hereby is signified from the Divine Love of the Lord, appears from the signification of making to burn, as denoting the kindling of Divine Love; and from the representation of the altar, as being a representative of the Lord as to the Divine Good of Love, see n. 9388, 9389, 9714. The reason why making to burn denotes the kindling of Divine Love is, because by the fire upon the altar was signified the Divine Love, n. 6832.

10,035. "And the flesh of the bullock"—that hereby is signified the evil of the former loves there, appears from the signification of flesh, as denoting the good of love, and in the opposite sense, the evil of love, of which we shall speak presently; and from the signification of the bullock, as denoting the external or natural principle, before treated of. By a bullock and a calf in a good sense the external or natural principle of man as to the good of innocence and of charity is signified, but in the opposite sense the external or natural principle of man as to the evil which is contrary to the good of innocence and of charity, for most expressions in the Word have also an opposite sense. The reason why the flesh of the bullock here signifies the evil of former loves in the external or natural man is, because by flesh is signified the will principle of man, thus his proprium, for what is of the will, that is proper to man [or his proprium]: and since by flesh is signified the will principle or the proprium, therefore also by it is signified the good of love or the evil of love; for there are two faculties appertaining to man, which are called the understanding and the will,—to the understanding appertain truths or falses,—but to the will goods or evils; thus to the understanding appertain those things which are of faith, and to the will those which are of love, for the things which are of love are perceived as goods, and the things which are of faith are perceived as truths; falses also are of faith, and evils are of love, with those who are in falses and in evils. Hence it may be manifest what is meant by the will proprium, which is signified by flesh in both senses. It is further to be noted, that all the will proprium of man is evil, because man of himself loves nothing but himself and the world, and if he loves his neighbor it is for the sake of himself; wherefore he must be regenerated, and by regeneration must receive a new will; but the will, which he receives by regeneration, is not of man, but of the Lord with man;—when this will, or this will principle, is meant by flesh, then flesh signifies the good of love. See however what has been before shown concerning flesh, and the proprium, namely, that flesh signifies the proprium of the Lord, which is Divine Good, and hence every good of love appertaining to the regenerate man, n. 3813, 7850, 9127; and that in the opposite sense it signifies the will proprium of man, which is the evil of love, n. 999, 3813, 8409. That the proprium of the Lord is Divine Good, and hence the good of love to Him, and towards the neighbor, since the proprium of the Lord is what gives the life of heaven to man when he is regenerating, may be seen, n. 1023, 1044, 1937, 1947, 3812, 5660, 5780, 8480; and that the proprium of man is nothing but evil, n. 210, 215, 694, 874, 875, 876, 987, 1047, 3812, 4328, 5660, 5780, 8480, 8497. That by the flesh of this bullock is signified the evil of love, is manifest from what follows in this verse, namely, that the flesh, the skin, and the dung, were to be burnt out of the camp, because they were sin. But what was represented by the flesh of the sacrifice being eaten by the priest and by the people in the holy place, will be seen below, n. 10,040.

10,036. "And his skin"—that hereby is signified what is false in ultimates, appears from the signification of the skin, as denoting truth in ultimates, and in the opposite sense what is false there; this signification of the skin is grounded in correspondence, for those who have reference to the skin in the GRAND MAN, or in heaven, are those who are in the truths of faith, and not so much in correspondent good, who are in the threshold of heaven, see n. 5552 to 5559;—hence by the skin in the abstract sense is signified truth in ultimates, n. 3540, 8980 The reason why by the skin is here signified what is false in ultimates, is, because by the flesh is signified the evil of love, treated of just above, n. 10,034, and when flesh signifies the evil of love, its skin signifies the false of faith thence derived.

10,037. "And his dung"—that hereby are signified all other unclean things, appears from the signification of dung, as denoting what is unclean. The reason why dung signifies what is unclean, consequently evil and the false, for these things in the spiritual sense are unclean, is, because every thing of food which is useless and obsolete passes off into dung [*fimum*] and ordure [*stercus*], and food in the spiritual sense is the truth and good of faith and love, see n. 4792, 5147, 5293, 5340, 5342, 5576, 5915, 8562, 9003; hence also it is that dung [*fimus*], ordure [*stercus*], and excrement, correspond to evils which are in hell, which also in the Word is called a jakes [*latrina*]; concerning this correspondence, see n. 954, 2755, 4948, 5394, 5395, 7161. Hence it is then that such things in the Word signify what is infernal, as may be manifest from the following passages, "He that is left in Zion, and he that remaineth in Jerusalem, shall be called holy, every one that is written for life in Jerusalem, *when the Lord hath washed the excrement of the daughters of Zion*, and hath washed away the bloods of Jerusalem," Isaiah iv. 3, 4. By Zion and Jerusalem is signified the church,—by Zion the church with those who are in the good of love, and by Jerusalem with those who are in truths derived from that good; to wash the excrement of the daughters of Zion, denotes to purify those in the church who are in the good of love from evils, and to wash away the bloods of Jerusalem, denotes to purify those in the church who are in truths from the falses of evil. And in Jeremiah, "They shall draw forth the bones of the kings of Judah, and the bones of his princes, and the bones of the priests, and the bones of the prophets, and shall spread them out to the sun, and to the moon, and to all the host of the heavens, which they had loved, and which they had served, they shall not be gathered together, neither shall they be buried, *they shall be for dung* [*stercus*] *on the faces of the earth*," viii. 1, 2. By these words is described the state of those who have profaned the goods and truths of the church, which state at that time was also represented by the drawing forth of bones from sepulchres. The bones of kings and of princes drawn forth from sepulchres signify truths profaned; the bones of priests and of prophets signify goods profaned; to be spread out to the sun, to the moon, and to all the host of the heavens, signifies removal from all good and truth; not to be gathered together, nor to be buried, signifies non-resurrection to life; to be dung on the faces of the earth, signifies to be nothing but what is infernal. Again, "They shall die by deaths of malignant diseases, so that they shall not be lamented, neither shall they be buried, *they shall be for dung* [*stercus*] *on the faces of the earth*," xvi. 4; chap. xxv. 33,—by dung on the faces of the earth, the like is signified as above. And in the Lamentations, "Those who did eat delicacies are devastated in the streets; *those who were educated upon purple have embraced dunghills*," iv. 5. Those who have eaten delicacies denote such as have the Word, and thence the knowledges of truth; those who were educated upon purple denote such as are in the knowledges of good; to embrace dunghills denotes instead of truth and good to learn and choose falsities. And in Malachi, "If ye will not hear, and if ye will not lay [it] on the heart, I will send into you a curse, and *will spread dung upon your faces, the dung of your festivals*," ii. 2, 3; to spread dung upon the faces denotes to defile the interiors of life with the falses of evil; the dung of festivals denotes to defile the holy things of worship. And in Ezekiel, "The prophet was commanded to make a cake of barley *with the ordure* [*stercus*] *of human dung* [*fimus*], because thus the sons of Israel eat their unclean bread: but he said, Ah, Lord Jehovah, my soul hath not been polluted, there hath not come into my mouth the flesh of abomination; then He answered, *I give thee the excrement of an ox for the dung of man* [*stercus*], that thou mayest make thy bread with it; for I will cause them to want bread and water, and a man and his brother shall be desolated, and shall consume away by reason of their iniquity," vi. 12 to 17. By these words was represented the quality of the good and truth of the church of the Jewish nation; a cake of barley with the ordure [*stercus*] of the dung [*fimus*] of man, signifies the interior good of the church defiled with the evils of the love of self; a cake with the excrements of an ox, signifies the external good of the church defiled with the evils of that love; inasmuch as those things are signified by the cake, it is said that they should want bread and water and should be desolated; bread and water denote good and truth; to want them and to be desolated denotes to be deprived of them. Inasmuch as such things were signified by dung [*fimus*], ordure [*stercus*], and excrement, it is evident what is signified by these words in Moses, "There shall be a space out of the camp, whither thou shalt go forth abroad, and thou shalt have a paddle, *with which thou shalt cover thine excrement;* for Jehovah God walketh in the midst of thy camp, that thy camp may be holy, and he may not see in thee the nakedness of any thing, and return from after thee," Deut. xxiii. 13—15. This was commanded, because what is unclean was represented by dung; for by the camp where the sons of Israel were, was represented heaven and the church, where the Lord is present by faith and love; wherefore by the place out of the camp, was represented where heaven and the church are not—thus where the Lord is not present by faith and love; wherefore it is said, that Jehovah walketh in the midst of the camp, that the camp may be holy, lest He see the nakedness of any thing, and return;—nakedness denotes what is unclean by reason of evils and falses. That the camp there signified heaven and the church, where the Lord is, will be seen in what now follows.

10,038. "Thou shalt burn with fire out of the camp"—that hereby is signified that those things are to be committed to hell, and to be defiled with the evils of self love, appears from the signification of burning with fire, as denoting to consume with the evils of self love; for by burning is signified to consume, and by fire the evil of self love; that those things are signified by burning and by fire, may be seen n. 1297, 5071, 5248, 6314, 6832, 7324, 7575, 9041, 9434; and from the signification of the camp, as denoting heaven and the church, and in the opposite sense where heaven and the church is not, thus hell, of which we shall speak presently. The reason why to be burnt with fire denotes to be consumed by the evils of self love is, because that love consumes all the goods and truths of faith:—that self love has this effect, scarce any one at this day knows, and hence neither is it known that this love is hell with man, and that it is meant by infernal fire. For there are two fires of the life appertaining to man, one is the love of self, the other is the love to God; those who are in the love of self cannot be in love to God, since they are opposite; the reason why they are opposite is, because the love of self produces all evils, which are contempt of others in comparison with itself, enmity against those who do not favor them, at length hatreds, revenges, savageness, cruelties, which evils altogether resist Divine influx, consequently extinguish the truths and goods of faith and of charity, for these are what flow in from the Lord. That every one's love is the fire of his life, every one may know who reflects, for without love there is no life, and such as the love is such is the life; and hence that self love produces evils of every kind, and that it so far produces them, as it is regarded as an end, that is, so far as it is the ruling love. The worst kind of self love is the love of dominion for the sake of self, that is, solely for the sake of honor and gain; those who are principled in that love, may indeed make a profession of faith and charity, but they do this with the mouth and not with the heart; yea, those who are the most abandoned of them, regard the things of faith and charity,—thus the holy things of the church, as means to accomplish their own ends. Concerning self love and its genera moreover, and concerning the evils therein originating, and their state in the other life, by the Divine Mercy of the Lord, we shall speak specifically in another place; these things are said, to the intent that it may be known what is meant by being burnt with fire out of the camp. That the camp, where the sons of Israel encamped, represented heaven and the church, and hence that out of the camp, denotes where heaven and the church are not, thus where hell is, may be manifest from those things in the Word which are related of the camp and of the encampment of the sons of Israel in the wilderness, as from these words in Moses, "*The sons of Israel shall encamp a man at his camp*, and a man at his standard, according to their armies: *And the Levites shall encamp around the habitation of testimony*, that there be not wrath upon the congregation of the sons of Israel," Numb. i. 52, 53; chap. ii. 2. And again, "The tribes of Judah, of Issachar, and of Zabulon, encamped to the east; the tribes of Reuben, of Simeon, and of Gad, to the south; the tribes of Ephraim, of Manasseh, and of Benjamin, to the west; and the tribes of Dan, of Ashur, and of Naphtali, to the north; but the Levites in the midst of the camp," Numb. ii. 1 to the end; chap. x. 1 to the end. The reason why their encampments were so ordained was, that they might represent heaven and the church, n. 9320; by the tribes also, according to which they encamped, were represented all the goods and truths of heaven and of the church in the complex, n. 3858, 3926, 3939, 4060, 6335, 6337, 6397, 6640, 7836, 7891, 7996, 7997; hence it is that we read, "*That Jehovah dwells in the midst of the camp*," Numb. v. 3. "*And that he walks in the midst thereof, and therefore it shall be holy*," Deut. xxiii. 14; and in the prophetic enunciation of Balaam, "When he saw Israel *dwelling according to tribes, he said, How good are thy tabernacles, O Jacob*, and thy habitations, O Israel," Numb. xxiv. 2, 3, 5. Inasmuch as by the camp was represented heaven and the church, it follows that by out of the camp was signified where heaven and the church are not,—thus where hell is; wherefore every one that was unclean, and also that was guilty, was sent forth thither, as may be manifest from the following passages, "Ye shall send forth out of the camp every one that is leprous, and every one that suffereth a flux, every one unclean, on account of the soul, from a male even to a female, *ye shall send them abroad out of the camp, that they may not pollute the camp*, in the midst of which Jehovah dwells," Numb. v. 2, 3; Levit. xiii. 15, 16. "A man who is not clean by chance of the night, *shall go forth abroad out of the camp*, *neither shall he come into the midst of the camp;* when he hath washed himself with waters, and the sun is set, he shall enter into the camp. There shall be a space for thee *out of the camp*, whither thou mayest go forth abroad, and by a paddle thou shalt cover thine excrement, because Jehovah walks in the midst of the camp, therefore the camp shall be holy," Deut. xxiii. 10 to 15; and that they should be stoned out of the camp, Levit. xxiv. 14; Numb. xv. 35, 36. From these passages it is now manifest that by burning with fire the flesh, the skin, and the dung of the bullock, out of the camp, is signified that the evils, which are signified by those things, were to be committed to hell. What was represented by the camp, and by out of the camp, was also represented by the land of Canaan, and by the countries [terræ] round about it, after that land had been distributed for inheritances amongst the sons of Israel; hence it is that by the land of Canaan, and simply by land [or earth, or country] in the Word, is signified heaven and the church, and by the sons of Israel, those who are in heaven and the church; that by land is signified heaven and the church, may be seen in what is cited, n. 9325; and that by the sons of Israel are signified those who are therein, n. 9340.

10,039. "This is sin"—that hereby is signified what is purified from evils and falses, appears from the signification of sin, when by it is meant sacrifice, as denoting purification from evils and falses; for in the original tongue *by sin*, where sacrifices are treated of, is meant *sacrifice for sin*, and by sacrifice is signified purification from evils and falses, n. 9990, 9991. That sacrifice for sin in the Word is called sin, may be seen Levit. iv. 3, 8, 14, 20, 21, 24, 25, 29, 33, 34; chap. v. 6, 8, 9; chap. xvi. 9, 25, and elsewhere.

10,040. Inasmuch as the flesh of the bullock with his skin and dung was to be burnt with fire out of the camp, it may be manifest that by the flesh was not signified the good, but the evil of love, according to what was said before concerning his flesh, n. 10,035, and concerning the camp just above, n. 10,039. But the reason why it was granted to eat the flesh of the sacrifice, as may be manifest from the passages which follow, was, because the Israelitish and Jewish nation, whilst in worship, was in an external principle without an internal, (see what is cited n. 9320, 9380); and an external principle without an internal is not at all holy, because in such case gesture alone acts, and the mouth speaks, but the heart and soul are absent. Nevertheless the external without the internal was called holy, because it represented holy internal things;—holy internal things are all those which are of love and faith from the Lord to the Lord. Now since that nation was of such a quality, it was not allowed them to eat blood and fat, inasmuch as by blood was signified the Divine Truth which is of faith, and by fat the Divine Good which is of love, each from the Lord, see above, n. 10,033; but they were allowed to eat the flesh of the sacrifice, because by it was signified the proprium of man, n. 10,035, and the proprium of that nation was to worship external things as holy, and to make no account at all of internal things, which worship, if we except its being representative, and thereby holy, was idolatrous, see n. 4281, 4311. The flesh also representatively was nothing else, when its blood represented Divine Truth, and its fat Divine Good, n. 10,033, for then the flesh represented something without life and soul, which is called dead, such as is an external principle without an internal, according to these words in Moses, "Thou shalt not eat the blood, because the blood is the soul; thou shalt not eat the soul with the flesh," Deut. xii. 23. *Nearly similar worship prevails with a nation of the Catholic religion as it is called, namely, external without internal [worship], for it is not given the common people to know the internal things of the Word, since they are forbidden to read the Word; on which account also by the Divine Providence of the Lord it has come to pass, that in the holy supper the bread was given, which is the flesh, and not the wine which is the blood; and yet the blood is what vivifies the flesh, as the wine the bread; for as bread without the wine [or some other liquid], does not afford nourishment to the body, so neither does the good of love, which is signified by bread and by flesh, without the truth of faith, which is signified by wine and by blood, give nourishment to the soul. By the Divine Providence of the Lord it has come to pass, that the priest should drink the wine, because by it is signified the nourishment of the soul by Divine Truth without the good of love, which is an external holy principle without an internal holy principle; that this has come to pass by the Divine Providence of the Lord, they do not know, by reason that they idolatrously adore things external, and thus do not apprehend things internal; wherefore if it had been otherwise, they would have profaned things holy, in like manner as the Jews:—by drinking the wine only is also signified to know Divine Truth only, whilst the vulgar do not know it, except according to the quantity and quality in which they will them to know it, as is also the case there. That in the holy supper the flesh and the bread denote the Divine Good of the Divine Love of the Lord towards the human race, and the reciprocal [love] of man to the Lord; and that the blood and the wine denote the Divine Truth proceeding from the Divine Good of the Lord, thus the truth of faith from the Lord to the Lord*, see n. 3464, 3813, 4211, 4217, 4735, 4796, 6135, 6189, 6377, 7850, 9127. In reference to the flesh of the sacrifices, when it was to be brought forth out of the camp, and to be burned with fire, may be seen Levit. iv. 11, 12, 21; and when and by whom it was to be eaten, Levit. vi. 19 to the end; chap. vii. 6, 15 to 19; chap. xix. 5, 6; Deut. xii. 7, 17, 18, 27; chap. xxvii. 6, 7.

10,041. Verses 15, 16, 17, 18. *And thou shalt take one ram, and Aaron and his sons shall put their hands upon the head of the ram. And thou shalt slay the ram, and shalt take the blood of it, and shalt sprinkle [it] upon the altar round about. And thou shalt cut the ram into his segments, and shalt wash his intestines, and his legs, and shalt give [them] upon his segments, and upon his head; and thou shalt cause the altar to burn with the whole ram; this is a burnt-offering to Jehovah, an odor of rest, this is an offering by fire to Jehovah.* And thou shalt take one ram, signifies the good of innocence in the internal man. And Aaron and his sons shall lay their hands, signifies the communication of power. Upon the head of the ram, signifies with the whole. And thou shalt slay the ram, signifies preparation for the purification of the internal man. And thou shalt take the blood, signifies Divine Truth; and shalt sprinkle it upon the altar round about, signifies conjunction with Divine Good. And thou shalt cut the ram into segments, signifies interior things to be distinctly arranged into order. And thou shalt wash the intestines, signifies purification of lowest things; and his legs, signifies the purification of the exterior things, which are of the natural man. And thou shalt give them upon his segments and upon his head, signifies the orderly arrangement of exterior things beneath internal and inmost things. And thou shalt cause the altar to burn with the whole ram, signifies the internal of the Lord's Divine Human united to the Divine Good of His Divine Love which was in Himself. This is a burnt-offering to Jehovah, signifies the glorification of the Lord's Human. An odor of rest, signifies perceptive of peace. This is an offering by fire to Jehovah, signifies all things from the Divine Love.

10,042. "And thou shalt take one ram"—that hereby is signified the good of innocence in the internal man, appears from the signification of a ram, as denoting the good of innocence and of charity in the internal man, of which we shall speak presently. Now as it treats in this chapter concerning the sacrifices and burnt-offerings of rams and of lambs, it may be expedient to say what was signified by the animals in general, which were offered for sacrifices and burnt-offerings. Those animals were oxen, bullocks, he-goats, rams, she-goats, he-kids; also he-lambs, she-lambs, and the female kids of she-goats. He who does not know what these animals signify, cannot in any wise know what is especially signified by the sacrifice and burnt-offerings of them. It is to be observed, that all animals, which are in the earths, signify such things as appertain to man, which in general have reference to the affections of his will, and to the thoughts of his understanding, thus to goods and to truths, for goods are of the will, and truths are of the understanding; and since they have reference to goods and truths, they have also reference to love and to faith, for all things which are of the love are called goods, and all things which are of the faith are called truths. This signification of animals of different kinds originates in representatives in the other life; for in that life there appears animals of numerous genera, and of innumerable species; such animals are appearances there which have an exact and living correspondence to the affections and the thoughts appertaining to spirits and angels. That this is the fact, may also be proved from the prophetic visions in the Word throughout; for all things which were seen by the prophets, are such as appear in heaven before the angels: hence it is that such frequent mention is made in the Word of beasts, and by every one of them is signtfied something which has reference to such things as appertain to man,—spoken of above. Nor is man himself any thing else but an animal as to his external man, but he is distinguished by the internal man, whereby both the latter and the former can be elevated towards heaven and to God, and thence receive faith and love;—hence it is that beasts were employed in sacrifices and burnt offerings. He who does not know these things, can in no wise know why it was commanded at one time to offer bullocks, rams, he-lambs, at another time oxen, she-goats, and she-lambs, at another time he-goats, he-kids, and she-kids of the she-goats; for otherwise to what purpose would such distinctions be made? That beasts in the Word signify goods and evils appertaining to man, and also truths and falses, see n. 142, 143, 246, 714, 715, 776, 1823, 2179, 2180, 2781, 3218, 3519, 5198, 7523, 7872, 9090, and that on this account they were employed in sacrifices, n. 1823, 2180, 2805, 2807, 2830. But as to what concerns sacrifices and burnt-offerings from them, it is to be noted, I. That representative worship with the Jewish and Israelitish nation consisted chiefly in sacrifices and burnt-offerings. II. That sacrifices and burnt-offerings in general signified the regeneration of man by the truths of faith and the goods of love from the Lord; and in the supreme sense, the glorification of the Lord's Human. III. That the all of worship was represented by sacrifices and burnt-offerings according to its various things [or principles], thus with all variety; and that on this account various kinds of animals were commanded. But to be more particular: I. *That representative worship with the Jewish and Israelitish nation consisted chiefly in sacrifices and burnt-offerings*, is manifest from the consideration that they were made use of for every sin and for all guilt; also for every consecration and inauguration; and further on every day, on every sabbath, on every new moon, and on every festival; and that on this account the altar was the most holy of all things. All other parts of worship with that nation depended upon these; therefore where the abolition of representative worship is treated of in Daniel, it is said that the *sacrifice and oblation* shall cease, chap. ix. 27; and the *continual* [sacrifice] shall be removed, chap. viii. 10, 11, 12, 13; chap. xi. 31; chap. xii. 11; by the continual [sacrifice] is specifically signified the sacrifice which was offered daily, and in general all worship. See moreover what has been shown before on this subject, namely, that sacrifices in general signify all representative worship, n. 923, 2165, 6905, 8680, 8936. That the altar was the principal representative of the Lord and hence of worship, n. 2777, 2811, 8935, 8940, 9388, 9389, 9714, 9964. That the ancients before Eber knew nothing of sacrifices, n. 2180. That from Eber, thus with the Hebrew nation, and thence with the posterity of Jacob, sacrifices were instituted, and why, n. 1178, 1343, 2180, 2818. That sacrifices were not commanded, but permitted, n. 2180. II. *That sacrifices and burnt-offerings in general signified the regeneration of man by the truths of faith and the goods of love to the Lord from the Lord*, is manifest from this consideration, that all things of worship have reference to purification from evils and falses, to the implantation of truth and good, and to their conjunction,—thus to regeneration, for by those three things man is regenerated; hence it is that sacrifices and burnt-offerings were offered for all sin and for all guilt; and when they were offered, it is said, that expiation was made and that pardon was granted, Levit. iv. 20, 26, 31, 35; chap. v. 6, 10, 13, 16, 18; chap. vi. 7; chap. vii. 7; chap. x. 17; chap. xiv. 18, 19; chap. xv. 30, 31; chap. xvi. 6, 24; chap. xvii. 11. The pardon of sins, expiation, propitiation, and redemption, are also nothing else but purification from evils and falses, the implantation of good and of truth, and their conjunction, thus regeneration, n. 9056, 9452, 9453, 9454, 9937, 9938. The entire process of regeneration is also described by each of [singular] the rituals of every sacrifice and burnt-offering, and is made manifest when the representatives are unfolded by the internal sense, n. 10,022. *The reason why sacrifices and burnt-offerings in the supreme sense signify the glorification of the Lord's Human [principle]* is, because all the rituals of worship instituted amongst the Israelitish and Jewish nation had reference to the Lord alone; thus sacrifices and burnt-offerings, by which in general was represented the all of worship, as was shown above, principally regarded Him; the regeneration of man also is from no other source than from the Lord, n. 9506, 9715, 9486, 9487, 9809, 10,019; wherefore where the subject treated of in the Word is the regeneration of man, in the supreme sense the glorification of the Lord's Human is treated of; for the regeneration of man is an image of the Lord's glorification; n. 3138, 3212, 3296, 3490, 4402, 5688. To glorify the Human [principle] is to make it Divine, but to regenerate man, is to make him celestial, that the Divine of the Lord may dwell in him. III. *That the all of worship according to its various particulars, was represented by sacrifices and burnt-offerings, thus with all variety, and that on this account different kinds of animals were commanded*, is manifest from the various things for which sacrifices and burnt-offerings were made, namely, for sins by error, and for sins not by error, for every prevarication and uncleanness, whether with the priest or with the whole assembly, or with the prince, or with any soul; for cleansing from the leprosy, for purification after the birth; for the consecration of the altar, of the tent of the congregation, and of all things therein; for the cleansing of the same when Aaron once every year entered into the holy of holies; for the inauguration of Aaron and of his sons into the priesthood; for the consecration of the Nazarites; and in general on the three festivals, on each of the new moons, on the sabbaths, and on days in the morning and between the evenings, besides votive and voluntary offerings. Because the sacrifices and burnt-offerings were for such various occasions, and because by them were represented the various particulars of worship, therefore also the different kinds of animals, which were to be offered, were expressly commanded, namely, bullocks, oxen, and he-goats, rams, she-goats and he-kids; he-lambs, she-lambs, and female-kids of the she-goats; and by the sacrifices and burnt-offerings of the bullock, the ox, and the he-goat were represented the purification and regeneration of the external or natural man; of the ram, the she-goat, and the he-kid, were represented the purification and regeneration of the internal or spiritual man; and of the he-lamb, the she-lamb, and the female-kid of the she-goats were represented the purification or regeneration of the inmost or celestial man. That there are three principles which have an orderly succession in man, the celestial, the spiritual, and the natural, may be seen, n. 9992, 10,005, 10,017; and that man must be regenerated as to internals and as to externals, before he can be a regenerate man, see what is cited, n. 9325 at the end. But what is specifically signified by the sacrifice and burnt-offering from the ram, which are treated of in this chapter, is manifest from the passages in the Word, where sacrifices and burnt-offerings from the ram are described, and where the ram is named; from which it is evident that by the ram is signified the good of innocence and of charity in the internal man, and by the sacrifice and burnt-offering from it the purification and regeneration of the internal man, thus the implantation of the good of innocence and of charity therein. That this is signified by a ram is manifest from the following passages, "All the flocks of Arabia shall be gathered together unto thee, *the rams of Nebaioth shall minister unto thee, they shall come up for what is well pleasing to My altar.*" Isaiah lx. 7. In this passage it treats of the Lord, and of His heaven and church;—the flocks of Arabia denote all the goods of the internal man;—and the rams of Nebaioth are the goods of innocence and of charity there. That flocks denote the goods of the internal man, may be seen, n. 8937, 9135; that Arabia denotes where good is, n. 3268; and that Nebaioth denotes those who are there in good, n. 3268, 3686, 3688. And in Ezekiel, "Arabia and all the princes of Kedar, the traders of thy hand by *cattle* and *rams* and *he-goats*," xxvii. 21, speaking of Tyre, by which is signified the church where the knowledges of good and of truth are, n. 1201; traders denote those who have those knowledges and communicate them, n. 2967, 4453; cattle the goods of love, rams the goods of charity, and he-goats the goods of faith. In the Word flocks, cattle [*pecora*], and cattle [*pecudes*] which in the original language are distinguished by their names; and by flocks are signified in general internal things, by cattle [*pecudes*] the same things specifically, and by cattle [*pecora*] inmost things specically; but by herds things external. And in Jeremiah, "I will cause them to descend as *cattle* [*pecora*] to be slaughtered, as *rams* with *he-goats*," li. 40; where by cattle, rams, and he-goats similar things are signified. And in Ezekiel, "Thus saith the Lord Jehovah, Behold I judge between *cattle* [*pecudes*] *and cattle* [*pecudes*], and between the *rams* and the *he-goats*," xxxiv. 17. Between cattle and cattle, denotes between those who are in the interiors of good and of evil; between the rams and the he-goats denotes between those who are in charity and thence in faith, and those who are in the truths of faith without charity;—rams in this passage signify the like as sheep, for rams are the males of sheep;—that sheep denote those who are in charity and thence in faith, may be seen, n. 4169, 4809; and that he-goats denote those who are in truths, which are called the truths of faith, without charity, n. 4169, 4769. Similar is the signification of the *ram* and the *he-goat* in Daniel, chap. viii. 1 to the end, and also of the *sheep* and the *he-goats* in Matthew, chap. xxv. 32. And in Moses, "If a soul shall sin through error, he shall bring his guilt to Jehovah *an entire ram of the flock*," Levit. v. 15, 18; chap. vi. 6. By sacrifices from a ram is signified the purification of the internal man, and the implantation of the good of innocence therein; for sin by error is sin grounded in ignorance wherein is innocence, and the innocence of ignorance is of the internal man. Again, "In the new moons they shall offer two *bullocks*, one *ram*, and seven *he-lambs*; and afterwards a *he-goat of the she-goats*. In like manner on every day of the passover: and in like manner *on the day of the first-fruits*," Numb. xxviii. 11, 15, 19, 22, 27. This was to represent the purification of the whole man, external, internal, and inmost; by the sacrifice and burnt-offering from bullocks the purification of the external man, from a ram the purification of the internal, and from lambs the purification of the inmost; and since purification was represented, so was also the implantation of the good of innocence, for a bullock denotes the good of innocence in the external man, a ram in the internal, and a he-lamb in the inmost, as was said above. The reason why the last of these was a he-goat was, because by a he-goat was signified the truth of faith in the external man, and the truth of faith there is the ultimate principle, n. 9959. Inasmuch as the goods and truths appertaining to man follow in that order, therefore also the presents of the princes of Israel, when the altar was anointed and the tent of the congregation, were *a bullock*, *a ram*, and a *he-lamb*, for burnt-offerings; and a *he-goat of the she-goat* for a sacrifice. Numb. vii. 15, 16, 17, 21, 22, 23, 27, 28, 29, 33 and following verses. From these considerations it may now be manifest, that a ram signifies the good of innocence and of charity in the internal man.

10,043. "And Aaron and his sons shall put their hands"—that hereby is signified communication of power, appears from the signification of laying on of hands, as denoting the communication of power,—see above, n. 10,023.

10,044. "Upon the head of the ram"—that hereby is signified with the whole, appears from the signification of the head, as denoting the whole man, thus the whole, see n. 10,011. The reason why the head denotes the whole is, because it is the highest, and therein is the inmost principle of man; and from what is supreme proceed all things which are beneath, as also from what is inmost proceed all things which are without, for the latter and former things are thence derived; the inmost principle appertaining to man is his will and understanding, these in their beginnings [*principia*] are in the head, and the things which thence proceed are acts [or deeds], which are effects of interior principles in the body; wherefore when mention is made of the will and the understanding, the whole man is meant, for thence man is a man. The acts of the body also have from the will all that belongs to them; hence it is, that man is not regarded from the acts of the body or works, but from the will in them; this being the case, by *soul* in the Word is meant the whole man, and man is called a soul, as in Levit. iv. 27; chap. v. 1, 4, 17; chap. vi. 2; chap. xvii. 10, 15, and elsewhere. There are two things which signify the whole, namely, what is highest and lowest. The reason why what is lowest or ultimate signifies also the whole is, because all interior things, even from the first to the highest, terminate in ultimates, and are there together, see n. 9828, 9836. Hence it is that the highest, by means of what is ultimate, holds together all the interior things which are intermediate in connection and in form, so that they look to one end, n. 9878. That what is ultimate also signifies the whole, is manifest from numerous passages in the Word, as when the whole man is called flesh, Gen.

vi. 12; Numb. xvi. 22; chap. xxvii. 16; Isaiah xl. 5; Zech. ii. 13, and elsewhere. Inasmuch as ultimates also signify all or the whole, therefore hair [*crinis*], hair [*pilus*], the beard, which are ultimates that are excrescent with man, are taken for all or the whole,—also the feet, yea the toes and fingers. That *hair* [*crinis*], *hair* [*pilus*], and *beard* are so, is manifest from Isaiah, "In that day the Lord *shall shave with a razor* by the king of Assyria *the head*, the hair [*pilus*] *of the feet* and also the *beard*," vii. 20; the king of Assyria denotes reasoning, such as is that of those who by it destroy things divine, n. 1186;—to shave the head, the hair of the feet, and the beard, denotes to take away ultimates, for when these are taken away interior things flow away, and perish; on this account also a priest was forbidden to *shave the head*, Levit. xxi. 10, and also a Nazarite, whose hair [*coma*] was called the Nazariteship of God, Numb. vi.; n. 6437, 9407, and is meant by *the crown of the head of the Nazarite* of the brethren, Gen. xlix. 25, 26; Deut. xxxiii. 16. Hence also it is said *that the hairs of the head are all numbered*, Matt. x. 30, by which is signified that each and every thing in man is so; also that *a hair of the head shall not perish*, Luke xxi. 18. That the feet also, and the toes, and fingers, signify all things, and thus the whole, is manifest from John, "Peter said, Lord, Thou shalt not wash my feet only, but also the hands and the head; Jesus said to him, *he who is washed hath no need to be washed but as to the feet, and the whole is clean*," xii. 9, 10; the feet denote the natural principle, which is the ultimate, n. 2162, 3147, 4938 to 4952, 9406. And in what follows in this chapter, "Thou shalt give of the blood of the ram upon the auricle of the ear of Aaron, and *upon the thumb of the right hand, and upon the great toe of the right foot*," verse 20; which denotes upon all and singular the things which are signified by the ear, the hand, and the foot. Inasmuch as what is highest and what is lowest, or what is the same, what is first and what is last, alike signify each and every thing, or the whole with its parts, therefore the omnipotence and omniscience of the Lord is described by His being *the first and the last, the beginning and the end, the alpha and omega*, Apoc. i. 8, 11; chap. xxi. 6; chap. xxii. 13; Isaiah xli. 4. That all things are held together in connection, and stand together from the first or highest by [or through] the last or lowest, is thus described in Isaiah, "*I am the first and I am the last*, also My hand hath founded *the earth*, and My right hand hath spanned *the heaven; I call them together, they stand together*," xlviii. 12, 13; where the hand and right hand of Jehovah, or of the Lord, denotes omnipotence; the earth which he hath founded is the ultimate; the heaven which he stretched out is what is between the first and the last; to call them together that they may stand together, denotes to hold together all interior things by what is last in connection and in form, that they may look to one end;—the one end to which they are to look is He who is the first and the last. That He is the Lord, is manifest from Isaiah, "Thus saith Jehovah, *the king of Israel and his Redeemer, I am the first and I the last,*" xliv. 6; where the king of Israel denotes the Lord, John xviii. 37; that the Redeemer is the Lord is evident. And in the Apocalypse, "These things saith *the first and the last*, who was dead and is alive again," ii. 8. That the first holds together all things in connection by means of the last, may be manifest from *the Word* and from *man*; the Word in ultimates is the sense of its letter, and the Word in first [principles] is the Lord, and the Word in interiors is its internal sense, which is perceived in the heavens, and has this effect, that the inhabitants look to one end, which is the Lord; concerning this arcanum, see n. 9560, 9824. As regards man, man in ultimates is the church in the earths, man in first [principles] is the Lord, man in interiors is heaven, for the church and heaven before the Lord is as one man, on which account heaven is called the GRAND MAN, treated of at the close of several chapters, (see what is cited at the end of n. 10,030). There is a continual connection and influx according to connection of all things from the Lord through the heavens to the church in the earths; by the heavens are meant the angels who are there, by the church the men who are true men of the church, and by man in first [principles] the Lord as to His Divine Human; that from the first by [or through] the last all things are held together in connection, and stand together, is meant by the Lord's words above quoted in Isaiah, "*I am the first and I am the last, also My hand hath founded the earth,* and My *right hand hath spanned the heaven, I call them together, they stand together,*" xlviii. 12, 13; that by the earth in the Word is meant the church, has also been abundantly shown,—see what is cited, n. 9325. An idea of this subject may be obtained from what is ultimate and what is inmost with man; the ultimate is the skin, the inmost is the heart, the things intermediate or interior are the viscera; from the heart even to the skin through the viscera there is a continuous connection by the blood vessels, for these proceed from the heart, and terminate in the skin;—that the skin is the ultimate, holding interior things in connection, is evident, for if the skin be taken away interior things flow forth. From these considerations it may be seen why it is, that as what is supreme or inmost signifies all and every thing [omnia et singula], so also does what is lowest or ultimate. From the same considerations also is discovered the arcanum, why the Lord glorified His Human even as to ultimates; the ultimates are called bones and flesh, wherefore the Lord said to His disciples, who supposed that they saw a spirit, "Behold

My hands and My feet, that I Am; *handle Me and see, for a spirit hath not flesh and bones as ye see Me have,*" Luke xxiv. 37, 39. That the Divine [principle] itself was the first in Him, is known well, for He was conceived from Jehovah, and what is conceived from the Father, this is the first [principle] of the man; that the Lord glorified even the ultimates of His Human, is evident from His words in the above passage, and also from this consideration, that He left nothing of His Human in the sepulchre. That interior things terminate and are at rest in ultimates, and are there together, and that ultimates hold interior things in connection, also in spiritual things, may be seen, n. 9216, 9828—that on this account strength and power are in ultimates, n. 9836—and that on this account sanctity is in ultimates, n. 9824—and that in ultimates there are revelations and responses, n. 9905.

10,045. "And thou shalt slay the ram"—that hereby is signified preparation for the purification of the internal man, appears from the signification of slaying, when spoken of the sacrifice or burnt-offering, as denoting preparation for purification, see n. 10,024; and from the signification of the ram, which is as to the internal man, see above, n. 10,042.

10,046. "And shalt take the blood of it"—that hereby is signified Divine Truth, see n. 10,026, 10,033; that all purification from evils and falses, and all regeneration, is effected by Divine Truth proceeding from the Lord, may be seen in what is cited, n. 9959.

10,047. "And shalt sprinkle [it] upon the altar round about" —that hereby is signified conjunction with Divine Good, appears from the signification of the blood, which was to be sprinkled upon the altar round about, as denoting the Divine Truth, see n. 10,026, 10,033; and from the representation of the altar, as being representative of the Lord as to Divine Good, see n. 9388, 9389, 9714, 9964; hence it is evident that to sprinkle the blood upon the altar round about denotes to unite Divine Truth with Divine Good in the Lord. The case herein is this; it was said above that the subject treated of in this chapter is the glorification of the Lord's Human, and in the representative sense the regeneration of man from the Lord. As to what concerns the glorification of the Lord's Human it was effected by the unition of Divine Truth with Divine Good; the Divine Good, which is Jehovah, was in the Lord, as the soul from the father is in man, for He was conceived of Jehovah, and made His Human Divine Truth by Divine means, especially by temptation-combats, and so much as He united, so much He glorified, that is, made Divine. This unition is what is signified in the supreme sense by the sprinkling of the blood round about the altar. That the Lord, when He was in the world, made His Human Divine Truth, and united it with Divine Good, which was in Himself, and thereby glorified His Human, may be seen in what is cited, n. 9199, 9315. And that Jehovah His Father is the Divine Good, which was in Him, n. 9194. As the Lord glorified His Human, so He also regenerates man; for the Lord with man flows in with good through the soul which is by an internal way, and with truth through the hearing and the sight, which is by an external way, and so far as man desists from evils, so far the Lord conjoins good with truth, and the good becomes [the good] of charity towards the neighbor and of love to God, and the truth becomes [the truth] of faith. Thus the Lord creates man anew, or regenerates him, for the regeneration of man, as was said above, is effected by purification from evils and falses, by the implantation of good and of truth, and by their conjunction; —the regeneration of man, and in the supreme sense the glorification of the Lord's Human, are what were represented by sacrifices and burnt offerings, n. 10,022. It is to be noted, that in the burnt-offerings the blood was sprinkled upon the altar round about; in like manner in the eucharistic sacrifices; but in the sacrifices for guilt and for sin the blood was sprinkled at the foundation of the altar. By the sprinkling of the blood on the altar round about was represented the unition of Divine Truth and Divine Good in every mode, both in the internal and external man,—and by the sprinkling of the blood at the foundation of the altar was represented the unition of Divine Truth and Divine Good in the external man only. With the regenerate, conjunction is effected in the external man, according to the Lord's words in John, "He who is washed, hath need only to be washed as to the feet, and is wholly clean," xii. 9, 10, washing signifies purification and regeneration, n. 3147, 9809, thus he that is washed signifies one who is purified and regenerated; and the feet signify the natural or external principle of man, n. 2162, 3147, 4938 to 4952, 9406. That in the burnt-offerings blood was sprinkled upon the altar round about, see Levit. i. 5, 11; also in the eucharistic sacrifices, Levit. iii. 2, 8, 13; and that in the sacrifices for guilt and for sin the blood was sprinkled at the foundation of the altar, Levit. iv. 7, 18, 25, 30, 34; chap. v. 9.

10,048. "And thou shalt cut the ram into his segments"—that hereby are signified interior things to be distinctly arranged into order, appears from the signification of the ram, as denoting the good of innocence and of charity in the internal man, see n. 10,052, here preparation for his purification, which is signified by the burnt-offering from the ram; and from the signification of cutting into segments, as denoting the orderly arrangement of interior things therein. The reason why preparation for the orderly arrangement of interior things is signified by cutting into segments, pieces, members, and parts is, because an orderly arrangement is described by the intestines and legs being given upon the segments and upon the head, and by the intestines are signified the lowest principles which are called external sensual, by the legs the proximately superior principles, which are called natural; thus by the segments, which were still superior, are signified interior principles, and by the head inmost principles. That such things are signified by the intestines, the legs, and the head, will be manifest from what follows;—that by the viscera and members of man such things are signified in order, may be seen above, n. 10,030. Inasmuch as in the representative sense by sacrifices and burnt-offerings is meant the regeneration of man, it may be expedient briefly to state how an orderly arrangement is effected therein. With those who are being regenerated, interior and exterior things are arranged in order by the Lord for all succeeding states, insomuch that present things involve those which are future, and things future, when they become present, do the same, and this to eternity; for the Lord foresees all things and provides all things, and His foresight and providence is to eternity, thus is eternal; for the Divine, which alone is His, is in itself infinite, and what is infinite in respect to duration is eternal; hence it is that whatsoever the Lord arranges and ordains is eternal. This is the case with those whom the Lord regenerates; the regeneration of man commences in the world, and continues to eternity, for man, when he becomes an angel, is always being perfected. There are in man things external, internal, and inmost; all these are arranged and restored to order together and successively for the reception of what is to succeed them to eternity. But in what order external, interior, and inmost things are regenerated, and how the unregenerate are circumstanced, will be shown, by the Divine Mercy of the Lord, in what follows.

10,049. "And shalt wash his intestines"—that hereby is signified the purification of lowest [things or principles], appears from the, signification of washing, as denoting to purify, see n. 3147, 5954, 9089. The purification, which was represented by washing, is purification from evils and falses, for these are filth in the spiritual sense; and from the signification of the intestines as denoting the lowest things, see above, n. 10,039. The reason why it is said that the intestines and the legs were to be washed is, because by them are signified lowest and natural [things], and lowest or natural [things] are more defiled with evils and falses than interior things; for the former are in the world, and sensual [things or principles], which are the lowest, are extant in the world, and therefore immediately receive those things which are in the world. Those things which they receive are the delights of the loves of self and of the world, together with the delights of the senses, and their fallacies. Interior [things or principles], however, are not so circumstanced, for these are not in the world, but in heaven; and those things which are of the world cannot enter into those which are of heaven, for physical influx is not given, but those things which are of heaven can enter into those which are of the world with man; wherefore as soon as the external man wishes to let himself into the internal,—which is effected by reasonings from the loves of self and of the world, and from the fallacies of the senses,—the internal man is closed; this is provided of the Lord: wherefore the purification of the internal man, during man's regeneration, is effected in heaven from the Lord. Hence it is that man, when he is in the world, does not perceive what is transacting in his internal man during regeneration; and these are the [arcana] which are meant by the Lord's words in John, "The spirit breatheth where it willeth, and thou hearest the voice thereof, but knowest not whence it cometh, and whither it goeth, so is every one who is born of the spirit," iii. 8;—the spirit is the life of charity by faith.

10,050. "And his legs"—that hereby is signified the purification of the exteriors which are of the natural man, is evident from the signification of washing the legs, as denoting the purification of the natural man;—that to wash denotes to purify, may be seen just above, n. 10,049;—and from the signification of the legs, as denoting the exterior [things or principles] which are of the natural man. The reason why the legs have this signification is, because the feet are meant at the same time, for the legs of beasts are four, and are continuous with the feet, and the feet from correspondence signify the natural or external principle of man, see n. 2162, 3147, 3765, 4938, to 4952. The same is signified by the legs in Amos, "As a shepherd snatched from the mouth of a lion *two legs*, or a portion of an ear, so shall the sons of Israel be snatched away that dwell in Samaria, in the corner of the bed, and in the extremity of a couch," iii. 12; by a lion those who vastate the church are here signified; by legs the external of a church, which also is of the natural man; by the auricle of the ear its perceptive principle; by the dwellers in Samaria those who are in external worship; the corner of a bed and the extremity of a couch denote the lowest natural principle, which is the external sensual principle, and its truth and good. By the legs, where the statue of Nebuchadnezzar is treated of in Daniel, where it is said, that its head was of pure gold, the breast and the arms of silver, the belly and the side of brass, the legs of iron, and the feet partly of iron, partly of clay," ii. 32, 33, the truth of faith in the external or natural man, which also is iron, is signified, may be seen, n. 10,030. The reason why the legs are here distinguished from the feet is, because the legs with man are otherwise circumstanced than with beasts.

10,051. "And shalt give [them] upon his segments and upon his head"—that hereby is signified the subordination of exterior things or principles to such as are interior and inmost, appears from the signification of the segments, as denoting interior things, as may be seen above, n. 10,048; from the signification of the head, as denoting what is inmost, n. 5328, 6436, 9656, 9913, 9914; and from the signification of the intestines and of the legs, which were to be given upon them, as denoting things outermost and exterior. That the intestines denote outermost or lowest things or principles may be seen, n. 10,030, and that legs denote exterior things, n. 10,050; and from the signification of giving the latter upon the former, as denoting to arrange into order. The reason why it denotes the orderly arrangement of exterior beneath interior things, and not upon them according to the sense of the letter is, because the altar and the fire upon the altar denote supreme or inmost things, for the altar represented the Divine Human of the Lord as to Divine Good, and the fire the Divine Love Itself, wherefore those parts of the ram and the burnt-offering, which were nearest to the fire of the altar, were superior or interior, and those which had a place above them, inasmuch as they were more remote from the fire of the altar, were inferior or exterior; for in the external sense, contrary to that of the letter, those things are regarded as superior or interior which are nearest to the supreme, and as inferior or exterior which are more remote from it. Whether we speak of things superior and interior, or of things inferior and exterior, it is the same; for what is superior, that is interior, and what is inferior, that is exterior, n. 2148, 3084, 4599, 5146, 8325. Hence now it is evident, that by giving the intestines and the legs upon the segments and the head, is signified that outermost or exterior things were to be arranged in subordination to interior or inmost things. That the altar was representative of the Divine Human of the Lord as to Divine Good, may be seen, n. 921, 2777, 2811, 9388, 9389, 9714, 9964; also that the fire of the altar denotes His Divine Love.

10,052. "And thou shalt cause the altar to burn with the whole ram"—that hereby is signified the internal of the Lord's Divine Human united to the Divine Good of His Divine Love which was in Himself, is evident from the signification of causing to burn, as denoting to unite to the Divine Good of the Divine Love, of which we shall speak presently; and from the signification of the ram, as denoting the internal principle appertaining to man, thus in the supreme sense the internal of the Lord's Divine Human, concerning which, see n. 10,042; and from the signification of the altar, as being the principal representative of the Lord's Divine Human as to His Divine Good, as was shown just above, n. 10,051 at the end. It is to be noted, that with every man there is an internal and an external, which are called his internal and external man, and that when man is regenerated he is regenerated both as to the internal and as to the external, and that regeneration is the conjunction of good and of truth in each. It was similar with the Lord as to His Human; yet it cannot be said of His Human that it was regenerated, but that it was glorified, for His inmost, which with man is called the soul from the father, was the Divine itself, inasmuch as He was conceived from Jehovah. The Divine itself is the Divine Good of the Divine Love; and since the Lord united His Human with this, and thereby made also His Human [principle] Divine, therefore it cannot be said that His Human was regenerated, but glorified, for to glorify is to make Divine, as may be seen just below, n. 10,053. The glorification of His internal man, or of His internal Human [principle], is described by representatives in the burnt-offerings from rams and from lambs. The reason why causing the altar to burn with the whole ram denotes to unite the Divine Good of the Divine Love with the internal of His Human principle is, because the altar was representative of the Lord's Divine Human, and the fire upon the altar, with which the burnt-offering was burned, signified the Divine Good of the Divine Love, as may be manifest from what was cited just above, n. 10,051 at the end; and because the ram, which was the burnt-offering and which was burned, signifies the internal principle appertaining to man, thus the internal of the Lord's Human, n. 10,042. From these considerations it is evident, that by causing the altar to burn with the whole ram for a burnt-offering, the internal of the Lord's Human united to the Divine Good of His Divine Love, which was in Himself, is signified.

10,053. "This is a burnt-offering to Jehovah"—that hereby is signified the glorification of the Lord's Human, is manifest from the representation of a burnt-offering, as denoting the glorification of the Lord's Human. With the Jewish nation there were sacrifices and burnt-offerings; the sacrifices signified purification from evils and falses, and the implantation of truth, but the burnt-offerings the conjunction of truth with good, thus plenary regeneration. In the supreme sense however, in which the Lord is treated of, sacrifices signified the ejection of evils and of falses from His Human which was from the mother, and the implantation of Divine Truth from the Divine Good which was in Himself, and burnt-offerings signified the unition of the Divine Truth with the Divine Good, which unition is what is meant by glorification; for the Lord, when He was in the world, made His Human Divine Truth, and successively also by unition with the Divine Good which was in Himself, and was the esse of His life, He made His Human Divine Good, thus one with Jehovah. The esse of His life was what with man is called the soul from the father, and this was Divine Good itself or Divine Love; but on these subjects, see what was shown in the passages cited, n. 9194, 9315, 9528; and that the Lord expelled all the Human which was from the mother, until at length he was not her son, n. 9315; and that the Son of Man, whom the Lord called Himself, is not the son of Mary but the Divine Truth, n. 9807. That glorification, where the Lord is treated of, denotes the unition of His Human with the Divine itself which was in Himself, thus with Jehovah His Father, by which unition He made His Human also Divine Good, is manifest from the passages in the Word where mention is made of glory and glorification, when spoken of Jehovah or the Lord, as in Isaiah, "The *glory of Jehovah* shall be revealed, and all flesh shall see together, because the mouth of the Lord hath spoken," xl. 5. Again, "I Jehovah have called thee in justice to open the blind eyes, to bring forth from the prison him that was bound, I [am] Jehovah, that is My name, and *My glory will I not give to another*," xlii. 6—8. And again, "On thee shall Jehovah arise, and *His glory shall be seen upon Thee;* the nations shall walk to Thy light," lx. 2, 3. In these passages the Lord is treated of, and by the glory of Jehovah is meant the Lord as to Divine Truth, for the Divine Truth proceeding from the Lord is the glory of Jehovah, n. 9429;—that Divine Truth is from no other source, the Lord teaches in John, "Ye have neither heard the voice of the Father at any time, nor have seen His shape," v. 37; and since it is the Lord, it is Jehovah Himself, for He saith, I am Jehovah, that is My name, and My glory will I not give to another. Hence also it is that the Lord is called the king of glory, as in David, "Lift up your heads, O ye gates, and be ye lifted up ye doors of the world, and *the King of Glory* shall enter in. *Who is this King of Glory?* Jehovah strong and a Hero, Jehovah the Hero of War," Psalm xxiv. 7 to 10. The Lord is here called the King of Glory from the Divine Truth, from which He fought, conquered, and subdued the hells. That this was done from His Human when He was in the world, may be seen, n. 9715, 9809, 10,019. Hence it is that He is called Jehovah Mighty and the Hero of War, also Hero in Isaiah, "Unto us a child is born, unto us a Son is given: His name is *God, Hero, the Father of eternity*," ix. 5. That the glory of Jehovah is the Lord as to the Divine Truth proceeding from His Divine Good, which is Jehovah or the Father, the Lord Himself teaches in John, "The Word was made flesh, and *we saw His glory, as the glory of the only-begotten of the Father*," i. 14; that the Lord is there meant by the Word which was made flesh, is evident; the Word is Divine Truth, and also glory. And in Matthew, "The Son of Man is about to come *in the glory of His Father*," xvi. 27. And in Luke, "Jesus said to the disciples, ought not Christ to suffer these things, and *to enter into His glory*," xxiv. 26. To enter into His glory is to be united to the Divine Good which was in Him, thus to Jehovah or His Father. Hence it is evident what is meant by being glorified in the following passages in John, "The Holy Spirit was not yet, *because Jesus was not yet glorified*," vii. 39. Again, "These things the disciples of Jesus knew not, but *when Jesus was glorified*, they then remembered. Jesus said, *the hour is come, that the Son of Man should be glorified.* And He said, Father, *glorify Thy name*, then came there a voice from heaven, *I have glorified it, and will again glorify*," xii. 16, 23, 27, 28. And again, "After that Judas was gone forth, Jesus said, *now is the Son of Man glorified, and God is glorified in Him, and God shall glorify Him in Himself, and shall straightway glorify Him*," xiii. 31, 32. Hence it is evident, that the unition of the Lord as to the Human with the Divine itself which was in Him, and which is called Jehovah the Father, is glorification, for it is said, that God will glorify Him in Himself; it is also evident, that that unition was fully made by the passion of the cross, which was the last of the temptations:—that the Lord by combats with the hells, which are temptations, glorified His Human, may be seen from what is cited, n. 9528, 9937. That when the Lord was glorified, the Divine Truth proceeds from Him, Himself teaches in John, "The Holy Spirit was not yet, *because Jesus was not yet glorified*," vii. 39. And again, "The Paraclete, the Spirit of Truth, whom I will send to you, shall not speak from Himself, *He shall glorify Me*, because He shall take of Mine, and shall announce it to you. *All things whatsoever the Father hath are Mine*," xvi. 13, 14, 15, 28; the Spirit of Truth is the Divine Truth proceeding from the Lord, n. 9818. The unition of the Human [principle] with the Divine in Himself is also here described by what is said, that all things which the Father hath are His; and in another place, that *the Father* and *He are one; and that the Father is in Him, and He in the Father*, John x. 30; chap. xiv. 10, 11; see n. 3704; thus that glorification or unition was reciprocal, which also the Lord teaches in John, "*Father glorify Thy Son, that Thy Son also may glorify Thee*," xvii. 1; where the Father is the Divine itself which was in Him, and the Son is the Divine Human: that the Father is the Divine Good which was in the Lord, may be seen, n. 3704, 7499. That Jehovah in the Word is the Lord, n. 2921, 6303, 8865; and that the Lord is the Divine itself or Jehovah under a human form, may be seen from what is cited, n. 9315.

10,054. "An odor of rest"—that hereby is signified perceptive of peace, appears from the signification of an odor, as denoting what is perceptive, is shown, n. 3577, 4624 to 4634, 4748; and from the signification of rest, as denoting peace. What Divine Peace is in the heavens, may be seen, n. 92, 93, 2780, 5662, 8455, 8665, 8722; that peace in the supreme sense is the Lord, and the Divine proceeding from Him effecting good in the heavens from what is inmost, n. 3780, 8517. The reason why a burnt-offering is called an odor of rest to Jehovah, is, because by the burnt-offering was represented the unition of the Lord's Divine Human with the Divine itself, as shown above, n. 10,053; and by that unition was acquired peace in the heavens; for all the hells were subjugated by the Lord, when He was in the world, and all the heavens were reduced into order, n. 9715, 9809, 9937, 10,019. Hence it is evident, why it is, that the burnt offering is called an odor of rest to Jehovah; as in several other places, where the burnt-offerings and the meat-offerings are treated of, as Levit. i. 9, 13, 17; chap. ii. 2, 9, 12; chap. iii. 5; chap. iv. 31; chap. vi. 6, 15; chap. viii. 28; chap. xxiii. 13, 18; Numb. xv. 3, 7, 13; chap. xxviii. 6, 8, 13; chap. xxix. 2, 6, 13.

10,055. "This is an offering by fire to Jehovah"—that hereby are signified all things from the Divine Love, is manifest from the signification of an offering by fire to Jehovah, as denoting that it is from the Divine Love, for fire in the Word signifies love in each sense, and when said of Jehovah or the Lord, it signifies the Divine Love. That fire denotes love in each sense, may be seen, n. 4906, 5215, 6314, 7324; and that in the supreme sense, in which it relates to Jehovah or the Lord, it denotes Divine Love, n. 6832, 6834, 6849. The burnt-offering is called an offering by fire to Jehovah, because the Divine [being] assumed the Human, and from the Human fought against the hells and subdued them, and at the same time united it to the Divine, to save the human race, out of pure love; that this unition is signified by the burnt-offering, may be seen, n. 10,042, 10,053.

10,056. Verses 19 to 35. *And thou shalt take the second ram, and Aaron and his sons shall put their hands upon the head of the ram. And thou shalt slay the ram, and shalt take of its blood, and shalt give [it] upon the auricle of the ear of Aaron, and upon the auricle of the right ear of his sons, and upon the thumb of their right hand, and upon the great toe of their right foot, and thou shalt sprinkle the blood upon the altar round about. And thou shalt take of the blood which is upon the altar, and of the oil of anointing, and shalt sprinkle [it] upon Aaron, and upon his garments, and upon his sons, and upon the garments of his sons with him; and he [shall be] holy, and his garments, and his sons, and the garments of his sons with him. And thou shalt take from the ram the fat, and the tail, and the fat that covers the intestines, and the caul of the liver, and the two kidneys, and the fat which is upon them, and the right flank, because it is the ram of fillings. And one piece of bread, and one cake of bread of oil, and one wafer, out of the basket of the unleavened things which are before Jehovah. And thou shalt put all the things upon the palms of the hands of Aaron, and upon the palms of the hands of his sons, and shalt shake them a shaking before Jehovah. And thou shalt receive them out of their hand, and shalt cause the altar to burn on the burnt-offering, for an odor of rest before Jehovah; this is an offering made by fire to Jehovah. And thou shalt take the breast of the ram of fillings, which is for Aaron, and shalt shake it a shaking before Jehovah, and it shall be to thee for a portion. And thou shalt sanctify the breast of shaking and the flank of up-lifting, which is shaken, and which is lifted up of the ram of fillings, of that which is for Aaron, and of that which is for his sons. And it shall be for Aaron, and for his sons for the statute of an age from with the sons of Israel, because this is the up-lifting, and the up-lifting shall be from with the sons of Israel of their peace-making sacrifices, their up-lifting to Jehovah. And the garments of holiness which are for Aaron shall be for his sons after him, to anointing in them, and to filling in them their hand. Seven days shall the priest after him of his sons put them on, who shall enter into the tent of the congregation to minister in the holy [place]. And thou shalt take the ram of fillings, and shalt boil his flesh in the holy place. And Aaron and his sons shall eat the flesh of the ram, and the bread which is in the basket at the door of the tent of the congregation. And they shall eat those things wherein is what is expiated, to fill their hand, to sanctify them; and a stranger shall not eat, because they are holy. And if there should have been left of the flesh of fillings, and of the bread until the morning, then thou shalt burn what is left with fire, it shall not be eaten, because it is holy. And thus thou shalt do to Aaron and to his sons, according to all which I have commanded thee; seven days thou shalt fill their hand.* And thou shalt take the second ram, signifies to the state following, which is of the Divine Truth proceeding from the Divine Good of the Lord in the heavens. And Aaron and his sons shall put their hands upon the head of the ram, signifies communication of power with the whole. And thou shalt slay the ram, signifies preparation. And thou shalt take of his blood, signifies the Divine Truth proceeding from the Divine Good of the Lord in the heavens. And thou shalt give it on the auricle of the ear of Aaron, and on the auricle of the right ear of his sons, signifies every thing perceptive of the Divine Truth proceeding from the Divine Good of the Lord in the heavens. And on the thumb of their right hand, signifies the intellectual principle thence derived in the middle heaven. And on the great toe of their right foot, signifies the intellectual principle in the ultimate heaven. And thou shalt sprinkle the blood upon the altar round about, signifies the unition of the Divine Truth with the Divine Good. And thou shalt take of the blood which is upon the altar signifies Divine Truth united to Divine Good in the Lord. And of the oil of anointing, signifies the Divine Good of the Divine Love which is in the Lord. And shalt sprinkle it upon Aaron and upon his garments, signifies the reciprocal unition of the Divine Good and the Divine Truth in the Lord's Divine Human in the superior heavens. And upon his sons, and upon the garments of his sons with him, signifies the reciprocal unition of the Divine Good and the Divine Truth in the Lord's Divine Human in the inferior heavens. And he [shall be] holy, and his garments, and his sons, and the garments of his sons with him, signifies thus all Divine Things in the heavens. And thou shalt take from the ram the fat, signifies good in the heavens. And the tail, signifies all truth there. And the fat that covers the intestines, signifies good in ultimates. And the caul of the liver, signifies interior purified good of the natural man. And the two kidneys and the fat which is upon them, signifies interior purified truth of the natural man and its good. And the right flank, signifies inmost good. Because it is the ram of fillings, signifies a representative of the Divine Power of the Lord in the heavens by Divine Truth from His Divine Good. And one piece of bread, signifies inmost celestial good from the Lord. And one cake of bread of oil, signifies middle celestial good. And one wafer, signifies ultimate celestial good. Out of the basket of the unleavened things, signifies which are together in the sensual principle. Which are before Jehovah, signifies from the Divine Good of the Lord. And thou shalt put all the things upon the palms of the hands of Aaron, and upon the palms of the hands of his sons, signifies acknowledgment in the heavens that those things are of the Lord and from the Lord. And shalt shake them a shaking before Jehovah, signifies hence Divine life. And thou shalt receive them out of their hand, and shalt cause the altar to burn upon the burnt-offering, signifies unition with the Divine Good of the Divine Love. For an odor of rest before Jehovah, signifies what is perceptive of peace. This is an offering made by fire to Jehovah, signifies from the Divine Love. And thou shalt take the breast, signifies the Divine spiritual principle in the heavens and its appropriation there. Of the ram of fillings, which is for Aaron, signifies a representative of the Divine Power of the Lord in the heavens by Divine Truth from His Divine Good. And shalt shake it a shaking before Jehovah, signifies vivification. And it shall be to thee for a portion, signifies communication with those who are in Divine Truths. And thou shalt sanctify the breast of shaking, signifies the Divine Spiritual [principle] acknowledged in heaven and in the church. And the flank of uplifting, signifies the Divine Celestial [principle], which is of the Lord alone, perceived in heaven and in the church. Which is shaken, and which is up-lifted, signifies which is acknowledged and which is received. Of the ram of fillings, of that which is for Aaron, and of that which is for his sons, signifies a representative of the Divine Power of the Lord in the heavens by Divine Truth from Divine Good. And it shall be for Aaron and for his sons for the statute of an age from with the sons of Israel, signifies the law of order in the representative church as to the Divine Good of the Lord and the Divine Truth thence proceeding. Because this is the up-lifting, signifies a representative of Divine Good and the Divine Truth thence proceeding. And the up-lifting shall be from with the sons of Israel of their peace-making sacrifices, their up-lifting to Jehovah, signifies reception in the heavens and in the church, and acknowledgment that it is of the Lord alone. And the garments of holiness which are for Aaron, signifies the Divine Spiritual [principle] immediately proceeding from the Divine Celestial. Shall be for his sons after him, signifies in the natural principle successively. To anointing in them, signifies to represent the Lord as to Divine Good. And to filling in them their hand, signifies a representative of Divine Truth proceeding from the Divine Good of the Lord in the heavens. Seven days shall the priest after him of his sons put them on, signifies plenary acknowledgement and reception. Who shall enter into the tent of the congregation to minister in the holy [place] signifies in all worship in heaven and in the church. And thou shalt take the ram of fillings, signifies a representative of the Divine Power of the Lord in the heavens by Divine Truth from Divine Good, and its communication and reception there. And shalt boil his flesh in the holy place, signifies the preparation of good for the use of life by truths of doctrine in illustration from the Lord. And Aaron and his sons shall eat the flesh of the ram, signifies the appropriation of spiritual good from the Lord. And the bread which is in the basket, signifies the appropriation of celestial good from the Lord. And they shall eat those things wherein is what is expiated, signifies the appropriation of good with those who are purified from evils and the falses thence derived. To fill their hand, signifies to receive Divine Truth. To sanctify them, signifies that they may be in truths grounded in good from the Lord. And a stranger shall not eat, signifies no appropriation with those who do not acknowledge the Lord. Because they are holy, signifies because they are Divine. And if there should have been left of the flesh of fillings and of the bread until the morning, signifies spiritual and celestial goods, which are not conjoined for a new state. Thou shalt burn what is left with fire, signfiies their dissipation. It shall not be eaten, signifies it shall not be appropriated. Because it is holy, signifies to which it shall not be conjoined, because thence it is profane. And thus thou shalt do to Aaron and to his sons, signifies this representative of the glorification of the Lord, and of His influx into the heavens and into the church. According to all which I have commanded thee, signifies according to the laws of Divine order. Seven days thou shalt fill their hand, signifies a representative of the plenary power of the Lord in the heavens by influx from the Divine Good of the Divine Love of His Human [principle].

10,057. "And thou shalt take the second ram"—that hereby is signified the following state, which is of Divine Truth proceeding from the Divine Good of the Lord in the heavens, appears from what precedes and follows. The subject treated of in what goes before was the sacrifices from the bullock, and the burnt-offering from the first ram; in what follows it treats of the second ram, and of the filling of the hand by it, and lastly of the sacrifice from the bullock, and of the daily burnt-offering from lambs. Who cannot see, if he thinks from reason at all enlightened, that in every particular of these things there lies concealed the arcana of heaven? For otherwise, to what purpose could the sacrifices and burnt-offerings have been instituted with so many ceremonials, as that the altar should be overflowed with blood, and that blood should be given upon the auricle of the ear, the thumb of the hand and the great toe of the foot, of Aaron and of his sons, and also upon their garments; and that in the sacrifice the fat of the intestines, of the liver, and of the kidneys, with the kidneys themselves, should be burnt upon the altar, and the rest of the parts burnt with fire out of the camp, or eaten; and in the burnt-offering that the intestines and the legs should be placed on the segments and the head burned; also that those things which were from the second ram should be first shaken upon the palms of the hands of Aaron and of his sons, and that some parts of it should be eaten? Let any one, who is so disposed, consider, whether such things would not have been merely terrestial, and of no account, if they had not involved holy arcana? And if they involve holy arcana, those arcana must be altogether such as relate to heaven and the church, and in the supreme sense to the Lord, for these alone are holy, because Divine. If it be a tenet of faith that the Word is holy and inspired by the Divine as to each and every expression [omnia et singula], it must be also a tenet of faith, that each and every thing, which was instituted concerning sacrifices and burnt-offerings, comprehend and contain in them inwardly such arcana. What they comprehend and contain in them, however, cannot at all be known in the earths, unless it be known what is signified by such things in the heavens; but, what is signified the internal sense of the Word alone teaches, since this sense unfolds correspondences; for all things which are in the natural world correspond to those which are in the spiritual world, by reason that the former world exists and subsists from the latter. But what the sacrifices and burnt-offerings, which are described in this chapter, involve, will be shown in a series from the unfolding of the correspondences by the internal sense. In the supreme sense, in which all holy things are Divine, the subject treated of is the glorification of the Lord's Human, and in the representative sense the regeneration of man; the process itself of the glorification of the Lord's Human, and of the regeneration of man is fully described by those things which were commanded concerning the sacrifices and burnt-offerings; and that this process may be apprehended, it is allowed to expound it by such things as can fall into the understanding. It is well known that the things seen by the eyes and heard by the ears are perceived inwardly with man, and as it were pass out of the world through the eyes or through the ears into the thought, thus into the understanding, for thought is of the understanding: and if they be such things as are loved, they pass thence into the will, and from the will by an intellectual way into the speech of the mouth, and also into the act of the body; such is the circle of things from the world through the natural man into his spiritual man; and from this again into the world. Let it be observed, however, that this circle is instituted from the will, which is the inmost principle of the life of man, and that it commences there, and is, thence accomplished, and the will of the man, who is in good, is ruled out of heaven by the Lord, although it appears otherwise; for there is an influx from the spiritual world into the natural, thus by the internal man into his external, but not *vice versa*; for the internal man is in heaven, but the external in the world. Inasmuch as this circle is the circle of the life of man, therefore when man is regenerated, he is regenerated according to the same, and when he becomes regenerate, he lives and acts according to the same; wherefore during man's regeneration, the truths, which are to be truths of faith, are insinuated by the hearing and the sight, and are implanted in the memory of his natural man; from that memory they are withdrawn into the thought which is of the understanding, and those which are loved become truths of the will; and so far as they become of the will, so far they become of the life, for the will of man is his very life, and so far as they become of the life, so far they become of his affection, thus of charity in the will, and of faith in the understanding. Afterwards man speaks and acts from that life, which is the life of charity and of faith; from charity which is of the will, goes forth the speech of the mouth and also the act of the body, each by an intellectual way, thus by the way of faith. From these considerations it is manifest that the circle of the regeneration of man is similar to the circle of his life in common; and that in like manner it is instituted in the will by an influx out of heaven from the Lord. Hence also it is evident, that there are two states appertaining to the man who is regenerating, the first when the truths of faith are implanted and are conjoined to the good of charity, the second when he speaks from the good of charity by the truths of faith, and acts according to them;—thus that the first state is from the world through the natural man into the spiritual; thus into heaven, and the second from heaven through the spiritual man into the natural, —thus into the world. The spiritual or internal man, as was said above, is in heaven, and the natural or external man in the world: this circle is the circle of the regeneration of man, and hence is the circle of his spiritual life; concerning this two-fold state of the man who is regenerating, see what is cited, n. 9274. From what has been said some idea may be formed concerning the glorification of the Lord's Human, for as the Lord glorified His Human, so He regenerates man; wherefore, as has been occasionally stated above, the regeneration of man is an image of the glorification of the Lord. Hence it is evident, that the first state of His glorification was to make His Human Divine Truth, and to unite it with the Divine Good which was in Himself; and that the second state was to act from Divine Good by Divine Truth, for by the Divine Truth proceeding from the Divine Good of the Lord heaven is builded and the church is builded; and by it all who are in the church are regenerated. These are the things which are described by the sacrifices and burnt-offerings, and their ceremonials, treated of in this chapter; by the sacrifice from the bullock, and by the burnt-offering from the first ram, is described the first state, and by the fillings of the hand from the second ram is described the second state; and lastly by the sacrifice from the bullock, and by the burnt-offerings is signified its continuity. It is to be noted, that with the man who is regenerating, purification from evils and the falses thence derived continually advances, for so far as man is purified from evils and falses, so far the truths which are of faith are implanted, and these are conjoined to the good which is of charity, and so far man then acts from the good of charity. Purification from evils and falses with man is not liberation from them, but is their removal, as may be seen, n. 868, 887, 894, 929, 1581, 2269, 2406, 4564, 8206, 8393, 8988, 9014, 9333, 9446 to 9451, 9938. But with the Lord there was not the removal, but the ejection of those things which He derived from the mother, thus a plenary liberation from them, insomuch that He was no longer the Son of Mary, as may be seen in what is cited, n. 9315, at the end. These things are premised, so that it may be known what is signified by the filling of the hand from the second ram, which is the subject of what now follows.

10,058. "And Aaron and his sons shall put their hands upon the head of the ram"—that hereby is signified the communication of power with the whole, appears from the signification of laying on the hands, as denoting the communication, translation, and reception of power, see n. 10,023; and from the signification of the head, as denoting the whole with the parts, see n. 10,011, thus all and every thing are represented by the second ram.

10,059. "And thou shalt slay the ram"—that hereby is signified preparation, is manifest from the signification of slaying, when relating to the sacrifice and burnt-offering, as denoting preparation, see n. 10,024.

10,060. "And shalt take of his blood"—that hereby is signified the Divine Truth proceeding from the Divine Good of the Lord in the heavens, is evident from the signification of blood, when relating to the sacrifice and burnt-offering, as denoting Divine Truth, as was shown above, n. 10,026, 10,033, in this case the Divine Truth proceeding from the Divine Good of the Lord's Divine Human, communicated and received in the heavens, for this is the subject treated of in what now follows. It was said above, n. 10,057, that there are two states appertaining to the man who is regenerating, the first when truth is implanted, and is conjoined to good, the second when man is in good and acts from good; when he is in this latter state, then the truths appertaining to him proceed from good, for from good he regards them, speaks them, and does them; in this case good is in every thing as the soul is in man, or the heart in the body, which is also perceived by a wise person from the discourses and actions of those who are in good. From this idea of the regeneration of man, some faint conception may be formed of the glorification of the Lord's Human, for in like manner as the Lord glorified His Human, He also regenerates man, n. 3130, 3212, 3296, 3490, 4402, 5680. For the first state of the glorification of His Human was the implantation of Divine Truth, and its unition with Divine Good: hence the Lord, when He was in the world, made His Human Divine Truth, and also by unition with Divine Good which was in Himself, made it Divine Good, as may be seen in what is cited, n. 9199, 9315. The second state of His glorification is, that from Divine Good proceeds Divine Truth, which is His Divine in the heavens. The first state of the glorification of the Lord's Human is decribed in the internal sense by those things which were said concerning the sacrifice from the bullock, and the burnt-offering from the first ram, treated of in this chapter, verses 10 to 18; but the second state is described by those things which now follow concerning the second ram, which is called the ram of fillings. Hence it is evident, that by blood is here signified the Divine Truth proceeding from the Divine Good of the Lord, communicated and received in the heavens.

10,061. "And thou shalt give [it] on the auricle of the ear of Aaron, and upon the auricle of the right ear of his sons"—that hereby is signified every thing perceptive of Divine Truth proceeding from the Divine Good of the Lord in the heavens, appears from the signification of the blood, which was given upon the auricle of the ear, as denoting Divine Truth in the heavens and in the church proceeding from the Divine Good of the Lord, as shown just above, n. 10,060; and from the signification of the ear, as denoting what is perceptive, see n. 9397,—here what is perceptive of Divine Truth in the heavens and in the church, for every thing perceptive therein is [perceptive] of that [truth]. It is here meant specifically what is perceptive in the celestial kingdom, for truth grounded in good is there perceived, as may be seen in what is cited, n. 9277; and from the signification of the auricle which is the outermost part of the ear, as denoting the whole or all, for as by what is first or supreme is signified the whole or all, so it is also by what is last or extreme, as may be seen above, n. 10,044; and from the signification of the right ear, as denoting what is perceptive of truth derived from good. The reason why the right ear has this signification is, because those things which are on the right side of man, correspond to the good from which truths are derived, and those on the left correspond to the truths by which good is procured, n. 9604, 9736; this is the case in the brain, also in the face, and in the organs of sense there, also in the breast, in the loins, and in the feet. He who does not know this arcanum, cannot in any wise know why it was commanded that the blood should be given upon the auricle *of the right ear*, upon the thumb *of the right hand*, and upon the great toe *of the right foot* of Aaron and of his sons; and that from this ram, besides the fat, *the right flank* should be burned upon the altar, treated of in what follows of this chapter, verses 22, 25. In like manner that the blood from the sacrifice should be given upon the auricle *of the right ear* of him that was to be cleansed from the leprosy, and upon the thumb *of the right hand*, and upon the great toe of his *right foot;* and that the priest should pour oil from the log* upon *the palm of his left hand*, and should dip *the right finger* in the oil which was *upon the palm of his left hand*, and should sprinkle it upon *his right finger* seven times before Jehovah, Levit. xiv. 14 to 18, 25 to 28. Nor can he know what is signified by what the Lord said to the disciples when they were fishing, that they should cast the net on *the right side of the ship*, and that when they cast it, they took so many, that they were not able to draw the net by reason of the multitude of fishes, John xxi. 6; by this was represented, that to act and teach from good is to comprehend innumerable things which are of truth, but not *vice versa*. Those also who are in truths derived from good, are meant *by the sheep which are on the right hand*, but those who are in truths not derived from good, are meant *by the goats, which are on the left hand*, Matt. xxv. 32. By the right hand are also meant those who are in the light of truth from good in David, "Thine are the heavens, and Thine the earth, Thou hast founded the world and

* The *log* was a Jewish measure of liquids, containing the 720th part of the *Homer* or *Cor*.

the fulness thereof, Thou hast created the north and the *right hand*," Psalm lxxxix. 11, 12; where by the heavens, the earth, and the world, is signified the church, n. 9325, by fulness all the truth and good, which constitute the church; by the north those therein who are in an obscure state as to truth, n. 3708, and by the right hand those who are in the light of truth from good, thus the like as by the south, n. 9642. Hence it may be manifest what is signified by sitting on the right hand of God, where it is said of the Lord, Psalm cx. 1, 5. Matt. xxvi. 63, 64. Mark xii. 36; chap. xiv. 61, 62. Luke xx. 42, 43; chap. xxii. 69, namely Divine Power by Divine Truth proceeding from His Divine Good, n. 3387, 4592, 4933, 7518, 8281, 9133. Since most of the expressions in the Word have also an opposite sense, so also have the right hand and the left, and in that sense the right hand signifies evil productive of the false, and the left hand the false productive of evil, as in Zechariah. "Woe to the shepherd of nought that forsaketh the flock, the sword is upon his arm, and *upon his right eye*, his arm withering shall wither, and *his right eye* darkening shall be darkened," xi. 17. The arm in this passage denotes the power of truth applied to confirm evil, concerning which power, since it is of nought, it is said that withering it shall wither; and the right eye denotes the science of good applied to confirm what is false, concerning which science, since it is of nought, it is said that darkening it shall be darkened; a shepherd denotes one who teaches truths, and thereby leads to good, n. 343, 3745, 6044; hence a shepherd of nought is one who teaches and leads to evil; the arm denotes the power which is of truth derived from good, n. 4931 to 4937, 7205; but the arm of a shepherd of nought denotes no power; the eye denotes the understanding and perception of truth, n. 4403 to 4421, 4523 to 4534, 9051: but the right eye of a shepherd of nought denotes the science of good without the understanding and perception of it, because it is applied to what is false; darkness denotes the false derived from evil, n. 7711. And in Matthew, "Jesus said, *if thy right eye shall scandalize thee*, pluck it out and cast it from thee; and *if thy right hand shall svandalize thee*, cut it off and cast it from thee; it is better for thee that one of thy members should perish, and not thy whole body be cast into hell [gehennah]," v. 29, 30. The right eye denotes the understanding and faith of what is false derived from evil, and the right hand denotes the false itself derived from evil. Every one may know that by eye is not here meant the eye, nor by right hand the right hand, and that the scandalizing eye is not to be plucked out, nor the scandalizing hand to be cut off, for nothing of salvation could thence be derived to man. And in the Apocalypse, "The beast gave to all a mark *on their right hand*, or on their foreheads," Apoc. xiii. 16; where the right hand denotes the false derived from evil, and the forehead denotes the love of evil from which the false is derived;—that the forehead denotes heavenly love, and hence in the opposite sense infernal love, may be seen, n. 9936.

10,062. "And on the thumb of their right hand"—that hereby is signified the intellectual principle thence derived in the middle heaven, is evident from the signification of the thumb, as denoting the power of good by truth, or truth in its power from good and the intellectual principle thence derived, of which we shall speak presently. The reason why it denotes the intellectual principle in the middle heaven is, because by the blood, which was given on the thumb, is signified the Divine Truth proceeding from the Divine Good of the Lord in the heavens, see above, n. 10,060, in this case therefore the intellectual principle thence derived; for by the blood on the auricle of the right ear is signified what is perceptive in the inmost heaven; hence by the blood on the thumb of the right hand is signified the intellectual principle in the middle heaven; and by the great toe of the right foot is signified the intellectual principle in the ultimate heaven; for those things which are of the inmost heaven are signified by the head, and by the things which are of the head, here therefore its perceptive principle by the right ear, for this is of the head;—and those which are of the middle heaven are signified by the body, and by the things which are of the body, in this case therefore the intellectnal principle by the right hand;—and those which are of the ultimate heaven are signified by the feet, and by the things which are of the feet. That such is the correspondence of the heavens with man, may be seen above, n. 10,030, and in the passages there cited. In the inmost heaven moreover there is a perceptivity of truth from good; but in the middle heaven, there is not what is perceptive of truth but what is intellectual concerning it, and in like manner in the ultimate heaven, as may be seen in the passages cited, n. 9277, 9596, 9684. That the thumb of the right hand should signifiy truth derived from good in its power, and thence the intellectual principle in the middle heaven, appears indeed [improbable] as being a part far too inferior and unimportant to signify heaven, for it may be asked whence has the thumb such and so important a signification? But let it be known, that the ultimate or extreme of any member signifies the same as the whole member, and the hand the whole power of the body; for the body has power by the arms and hands; that what is ultimate or extreme signifies all and the whole, in like manner as what is first and highest, may be seen above, n. 10,044. That the hands signify power, and that all power is of truth derived from good, may be seen in what is cited, n. 10,019, and that the right hand signifies the power of truth derived from good, and the left hand truth productive of good, n. 10,061. The reason why the intellectual principle is what is meant is because every thing intellectual is formed from truths, but every thing voluntary from goods, for all things in the world and in heaven have reference to truth and to good, and the understanding of man was given for truths, and the will for goods; therefore since by the hands is signified truth in its power, the intellect is also signified. Inasmuch as the thumb, like the hand itself, signified the power which is of truth derived from good, therefore in ancient times amongst the Gentiles, and also with the Israelitish people, it was usual to cut off the thumbs and the great toes of their enemies, Judges i. 6, 7; by which was represented the taking away of all power; in the thumb also is the chief power of the hand, for when that is cut off the hand is of no avail in battle. As the thumb, so also the fingers signify power, as in David, "Jehovah teacheth my hands to war, and *my fingers to fight*," Psalm cxliv. 1. Again, "When I look at the heavens *the work of Thy fingers*," Psalm viii. 3. And in Luke, "Jesus said, if *by the finger of God* I cast out demons, certainly the kingdom of God is come unto you," xi. 20.

10,063. "And upon the great toe of their right foot"—that hereby is signified the intellectual principle in the ultimate heaven, appears from what was said and shown just above, n. 10,062.

10,064. "And thou shalt sprinkle the blood upon the altar round about"—that hereby is signified the unition of the Divine Truth with Divine Good, appears from the signification of blood, when relating to the sacrifice and burnt-offering, as denoting the Divine Truth, shown above, n. 10, 026, 10,033; and from the signification of the altar, as being representative of the Lord as to Divine Good, n. 9964. When it is said Divine Good, the Divine Love is also meant, since all good is of love, for whatsoever is loved, that is perceived as good, and hence is also called good; but all truth is of faith, for whatsoever is believed, this is perceived and is also called truth; hence it follows that those things which form the understanding of man, are of faith, and those which form the will, are of love, for the understanding of man is dedicated to the reception of the truths which are of faith, and his will is dedicated to the reception of the goods which are of love. The understanding of man therefore is of such a quality, as are the truths which form it, and as is the faith of those truths; and the will of man is of such a quality, as are the goods which make it, and as is the love of those goods. In the opposite sense there is a love of evil and a faith in what is false, hence also a will and an understanding; but the understanding is of such a quality as is the false which forms it, and as is the faith in what is false; and the will is of such a quality, as is the evil which makes it, and as is the love of evil; that the will of evil, and the understanding of what is false are from hell, and that they are hell with man, is evident, since they are opposite to the understanding of truth and to the will of good, which are out of heaven from the Lord, and thus which constitute heaven with man.

10,065. "And thou shalt take of the blood which is upon the altar"—that hereby is signified Divine Truth united to Divine Good in the Lord, appears from the signification of the blood on the altar, as denoting the Divine Truth united to the Divine Good, as was shown just above, n. 10,064. How the case herein is, will be shown in what presently follows.

10,066. "And of the oil of anointing"—that hereby is signified the Divine Good of the Divine Love which is in the Lord, appears from the signification of the oil of anointing, as being a representative of the Divine Good of the Divine Love which is in the Lord, see n. 9954, 10,019.

10,067. "And thou shalt sprinkle [it] upon Aaron, and upon his garments"—that hereby is signified the reciprocal unition of the Divine Good and the Divine Truth in the superior heavens, is evident from the representation of Aaron, as denoting the Lord as to Divine Good, as may be seen n. 9806, which is the Divine Good of the Lord in the celestial kingdom, as shown n. 9966, or what is the same in the superior heavens; and from the signification of the garments of Aaron, as being representative of the Lord's spiritual kingdom adjoined to His celestial kingdom, spoken of in n. 9814; and from the signification of sprinkling upon them, as denoting to unite, for what was sprinkled and poured upon any one, this represented unition, as also above, where it is said that the blood was to be sprinkled upon the altar round about, n. 10,064. The reason why the Lord's Divine Human in the heavens is what is meant, is, because in this passage and in what now follows the subject treated of is concerning the Divine of the Lord in the heavens, and concerning His unition with the angels there, thus concerning the second state of the glorification of the Lord's Human, see n. 10,057, therefore here by Aaron is represented the Lord as to the Divine Good in the celestial kingdom, and by His garments as to the Divine Truth in the spiritual kingdom adjoined to the celestial kingdom, thus as to each in the superior heavens. The reason why it is the Divine Human from which those things are derived is, because no other Divine [principle]is acknowledged and worshiped in the heavens,except the Divine Human of the Lord, for the Divine, which the Lord called His Father, was the Divine in Himself. That in the heavens no other Divine [being or principle] is acknowledged and worshiped except the Lord as to the Divine Human, may be manifest from the Lord's words on numerous occasions in the evangelists, as from these, "*All things are delivered to Me by the Father*," Matt. xi. 27; Luke x. 22. "*The Father hath given all things into the hand of the Son,*" John iii. 34, 35. "*The Father hath given to the Son the power of all flesh,*" John xvii. 2. "*Without Me ye can do nothing,*" xv. 5. *Father, all Mine are Thine, and all Thine are Mine,*" John xvii. 10. "*All power is given to Me in the heavens and in the earths,*" Matt. xxviii. 18. Jesus said to Peter, "*I will give to thee the keys of the kingdom of the heavens, and whatsoever thou shalt bind on earth, shall be bound in the heavens, and whatsoever thou shalt loosen on earth shall be loosened in the heavens,*" Matt. xvi. 19. That this is the case, is also evident from this consideration, that no one can be conjoined by faith and love to the Divine itself without the Divine Human; for the Divine itself, which is called the Father, cannot be thought of, because it is incomprehensible, and what cannot be thought of cannot enter into the mind as an object of faith, thus neither as an object of love, when yet the principal of all things of worship is to believe in God, and to love Him above all things. That the Divine itself, which is the Father, is incomprehensible, the Lord also teaches in John, "*No one hath seen God at any time,* the only-begotten Son, who is in the bosom of the Father, He hath brought Him forth to view," i. 18. Again, "*Ye have neither heard the voice of the Father at any time, nor seen his shape,*" v. 37. And that the Divine itself, which is the Father, is comprehensible in the Lord by His Divine Human, He again teaches in John, "*He that seeth Me, seeth Him who sent Me,*" xii. 45. Again, "*If ye have known Me, ye have known My Father also, and henceforth ye have known Him and have seen Him. He that seeth Me, seeth the Father,*" xiv. 6 to 11. And in Matthew, "*All things are delivered to Me from my Father, and no one knoweth the Son but the Father, neither doth any one know the Father but the Son,* and he to whom the Son shall reveal Him," xi. 27; Luke xi. 22. The reason why it is also said, that no one knoweth the Son but the Father, is, because by the Son is meant the Divine Truth, and by the Father the Divine Good, each in the Lord, and the one cannot be known but from the other, wherefore the Lord first says, that all things are delivered to Him from the Father, and afterwards that he knoweth [the Father] to whom the Son is willing to reveal Him;—that the Son is the Divine Truth, and the Father the Divine Good, each of the Lord, may be seen, n. 2803, 2813, 3704, 7499, 8328, 8897, 9807. From these considerations it is now evident that the Divine in the heavens is the Divine Human of the Lord. We now proceed to show what was represented by the blood from the second ram being sprinkled upon the altar round about, and by taking from that blood and from the oil of anointing, and sprinkling it upon Aaron and upon his garments; that these things signified the unition of Divine Truth with Divine Good, and of Divine Good with Divine Truth in the Divine Human of the Lord, is evident from what was said and shown above, n. 10,064, 10,065, 10,066, 10,067; but the arcanum which lies concealed herein, has not yet been discovered; this arcanum is, that there was a reciprocal unition of Divine Good and Divine Truth, thus of the Divine itself, which is called the Father, and of the Divine Truth which is the Son. The unition of Divine Truth with Divine Good is signified by the sprinkling of the blood upon the altar, n. 10,064; these united are signified by the blood upon the altar, from which it was to be taken, n. 10,065; and the oil of anointing, by which was signified the Divine Good, n. 10,066; hence the reciprocal unition of Divine Truth and Divine Good in the Divine Human of the Lord is signified by the sprinkling of that blood, and at the same time of the oil of anointing, upon Aaron and upon his garments, as shown in the former part of this paragraph. That the unition was reciprocal, is manifest from the Lord's words in the following passages. "*The Father and I are one.* If therefore ye believe not Me, believe the works, that ye may know and believe, *that the Father is in Me, and I in the Father*," John x. 30, 38. Again, "*Believest thou not that I am in the Father and the Father in Me?* Believe Me, that *I am in the Father and the Father in Me*," xiv. 6 to 11. Again, "Jesus said, Father, the hour is come, *glorify Thy Son, that Thy Son also may glorify Thee; all Mine are Thine, and all Thine Mine*," xvii. 1, 10. Again, "Now is the Son of Man glorified, and *God is glorified in Him, and God shall glorify Him in Himself*," xiii. 31, 32. From these passages it may be manifest, that the Divine Good of the Divine Love, which is the Father, was united to the Divine Truth, which is the Son, reciprocally in the Lord; and hence that His Human itself is the Divine Good; the like is also signified by His *coming forth from the Father, and coming into the world, and going to the Father*, John xvi. 27, 28; and *that all things of the Father are His*, John xvi. 15, and *that the Father and He are one*, John x. 30. But these things may be better apprehended from the reciprocal conjunction of good and truth with the man who is regenerated by the Lord, for, as was before said, the Lord regenerates man as He glorified His Human, n. 10,057. When the Lord regenerates man, He insinuates the truth which is to be of faith into the man's intellectual principle, and the good which is to be of love into his will principle, and therein conjoins them, and when they are conjoined, then the truth which is of faith has its life from the good which is of love, and the good which is of love has its quality of life from the truth which is of faith:—thus conjunction is effected reciprocally by good, and is called the heavenly marriage, and is heaven with man. In that heaven the Lord dwells as in His own, for all the good of love is from Him, and also all the conjunction of truth with good; the Lord cannot dwell in any proprium of man because it is evil; this reciprocal conjunction is what is meant by the Lord's words in John, "In that day ye shall know that I am in My Father, and *ye in Me, and I in you*," xiv. 20. And again, "All Mine are Thine, and Thine Mine, but I am glorified in them, that they all may be one, as thou Father in Me, and *I in them, that they may be one in us*," xvii. 10, 21. Reciprocal conjunction is thus described, nevertheless it is not meant that man conjoins Himself to the Lord, but that the Lord conjoins to Himself the man who desists from evils; for to desist from evils is left to the determination of man, and when he desists, then is effected the reciprocal conjunction of the truth which is of faith and of the good which is of love from the Lord, and not at all from man; for that man from himself cannot do any thing of good, and thus cannot receive any thing of truth in good, is a known thing in the church; this also the Lord confirms in John, "*Abide in Me, and I in you; he that abideth in Me, and I in him*, the same beareth much fruit; for *without Me ye can do nothing*," xv. 4, 5. This reciprocal conjunction may be illustrated by the conjunction of the understanding and of the will with man; his understanding is formed from truths, and his will from goods, and truths are of the faith appertaining to him, and goods are of the love: man imbibes truths from hearing by the sense of hearing, and from reading by the sight, and stores them up in the memory; those truths relate either to the civil state or to the moral state, and are called scientifics; the love of man, which is of his will, through the understanding, looks into those truths in the memory, and thence selects such as are in agreement with the love, and those which it selects, it brings near to itself, and conjoins to itself, and by them strengthens itself every day. Truths thus vivified by love constitute his intellectual principle, and goods themselves which are of the love constitute his will principle; the goods of love are also as fires there, and truths in the circumferences round about vivified by love are as light from that fire; by degrees, as truths are enkindled from that fire, there is kindled in them a desire of conjoining themselves reciprocally; hence the reciprocal conjunction, which is of perpetual duration. From these considerations it is manifest, that the good which is of love is the conjoining principle itself, but not the truth which is of faith, only so far as this partakes of the good of love in itself; whether we speak of love or of good, it is the same thing, for all good is of love, and what is of love that is called good; and also whether we speak of love or of the will, it is likewise the same, for what a man loves that he wills. It is to be noted, that those things which relate to the civil and moral state, just now spoken of, conjoin themselves in the external man; but those which are of the spiritual state, before treated of, conjoin themselves in the internal man, and afterwards by the internal in the external; for those which are of the spiritual state, which are the truths of faith and the goods of love to the Lord, and which respect eternal life, communicate with the heavens, and open the internal man, and they open it so far and in such a manner, as the truths which are of faith are received in the goods which are of love to the Lord and towards the neighbor, from the Lord. Hence it is evident, that those are only external men, who do not at the same time imbibe those things which are of the spiritual state, and that those are merely sensual men who deny those things, however intelligently they may appear to discourse.

10,068. "And upon his sons, and upon the garments of his sons"—that hereby is signified the reciprocal unition of Divine Good and Divine Truth from the Lord's Divine Human in the inferior heavens, appears from this consideration, that when by the sprinkling of blood from the altar and the anointings of oil upon Aaron, is signified the reciprocal unition of the Divine Good and the Divine Truth from the Lord's Divine Human in the superior heavens, n. 10,067, by similar things upon the sons of Aaron and their garments is signified such unition in the inferior heavens; for the Divine of the Lord in the inferior heavens is represented by the sons of Aaron, when the Divine of the Lord in the superior heavens is represented by Aaron himself; the reason of this is, because the inferior heavens are born from the superior as sons from a father, see n. 9468, 9473, 9680, 9683, 9780. It is to be noted, that by the superior heavens is meant the celestial kingdom of the Lord, and by the inferior heavens His spiritual kingdom. That the heavens are distinguished into two kingdoms, has been frequently said and shown. In each kingdom the Divine of the Lord is similar, but as to reception by the angels it is dissimilar.

10,069. "And he [shall be] holy, and his garments, and his sons, and the garments of his sons"—that hereby are signified thus all things Divine in the heavens, appears from the signification of what is holy, as denoting what proceeds from the Lord, since He alone is holy, see n. 9229, 9479, 9680, 9818, 9820, 9956, 9980, thus denoting what is Divine; and since by Aaron and by his garments, and by his sons and by their garments were represented holy or Divine things in the heavens, treated of above, n. 10,067, 10,068, therefore by them are signified all things Divine in the heavens. That Aaron, his sons, and their garments were called holy, by reason that they represented holy Divine things, is manifest, for every one, who exercises due consideration may know, that neither the blood of a ram, nor the oil of anointing, can sanctify any one; for blood and oil are dead things, and thus cannot affect the interiors of man. The interiors themselves of man are only affected by virtue of the truths of faith and of the good of love from the Lord, to the Lord, thus by virtue of things Divine, and these are the things which sanctify, because these alone are holy.

10,070. "And thou shalt take the fat of the ram"—that hereby is signified good in the heavens, appears from the signification of fat, as denoting good, see n. 10,033; the reason why it denotes in the heavens is, because by the filling of the hand from the second ram is signified the Divine [proceeding] from the Lord in the heavens, n. 10,057.

10,071. "And the tail"—that hereby is signified every truth there, is evident from the signification of the tail of the ram, as denoting truth; the reason why the tail denotes truth is, because it is an ultimate, and truth is in ultimates, n. 9959; the tail also is the ultimate of the cerebrum and cerebellum, for these are continued into the spinal marrow, which also terminates in the tail, and which thus is their ultimate appendix; therefore it is said that in the sacrifices "*the tail was to be removed near the spine of the back*," Levit. iii. 9. That the tail signifies truth in ultimates, and in the opposite sense the false, is manifest from the following passages, "Jehovah shall cut off from Israel *the head and the tail*, the old man and the honored is *the head*, but *the prophet, the teacher of a lie, is the tail*," Isaiah ix. 13, 14. To cut off the head and the tail in the spiritual sense denotes good and truth, for the subject treated of is the church, which being devastated, the head signifies what is evil, and the tail what is false; that the head denotes good, may be seen, n. 4936, 4939, 5328, 9913, 9914; in like manner an old man, n. 6523, 9404. That a prophet is one who teaches truth, thus abstractedly a prophet is truth, n. 2534, 7269; in the opposite sense therefore the head denotes evil, likewise the old man and the honored who do it; and the tail denotes the false, in like manner the prophet, whence he is called the prophet of a lie, for a lie is what is false. Again in the same prophet, "There shall not be work for Egypt, *which may make the head and the tail*," xix. 15. Egypt denotes those who by reasonings from scientifics are desirous of entering into the truths and goods of faith, and not from what is revealed, thus not from faith in what is revealed, n. 1164, 1165, 1186; no work which makes the head and the tail denotes that they have neither good nor truth; that the tail denotes truth in ultimates is evident from the signification in the opposite sense, in which the tail denotes what is false, as in the Apocalypse, "*The locusts had tails like unto scorpions, and stings were in their tails*, and their power was to hurt men," ix. 10; where tails like unto scorpions, and stings in the tails, denote cunning reasonings from falses by which they persuade, and thereby hurt, wherefore it is said, that their power is to hurt men; that a locust also denotes the false in what is outermost may be seen n. 7643. Again, "*The tails of the horses* were like unto serpents, having heads, and by them they do hurt," Apoc. ix. 19; where tails like unto serpents also denote reasonings from falses, whereby hurt is done. Again, "*The tail of the dragon drew the third part of the stars of heaven*, and cast them to the earth," Apoc. xii. 3. The tail of the dragon denotes truths falsified, especially by application to evils; the stars denote the knowledges of truth and good, which are falsified; to cast to the earth denotes to destroy.

10,072. "The fat covering the intestines"—that hereby is signified good in ultimates, appears from the signification of fat, as denoting good, see n. 10,033; and from the signification of the intestines, as denoting ultimates and lowest principles, shown n. 10,030, 10,049.

10,073. "And the caul of the liver"—that hereby is signified the interior good of the natural man purified, is manifest from the signification of the caul of the liver, as denoting the interior good of the external or natural man, shown n. 13,031; the reason why it denotes good purified is, because the liver is a purificatory organ, n. 10,031; and because by the kidneys truth purified is signified, n. 10,032, hence also it is said that that caul shall be removed near the kidneys, Levit. iii. 4, 10, 15.

10,074. "And the two kidneys, and the fat which is upon them"—that hereby is signified the interior truth of the natural man purified, and its good, is evident from the signification of the kidneys, as denoting the interior truth of the external or natural man; and from the signification of the fat which is upon them, as denoting its good, shown n. 10,032. The reason why it is truth purified, which is signified by the kidneys, is, because the kidneys are organs purifying the blood, n. 10,032, and the blood denotes truth, n. 9393, 10,026.

10,075. "And the right flank"—that hereby is signified inmost good, appears from the signification of the right flank, as denoting inmost good. The reason why the right flank denotes inmost good is, because the flanks of animals signify the same as the loins and thighs appertaining to man, and the loins and thighs appertaining to man signify conjugial love, and hence the good of celestial love, which good is the good of the inmost heaven, as may be seen, n. 3021, 4277, 4280, 4575, 5050 to 5062, 9961, and the right loin and the right thigh signify inmost good there; for the things which are on the right side of man from correspondence signify the good productive of truth, and those which are on his left the truth productive of good; and hence those which are in the midst signify the conjunction of both good and truth. Hence also it may be manifest, that the flanks are the hinder parts of the animal, where the genitals are, but not the fore parts, for these are called the breast. Inasmuch as the right flank signifies inmost good or celestial good, therefore when it was taken up from the sacrifice, and given to Aaron, it was called his anointing, in Moses, "*The right flank* ye shall give an up-lifting to the priest of your eucharistic sacrifices; the breast of shaking and *the flank of up-lifting* I have taken from [being] with the sons of Israel of their eucharistic sacrifices; I have given them to Aaron the priest, and to his sons for the statute of an age; *this is the anointing of Aaron, and the anointing of his sons* from the offerings by fire to Jehovah," Levit. vii. 32, 34, 35; the breast and the flank are called the anointing, by reason of the representation of spiritual good and celestial good, for the breast from correspondence signifies spiritual good, which is the good of the middle or second heaven, and the right flank celestial good, which is the good of the inmost or third heaven, and the anointing is a representation of the Lord as to Divine Good, n. 9954, 10,019. *The breast and right flank* were also given to Aaron from the sacrifices of the first-born of an ox, of a sheep, and of a goat. That the right flank signifies inmost good, is also evident from this consideration, that it is named in the last place; for the tail is first named and the intestines, afterwards the caul of the liver and the kidneys, and lastly the right flank; the things which are named in the first place are most external, those in the second are more inward, and that in the last place is inmost.

10,076. "Because it is the ram of fillings"—that hereby is signified a representative of the Divine Power of the Lord in the heavens by Divine Truth from Divine Good and its communicative and receptive principle there, appears from the signification of a ram, as denoting the internal of man as to the good of innocence and of charity, shown above, n. 9991. For all beasts signify something of affection or of inclination appertaining to man, n. 9280; hence it is that those who are in charity and in innocence are called sheep and lambs; the ram therefore, which is the male of the sheep, signifies the good of charity and of innocence in the internal man, and in the supreme sense the same in the internal of the Lord's Human. For that which in the internal sense signifies any thing of man, thus any thing of the church or heaven appertaining to man, in the supreme sense signifies such a principle eminently appertaining to the Lord when He was in the world; all things also of the Word in the inmost sense treat of the Lord, whence comes the holy principle of the Word. And from the signification of the fillings of the hand, as being representative of Divine Truth from the Divine Good of the Lord in the heavens, and its communicative principle with the angels there, and the principle of recipiency by them; for, according to what was previously shown, as with man who is regenerating there are two states; the first when the truths which are of faith are implanting in the good which is of love, and are conjoining, and the second when he acts from the good of love, the like was eminently the case in the Lord; the first state of the glorification of His Human was to make it Divine Truth, and to conjoin it with the Divine Good which was in Him, and was called the Father, and thereby to make it the Divine Good of the Divine Love, which is Jehovah; the second state of His glorification was to act from the Divine Good of the Divine Love, which is effected by the Divine Truth proceeding from that good. As respects man, in the first state, he is imbued with those things which are to be of faith, and as he is imbued with them from good, that is, by good from the Lord, so is his intellectual principle formed; when those truths which are of the intellectual principle, have been implanted in and conjoined with good, then he comes into the second state, which consists in acting from good by truths. Hence it is evident what is the quality of the second state of the man who is regenerated, namely, that it consists in thinking and acting from good, or, what is the same thing, from love, or, what is also the same, from the will, for what a man wills, this he loves, and what he loves, this he calls good. But man then first comes into the second state, when he is wholly from the head even to the heel such as his love is, thus such as his will is and the understanding thence derived. Who can at all believe, that the whole man is a resemblance of his will and of his understanding thence derived, consequently a resemblance of his good and the truth thence derived, or a resemblance of his evil and of the false thence derived, for good or evil form the will, and truth or the false form the undertanding? This arcanum is known to all the angels in the heavens; but the reason why man does not know it is, because he has no knowledge of his soul, and consequently no knowledge that the body is formed after its likeness, and hence that the whole man is of such a quality as his soul is. That this is the case appears manifestly from spirits and angels in the other life; for they are all of them human forms, and such forms as their affections are, which are of love and of faith; and this to such a degree that those who are in the good of love and charity may be said to be loves and charities in form; and *vice versa*, those who are in evils grounded in the loves of self and of the world, thus in hatreds and the like, are hatreds in form. That this is so, may be also manifest from these three things, which in universal nature follow in order, namely, effect, cause, and end; the effect derives its all from the cause, for an effect is nothing else but a cause in an external form, since when a cause becomes an effect, it clothes itself with such things as are in externals, that it may appear in a lower sphere, which is the sphere of effects. The case is similar with the cause of a cause, which in the superior sphere is called a final cause, or an end; this end is the all in the cause, that the cause may be for the sake of something; for a cause, which is not for the sake of something, cannot be called a cause, for otherwise to what purpose would it be? This for the sake of *something* is the end, which is the first [principle] in the cause, and also its last; hence it is evident, that the end is as it were the soul of the cause, and as it were its life, consequently also the soul and life of the effect. For if in the cause and in the effect there is not that which produces an end, it is not any thing, because it is not for the sake of any thing, thus it is as a dead thing without soul or life, and such a thing perishes like the body when the soul departs from it. The case is similar with man, his soul itself is his will; the proximate cause, by which the will produces effect, is his understanding, and the effect which is produced is in the body, thus of the body; that this is the fact is manifest from this consideration, that what a man wills, and thence thinks, presents itself suitably in an effect in the body,—when as he speaks and when he acts. From these considerations it is further evident, that such as the quality of man's will is, such is the quality of the whole man; whether we speak of the will, or of the end, or of the love, or of the good, it is the same, for all that a man wills is regarded as an end, and is loved, and is called good: in like manner whether we speak of the understanding, or of the cause of an end, or of faith, or of truth, it is also the same, for what a man from will understands or thinks, this he takes for a cause, and believes, and calls true. When these things are apprehended, it may be known what is the quality of the man who is regenerating, in his first state, and what is his quality in the second. From these observations some idea may be had how it is to be understood, that the Lord when He was in the world, and glorified His Human, first made it Divine Truth, and by degrees the Divine Good of the Divine Love; and afterwards that from the Divine Good of the Divine Love He acts in heaven and in the world, and gives them life, which is effected by the Divine Truth which proceeds from the Divine Good of the Divine Love of His Divine Human, for from it the heavens existed, and from it perpetually exist, that is, subsist; or what is the same, from it the heavens were created, and from it they are perpetually being created, that is preserved, for preservation is perpetual creation, as subsistence is perpetual existence. Such [truths] are also involved in these words in John, "In the beginning was the Word, and the Word was with God, and God was the Word. All things were made by Him, and without Him was not any thing made that was made:—and the Word was made flesh," i. 1, 3, 14. The Word is the Divine Truth; the first state is described by the Word being in the beginning, and the Word being with God, and God being the Word; the second state by all things being made by Him, and by nothing which was made being made without Him. The case was similar when the Lord came into the world, and reduced the heavens into order, and as it were created them anew. That the Lord is there meant by the Word, is manifest, for it is said, that the Word was made flesh. The communicative and perceptive principle of the Divine Truth proceeding from the

Divine Good of the Divine Love of His Divine Human, is what is meant by the filling of the hand, and is described by representatives in this passage concerning the second ram. Inasmuch as the Lord as to Divine Good is represented by Aaron, n. 9806, therefore the glorification of the Lord as to His Human is representatively described in the process of the inauguration of Aaron and of his sons; the first state of glorification by what was said of the sacrifice from the bullock, and of the burnt-offering from the first ram, and the second state of glorification by what was said of the second ram, which is called the ram of fillings. The first state is called anointing, and the second state is called the filling of the hand; hence when Aaron and his sons were inaugurated into the priesthood by anointing and by filling of the hand, they were said to be anointed, and those whose hand he has filled, as in Moses, "The Great Priest, *upon whose head is poured forth the oil of anointing*, and *he hath filled his hand* to put on garments, shall not shave his head, and his garments he shall not unsew," Levit. xxi. 10. From these considerations it is also evident, that the filling of the hand is representative of the communication and reception of Divine Truth proceeding from the Divine Good of the Lord in the heavens, for it is said, he hath filled his hand, and not he is filled in the band, and also he hath filled the hand to put on garments; for by Aaron and by his anointing, is represented the Lord as to Divine Good, and by his garments the like as by the filling of the hand, namely, the Divine Truth proceeding from the Divine Good of the Lord; that this is represented by garments, see n. 9814; its dissipation is signified by unsewing them, and the dissipation of Divine Good in the heavens by shaving the head. Now, as the influx and communication of Divine Truth from the Lord, and its reception in the heavens, is signified by the filling of the hand, therefore by it is also signified purification from evils and falses; for so far as a man or an angel is purified from these latter, so far he receives Divine Truth from the Lord; in this sense the filling of the hand is meant by these words in Moses, "The sons of Levi smote of the people three thousand men; and Moses said, *fill your hand to-day to Jehovah*, to give a blessing to-day upon you," Exod. xxxii. 28, 29; to be blessed, in the spiritual sense, denotes to be gifted with the good of love and of faith, thus to receive the Divine proceeding from the Lord, n. 2846, 3017, 3408, 4981, 6091, 6099, 8939. Mention also is made of filling after Jehovah, and by it is signified to do according to Divine Truth, thus also by it is signified the receptive principle of truth, as in Moses, "Another spirit was with Caleb, and *he hath filled after Jehovah*," Numb. xiv. 24; Deut. i. 36; and in another place, "Jehovah sware, saying, surely none of the men, from a son of twenty years and upwards, shall see the land which I have sworn to Abraham, to Isaac, and to Jacob, because they *have not filled after Me*, except Caleb and Joshua, *who have filled after Jehovah*," Numb. xxxii. 11, 12.

10,077. "And one piece of bread"—that hereby is signified inmost celestial good, from the Lord, is evident from the signification of bread, as denoting celestial good, see n. 2165, 2177, 3478, 9545. Celestial good is the good of love to the Lord; this good, because it is the good of the celestial kingdom, is therefore called celestial good.

10,078. "And one cake of the bread of oil"—that hereby is signified middle celestial good, appears from the signification of a cake of the bread of oil, as denoting middle celestial good, see above, n. 9993.

10,079. "And one wafer"—that hereby is signified ultimate celestial good, appears from the signification of a wafer, as denoting celestial good in the external man, see n. 9994,—thus ultimate good. In the heavens there are two distinct kingdoms, one is called the celestial kingdom, the other the spiritual kingdom; each kingdom is tripartite, having its inmost, its middle, and its ultimate; the inmost good of the celestial is signified by bread, the middle good by cakes, and the ultimate good by wafers, as may be seen above, n. 9993. It is said that they should take one piece of bread and one cake, and one wafer, and that they should burn them, after they were shaken, upon the burnt-offering, and that Aaron and his sons should eat the residue of the bread in a basket at the door of the tent of the congregation; by these things were signified the communicative principle of the good of love from the Lord, and its receptive principle in the superior heavens, or in the celestial kingdom, the communicative principle by those kinds of bread [panes] which, after being shaken, were burnt on the burnt-offering, and its receptive principle by the bread which was eaten. It is said one piece of bread, one cake, and one wafer, because the Divine Good in itself is one. It may here be expedient also to remark why it was appointed, that not only the fat of the ram and the right flank should be burned upon the altar, but also the kind of bread which was called cakes, when yet by the fat and by the flank good is alike signified as by the bread or cakes; unless the reason be known why it was so done, it may seem superfluous; the reason however was, that sacrifices and burnt-offerings were not commanded, but permitted, and that on this account there was nothing in them well pleasing in the heavens; therefore cakes, which were a kind of bread, were also employed, and likewise libations of wine, in which was something well pleasing, for bread signifies all celestial good, and wine all its truth. Hence also it is that sacrifices and burnt-offerings were called bread, and also cakes or presents, for in the original tongue cakes are presents; but see what has been previously shown on these subjects,—namely that sacrifices and burnt-offerings were first instituted by Eber, and that they thence descended to the posterity of Jacob, n. 1128, 1343, 2818, 4874, 5702;—that sacrifices and burnt-offerings were not commanded, but permitted, n. 2180;—that sacrifices and burnt-offerings were called bread, n. 2165;—that bread denotes celestial good, and wine its truth, n. 276, 680, 2165, 2177, 3735, 4217, 4735, 4976, 5195, 6118, 6377, 8410, 9323, 9545; in like manner a meat-offering and libation, n. 4581. Hence it is evident that for this reason also burnt-offerings and sacrifices were abrogated by the Lord, and bread and wine retained. But it is to be noted, that the flesh of the sacrifice and burnt-offering specifically signified spiritual good, whereas the bread of the meat-offering signified celestial good, and that on this account not only flesh but also bread was offered.

10,080. "Out of the basket of the unleavened things"—that hereby is signified which are together in the sensual principle, appears from the signification of the basket, in which the different kinds of bread were, by which are signified goods, as denoting the external sensual principle, in which those things are together, see n. 9996; and from the signification of things unleavened, as denoting which are purified, see n. 9992.

10,081. "Which are before Jehovah"—that hereby is signified from the Divine Good of the Lord, is evident from this consideration, that Jehovah in the Word is the Lord, who is called Jehovah from the Divine Good, and God from the Divine Truth. That all those things which are here stated concerning the second ram, and are called fillings of the hand, signify the Divine of the Lord in the heavens proceeding from the Divine Good of His Divine Love, is evident from what has been shown above. That Jehovah in the Word is the Lord, may be seen in what is cited, n. 9373; and that the Lord is called Jehovah where the Divine Good is treated of, and God where the Divine Truth, n. 2769, 2870, 2822, 4022, 6303, 9167.

10,082. "And thou shalt put all the things on the palms of the hands of Aaron, and on the palms of the hands of his sons"—that hereby is signified acknowledgment in the heavens that those things are of the Lord and from the Lord, appears from the signification of all things which are from the ram, as the fats, the kidneys, and the right flank, and of all which were in the basket, as the bread, the cake, the wafer, as denoting Divine Goods and Divine Truths which are of the Lord because from the Lord, on which see n. 10,070 to 10,080; and from the signification of the palms of the hands, as denoting those things which are from proper power,—thus the proprium, of which we shall speak presently; and from the representation of Aaron and of his sons, as denoting the Lord as to the Divine Good and the Divine Truth thence proceeding, see n. 9806, 9807, 10,017. The reason why the palms of the hands denote those things which are from proper power, and hence why to be put on the palms denotes acknowledgment that all those things are of the Lord and from the Lord, is, because the palms are the palms of the hands, and by the hands power is signified, and to put any thing upon them denotes to ascribe it, thus to acknowledge; for it follows, that they were to be shaken upon them, by which is signified life thence derived from the Divine, and life from the Divine is given by faith, the first principle of which is acknowledgment. Inasmuch as by the hands is signified power, it follows that by the palms is signified full power, since the palms of the hands comprehend fully; hence when the palms of the hands are predicated of the Lord, and of the Divine Truth proceeding from His Divine Good, as in this passage, Omnipotence is signified. Hence it is evident, that by putting on the palms of the hand of Aaron and of his sons, is signified the acknowledgment of the Lord's omnipotence,—thus that all things are His, because all things in the heavens are from Him. That the hands denote power, may be seen, n. 4931 to 4937, 5327, 5328, 6947, 7188, 7189, 7518;—that the hand and right hand, when applied to the Lord, denote omnipotence, n. 3387, 4592, 4933, 7518, 7673, 8050, 8153, 8281, 9133; and that the Divine Truth proceeding from the Divine Good of the Lord has all power, n. 6948, 8200, 9327, 9410, 9639, 10,019.

10,083. "And thou shalt shake them a shaking before Jehovah"—that hereby is signified hence Divine life, appears from shaking a shaking, as denoting to vivify, thus denoting life; and because it is said before Jehovah, Divine life is signified. That to shake a shaking denotes to vivify, or to give Divine life, is manifest from the passages in the Word, where mention is made of shaking a shaking, as in Moses, "When ye bring a sheaf of the first-fruits of your harvest to the priest, *ye shall shake the sheaf before Jehovah* to your well pleasing; on the morrow of the sabbath *ye shall shake it*," Levit. xxiii. 10, 11. By the harvest is signified the state of the truth of faith derived from good, thus the state of good, n. 9295; by the sheaf of the first-fruits is signified the state thereof collectively; hence by being shaken by the priest is signified to be verified to receive a blessing; for every blessing, to be a blessing, must have life in it from the Divine. Again, "*Aaron shall shake the Levites a shaking before Jehovah* from being with the sons of Israel, that they may be to minister a ministry to Jehovah. Thou shalt set the Levites before Aaron, and before his sons, and *shalt shake them a shaking to Jehovah;* afterwards the Levites shall come to minister in the tent of assembly, and thou shalt purify them, and *shalt shake them a shaking:* and when the Levites are purified, and *Aaron hath shaken them a shaking before Jehovah*, and hath expiated them to purify them," Numb. viii. 11, 13, 15, 21. From these considerations it may be manifest what is meant by shaking a shaking, namely, that it denotes to vivify by acknowledgment, which is the first principle of life from the Divine appertaining to man ; knowledge indeed precedes acknowledgment, but there is nothing of Divine life in knowledge, until it becomes acknowledgment, and afterwards faith. The Levites represented truths ministering to good, and Aaron represented the good to which they ministered, therefore the former were shaken, that is, were vivified ; on which account it is also said that they were to be purified, for life from the Divine must be in truths that they may minister to good, and that life first flows in by acknowledgment. The like is signified by the shaking of gold in Moses. "The men came with the women and brought the clasp, the necklace, the ring, the girdle, all the vessels of gold, every man who *shook a shaking of gold to Jehovah*," Exod. xxxv. 22 ; where to shake a shaking of gold to Jehovah denotes to vivify by the acknowledgment that it was Jehovah's, that is, the Lord's. This signification of shaking a shaking, is grounded in correspondence, for all motion corresponds to a state of thought ; hence progressions, journeyings, and the like, which relate to motion in the Word, signify states of life, see n. 3335, 4882, 5493, 5606, 8103, 8417, 8420, 8557. And in John, "At the pool Bethesda lay a great multitude of sick people, and an angel at certain times descended into the pool, *and put the water in motion ;* whosoever then first entered after *the motion of the water* was made sound, whatsoever the disorder was by which he was held," v. 2 to 7. By putting the water in motion was here in like manner signified vivification by acknowledgment and faith, thus also purification by truths. That motion signifies states of life may be seen, n. 2837, 3356, 3387, 4321, 4882, 5604, 7381, 9440, 9967 ; and that waters denote the truths of faith, n. 2702, 3058, 3424, 4976, 8568, 9323 ; that all purifications are effected by the truths of faith, n. 2799, 5954, 7044, 7918, 9089 ; and that healings represented the restorations of spiritual life, n. 8365, 9031. Now as by shaking upon the palms of the hands of Aaron is signified vivification by acknowledgment of the Lord, and that all things are from Him, therefore it may be expedient to speak briefly concerning the acknowledgment and the faith thence derived. It was often said by the Lord, when the sick were healed, that they should have faith, and that it should be done to them according to their faith, as Matt. viii. 10 to 13 ; chap. ix. 2, 22, 27, 28, 29 ; chap. xiii. 57, 58 ; chap. xv. 28 ; chap. xxi. 21, 22, 31, 32 ; Mark v. 34, 36 ; chap. x. 49, 52 ; Luke vii. 9, 47, 48, 49, 50 ; chap. viii. 48 ; chap. xvii. 19 ; chap. xviii. 42, 43 ; the reason was, because the first principle of all is to acknowledge that the Lord is the Saviour of the world, for without that acknowledgment no one can receive any thing of good and of truth from heaven,—thus not faith,—and because it is the first and most essential [principle] of all, therefore, that the Lord might be acknowledged when He came into the world, in healing the sick, He questioned them concerning their faith, and those who had faith were healed; the faith was that He was the Son of God about to come into the world, and that He had the power of healing and of saving. All healings also of diseases by the Lord, when He was in the world, signified the healings of spiritual life, thus the things which are of salvation, n. 8364, 9086, 9031. Inasmuch as the acknowledgment of the Lord is the first of all [the principles] of spiritual life, and the most essential [principle] of the church, and since without it no one can receive from heaven any thing of the truth of faith and of the good of love, therefore the Lord also often says, that whosoever believeth in him hath eternal life, and whosoever doth not believe hath not life, as John i. 1, 4, 12, 13; chap. iii. 14, 15, 16, 36; chap. v. 39, 40; chap. vi. 28, 29, 30, 34, 35, 40, 47, 48; chap. vii. 37, 38; chap. viii. 24; chap. xi. 25, 26; chap. xx. 30, 31; but He also teaches at the same time, that those have faith in Him, who live according to His precepts, so that life thence enters into faith. These observations are made to illustrate and confirm [the doctrine] that the acknowledgment of the Lord, and that from Him is all salvation, is the first [principle] of life from the Divine appertaining to man;—this first [principle] of life is signified by the shakings upon the palms of the hands of Aaron.

10,084. "And thou shalt receive them out of their hand, and shalt cause the altar to burn on the burnt-offering"—that hereby is signified unition with the Divine Good of the Divine Love, is manifest from the signification of taking out of their hand, as denoting the state after acknowledgment, for since by shaking on the palms of the hands of Aaron and of his sons is signified acknowledgment whereby is Divine life, by taking those things out of their hand, is signified the state after acknowledgment, which is a state of conjunction with good, signified by causing the altar to burn on the burnt-offering; for by causing the altar to burn is signified to be conjoined to good, n. 10,052; and by the burnt-offering is signified and described the conjunction itself.

10,085. "For an odor of rest before Jehovah"—that hereby is signified what is perceptive of peace, appears from the signification of an odor of rest, when it is predicated of Jehovah or the Lord, as denoting what is perceptive of peace, as shown, n. 10,054.

10,086. "This is an offering made by fire to Jehovah"—that hereby is signified from the Divine Love, appears from the signification of an offering by fire to Jehovah, as denoting the Divine Love, concerning which, see n. 10,055.

10 087. "And thou shalt take the breast"—that hereby is

signified the Divine Spiritual [principle] in the heavens, and appropriation there, appears from the signification of the breast, as denoting the good of charity, and in the supreme sense the Divine Spiritual [principle], of which we shall speak presently. The reason why it denotes the appropriation thereof in the heavens is, because the subject of what now follows is the flesh from the ram, and the bread from the basket, which were not burnt on the altar, but were given up to Moses, to Aaron, and his sons, for a portion, and were eaten, whereby appropriation is signified, the process of which is described in what now follows. That by the breast is signified the good of charity and in the supreme sense the Divine Spiritual [principle], is grounded in correspondence; for the head with man corresponds to the good of love to the Lord, which good is the good of the inmost heaven, and is called the Divine Celestial; but the breast corresponds to the good of charity, which is the good of the middle or second heaven, and is called the Divine Spiritual; and the feet correspond to the good of faith, thus to the good of obedience, which is the good of the ultimate heaven, and is called the Divine Natural, concerning which correspondence may be seen what was shown above, n. 10,030. Inasmuch as the breast from correspondence denotes the good of charity, and the good of charity consists in doing good from willing it, therefore John, who represented that good, *lay at the breast* or *in the bosom of the Lord*, John xiii. 23, 25; by which is signified, that it was loved by the Lord; for to lie at the breast and in the bosom denotes to love. He who knows this, may also know what is signified by these words of the Lord to Peter and to John, "Jesus said to Simon Peter, Simon of Jonah, lovest thou Me? he saith, yea Lord, Thou knowest that I love Thee; He saith unto him, Feed My lambs: He saith unto him again, Simon of Jonah, lovest thou Me? he saith, yea Lord, Thou knowest that I love Thee; He saith unto him, Feed My sheep: He said to him the third time, Simon of Jonah, lovest thou Me? Peter was sorrowful, therefore he said, Lord, thou knowest all things, Thou knowest that I love Thee; Jesus saith unto him, Feed My sheep: verily I say unto thee, when thou wast young, thou girdest thyself and walkedst whither thou wouldest; but when thou art old, thou shalt stretch out thy hands, and another shall gird and lead thee whither thou wouldest not. When He had said these things, He said unto him, Follow Me; Peter being turned *saw the disciple whom Jesus loved following*, who also *lay on His breast at supper*: Peter seeing him, saith, Lord, what is he? Jesus said, If I will that he remain till I come, what is it to thee, *follow thou Me*" John xxi. 15 to 21. What these words signify, no one can know except by the internal sense, which teaches that the twelve disciples of the Lord represented all the things of faith and of love in the complex, after the manner of the twelve tribes of Israel, and that Peter represented faith, James charity, and John the works or goods of charity. That the twelve disciples of the Lord represented all the things of faith and love in the complex, may be seen n. 3488, 3858, 6397 ; in like manner the twelve tribes of Israel, n. 3858, 3926, 4060, 6335, 6640. That Peter represented faith, James charity, and John the works of charity, see preface to chap. xviii. and xxii. of Gen., n. 3750, 4738, 6344 ; and that Petra, as Peter is also called, denotes the Lord as to faith, n. 8581. Now as faith without charity does not love the Lord, and still can teach such shings as relate to faith and love, and as relate to the Lord, therefore the Lord says three times, Lovest thou Me, feed My lambs, and feed My sheep, and on this account the Lord says, when thou wast young, thou girdedst thyself, and walkedst whither thou wouldest, but when thou shalt be old, thou shalt stretch out thy hands, and another shall gird thee and lead thee whither thou wouldest not; by which is signified that the faith of the church, in its rising, is in the good of innocence as an infant, but when it is in its setting, which is in the end of the church, faith would be no longer in that good, nor in the good of charity; and that then evil and the false would lead, which are signified by when thou shalt be old, thou shalt stretch out thy hands, and another shall gird thee and lead thee whither thou wouldest not; thus from being free it would become a servant. To gird is to know and perceive truths in light from good, n. 9952 ; to walk, is to live according to them, n. 8417, 8420 ; hence to gird himself and walk whither he would, is to act from freedom, and to act from freedom is to act from the affection of truth grounded in good, n. 2870 to 2893, 9585 to 9591 ; and is to be led of the Lord, n. 9096, 9586, 9589, 9590, 9591. But to be girded by another, and to be led whither he would not, is to be a slave, and to be a slave is to act from evil, thus to be led of hell, n. 9096, 9586, 9589, 9590, 9591. That lambs, of which the Lord first speaks, denote those who are in the good of innocence, may be seen n. 3994 ; that sheep, of which the Lord speaks in the second and third place, denote those who are in the good of charity and thence in faith, n. 4169, 4809 ; and that *three* denote a whole period from beginning to end, n. 2788, 4495, 7715, 9198, therefore, because He spake to Peter concerning the church from its rising to its sitting, He said three times, Lovest thou Me. By John's following the Lord was signified, that those who are in the goods of charity follow the Lord, and are loved by the Lord, neither do they fall away; but that those who are in faith separate [from charity], not only do not follow the Lord, but are also indignant on the occasion, like Peter in this passage ; not to mention numerous other arcana, which are contained in the above words. From these considerations it is also evident, that *to lie on the breast and in the bosom of the Lord* denotes to be loved by Him, and that this is said of those who are in the goods of charity, in like manner as *carrying in the bosom*, Isaiah xl. 10, 11, and *lying in the bosom*, 2 Samuel xii. 3.

10,088. "Of the ram of fillings, which is from Aaron"—that hereby is signified a representative of the Divine Power of the Lord in the heavens by the Divine Truth from His Divine Good, and the communicative and receptive [principle] thereof in the heavens, was shown above, n. 10,076.

10,089. "And thou shalt shake it a shaking before Jehovah" —that hereby is signified vivification, appears from the signification of shaking a shaking before Jehovah, as denoting vivification by the acknowledgment of the Lord, and that He has all power in the heavens and in the earths, may be seen above, n. 10,083. That the first principle of the church is to acknowledge the Lord, is known, for the doctrine of the church teaches, that without the Lord there is no salvation. That He has all power, the Word teaches in many passages, and the Lord Himself in those which follow, "*All things are delivered to Me of the Father*," Matt. xi. 27; Luke x. 22. "*The Father hath given all things into the hand of the Son*," John iii. 34, 35. "*The Father hath given to the Son power over all flesh*," John xvii. 2. "*Without Me ye can do nothing*," John xv. 5. "*All power is given unto Me in heaven and in earth*," Matt. xxviii. 18. "Jesus said to Peter, thou art Petra [a rock], *I will give to thee the keys of the kingdom of the heavens, that whatsoever thou shalt bind on earth shall be bound in the heavens, and whatsoever thou shalt loosen on earth shall be loosened in the heavens*," Matt. xvi. 19. That by Peter in this passage is meant faith from the Lord, thus the Lord as to faith, which has that power, may be seen in the preface to chap. xxii. Gen., n. 4738, 6344; and that Petra, as he is there called, denotes the Lord as to faith, n. 8581.

10,090. "And it shall be to thee for a portion"—that hereby is signified communication with those who are in Divine Truths, is evident from the representation of Moses, who was to have the breast for a portion, as denoting the Lord as to Divine Truth, thus the Divine Truth which is from the Lord, is shown n. 6752, 7010, 7014, 9372; and from the signification of being for a portion, as denoting communication, for what was given from the sacrifices to Moses, to Aaron, to his sons, and to the people, signified communication of a Holy Divine [principle] with them; and all communication is effected according to the quality of him who receives, thus according to the quality of the representation appertaining to those who receive it. The reason why the breast was given to Moses for a portion, and the flank to Aaron, subsequently spoken of, was, because the subject here treated of is the communication and appropriation of

Divine Truth and Divine Good from the Lord in heaven and in the church ; and there are two things which are received there, namely, Divine Truth and Divine Good, both from the Lord: —Divine Truth by those who are in the Lord's spiritual kingdom, and Divine Good by those who are in the celestial kingdom, as may be seen from what is cited, n. 9277, 9684, therefore the breast was given to Moses for a portion, and the flank to Aaron, for by the breast is signified the Divine Truth in the Lord's spiritual kingdom, n. 10,087 ; and by the flank, the Divine Good in the celestial kingdom, n. 10,075 ; and also by the different kinds of bread in the baskets, which likewise were given to Aaron, n. 10,077. That Moses represented the Lord as to Divine Truth, was shown above ; and that Aaron, when he was inaugurated into the priesthood, represented the Lord as to Divine Good, may be seen n. 9806. That the breast was given to Moses for a portion, is manifest from Leviticus, where also it treats of the inauguration of Aaron, and of his sons, into the priesthood, "*Moses took the breast*, and shook it a shaking before Jehovah, of the ram of fillings, *and it was to Moses for a portion*, as Jehovah commanded Moses," viii. 29.

10,091. "And thou shalt sanctify the breast of shaking"—that hereby is signified the Divine Spiritual [principle] acknowledged in heaven and in the church, appears from the signification of sanctifying, as denoting to represent the Lord and the holy things which are from Him, as shown n. 9956, 9988 ; and from the signification of the breast, as denoting the Divine Spiritual [principle] in heaven, n. 10,087 ; and from the signification of shaking, as denoting vivification by acknowledgment, n. 10,083, 10,089 ; the Divine Spiritual [principle] is the Divine Truth in the middle or second heaven, which heaven is called the spiritual kingdom.

10,092. "And the flank of up-lifting"—that hereby is signified the Divine Celestial [principle] which is of the Lord alone, perceived in heaven and the church, is manifest from the signification of the flank, as denoting the Divine Celestial in heaven and in the church, respecting which, see n. 10,075 ; and from the signification of up-lifting, as denoting what is given and received, of which we shall speak presently. The Divine Celestial is the Divine Good from the Lord received in the inmost heaven, which heaven is also the celestial kingdom ; hence the Divine Good received in the inmost heaven is called celestial good.

10,093. "Which is shaken, and which is up-lifted"—that hereby is signified which is acknowledged and which is perceived, appears from the signification of being shaken, when it is said of the breast, as denoting what is vivified by acknowledgment, as shown above, n. 10,091 ; and from the signification of up-lifted, as denoting the Divine Celestial [principle], which is of the Lord alone, perceived in heaven and in the church, of which we shall speak presently. It may be expedient briefly to say how the case herein is; there are two kingdoms of which the heavens consist, the celestial kingdom and the spiritual kingdom. The Divine Truth in the spiritual kingdom is acknowledged, but in the celestial kingdom it is perceived; the reason is, because Divine Truth in the spiritual kingdom is received in the intellectual part, but in the celestial kingdom in the voluntary [or will] part; what is received in the intellectual part is said to be acknowledged, but what is received in the voluntary part is said to be perceived. That the former also have only an acknowledgment of Divine Truth, but the latter a perception of it, may be seen from what was copiously shown concerning those two kingdoms in the passages cited, n. 9277, 9596, 9684. As regards up-lifting, that is called an up-lifting, which was Jehovah's or the Lord's, and is given to Aaron for the sake of the representation; and as Aaron represented the Lord as to Divine Good, n. 9806, therefore what was up-lifted from the sacrifices, and given to Aaron, represented the Divine of the Lord, and is also called the anointing in Moses, "*The breast of shaking, and the flank of up-lifting,* I have received from [being] with the sons of Israel of their eucharistic sacrifices, and have given them to Aaron the priest and to his sons for a statute of eternity from [being] with the sons of Israel; this is *the anointing of Aaron, and the anointing of his sons* of the offerings by fire to Jehovah, on the day in which I caused them to approach to perform the office of the priesthood to Jehovah," Levit. vii. 34, 35. The reason why it is called the anointing is, because anointing is inauguration to represent the Lord as to Divine Good, as may be seen, n. 9954, 10,019. Again, "Jehovah spake to Aaron, behold I have given thee *the keeping of mine up-liftings,* as to all the holy things of the sons of Israel *I have given them to thee for the anointing,* and to thy sons for thee *the up-lifting of the gift as to every shaking of the sons of Israel, all the fat of pure oil, and all the fat of new wine and corn, of the first fruits, and as to all the first fruits,* which they shall give to Jehovah, they shall be for thee; as to every thing *devoted;* every *opening of the womb, and as to all flesh,* which they shall bring to Jehovah, *of the first born of the ox, of the sheep, and of the goat,* the flesh shall be for thee, as the *breast of shaking,* and as *the right flank:* every *up-lifting of holy things.* Thou shalt not have part nor inheritance in the land, because Jehovah is thy part and inheritance; also every *up-lifting from the tenths and from the gifts, which are given to the Levites,*" Numb. xviii. From these considerations it is evident, what is meant by up-liftings, namely, that all things were so called which are Jehovah's, that is, the Lord's. And whereas the Levites represented Divine Truths in heaven and in the church serviceable to Divine

Good, they were also given to Aaron in the place of all the first born, which were Jehovah's, that is, the Lord's, concerning which it is thus written in Moses, "I have taken the Levites out of the midst of the sons of Israel, in the place of every first born, the opening of the womb, from the sons of Israel, that the Levites may be Mine, because every first born is Mine, and because the Levites were given to Me, I have given those that were given to Aaron and to his sons," Numb. iii. 12, 13, chap. viii. 16—18. Up-liftings are called gifts given to Jehovah, that is, to the Lord, from [being] with the sons of Israel; but hereby is meant that they are Jehovah's, not from any gift, but from possession, since every thing holy or Divine appertaining to man is not of man, but is of the Lord with him. That every thing good and true, thus every holy Divine thing is from the Lord God, and nothing from man, is known in the church, whence it is evident that it is from appearance that it is called a gift from man; wherefore also in what presently follows it is said, "Because this is the up-lifting, and the up-lifting shall be from [being] with the sons of Israel, *it is an up-lifting to Jehovah*," by which is signified that the up-lifting from the sons of Israel is Jehovah's uplifting, thus that the gift from them is a gift from the Lord. Hence it is evident what is meant by up-lifting.

10,094. "Of the ram of fillings of that which is for Aaron, and of that which is for his sons"—that hereby is signified a representative of the Divine Power of the Lord in the heavens, by Divine Truth derived from Divine Good, is evident from what was shown above, n. 10,076.

10,095. "And it shall be for Aaron and for his sons for the statute of an age from with the sons of Israel"—that hereby is signified the law of order in the representative church as to the Divine Good of the Lord and the Divine Truth thence proceeding, appears from the representation of Aaron and of his sons, as denoting the Lord as to Divine Good and the Divine Truth thence proceeding, as shown n. 9806, 9807, 10,068; and from the signification of the statute of an age, as denoting the law of Divine Order, see n. 7884, 7995, 8357; and from the representation of the sons of Israel, as denoting the church, n. 4286, 6426, 6637, 9340. The reason why it denotes the representative church is, because with the sons of Israel that church was instituted, as may be seen in what is cited, n. 9320.

10,096. "Because this is the up-lifting"—that hereby is signified a representative of Divine Good and of the Divine Truth thence proceeding, is evident from what was shown just above, n. 10,093.

10,097. "And the up-lifting shall be from with the sons of Israel of their peace-making sacrifices, their up-lifting to Jehovah"—that hereby is signified reception in the heavens and in the church, and acknowledgment that it is of the Lord alone, appears also from what was shown above, n. 10,093. It is said from the peace-making sacrifices, because by them is signified worship which is from freedom; for the peace-making or eucharistic sacrifices were voluntary sacrifices, and those things which are voluntary are from man's freedom; that is called free which is done from the love, thus which is done from the will, for what a man loves, that he wills. The Lord flows in with man into his love, thus into his will, and produces the effect, that what a man receives is in freedom; and what is received in freedom, this also becomes free, and he loves it, consequently it is of his life. Hence it is evident what is meant by worship from freedom, which is signified by the peace-making or voluntary sacrifices; thus also what is meant by an up-lifting from them, namely, that it denotes what is of the Lord alone. That sacrifices signify all worship in general, may be seen n. 6905, 8936, 10,042; and that the freedom of man is what is of his love, n. 2870 to 2893, 3158, 4031, 7439, 9096, 9585 to 9591.

10,098. "And the garments of holiness which are for Aaron" that hereby is signified the Divine Spiritual immediately proceeding from the Divine Celestial, appears from the signification of the garments of Aaron, as being representative of the Lord's spiritual kingdom adjoined to His celestial kingdom, shown n. 9814; thus also denoting the Divine Spiritual, for the Lord's spiritual kingdom exists from His Divine there, which is called the Divine Spiritual; neither is the universal heaven any thing else but the Divine of the Lord, for the angels who are there, know, acknowledge, believe, and perceive, that all the good of faith and the good of love, which constitute heaven, are from the Lord, and nothing from themselves. Those garments are called the garments of holiness, because they represented the holy Divine things which are from the Lord. That the Lord alone is holy, and that every holy thing is from Him, and that all sanctification represented Him, may be seen n. 9229, 9680, 9818, 9820, 9956, 9988; and that heaven is hence called the sanctuary, n. 9479.

10,099. "Shall be for his sons after him"—that hereby is signified in the natural principle successively, appears from the signification of the sons of Aaron, as denoting those things which proceed from Divine Good, as from a father, as was shown n. 9807, 10,068; and from the signification of after him, as denoting successively or in successive order; and since those things are said of the garments of Aaron, by which was represented the Divine Spiritual, n. 10,098, therefore by being for his sons after him is signified the Divine Spiritual in the natural successively. For there are three [things or principles], which succeed [each other] in heaven, which, that they may be distinctly conceived, are to be called by their names, which are celestial, spiritual, and natural; these three proceed there in order, the one from the other, and by the influx of the one into the other successively, they are connected together, and thereby make a one. The Divine of the Lord in the heavens, from the difference of reception, is called by those names. Now, as the subject here treated of is the second ram, which is called the ram of fillings, and by the filling of the hand is signified inauguration to represent the Divine of the Lord in the heavens, and its communicative and receptive principle there, n. 10,019, therefore, that its reception in the natural principle may likewise be described, it here now treats of the successive putting on of the garments of Aaron by his sons after him, whereby is meant the succession of that thing in the heavens, which is signified by the filling of the hands. Hence it is evident, that in the internal sense these cohere by continuity, although in the sense of the letter the series of the things treated of, which is concerning the ram, here appears disjoined. Inasmuch as the subject here treated of is concerning things successive in heaven, it may be expedient to say also what is meant by what is successive. Most of the learned in the present day have no other idea respecting things successive, than as of what is continuous, or as of what coheres by continuity; and because of this idea concerning the succession of things, they cannot conceive the distinction between the exteriors and interiors of man, consequently neither between the body and the spirit of man; wherefore when they think of them from those ideas, they cannot at all understand, that the spirit of man, after the dissipation or death of the body, can also live under a human form. But things successive are not connected continuously, but discretely, that is distinctly according to degrees; for interior things are altogether distinct from exterior, insomuch that exterior things may be separated, whilst interior things still continue in their life; hence it is that man can be withdrawn from the body, and think in his spirit, or, according to a form of speaking in use amongst the ancients, can be withdrawn from things sensual, and elevated towards things interior. The ancients moreover knew, that when man is withdrawn from the sensual things which are of the body, he is withdrawn or elevated into the light of his spirit, thus into the light of heaven; hence also the learned ancients knew, that when the body was dissipated, they should live an interior life which they called their spirit; and as they regarded that life as the very human life itself, they thence also knew that they should live under a human form. Such was the idea which they had concerning the soul of man; and since that life was in affinity with Divine life, they hence perceived that their soul was immortal; for they knew that that part of man, which was in affinity with Divine life, and thus conjoined to it, cannot in any wise die. But this idea concerning the soul, and concerning the spirit of man, after those ancient times disappeared, by reason, as was said above, of the want of a just idea of things successive; hence also it is, that those who think from modern erudition, do not know that there is a spiritual principle, and that this is distinct from what is natural, for those who have an idea of things successive, as of what is continuous, cannot conceive of what is spiritual any otherwise than as of something more purely natural, when yet they are distinct from each other, like what is prior and what is posterior, thus as that which begets and that which is begotten. Hence it is that by persons of such erudition the difference is not apprehended between the internal or spiritual man, and the external or natural, thus neither between man's internal thought and will, and his external thought and will; hence also they are unable to comprehend any thing concerning faith and love, heaven and hell, and the life of man after death. Whereas those who have a just and distinct idea concerning things successive, are able in some manner to comprehend, that with the man who is regenerating, the interiors are successively opened, and that as they are opened, they are also elevated into interior light and life, and nearer to the Divine; and that such opening and consequent elevation is effected by Divine Truths, which are vessels recipient of the good of love from the Divine. The good of love is what immediately conjoins man to the Divine, for love is spiritual conjunction. Hence it follows, that man can thus be more and more interiorly opened and elevated, in proportion as he is in the good of love from the Divine; and that on the contrary, there is no opening and consequently no elevation with the man who does not receive Divine Truths, as is the case with every one who is in evil. But concerning this successive order, and its arcana, by the Divine Mercy of the Lord, we shall speak more fully in another place.

10,100. "To anointing in them"—that hereby is signified to represent the Lord as to Divine Good, is manifest from the signification of anointing, as denoting inauguration to represent the Lord as to the Divine Good, as shown, n. 9954, 10,019, in this case by those who receive the Divine of the Lord in the natural principle, for by the garments of Aaron being for his sons after him, is signified the Divine Spiritual of the Lord in the natural, n. 10,098, 10,099.

10,101. "And to filling in them their hand"—that hereby is signified a representative of Divine Truth proceeding from the Divine Good of the Lord in the heavens, appears from the signification of the filling of the hand, as denoting inauguration to represent Divine Truth proceeding from the Divine Good of the Lord, and its communicative and receptive principle in the heavens, as shown, n. 10,019, hereby those who are in ultimates there.

10,102. "Seven days shall the priest after him of his sons

put them on"--that hereby is signified plenary acknowledgment and reception, is evident from the signification of seven days, as denoting a full state, shown n. 6508, 9228, thus what is plenary; and from the signification of putting on garments after Aaron of his sons, as denoting to represent the reception of the Divine Spiritual in the natural, shown above, n. 10,098, 10,099.

10,103. "Who shall enter into the tent of the congregation to minister in the holy [place]"—that hereby is signified in all worship in heaven and in the church, appears from the signification of the tent of the congregation, as being a representative of heaven and of the church, shown n. 9457, 9481, 9485; and from the signification of entering-in thither to minister in the holy [place], as denoting worship, see n. 9963, 9964.

10,104. "And thou shalt take the ram of fillings"—that hereby is signified a representative of Divine power in the heavens by Divine Truth from the Divine Good, and its communicative and receptive principle there, as shown above, n. 10,076.

10,105. "And shalt boil his flesh in the holy place"—that hereby is signified preparation of good for uses of life by truths of doctrine in illustration from the Lord, is evident from the signification of boiling, as denoting to prepare for use of life by truths of doctrine; and from the signification of flesh, as denoting good, see n. 7850, 9127; and from the signification of in the holy place, as denoting from Divine illustration, for the holy place is where the Divine of the Lord is present, thus in application to the truths of doctrine, where there is Divine illustration, for where the Divine of the Lord is present, there is illustration. The reason why boiling the flesh of the sacrifice denotes to prepare good for the use of life by truths of doctrine is, because the flesh, by which is signified good, is thus prepared for the use of the body, hence in the spiritual sense for the use of life; that preparation is effected by the truths of doctrine, is evident, inasmuch as they teach use; by waters also, in which boiling is effected, are signified truths, may be seen, n. 2702, 3058, 3424, 5668, 8568, 9323. It is said by truths of doctrine in illustration from the Lord, since truths derived from the Word are to be fashioned into doctrine that they may be serviceable for use, and this must be effected by those who are in illustration from the Lord; and those are in illustration, when they read the Word, who are in the affection of truth for the sake of truth, and for the sake of the good of life, and not those who are in the affection of truth for the sake of self-glory, of reputation, or of gain. That doctrine ought to be altogether derived from the Word, that the Word may be understood, may be seen, n 9025, 9409, 9410, 9424, 9430; and that those who collect doctrine from the Word, must be in illustration from the Lord, n. 9382, 9424. That to boil in waters denotes to reduce truths into doctrine, and thereby to prepare for the use of life, appears at first sight as a groundless and far-fetched interpretation; nevertheless that this is the case, may be manifest from the passages in the Word, where mention is made of boiling in waters, and also where the pot is spoken of, in which the boiling takes place, as in the Second Book of Kings, "Elisha returned to Gilgal, when a famine was in the land; when the sons of the prophets sat before him, he said to his boy, *set on the great pot, and boil pottage for the sons of the prophets;* one went out into the field to gather herbs, and found a wild vine, and gathered from it wild gourds and *cut them together into the pot of pottage;* when they did eat of the pottage, they cried, *there is death in the pot, O man of God;* wherefore he said, that they should take *fine flour, which he cast into the pot,* and said, pour for the people that they may eat, *then there was no evil thing in the pot,*" iv. 38 to 42. This miracle, like all the others in the Word, involves holy things of the church, which are discoverable by the internal sense; from this sense it is known, that Elisha represented the Lord as to the Word, in like manner as Elias. That the sons of the prophets denote those who teach truths from the Word; that the pot, which was set on by order of Elisha, denotes doctrine thence derived. That a wild vine and the gourds thence gathered denote falses; hence it is evident what is meant by death in the pot. The fine flour, which he cast into the pot, denotes truth derived from good, and since doctrine is amended by such truth, it came to pass that there was no evil thing in the pot; hence also it is evident, that to boil in a pot denotes to bring together into doctrine, and thus to prepare for use. That all the miracles in the Word involve holy things of the church, may be seen, n. 7337, 8364, 9086; that Elisha represented the Lord as to the Word, n. 2762; that prophets denote those who teach truths, thus, abstractedly from persons, the truths of doctrine, n. 2534, 7269; that a vine denotes the truth of the church, and grapes its good, n. 5113, 5117, 9277; hence a wild vine and wild gourds denote falses and evils. That fine flour denotes the genuine truth of faith derived from good, n. 9995; that the pottage, which they were to boil, denotes a mass of doctrinals, such as was that of the Jews, n. 3316; hence may be concluded what is meant by boiling, and what by a pot. And in Ezekiel, "Parabolize a parable against the house of rebellion; *set on a pot,* set on, and also *pour into it waters;* by gathering pieces into it, every good piece, the thigh and the shoulder, fill with the choice of bones, and *let the bones be boiled in the midst of it;* thus saith the Lord Jehovah, woe to the city of bloods, *to the pot* whose scum is in her, and whose scum is not gone out of her," xxiv. 3 to 7. In this passage is described the Word such as it is as to doctrine, namely, that

Divine Truths derived from Divine Good are therein; and afterwards is described the doctrine derived from the Word, such as prevailed with the Jewish nation, that it was full of uncleannesses and falses. The pot denotes doctrine; the thigh, the shoulder, and the choice of bones, denote Divine Truths derived from Divine Good in successive order; the city of bloods denotes the Jewish nation in respect to the truths of doctrine appertaining to them, thus abstractedly from nation or person, it denotes the doctrine which destroys good; the scum therein is the external principle favoring filthy loves, which not being removed, the truth is defiled. Hence also it is evident, that a pot denotes doctrine, and that to boil denotes to prepare for use. Again, in the same prophet, "The spirit said to me, Son of Man, these men think iniquity, and consult the counsel of wickedness in the city, saying it is not near to build houses, *it is the pot, and we are the flesh,*" xi. 2, 3, 7. In this passage also the pot denotes the doctrine of the false derived from evil, for so the city is called where iniquity is thought of, and the counsel of wickedness consulted; that a city also denotes doctrine, may be seen, n. 402, 2712, 2943, 3216, 4492, 4493; here doctrine of such a quality. And in Jeremiah, "Jehovah said, what seest thou; he said, *I see a pot boiling*, the face of which is towards the north: Jehovah said, from the north shall be opened evil upon all the inhabitants of the earth," i. 13, 14. In this passage also a boiling pot denotes the doctrine of the false derived from evil; the north denotes an obscure state as to the truth of faith, and also thick darkness derived from falses, n. 3708; hence it is evident, what this prophetic vision involves. And in Zechariah, "In that day *every pot in Jerusalem and in Judah shall be holiness to Jehovah Zebaoth*, and all that sacrifice shall come and shall take from them, and *shall boil in them*," xiv. 21; where pot signifies the doctrine of charity and of faith, thus the doctrine of truth derived from good; Jerusalem denotes the church of the Lord; those who sacrifice denote those who are in Divine worship; hence it is evident, that to boil in pots denotes to prepare for the use of spiritual life. And in Moses, "Every vessel of earthenware, *in which the flesh is boiled* of a sacrifice of guilt and of sin, *shall be broken;* but if it *hath been boiled* in a vessel of brass, it shall be scraped, and plunged in waters," Levit. vi. 28. The vessel of earthenware, in which the boiling is effected, denotes the false, which does not cohere with good; a vessel of brass denotes the doctrinal wherein is good; the boiling of the flesh of the sacrifice of guilt and of sin, in them, denotes preparation for purification from evils and the falses thence derived. Hence it is evident what was represented by the law requiring that every vessel of earthenware should be broken, and that a vessel of brass should be scoured and immersed in waters.

10,106. "And Aaron and his sons shall eat the flesh of the ram"—that hereby is signified the appropriation of spiritual good with those who are in internal things from the Lord, is evident from the signification of eating, as denoting appropriation, see n. 3168, 3513, 3596, 4745; and from the representation of Aaron and his sons, as denoting the Lord as to Divine Good and Divine Truth, see n. 9806, 9807, 10,068, in this case in the heavens, because the subject treated of is the filling of the hand, by which is signified their communicative and receptive principle there; and from the signification of the flesh of the ram as denoting the good of the internal man, or good in internals; that flesh denotes good, may be seen, n. 3813, 7850, 9127; and that a ram denotes the good of innocence and of charity in the internal man, n. 9991, 10,042. It is said the Lord as to the Divine Good and Divine Truth in the heavens, and its communicative and receptive principle there, inasmuch as the Lord is above the heavens, for He is the sun of heaven, and actually appears also as the sun to those who are in heaven; all the light likewise of the heavens is thence derived; by the light and heat thence derived He is present in the heavens, and so present as if He were altogether there, for He fills the heavens and makes them. The light proceeding from Him as a sun is in its essence Divine Truth, and hence come the wisdom and intelligence appertaining to the angels; and the heat proceeding from Him as a sun is the Divine Good of His Divine Love there. The communication and reception of this Divine Good and of that Divine Truth, in the heavens, is what is signified by the filling of the hand. That the Lord is the sun of heaven, and that hence come light and heat in the heavens, from which the angels derive life, that is, wisdom and love, may be seen, n. 3636, 3543, 4321, 5097, 7078, 7083, 7171, 7173, 7270, 8644, 8812.

10,107. "And the bread which is in the basket"—that hereby is signified the appropriation of celestial good from the Lord, appears from the signification of eating, in this case bread, as denoting appropriation, as just above, n. 10,106; and from the signification of bread, as denoting the good of love and charity, see n. 2165, 2177, 3464, 3478, 3735, 3813, 4217, 4735, 4976, 5915, 6118, 9323, 9545; and from the signification of a basket, as denoting the external sensual principle, see n. 9996; hence it is evident, that by eating the bread which was in the basket, is signified the appropriation of good from the Lord in things external. The bread which was in the basket was unleavened bread, unleavened cakes, and unleavened wafers, and by them are signified goods purified, both internal and external, n. 9992, 9993, 9994; when therefore it is said bread in the basket, all those things are signified in the external sensual principle, and the external sensual principle is the ultimate of the life of man, containing all interior things together in itself. That the external sensual principle is the ultimate of the life of man, may be seen, n. 5077, 5081, 5094, 5125, 5128, 5767, 6183, 6311, 6313, 6318, 6564, 7645, 9212, 9216, 9730, 9996; and that it contains all interior things, as being the ultimate, n. 6451, 6465, 9216, 9828, 9836, 10,044.

10,108. "At the door of the tent of the congregation"—that hereby is signified to enter into heaven, appears from the signification of a door, as denoting entrance, see n. 2145, 2152, 2356, 2385; and as denoting introduction, n. 8989; and from the representation of the tent of the congregation, as denoting heaven where the Lord is, see n. 9457, 9481, 9485, 9963.

10,109. "And they shall eat those things wherein is what is expiated"—that hereby is signified the appropriation of good with those who are purified from evils and the falses thence derived, appears from the signification of eating, as denoting appropriation, see above, n. 10,106, and from the signification of what is expiated, as denoting what is purified from evils and the falses thence derived, see n. 9506. It is said, purified from evils and the falses thence derived, because there are falses, and also truths, appertaining to those who are in evil, and likewise falses and truths appertaining to those who are in good; the falses appertaining to those who are in evil are the falses of evil, and the truths appertaining to them, are truths falsified, which are dead; but the falses appertaining to those who are in good, are accepted as truths, for they are moderated by the good, and are applied to good uses, and the truths appertaining to them are truths of good, which are alive; concerning both kinds of the false and of the true, see what was shown, n. 2243, 2488, 2863, 4736, 4822, 6359, 7272, 7437, 7574, 7577, 8051, 8137, 8138, 8149, 8298, 8311, 8318, 9258, 9298. Since by eating the holy things, wherein is what is expiated, is signified the appropriation of good with those who have been purified from evils and the falses thence derived, therefore it was strictly forbidden, that any unclean person should eat of them, for by uncleanness is signified the defilement arising from evils and from the falses thence derived. For the case herein is this; so long as a man is in evils and in the falses thence derived, it is impossible for any good to be appropriated to him, for evil ascends from hell, and good descends from heaven; and where hell is, there heaven cannot be, for they are diametrically opposite; to the intent therefore that heaven may have place, that is, good from heaven, hell must be removed, that is, evil from hell. Hence it may be manifest, that good cannot in any wise be appropriated to man so long as he is in evil. By the appropriation of good, is meant the implantation of good into the will, for good cannot be said to be appropriated to man, until it becomes of his will, since the will of man is the man himself, and his understanding is only so far the man, as it partakes of the will; for what is of the will, that is of man's love, and thence of his life, for what a man wills, that he loves, and calls good, and also when it is done he feels it as a good; it is otherwise with those things which are of the understanding, and not at the same time of the will. It is also to be observed, that by the appropriation of good with man is meant only the faculty of receiving good from the Lord, with which faculty he is gifted by regeneration. Hence the good appertaining to man is not of man, but is of the Lord with him, and man is held in it so far as he suffers himself to be withheld from evils. Inasmuch as good cannot be appropriated, that is, be communicated to man so long as he is in evil, therefore it was forbidden that an unclean person should eat the flesh and bread of the sacrifice, for by that eating was represented the appropriation of good, as was said above. That the unclean were forbidden under penalty of death to eat of the sanctified things, is manifest from Moses, "Every one that is clean shall eat flesh; the soul which would eat the flesh of the sacrifices, whilst *uncleanness is upon him, shall be cut off from his people.* The soul which hath touched any unclean thing, *the uncleanness of man*, or an *unclean beast*, or *any unclean creeping thing*, and shall eat of the flesh of the eucharistic sacrifice, *shall be cut off from the people*," Levit. vii. 18, 19, 20, 21; all those external uncleannesses represented internal uncleannesses, which are evils appertaining to man, and such evils as are of his will, appropriated by actual life. This is further described in another passage in Moses, "No man of the seed of Aaron, who is *leprous* or *suffers a flux*, shall eat of the holy things, until he be cleansed: he who hath touched any one *unclean* on account of the soul, the man from whom hath gone forth *seed*, or the man who hath touched any *creeping thing*, with which he is polluted, or the man who has polluted himself as to all his *uncleanness*, the soul which hath touched it shall be unclean to the evening, and shall not eat of the holy thing; but when he hath washed his flesh with waters, and the sun is set, he shall be clean, and afterwards shall eat of the holy things, because this is his bread. No stranger shall eat what is holy; a lodger of a priest and a hireling shall not eat what is holy. If a priest shall buy a soul with the purchase of his silver, he may eat of it; and he that is born of his house, these shall eat of his bread. When the daughter of a priest shall marry a strange man [*vir*], she shall not eat of the uplifting of the holy thing; but if the daughter of a priest shall become a widow, or be divorced, and she hath no seed, and shall therefore return to the house of her father according to her youth, she shall eat the bread of her father," Levit. xxii. 1 to 16. That all these things are significative of interior things, is very manifest, thus that they involve the communication and appropriation of holy things with those who are in a state of reception; by no stranger eating, was signified that those should not who do not acknowledge the Lord within the church, thus who are not in the truths and goods of the church; by a lodger and a hireling not being allowed to eat was signified, that neither should those who are in natural good without the good of faith, and also those who do good for the sake of recompense; by those who were bought with silver and born in the house being allowed to eat was signified, that those should who are converted, and who are in the truth and good of the church from faith and love; by the daughter of a priest married to a strange man not being allowed to eat was signified, that the holy things of the church cannot be appropriated to the good which is not conjoined with the truths of the church; but by a widow and one that is divorced, if she hath no seed, being allowed to eat, was signified the appropriation of good after those things are removed which are not of the church, if from their conjunction nothing has proceeded or been born, which has been made a principle of faith; that these things are signified is evident, from the internal sense of each expression. That hereditary evils do not hinder the appropriation of good, is also described in Moses, "Every man [*vir*] of the seed of Aaron, in whom there is a spot, shall not come near to offer the bread of God; a man that is blind, lame, or a dwarf, or too tall, who hath a breach of the foot, or of the hand, is hump-backed, bruised, that hath a blemish in the eye, is scabby, full of warts, or bruised in the testicle, the bread of his God he shall not come near to offer, but the bread of the holies of holies, and of the holy things he may eat," Levit. xxi. 17 to 23; by these words, as was stated, are signified hereditary evils, and some specific evil by each. The reason why the persons above described should not bring bread, and come near to the altar, like the priests, was, because those vicious principles, or those evils thereby became manifest to the people, and what was manifested fell into a species of representation, but not those which lay concealed; for although the priest, the Levite, or the people were unclean as to the interiors, they were still called clean, and were also believed to be sanctified if they only appeared outwardly washed and clean.

10,110. "To fill their hand"—that hereby is signified to receive Divine Truth, is evident from the signification of filling the hand, as denoting to represent the Lord as to the Divine Truth, and its communicative and receptive principle there, n. 2076. It is said that they should eat the holy things in which is what is expiated to fill their hand, and that by them is signified the appropriation of good with those who are purified from evils and the falses thence derived, thus [who are prepared] to receive Divine Truth. The case herein is this; the first principle of all which is appropriated to man is good, and subsequently truth; the reason is, because good is the ground, and truth is the seed, thus in like manner good adopts truth, and conjoins it to itself, because it loves it as a parent; for there is a celestial conjugial principle subsisting between good and truth; and good is what makes the life appertaining to man, inasmuch as good is of the will, and the will of man is the man himself; whereas truth does not make the life appertaining to man, only so far as it is derived from good, since truth is of the understanding, and the understanding without the will is not the man himself, it is only an entrance to the man, for he is entered through the understanding. Man may be compared with a house, in which are numerous chambers, one of which leads into another; those who are in truths only as to the understanding are not in any chamber of the house, but only in the court [atrium]; but so far as truth by the understanding enters into the will, so far it enters into the chambers, and dwells in the house; man also in the Word is compared to a house, and the truth which is of the understanding alone is compared to a court; but the truth which has been made also of the will, and is there become good, is compared to an inhabited chamber and to a bed-chamber itself. That good is the principle which first of all is appropriated to man from the Lord, is manifest from his infancy and early childhood; for it is well known that at that time he has the good of innocence and the good of love towards parents and towards his nurse, and the good of charity towards infant companions; the good flows-in from the Lord with infants, that it may serve in advancing age for the first [principle] of the Lord's life appertaining to man, and thereby for a plane to receive truths; this is also preserved with man, when he grows up, if he does not destroy it by a life of evil and the faith of the false thence derived. When mention is made of good, thereby is meant charity towards the neighbor, and love to the Lord, for all that which is of love and charity is good. That good is in the first place, and truth in the second, with those who are regenerating, although it appears otherwise, may be seen n. 3325, 3494, 3539, 3548, 3556, 3563, 3570, 4925, 4926, 4928, 4930, 6258, 6269, 6272, 6273.

10,111. "To sanctify them"—that hereby is signified that they may be in truths from good derived from the Lord, appears from the signification of being sanctified, as denoting to represent the Lord and the holy things which are from Him, see n. 9956, 9988, thus in the spiritual sense it denotes to be led by the Lord, since the Lord alone is holy, and every thing holy proceeds from Him, n. 8806, 9229, 9479, 9688, 9818, 9820; hence it is evident that to receive truths by good from the Lord, thus faith by love from Him to Him, is to be sanctified; not that man considered in himself is on this account holy, but the Lord with him, for faith and love are the Lord with man, because they are continually from Him.

10,112. "And a stranger shall not eat"—that hereby is signified no appropriation of good with those who do not acknowledge the Lord, is manifest from the signification of a stranger, as denoting those who are out of the church, see n. 2049, 2115, 7996; and those are said to be out of the church, who do not acknowledge the Lord. With the Israelitish nation, those were said to be out of the church who did not acknowledge Jehovah for their God, and suffer themselves to be instructed in the rituals of the church; those who acknowledged, and suffered themselves to be instructed, were called sojourners, who had the same privilege with the home-born, as may be seen, n. 8007, 8013, 9196; and from the signification of eating, as denoting the appropriation of good, see n. 10,109. The reason why there is no appropriation of good with those who do not acknowledge the Lord is, because for man to acknowledge his God is the first [principle] of religion, and with Christians to acknowledge the Lord is the first [principle] of the church, for without acknowledgment there is no communication given, consequently no faith, thus no love; hence the primary [tenet] of doctrine in the Christian church is, that without the Lord there is no salvation: for whatsoever a man calls true and believes, and whatsoever he calls good and loves, cannot be called true and good, unless it be from the Divine, thus unless it be from the Lord; for that man from himself cannot believe, and do good, but that all truth and all good comes from above, is also well known. Hence it is manifestly evident that those within the church who do not acknowledge the Lord, cannot have faith, thus neither can they have love to God, consequently neither can they be saved. This was represented amongst the Israelitish nation by their acknowledging Jehovah for their God, and by their worship being accepted and called holy, and they were then sanctified, whatsoever was their quality as to the interiors; for representatives were only external, and with that nation it was sufficient to be in externals, as may be seen in what is cited, n. 9320; those therefore of that nation who did not acknowledge Jehovah, but another God, notwithstanding they sacrificed in like manner, and in like manner worshiped, were still rejected from the church, as those who worshiped Baal, and other gods. Hence it may be manifest what is the lot of those in the other life, who have been born within the church, and yet in heart deny the Lord, whatsoever may be their quality as to moral life; by abundant experience also it has been given me to know, that they cannot be saved; which the Lord also teaches openly in John, "*He that believeth in the Son, hath eternal life, but he who believeth not the Son, shall not see life, but the wrath of God abideth in him,*" iii. 36. But as to what concerns the nations out of the church, those who from their religious principle have lived in any species of charity towards their neighbor, and in any species of love to God the Creator of the universe under a human form, are in the other life accepted by the Lord and saved; for, when instructed by the angels, they acknowledge the Lord, and believe in Him, and love Him, as may be seen n. 2589 to 2604.

10,113. "Because they are holy"—that hereby is signified because they are Divine, appears from the signification of holy things, as denoting what are from the Lord, see above, n. 10,111, —thus what are Divine.

10,114. "And if there should have been [any thing] left of the flesh of fillings and of the bread until the morning"—that hereby are signified the spiritual and celestial goods, which were not conjoined to the new state, appears from the signification of what was left of the flesh and of the bread, as denoting that it was not appropriated, for by eating is signified to appropriate, n. 10,109, thus by what was not eaten, is signified what was not appropriated; and from the signification of flesh, as denoting good, see n. 7850, 9127; and from the signification of fillings, as denoting what is receptive, see n. 10,076, 10,110; hence by the flesh of fillings is signified the reception of truth in good, consequently their conjunction; but in this case non-reception and non-conjunction, because what was left of the flesh is understood; and from the signification of bread, as denoting celestial good, which is inmost good, see n. 10,077; and from the signification of morning, as denoting a new state, see n. 8211, 8427; from which considerations it is evident, that by what was left of the flesh of fillings and of the bread until the morning, are signified the spiritual and celestial goods, which were not conjoined to a new state; for by the flesh of the sacrifice is signified spiritual good, which is the good of charity towards the neighbor, and by the bread of the sacrifice celestial good, which is the good of love to the Lord. What is further meant by non-conjunction to a new state, it may be expedient briefly to relate. A new state is every state of the conjunction of good and truth, which occurs when the man, who is being regenerated, acts from good, thus from the affection of the good which is of love, and not as heretofore from truth, or from obedience only; it is also a new state, when those who are in heaven are in the good of love, which state is there called morning, for the states of love and of faith vary there, as mid-day, evening, twilight, and morning, in the earths, and it is also a new state, when an old church ceases, and a new one commences; all these new states in the Word are signified by morning; each of them has been treated of in the above explications of Genesis and Exodus throughout. Similar things are signified by the law, that nothing should be left of the flesh of the paschal cattle *until the morning*, and that the residue of it *should be burned with fire*, Exod. xii. 10; also by the law, that the fat of the feast should not be kept all night *until the morning*, Exod. xxiii. 18. Similar things are also signified by the law, that the residue of the flesh of the eucharistic sacrifice should be likewise eaten on the following day, but *should be burnt on the third day*, Levit. vii. 16, 17, 18; chap. xix. 6, 7; by the third day is also signified a new state, as may be seen, n. 4901, 5123, 5159. The reason why it was so granted was, because the eucharistic sacrifices were votive and voluntary sacrifices, not so much for the sake of purification and sanctification as the rest, but that they might eat together in the holy place, and testify joy of heart from Divine worship; and those meals, which they called holy, excited gladness in them more than all other worship. Similar things are also signified by the law respecting the manna, that they should not leave any thing of it until the morning, on which subject it is thus written in Moses, "Moses said, *let not a man* [vir] *leave of the manna until the morning;* but they obeyed not Moses, for they left of it until the morning, and it produced worms and stank," Exod. xvi. 19, 20.

10,115. "Then thou shalt burn what is left with fire"—that hereby is signified their dissipation, appears from the signification of what is left of the flesh and of the bread, as denoting what was not appropriated, as above, n. 10,114; and from the signification of burning with fire, as denoting to dissipate, in this place by the loves which are of man's proprium,—thus by the evils which are of those loves. For by fire is signified love in each sense, in this case proper love, which is the love of self. That this love is signified by fire, may be seen n. 1297, 2446, 5071, 5215, 6314, 6832, 7575; and that the proprium of man is nothing but evil, n. 210, 215, 694, 874, 875, 876, 987, 1023, 1044, 3812, 5660; that proper love [or the love peculiar to the proprium] is here signified, is, because by what was left until the morning is signified that which was not conjoined to good, n. 10,114; and what cannot be conjoined, this is not from the Divine but from the proprium. That this was unclean, thus evil, is manifest from Moses, "He who *eateth what is left until the morning*, shall bear his iniquity, and that soul shall be cut off from his people," Levit. xix. 7, 8. Again, "If in eating *there be eaten of the flesh of the eucharistic sacrifice on the third day*, he that offereth it shall not be accepted, nor shall it be imputed unto him, it shall be an abomination, and the soul which hath eaten of it shall bear its iniquity," Levit. vii. 16, 17, 18; in like manner it is manifest from this consideration, that what was left of the manna "produced worms and stank," Exod. xvi. 20.

10,116. "It shall not be eaten"—that hereby is signified it shall not be appropriated, is evident from the signification of eating, as denoting to appropriate, see above, n. 10,106.

10,117. "Because it is holy"—that hereby is signified what is Divine, to which it shall not be conjoined, because hence comes what is profane, appears from the signification of what is holy, as denoting what is Divine, see above, n. 10,111. The reason why it is not conjoined to it is, because by what was left of the flesh and of the bread, is signified that it was not conjoined, n. 10,114, thus also that it ought not to be conjoined; that this is the proprium of man, which is nothing but evil, may be seen above, n. 10,115, and to conjoin what is Divine with the proprium of man, thus with evil, is to profane it, n. 6348, 9298. Hence it is said, that whosoever eateth of what is left until the morning, *profanes the holy thing of Jehovah*, and that that soul shall be cut off from his people, Levit. xix. 7, 8; and *also that the flesh of the sacrifice*, which touched any unclean thing, *should be burnt with fire*, Levit. vii. 19. From these considerations it is now evident, that the profanation of what is holy is signified by eating the flesh and bread of the sacrifice on the day following.

10,118. "And thus thou shalt do to Aaron and to his sons"—that hereby is signified this representative of the glorification of the Lord, and His influx into the heavens and into the church, appears from the representation of Aaron, as denoting the Lord as to Divine Good, see n. 9809; and from the representation of his sons, as denoting the Lord as to Divine Spiritual Good, see n. 10,068; and from the signification of doing thus, that is, anointing them and filling their hands, and thereby inaugurating them into the priesthood, as denoting that they may represent the Lord as to the glorification of His Human, and influx thence into the heavens and into the church; for anointing was a representative of the glorification of His Human, and the filling of the hand was a representative of His influx thence into the heavens and into the church. That anointing represented the Divine Good of the Lord in His Divine Human, see n. 9954, consequently glorification, which is the unition of the Divine Human with the Divine Itself, which is called the Father, n. 10,053; and that the filling of the hand represented the Divine Power of the Lord by Divine Truth in the heavens and in the church, and its communicative and receptive [principle] there, n. 10,019,—thus its influx.

10,119. "According to all which I have commanded thee"—that hereby is signified according to the laws of Divine Order, is manifest from the signification of commanding, when concerning Jehovah, that is, the Lord, as denoting according to the laws of Divine Order, for whatsoever the Lord commands is according to Divine Order, thus according to its laws, for the

Divine Truth proceeding from the Divine Good of the Lord in the heavens, thus the Lord there, is order itself; wherefore every thing which the Lord commands is a law of order; that the laws of order are the Divine Truths of the Lord, may be seen n. 1728, 2247, 2258, 5703, 7995, 8512, 8700, 8988.

10,120. "Seven days thou shalt fill their hand"—that hereby is signified a representative of the plenary power of the Lord in the heavens by influx from the Divine Good of the Divine Love of His Divine Human, appears from the signification of seven days, as denoting a full state or what is plenary, see n. 6508, 7228; and from the signification of filling the hand, as being a representative of the Divine Power of the Lord in the heavens, and the communicative and receptive principle there, see n. 10,019; and since this is effected by influx from the Divine Good of His Divine Love from His Divine Human, therefore this also is signified.

10,121. Verses 36 to 46. *And a bullock of sin thou shalt offer every day on the propitiations, and thou shalt cleanse from sin upon the altar in propitiating thyself upon it, and thou shalt anoint it to sanctify it. Seven days thou shalt propitiate upon the altar, and shalt sanctify it, and the altar shall be the holy of holies; every one touching the altar shall be sanctified. And this is what thou shalt offer upon the altar; two lambs the sons of a year every day, continually. One lamb thou shalt offer in the morning, and the other lamb thou shalt offer between the evenings. And a tenth of fine flour mixed with bruised oil, the fourth of a hin, and a libation of the fourth of a hin of wine with the first lamb. And the second lamb thou shalt offer between the evenings, according to the morning meat-offering, and according to the libation thereof thou shalt offer it, for an odor of rest, an offering made by fire unto Jehovah; and a burnt-offering continually throughout your generations, at the door of the tent of the congregation before Jehovah, where I will meet you to speak there unto thee. And there I will meet the sons of Israel, and he shall be sanctified with My glory. And I will sanctify the tent of the congregation and the altar, and Aaron and his sons, to perform the office of the priesthood to Me. And I will dwell in the midst of the sons of Israel, and I will be to them for a God. And they shall know that I am Jehovah their God, who brought them forth out of the land of Egypt, to dwell Myself in the midst of them: I am Jehovah their God.* And a bullock of sin thou shalt offer every day on the propitiations, signifies the continual removal of evils and thence of falses in the natural man by the good of innocence from the Lord. And thou shalt cleanse from sin upon the altar, signifies purification from evils in heaven and in the church. In propitiating thyself upon it, signifies thereby the faculty of receiving good from the Lord. And thou shalt anoint it, signifies inauguration to represent the

Divine Good of love from the Lord in heaven and in the church. To sanctify it, signifies thereby the Lord there. Seven days thou shalt propitiate upon the altar, signifies what is full as to influx into heaven and into the church. And shalt sanctify it, signifies to receive the Lord. And the altar shall be the holy of holies, signifies the celestial kingdom, where the Lord is present in the good of love. Every one touching the altar shall be sanctified, signifies every one who receives the Divine principle of the Lord. And this is what thou shalt offer upon the altar, signifies what in general concerns the reception of the Lord in heaven and in the church. Two lambs the sons of a year every day, signifies the good of innocence in every state. Continually, signifies in all Divine worship. One lamb thou shalt offer in the morning, signifies the removal of evils by the good of innocence from the Lord in a state of love and of light thence derived in the internal man. And the other lamb thou shalt offer between the evenings, signifies the like in a state of light and of love in the external man. And a tenth of fine flour mixed with bruised oil, the fourth of a hin, signifies spiritual good derived from celestial, as much as [is needful] for conjunction. And a libation of the fourth of a hin of wine, signifies spiritual truth as much as [is needful] for conjunction. With the first lamb, signifies this is in the internal man. And the second lamb thou shalt offer between the evenings, signifies the removal of evils by the good of innocence from the Lord in a state of love and of light thence derived in the external man. According to the morning meat-offering, and according to the libation thereof thou shalt offer it, signifies spiritual good derived from celestial and the truth thereof, so much as [is needful] for conjunction. For an odor of rest, signifies what is perceptive of peace. An offering made by fire unto Jehovah, signifies from the Divine Love of the Lord. And a burnt-offering continually, signifies all Divine worship in general. Throughout your generations, signifies what is perpetual in the church. At the door of the tent of the congregation, signifies the conjunction of good and of truth. Before Jehovah, signifies from the Lord. Where I will meet you to speak there unto thee, signifies His presence and influx. And there I will meet the sons of Israel, signifies the presence of the Lord in the church. And he shall be sanctified with My glory, signifies what is receptive of Divine Truth from the Lord. And I will sanctify the tent of the congregation, signifies what is receptive of the Lord in the inferior heavens. And the altar, signifies what is receptive of the Divine from the Lord in the superior heavens. And Aaron and his sons to perform the office of the priesthood to Me, signifies a representative of the Lord in both as to the work of salvation. And I will dwell in the midst of the sons of Israel, signifies the presence of the Lord and His influx by good in heaven and in the church; and I will be to them for a God, signifies the presence of the Lord and His influx into truth in the church. And they shall know that I am Jehovah their God, signifies a perceptive principle that from the Lord is all good and all truth. Who brought them forth out of the land of Egypt, signifies salvation from hell by the Lord. To dwell Myself in the midst of them, signifies the Divine of the Lord, that it is the all in all of heaven and of the church. I am Jehovah their God, signifies from which is all the good of love and the truth of faith.

10,122. "And a bullock of sin thou shalt offer every day on the propitiations"—that hereby is signified the continual removal of evils and of the falses thence derived in the natural man by the good of innocence from the Lord, appears from the signification of a bullock, as denoting the good of innocence, see n. 9391, 9990; and from the signification of sin, as denoting purification from evils and the falses thence derived, for by sin is meant the sacrifice of sin, n. 10,039, and by the sacrifice of sin is signified purification from evils and falses, n. 9939, 9990, 10,022, 10,053. The reason why it is called the removal of evils and the falses thence derived is, because the evils and falses appertaining to man are not ejected, but are only removed, as may be seen in what is cited, n. 10,057; and from the signification of every day as denoting continually; and from the signification of propitiations, as denoting the reception of the good of love and of faith from the Lord after the removal of evils and of the falses thence derived, see n. 9506. It is said the removal of evils and of the falses thence derived, inasmuch as all falses are from evil, wherefore so far as evil is removed, so far falses are removed. The case herein is this; all things in heaven have reference to good and the truth thence derived; but all things in hell have reference to evil and the false thence derived; hence. in like manner in man, all things appertaining to him, which are from heaven, have reference to good and truth, but all things appertaining to him, which are from hell, have reference to what is evil and false: or what is the same thing, all things appertaining to man, which are from the Lord, have reference to what is good and true; but all things which are from the man himself have reference to what is evil and false. Now as those are the principles, to which all things in the universe have reference, and man is a receptacle of them, therefore there are two things appertaining to man which receive them, one is called the will, and the other the understanding: the will is the receptacle of what is good or of what is evil, and the understanding is the receptacle of what is true or what is false; the will which is from the Lord, which is also called the new will, is the receptacle of what is good; and the understanding which is from the Lord, which is also called the new understanding, is the receptacle of what is true; but the will, which is from the proprium of man, and is also called the old will, is the receptacle of what is evil, and the understanding which is from the proprium of man and is also called the old understanding, is the receptacle of what is false; into this latter understanding, and into this latter will, man is born from his parents; but into the former understanding and into the former will, man is born from the Lord, as is the case when he is regenerating, for when man is regenerating, he is conceived and born anew. Man is so created, that the will and the understanding make a one, so that those two principles together constitute one man; for the understanding is given to man that he may understand truth, but to the end that it may be implanted in the will and become good, and so far as it becomes of the will, so far it is in the man, for the will is the inmost principle of man, and is the esse of his life, but the understanding is an exterior principle, and exists thence; for what a man wills, that he loves, and what he loves, that he feels to be delightful, and therefore calls it good; the understanding favors it, and confirms it by reasons, and these he calls truths; hence it is that the will and the undestanding in reality make a one, but that it appears otherwise, as is the case when the man understands what is true, and yet wills what is evil; nevertheless that same man, when he is left to himself, and thinks from himself, understands altogether as he wills, that is, as he loves. The reason why a man who wills what is evil, can still speak what is true, and also do what is good, is grounded in hypocrisy, to which truth and good are subservient as means; such a man, if those means are taken away from him, and he is left in freedom, rushes into evils according to the lusts of his will and favors them by his intellectual faculty: this is especially evident from persons of like character in the other life, where every one comes into a state similar to that of his will; and on this occasion those who have not received a new will from the Lord, rush into evils of every kind, and think such things as favor evils, howsoever in the world they have spoken and acted altogether otherwise: for the law of Divine Order is, that the will and the understanding should make one mind, thus one man, consequently that the whole man should be either in heaven or in hell, and not hang between both, that is, with the eye look to those things which are of heaven, and with the heart to those things which are of hell;—by the heart is meant the will and by the eye the understanding.

10,123. "And thou shalt cleanse from sin upon the altar"—that hereby is signified purification from evils in heaven and in the church, appears from the signification of cleansing, as denoting to purify; and from the signification of sin, as denoting evil, for all evil from man is called sin; and from the signification of the altar, as being a representative of the Lord as to

Divine Good and the worship of Him, see n. 9714, 9964; here as to Divine Good in heaven and in the church: since the subject of the influx, the presence, and the reception of the Lord there is still continued, it is from this ground that by the altar is also signified heaven and the church as to the reception of Divine Good from the Lord there; for it is the Divine of the Lord which makes heaven and the church, inasmuch as the Lord dwells there in His own, and not in man's proprium. Hence also it is, that by the altar is likewise signified the man himself in whom is heaven, or in whom is the church, thus in whom is the Lord, and abstractedly from person the altar denotes the good itself, which from the Lord appertains to the angels of heaven and to the men of the church. In these senses the altar is spoken of in the Apocalypse, "There was given to me a reed like unto a staff, and the angel stood near, and said, *measure the temple of God and the altar*, and those who worship in it," Apoc. xi. 1. In this passage the temple of God and the altar denote heaven and the church, the temple denotes the spiritual church, and the altar the celestial church; to measure denotes to know the quantity and quality of truth and of good, wherefore it is not only said, measure the temple and the altar, but also those who worship in it; that the temple denotes the spiritual church, may be seen, n. 3720; and that to measure denotes to know the state of a thing as to truth and good n. 9603. Again, "I heard another angel *from the altar* say, Lord God Omnipotent, true and just are thy judgments," Rev. xvi. 7. From the altar denotes from the inmost heaven, where celestial good reigns,—celestial good is the good of love to the Lord. And in Jeremiah, "*The Lord hath forsaken His altar*, He hath abominated His sanctuary," Lam. ii. 7; where to forsake the altar and the sanctuary denotes every thing of the church, the altar every thing of the church as to good, and the sanctuary every thing of the church as to truth.

10,124. "In propitiating thyself upon it"—that hereby is signified thus the faculty of receiving good from the Lord, is evident from the signification of propitiating upon the altar, as denoting the implantation of good from the Lord, and its reception by a man of the church, and by an angel of heaven, subsequent to the removal of evils and of the falses thence derived, see n. 9506; for by the altar, as was shown just above, n. 10,123, is signified heaven and the church as to the reception of good from the Lord. Now as by the altar is signified heaven and the church where celestial good reigns, which is the good of love from the Lord to the Lord, it may be expedient briefly to state how it is with the reception of good in the celestial kingdom. That heaven is distinguished into two kingdoms, one of which is called the celestial kingdom, and the other the spiritual kingdom, has been frequently said above; in each kingdom good is implanted by truth, but with those who are in the spiritual kingdom, good is implanted by truth in the intellectual part, whereas with those who are in the celestial kingdom, good is implanted by truth in the will part. The implantation of good by truth, with those who are in the spiritual kingdom, is effected in another manner, than with those who are in the celestial kingdom; with those who are in the spiritual kingdom, truth is implanted in the external or natural man, and there first becomes science, and so far as man is affected by it, and forms his life according to it, it is called forth into the intellectual principle, and becomes faith and at the same time charity towards the neighbor; this charity constitutes his new will principle, and this faith his new intellectual principle, and both his conscience. But with those who are in the celestial kingdom, truth does not become science, nor faith, nor conscience, but it becomes reception in the good of love, and so far as the life is formed according to it, it becomes perception, which grows and is perfected with them according to love; this is effected every day, whilst they are ignorant of it, almost as in the case of infants. The reason why it is effected whilst they are ignorant is, because it does not remain as science in their memory, neither does it tarry as something intellectual in the thought, but it passes immediately into the will principle and becomes incorporated into the life. Wherefore these latter do not see truth, but perceive it; and they perceive it in such a degree and according to such a quality, as is in agreement with the good of love from the Lord to the Lord in which they are principled; hence much difference prevails herein amongst them. And since they perceive truth from good, they in no wise confirm it by reasons, but when truths are treated of, they say only, either yea, yea, or nay, nay. These are they who are meant by the Lord in Matthew, "*Let your discourse be yea, yea, nay, nay, what is beyond these is from evil,*" v. 36; for to reason about truths whether they be so, is not from good, since in such case truth is not perceived, but is only believed from authority, and thence from self-confirmation; and what a man believes from authority, is the [belief] of others in himself, and is not his own; and what is only believed thence from confirmation, this appears after confirmation as truth, although it be false; as may evidently appear from the faith of every religious person, and from the variety thereof in the universal world. Hence it is evident what is the difference, and what the quality of the difference between those who are of the Lord's celestial kingdom, and those who are of His spiritual kingdom. The cause of the difference is, because the former turn the truths of the church immediately into goods by life, but the latter abide in truths and prefer faith to life. Those who turn the truths of the church immediately into goods by life, thus who are of the celestial kingdom, are described by the Lord in Mark, chap. iv. 26, 27, 28, 29, and in numerous other passages. Concerning the difference between the celestial kingdom and the spiritual kingdom, see what is cited, n. 9277.

10,125. "And shalt anoint it"—that hereby is signified inauguration to represent the Divine Good of love from the Lord in heaven and in the church, appears from the signification of anointing, as denoting inauguration to represent the Lord as to the Divine Good of the Divine Love from His Divine Human, see n. 9474, 9954, 10,019, in this place from the Lord in heaven and in the church, for the subject treated of is His influx and reception there. Whatsoever represents the Lord, represents Him also with the men of the church, and with the angels of heaven,—thus heaven and the church, since the men in whom the church is, constitute the church in general, and the angels in whom heaven is, constitute heaven in general; nevertheless the men themselves, viewed in themselves, do not constitute the church, but the Lord with them; so neither do the angels, viewed in themselves, constitute heaven, but the Lord with them; for the Lord does not dwell in any proprium of man and of angel, but in His own appertaining to them; hence it is, that when mention is made of the church and of heaven, the Divine of the Lord is meant appertaining to those who are there. From these considerations it is evident in what manner it ought to be apprehended, that the Lord is the all in all of heaven and of the church, and that the Lord Himself is heaven and the church. This is also manifest from the doctrine known and received in the Christian world, that all the good of faith and of love is from God, and nothing from man, and that whatever is from man, as from himself, is not good; hence also it is, that no one has merit, nor justice, from any thing of his own. These observations are made to the intent that it may be known what the Lord is in heaven and in the church, thus what heaven and the church are; and hence what representative of Him is denoted by the altar and its anointing, which is the subject here treated of. All things were anointed which were to represent the Lord, and the Divine things which are from the Lord, as the altar, the tent of the congregation, the tables which were therein, the candlestick, the ark, Aaron himself, his sons, and their garments, and when they were anointed, they were called holy; not that the oil induced any holiness, but because they thus represented Divine things from the Lord, which alone are holy. The reason why oil was applied to that use, was, because oil signified the good of love, and the Divine Good of the Divine Love is the Divine itself, for it is the esse itself of all things; thus to represent it, inauguration was effected by oil. The Divine itself, which is the esse of all things, was in the Lord alone, for He was conceived of Jehovah; and every man has from his father the esse of his life, which is called his soul; hence it is manifest that the Divine Good of the Divine Love was in the Lord's Human, as the soul of a father in a son; and as with man nothing lives but his soul, for the body without the soul does not live, and as every thing of the body is produced from the soul, thus to a resemblance of it, that the soul may be in an adequate state and accommodated to functions in the ultimates of order, which are in the world, it hence follows, that the esse itself in the Human of the Lord was Jehovah, which is the Divine Good of the Divine Love; and the esse of life makes every thing which thence exists to its own likeness; thus the Lord, from the Divine which was in Himself, thus which was of Himself, made also His Human the Divine Good of the Divine Love. In the Athanasian creed, moreover, which contains the faith received throughout the Christian world, it is said, *As the body and soul is one man, so the Divine and the Human in the Lord is one Christ;* he therefore who is acquainted with the union of the soul in the body, and the resemblance of the former to the latter, may in some measure know the union of the Divine and the Human in the Lord, and the resemblance of the one to the other, and hence might know, that the Divine [principle] which is called the Father, and the Human which is called the Son, were one, and one in the other, that is, the Father in Him and He in the Father, according to the Lord's words in John, chap. x. 30; chap. xiv. 10, 11. But since at this day it is not known what the soul is, and scarcely that it is from the Father, and that the body is its resemblance, and that those two are one as what is prior and what is posterior, or as an esse and what thence exists, therefore man has separated the Divine from the Human in the Lord, and has distinguished them into two natures, and hence has conceived no other idea of the Lord's Human than as of the human of a man; when yet the soul of a man derived from his father is finite, and has evil in it hereditarily, whereas the soul of the Lord, as being from Jehovah, was infinite, and was nothing but the Divine Good of the Divine Love, and hence His Human after glorification was not as the human principle of a man. For the same reason the Lord took up into heaven His Human glorified, that is, made Divine from Himself, and left nothing of it in the sepulchre, otherwise than is the case with man. That the Lord glorified His body itself, even to its ultimates which are bones and flesh, the Lord also manifested to His disciples, saying, "Behold My hands and My feet, that I Myself am, handle Me and see, *for a spirit hath not flesh and bones as ye see Me have*," Luke xxiv. 39; and still He entered through the doors that were shut, and after that He had manifested Himself, became invisible, John xx. 19; Luke xxiv. 31. These observations are made to the intent that it may be known, that the Lord alone as to His Human was the anointed of Jehovah, yet not anointed with oil, but with the Divine Good itself of the Divine Love, which is signified by oil, and which was represented by anointing, as may be seen, n. 9954.

10,126. "To sanctify it"—that hereby is signified thus the Lord there, appears from the signification of sanctifying, as denoting to represent the Lord and the holy things which are from Him, thus His presence in heaven and in the church, as may be seen above, n. 10,111. What is represented, that in the internal sense is signified; the Word in the letter consists of representatives of things celestial and spiritual, which are of heaven and of the church, and therefore in the internal sense those things are signified; hence the Word of the Lord may be called as it were heaven in ultimates, for in the ultimates of heaven all things which are seen and heard are representative of such things as the angels in the superior heaven speak and think, all which have reference to the truths of faith and to the goods of love. The reason why in the ultimates of heaven such things are representative is, because those who are in the ultimates of heaven do not apprehend the interior things of angelic wisdom, but only such things as represent them; it is also according to Divine Order, that when superior things flow down into inferior, they are turned into similar things, and are thereby presented before the external senses, thus accommodated to the apprehension of every one; hence it is that the Word in ultimates, that is, in the sense of the letter, is representative, and thence significative of the celestial and spiritual things which are in the superior heavens, and hereby is also presented in a way of accommodation to the apprehensions of men; thus also it serves the heavens for a basis and foundation.

10,127. "Seven days thou shalt propitiate upon the altar"—that hereby is signified what is full as to influx into heaven and into the church, appears from the signification of seven days, as denoting what is full, of which we shall speak presently; and from the signification of propitiating, as denoting purification from evils and the falses thence derived, of which also we shall speak presently; and from the signification of the altar, as being a representative of the Divine Human of the Lord as to Divine Good, as may be seen, n. 9388, 9389, 9714, 9904, here in heaven and in the church, n. 10,123. The reason why the sacrifice from the bullock to propitiate and sanctify the altar was to be offered seven days was, because seven days, like a week, signified an entire period from beginning to end, greater or lesser; hence also seven days signify what is full. The number three likewise signifies an entire period from beginning to end, and hence also what is full, but with this difference, that seven is applied where the subject treated of is concerning any thing holy, but three when the subject treated of is concerning any thing whatsoever. It is to be observed that all numbers in the Word signify things, which is very well known in the other life, where occasionally papers are let down from heaven to the spirits beneath full of numbers, and such spirits as receive influx from the Lord know thence the things which are signified, in a continual series, as if they were written with letters; such papers it has also been given to myself occasionally to see. And it was stated, moreover, that some of the most ancient people, who as to their interiors were in consort with the angels, involved in numbers the things of their church, and heavenly arcana, and stored them up as a memorial for themselves. Hence it may be manifest, that all numbers in the Word are significative of things, for in the Word there is not the smallest expression which is not significative, since it was written not only for men, but also at the same time for the angels in heaven; hence the Word is the Divine passing through all the heavens. That all numbers in the Word signify things, may be seen, n. 575, 1963, 1988, 2075, 2252, 3252, 4364, 4495, 4670, 5265, 6175, 9659. That seven in the Word involves things holy, n. 395, 433, 716, 881, 5265, 5268; and that it signifies an entire period from beginning to end, thus a full state, n. 6508, 9228. In like manner a week, n. 2044, 3845. And also the number three, n. 2788, 4495, 4901, 5123, 5159, 7715, 9198, 9488, 9489, 9825. As to what concerns propitiating, it signifies purification from evils and the falses thence derived, or what is the same thing, their removal. And, since to propitiate and to expiate has this signification, therefore also it involves the implantation of good and of truth, and the conjunction of both from the Lord. The reason why these things are involved is, because so far as man is purified from evils and falses, so far good and truth are implanted and conjoined from the Lord; wherefore taking the first for granted, the second is taken for granted also; for the Lord is present with every man with the good of love, inasmuch as He loves all, and from love is willing to conjoin them to Himself, which is effected by the good of love and the truth of faith; but evils and the falses thence derived, which man appropriates to himself by a life of evil, oppose and hinder influx; hence it is evident what is meant by propitiation and expiation, see also n. 9506.

10,128. "And shalt sanctify it"—that hereby is signified to receive the Lord, appears from the signification of being sanctified, as denoting the reception of the Lord. The reason why being sanctified denotes the reception of the Lord is, because the Lord alone is holy, and hence whatsoever proceeds from the Lord is holy, therefore so far as man receives good, and with good truth from the Lord, which are holy things, so far he receives the Lord; for whether we speak of receiving good and truth from the Lord, or the Lord, it is the same thing; for good and truth are of the Lord, because from Him, thus they are the Lord in heaven and in the church. That the Lord alone is holy, and that every holy thing proceeds from Him, and hence that to receive Him is to be sanctified, may be seen, n. 9229, 9479, 9680, 9818, 9820, 9956, 9988, 10,069. That to be sanctified denotes the reception of the Lord, is also evident from this consideration, that it is said thou shalt propitiate and sanctify, for by propitiating or expiating is signified purification from evils and the falses thence derived, and at the same time the implantation of truth and of good from the Lord, n. 10,127; the implantation of good and of truth from the Lord is the reception of Him, thus sanctification. In like manner as above, it is said, in this chapter, "They shall eat those things *in which is what is expiated*, to fill their hand, *to sanctify them*," verse 33; where by what is expiated is signified what is purified from evils and the falses thence derived, n. 9056, 10,105; by filling the hand is signified to implant good and truth, and to conjoin them, n. 10,075; thus by being sanctified is signified to receive those things from the Lord, n. 10,111.

10,129. "And the altar shall be the holy of holies"—that hereby is signified the celestial kingdom, where the Lord is present in the good of love, is manifest from the signification of the altar, as a representative of the Lord as to Divine Good, see n. 9388, 9389, 9714, 9964; in this place as to Divine Good in heaven and in the church, n. 10,123; and from the signification of the holy of holies, as denoting celestial good, or the good of love from the Lord. The reason why it is the celestial kingdom, which is here signified by the altar, and the good in that kingdom which is signified by the holy of holies, is, because in that kingdom is received the good of love from the Lord to the Lord, which is celestial good; for there are two kingdoms into which the heavens are divided, the celestial kingdom and the spiritual kingdom; in the celestial kingdom is received the good of love from the Lord to the Lord; and in the spiritual kingdom is received the good of charity towards the neighbor from the Lord, as may be seen in what is cited, n. 9277, 9680, 10,068; by the altar is represented the celestial kingdom, or what is the same thing, is represented the Lord where He is present in the good of love. And by the tent of the congregation out of the vail is represented the spiritual kingdom, or what is the same, the Lord where He is present in the good of charity towards the neighbor; the good of the spiritual kingdom or spiritual good is called holy, but the good of the celestial kingdom, or celestial good, is called the holy of holies. The reason why celestial good, which is the good of love from the Lord to the Lord, is called the holy of holies is, because the Lord by that good immediately flows-in into the heavens, but by spiritual good, which is the good of charity towards the neighbor, mediately, see n. 9473, 9683, 9873, 9992, 10,005. It is said flows-in, because the Lord is above the heavens, and thence flows-in, n. 10,106; nevertheless, He is as it were present in the heavens. That celestial good, which is the good of love from the Lord to the Lord, is meant by the holy of holies, is manifest from the passages in the Word where mention is made of the holy of holies, as in Moses, "The vail shall distinguish for you *between the holy and the holy of holies;* and thou shalt give the propitiatory upon the ark of the testimony in *the holy of holies,*" Exod. xxvi. 33, 34; hence it is evident that that [part] of the tent is called holy, which was out of the vail, and that holy of holies which was within the vail. That the tent or habitation out of the vail represented the Lord's spiritual kingdom or the middle heaven, and that the tent or habitation within the vail represented the Lord's celestial kingdom, may be seen n. 9457, 9481, 9485, 10,001, 10,025; that [part] of the tent which was within the vail, is called the *sanctuary of holiness,* Levit. xvi. 33. Now as by the ark, in which was the testimony, and upon which was the propitiatory, was represented the inmost heaven, where celestial good reigns, therefore *the secret place of the temple,* where the ark of the covenant was, is also called *the holy of holies,* 1 Kings vi. 16; chap. viii. 6. The bread and the meat-offering, inasmuch as they signified the good of love from the Lord to the Lord, which is celestial good, are also called the holy of holies in Moses, "*The bread of faces or of proposition* shall be eaten by Aaron and his sons in the holy place, because *it is the holy of holies* of the offerings made by fire to Jehovah," Levit. xxiv. 9; that the bread of faces, or of proposition, signifies celestial good, may be seen n. 9545. Again, "*The residue of the meat-offering* shall be for Aaron and his sons, *the holy of holies* of the offerings made by fire to Jehovah," Levit. ii. 3, 10; that the meat-offering, which was unleavened bread,cakes, and unleavened wafers mixed with oil, denotes celestial good, or the good of love, may be seen n. 4581, 9992, 10,109. Again, "Every meat-offering, the sarifice of sin and of guilt, which is for Aaron and his sons, is *the holy of holies to Jehovah,*" Numb. xviii. 9. The reason why those things were called the holy of holies was, because those sacrifices signified purification from evils, and all purification from evils is effected in a state of the good of innocence, which good is also celestial good; wherefore in the sacrifices of sin and of guilt were offered she-lambs or he-lambs, or rams, or bullocks, or turtle doves, as is manifest from Leviticus, chap. iv. v., and by those animals that good is signified. That it is signified by lambs, may be seen n. 3994, 3519, 7840;—by rams, n. 10,042;—by bullocks, n. 9391; and by turtle doves, is evident from the passages in the Word where they are named; that purification from evils and regeneration is effected in a state of innocence, may be seen, n. 10,021: on this account those sacrifices are called the holy of holies also in Leviticus vi. 17; chap. vii. 6; chap. x. 17; chap. xiv. 13. That the altar of burnt-offering represented the Lord as to the good of love, and its receptive principle by angels and men, was shown above, therefore it is thus said of it in Moses, "*Thou shalt anoint the altar of burnt-offering*, and all its vessels, its laver, and its bases, and shalt sanctify them *that they may be the holy of holies;* every one who toucheth them shall sanctify himself," Exod. xxx. 29. *The incense*, [a portion] of which was given before the testimony in the tent of the congregation, is also called *the holy of holies*, Exod. xxx. 36, because it signified celestial good in ultimates, and also those things which proceed from that good, n. 9475. And in Ezekiel, "This is the law *of the house*, on *the head of the mountain* all its border round about, shall be *the holy of holies*," xliii. 12; the reason why the house with the border around it is called the holy of holies is, because by the house of God is signified the celestial kingdom, and in the supreme sense the Lord as to the good of love, n. 3720; hence also it is said on the head of the mountain, for by the head of the mountain the like is signified, n. 6435, 9422, 9434. And in Daniel, "Seventy weeks are decided on the people and on the holy city, to sign the vision and prophet, and *to anoint the holy of holies*," ix. 24; speaking of the coming of the Lord, who alone is the anointed of Jehovah, and alone holy, and also as to His Human is the Divine Good of the Divine Love, thus the holy of holies. That the Lord as to the Divine Human is alone the anointed of Jehovah, may be seen n. 9954; that He alone is holy, n. 9229; and that He is the Divine Good of the Divine Love, in what is cited, n. 9199. The reason why celestial good is the holy of holies, but spiritual good, holy, is, because celestial good is inmost good, therefore also that good is the good of the inmost heaven; whilst spiritual good is the good thence proceeding, and on that account is the good of the middle heaven, and this good is so far good, and hence is so far holy, as it has in it celestial good, for this latter flows-in into the former, and conceives it, and begets it, as a father a son. By celestial good is meant the good of love from the Lord to the Lord, and by spiritual good is meant the good of charity towards the neighbor from the Lord; the good itself of love to the Lord from the Lord is the holy of holies, because the Lord by it conjoins Himself immediately, but the good of charity towards the neighbor is holy, because the Lord by it conjoins Himself mediately, and so far conjoins Himself, as it has in it the good of love from the Lord. The good of love to the Lord from the Lord is in all the good of charity which is genuine, and likewise in all the good of faith which is genuine, for it flows-in from the Lord; for no one can love the neighbor, and from love do good to him from himself, but from the Lord, and no one can believe in God from himself, but from the Lord; therefore when the Lord is acknowledged, and the neighbor is loved, then the Lord is in the love towards the neighbor whether man knows it or not; this also is meant by the Lord's words in Matthew, "The just answered, Lord, *when saw we Thee* hungry, and fed Thee, or thirsty and gave Thee to drink; *when saw we Thee* sick and in prison and came to Thee; but the king shall say unto them, verily I say unto you, *inasmuch as ye have done it unto one of these least brethren ye have done it unto Me*," xxv. 37, 38, 39, 40. Hence it is evident that the Lord is in the good of charity, and is that good, although those who are in that good are ignorant of it. By brethren in the proximate sense are meant those who are in the good of charity, and in the sense abstracted from person, the brethren of the Lord are the goods themselves of charity, as may be seen n. 5063 to 5071.

10,130. "Every one touching the altar shall be sanctified"—that hereby is signified every one who receives the Divine of the Lord, appears from the signification of touching, as denoting communication, translation, reception, of which we shall speak presently; and from the signification of the altar, as being representative of the Lord as to the good of love, here in heaven and the church, as may be seen above, n. 10,129; and from the signification of being sanctified, as denoting to receive the Divine of the Lord, see also above, n. 10,128. The reason why to touch denotes communication, translation, and reception is, because the interiors of man put themselves forth by external things, especially by the touch, and thereby communicate themselves with another, and transfer themselves to another, and so far as the will is in further agreement, and makes one, they are received; whether we speak of the will or the love, it is the same thing, for what is of the love of man, this also is of his will. Hence also it follows that the interiors of man, which are of his love and of the thought thence derived, put themselves forth by the touch, and thus communicate themselves with another, and transfer themselves into another; and so far as another loves the person or the things which the person speaks or acts, so far they are received. This especially manifests itself in the other life, for all in that life act from the heart, that is, from the will or love, and it is not allowed to act from gestures separate from thence, nor to speak from the mouth according to pretence, that is, separately from the thought of the heart; it is there evident how the interiors communicate themselves with another, and transfer themselves into another by the touch; and how another receives them according to his love. The will or love of every one constitutes the whole man there, and the sphere of the life thence flows forth from him as an exhalation or vapor, and encompasses him, and makes as it were himself around him; resembling in a great measure the effluvia encompassing vegetables in the world, which is also made sensible at a distance by odors; also that encompassing beasts, of which a sagacious dog is exquisitely sensible; such an effluvium also diffuses itself from every man, as is moreover known from much experience. When, however, man lays aside the body, and becomes a spirit or an angel, then the effluvium or expiatory principle is not material, as in the world, but is spiritual, flowing forth from his love; this then forms a sphere around him, which causes his quality to be perceived at a distance by others. Concerning this sphere see what was shown in the passages cited, n. 9606. Now as this sphere communicates with another, and is there transferred into him, and is received by another according to his love, hence many wonderful things there exist which are unknown to man in the world; as 1st, That all presence is according to similitudes of loves, and all absence according to their dissimilitudes. 2dly, That all are consociated according to loves; those who are in love to the Lord from the Lord, consociate in the inmost heaven; those who are in love towards the neighbor from the Lord, consociate in the middle heaven; those who are in the obedience of faith, that is, who do the truth for the sake of the truth, consociate in the ultimate heaven; but those who are in the love of self and of the world, that is, who do what they do for the sake of themselves and the world as ends, consociate in hell. 3dly, That all turn their eyes to those whom they love; those who love the Lord, turn their eyes to the Lord as a sun; those who love the neighbor from the Lord, turn their eyes to the Lord as the moon; in like manner those who do the truth for the sake of the truth; (concerning the Lord as the sun and as the moon, see what was shown, n. 1521, 1529, 1530, 1531, 3636, 3643, 4060, 4321, 5097, 5377, 7078, 7083, 7171, 8644, 8812;) and what is wonderful, in whatsoever direction they turn themselves, or to whatsoever quarter, they still view the Lord before them. The contrary is the case with those who are in hell, since the more they are in the love of self, and in the love of the world, the more they avert themselves from the Lord, and have Him to the back; and this in whatsoever direction or to whatsoever quarter they turn themselves. 4thly, When an angel of heaven determinates his sight to others, in such case his interiors are communicated and transferred into them, according to the quantity and quality of his love; and are received by them according to the quality and quantity of their love; wherefore if by an angel of heaven the sight be determined to the good, the effect is gladness and joy; but if to the evil, the effect is grief and torment. The reason, moreover, why by the touch of the hand is also signified communication, translation, and reception, is, because the active principle of the whole body is brought together into the arms and into the hands, and interior things are expressed in the Word by exterior. Hence it is that by the arms, by the hands, and especially by the right hand, is signified power, as may be seen in what was cited, n. 10,019, 10,023, 10,076; and hence by the hands whatever appertains to the man is signified, thus the whole man so far as he is an agent, see what was cited, n. 10,019. Moreover, that all the external senses, as sight, hearing, taste, and smell, have relation to the touch, and are species of touch, is well known in the learned world. That by touching is signified communication, translation, and reception, is manifest from numerous passages in the Word, of which it is allowed to adduce the following, "Thou shalt anoint the tent of the congregation, and the ark of the testimony, and the table, and all its vessels, and the candlestick and its vessels, and the altar of incense, and the altar of burnt-offering, and all its vessels, and the laver and its base, and shall sanctify them, that they may be the holy of holies; *every one who toucheth those things shall be sanctified*," Exod. xxx. 26 to 29. Again, "*Every thing which hath touched the residue of the meat-offering, and the residue of the flesh of the sacrifices*, which are for Aaron and his sons, *shall be sanctified*," Levit. vi. 18, 27. And in Daniel, "*The angel touched Daniel*, and restored him on his station and lifted him up on his knees; *and touched his lips*, and opened his mouth; and *added to touch him*, and strengthened him," x. 10, 16, 18. And in Isaiah, "One of the seraphim *touched my mouth with a burning coal*, and said, behold *this hath touched thy lips*, therefore thine iniquity hath departed, and thy sin is expiated," vi. 7. And in Jeremiah, "Jehovah put forth His hand, and *touched my mouth*, and said, I give My words into thy mouth," i. 9. And in Matthew, "Jesus stretching out the hand to the leper, *touched him*, saying, I will, be thou cleansed, and immediately his leprosy was cleansed," viii. 3. Again, "Jesus saw Peter's wife's mother afflicted with a fever, and *He touched her hand*, and the fever left her," Matt. viii. 14, 15. Again, "*Jesus touched the eyes of the blind*, and their eyes were opened," Matt. ix. 29, 30. Again, "*Jesus touched the eyes of the two blind men*, and they immediately received sight," xx. 34. And in Luke, "*Jesus touched the ear of the wounded man*, and healed him," xxii. 51. And in Mark, "They brought to Jesus those who were sick, *that at least they might touch the hem of His garment*, and as many as *touched* were made whole," vi. 56; Matt. xiv. 36. And in Luke, "A woman laboring under a flux of blood *touched the hem of the garm ent of Jesus;* and immediately the flux of blood was staunched; Jesus said, *who is it that hath touched Me; some one hath touched Me, I know that virtue hath gone forth from Me*," viii. 44 to 48. And in Mark, "They brought infants to Jesus, that he should touch them; and *He took them up in his arms, laid His hands on them, and blessed them*," x. 13, 16. From these passages it is evident, that by touching is signified communication, translation, and reception. In like manner where it treats of things unclean, by which in the internal sense are signified evils and falses which are from the hells, as in Moses, "*He that toucheth one that is dead*, as to every soul of man, shall be unclean seven days. *Every one that toucheth one that is dead*, as to the soul of the man who dies, and hath not expiated himself, *hath polluted the habitation of Jehovah*, therefore this soul shall be cut off from Israel. *Every one who hath touched on the surface of a field one thrust through with a sword*, or *one that is dead*, or *the bone of a man*, or a *sepulchre*, shall be unclean seven days. *He that toucheth the waters of separation* shall be unclean to the evening. *Every thing which an unclean person hath touched* shall become unclean; and *the soul which hath touched it* shall be unclean until the evening," Numb. xix. 11, 13, 16, 21, 22. Again, "*He who toucheth unclean beasts, unclean creeping things*, shall be unclean until the evening; *every thing on which he shall fall shall be unclean*, whether vessel of wood, garment, waters, earthen vessel, meat, drink, an oven, a fountain, a cistern, a receptacle of waters, they shall be unclean," Levit. xi. 31 to 36; in like manner, chap. v. 2, 3; chap. vii. 21. Again, "He that is in a flux, is unclean; *the man who shall touch his bed*; if he shall sit upon a vessel on which he that hath a flux hath sat; he who shall touch his flesh, or his garments; if he that is affected with a flux *shall spit* upon one that is clean; *the chariot* on which he is carried, *the earthen vessel, the vessel of wood*, shall be unclean," Levit. xvi. 1 to the end. Also he *who touched a leper*, Levit. xxii. 4. Again, "*If there shall fall any thing from a dead body upon all seed of the sower*, which is sown, it shall be clean; but if water hath been given upon the seed, and *a dead body shall fall upon it*, it shall be unclean," Levit. xi. 37, 38. By those unclean things are signified various kinds of evils and of falses thence derived, which are from hell, and which are communicated, transferred and received; each of the unclean things signifies some specific evil; for evils are what render man unclean, inasmuch as they infect his soul; also from evil spirits and genii flow forth the evils of their hearts, and according to the persuasions of evil they infect those who are present; this contagion is what is signified by the touch of unclean things. And in Moses, "Of the fruit of the tree, which is in the midst of the garden, ye shall not eat, *neither shall ye touch it*, lest ye die," Gen. iii. 3. Again, "The angel, who wrestled with Jacob, seeing that he did not prevail over him, *touched the hollow of his thigh*, and the hollow of the thigh shrank," Gen. xxxii. 26 Again, "Moses said, *that they should not touch any thing* which belonged to Korah, Dathan, and Abiram, lest they should be consumed for all their sins," Numb. xvi. 26. And in Isaiah, "Depart ye, depart ye, *touch not the unclean thing*, go forth from the midst of her, be ye purified that carry the vessels of Jehovah," lii. 11. And in Jeremiah, "They have wandered blind in the streets, they are polluted with blood, those things which they cannot [pollute], *they touch with their garments:* recede, he is unclean, they cry to them, recede, *touch not*," Lam. iv. 14, 15. And in Haggai, "Behold a man [*vir*] shall carry the flesh of holiness in the hem [the wing] of his garment, and *his hem toucheth bread, or wine, or oil, or any food whatsoever*, still it shall not be sanctified: *If one unclean in soul shall touch any of those things*, still he shall be unclean," ii. 12, 13, 14. And in Hosea, "To forswear, and to lie, and to kill, and to steal, and to commit adultery, they commit robbery, *and bloods touch bloods;* therefore the land shall mourn," iv. 2, 3.

10,131. "And this is what thou shalt offer upon the altar"—that hereby is signified what in general concerns the reception of the Lord in heaven and in the church, is evident from the signification of this is what thou shalt offer upon the altar, as denoting what in general concerns the reception of the Lord in the heavens; for by the altar is signified the Divine of the Lord in the heavens, n. 10, 129, thus also the reception of Him; and by this thou shalt offer upon it is signified what in general concerns. For what follows is concerning the daily burnt-offerings, and by them is represented in general what concerns the reception of the Lord, for by the lambs is signified the good of innocence, and the good of innocence is the only [principle or good] which receives the Lord, for without the good of innocence love to the Lord is not given, neither is charity towards the neighbor, nor faith which has life in it, nor in general any good containing what is Divine, as may be seen in what is cited, n. 10,021. Hence it is, that by this thou shalt offer upon the altar, is signified what in general concerns the reception of the Lord in heaven and in the church. When it is said heaven, the church is also meant, for the heaven of the Lord in the earths is the church, and in whomsoever the church is, in him also is heaven, for the Lord is in him, and where the Lord is, there is heaven; the church also makes one with heaven, for the one hangs from the other by an inseparable connection; the Word is what conjoins, in the Word is the Lord, and the Lord is the Word, John i. 1 and following verses.

10,132. "Two lambs the sons of a year every day"—that hereby is signified the good of innocence in every state, appears from the signification of lambs, as denoting the good of innocence, of which we shall speak presently, and from the signification of the sons of a year, as denoting the quality of infancy, in which however truths are implanted, of which also we shall speak presently; and from the signification of every day, as denoting in every state, for by day is signified state, and by the morning of the day, and by its evening, in which the burnt-offerings of lambs were offered, is signified every state. That day denotes state, may be seen, n. 893, 2788, 3462, 3785, 4850, 7680; and that changes of states are as the changes of the day as to morning, mid-day, evening, night, and again morning, n. 5672, 5962, 6110, 8426. That lambs denote the good of innocence, is manifest from the passages in the Word where lambs are mentioned, as in Isaiah, "The wolf shall dwell together *with the lamb*, and the leopard shall lie down *with the kid*, and *the calf* and the young lion, and the fatling together; and *a little child shall lead them;* the *suckling* shall play on the hole of the viper, and the *weaned child* shall lay his hand on the den of the basilisk; they shall not corrupt themselves in the whole mountain of My holiness. And it shall come to pass in that day, the nations shall seek the root of Jesse, which standeth for a sign for the people; and His rest shall be glorious," xi. 6, 8, 9, 10. In this passage is described the state of peace and innocence in the heavens and in the church, after that the Lord came into the world; and because a state of peace and innocence is described, mention is made of a lamb, of a kid, and of a calf, also of a little child, a suckling, and a weaned child, and by them all is signified the good of innocence, the inmost good of innocence by a lamb, the interior good of innocence by a kid, and the exterior good of innocence by a calf; in like manner by a child, a suckling, and a weaned child. The mountain of holiness denotes heaven and the church, where the good of innocence prevails; the nations are those who are in that good; the root of Jesse is the Lord from whom that good is derived; the good of love from Him to Him, which is also called celestial good, is the good of innocence. That a lamb denotes the good of innocence in general, and specifically the inmost good of innocence, is manifest from this consideration, that it is named in the first place, as well as from the fact, that the Lord Himself is called a lamb, as will be seen in what follows. That a kid denotes the interior good of innocence, may be seen, n. 3519, 4871; that a calf or a bullock denotes the exterior good of innocence, n. 430, 9391; that a child denotes innocence, n. 5236; and in like manner a suckling, a weaned child, or infant, n. 430, 2280, 3183, 3494, 5608. That the mountain of holiness is where the good of love to the Lord is, n. 6435, 8758; and that nations are those who are in that good, n. 1416, 6005. That the good of love to the Lord, which is called celestial good, is the good of innocence, is manifest from those who are in the inmost heaven, who, because they are in that good, appear naked and as infants, by reason that nakedness denotes innocence, in like manner infancy, as may be seen in what is cited, n. 9277: and n. 3887, 9680. It is said that the wolf shall dwell with the lamb, because by the wolf are signified those who are opposed to innocence, as also in the same prophet, "*The wolf and the lamb* shall feed together, they shall not do evil, neither shall they destroy in the whole mountain of My holiness," lxv. 25; and in Luke, "Jesus said to the disciples, whom He sent forth, *behold I send you as lambs in the midst of wolves*," x. 3. Inasmuch as the Lord, when in the world, was, as to His Human, innocence itself; and because thence the all of innocence proceeds from Him, therefore the Lord is called the lamb, and the lamb of God; as in Isaiah, "*Send the lamb of the Governor of the earth* from the rock towards the wilderness to the mountain of the daughter of Zion," xvi. 1. Again, "He hath endured exaction, and was afflicted, yet He opened not His mouth, *as a lamb He is led to the slaughter*," liii. 7. And in John, "John the Baptist saw Jesus coming, and said, *behold the lamb of God*, who taketh away the sin of the world," i. 29, 36. And in the Apoc., "*The Lamb who is in the midst of the throne shall feed them*, and shall lead them to living fountains of water," vii. 17; and in another place, "These are they who have not been polluted with women, *these are they who follow the Lamb whithersoever He goeth;* these were brought from men, *the first-fruits to God and the Lamb*," xvi. 4; besides numerous other passages in the Apoc., as chap. v. 6, 8, 12, 13; chap. vi. 1, 16; chap. vii. 9, 10, 14; chap. xii. 11; chap. xiii. 8; chap. xiv. 1; chap. xv. 3; chap. xvii. 14; chap. xix. 7, 9; chap. xxi. 9, 14, 22, 23, 26; chap. xxii. 1, 3. Now as lambs denote those who are in innocence, therefore the Lord said to Peter, first, *feed My lambs*, and afterwards, *feed My sheep*, and again, *feed My sheep*," John xxi. 15, 16, 17. Lambs in this passage denote those who are in the good of love to the Lord, for these are in the good of innocence more than others; but sheep denote those who are in the good of charity towards the neighbor, and those who are in the good of faith. The like is signified by lambs in Isaiah, "Behold the Lord Jehovih cometh in might, and His arm ruleth for Him; as a shepherd He shall feed His flock, *into His arms He shall gather the lambs*, in His bosom He shall carry [them], *the sucklings He shall gently lead*," xl. 10, 11; that these things were said of the Lord, is evident. Inasmuch as by lambs are meant those who are in love to Him, thus in the good of innocence, therefore it is said that He will gather them into His arms, and carry them in His bosom; for they are conjoined to the Lord by love, and love is spiritual con junction; and on this account it is also added, that He will gently lead the sucklings, for sucklings and infants denote those who are in the good of innocence, n. 430, 2280, 3183, 3494 From these considerations it may now be manifest what is signified by the burnt-offerings and sacrifices of lambs, and why they were to be made every day, every Sabbath, every new moon, and every festival, and every day on the feast of the passover; and why at the feast of the passover, the lamb which was called the paschal lamb was to be eaten, concerning which it is thus written in Moses, "This month is to you the head of months, this is to you the first of the months of the year; ye shall take *cattle a male of the lambs or of the kids;* and they shall take of the blood and shall give it upon the door posts; and on the threshold, and on the houses in which they shall eat it; they shall not eat of it raw, or boiled in waters, but roast with fire," Exod. xii. 1 and following verses. By the feast of the passover was signified the liberation of those from damnation, who receive the Lord in love and faith, n. 9286, 9287 to 9292, thus who are in the good of innocence, for the good of innocence is the inmost principle of love and of faith, and is their soul; wherefore it is said, that they should give the blood thereof upon the door posts, the threshold, and the houses, for where the good of innocence is, thither hell cannot enter; the reason why they were to eat it roast with fire was, because by it was signified the good of celestial love, which is the good of love to the Lord from the Lord. Now because a lamb signified innocence, therefore when the days were fulfilled after child-birth, *a lamb the son of a year was offered for a burnt-offering*, and the son of a dove or a turtle for sacrifices, Levit. xii. 6. By the son of a dove, and by a turtle, in like manner as by a lamb, was signified innocence; by child-birth in the spiritual sense is signified the birth of the church, which is that of the good of love, for no other birth is understood in heaven; and by the burnt-offering and sacrifice from those things is signified purification from evils by the good of innocence; for this good is that into which the Divine flows-in, and by which it purifies. The reason why he who sinned through error *was to offer a lamb*, or *a she-goat of the goats*, or *two turtles*, or *two sons of the doves*, according to the offence, Levit. v. 1 to 13, was, because sin through error is sin from ignorance, and if in ignorance there is innocence, purification is effected. Concerning the Nazarite also it is said, that when he hath fulfilled his Nazariteship, *he shall offer a he-lamb the son of a year* for a burnt-offering, and a she-lamb the daughter of a year for a sacrifice of sin, and *one ram* for an eucharistic sacrifice, also a basket of things unleavened, cakes mixed with oil, and wafers of things unleavened anointed with oil, Numb. vi. 13, 14, 15. By all those things, namely, by a he-lamb, a she-lamb, a ram, unleavened bread, cakes, wafers, and oil, are signified celestial things, that is, those which are of love to the Lord from the Lord. The reason why those things were to be sacrificed by the Nazarite after the fulfilling of the days of the Nazariteship, was, because the Nazarite represented the celestial man, or the Lord as to the Divine Celestial; the Divine Celestial is the Divine of the Lord in the inmost heaven; and this Divine [principle] is innocence. From these considerations it may be manifest, that by a lamb is signified the good of innocence, for by all the beasts which were sacrificed something of the church was signified, which is especially evident from this consideration, that the Lord Himself is called a lamb, as is plain from the passages above cited; and likewise that they are called lambs, who love the Lord, as in Isaiah, chap. xl. 10, 11.; and in John, chap. xxi. 15; and that well-disposed men are also called sheep, as Matt. xv. 21 to 29; chap. xxv. 31 to 41; John x. 7 to 16, 26 to 31; chap. xxi. 16, 17, and in other places; whilst evil men are called goats, Matt. xxv. 31; Zech. x. 3; Dan. viii. 5 to 11, 25. That all the useful and tame beasts signify good affections and inclinations, but that the useless and untame signify evil affections and inclinations, may be seen in what is cited, n. 9280. The good of innocence is signified not only by a lamb, but also by a ram, and by a bullock, but with the difference, that by a lamb is signified the inmost good of innocence, by a ram the interior or middle good of innocence, and by a bullock the external good of innocence. The good of innocence in every one must be external, internal, and inmost, that man may be regenerated, for the good of innocence is the very essence of all good; and since these three degrees of innocence are signified by a bullock, a ram, and a lamb, therefore those three [animals] were offered in sacrifice and for the burnt-offering, when purification was represented by that good, as was the case at each of the new moons, the festivals, the day of first fruits, when the altar was inaugurated, as is evident from Numb. vii. 15, 21, 27, 33; chap. xxviii. 1 to the end; chap. xxix. 1 to the end. That a bullock denotes the external good of innocence, may be seen, n. 9391, 9990; and that a ram denotes the internal good of innocence, n. 10,042. What innocence is, and what is its quality with infants, with the simple who are in ignorance, and with the wise, may be seen in what is cited, n. 10,021. By its being said that the lamb, which was to be offered for a burnt-offering, should be the son of a year, was signified that it then was a lamb, for when it exceeded a year, it became a sheep; and since a lamb was an infant sheep, by it was signified such good as is of infancy, which is the good of innocence; hence also it was that lambs were to be offered for a burnt-offering in the first month of the year, at the passover, Exod. xii. 2, and following verses; Numb. xxviii. 16, 19: also on the day of the first fruits, Numb. xxviii. 26, 27: and on the day in which they shook the sheaf of corn, Levit. xxiii. 11, 12; for by the first month of the year, by the day of the first fruits, and by the day of the shaking of the sheaf, was also signified a state of infancy, thus a state of innocence.

10,133. "Continually"—that hereby is signified in all Divine Worship, appears from the signification of continually, when applied to such things as relate to Divine Worship, as denoting all and in all; for the subject treated of is purification from evils and falses by the good of innocence, for this good is signified by lambs, and purification from evils and the falses thence derived by the burnt-offering of them. This is said to be continual, because in all Divine Worship. Therefore also it was offered twice every day, in the morning and in the evening; and what was offered in the morning and in the evening represented in general all worship, and in all worship; for the good of innocence must be in all good, and thence in all truth, to the intent that it may be good and truth, in which there is life from the Divine; thus it must be in all worship, for all worship ought to be grounded in the good of love and in the truths of faith to make it worship. That all the good of the church and of heaven has in it innocence, and that without innocence good is not good, thus neither is worship worship, may be seen, n. 2736, 2780, 6013, 7840, 7262, 7887; and what innocence is, n. 3994, 4001, 4797, 5236, 6107, 6765, 7902, 9262, 9936, and what is cited, n. 10,021 at the end. The reason why continually denotes all and in all, namely, the all of worship and in all worship, is because it involves time; and in the heavens, where the Word is not understood in a natural sense, but in a spiritual sense, there is not any notion of time, but instead of times are perceived such things as relate to state; here therefore by continually is perceived a perpetual state in worship, thus the all of worship and in all worship. It is so likewise with all the other expressions in the Word which involve any thing of time, as by yesterday, to-day, to-morrow, two days, three days, a day, a week, a month, and a year, also by the times of the day and of the year, as by morning, mid-day, evening, night, spring, summer, autumn, and winter; wherefore, that the spiritual sense of the Word may be understood, every thing which relates to time, and also which relates to place, and likewise every thing which relates to person, must be rejected from its natural sense, and instead thereof are to be conceived the states of things. From which considerations it may be manifest how pure the Word is in the internal sense, thus how purely it is perceived by the angels in the heavens, consequently how eminent the wisdom and the intelligence of the angels is, in comparison with the intelligence and wisdom of men, who think only from the natural principle determined to things most finite in the world and the earth. That times in the heavens denote states, may be seen, n. 1274, 1382, 2625, 2788, 2837, 3254,

3356, 3404, 3827, 4814, 4882, 4901, 4916, 6110, 7218, 7381, 8070; and what is meant by states, n. 4850. From these considerations it is evident what is signified by the continual burnt-offering of lambs; thus what by continual and continually in other places, as that the fire should burn *continually* upon the altar, Levit. vi. 13; and "that *continual bread* should be upon the table," Numb. iv. 7. By fire and by bread is here signified the good of love from the Lord to the Lord. That fire has this signification, may be seen, n. 4906, 5215, 6314, 6832, 6834, 6849, 7324, 7852, 10,055; and also bread, n. 2165, 2177, 3478, 3735, 3813, 4211, 4217, 4735, 4976, 9323, 9545. By *continual* is here also signified that that good should be in all worship; and that from that good, as from its own fire, the truth of faith should give light, is signified by *making the lamp to ascend continually*, Exod. xxviii. 20; that lamp denotes the truth and good of faith, may be seen, n. 9548, 9783.

10,134. "One lamb thou shalt offer in the morning"—that hereby is signified the removal of evils by the good of innocence from the Lord in a state of love and of light thence derived in the internal man, is evident from the signification of offering a lamb, or sacrificing it, as denoting the removal of evils by the good of innocence from the Lord, of which we shall speak presently; and from the signification of morning, as denoting a state of love and of light thence derived in the internal man, of which also we shall speak presently. The reason why by offering, or sacrificing a lamb, is signified the removal of evils by the good of innocence from the Lord is, because by burnt-offerings and sacrifices purification from evils and the falses thence derived was signified, or, what is the same thing, their removal, and the implantation of good and of truth, and their conjunction by the Lord, n. 9990, 9991, 10,022, 10,042, 10,053. That purification from evils is their removal, may be seen in what is cited, n. 10,057; and that a lamb denotes the good of innocence, n. 10,132. The reason why the removal of evils, and the implantation of good and of truth, and their conjunction, is effected by the good of innocence from the Lord is, because in all good there must be innocence to make it good, and because without innocence good is not good; for innocence is not only the plane in which truths are inseminated, but is also the very essence of good; so far therefore as man is in innocence, so far good becomes good, and truth lives from good, consequently so far man becomes alive, and so far the evils appertaining to him are removed, and in proportion as they are removed, in the same proportion goods and truths are implanted and conjoined by the Lord; hence it is that the continual burnt-offering was made by lambs. That every good of heaven and of the church has innocence in it, and that without innocence good is not good, may be seen, n. 2736, 2780 6013, 7840, 7887; and what innocence is, n. 3994, 4001, 4797, 5236, 6107, 6765, 7902, 9262, 9936. The reason why morning denotes a state of love and of light thence derived in the internal man is, because in the heavens, with the angels, the states vary as to love and the faith thence derived; as, in the world, times, with men, vary as to heat, and at the same time light; those times are, as it is well known, morning, mid-day, evening, and night; hence in the Word by morning is signified a state of love, by mid-day a state of light in clearness, by evening a state of light in obscurity, and by night or twilight a state of love in obscurity. That there are such variations of states in the heavens, may be seen, n. 5672, 6110, 7218, 8426; that morning there denotes a state of peace and innocence, thus a state of love to the Lord, n. 2405, 2780, 8426, 8812, 10,114; that mid-day denotes a state of light in clearness, n. 3708, 5672, 9642; that evening denotes a state of light in obscurity, n. 3056, 3833, 6110; and that there is no night in heaven, but twilight, n. 6110, by which is signified a state of love in obscurity. The reason why by morning is signified a state of love and of light thence derived *in the internal man* is, because when an angel is in a state of love and light, he is then in his internal man; but when he is in a state of light and of love in obscurity, he is then in the external; for angels have an internal and an external, but when they are in the internal, the external is almost quiescent, and when they are in the external they are in a more gross and obscure state. Hence it is that when they are in a state of love and of light, they are in their internal, thus in their morning; and when in a state of light and of love in obscurity, they are in the external, thus in their evening; hence it is evident that variations of state are effected by elevations towards things interior, thus into a superior state of heavenly light and heat, consequently into one nearer to the Lord, and by depressions towards exterior things into an inferior sphere of heavenly light and heat, consequently one more remote from the Lord. It is to be observed, that interior things are superior, thus nearer to the Lord, and that exterior things are inferior, thus more remote from the Lord; and that light in the heavens is the Divine Truth which is of faith, and heat in the heavens is the Divine Good which is of love, each proceeding from the Lord; for the Lord in heaven is the Sun, from which the angels derive every thing of life, and hence man derives every thing of spiritual and celestial life, as may be seen in what is cited, n. 9548, 9684; and that interior things are superior, thus nearer to the Lord, n. 2148, 3084, 4599, 5146, 8325. The man who is regenerating, and likewise the man who is regenerated, undergoes also variations of state as to love and as to faith, by elevations towards interior things, and by depressions towards exterior things; but there are few capable of reflecting upon it, because they do not know what it is to think and to will in the internal man and in the external, nor even indeed what the internal man is, and what the external. To think and to will in the internal man, is to think and to will in heaven, for the internal man is there, but to think and to will in the external man is to think and to will in the world, for the external man is there; wherefore when man is in love to God, and in faith thence derived, then he is in the internal, because he is in heaven; but when he is in obscurity as to love, and the faith thence derived, then he is in the external, because in the world. These states also are meant by morning, mid-day, evening, and night, or the twilight, in the Word; as likewise states of the church, the first state of which is moreover called morning in the Word, the second state mid-day, the third evening, and the fourth or last night. But when the church is in its night, in which it is when no longer in love to God and in faith, then morning commences from the twilight with another nation, where a new church is established. For it is with the church in general as with man in particular; his first state is a state of innocence, thus also of love towards parents, towards his nurse, and also towards his infant companions; his second state is a state of light, for when the infant becomes a boy, he learns those things which are of light, that is, the truths of faith, and believes them; the third state is when he begins to love the world and to love himself, as is the case when he becomes a youth, and when he thinks from himself, and in proportion as these loves increase, in the same proportion faith decreases, and with faith charity towards the neighbor, and love to God; the fourth and last state is when he has no concern about truths, and especially when he denies them. Such states also are the states of every church from its beginning to its end; its first state is likewise a state of infancy, thus also of innocence, consequently of love to the Lord, this state of it is called morning; the second state is a state of light; the third state is a state of light in obscurity, which is its evening; and the fourth state is a state of no love and thence of no light, which is its night. The reason of this is, because evils increase every day, and so far as they increase, so far one infects another like a contagion, especially parents their children; besides that, hereditary evils are successively concentrated, and thus transmitted. That morning signifies the first state of the church, and also a state of love, is manifest from Daniel, "The holy One said, how long is this vision, the continual [sacrifice] and the vastating prevarication; he said to me *even to the evening, morning*, two thousand and three hundred; then shall what is holy be justified," viii. 13, 14. The subject here treated of is the coming of the Lord; evening is the state of the church before His coming, but morning is the first state of the church after His coming, and in the supreme sense it denotes the Lord Himself. The reason why the Lord, in the supreme sense, is the morning, is, because He is the sun of heaven, and the sun of heaven never sets, but is always rising; hence also the Lord is called the east [oriens], consequently also the morning, as may be seen n. 2405, 2780, 9668. And in Isaiah, "He calleth to me out of Seir, watchman, what *of the night*, what *of the night;* the watchman said, *the morning cometh and also the night*," xxi. 11, 12. By watchman, in the internal sense, is meant one who observes the states of the church and its changes, thus every prophet; by night is meant the last state of the church, by morning its first state; by Seir, from which the watchman cries, is signified the illumination of the nations which are in darkness; that Seir has this signification, may be seen, n. 4240; and that night denotes the last state of the church, n. 6000; the morning cometh and also the night, signifies, that although those have illumination who are of the New Church, yet that it is still night to those who are in the old. The like is signified by morning in David, "*In the evening* weeping will continue all night, *in the morning* will be singing," Psalm xxx. 5. And in Isaiah, "*About the time of evening* behold terror, *before the morning* it is not," xvii. 14. Inasmuch as morning signifies the Lord in the supreme sense, and thence love from Him to Him, therefore the manna, which was heavenly bread, *rained down every morning*, Exod. xvi. 8, 12, 13, 21. That the Lord is the bread which comes down from heaven, thus the manna, may be seen in John, vi. 33, 35, 48, 50; and that bread denotes celestial love, which is love from the Lord to the Lord, n. 2165, 2177, 3464, 4217, 4735, 5405, 5915, 9545. And whereas the Lord is the east [oriens] and the morning, and the all of celestial love is from Him, therefore also He rose *in the morning on the day of the Sabbath*, Mark xvi. 9; and therefore also the day before the passover was called evening; for by the feast of the passover was signified the Lord's presence, and the liberation of the faithful from damnation by Him, n. 7867, 9286, 9287 to 9292. He who is acquainted with the internal sense of the Word, may know what is involved in Peter's thrice denying the Lord, before the cock crew twice, Matt. xxvi. 34, 74, 75; Mark xiv. 30, 68, 72; Luke xxii. 34, 60, 61; John xviii. 27; for by Peter was represented the faith of the church, or what is the same thing, the church as to faith; by the time when the cock crew was signified the last state of the church, which time was also called cock-crowing; by triple denial was signified the plenary denial of the Lord in the end of the church. That Peter represented the faith of the church, thus the church as to faith, may be seen in the preface to chap. xviii. Gen. and to chap. xxii.; also n. 3750, 4738, and that those words to Peter signified the denial of the Lord in the church when its end is, n. 6000, 6073, 10,087; for the Lord is denied, when there is no longer any faith, and there is no faith when there is no longer any charity. That three signifies what is plenary, may be seen, n. 2788, 4495, 7715, 8347, 9198, 9488, 9489. It is from this ground that it was said, that he should thrice deny. That this was done in the twilight, when morning was about to appear, is manifest from John, chap. xviii. 28; and that *cock-crowing* and twilight denote the same thing, is evident from Mark, "Watch ye, for ye know not when the Lord of the house is about to come, in the evening, or at midnight, or at *cock-crowing*, or in the morning," xiii. 35. From these considerations it may now be manifest what is signified by morning.

10,135. "And the other lamb thou shalt offer between the evenings"—that hereby is signified the like in a state of light and of love in the external man, appears from the signification of offering a lamb or sacrificing him, as denoting removal from evils by the good of innocence from the Lord, as described just above, n. 10,134; and from the signification of between the evenings, as denoting in a state of light and of love in the external man; for by evening in the Word is signified a state of the interiors when the truths of faith are in obscurity, and the goods of love in some degree of cold; for the states of love and of light vary with angels, as in the world the states of the times of the day vary, which are morning, mid-day, evening, night or the twilight, and again morning. When the angels are in a state of love, then it is morning to them, and then the Lord appears to them as the rising sun; when they are in a state of light, then it is mid-day to them; but when they are in a state of light in obscurity, then it is evening to them; and afterwards when they are in a state of love in obscurity or in some degree of cold, then it is night to them, or rather the twilight preceding the morning. Such states succeed continually with the angels, and by them they are continually perfecting. Those variations however do not exist from the sun there, and from its rising and setting, but from the state of the interiors of the angels themselves; for they desire, like men, to be at one time in their internals, and at another in externals; when they are in internals, then they are in a state of love, and of light thence derived in clearness, and when in externals, then they are in a state of love and of light thence derived in obscurity, for such is the external in respect to the internal. This is the origin of the variations of the states of the angels. The reason why they have such states, and such variations, is, because the Sun of heaven, which is there the Lord, is the Divine Love itself; wherefore the heat which thence proceeds is the good of love, and the light which thence proceeds is the truth of faith; for all things which proceed from that Sun are alive, and not like the things which proceed from the sun of the world which are dead. Hence it may be manifest what heavenly heat is, and what heavenly light; and whence it is that by heat, flame, and fire, in the Word, is signified the good of love, and by light and its splendor the truth of faith, and by the Sun the Lord Himself as to Divine Love. That the Lord in the heavens is a Sun, may be seen, n. 3636, 3643, 4321, 5097, 7078, 7083, 7171, 7173, 8812; that the heat thence derived is the good of love, n. 3338, 3339, 3636, 3693, 4018, 5125, 6032, 6314; and that the light from that Sun is Divine Truth, from which comes faith, intelligence, and wisdom, in what is cited, n. 9548, 9684. From these considerations it may now be manifest what is signified by morning, and what by evening. But let it be observed, that this morning involves also mid-day, and that evening involves also the twilight; for when mention is made in the Word of morning and evening, in such case the whole day is meant, thus by morning also mid-day, and by evening also night or twilight; hence it is that by morning is here signified a state of love and also of light in clearness, and by evening a state of light and also of love in obscurity, or in the external man. That by between the evenings is not meant the time between the evening of one day and the evening of another day, but the time between evening and morning, thus inclusively night or twilight, is evident from this consideration, that the continual burnt-offering from a lamb was not only made in the evening, but also in the morning. Hence it may be manifest that the like is signified in other places by between the evenings, as where it is said that they should offer the passover *between the evenings*, Exod. xii. 6; Numb. ix. 5, 11; which is also explained elsewhere in these words, "*Thou shalt sacrifice the passover in the evening*, when the sun hath set, at the stated time of departure out of Egypt, afterwards thou shalt roast and eat it in the place which Jehovah thy God shall choose, *and thou shalt respect the morning*, and shalt go into thy tents," Deut. xvi. 6, 7. That evening in general signifies a state of light in obscurity, is manifest from Jeremiah, "Arise, and let us go up at mid-day; woe unto you because the day departeth, because *the shades of evening are inclined*; arise, let us go up *in the night*, and let us destroy the palaces," vi. 4, 5; in this passage evening and night signify the last times of the church, when all things of faith and of love are destroyed. And in Zechariah, speaking of the coming of the Lord, "The day shall be one, which is known to Jehovah, *when about the time of evening shall be light.* In that day, living waters shall go forth from Jerusalem, and Jehovah shall be for a King over the whole earth," xiv. 7, 8. The end of the church is the time of evening; light is the Lord as to Divine Truth. In like manner in Daniel, "One saint said to me, *even to the evening, morning*, two thousand three hundred," viii. 13, 14.

10,136. "And a tenth of fine flour mixed with bruised oil,

the fourth of a hin"—that hereby is signified spiritual good from what is celestial as much as [is necessary] for conjunction, appears from the signification of the tenth of an ephah, as denoting so much as is sufficient, and so much as is for uses; see n. 8468, 8540, 9757; and from the signification of fine flour, as denoting truth from good, see n. 9995, in this case truth from celestial good, which truth is called spiritual good; and from the signification of oil, as denoting celestial good, see n. 886, 3728, 4582, 4638, 9474, 9780; and from the signification of the fourth of a hin, as denoting so much as [is required] for conjunction, for by four is signified conjunction, n. 9601, 9674; and hence a fourth or fourth part denotes so much as is sufficient for that purpose. An ephah and a hin were measures, and by measures is signified the quantity of a thing treated of; by an ephah, which was a measure of fine flour, of wheat and of barley, the quantity of good, and by a hin, which was a measure of wine and of oil, the quantity of truth; that the tenth of an ephah is what is meant, is manifest from Leviticus vi. 20, and other passages. Hence it is evident, that by a tenth of fine flour mixed with bruised oil, the fourth of a hin, is signified spiritual good from celestial, so much as [is necessary] for conjunction. What is meant by spiritual and what by celestial, may be seen in the passages cited, n. 9277.

10,137. "And a libation of the fourth of a hin of wine"—that hereby is signified spiritual truth so much as [is expedient] for conjunction, appears from the signification of wine, as denoting truth, see n. 1071, 1798, 6377, in this case spiritual truth corresponding to spiritual good derived from celestial, which is signified by fine flour mixed with oil, see just above, n. 10,136. For, in the Word, where good is treated of, truth is treated of also, and indeed truth of the same genus with that from which the good is derived, by reason that each and every thing in heaven, and likewise in the world, has reference to good and to truth, and to both that they may be something, for good without truth is not good, and truth without good is not truth, as may be seen in what was cited, n. 9263, 9314. Hence it is that when the meat-offering was offered, which was bread, a libation was also offered, which was wine; in like manner in the holy supper. Hence it is that by a libation of wine is here meant truth corresponding with the good, signified by the meat-offering spoken of just above; and from the signification of the fourth of a hin, that it was as much as was sufficient for conjunction, see just above, n. 10,136. Every one may see, that by a meat-offering which was bread, and by a libation which was wine, is not meant merely bread and wine, but something of the church and of heaven, thus things spiritual and celestial, which are of heaven and of the church; otherwise to what purpose could bread and wine be put upon the fire of the altar?

could this have been grateful to Jehovah? or could this have been to Him an odor of rest, as it is called, and could this expiate man? He who thinks holily of the Word, can never suppose that such an earthly thing would be well pleasing to Jehovah, unless something higher and more interiorly Divine was contained in it. He who believes that the Word is Divine and spiritual throughout, ought to believe fully that in each of its expressions there lies concealed an arcanum of heaven. The reason, moreover, why heretofore it has not been known where that arcanum lies concealed is, because it has not been known that there is an internal sense, which is spiritual and Divine, in every portion of the Word; also that angels are attendant upon every man, who perceive what he thinks, and apprehend the Word spiritually whilst he is reading it, and that through them from the Lord a holy principle then flows in, and thus that by them there is conjunction of heaven with man, consequently conjunction of the Lord by the heavens with him. For this reason such a Word has been given to man, by which his salvation may be thus provided for by the Lord, and no otherwise. That the meat-offering, which was bread, signifies the good of love, and that the libation, which was wine, signifies the good of faith, and that they are so perceived by the angels, may be manifest from all those things which are mentioned in the Word concerning the meat-offering and concerning the libation, as in Joel, "*The meat-offering is cut off and the libation from the house of Jehovah;* the priests, the ministers of Jehovah have mourned, the field is devastated, the earth hath mourned, because the corn is devastated, the new wine is dried up, the oil languisheth, the vine is dried up, and the fig-tree languisheth; howl, ye ministers of Jehovah, *because the meat-offering and the libation is withholden from the house of our God;* because the day of Jehovah is near, and cometh as devastation from Schaddai," i. 9 to 15. The subject here treated of is the last time of the church, when there is no longer in it the good of love and the truth of faith, which is signified by the day of Jehovah being near, and coming as a devastation from Schaddai. Hence it is evident that by the meat-offering and libation, which were cut off from the house of Jehovah, by the field which was devastated, by the earth which mourned, by the corn which was also devastated, by the new wine which was dried up, by the oil which languisheth, and by the vine and fig-tree, are signified such things as are of the church and of heaven. What is signified, however, the internal sense teaches; and hence it is evident, that by field is signified the church as to the reception of truth, as may be seen, n. 3766, 4982, 7502, 7571, 9295; by earth the church as to good, in what is cited, n. 9325; by corn every good of the church, n. 5295, 5410, 5959; by new wine every truth of the church, n. 3580; by oil the good of love, n.

4582, 4638, 9780; by vine the interior good of the Spiritual Church, n. 5113, 6376, 9277; and by fig-tree exterior good, n. 217, 4231, 5113. Hence it is evident, that a meat-offering and libation denote worship grounded in the good of love and in the good of faith. And in Malachi, "*The meat-offering I will not accept* from your hands; for from the rising of the sun even to its setting the name of Jehovah is great among the nations; and in every place incense is brought to My name, and *a clean meat-offering*," i. 10, 11. That in this passage by a meat-offering is not meant a meat-offering, nor by incense incense, is evident, for the subject treated of is the church amongst the Gentiles, with whom there was yet no meat-offering; for it is said, from the rising of the sun to its setting the name of Jehovah is great amongst the nations, and in every place is a clean meat-offering and incense; that incense denotes adoration from the good of faith, may be seen, n. 9475. In like manner in David, "My prayers are accepted, [they are] *incense before Thee*, the lifting up of my hands is *the meat-offering of the evening*," Psalm cxli. 2; the meat-offering of the evening is the good of love in the external man. And in Isaiah, "Ye are inflamed with gods under every green tree, also *thou hast poured forth a libation* to them; thou hast made a present to ascend, *thou offerest a present to the king in oil*; and thou multipliest thy spices; and humblest thyself to hell," lvii. 6, 9. It here treats of worship grounded in evils and falses, which are from hell; gods in the internal sense denote falses, for those who worshiped other gods called them indeed by name, but still they were falses derived from the evils which they worshiped. That strange gods in the Word denote falses, may be seen, n. 4402, 8941. A green tree denotes every principle that is perceptive, has knowledge of, and tends to confirm what is false, n. 2722, 2972, 4552, 7692. Green denotes what is sensitive, n. 7691. To be enflamed denotes the ardor of worship, for fire, from which the enflaming comes, denotes love in both senses, n. 5215, 6832, 7575. To pour forth a libation denotes worship grounded in the falses of evil. To offer a present to a king in oil, denotes to worship Satan from evils. A present in oil is a meat-offering. To multiply spices is to multiply incense, by which are signified adorations, n. 9475; wherefore also it is said, that he humbles himself to hell. From these considerations it may be manifest that the meat-offering, which was bread, and the libation, which was wine, signify such things as are of the church and of heaven, namely, heavenly meat and drink, in like manner as the bread and wine in the holy supper; for the reason above mentioned, that heaven may conjoin itself with man by the Word, consequently the Lord through heaven by means of the Word. When the Divine of the Word consists in such things, then it not only nourishes human minds, but also angelic minds, and causes heaven and the world to be a one. From these considerations it may also be manifest that each and every thing which was said and commanded in the Word concerning the meat-offering and libation, or concerning bread and wine, contains inwardly in it Divine arcana; as that the meat-offering should be fine flour, on which should be poured oil and also frankincense, and that it should be wholly salted, and that it should be unleavened; also that there should be one rule for its composition when a lamb was sacrificed, another when a ram, another when a bullock, and also a different one in the sacrifices of guilt and of sin from that used in the other sacrifices; in like manner the rule of the composition of the wine was various in the libation; unless each had involved arcana of heaven, such things would never have been commanded in the way of application to the various things of worship. That these various things may be presented under one view, it is allowed to offer them in their order, "In the eucharistic sacrifices and burnt-offerings there was for *every lamb* a meat-offering *of one tenth of an ephah of fine flour* mixed *with the fourth of a hin of oil;* and wine for a libation *the fourth of a hin.* For *every ram* there was a meat-offering *of two tenths of fine flour* and *a third of a hin of oil;* of wine for a libation *the third of a hin.* For *every bullock* there was a meat-offering *of three tenths of fine flour* mixed with oil *the half of a hin;* and of wine for a libation *the half of a hin,*" Numb. xv. 4 to 12; chap. xxviii. 10, 11, 12, 20, 21, 28, 29; chap. xxix. 3, 4, 9, 10, 14, 15, 18, 21, 24, 27, 30, 33, 37. The reason why there was a different proportion of the quantity of fine flour of oil, and of wine, for a lamb, than for a ram and a bullock, was, because a lamb signified the inmost good of innocence, a ram the middle good of innocence, and a bullock the ultimate or external good of innocence; for there are three heavens, the inmost, the middle, and the ultimate, hence also there are three degrees of the good of innocence; its increase from first to last is signified by the increasing proportion of fine flour, of oil, and of wine. It is to be observed, that the good of innocence is the very soul of heaven, because this good is alone receptive of love, of charity, and of faith, which make the heavens. That a lamb denotes the inmost good of innocence, may be seen, n. 3994, 10,132; that a ram denotes the middle or interior good of innocence, n. 10,042; and that a bullock denotes the ultimate or external good of innocence, n. 9391, 9990. But in the sacrifices for confession there *was a meat-offering of unleavened cakes mixed with oil, of unleavened wafers anointed with oil, of fine flour puffed up for the cakes mixed with oil; besides leavened cakes of bread,* Levit. vii. 11, 12; and in the sacrifices of guilt and of sin there was a meat-offering of *the tenth of an ephah of fine flour, but no oil and frankincense upon it,* Levit. v. 11. The reason why no oil and frankincense was to be put upon the meat-offering of the sacrifice of sin and of guilt was, because by oil is signified the good of love, and by frankincense the truth of that good, and by the sacrifice of sin and of guilt is signified purification and expiation from evils and the falses thence derived, which on that account were not to be commixed with good and the truth thence derived. Moreover concerning the meat-offering of Aaron and of his sons on the day in which they were anointed, may be seen, Levit. vi. 13, 14, 15; concerning the meat-offering of the first-fruits of the harvest, Levit. ii. 14, 15; chap. xxiii. 10, 12, 13, 17; the meat-offering of the Nazarite, Numb. vi.; the meat-offering of jealousy, Numb. v.; and the meat-offering of one that was cleansed from the leprosy, Levit. xiv.; and concerning the meat-offering baked in an oven; the meat-offering of the frying-pan; and the meat-offering in the kettle, Levit. ii. 3, 4, 5, 6, 7; that no leaven was to be in the meat-offering, nor any honey: and that the meat-offering was to be wholly salted, verses 10, 11, 13, of the same chapter. The reason why no leaven and honey were to be in the meat-offering was, because leaven in the spiritual sense denotes the false derived from evil, and honey denotes external delight thus commixed with the delight of the love of the world, by which also celestial goods and truths ferment, and are thereby dissipated; and the reason why it was to be wholly salted was, because salt signified truth desiring good, thus conjoining both. That leaven denotes the false derived from evil, may be seen, n. 2342, 7906, 8051, 9992; that honey denotes external delight, thus the delight of love in both senses, n. 5620; and that salt denotes truth desiring good, n. 9207.

10,138. "With the first lamb"—that hereby are signified these things in the internal man, appears from the signification of the first lamb, or what was offered for a burnt-offering in the morning, as denoting the good of innocence in the internal, see above, n. 10,134.

10,139. "And the second lamb thou shalt offer between the evenings"—that hereby is signified the removal of evils by the good of innocence from the Lord in a state of love and of light thence derived in the external man, is evident from what was explained above, n. 10,135, where similar words occur.

10,140. "According to the morning meat-offering, and according to the libation thereof, thou shalt offer it"—that hereby is signified spiritual good derived from celestial, and its truth so much as is sufficient for conjunction, appears from the signification of the morning meat-offering, or of the meat-offering for the second lamb, as denoting spiritual good derived from celestial, and its truth so much as is sufficient for conjunction, see also above, n. 10,136, 10,137.

10,141. "For an odor of rest"—that hereby is signified a principle perceptive of peace, is manifest from the signification of an odor of rest, as denoting what is perceptive of peace, see n. 10,054.

10,142. "An offering made by fire unto Jehovah"—that hereby is signified from the Divine Love of the Lord, is evident from what was said and shown also above, n. 10,055.

10,143. "And a burnt-offering continually"—that hereby is signified all Divine Worship in general, appears from the signification of a burnt-offering, as denoting Divine Worship, of which we shall speak presently; and from the signification of continual, as denoting all and in all, see above, n. 10,133; hence by a burnt-offering continually is signified all Divine Worship in general, and when the lamb is understood, of which the burnt-offering consists, by which is signified the good of innocence, that also is signified in all worship; for all worship, which is truly worship, will be from the truths of faith and the goods of love, and in every good of love, and hence in every truth of faith, there will be the good of innocence, n. 10,133; hence it is that by the continual burnt-offering is also signified in all worship. The reason why a burnt-offering denotes all worship is, because burnt-offerings and sacrifices were the principal things of representative worship with the Israelitish and Jewish nation, and all things have reference to their principal, and are hence denominated. That the principal of worship with that nation consisted in sacrifices and burnt-offerings, and that hence by those things is signified the all of worship in general, may be seen, n. 922, 1343, 2180, 6905, 8680, 8936, 10,142. It may, however, be expedient briefly to state what the Divine Worship is, which is signified by sacrifices and burnt-offerings; by sacrifices and burnt-offerings were specifically signified purification from evils and falses, and then the implantation of good and of truth, and the conjunction of both, thus regeneration, as may be seen, n. 10,022, 10,053, 10,057. The man who is principled in these is in genuine worship, for purification from evils and falses consists in desisting from them, and in shunning and holding them in aversion; and the implantation of good and of truth consists in thinking and willing what is good and true, and in speaking and doing them; and the conjunction of both consists in living from them; for when good and truth are conjoined with man, he has then a new will and a new understanding, consequently a new life. When man is of such a quality, then in every employment in which he is engaged there is Divine Worship, for he then has respect to the Divine in every thing, he venerates it, and he loves it, consequently he worships it. That this is genuine Divine Worship, is unknown to those who place all worship in adoration and in prayers, thus in such things as are of the mouth and of the thought, and not in such as are of the work grounded in the good of love and in the good of faith; when yet the Lord regards nothing else in the man, who is in adoration and in prayers, than his heart, that is, his interiors, as to their quality in regard to love and the faith thence derived; wherefore if these things are not inwardly in adoration and in prayers, there is no soul and life in these latter, but it is an external, like that of flatterers and pretenders, who it is well known, are not pleasing even to a wise man in the world. In a word, to act according to the precepts of the Lord is truly the worship of Him, yea it is truly love and truly faith; which may be manifest to every considerate person; for he who loves any one, and who believes any one, wishes for nothing more than to will and to do what the other wills and thinks, for he only desires to know his will and thought, thus his good pleasure; it is otherwise with him who does not love, or believe. It is similar with love to God, which also the Lord teaches in John, "*He that hath My precepts, and doeth them, he it is who loveth Me; but he who doth not love Me, keepeth not My words*," xiv. 21, 24. And again, "*If ye keep My commandments, ye shall abide in My love; My commandment is that ye love one another*," xv. 10, 12. That external worship without such an internal is not worship, is also signified by what is said of burnt-offerings and sacrifices in Jeremiah, "I spake not with your fathers upon the words of a burnt-offering and sacrifice, but this word I commanded them, saying, *obey My voice*, and I will be to you for a God," vii. 21, 22, 23. And in Hosea, "*I will mercy, and not sacrifice, and the knowledges of God more than burnt-offering*," vi. 6. And in Micah, "Shall I come before Jehovah with burnt-offering, will Jehovah be pleased with thousands of rams; he hath declared to thee what is good, and what doth Jehovah require from thee, *only to do judgment, and love mercy*, and to humble thyself, *by walking with thy God*," vi. 6, 7, 8. And in the 1st book of Samuel, "Hath Jehovah pleasure in burnt-offerings and sacrifices, *behold to comply is better than the sacrifice of oxen, obedience is better than the fat of rams*," xv. 22. That the veriest worship of the Lord itself consists in a life of charity, and not in a life of piety without that, may be seen, n. 8252 to 8257.

10,144. "Throughout your generations"—that hereby is signified what is perpetual in the church, appears from the signification of generations, when [spoken] concerning the sons of Israel, as denoting what is successive in the church, for by the sons of Israel the church is signified, and by generations what is successive in it. By generations are also signified the spiritual generations which are of faith and of love, thus which are of the church; and by into [or throughout] generations is also signified what is perpetual, thus likewise what is successive. That by the sons of Israel the church is signified, may be seen in what is cited, n. 9340; that by generations are signified those things which are of faith and of love, n. 2020, 2584, 6239; that they denote what is perpetual and eternal, n. 9789; thus what is successive, n. 9845.

10,145. "At the door of the tent"—that hereby is signified the conjunction of good and of truth, is manifest from the signification of the door of the tent, as denoting the conjunction of good and of truth, see n. 10,001, 10,025.

10,146. "Before Jehovah"—that hereby is signified from the Lord, is evident from this consideration, that Jehovah in the Word is the Lord, as may be seen in what is cited, n. 9373. The reason why before Jehovah denotes from the Lord is, because before signifies presence, and the presence of the Lord is as the quantity received of the good which is of love and of the truth which is of faith from Him; hence it is that before the Lord denotes from the Lord. The Lord indeed is present with every man, but he is present with the good in one way and with the evil in another; with the good He is present in every thing which they think from the truths of faith, and which they will from the good of love; and so present that He Himself is faith, and He Himself is love to them; consequently He is as dwelling with them, according to the words of the Lord Himself in John, "*The Spirit of Truth shall abide with you, and shall be in you; and ye shall know that I am in My Father, and ye in Me, and I in you; he that hath My precepts, and doeth them, he it is who loveth Me; to him we will come, and make our abode with him*," xiv. 17, 18, 20, 21, 23. But with the evil the Lord is not present in every thing, because they have not faith nor charity, but He is present in a general way, by which presence they have the faculty of thinking and of willing, and also of receiving faith and charity, but only so far as they desist from evils; but so far as they do not desist from evils, so far He appears absent; the degrees of his absence are according to the absence of the truth and the good of faith and of love. Hence it is that those who are in heaven are in the presence of the Lord, but those who are in hell are in His absence. Nevertheless the case is this, the Lord is not absent from man, but man is absent from the Lord, for the man who is in evils looks backward from Him; and the things which are then before his eyes are present to him, according to the affinities of the evils in which he is; for in the other life there is not space, but only an appearance of space according to the affinities of the thoughts and affections; those things are almost like the presence of the sun of this world as to light and as to heat; the sun is equally present at all times; but when the earth averteth itself from the sun, then the light perishes, and is succeeded by shade, first by the shade of evening, and next by the shade of night; and when the earth does not look directly to the sun, but obliquely, as occurs in the time of winter, then the heat perishes, and is succeeded by cold, and in consequence thereof all things of the earth grow torpid and die; this also is called the absence of the sun, when nevertheless it is the absence of the earth from the sun, not as to space, but as to a state of light and of heat. These observations are made for the sake of illustration.

10,147. "Where I will meet you to speak there unto thee"—that hereby is signified His presence and influx, appears from the signification of meeting to speak, as denoting presence and influx; for to meet denotes presence, and to speak, when concerning Jehovah, that is, the Lord, denotes influx. That to speak denotes influx, may be seen n. 2951, 5481, 5797, 7270. What the presence of the Lord is, was shown above, n. 10,146; but what His influx is, may be seen in the passages cited, n. 9223, 9276, 9682.

10,148. "And there I will meet the sons of Israel"—that hereby is signified the presence of the Lord in the church, appears from the signification of meeting, as denoting presence, as just above, n. 10,147; and from the representation of the sons of Israel, as denoting the church, see n. 9340.

10,149. "And he shall be sanctified with My glory"—that hereby is signified what is receptive of Divine Truth from the Lord, is evident from the signification of being sanctified, as denoting what is receptive of the Divine from the Lord, of which we shall speak presently; and from the signification of glory, as denoting Divine Truth, see n. 4809, 5922, 8627, 9427. The reason why to be sanctified denotes what is receptive of the Divine from the Lord is, because the Lord alone is holy, and hence every thing holy is from Him, n. 9229; and because the Divine Truth proceeding from Him, is what in the Word is meant by holy, n. 9818. Here, however, where it treats of the sons of Israel, of burnt-offerings and sacrifices, of the tent of the congregation, and of the altar, by what is holy and by being sanctified is signified the representative thereof; by reason that with the Israelitish and Jewish nation all things were representative of the interiors of the church, which are of faith and love from the Lord to the Lord, for the church instituted amongst that nation was a representative church. Hence all external things signified and represented such things as the internal sense teaches, on which account they were called holy,—as the altar, the fire upon it, the burnt-offering, the fat, the blood; the tent of the congregation; the table there on which were the breads of faces, the table of incense, the candlestick, and all their vessels; especially the ark in which was the testimony; besides the breads, the cakes, the wafers, which were called the meat-offering, the oil, the frankincense, also the garments of Aaron, as the ephod, the robe, the tunic, the turban, especially the breast-plate, and likewise Aaron himself was called holy, and also the sons of

Israel; but all those things were not holy from any other source than because they represented, and thereby signified holy things; that is, Divine things which are from the Lord, for these alone are holy. He who is in external things without internal, believes that such things were holy, not representatively but essentially, after that they were initiated; but they are altogether deceived. If they worship those things as essentially holy, in such case they worship terrestrial things, nor do they much differ from those who worship stones and wood, as the idolaters, but those who worship those things which are represented or signified, which are holy Divine things, they are in genuine worship, for external things to them are only mediate causes leading to think of such things, and to will such things, as are essential to the church, which, as was said above, are the things of faith and of love from the Lord to the Lord. It is similar at the present day with the holy supper; those who, when they frequent it, do not think from a principle of faith of the Lord, of His love towards the human race, and of renovation of life according to His precepts, worship only bread and wine in the holy supper, and not the Lord, and believe external things holy, which yet are not holy in themselves, but from those things which they signify, for the bread there signifies the Lord as to the good of love, and the wine the Lord as to the truth of faith, and at the same time receptivity by man, which two things are the very essentials of the church, thus the very essentials of worship, as may be seen n. 4211, 4217, 4735, 6135, 6789, 7850, 8682, 9003, 9127, 10,040. From these considerations it may now be manifest what is signified in the Word by holy, and by being sanctified [or made holy].

10,150. "And I will sanctify the tent of the congregation"—that hereby is signified what is receptive of the Lord in the inferior heavens, is evident from the signification of sanctifying, as denoting the receptivity of the Divine of the Lord, as may be seen just above, n. 10,149; and from the signification of the tent of the congregation, as denoting the heavens, see n. 3478, 9457, 9481, 9485, 9963; the reason why it denotes the inferior heavens is, because by the altar are signified the superior heavens, as may be seen just below, n. 10,151. It may be expedient briefly to state what is meant by the inferior heavens and the superior heavens. The heavens are distinguished into two kingdoms, the celestial and the spiritual; the celestial kingdom makes the superior heavens, and the spiritual kingdom the inferior heavens; the essential good of the celestial kingdom is the good of love to the Lord, and the good of mutual love; but the essential good of the spiritual kingdom is the good of charity towards the neighbor, and the good of faith: these kingdoms differ from each other as the intellectual principle and the will principle with the regenerate man,—in general as good and truth; but what the quality of that difference is, may be manifest from what was shown concerning those two kingdoms in the passages cited, n. 9277; also at n. 9543, 9688, 9992, 10,005, 10,068. The will principle moreover is the inmost principle of man, for it is the man himself; but the intellectual principle is adjacent and subservient, thus it is exterior; what is interior is also called superior, and what is exterior is called inferior; that the celestial kingdom corresponds to the will principle, and the spiritual kingdom to the intellectual principle appertaining to the regenerate man, may be seen n. 9835. From these considerations it is evident what is meant by the inferior heavens, and what by the superior heavens.

10,151. "And the altar"—that hereby is signified what is receptive of the Divine from the Lord, in the superior heavens, appears from the signification of sanctifying, as denoting what is receptive of the Divine from the Lord, shown above, n. 10,149; and from the signification of the altar, as being a representative of the Lord as to Divine Good, see n. 9964, here as to the Divine Good proceeding from Him in the heavens, where it is received, thus in the superior heavens, for there the Lord is received as to the Divine Good; but in the inferior heavens the Lord is received as to Divine Truth, according to what was shown just above, n. 10,150. It is to be noted, that whatsoever represented the Lord Himself, this also represented heaven, for the Divine proceeding from the Lord, received by the angels, makes heaven; the angels themselves as to their proprium do not constitute heaven, but as to the Divine which they receive from the Lord. That this is the fact, may be manifest from this consideration, that every one of them there acknowledges, believes, and also perceives, that there is nothing of good from themselves, but from the Lord; and that whatsoever is from themselves is not good; thus altogether according to the doctrinal of the church, that every thing good comes from above. This being the case, it follows, that the Divine of the Lord is what makes celestial life in them, consequently what makes heaven. Hence it may be manifest how it is to be understood that the Lord is the all in all of heaven; also that the Lord dwells there in His own; and likewise that by an angel in the Word is signified somewhat of the Lord, which subjects have been treated of in the preceding pages throughout. It is similar with the church; the men of the church as to their proprium do not constitute the church, but as to the Divine which they receive from the Lord; for every one in the church, who does not acknowledge and believe, that all the good of love and the truth of faith is from God, is not of the church; for he wills to love God from himself, and to believe in God from himself, which yet no one can do; hence also it is evident that the Divine of the Lord constitutes the church, as it constitutes heaven;—

the church is moreover the Lord's heaven in the earths. Hence also the Lord in the church is the all in all, as in heaven, and dwells in His own with men, as with the angels in heaven; and the men of the church who thus receive the Divine by love and faith, become angels of heaven after the life in the world; and none else. That the Divine of the Lord constitutes His kingdom, that is, heaven and the church with Him, the Lord also teaches in John, "The Spirit of Truth shall abide with you, and *shall be in you;* and ye shall know that I am in the Father, and *ye in Me, and I in you,*" xiv. 20; the Spirit of Truth is the Divine Truth proceeding from the Lord, of which it is said that it shall abide in you; and afterwards that He is in the Father, and they in Him, and He in them, whereby is signified that they should be in the Divine of the Lord, and the Divine of the Lord in them: that the Divine Human is what is there meant, is evident. And again in the same evangelist, "*Abide in Me, and I also in you,* as the branch cannot bear fruit of itself, except it abide in the vine, so neither can ye except ye abide in Me; *he that abideth in Me, and I in him,* the same beareth much fruit, for without Me ye can do nothing," xv. 4.

10,152. "And Aaron and his sons I will sanctify to perform the office of the priesthood to Me"—that hereby is signified a representative of the Lord in both as to the work of salvation, appears from the representation of Aaron, as denoting the Lord as to celestial good, see n. 9806, 9966, 10,068; and from the representation of the sons of Aaron, as denoting the Lord as to spiritual good, see n. 10,017, 10,068, thus in both heavens, as well the superior as the inferior; for whether we speak of celestial good, or of the celestial kingdom, or of the superior heaven, it is the same; and also whether we speak of spiritual good, or of the spiritual kingdom, or of the inferior heaven it is the same: concerning the inferior and superior heavens, see what was said just above, n. 10,150, 10,151; and from the representation of the priesthood, as denoting the Lord's work of salvation, see n. 9809, 10,017. Hence it is evident, that by sanctifying Aaron and his sons to perform the office of the priesthood to Jehovah, is signified a representative of the Lord in both heavens as to the work of salvation. It is allowed to me to make some further observations on the Lord's work of salvation. It is known in the church, that the Lord is the Saviour and Redeemer of the human race, but it is known to few in what manner this is to be understood. Those who are in the externals of the church, believe that the Lord redeemed the world, that is, the human race, by His blood, by which they mean the passion of the cross; but those who are in the internals of the church, know that no one is saved by the blood of the Lord, but by a life according to the precepts of faith and of charity from the Word of the Lord; those who are in the inmost of the church, by the blood of the Lord understand the Divine Truth proceeding from Him, and by the passion of the cross they understand the ultimate of the Lord's temptation, by which He entirely subjugated the hells, and at the same time glorified His Human, that is, made it Divine; and that hereby He redeemed and saved all, who suffer themselves to be regenerated by a life according to the precepts of faith and charity from His Word. By the blood of the Lord moreover in the internal sense, according to which the angels in the heavens perceive the Word, is meant the Divine Truth proceeding from the Lord, as may be seen, n. 4735, 4978, 5476, 7317, 7326, 7850, 9127, 9397, 10,026, 10,033. But how man was saved and redeemed by the Divine, through the subjugation of the hells, and the glorification of His Human, no one can know, unless he knows that there are attendant upon every man angels from heaven, and spirits from hell, and that unless these are present with man continually, he cannot think any thing, nor will any thing; and thus that man as to his interiors is either under the dominion of spirits who are from hell, or under the dominion of angels who are from heaven. When this is previously known, then it may be known, that unless the Lord had altogether subdued the hells, and reduced all things both there and in the heavens into order, no one could have been saved; in like manner, unless the Lord had made His Human Divine, and had thereby acquired to Himself Divine Power over the hells and over the heavens to eternity; for without Divine Power neither the hells nor the heavens can be kept in order, since the power, by which any thing exists, must be perpetual that it may subsist, for subsistence is perpetual existence. The Divine itself, which is called the Father, without the Divine Human which is called the Son, could not produce this effect, inasmuch as the Divine itself, without the Divine Human, cannot reach to man, nor even to an angel, when the human race have altogether removed themselves from what is Divine, as occurred in the end of times, when there was no longer any faith or any charity; wherefore the Lord then came into the world, and restored all things, and this by virtue of His Human, and thus saved and redeemed man by faith and love to the Lord from the Lord: for such the Lord can withhold from the hells and from eternal damnation, but not those who reject faith and love from Him to Him, for these reject salvation and redemption. That the Divine itself produces this effect by the Divine Human, is manifest from numerous passages in the Word, as from those where the Divine Human, which is the Son of God, is called the right hand and arm of Jehovah; and where it is said, that the Lord has all power in the heavens and in the earths. That the Lord is called the right hand and arm of Jehovah, may be seen, n. 10,019; and that He has all power in the heavens and in the earths, 10,089. That the Lord from the Divine Human subdued the hells, ana reduced all things therein and in the heavens into order; and then at the same time glorified His Human, that is, made it Divine, is shown, n. 9528 and 9715, 9809, 9937, 10,019; and that the Divine itself, which is called the Father, effected this by the Divine Human, is evident from John, "In the beginning was the Word, and the Word was with God, and God was the Word; *all things were made by Him, and without Him was not any thing made that was made; and the Word was made flesh, and dwelt amongst us*," i. 1, 2, 3, 14. That in this passage the Lord as to the Divine Human is He who is called the Word, is evident, for it is said, the Word was made flesh. And again, "*No one hath seen God at any time, the only-begotten Son, who is in the bosom of the Father, He hath brought Him forth to view*," verse 20. And again in the same evangelist, "*Ye have never heard the voice of the Father at any time, nor seen his shape*," v. 37. And again, "*I am the way, the truth, and the life, no one cometh to the Father but by Me; henceforth ye have known the Father, and have seen Him; he who seeth Me seeth the Father*," xiv. 6, 7, 9. And in Matthew, "*No one knoweth the Father, but the Son, and he to whom the Son shall be willing to reveal Him*," xi. 27. From these considerations it may now be manifest what the work of salvation and redemption is, and that it is effected from His Divine Human.

10,153. "And I will dwell in the midst of the sons of Israel"—that hereby is signified the presence of the Lord and His influx by good in heaven and in the church, is evident from the signification of dwelling, when concerning the Lord, as denoting to be present and to flow in. The reason why it is effected by Divine Good is, because to dwell is predicated of good, as may be seen, n. 2268, 2451, 2712, 3613, 8269, 8309; therefore also it is said in the midst, because by the midst is signified the inmost, and in the inmost principle is good; that this is signified by the midst, may be seen, n. 2940, 5897, 6084, 6103; and from the representation of the sons of Israel, as denoting the church, see n. 9340. The reason why by dwelling in the midst, when it relates to the Lord, is signified His presence and influx by Divine Good is, because the Lord flows in and is present with man in this good, which he receives from the Lord; for good makes the man himself, since every one is such as his good is; by good is meant the love, for every thing which is loved is called good. That his love or good constitues the man, is known to every one who explores another, for when he has explored him, he leads him by his love whithersoever he wills, insomuch that when he is held in his love, he is no longer master of himself, and then the reasons, which are against the love, are of no avail, but those which are with the love are all powerful. That this is the case, is also very manifest in the other life; all spirits are there known from their loves, and when they are held in them, they cannot do any thing contrary to them, for to act contrary to them is to act contrary to themselves; they are therefore the forms of their loves. Those who are in the heavens, are forms of celestial charity and love, of such beauty as cannot be described; but those who are in the hells, are forms of their loves, which are the loves of selt and of the world, consequently also they are forms of hatred and revenge, thus such monsters as cannot be described. Since therefore the whole man is such as his love is, it is evident that the Lord cannot be present in evil love, but in the good love appertaining to man, thus in his good. It is believed that the Lord is present in the truth which is called the truth of faith; but He is not present in truth without good, but where good is, there He is present in truth by good, and so far present in truth as it leads to good, and as it proceeds from good. Truth without good cannot be said to be inwardly in man, it is only in his memory as something scientific, which does not enter the man, and constitute him a man, until it becomes of the life; and it becomes of the life when he loves it, and from love lives according to it; when this is the case, then the Lord dwells with him. This also the Lord teaches in John, "He that hath My precepts, and *doeth them, he it is who loveth Me, and I will love him*, and will manifest Myself unto him; and My Father will love him, and we will come to him, and *make our abode with him*," xiv. 21, 23. To manifest Himself denotes to enlighten by the truths of faith from the Word; to come to him denotes to be present; and to make abode with him denotes to dwell in his good.

10,154. "And I will be to them for a God"—that hereby is signified the presence of the Lord and His influx into truth in the church, appears from the signification of being for a God, as denoting the presence of the Lord and His influx into truth. The reason why it denotes into truth is, because the Lord in the Word of the Old Testament is called God, where the subject treated of is truth, and Jehovah where it is good; hence also it is that the angels are called gods from the reception of Divine Truth from the Lord; hence too it is that in the original tongue God is called Elohim in the plural, for truths are numerous, but good is one, Matt. xix. 16, 17. That the Lord is called God where truth, and Jehovah where good is treated of, may be seen, n. 2586, 2769, 2807, 2822, 3921, 4287, 4402, 7010, 9167. And that the angels are called gods from the reception of Divine Truth from the Lord, n. 4295, 4402, 7268, 7873, 8192, 8302, 8867, 8941; and that the Lord is the Jehovah of the Word, in what is cited, n. 9373. That He is called the Father from eternity, and also God, is manifest in Isaiah, "A child is born to us, a Son is given to us, on whose shoulder is the government, His name shall be called *God*, Hero, *the Father of eternity*, the Prince of Peace," ix. 6. And again, "A virgin shall conceive, and shall bring forth, and His name shall be called *Immanuel*, which is, *God with us*," vii. 14; also Matt. i. 23. That in this passage by I will be to them for a God, is signified the presence and influx of the Lord into truth, is evident also from this consideration, that by I will dwell in the midst of the sons of Israel is signified the presence of the Lord and His influx by good; for in the Word, where good is treated of, truth is also treated of, on account of the heavenly marriage, which is that of good and truth, in every part of the Word, as may be seen in what is cited, n. 9263, 9314.

10,155. "And they shall know that I am Jehovah their God"—that hereby is signified a perceptive principle that from the Lord is all good and all truth, is evident from the signification of knowing, as denoting to understand, to believe, and to perceive, of which we shall speak presently. The reason why it denotes to perceive that from the Lord is all good and all truth is, because it is said Jehovah God, and the Lord is called Jehovah from good, and God from truth, as may be seen, n. 2586, 2769, 2807, 2822, 3921, 4287, 4402, 7010, 9167. The reason why to know denotes to understand, to believe, and to perceive, is, because it is said both of man's intellectual principle, and of his will; when it is said of the intellectual principle only, it denotes to understand; when of the intellectual principle and at the same time of the will, it denotes to believe; and when of the will principle alone, it denotes to perceive; wherefore with those who are only in the science of a thing, and hence in thought concerning it, to know denotes to understand; but with those who are in faith, to know denotes to believe; whereas with those who are in love, to know denotes to perceive. When however knowing is conjoined with understanding, seeing, and believing, then to know denotes to perceive, since understanding, seeing, and believing, have reference to the intellect, consequently to truth, whereas perceiving has reference to the will, consequently to good; as in John, "Peter said, *we have believed and known*, that Thou art the Christ the Son of the living God," vi. 69. Again, "Jesus said, believe the works, that ye *may know and believe*, that the Father is in Me, and I in the Father," x. 38. Again, "Jesus said, *if ye have known Me*, *ye have known My Father;* and henceforth *ye have known* Him, and *have seen* Him," xiv. 7. Again, "The Spirit of Truth will be sent, whom the world cannot receive, *since it seeth Him not*, *neither knoweth Him;* but *ye know Him*, because He abideth with you, and shall be in you," xiv. 17. And in Mark, "Jesus spake in parables, that *seeing they may see*, *and not know*," iv. 11, 12. And in Jeremiah, "That thou *mayest know and see* that it is evil and bitter to forsake Jehovah thy God," ii. 19. Again, "Let him who glorieth, glory in this, *to understand and know Me* that I am Jehovah," ix. 24. And in Hosea, "I will betroth thee unto me in *faith*, and *thou shalt know Jehovah*," ii. 20. In these passages to know denotes to perceive, and to perceive is from good; but to understand and to see is from truth; for those who are in good or in love, perceive inwardly in themselves that a thing is so; whilst those who are in truth or in faith, see inwardly in themselves; wherefore those who are in the Lord's celestial kingdom, have a perception that it is so, but those who are in the Lord's spiritual kingdom, have faith that it is so, as may be seen in the passages cited n. 9277; as well as at n. 9992, 9995, 10,105; and what perception is, n. 125, 371, 483, 495, 503, 521, 536, 597, 607, 1121, 1384, 1387, 1398, 1442, 1919, 2144, 2515, 2831, 3528, 5121, 5145, 5227, 7680, 7977, 8780. Since to know in the proper sense signifies to perceive from good, therefore, also it is said, "*it is known from the heart*," Deut. viii. 5: for from the heart denotes from the good of love, n. 3883 to 3896, 7542, 9050, 9300, 9494: and therefore to do good is called *to know Jehovah*, Jer. xxii. 16. Hence it is evident that by they shall know that I am Jehovah their God, is signified a perceptive principle that from the Lord is all good and truth.

10,156. "Who brought them forth out of the land of Egypt"—that hereby is signified salvation from hell by the Lord, appears from the signification of being brought forth out of the land of Egypt, as denoting to be liberated from hell, see n. 8866, 9197, thus to be saved. The reason why by the land of Egypt is signified hell is, because by that land, in the genuine sense, is signified the natural principle and its scientific principle; and to be brought forth from the natural man, and his scientific principle, and to be elevated into the spiritual man, and into his intelligence and wisdom, is also to be brought forth out of hell. For man is born natural, but is made spiritual by regeneration; and if he be not made spiritual, he is in hell; for the science of the natural man, that is of a man not regenerated, is in the light of the world; but the intelligence of the spiritual man, that is, of the regenerate man, is in the light of heaven; and so long as a man is only in the light of the world, he is in hell; but when he is at the same time in the light of heaven, he is in heaven. Those moreover who are only in natural science, and thence in no other light than in that of the world, cannot in any wise believe those things which are of heaven; and even if they be willing to enter into those things by their lumen, which is called natural lumen, there comes over them as it were a thick darkness, which blinds them, and makes what is heavenly appear as nothing; for such is the quality of what appears in the mind as thick darkness. Hence it is that the merely natural man, although he may believe himself to excel others in lumen, in heart he denies Divine and celestial things; which also is the cause why so many of the learned reduce themselves by their sciences to such insanity, for many more of them deny the things relating to the faith of the church and of heaven than of the simple. It is otherwise with those who suffer themselves to be elevated by the Lord into the light of heaven; for these are first elevated above the scientifics which are of the natural man; and then from the light of heaven they see those things which are in their natural man, which are called scientifics, and well discern them, adopting such as they apprehend and which are in congruity, and rejecting or laying aside those which they do not comprehend and which are incongruous. In a word, the case herein is this; so long as man is merely natural, so long his interiors, which see from the light of heaven, are closed; and the exteriors, which see from the light of the world, are open, and then man looks downwards, that is, into the world, and to himself, for such is the direction of all things which are of his will and thought; and whither the man looks, thither also his heart turns itself, that is, his will and his love. When however man becomes spiritual, then his interiors, which see from the light of heaven, are opened, and then the man looks upwards, which is effected by elevation from the Lord, thus he looks into heaven and to the Lord; thither also are elevated all things which are of his will and of his thought,—thus his heart, that is, his love. For man is so created, that as to his internal he is formed to the image of heaven, and as to his external to the image of the world, n. 6057, 9279; to the intent that heaven and the world with man may be conjoined, and that thus the Lord by [or through] man may flow in out of heaven into the world, and govern it, in particular with every one, and in general with all, and thus conjoin both, and thereby make a resemblance of heaven to exist also in the world. When however man makes the world his sole concern, heaven is closed with him; but when he suffers himself to be elevated by the Lord, then heaven is opened with him and the world is subjected to him; and when this is the case, hell is separated and removed from him: and then man first knows what good is and what evil is, but not before. This is what is called the image of God with man, Gen. i. 27, 28. These observations are made, to the intent that it may be known what the spiritual man is, and what the natural, and that the merely natural man, unless he be made spiritual by the Lord, is a hell; consequently that it may be known why by Egypt is signified hell, since also the natural principle and its scientific principle is signified. That by Egypt is signified the scientific principle, may be seen in what is cited, n. 9340; and thence the natural principle in what is cited, n. 9391; and hell, n. 8866, 9197.

10,157. "To dwell Myself in the midst of them"—that hereby is signified the Divine of the Lord, that it is the all in all of heaven and of the church, is evident from the signification of dwelling in the midst of the sons of Israel, when relating to Jehovah, as denoting the presence of the Lord, and His influx by good in heaven and in the church, shown, n. 10,153. And because His presence is there, His Divine is likewise the all in all there, for the Lord is present with the angels of heaven and with the men of the church, not in their proprium, but in what is of Himself appertaining to them, thus in what is Divine, according to what was shown above, n. 10,151; and when the Lord is present in His own Divine in the heavens and in the church, He is likewise the all in all there. Hence he is heaven itself; and also hence it is that the whole heaven has reference to the Lord as to His Divine Human; and that heaven in the complex is a man, which is called the GRAND MAN, treated of at the close of many chapters, as may be seen in what is cited at the end of n. 9276, 10,030. Hence also it is that by a man in the Word is signified the church, and likewise heaven, n. 478, 768, 3636; and that those who are in heaven, and truly in the church, are said to be in the Lord, n. 3637, 3638, when in the good of love and in the truth of faith in Him from Him.

10,158. "I am Jehovah their God"—that hereby is signified from whom is all the good of love and the truth of faith, appears from this consideration, that Jehovah is the Divine Esse, and the Divine Esse is the Divine Love, thus the Divine Good; and that God is the Divine Existere, and the Divine Existere is the Divine of faith, thus the Divine Truth; for all truth exists from good, truth being the form of good. From these considerations it is evident, that when the Lord is called Jehovah God, thereby is meant all the good of love and the truth of faith; and when Jehovah God is said to be in the midst of the sons of Israel, thereby is meant the perceptive principle, that from the Lord is every good which is of love and truth which is of faith, as shown above, n. 10,155.

CONTINUATION RESPECTING THE SECOND EARTH SEEN IN THE STARRY HEAVENS.

10,159. *INASMUCH as I have discoursed with those of that earth, concerning the invisible and visible God, it is allowed to mention, that almost all in the universe worship God under a visible form, and indeed in their idea under a human form, and that this is an ingrafted principle. It is ingrafted by virtue of influx from heaven, for, what is remarkable, the angels who are elevated even into the sphere of the third heaven, come into mani-*

fest perfection on the subject. The reason is, because all in that heaven are in the love of the Lord, and hence as it were in the Lord; and because all perception, such as the angels have there, is from the order and from the flux of heaven; for heaven in its whole complex resembles one man, as may be manifest from what has been shown concerning heaven, as the GRAND MAN, *at the close of several chapters, as may be seen in the passages cited, n.* 10,030. *This resemblance of heaven in its whole complex, to one man, is from the Divine Human of the Lord; for from this the Lord flows-in into heaven, makes it, and forms it to a likeness of Himself. But this arcanum can hardly be apprehended by those who have extirpated from themselves this ingrafted principle by their own proper intelligence.*

10,160. *The question was asked them, whether in their earth they live under the government of princes or of kings; to which they replied, that they do not know what governments are, and that they live under themselves, distinguished into nations, families, and houses. They were further questioned whether they are thus secure, they said that they were secure, since one family in no respect envies another, and in no respect is willing to derogate from another. They were indignant that such questions were asked them, as if they contained a charge of hostility, and of some sort of protection against robbers. What more have we need of, said they, than food and raiment, and thus to dwell content and quiet under ourselves? It was perceived from the most ancient people who were from our earth, that they had lived in like manner in their time, and that they then knew not what it was to rule over others from a principle of self-love, and to heap together wealth beyond necessity, from a principle of worldly love; and that then they had internal peace, and at the same time external, and hence heaven was with man. Those times were therefore called by ancient writers the golden ages and were described by their doing what was just and equitable, from a law inscribed on their hearts. The state of life of those times is described in the Word by dwelling under themselves securely and solitarily, without doors and bars. And whereas their habitations were tents, therefore, as a record, a tent was constructed, which was for the house of God, and afterwards the feast of tents was instituted, in which they were gladdened from the heart; and since those who thus lived were free from the insane love of ruling for the sake of themselves, and of gaining the world for the sake of the world, therefore heaven then let itself down to them, and the Lord was seen by many in a human form.*

10,161. *Being questioned concerning their earth, they said, that they have meadows, shrubberies, forests full of trees bearing fruit, and also lakes, in which are fishes ; and that they have birds of a blue color with golden feathers, and that there are greater and lesser animals, and among the lesser they mentioned some which had an elevated back, like that of camels in our earth ; nevertheless that they do not feed on their flesh, but only on the flesh of fish ; and also on the fruits of trees, and on leguminous vegetables. They said further, that they do not build in houses raised for the purpose, but in groves, in which amongst the leaves they make for themselves coverings to defend them from the rain and the heat of the sun.*

10,162. *Being asked concerning their sun, which is a star visible from our earth, they said that it was of a fiery color, to appearance no larger than a man's head. I was told by the angels that the star, which was to them a sun, was amongst the lesser stars, not far distant from the equator.*

10,163. *Spirits were seen, who were similar to themselves when they were men in their earth; their faces were not unlike the faces of the men of our earth, except that their eyes were small, and also the nose small, and as this appeared to me to be a sort of deformity, they said that small eyes and a small nose are accounted beautiful amongst them. A female was seen, clad in a gown in which were roses of various colors. I asked whence they prepare their garments in that earth; they replied, that they gather from certain herbs such substances as they spin into threads, and that they afterwards lay the threads in rows, in a double and triple order, and moisten them with a glutinous water, and thereby induce consistence, coloring the substance afterwards with juices derived from herbs.*

10,164. *It was also shown how they make the threads. The women sit down on the ground, and wind them by means of their toes, and when wound, they draw the thread towards them, and with the hand spin it out to any fineness they please.*

10,165. *They said also, that on that earth every husband has no more than one wife ; and that the number of children in a family is from ten to fifteen. They added that there are found likewise harlots amongst them, but that all such, after the life of the body, when they become spirits, are magicians, and are cast into hell.*

10,166. *An account of the third earth in the starry heavens will be given at the close of the following chapter.*

EXODUS.

CHAPTER THE THIRTIETH.

THE DOCTRINE OF CHARITY AND OF FAITH.

10,167. FEW know from what origin conjugial love exists; those who think from the world, believe that it is from nature; but those who think from heaven, that it is from the Divine there.

10,168. Love truly conjugial is the union of two minds, which is spiritual union; and all spiritual union descends from heaven; hence it is that love truly conjugial is from heaven, and that its first esse is from the marriage of good and of truth there. The marriage of good and of truth in heaven is from the Lord; wherefore the Lord in the Word is called the bridegroom and husband, and heaven and the church is called the bride and wife; and on this account also heaven is compared to a marriage.

10,169. From these considerations it is evident, that love truly conjugial is the union of two as to the interiors which are of the thought and of the will,—thus which are of truth and of good—for truth is of the thought, and good is of the will. For he who is principled in love truly conjugial, loves what another thinks, and what another wills; thus also he loves to think as another; and he loves to will as another,—consequently to be united to another, and to become as one man. This is what is meant by the Lord's words in Matthew, "*And two shall be one flesh, wherefore they are no longer two, but one flesh*," xix. 4, 5; also Gen. ii. 24.

10,170. The delight of love truly conjugial, is an internal delight, because it is of the mind, and it is also an external delight thence derived, which is of the body; but the delight of love not truly conjugial is only external delight without being internal, which is that of the body, not of the mind. This latter delight moreover is terrestrial, almost like that of animals, and therefore in time perishes; but the former is celestial, such as that of men should be, and therefore it is permanent.

10,171. No one can know what love truly conjugial is, and what is the quality of its delight, unless he be in the good of love and in the truths of faith from the Lord, since, as was said, love truly conjugial is from heaven, and originates in the marriage of good and of truth there.

10,172. From the marriage of good and of truth in heaven and in the church, we may be instructed what ought to be the quality of marriages in the earths, namely, that they ought to be between two, one husband and one wife, and that love truly conjugial is in no case given, if one husband has a plurality of wives.

10,173. What is done from a principle of love truly conjugial, this is done from freedom on both sides, for all freedom is from love, and each party has freedom when one loves what the other thinks and what the other wills. Hence it is that to be willing to exercise rule in marriages destroys genuine love, for it takes away its freedom, thus also its delight; the delight of exercising rule, which succeeds in its place, begets disagreements, and sets minds at enmity, and causes evils to take root according to the quality of dominion on one part, and the quality of servitude on the other.

10,174. From these considerations it may be manifest, that marriages are holy, and that to do violence to them is to do violence to that which is holy: consequently that adulteries are profane; for since the delight of conjugial love descends from heaven, the delight of adultery ascends out of hell.

10,175. Those, therefore, who take delight in adulteries, cannot any longer receive any good and truth from heaven. Hence it is that those who have taken delight in adulteries, afterwards make light of and also in heart deny those things which are of the church and of heaven. The reason is, because the love of adultery is from the marriage of what is evil and false, which is the infernal marriage.

CHAPTER XXX.

1. AND thou shalt make an altar of the fuming of incense; of shittim-wood thou shalt make it.

2. A cubit the length thereof, and a cubit the breadth thereof; it shall be square; and two cubits the height thereof; out of it shall be its horns.

3. And thou shalt cover it over with pure gold, its roof and its walls round about, and its horns; and thou shalt make for it a border of gold round about.

4. And two rings of gold thou shalt make for it from beneath its border, upon its two ribs, thou shalt make them upon its two sides; and it shall be for receptacles to the staves, to carry it in them.

5. And thou shalt make the staves of shittim-wood; and shalt cover them over with gold.

6. And thou shalt give it before the vail, which is over the ark of the testimony, before the propitiatory which is over the testimony, where I will meet thee there.

7. And Aaron shall cause to fume upon it incense of spices in the morning in the morning, in adorning the lamps he shall cause it to fume.

8. And in Aaron causing the lamps to ascend between the evenings he shall cause it to fume; continual incense before JEHOVAH to your generations.

9. Ye shall not make to ascend upon it strange incense, and a burnt-offering, and a meat-offering; and a libation ye shall not offer upon it.

10. And Aaron shall expiate upon its horns once in a year from the blood of the sin of expiations: once in a year he shall expiate upon it to your generations; this is the holy of holies to JEHOVAH.

11. And JEHOVAH spake to Moses, saying,

12. When thou shalt take the sum of the sons of Israel as to those that are numbered of them, and they shall give every one an expiation of his soul to JEHOVAH in numbering them; and let there be no plague in them in numbering them.

13. This they shall give every one that passeth upon the numbered; half a shekel in the shekel of holiness: a shekel is twenty oboli; the half of a shekel an up-lifting to JEHOVAH.

14. Every one passing upon the numbered, from a son of twenty years and upwards, shall give an up-lifting to JEHOVAH.

15. A rich man shall not give more, and a poor man shall not give less, from the half of a shekel to give an up-lifting to JEHOVAH to expiate on your souls.

16. And thou shalt take silver of expiations from [being] with the sons of Israel, and thou shalt give it for the work of the tent of the congregation; and it shall be to the sons of Israel for remembrance before JEHOVAH to expiate on your souls.

17. And JEHOVAH spake to Moses saying,

18. And thou shalt make a laver of brass, and its base of brass, to wash; and thou shalt give it between the tent of the congregation and between the altar, and thou shalt give waters there.

19. And Aaron and his sons shall wash out of it their hands and their feet.

20. In their entering-in into the tent of the congregation, they shall wash with waters lest they die; or in their coming near to the altar to minister, to cause to burn an offering made by fire to JEHOVAH.

21. And they shall wash their hands and their feet, lest they die; and it shall be to them a statute of an age to him and to his seed, to their generations.

22. And JEHOVAH spake to Moses, saying,

23. And do thou take to thyself chief spices, the best myrrh five hundred, and aromatic cinnamon the half thereof, fifty and two hundred, and aromatic calamus fifty and two hundred.

24. And cassia five hundred, in the shekel of holiness; and oil of olive a hin.

25. And thou shalt make it oil of anointing of holiness, an ointment of ointment, the work of an ointment dealer, it shall be the oil of anointing of holiness.

26. And thou shalt anoint with it the tent of the congregation, and the ark of the testimony.

27. And the table and all its vessels, and the candlestick and its vessels, and the altar of incense.

28. And the altar of burnt-offering and all its vessels, and the laver and its base.

29. And thou shalt sanctify them, and they shall be the holy of holies; every one that toucheth them shall be sanctified.

30. And Aaron and his sons thou shalt anoint, and shalt sanctify them to perform the office of the priesthood to Me.

31. And to the sons of Israel speak, saying; this shall be to Me the oil of anointing of holiness to your generations.

32. Upon the flesh of man it shall not be poured; and in its quality ye shall not make like it, it is holy, it shall be holy to you.

33. The man [*vir*] who shall make ointment like it, and who shall give of it upon a stranger, shall be cut off from his people.

34. And JEHOVAH said to Moses; take to thee fragrant spices, stacte, and onycha, and galbanum [which are] fragrant, and pure frankincense; so much shall be in so much.

35. And thou shalt make it incense, an ointment the work of an ointment dealer, salted, pure, holy.

36. And thou shalt bruise of it into small pieces, and shalt give of it before the testimony in the tent of the congregation, where I will meet thee there; the holy of holies it shall be to you.

37. And the incense which thou makest in its quality, ye shall not make to yourselves; it shall be holy to thee to JEHOVAH.

38. The man [*vir*] who shall make like it, to make an odor with it, shall be cut off from his people.

THE CONTENTS.

THE subject treated of in this chapter is the altar of fuming incense; the expiation of every one by silver; the laver and washing thence derived; and the preparation of the oil of anointing, and of incense. By fuming incense in the internal sense is signified the hearing and reception of all the things of worship, which are from love and charity by the Lord. By the expiation of every one by silver, is signified the ascribing of all the things of worship to the Lord, and nothing to self, that no one may have merit. By the laver and washing is signified purification from evils first in all worship. By the preparation of the oil of anointing, is signified the quality of love in worship; and by the preparation of incense, the quality of worship thence derived.

THE INTERNAL SENSE.

10,176. VERSES 1 to 10. *And thou shalt make an altar of the fuming of incense; of shittim-wood thou shalt make it. A cubit the length thereof, and a cubit the breadth thereof; it shall be square; and two cubits the height thereof; out of it shall be its horns. And thou shalt cover it over with pure gold, its roof, its walls round about, and its horns; and thou shalt make for it a border of gold round about. And two rings of gold thou shalt make for it from beneath its border, upon its two ribs, thou shalt make them upon its two sides; and it shall be for receptacles to the staves, to carry it in them. And thou shalt make the staves of shittim-wood; and shalt cover them over with gold. And thou shalt give it before the vail, which is over the ark of the testimony, before the propitiatory, which is over the testimony, where I will meet thee there. And Aaron shall cause to fume upon it incense of spices in the morning in the morning, in adorning the lamps he shall cause it to fume. And in Aaron causing the lamps to ascend between the evenings, he shall cause it to fume; continual incense before Jehovah to your generations. Ye shall not make to ascend upon it strange incense, and a burnt-offering, and a meat-offering; and a libation ye shall not offer upon it. And Aaron shall expiate upon its horns once in a year from the blood of the sin of expiations; once in a year he shall expiate upon it to your generations. This is the holy of holies to Jehovah.* And thou shalt make an altar of the fuming of incense, signifies a representative of the hearing and grateful reception of all the things of worship, which are from love and charity, by the Lord. Of shittim-wood thou shalt make it, signifies from Divine Love. A cubit the length thereof, and a cubit the breadth thereof, signifies what is equally from good and from truth. It shall be square, signifies thereby perfect. And two cubits the height thereof, signifies the degrees of good and truth, and their conjunction. Out of it shall be its horns, signifies the powers of truth derived from the good of love and charity. And thou shalt cover it over with pure gold, signifies a representative of all the things of worship grounded in good. Its roof signifies the inmost principle. And its walls, signifies interior principles. And its horns, signifies exterior principles. And thou shalt make a border of gold round about, signifies termination from good lest they should be approached and hurt by evils. And two rings of gold thou shalt make for it from beneath the border, signifies the sphere of Divine Good, by which is conjunction and conservation. On its two ribs, signifies with truths on one part. Thou shalt make them on its two sides, signifies with good on the other part. And it shall be for receptacles to the staves, signifies the power of truth derived from good there. To carry it in them, signifies hence conservation in its state. And thou shalt make the staves of shittim-wood, signifies power derived from the good of the Lord's love. And shalt cover them over with gold, signifies the foundation of all things on good. And shalt give it before the vail which is over the ark of the testimony, signifies in the interior heaven, where it is conjoined to the inmost heaven. Before the propitiatory which is above the testimony, signifies where there is hearing and reception of all the things of worship grounded in the good of love from the Lord. Where I will meet thee there, signifies thus the presence and influx of the Lord. And Aaron shall fume incense upon it, signifies the elevation of worship by virtue of love and charity from the Lord. Incense of spices, signifies grateful hearing and reception. In the morning in the morning, signifies when the state of love is in clearness. In adorning the lamps he shall fume it, signifies when truth also comes into its light. And in Aaron causing the lamps to ascend between the evenings he shall fume it, signifies elevation also in an obscure state of love when truth is likewise in its shade. Continual incense before Jehovah, signifies in all worship grounded in love from the Lord. To your generations, signifies to eternity to those who are in faith grounded in love. Ye shall not make to ascend upon it strange incense, signifies no worship from any other love than of the Lord. And the burnt-offering and meat-offering, signifies no representative there of regeneration by truths and goods of celestial love. And a libation ye shall not offer upon it, signifies no representative there of regeneration by the truths and goods of spiritual love. And Aaron shall expiate on its horns, signifies purification from evils by the truths of faith which are from the good of love. Once in a year, signifies perpetually. Of the blood of the sin of expiations, signifies by truths which are from the good of innocence. Once in a year he shall expiate upon it, signifies the perpetual removal of evils. To your generations, signifies those of the church who are in the truths and goods of faith. This is the holy of holies to Jehovah, signifies since grounded in the celestial Divine [principle]

10,177. "And thou shalt make an altar of the fuming of in

cense"—that hereby is signified a representative of the grateful hearing and reception of all things of worship grounded in love and charity by the Lord, appears from the signification of the altar of the fuming of incense, as being representative of such things of worship as are elevated to the Lord ; that those things are what are grounded in love and charity, will be evident from what follows. By the altar is signified the like as by that which is upon it, since the altar is the continent, and that which is upon it is the thing contained, and the continent and the thing contained make one thing, as a table and the bread which is upon it, a cup and the wine which is in it. The reason why an altar was made for the fuming of incense, and not a table, was, because altars with the Israelitish nation were the principal representatives of worship, grounded in love, for fire was upon them, and by fire is signified love and charity, in which worship is grounded ; that altars were the principal representatives of worship, see n. 4192, 4541, 8623, 8935, 8940, 9714. The reason why the altar of fuming incense represented the hearing and reception of all things of worship which are grounded in love and charity, was, because by fume and hence by fumigation were signified that which is elevated on high, and by the odor of fume that which is grateful, consequently that which is heard and received by the Lord ; and that alone is grateful, and is received by the Lord which is grounded in love and charity; hence also it was, that the altar was covered over with gold, and was called the golden altar, for gold signifies the good of love and charity, as may be seen in what is cited, n. 9874, 9881. The reason why that alone is grateful, and is therefore heard and received by the Lord, which is grounded in love and charity is, because love makes the whole man, every man being such as his love is ; hence it is that the angels in the heavens are loves and charities in form ; the form itself which they thence have is the human form, inasmuch as the Lord, who is in them, and forms them, as to the Divine Human [principle] is the Divine Love itself; hence it is, that from their faces, from their discourse, from their gestures, and especially from the spheres of affections, which flow forth from them to a distance, is clearly perceived what is their quality as to love. And whereas love to the Lord and charity towards the neighbor are from the Lord, and love is spiritual conjunction, therefore whatsoever proceeds is heard and received by the Lord : but what is holy and pious, which is not grounded in love, is indeed heard, but is not received gratefully, for it is an hypocritical sanctity and piety, being only external without an internal principle ; and a holy external principle without an internal penetrates no further than to the first threshold of heaven, and is there dissipated ; but a holy external principle derived from an internal penetrates even into heaven, according to the quality of the internal, thus to the Lord ; for a holy external principle without an internal is merely from the mouth and gestures, whereas a holy external principle derived from an internal is at the same time from the heart; concerning the latter and the former holy principle, see what was said and shown, n. 8252 to 8257. In the tent out of the vail was the table, on which were the breads of faces, there was also the candlestick with lamps, and there was the altar of incense; by the breads of faces was represented love to the Lord; by the lamps of the candlestick, charity and faith; and by the incense upon the altar, the worship thence derived; wherefore it was fumed every morning, and every evening when the lamps were adorned; hence also it is evident, that by the fuming of incense was represented the worship of the Lord, grounded in love and charity; by the tent itself, in which that fuming was performed, heaven, where all worship is of such a quality. That the breads represented celestial good, which is the good of love to the Lord, may be seen in n. 9545; that the candlestick represented spiritual good, which is the good of charity towards the neighbor and the good of faith, in n. 9548 to 9561; and that the tent represented heaven, in n. 9457, 9481, 9485, 9784, 9963. When mention is made of worship, thereby is meant that holy principle, which is wrought by prayers, adorations, confessions, and the like, which proceed from the internal principles that are of love and charity; those things constitute the worship, which is meant by burning of incense, as may be manifest from the following passages: "My prayers are accepted, they are *incense before Thee*," Ps. cxli. 2. And in the Apocalypse, "The four animals and the four-and-twenty elders fell down before the Lamb, having each of them harps, and *golden vials full of incenses, which are the prayers of the saints*," Apoc. v. 8. Again, "An angel having *a golden censer, and there were given to him there many incenses, that he might give them to the prayers of all the saints on the golden altar*, which is before the throne; *the fume of the incenses from the prayers of the saints ascended*," Apoc. viii. 3, 4. Inasmuch as by incense was signified worship and its elevation, thus hearing and reception by the Lord, therefore it was commanded by Moses, *that they should take censers with incense, and fume it before Jehovah*, that they might thence know whom Jehovah would choose, thus whom He would hear, Numb. xvi. 1 and following verses; and when the people murmured, that Aaron ran into the midst of the congregation *with incense*, when the plague began, and thereby appeased it, Numb. xvi. 44 to 49. And in Malachi, "From the rising of the sun even to the setting, the name of Jehovah shall be great amongst the nations, and in every place *incense shall be brought to My name* and a clean meat-offering," i. 11; a clean meat-offering is added, because by it is signified the good of love, n. 10,137. And in Moses.

"The sons of Levi shall teach Jacob judgments, and Israel Thy law, *they shall put incense into Thy nose*, and a burnt-offering upon Thine altar," Deut. xxxiii. 10; it is said shall put incense into the nose, because by the nostrils is signified perception, n. 4624 to 4634; a burnt offering is here added, because by it also is signified what is from the good of love. But by fuming incense, in the opposite sense, is signified worship derived from contrary loves, which are the loves of self and of the world, as by *fuming incense to other gods*, Jer. i. 16; chap. xliv. 3, 5. By *fuming incense to idols*, Ezek. viii. 11; chap. xvi. 18: and by *burning incense to Baalim*, Hosea ii. 13. Inasmuch as the fuming of incense signified such things as are elevated upwards, and are accepted by the Divine [being], therefore also they were applied by the Gentiles in their religious ceremonies; that frankincense, censers [*thuribula*], and censers [*acerræ*], were in use amongst the Romans, and amongst other nations, is known from history; such religious ceremony was derived from the ancient church, which was extended through several regions of Asia, as through Syria, Arabia, Babylon, Egypt, Canaan; this church had been a representative church, thus consisting in externals, which represented things internal, which are celestial and spiritual things; from this church several religious ceremonies were translated to the nations round about, and amongst others the fumings of incense also; hence through Greece into Italy; in like manner also perpetual fire, for the guarding of which chaste virgins were appointed, whom they called vestal virgins. The fumings of incense in the ancient church, and thence in the Israelitish, were prepared from fragrant substances, as from stacte, onycha, galbanum, and frankincense, because odor signified perception, and fragrant odor grateful perception, see n. 925, 1514, 1517, 1518, 1519, 3577, 4624 to 4634, 4748, 10,054. But frankincense specifically signifies the truth of faith, therefore when frankincense is named in the Word there is adjoined also oil, bread, a meat-offering, or gold, by which is signified the good of love, as in Isaiah, "All shall come from Sheba, *they shall carry gold and frankincense*, and shall announce the praises of Jehovah," lx. 6. In like manner those who came from the east, of whom it is written in Matthew, "There came wise men from the east, seeking the Lord at that time born, opening their treasures, and *they offered gold, frankincense*, and myrrh," ii. 1, 2, 11. That those who were from the east, and were called sons of the east, in the Word signify those who were in the knowledges of good and truth, may be seen in n. 3249, 3762; in like manner Sheba, n. 1171, 3240; that gold signifies the good of love, may be seen in what is cited, n. 9874, and n. 9881. And in Jer., "They shall bring a burnt-offering and sacrifices, and *a meat-offering and frankincense*," xvii. 26; by a meat-offering in like manner is signified the good of love, see n. 9992, 10,137; hence it is evident, that by frankincense in the Word is signified the truth which is of faith, for in the Word, where good is spoken of, truth is also spoken of, on account of the celestial marriage, which is that of good and truth, in all things therein, see what is cited, n. 9263, 9314; hence also it was, that upon the meat-offering was *oil*, and also frankincense, Levit. ii. 1, 2, 15, but not on the meat-offering which was for sin, Levit. v. 11; nor on the meat-offering of jealousy, Numb. v. 15; the reason why there was no oil and frankincense on these latter meat-offerings, was, because they were given for expiation from evils, and so long as man is in expiation, he cannot receive the good of love and the truth of faith, for evils oppose; it is otherwise after expiation or the removal of evils. Inasmuch as the good which is of love cannot be given but together with the truth which is of faith, since good produces truth, and in truth procures to itself its quality, and forms itself, it was from this ground that upon *every meat-offering there was frankincense;* and also *on the breads of faces*, which were on the table in the tent of the congregation, Levit. xxiv. 7; for breads signified the good of love, n. 3478, 3813, 4211, 4217, 4735, 4976, 8410, 9323, 9545, 10,040, 10,137.

10,178. "Of shittim-wood thou shalt make it"—that hereby is signified from Divine Love, appears from the signification of shittim-wood, as denoting the good of merit and of justice, which is of the Lord alone, see n. 9472, 9486, 9715. The reason why it also denotes love is, because the Lord, when He was in the world, from Divine Love fought against all the hells, and subdued them, and thereby saved the human race, and hence alone had merit, and was made justice, see n. 9486, 9715, 9809, 10,019, 10,152; wherefore the good of the Lord's merit is His Divine Love. The reason why shittim-wood is of such and of so great signification is, because all things, which are in the triple kingdom of the earth, namely, in the animal kingdom, the vegetable, and the mineral, signify spiritual and celestial things, and also the things opposite to them, for universal nature is a theatre representative of the Lord's kingdom, see what is cited, n. 9280; and wood in general signifies the good of love, and specifically the good of merit, n. 2784, 2812, 3720, 4943, 8354, 8740; hence it is that wood in the supreme sense signifies Divine Good, since all things, which in the internal sense signify things relating to the church and heaven, in the supreme sense signify Divine things.

10,179. "A cubit the length thereof, and a cubit the breadth thereof"—that hereby is signified what is equally from good and from truth, appears from the signification of length, as denoting good, and of breadth as denoting truth, see n. 1613, 3433, 3434, 4482, 9487. Equally from both is signified by the former being a cubit, and the latter a cubit, thus by the measure being equal, because by measures in the Word a thing is determined as to its quantity and quality, and the determination is made by number; the thing which is here determined by the measure, which is a cubit, is good and truth, the former by length, and the latter by breadth. The reason why length denotes good, is, because it is reckoned from east to west, and by east and west is signified good from one boundary to another; and breadth from south to north, and by south and north is signified truth from one boundary to another; for so the case is in heaven, where the Lord is the sun, and also the east, from which all determinations are there made. Those who are in front there, are in the perception of good according to distance; those who are in clear perception of good are in the east, n. 3708, 9668; those who are in obscure perception of good, are in the west, n. 3708, 9653; but those who are in the clear light of truth are in the south, n. 9642; and those who are in the obscure light of truth are in the north, n. 3708. Hence it is that by those four quarters in the Word such things are signified; and that by length is signified good, and by breadth truth.

10,180. "It shall be square"—that hereby is signified thus perfect, appears from the signification of square, as denoting what is just, and also what is perfect, see n. 9177, 9861.

10,181. "And two cubits the height thereof"—that hereby are signified degrees of good and of truth, and their conjunction, appears from the signification of two, as denoting conjunction, see n. 1686, 5194, 8423; and from the signification of height, as denoting degrees of good and of truth thence derived, see n. 9489, 9773. By degrees of height are meant degrees from things interior to things exterior, or from inmost things to outermost, the nature and quality of which degrees may be seen illustrated and shown in n. 3405, 3691, 4145, 5114, 5146, 8603, 8945, 10,099. There are degrees of two kinds, namely, degrees into length and breadth, and degrees as to height and depth; the latter degrees differ exceedingly from the former. The degrees of length and breadth are those which succeed from the midst to the circumference; but degrees of height proceed from things interior to things exterior; the former degrees, namely, of length and breadth, are degrees which decrease from the midst continually to the circumferences, as light decreases from flame even to its obscurity, and as the sight of the eye from nearest objects to the most remote, and as the intellectual sight from those things which are in light to those which enter into shade; but degrees of height, which proceed from things inmost to outermost, or from highest things to lowest, are not continuous, but discrete; for they are like the inmost principles of a seed to its exteriors; and as the inmost principles of man to his outermost; and as the inmost principle of the angelic heaven to its outermost, these degrees are discriminate, thus distinct, as the thing producing and the thing produced. Those things which are in an interior degree are more perfect than those which are in an exterior degree, and no other similitude exists between them but by correspondences; hence it is that those who are in the inmost heaven, are more perfect than those who are in the middle heaven, and these latter more perfect than those who are in the ultimate heaven. The case is the same with man in whom heaven is formed, his inmost principle is in a more perfect state than the middle, and this latter in a more perfect state than the ultimate; and they have consociation with each other in no other way than by correspondences; what the nature and quality of those correspondences is, has been abundantly shown in the preceding explications. He who does not procure to himself a perception of these degrees, cannot in anywise know the distinctions of the heavens, and the distinctions of the interior and exterior faculties of man, thus neither the distinction between soul and body; he is also incapable of comprehending what the internal sense of the Word is, and its distinction from the external sense, also the distinction between the spiritual world and the natural world; neither can he understand what and whence correspondences and representations are, and scarcely what influx is; sensual men do not comprehend these distinctions, for they make increase and decrease according to these degrees continuous, thus, they make these degrees like the degrees of length and breadth, wherefore also they stand without, and at a distance from intelligence. These degrees are degrees of height, therefore by what is high in the Word is meant what is interior, n. 2146, 4210, 4599, and because what is interior, also what is more perfect; hence it is that the Lord in the Word is called the Highest, because He is Perfection Itself, Intelligence Itself, and Wisdom and Good and Truth Itself; and hence it is that heaven is said to be on high, because in perfection, intelligence, wisdom, good, and truth, from the Lord; and therefore hell is said to be in the deep, because therein is no perfection, intelligence, and wisdom, and no good and truth.

10,182. "Out of it shall be its horns"—that hereby are signified the powers of truth from the good of love and charity, appears from the signification of horns, as denoting the powers of truth, see n. 2832, 9719, 9720, 9721. The reason why it denotes from the good of love and charity is, because all the power of truth is from that source, wherefore also the horns were continued to the altar itself, or were out of it; for this altar was representative of the hearing and reception of all things of worship grounded in love and charity from the Lord, n. 10,177. That all the power of truth is from the good of love cannot be apprehended by those who have only a material idea concerning power, wherefore it may be expedient to say how the case herein is: in the heavens all power is derived from Divine Truth proceeding from the Divine Good of the Lord, hence the angels have power, for the angels are receptions of Divine Truth from the Lord, n. 1752, 4295, 8192; by the power thence derived they protect man, removing the hells from him, for one angel prevails against a thousand who are from the hells: this power is what is meant by the keys of Peter, but by Peter, who is there called Petra [a rock], is meant the Lord as to the truth of faith derived from the good of love, see preface to chap. xxii. Gen. and n. 4738, 5150, 6000, 6073, 6344, 10,087; and that Petra [a rock] denotes the Lord as to the truth of faith, see n. 8581. The power of Divine Truth is also meant by the voice of Jehovah, in David, "*The voice of Jehovah* is on the waters; *the voice of Jehovah* is in virtue; *the voice of Jehovah* breaketh the cedars; *the voice of Jehovah* cuts [or divides] the flame of fire; *the voice of Jehovah* maketh the wilderness to tremble; *the voice of Jehovah* maketh bare the forests; Jehovah giveth *strength* to His people," Psalm xxix. That the voice of Jehovah is the Divine Truth proceeding from His Divine Good, see n. 9926. The power of Divine Truth is also meant by the Word in John, "*All things were made by the Word*, and without Him was not any thing made which was made," i. 3. That the Word is the Divine Truth proceeding from Divine Good, see n. 9987. On this account also the Lord, when He was in the world, first made Himself the Divine Truth, which is also meant by "*the Word being made flesh*," verse 14 of the same chapter. The reason why the Lord then made Himself Divine Truth was, that He might fight against all the hells, and subdue them, and thus reduce all things therein, and at the same time all things in the heavens, into order, n. 9715, 8809, 10,019, 10,052. That truths derived from good have all power, and *vice versa*, that falses derived from evil have no power, is a thing most known in the other life; hence it is that the evil, who come thither from the world, are deprived of persuasive faith, and likewise of all knowledge of truth, and are thus left to the falses of their own evil. That truths derived from good have such power, cannot be apprehended by those who have an idea of truth and of its faith as of a principle of thought alone, when yet man's principle of thought derived from his will principle makes all the strength of his body, and if it was inspired from the Lord by His Divine Truth, man would have the strength of Sampson; but it is the Lord's good pleasure that man should have strength by faith derived from love as to those things which relate to his spirit, and which conduce to eternal salvation. From these considerations it may be manifest what is meant by the power of truth derived from good, which is signified by the horns of the altars both of burnt-offering and of incense. That horns signify that power, is manifest from the passages in the Word where horns are named, as in Ezekiel, "In that day *I will make a horn to grow* for the house of Israel," xxix. 21. And in Amos, "*Have we not taken to ourselves horns by our fortitude*," vi. 13. And in the 1st book of Samuel, "Jehovah *will give strength* to our king, *and will exalt the horn of His anointed*," ii. 10. And in David, "Jehovah *hath exalted the horn of His people*," Psalm cxlviii. 14. Again, "*All the horns of the wicked I will cut off; let the horns of the just one be exalted*," Psalm lxxv. 10. And in Jeremiah, "The Lord *hath cut off* in the wrath of His anger *all the horn of Israel;* and hath *exalted the horn of thy foes*," Lamen. ii. 3, 17. And in Ezekiel, "Ye push with side and shoulder, and *with your horns* ye strike all the infirm sheep until ye have dispersed them abroad," xxxiv. 21. And in Zechariah, "I saw *four horns;* the angel said, *these are the horns* which have dispersed Judah, Israel, and Jerusalem: the smiths came *to cast down the horns of the nations that lifted up the horn* against the land of Judah," i. 18 to 21. And in Moses, "*The horns of the unicorn are his horns*, with these he shall strike the people together to the ends of the earth," Deut. xxxiii. 17. That in these passages by horns is signified power, is evident, and indeed power in each sense, namely, the power of truth against the false, and of the false against truth; for the subject treated of in the internal sense of the Word throughout is concerning the state of the church. In like manner in Amos, "In that day I will visit upon the altars of Bethel, and *the horns of the altar shall be cut off*, and they shall fall to the earth," iii. 14. By the altars of Bethel, and by its horns, are signified evils and falses destroying the good and truth of the church, of which it is said that they shall be cut off. From these considerations it may be manifest what is meant by the horns, of which so frequent mention is made in Daniel and in the Apocalypse; in Daniel where it is said, "That the beast had *ten horns*, and also *a horn speaking* to it," vii. 8, 11, 20; that *the horn made war with the saints and prevailed*, until the Son of Man came, verses 11, 24; and *concerning the horns of the ram*, and *concerning the horns of the he-goat of the she-goats*, by which they made war with each other, viii. 3 to 21. And in the Apocalypse, "That *the dragon had ten horns*," xii. 3. In like manner *the beast ascending out of the sea*, xiii. 1. Also the *scarlet beast*, xvii. 3; where also it is said, that *the horns are ten kings*, verses 12, 13; in like manner in Daniel, chap. vii. 24. That by kings in the Word are signified truths, and in the opposite sense falses, see n. 1672, 2015, 2069, 3009, 4575, 4581, 4966, 5044, 5068, 6148. Inasmuch as by horns is signified truth in its power, and in the opposite sense the false destroying the truth, therefore speech is attributed to a horn, Apoc. ix. 13; Dan. vii. 8; Psalm xxii. 21. That kings were anointed with oil from a horn, 1 Samuel xvi. 1, 13; 1 Kings i. 39, represented truth derived from good in its power, for horns denote truths in their power, oil denotes good, and kings those who are in truths derived from good; that oil denotes good, see n. 886, 9780; and that kings denotes those who are in truths derived from good, thus abstractedly truths derived from good, n. 6148; hence also it is that *a horn is said to bud forth*, Psalm cxxxii. 17; since all spiritual budding is of truth derived from good, wherefore also formerly they made horns budding forth. That good has all power by truth, or what is the same thing, that all power is of truth derived from good, see what is cited, n. 10,129.

10,183. "And thou shalt cover it over with pure gold"—that hereby is signified a representative of all the things of worship grounded in good, appears from the signification of gold, as denoting the good of love, see n. 9874; and that covering over with gold denotes to found upon that good, see n. 9490; but that it is representative thereof, is evident.

10,184. "Its roof"—that hereby is signified what is inmost, appears from the signification of a roof, as denoting what is inmost. The reason why a roof denotes what is inmost is, because it is supreme or highest, and what is supreme or highest signifies what is inmost, according to what was shown above, n. 10,181; and because a roof signifies the like as the head with man; for all representatives in nature have reference to the human form and have a signification according to that reference, n. 9496. That the head signifies what is inmost, see n. 5328, 6436, 7859, 9656, 9913, 9914. The inmost [principle] which is here signified by the roof of the altar of incense, is the inmost [principle] of worship; for there are in worship similar things in the man himself from whom worship proceeds, namely, what is internal, what is middle, and what is external; the inmost is called celestial, the middle spiritual, and the external natural, n. 4938, 4939, 9992, 10,005, 10,017, 10,068. These degrees from correspondence are signified by the head, the breast, and the feet; in like manner by the roof, the walls, and the horns of the altar of incense. Inasmuch as by the roof is signified what is celestial, which is inmost, good is also signified, for good is every where inmost, and truth proceeds from it, comparatively as light from flame. This is meant by the roof in Matthew, "Then he who is *on the roof of the house*, let him not come down to take any thing out of the house," xxiv. 17; Mark xiii. 15; Luke xvii. 31. The subject there treated of is concerning the last times of the church, and by being on the roof is signified the state of a man who is in good; and by going down to take any thing out of the house is signified return to a former state, see n. 3652. And in Jeremiah, "*On all the roofs of Moab* and in the streets thereof, the whole is mourning," xlviii. 38. By mourning on all roofs, is signified the vastation of all goods with those who, in the representative sense, are meant by Moab, namely, those who are in natural good, who suffer themselves easily to be seduced, n. 2468. And by mourning in the streets, is signified the vastation of all truths; that streets denote truths, see n. 2336. Inasmuch as a roof signified good, therefore the ancients had roofs on their houses where they walked, and also where they offered adoration, as may be manifest from 1 Samuel ix. 25, 26; 2 Samuel xi. 2; Zeph. i. 5. And in Moses, "When thou shalt build a new house, *thou shalt make a compass for thy roof*, lest thou set bloods in thine house, if any one falling shall fall from it. Thou shalt not sow thy vineyard mixedly, lest the gathering of the seed which thou hast sowed, and from the produce of the vineyard, become holy. Thou shalt not plow with an ox and an ass together. Thou shalt not put on a garment mixed with wool and linen together," Deut. xxii. 8, 9, 10, 11. From these considerations also it is evident, that by a roof is signified the good of love; for each of these precepts, involve similar things, which are not discoverable but by the internal sense, which is, that he who is in good, which state is the state of a regenerate man, shall not return into a state of truth which is his prior state, namely, during regeneration; for in this latter state man is led by truth to good, thus partly by himself, but in the former or posterior state, namely, when he is regenerated, he is led of good, that is, by good from the Lord; this is the arcanum which lies interiorly concealed in each of those precepts; thus like to what is contained in the Lord's words in Matthew, "Then he who is on the house, let him not go down to take any thing out of his house: and he who is in the field, let him not return back to take his clothes," xxiv. 17, 18. And in Mark, "He who is on the roof, let him not go down into the house, neither let him enter to take away any thing out of his house; and he who shall be in the field, let him not turn himself any longer back to take away his raiment," xiii. 16. And in Luke, "In that day whosoever shall be on the house, and his vessels in the house, let him not go down to take them away; and whosoever shall be in the field, in like manner let him not return to the things behind him: remember Lot's wife," xvii. 31, 32. Who cannot see that in the above passages are contained the arcana of heaven?—for otherwise, to what intent could it be said that they should not go down from the house, and return back from the field, and that they should remember Lot's wife? In like manner in what was said in Moses, that they should make a compass about the roof lest blood should be shed in falling; and presently that a field should not be sown mixedly with the seed and produce of a vineyard; nor that they should plow with an ox and an ass together; nor should wear a garment mixed with wool and linen together: for by the roof is signified good, and by being upon the house or upon the roof, a state when man is in good; by falling thence is signified a relapse to a former state; and by bloods is signified violence in such case offered to good and truth, n. 375, 1005, 4735, 4978, 7317, 7326. By vineyard is signified the church with man; by the produce of the vineyard, a state of truth, n. 9139; by the seed of wheat or of barley, a state of good, n. 3941, 7605. By an ox also is signified good; and by plowing with an ox, a state of good, n. 2781, 9135; in like manner by wool, and by wearing a garment of wool, n. 9470; and by an ass is signified truth, n. 2781, 5741, and also by linen, n. 7601, 9959: but how the case is with this arcanum in other respects may be seen explained in the passages cited, n. 9274.

10,185. "The walls thereof"—that hereby are signified interior things, appears from the signification of walls or sides, as denoting things interior; for when a roof signifies what is inmost, the walls which are beneath signify interior things. By interior things are meant those which are beneath the inmost and above the ultimate, thus which are middle. The reason why walls signify interior things is, because the sides and breasts appertaining to man signify things interior: for all the representatives in nature have reference to the human form, and are significative according to that reference, n. 9496; as a house, the highest part whereof, which is called the roof, signifies the like with the head; the interior things, which are below the highest, signify the like with the breast and sides; and the foundation thereof the like with the feet and the soles of the feet. The reason of this is, because the universal heaven resembles one man, and hence there is an influx into universal nature, for the natural world exists from the spiritual world. When it is said the spiritual world, the Divine [principle] of the Lord, which is therein, is meant. That all things in nature have reference to the human form, is also manifest from all things in the vegetable kingdom, in which kingdom all things are clothed with leaves, bearing flowers before they bring forth fruits, whilst fruits are the ultimate ends for the sake of which prior things existed, and to which they all tend; for leaves in that kingdom have reference to the lungs, and are as it were in the place of respiration, for by their means juice is attracted, wherefore a tree spoiled of its leaves bears no fruit; hence also it is that leaves in the Word signify the truths which are of faith, n. 885, for in like manner by them is conveyed the vital principle, whereby good is formed. The blossoming before fruit, corresponds to the state of that age with man, when the conjugial principle enters the mind, and gladdens it, thus when truth is conjoining to good; but fruit corresponds to the good itself, which, so far as it ripens like fruit, so far it puts itself forth into works; hence it is that fruits in the Word signify works of charity; and that the blossoming before fruit, is compared to the voice and joy of the bride and bridegroom; so in all other cases. Wherefore he who can reflect wisely, will observe very clearly, that the celestial paradise is represented in the terrestrial paradise, and hence that all things in nature have reference to such things as are in the spiritual world; and he who is able to form further conclusions, will perceive that nature doth not subsist from itself, but by influx from heaven, that is, from the Divine [being] there, insomuch that if the communication were taken away, all things of the earth would be annihilated. That this is the case, the simple apprehend, but not so the wise ones of the world; the reason is, because the simple attribute all those things to the Divine [being], but the worldly-wise to nature.

10,186. "And the horns thereof"—that hereby are signified things exterior, appears from the signification of horns, as denoting the powers of truth derived from good, see above, n. 10,182; the reason why they also denote exterior things is, because in things outermost or ultimate, truth derived from good is in its power, n. 9836; and because the horns of the altar have also reference to the arms and hands appertaining to man, by which also is signified truth in its power, in things ultimate or outermost, see what is cited, n. 10,019, 10,062, 10,076, 10,082.

10,187. "And thou shalt make a border of gold round about"—that hereby is signified termination from good to prevent their being approached and hurt by evils, appears from the signification of a border, as denoting termination to prevent being approached and hurt by evils, see n. 9492; and from the signification of gold, as denoting good, see n. 9874, 9887. The reason why the border was made of gold was, because it represented a closure derived from good; for good cannot be approached by evils, for evils cannot sustain in any measure the sphere of good. When evils, that is, they who are in evils, or they who are from hell, come into that sphere, which sphere is the sphere of heaven, they are direfully tormented, and so far as they enter into that sphere, so far they are made sensible of infernal tortures in themselves, and become thence like those who lie in the agony of death, wherefore they cast themselves down instantly into hell, and dare not any longer lift up their heads; this is the reason why they who are in heaven are in security from the infestation of the hells: this is meant by the words of Abraham to the rich man in hell, "*Between us and you is a great gulf fixed, that they who would pass over from hence to you cannot, neither can they who are there pass to us*," Luke xvi. 26; and by these words, "*They shall say to the mountains and to the rocks, fall on us, and hide us from the face of Him that sit-*

teth on the throne, and from the anger of the Lamb," Apoc. vi. 16; Hosea x. 8. But as to what concerns truth, this may be approached by the evil, by reason that the evil pervert truths by sinister interpretations, and thereby apply them to favor their own lusts; but in proportion as good is present in truths, in the same proportion truths cannot be approached. Hence it may be manifest what protection they can have in the other life, who are only in truths, which are called the truths of faith, and not at the same time in good; by good is meant the good of charity towards the neighbor, and love to the Lord, for all goods are thence derived. From these considerations it is now evident why a border was made round about the walls of the altar of incense.

10,188. "And thou shalt make two rings of gold for it from beneath the border"—that hereby is signified the sphere of Divine Good, by which is conjunction and conservation, appears from the signification of two, as denoting conjunction, see n. 5194, 8423; and from the signification of gold, as denoting good, see n. 9874, 9881; and from the signification of border, as denoting a termination to prevent their being approached and hurt by evils, see just above, n. 10,187. From these considerations it is evident, that by two rings of gold from beneath the border is signified the sphere of Divine Good by which is conjunction; the reason why conservation is also signified is, because it was carried by staves inserted in the rings, and by carrying is signified conservation, n. 9900. It may be expedient here briefly to say what is meant by the sphere of Divine Good. The sphere of Divine Good fills the universal heaven, and also extends itself into hell, for it is like the sphere of the sun's heat in the world, which in summer penetrates even into dark places where the sun does not appear. This Divine sphere was likened by the ancients to circular rays, in the midst of which was God, and round about which were angels; those therefore who suffer themselves to be led of the Lord, thus who receive the Divine [principle] from Him, are in the sphere of the Divine Good in proportion as they receive; but those who do not receive, are indeed in the same sphere, but their interiors are so far closed that they are not sensible of the influx; for those who are in hell are in things external, and not in things internal; from their externals also exhale evils and the falses thence derived, which appear around them like smoke from a furnace. Hence the external sphere of the Divine Good is there made dull, the internal still remaining, which is not received, because every thing is closed against it, nevertheless the Lord by it rules the hells. The reason why there is a sphere of Divine Good, which proceeds from the Lord, is, because the sun of heaven, which is the Lord, is the Divine Love itself, for this so appears; the heat thence proceeding is the good of love, and the light thence proceeding is the truth of faith; hence in the Word by the sun is meant Divine Love, by fire and heat the good of love, and by light the truth of faith. Moreover, from every angel proceeds a sphere derived from his love, also from every good and evil spirit according to their loves; but the spheres proceeding from them do not extend themselves far, whereas the Divine sphere extends into the universe, for it proceeds from what is inmost, and what is inmost is all in all in things which thence succeed. Concerning those spheres, see what was shown above in part also from experience, n. 1048, 1053, 1316, 1504 to 1512, 1695, 2401, 4464, 5179, 6206, 7454, 8598, 8063, 8630, 8794, 8797, 9490, 9491, 9492, 9498, 9499, 9534, 9606, 9607.

10,189. "On the two ribs thereof"—that hereby is signified with truths on one part, namely, conjunction, and by them conservation, appears from the signification of ribs, when by them are meant sides, as denoting truths; for the sides, which are called ribs, have respect to the south and the north, and by the south is signified truth in light, n. 9462, and by the north truth in shade, n. 3708; but by sides, which are properly called sides, is signified good, since they have respect to the east and the west, and by the east is signified good in clearness, and by the west good in obscurity, n. 3708, 9653; therefore it is here said, "Two rings of gold thou shalt make for it from beneath the border, *on the two ribs thereof thou shalt make them, on the two sides thereof.*" That the sides, which are properly sides, have respect to the east and west, but that the sides, which are called ribs, have respect to the south and north, is evident in Exodus, chap. xxvi. 13, 26, 27, 35; also by ribs, since they are the supports of the breast, are signified truths sustaining good. But in heaven the case is this; to the right are those who are in the light of truth, thus who are in the south; but to the left those who are in the shade of truth, thus who are in the north; before the face are those who are in the clear perception of good, thus who are in the east; but to the back are those who are in the obscure perception of good, thus who are in the west; these latter who are in good constitute the Lord's celestial kingdom, but the former who are in truths constitute the Lord's spiritual kingdom. This appearance is presented to the angels there in whatsoever direction they turn themselves, for the angels have continually before the face the Lord, who is the east itself; but the contrary is the case with those who are in hell, for they have the Lord continually to the back; for in the other life there are not quarters, as in the world, determined to stated regions, but according to stated and ruling loves; for an angel and a spirit is his own love, and where it is, thither he turns himself. Those who are in love to the Lord, and in charity towards the neighbor, and thence in faith, behold the Lord before them in every turning of their body with their face; for the Lord turns them to Himself, for He enters by the way of the east to them, and keeps them continually in a determination to Himself; hence their external sight is determined from the internal sight, which is of the understanding, and this from the love which is of the will, looks where the love carries it. The case is similar with men in the world as to their interiors, which are their spirits. From the turning of every one also all in the other life are known asunder. That spaces and places in the other life are so circumstanced, and that hence they signify states, see n. 2625, 2837, 3256, 3387, 4321, 4882, 5604, 7381, 9440, 9667, 10,146.

10,190. "Thou shalt make on the two sides thereof"—that hereby is signified with good on the other [part], namely, conjunction and by it conservation, is manifest from what was said and shown just above, n. 10,189. From thence also it may be manifest how the case is with the Divine sphere round about, namely that it is a sphere of the good of love from the Lord as a sun from the east even to the west, and a sphere of truth derived from good from the south to the north; thus the sphere of Divine Good in the midst is as an axis, and the sphere of Divine Truth thence proceeding is on both sides, on the right and the left.

10,191. "And it shall be for receptacles for the staves"—that hereby is signified the power of truth derived from good there, appears from the signification of receptacles or rings, for these latter were the receptacles, as denoting a Divine sphere, see just above, n. 10,188; and from the signification of staves, as denoting the power of truth from good, see n. 9496.

10,192. "To carry it in them"—that hereby is signified hence conservation in state, appears from the signification of carrying, as denoting to hold together in a state of good and of truth, thus to exist and subsist, see n. 9500, 9737, and to preserve together, n. 9900.

10,193. "And thou shalt make staves of shittim-wood"—that hereby is signified power derived from the good of the Lord's love, appears from the signification of staves, as denoting power, see n. 9496; and from the signification of shittim-wood, as denoting the good of the Lord's love, see above, n. 10,178.

10,194. "And thou shalt cover them over with gold"—that hereby is signified the foundation of all things on good, appears from the signification of covering over with gold, as denoting to found upon good, see n. 9490. It may be expedient briefly to say what is meant by being founded on good. It is believed by some, that truth is [that principle] on which all things are founded, but they are greatly deceived; for there is no truth given with man unless he be in good; the truth appertaining to man which is without good, is external without internal, thus as a shell without a kernel, residing solely in the memory. This truth may be likened to a picture, either of a flower, or of a tree, or of an animal, in which inwardly there is only mud; but truth derived from good not only resides in the memory, but is also rooted in the life, and may be likened to the flower itself, or to the tree, or to the animal, the perfection whereof increases towards the interiors, for what is created from the Divine [being] is the more perfect as it is more interior. This may be very manifest from representatives in the other life; representatives are there presented according to states of the interiors appertaining to spirits, for they are correspondences. Around spirits, who are in truths derived from good, appear the most beautiful representatives, namely, houses and palaces glittering with gold and precious stones, also gardens and paradises of ineffable beauty; all these from correspondence; but around those who are in truths, and not derived from good, there appear nothing but craggy places, rocks, and bogs, and sometimes shrubberies, but unpleasant and barren; these also are from correspondence; but around those who are in falses derived from evil, there appear fens, jakes, and several monstrous objects; the reason of this is because all representatives in the other life are external things figured according to states of the interiors, for thus the spiritual world presents itself visible there. Hence it may be manifest what is meant by being founded on good.

10,195. "And thou shalt give it before the vail, which is above the ark of the testimony"—that hereby is signified in the interior heaven where it is conjoined to the inmost heaven, appears from the signification of the vail, which was between the holy and the holy of holies before the ark, as denoting a medium uniting the second and third heaven, see n. 9670, 9671; and from the signification of the ark of the testimony, as denoting the inmost heaven, see n. 9485. That the tent, with the place within the vail, and out of the vail, and with the court, represented the three heavens, see n. 9457, 9481, 9485, 9741.

10,196. "Before the propitiatory which is above the testimony"—that hereby is signified where there is hearing and reception of all things of worship grounded in the good of love from the Lord, appears from the signification of the propitiatory, as denoting the hearing and reception of all things of worship grounded in the good of love from the Lord, see n. 9506; and from the signification of the testimony, as denoting the Lord as to the Word, see n. 8535, 9503, thus as to Divine Truth, for the Lord as to Divine Truth is the Word, n. 9987. It may be expedient here to make a few observations concerning the Divine Good and the Divine Truth. The Lord as to the Divine [principle] itself, which is called the Father, and as to the Divine Human, which is called the Son, is the Divine Love itself, thus the Divine Good itself; but the Lord as heaven, which is beneath the Lord as a sun, is the Divine Truth; but this Divine Truth has in it Divine Good accommodated to the reception of angels and spirits; this Divine [principle] is what is called the spirit of Jehovah and the holy. The reason why this [principle] is called Divine Truth, and not Divine Good, is, because angels and spirits are created, and thence are receptions of Divine Truth proceeding from Divine Good; they, like men, enjoy two faculties, namely, understanding and will, and the understanding is formed to receive Divine Truth, and the will to receive Divine Good; the understanding serves them for reception, and also for perception. An idea of this subject may be apprehended by the simple from comparison with the sun of the world, and with the world thence existing. In the sun of the world is fire, but what proceeds thence is heat and light; that light is not in the sun itself, may be known to every one, but that light thence proceeds; and in proportion as the light proceeding from the sun has in it heat, in the same proportion vegetables live and grow, and in the same proportion they bring forth fruits and seeds. These things are said comparatively, since universal nature is a theatre representative of the Lord's kingdom; and it is a theatre representative, inasmuch as the natural world by the spiritual world from the Divine [being] first existed, and perpetually exists, that is subsists. Hence it is that in the Word, by the sun is meant the Lord as to Divine Love; in like manner by fire; and that by light is meant the Lord as to Divine Truth, as in John i. 9; chap. iii. 19; chap. ix. 5; chap. xii. 46.

10,197. "Where I will meet thee there"—that hereby is signified thus the presence and influx of the Lord, appears from the signification of meeting, when concerning Jehovah, as denoting the presence and influx of the Lord, see n. 10,147, 10,148.

10,198. "And Aaron shall cause to fume incense upon it"—that hereby is signified the elevation of worship by virtue of love and charity from the Lord, appears from the signification of causing incense to fume, as denoting an elevation of all things of worship by virtue of love and charity, see above, n. 10,177; and from the representation of Aaron as the chief priest, as denoting the Lord as to Divine Good, and as to the work of salvation, see n. 9806, 9966, 10,168. The reason why causing incense to fume signifies elevation of worship is, because fire signified the good of love, hence all things which came forth from fire signified such things as proceed from love; from which ground it is that not only light, but also smoke, were representative. That by fire is signified the good of love, see n. 4906, 5215, 6314, 6832, 6834, 6849, 7324, 10,055; that smoke also represented, is manifest from Isaiah, "Jehovah will create upon every habitation of Zion a cloud in the day, and *smoke and the splendor of a flame of fire by night*," iv. 5. And in the Apocalypse, "*the temple was filled with smoke* from the glory of God and His virtue," xv. 8. That the smoke of incenses denotes an elevation of prayers, thus in general the elevation of all things of worship, is manifest also from the Apocalypse, "*the smoke of incenses ascended from the prayers of the saints*," viii. 4.

10,199. "The incense of spices"—that hereby is signified hearing and reception grateful, appears from the signification of incense, as denoting the hearing and reception of all things of worship, which are grounded in love and charity from the Lord, see n. 10,177; and from the signification of spices, as denoting things grateful. The reason why spices denote things grateful is from their odor, for odor signifies what is perceptive, hence a sweet odor grateful perceptivity, and a disagreeable odor a perceptivity not grateful. For all things which are perceived of man by the sensory organs signify spiritual things, which have relation to the good of love and the truths of faith, as the smell, the taste, the sight, the hearing, and the touch; hence smell signifies the perceptivity of interior truth derived from the good of love; the taste, the perception and affection of knowing and growing wise; the sight, the understanding of the truths of faith; the hearing, perceptivity grounded in the good of faith and in obedience; and the touch in general communication, translation, and reception. The reason of this is, because all external sensations derive their origin from internal sensations, which are of the understanding and will, thus in man from the truths of faith and from the good of love; for these constitute the intellectual and voluntary principle of man. But the internal sensations, which are proper to the understanding and will appertaining to man, have not that sense which the external sensations have, but are turned into such things when they flow in. For all the things which are made sensible to man by the external sensory organs, flow in from things internal, since all influx is from internal things into external, but not *vice versa*, inasmuch as physical influx is not given, that is, influx into the natural world from the spiritual, but from the spiritual world into the natural. The interiors of man, which are proper to his understanding and will, are in the spiritual world, and his externals, which are proper to the senses of the body, are in the natural world; hence also it may be manifest what correspondence is, and what its quality. That the smell in general corresponds to perception according to the quality of a thing, see n. 1514, 1517, 1518, 1519, 3577, 4624 to 4634, 10,054. That taste corresponds to the perception and affection of knowing and of growing wise, n. 3502, 4791, 4085. That the sight corresponds to the understanding of the truths of faith, n.

3863, 4403 to 4421, 4567, 5114, 5400, 6805. That hearing corresponds to the perception of the good of faith and to obedience, n. 3869, 4652, 4660, 7216, 8361, 9311, 9326. And that the touch denotes communication, translation, and reception, n. 10,130. From these considerations it is evident that spices signify such things as are gratefully perceived, such as are the things derived from love and charity, specifically interior truths, because these are from that source, as appears from the following passages in the Word, "*Instead of spice shall be infection*, and instead of a girdle, a rent; and instead of twined work, baldness," Isaiah iii. 24; where the subject treated of is concerning the daughters of Zion, by whom is signified the celestial church, which church is in interior truths derived from the good of love to the Lord; spice denotes interior truth, infection the privation thereof; a girdle denotes conjunction, and a rent denotes the dissipation of connection and of order; twined [or twisted] work denotes scientific truth, which is exterior truth, or truth of the external man, and baldness the deprivation thereof. That a girdle denotes conjunction and a bond to keep all things in connection that they may look to one end, see n. 9828. That twined [or twisted] work denotes scientific truth, n. 2831. And that baldness denotes its deprivation, n. 9960. And in Ezekiel, "An eagle great with wings came into Lebanon, and thence brought away a small branch of a cedar into the land of Canaan, *in a city of those who deal in spices* he set the head thereof," xvii. 3, 4. The subject here treated of, in the internal sense, is concerning the beginning of a spiritual church and its growth, and next concerning its perversion and end; by an eagle great with wings is signified the interior truth of that church, n. 3901, 8764; wings denote exterior truths, n. 8764, 9514; Lebanon denotes that church; the cedar there denotes the truth of the spiritual church; the city of those who deal in spices, where the doctrine of interior truth is. That cities in the Word denote doctrines, see n. 402, 2450, 3216, 4492, 4493. It is called the city of those who deal in spices from interior truths. Again, "The traders of Sheba and Raamah *by the chief of spice*, and by every precious stone and gold gave their tradings," xxvii. 22. The subject here treated of is concerning Tyre, by which is signified the church as to the knowledges of good and truth; traders denote those who have those knowledges and communicate them; Sheba and Raamah, those who are in the knowledges of things celestial and spiritual; the chief of spice, what is grateful from interior truths; precious stones, those truths themselves; and gold, their good; that Tyre denotes the church as to the interior knowledges of good and truth, and in the abstract sense those knowledges themselves, see n. 1201; that traders denote those who have those knowledges and communicate them, n. 2967, 4453; that Sheba and Raamah denote those who are in the knowledges of things celestial and spiritual, n. 1171, 3240; that a precious stone denotes interior truth, n. 9863, 9865, 9873, 9874; and that gold denotes its good, see what is cited, n. 9874, 9881. Hence it is evident what was represented by the Queen of Sheba coming to Jerusalem to Solomon, *with camels carrying spices*, and gold, and precious stones, 1 Kings x. 1, 2; and by the wise men from the east offering to the child Jesus, *gold, frankincense and myrrh*, Matt. ii. 11. Inasmuch as spices signify interior truths, thus such as are grateful, therefore incense was made of spices, and also the oil of anointing, treated of in what follows of this chapter. By interior truths are meant those truths which are made [truths] of man's life and affection, thus which inwardly appertain to him, but not the truths which are only in the memory and are not made truths of the life, for these truths are called external truths respectively, since they are not inscribed on the life, but only on the memory, for they reside in the external man, and not in the internal. The truths of faith, which are inscribed on the life, are in the will, and those things which are in the will are in the internal man, for by the truths of faith the internal man is opened, and communication is effected with the heavens. Hence it is evident that the interior truths appertaining to man are those which are derived from the good of love and charity; whether we speak of the will, or of the love, it is the same thing, for what is of man's will is of his love; wherefore truths inscribed on the life, which are called interior truths, are those which are inscribed on the love, thus which are inscribed on the will, from which they afterwards proceed, when they come into speech and act; for heaven, in which the internal man is who is opened, does not flow in immediately into truth, but mediately by the good of love; but heaven cannot enter with man when the internal man is closed, since there is not any good of love there which receives; wherefore with those with whom the internal man is not opened by truths received from the good of love and charity, hell flows in with falses derived from evil, howsoever the truths of faith, even interior truths, reside solely in the external man, that is, in the memory. From these considerations it may now be manifest what is meant by interior truths, which are grateful, and are signified by spices, namely, those which are derived from the good of love and charity.

10,200. "In the morning in the morning"—that hereby is signified when the state of love is in clearness, appears from the signification of morning, as denoting when the state of love is in clearness, see n. 10,134. Hence in the morning in the morning, or every morning, denotes when that state is. That in the heavens there is a succession of states of love and light, that is, of good and truth, continually, as in the earth of morning, mid-day, evening and twilight, and as of spring, summer, autumn, and winter, has been occasionally shown above; also that hence those times of the day and of the year derive their origin; for those things which exist in the world are images of things which are in the heavens, by reason that every thing natural exists from what is spiritual, that is, from the Divine [principle] in the heavens. Hence it is evident what is the quality of the variations of states in the heavens, for they are known from comparison with the states of heat and light in the world; for heat in the heavens is the good of love from the Lord, and the light there is the truth of faith from the Lord. The reason why such successions of states exist there, is, that the angels there may be continually perfecting; for thus they pass through all the varieties of good and truth, and imbue them. The differences of the varieties of the good of love and of the truth of faith in the heavens, are also like the differences of heat and light in all the regions or climates of the earth, namely, of one sort nearer to the equator, and of another sort at a more remote distance from the equator, on each side; and of one sort in every day of every year, and also of another sort in every year; for there is never a return of what is absolutely like, or the same; for it is provided that what is absolutely the same is never given either in the spiritual world or in the natural world; hence perfection continually increases.

10,201. "In adorning the lamps he shall cause it to fume"—that hereby is signified when truth also comes into its light, appears from the signification of lamps, as denoting Divine Truth, and hence intelligence and wisdom, see n. 9548, 9783. That to adorn or kindle them denotes when those things come into their light, is evident; and from the signification of causing to fume, as denoting the hearing and reception of all things of worship, see above, n. 10,177, 10,192. Hence it is manifest that by causing it to fume every morning, when the lamps were adorned, is signified that the hearing and reception of all things of worship, is principally when they are in a clear state of love, and thence in the intelligence and wisdom of truth. It is said thence in the intelligence of wisdom and truth, inasmuch as the light of truth with man is altogether according to the state of his love; in proportion as the love is kindled, in the same proportion the truth shines bright, for the good of love is the vital fire itself, and the truth of faith is the intellectual light itself, which is intelligence and wisdom; those two principles proceed by like degrees. By intelligence and wisdom, is not meant the faculty of thinking and reasoning on any subject, for this is given alike with the evil as with the good; but by intelligence and wisdom is meant the faculty of seeing and perceiving the truths and goods which are of faith and charity, and which are of love to the Lord: this faculty is not given except with those who are in illustration from the Lord, and they are so far in illustration as they are in love to him and in charity towards the neighbor; for the Lord enters by good, thus by the love and charity appertaining to man, and leads into truths corresponding to good; but when the loves are strange, as is the case with those that are turned from the Lord and the neighbor to self and the world, then those loves lead him, but from truths into falses, whilst the faculty of thinking and reasoning still remains; the reason is, because they are not in illustration from the Lord, but from self and the world, which illustration is mere thick darkness in things spiritual, that is, in those which relate to heaven and the church; for with such persons the internal man is closed, which sees from the light of heaven, and the external is opened, which sees from the light of the world; and to see any thing from the light of the world without an influx of light from heaven, is to see in thick darkness those things which are of heaven; yea, in proportion as man in such case has kindled natural lumen by the loves of self and the world, in the same proportion he rushes into falses, consequently in the same proportion he extinguishes the truths of faith: hence it is that those who are distinguished by worldly learning, who are in the love of self, and have a greater opportunity of confirming falses, are more blind than the simple. These observations are made to the intent that it may be known that the faith of every one is as his love; and that it may be understood how it is that truth comes into its light, when love comes into its clearness, which things are signified by causing the incense to fume every morning when the lamps were adorned.

10,202. "And in causing the lamps to ascend between the evenings Aaron shall make it to fume"—that hereby is signified elevation also in an obscure state of love when truth likewise is in its shade, appears from the signification of causing to ascend or kindling the lamps, as denoting to illustrate with Divine Truth, and hence with intelligence and wisdom, see just above, n. 10,195; and from the representation of Aaron, as denoting the Lord as to Divine Good, and as to the work of salvation, see n. 9806, 9966, 10,068; and from the signification of between the evenings, as denoting an obscure state of love, and hence a state of truth in the shade, see n. 10,134, 10,135; and from the signification of making to fume, as denoting elevation of worship, see above, n. 10,198; hence it is evident that by Aaron making it to fume in causing the lamps to ascend between the evenings, is signified the elevation of all things of worship by the Lord in an obscure state of love, when also truth is in its shade. How the case herein is, may be manifest from what was said just above, n. 10,200, 10,201, namely, that states of love in the heavens vary as the times of the day and of the year in the world, and that truth is in its light as good is in its heat, that is, in its love; wherefore when the love is not so much in its heat, neither is the truth also in its light. This being the case, mention is made of adorning the lamps in the morning and causing the lamps to ascend in the evening, for to cause to ascend is to elevate and increase the light of truth on the occasion as much as possible.

10,203. "Continual incense before Jehovah"—that hereby is signified in all worship grounded in love from the Lord, appears from the signification of incense, as denoting worship grounded in love, see n. 9475; and from the signification of continual, as denoting all in all, see n. 10,133; and from the signification of before Jehovah, as denoting from the Lord, see n. 10,146. It is called worship grounded in love from the Lord, since from the Lord is both love and faith, which are the essentials of worship, and also from the Lord is the elevation of all things of worship to Himself. The man who is not acquainted with the arcana of heaven, supposes that worship is from himself, because he thinks and adores; yet the worship which is from man himself is not worship, but that which is from the Lord with man. For love and faith constitute worship, and since love and faith are from the Lord, worship also is from Him; neither can man elevate any thing from himself into heaven, but the Lord elevates it; in man is merely the faculty that it may be effected, with which faculty he is gifted during regeneration, n. 6148, but all the active and living principle of that faculty is from the Lord. That life itself is from the Lord, and that man and angels are recipient forms, see n. 1954, 2021, 2536, 2706, 3001, 3318, 3484, 3741, 3742, 3743, 4151, 4249, 4318, 4319, 4320, 4417, 4523, 4524, 4882, 5847, 5986, 6325, 6467, 6468, 6470, 6472, 6479, 9338.

10,204. "To your generations"—that hereby is signified to eternity for those who are in faith grounded in love, appears from the signification of generations, as denoting those things which are of faith and love, see n. 613, 2020, 2584, 6239, 9042, 9079, 9845; and that to generations denotes to eternity, see n. 9789.

10,205. "Ye shall not cause to ascend upon it strange incense"—that hereby is signified no worship from any other love than of the Lord, appears from the signification of incense, as denoting worship grounded in love, see n. 9479; and from the signification of strange, as denoting one who is within the church, and does not acknowledge the Lord, see n. 10,112; hence it is evident that by not making strange incense to ascend is signified that worship grounded in any other love than that of the Lord, is not worship. The case herein is this: acknowledgment, faith, and love to the Lord, are the principals of all things of worship within the church, for acknowledgment, faith, and love conjoin; acknowledgment and faith conjoin therein the intellectual principle, and love the will principle; and these two principles make the whole man. He therefore who does not acknowledge the Lord within the church, has not any conjunction with the Divine [being], for all the Divine is in the Lord, and from the Lord; and when there is not any conjunction with the Divine, there is not any salvation; hence it is that worship from any other faith and from any other love than of the Lord, is not worship. The case is otherwise with those who are out of the church; for since they are in ignorance concerning the Lord, worship is still accepted of the Lord from them, when from their religious principle they live in any mutual charity, and in any faith and love to God, whom several of them worship under a human form. They also in the other life, when they are informed by the angels concerning the Lord, that He is the Divine Itself in a human form, acknowledge Him; and so far as they had been in good of life, so far they worship Him from faith and love, see n. 2589 to 2604.

10,206. "And the burnt-offering and meat-offering"—that hereby is signified that there was not there a representative of regeneration by the truths and goods of celestial love, appears from the signification of a burnt-offering, as being representative of purification from evils, of the implantation of good and truth, and their conjunction, thus of regeneration, see n. 10,042, 10,053, 10,057; and from the signification of a meat-offering, as denoting the celestial good, into which man is introduced by regeneration, see n. 4581, 9992, 10,079, 10,137; and also being representative of regeneration, n. 9993, 9994; hence it is evident that by not causing the burnt-offering and meat-offering to ascend on the altar of incense, is signified, that there was not a representative there of regeneration by the truths and goods of faith and love, but a representative of the worship of the Lord from them; for regeneration is one thing, and worship another. For regeneration is the first thing, and according to the quality thereof with man there is worship; for in proportion as man is purified from evils and consequent falses, and in this case in proportion as the truths and goods of faith and love are implanted, in the same proportion worship is accepted and is pleasing; for by worship is meant all that proceeds from love and faith with man, and is elevated to the Lord from the Lord. Inasmuch as this is the completion, therefore the altar of incense, by which worship was represented, is described in the last place; for all things follow in order according to the series in which they are described; for first is described the testimony, by which is meant the Lord; next the ark, in which was the testimony, by which is signified the inmost heaven where the Lord is; afterwards the table on which were the breads, by which is signified the good of love thence derived; also the candlestick with the lamps, by which is signified the Divine Truth proceeding from the Divine Good of the Lord; then the tent itself, by which is signified heaven and the church which are derived from those Divine principles; at length the altar of burnt-offering, by which is signified regeneration by truths derived from good; and lastly the altar of incense, by which is signified worship from all those things in heaven and in the church.

10,207. "And a libation ye shall not offer upon it"—that hereby is signified that there was not a representative there of regeneration by the truths and goods of spiritual love, appears from the signification of a libation, as being a representative of regeneration by the truths and goods of faith and charity, see n. 10,137; which are the truths and goods of spiritual love; for love to the Lord is called celestial love, but charity towards the neighbor is called spiritual love; the former love reigns in the inmost heaven, but the latter in the middle and last heaven, see what is cited, n. 9277, 9596, 9684.

10,208. "And Aaron shall expiate on its horns"—that hereby is signified purification from evils by the truths of faith which are from the good of love, appears from the signification of expiating, as denoting purification from evils, see n. 9506; and from the representation of Aaron, as denoting the Lord as to Divine Good, and as to the work of salvation, see n. 9806, 9966, 10,017; and from the signification of horns, as denoting powers, see n. 10,182, and also exterior things, n. 10,186. The reason why it denotes purification by the truths of faith which are derived from the good of love was, because expiation was made by blood, and by blood is signified the truth of faith which is from the good of love, n. 4735, 7317, 7326, 7846, 7850, 9127, 9393, 10,026, 10,033, 10,047; and all purification from evils is effected by the truths of faith which are from the good of love, n. 2799, 5954, 7044, 7918, 7089. That expiations were made with blood on the horns of the altar of burnt-offerings and of the altar of incense, is manifest in Levit. chap. iv. 3, 7, 18, 25, 30, 34; chap. xvi. 18. The reason why altars were thus expiated was, because holy things were polluted by the sins of the people, for the people represented the church, wherefore those things which were of the church and were called its sanctuaries, as the altar and the tent, together with the things which were therein, were defiled when the people themselves sinned; for those sanctuaries were of the church. This also may be manifest from Moses, "Ye shall separate the sons of Israel from their uncleanness, that they may not die in their uncleanness, *in polluting My habitation*, which is in the midst of them," Levit. xv. 31. And again, "*Aaron shall expiate what is holy from the uncleanness of the sons of Israel;* thus he shall expiate the sanctuary of holiness, and the tent of assembly, and the altar," Levit. xvi. 16, 33. The case herein is this; those things which are called the holy things of the church are not holy unless they be holily received; for unless they be holily received, the Divine does not flow-in into them, and all holy things with man are not holy but from Divine influx. For instance, sacred buildings, altars therein, the bread and wine for the holy supper, become holy solely by the presence of the Lord; wherefore if the Lord cannot be present there by reason of the sins of the people, the holy principle is absent, because the Divine is absent; also the holy things of the church are profaned by sins, since they remove thence the Divine. This now is the reason why the sanctuaries are said to be polluted by the uncleanness of the people, and why on this account they were to be expiated every year. The reasons why expiations were made by blood on the horns of the altars, and not on the altars themselves, was, because the horns were their extremes, and nothing of man is purified unless the extremes be purified; for the extremes are those into which interior things flow in, and according to their state the influx is effected; wherefore if the extremes be perverted, interior things are perverted therein, for when they flow in, the forms receptive of interior things accommodate themselves to the state of the extremes. The case herein is as when the eye is disordered, on which occasion the sight which comes from within sees no otherwise than according to the state of the eye; or as when the arms are disordered, on this occasion the powers which come from within must needs exert themselves accordingly, and in no other way; wherefore if the natural man is perverted, in this case the spiritual has no opportunity of acting into him but in a perverse manner: hence it is, that in such case the spiritual or internal man is closed: but see what has been shown above on these subjects, namely, that in order to man's purification he ought to be purified as to the natural or external man, n. 9325; by reason that all influx is from the internal into the external, and not *vice versa*, n. 5119, 6322; for the natural principle of man is the plane wherein influx from the spiritual world terminates, n. 5651. That the externals of man are formed to serve internals, n. 5947, 9216, 9828. Thus the external man ought to be altogether subject to the internal, n. 5786, 6275, 6284, 6299; by reason that the internal man is in heaven, and the external in the world, n. 3167, 10,156; and the external man of himself, or left to himself alone, is opposite to the internal, n. 3913, 3928. Moreover what the internal man is, and what the external, may be seen in n. 9701 to 9709.

10,209. "Once in a year"—that hereby is signified perpetually, appears from the signification of once in a year, as denoting for the whole year, for expiations on the horns of the altar of incense once in the year, involved expiation for the whole year; and the year, like all things which are of time, signifies a state and its duration, and also perpetuity; in this case a state of purification from evils by the truths of faith, for this state is signified by expiation on the horns of the altar of incense once in a year; and all purification from evils, or regeneration, continues not only perpetually in the world, but also perpetually in the other life. That a year signifies what is perpetual and eternal, see n. 2906, 7828; and that the same is also signified by yesterday, to-day, to-morrow, and similar things which are of time, n. 2838, 3998, 4304, 6165, 6984, 9939; and that purification from evils or regeneration persists to eternity, see what is cited, n. 9334, 10,048.

10,210. "Of the blood of the sin of expiations"—that hereby is signified by the truths which are from the good of innocence, appears from the signification of blood, as denoting Divine Truths, see n 4735, 4998, 7317, 7326, 7846, 7850, 9127, 9393, 10,026, 10,033, 10,047; and from the signification of the sin of expiations, or of the sacrifice of sin by which expiation is effected, as denoting purification from evils and consequent falses; that by sin is meant sacrifice for sin, see n. 10,039; and that expiation denotes purification from evils and consequent falses, n. 9506. The reason why such purification is effected by truths which are from the good of innocence is, because the blood by which expiation was effected, was from a bullock or a lamb, and by a bullock is signified the good of innocence in the external man, n. 9391, 9990, 10,132; and by a lamb the good of innocence in the internal man, n. 10,132, and there must be innocence to the intent that truth and good may be received, n. 3111, 3994, 4797, 6013, 6765, 7836, 7840, 9262, 10,134; also what is cited, n. 10,021; for the good of innocence consists in acknowledging that all goods and truths are from the Lord, and nothing from the proprium of man; thus it consists in being willing to be led of the Lord, and not of self. Hence it is evident, that the more man confides and believes in himself, thus the more he is in self-love, the less he is in the good of innocence; hence it is, that man cannot be purified from evils, unless he be in the good of innocence; for if he be not in that good, he is not led of the Lord, but of self; and he who is led of self, is led of hell, for the proprium of man is nothing but evil, and all evil is of hell. That all expiation was made by blood, either of a bullock, or of a lamb, or of turtles, or of young doves, is manifest from Moses, Exod. xxix. 36; Levit. iv. 1 to 7, 13 to 18, 27 to the end; chap. v. 1 to 7; chap. xv. 14, 28 to 31; Numb. vi. 9, 10, 11. By turtles and by young doves is also signified the good of innocence.

10,211. "Once in a year he shall expiate upon it"—that hereby is signified the perpetual removal of evils, appears from the signification of once in a year, as denoting what is perpetual, see above, n. 10,203; and from the signification of expiating, as denoting purification from evils and consequent falses, see n. 9506; and purification from evils is nothing but a withholding from them, or their removal, see what is cited, n. 10,057.

10,212. "To your generations"—that hereby are signified those of the church who are in the truths and goods of faith, appears from the signification of generations, as denoting those things which are of faith and charity, see what is cited, n. 10,194. The reason why they denote those who are of the church is, because the genuine truths and goods of faith and love are given only with them, for with them is the Word; and by the sons of Israel, whose generations are here meant, is signified the church, see what is cited, n. 9346.

10,213. "This is the holy of holies to Jehovah"—that hereby is signified since from the Divine celestial [principle], appears from the signification of the holy of holies, as denoting the Divine celestial [principle], see n. 10,129. What the Divine celestial [principle] is, and the Divine spiritual, and what is the difference, see what is cited, n. 9277, 9599.

10,214. Verses 11 to 16. *And Jehovah spake to Moses, saying, when thou shalt take the sum of the sons of Israel, as to those that are numbered of them, and they shall give every one an expiation of his soul to Jehovah in numbering them; and let there be no plague in them in numbering them. This they shall give every one that passeth upon the numbered; half a shekel in the shekel of holiness; a shekel is twenty oboli; the half of a shekel an up-lifting to Jehovah. Every one passing upon the numbered, from a son of twenty years and upwards, shall give an up-lifting to Jehovah. A rich man shall not give more, and a poor man shall not give less, from the half of a shekel to give an up-lifting to Jehovah, to expiate on your souls. And thou shalt take silver of expiations from [being] with the sons of Israel, and thou shalt give it for the work of the tent of the congregation; and it shall be to the sons of Israel for remembrance before Jehovah, to expiate on your souls.* And Jehovah spake to Moses, saying, signifies illustration by the Word from the Lord. When thou shalt take the sum of the sons of Israel, signifies all things of the church. As to those that are numbered of them, signifies as to ordination and arrangement, and they shall give every one an expiation of his soul in numbering them, signifies purification or liberation from evil by the acknowledgment and faith that all the goods and truths of faith and love, and their ordination and arrangement, are from the Lord, and nothing from man. And let there be no plague in them in numbering them, signifies lest there should be the punishment of evil in doing goods as from self. This they shall give every one that passes upon the numbered, signifies the ascribing of all things which are of faith and love to the Lord. The half of a shekel in the shekel of holiness, signifies all things of truth derived from good. Twenty oboli are a shekel, signifies all things of good. The half of a shekel an up-lifting to Jehovah, signifies that all things of truth derived from good are of the Lord alone. From a son of twenty years and upwards, signifies a state of intelligence, of truth, and of good. Ye shall give an up-lifting to Jehovah, signifies ascribing to the Lord alone. A rich man shall not give more, and a poor man shall not give less, from the half of a shekel to give to Jehovah, signifies that all, of whatsoever faculty they be, ought to ascribe all things of truth and good to the Lord. To expiate on your souls, signifies that evils may be removed. And thou shalt take the silver of expiations from [being] with the sons of Israel, signifies truths derived from good purifying, which are of the church. And thou shalt give for the work of the tent of the congregation, signifies conjunction with heaven by the acknowledgment that all truths and goods are from the Lord. And it shall be to the sons of Israel for remembrance before Jehovah, signifies thereby the preservation of the church and of all things of the church by the Lord. To expiate on your souls, signifies since thus evils are removed.

10,215. "And Jehovah spake to Moses, saying"—that hereby is signified illustration by the Word from the Lord, appears from the signification of speaking, when from Jehovah to Moses, as denoting illustration from the Lord by the Word, for Jehovah in the Word is the Lord, and by Moses is represented the Word; for by speaking is signified influx, perception, and instruction, see n. 2951, 5481, 5743, 5797, 7226, 7241, 7270, 8127, 8128, 8221, 8262, 8660, consequently also illustration, for illustration is influx, perception, and instruction, from the Lord, whilst the Word is reading. That Jehovah in the Word is the Lord, see the passages cited, n. 9373; and that Moses is the Word in the representative sense, n. 9372. The reason why these things are signified by Jehovah speaking to Moses, is, because those words are not perceived in heaven as in earth; for in heaven the words are perceived according to the internal sense, but in earth according to the external sense, for in heaven all things are spiritually understood, but in earth naturally; the former understanding is momentaneous, without the knowledge of what is understood in the external or literal sense by man. Such is the consociation of the angels of heaven with man, by reason that the all of man's thought flows in from the spiritual world, and thus that his thought in its first origin is spiritual, and becomes natural in the external man by influx.

10,216. "When thou shalt take the sum of the sons of Israel"—that hereby are signified all things of the church, appears from the signification of a sum, as denoting all; and from the representation of the sons of Israel, as denoting the church, see what is cited, n. 9340. The reason why all things of the church are signified by the sum of the sons of Israel is, because the internal sense of the Word is such as its sense is in heaven; thither names do not pass, as the names of Israel, Moses, Aaron, and several others, for those names are amongst material things, which are only for the corporeal sensual man, but in their place are perceived things spiritually relating to heaven and to the church; for the angels of heaven are spiritual, and apprehend names which occur according to their essence, that is, spiritually. The reason why in heaven instead of the sons of Israel they understand the church is, because in the inmost heaven, where the Lord is more present than in the heavens beneath, by names in the Word, in the good sense, is understood the Lord Himself, as by Abraham, Isaac, Jacob, Moses, Aaron, David, Joseph, Judah, Israel; and since by them is understood the Lord there, hence the Divine things which are of heaven and of the church, which are from the Lord, are perceived by the same, according to the series of things treated of in the Word; the perception flows in from the Lord, who is the Word, for from the Lord is the all of intelligence and of wisdom, and without Him is nothing.

10,217. "As to those that are numbered of them"—that hereby is signified as to ordination and arrangement, appears from the signification of numbering when relating to all things of the church, which are the truths and goods of faith and love, as denoting their ordination and arrangement; hence those that are numbered denote the things which are ordained and arranged. The reason why numbering has this signification is, because numbering involves a survey, and what is surveyed by the Lord, this also is ordained and arranged; the term also, by which numbering is here expressed in the original tongue, signifies to survey, to take an estimate of, to observe, and also to visit, to command, to preside, thus to ordain and arrange. The reason why these significations belong to that term is, because one thing involves another in the spiritual sense, and the spiritual sense is the interior sense of terms, which sense is for the most part in the terms of languages, especially of the oriental. That to number in the spiritual sense, in which sense the truths and goods of faith and love are treated of, denotes to ordain and to arrange, is manifest also from the passages in the Word, where mention is made of numbering, and also of number, as in Isaiah, "The voice of a tumult of kingdoms of nations gathered together, *Jehovah Zebaoth numbereth* [ordaineth] *the army of war*," xiii. 4. Again, "Lift up your eyes on high, and see who hath created these, *who hath brought forth into number their army;* He calleth all by name; of the multitude of the powerful and mighty in strength a man is not wanting," xl. 26. And in David, "*Jehovah who numbereth the army of the stars*, He calleth all by names," Psalm cxlvii. 2; that by numbering in these passages is signified to ordain and to arrange, is evident, for the subject treated of is concerning Jehovah, that is, the Lord, who does not number any army, nor stars, but ordains and arranges those things which are signified by an army and by stars, which are the truths and goods of faith and love; for the subject treated of is not concerning wars in the natural world, but concerning wars in the spiritual world, which are wars or combats of truths derived from good against falses derived from evil; that wars in the spiritual sense are such combats, see n. 1664, 2686, 8273, 8295; that an army denotes the truths and goods of the church and of heaven, n. 7988, 8019; and that stars denote the knowledges of truth and good, n. 2495, 2849, 4697. When it is known what is signified by numbering, and what by the sons of Israel, it may be manifest why it was not lawful for David to number the people, and why after that he numbered them, Gad the prophet being sent to him denounced punishment, 2 Sam. xxiv. 1 to 15; and why it is here said, that every one should give an expiation of his soul, *lest there be in them a plague in numbering them.* For by the sons of Israel are signified the truths and goods of the church, and by numbering is signified to ordain and to arrange; and since it is of the Lord alone to ordain and arrange the truths and goods of faith and love appertaining to every one in the church and in heaven, therefore when this is done by man, as it was done of David by Joab, it then signified the ordination and arrangement of such things by man and not by the Lord, which is not to ordain and arrange, but to destroy. If the numbering of the sons of Israel had not involved such things, there would not have been any thing of sin or of guilt in numbering them. That by the sons of Israel are signified spiritual truths and goods, which are the truths and goods of the church and of heaven, see n. 5414, 5801, 5803, 5812, 5817, 5819, 5826, 5833, 5879, 5981, 7956, 8234, 8805, in like manner by the tribes, into which the sons of Israel were distinguished, n. 3858, 3926, 4060, 6335, 6397. Inasmuch as by the sons of Israel and by the tribes such things are signified, and those things are innumerable, therefore in the Word it is said of them, "*That their number was as the sand of the sea, which shall not be mea-*

sured neither shall be numbered," Hosea ix. "*Who shall number the dust of Jacob, and the number of Israel?*" Numb. xxiii. 10. Jehovah said to Abraham, "*I will set thy seed as the dust of the earth, that if ye can number the dust of the earth it will also come to pass that thy seed may be numbered,*" Gen. xiii. 16; chap xvi. 10. And in another place, "*Look up towards heaven, and number the stars, whether thou canst number them, so shall thy seed be,*" Gen. xv. 5. That by the sons of Israel and by the seed of Abraham was not meant his posterity, but spiritual truths and goods, which are innumerable, and also for the most part ineffable, may be manifest from this consideration, that there was not a greater multitude of them than of other nations, which also Moses testifies, "*Not because of your multitude above all people hath Jehovah desired you, that He might choose you, for ye were fewer than all people,*" Deut. vii. 7. Also by numbering is signified to ordain and to arrange in Jeremiah, "In the cities of Jerusalem and of Judah shall flocks yet pass *according to the hands of him that numbereth,*" xxxiii. 13; flocks denote also the goods and truths of the church, n. 6048, 8937, 9135; according to the hands of him that numbereth, denotes according to the arrangement of the Lord. And in David, "Who knoweth the vehemence of Thine anger, *to number our days*, make known what is right, that we may put on a heart of wisdom," Psalm xc. 12; to number days denotes to ordain and arrange states of life; and days are said to be numbered when they are ordained and arranged, thus when they are finished, as in Isaiah, "By the discharge of my days I was about to go away to the gates of hell; *I was numbered*, the residue of my years," xxxviii. 10. And in Daniel, "A writing appeared before king Belshazzar, *numbered*, weighed, and divided," v. 25; for when to number signifies to ordain and arrange, then what is numbered signifies what is completed, as when a line is drawn under a number on finishing a calculation. The reason why by numbering is signified to ordain and arrange is, because by number is signified the quality of a thing and of a state, and the quality is determined by the number adjoined; hence to number denotes to qualify, and the qualification of a thing in spiritual things is effected by ordination and arrangement from the Lord; this is signified by number in the Apocalypse, "He caused all to receive a mark on the right hand or on their foreheads; and that no one might buy or sell but he who had the mark or name of the beast, *or the number of his name;* this is wisdom, he who hath intelligence *let him compute the number of the beast, for it is the number of a man*, namely, *the number six hundred sixty-six,*" chap. xiii. 16, 17, 18; the subject treated of in this chapter, is concerning the beast out of the sea, and concerning the beast out of the earth. By the beast out of the sea is meant the truth of the church falsified by scientifics, which are from the world. And by the beast out of the earth is meant the truth of the church falsified by the literal sense of the Word applied to favor the evils of self-love and of the love of the world, for the earth denotes the church as to good and truth, see what is cited, n. 9325; and the sea denotes the scientific principle in general, n. 28, 2850, 3120; to have his mark upon the hand and upon his forehead denotes to acknowledge all things of whatsoever kind they are; for the forehead signifies love, n. 9936; a name signifies all the quality of that which is treated of, n. 3006, 3421, 6674, 8274, 9310; to compute the number of the beast denotes to explore and know those falsified truths of the church; the number of a man signifies the thing and state of that church; six hundred sixty-six signify its quality as to all truths falsified, and falses derived from evil, and also the profanation of what is holy, and likewise the end; to know those things and to explore them is the part of a wise and intelligent person, wherefore it is said, this is wisdom, he that has intelligence let him compute its number; for the number six signifies the same with the number twelve, because it is the half thereof, n. 3960, 7973, 8148; and twelve signifies all the truths and goods of the church in the complex, n. 2129, 2130, 3272, 3858, 3913, 7973. Hence also in the opposite sense all falses and evils in the complex; the triplication of the number six involves also the end, and the end is when truth is altogether profaned. From these considerations it is very evident, that numbers in the Word involve things and states, and signifies quality according to the determinate numbers, as also in the following words in the Apocalypse, "The angel measured the wall of the holy Jerusalem, *a hundred forty-four cubits*, which is the *measure of a man*, that is, *of an angel*," xxi. 17. By the determinate number in this passage are also signified all truths and goods in the complex, for a hundred forty-four signifies the same with twelve, n. 7973, for it arises out of twelve multiplied into itself; wherefore also it is here said, that its measure is the measure of a man, as above, that that number is the number of a man; but whereas truths derived from good are here signified, it is added that that measure is also the measure of an angel, for an angel in the Word signifies truths derived from good, since he is the recipient of Divine Truth from the Lord, n. 8192.

10,218. "And they shall give every one the expiation of his soul in numbering them"—that hereby is signified purification or liberation from evil by the acknowledgment and faith, that all the truths and goods of faith and of love, together with their ordination and arrangement, are from the Lord, and nothing from man, appears from the signification of giving the expiation of his soul, as denoting to be purified or liberated from evil by the truth of faith, which is here to acknowledge that all truths and goods are from the Lord; and from the signification of numbering Israel, as denoting the ordination and arrangement of those principles by the Lord alone, and not by man. That these things are signified, is manifest from all that is here said concerning the half of a shekel which was to be given to Jehovah, and the expiation by it in numbering the people; for by the shekel of holiness is signified truth which is of the Lord alone, and by expiation thereby, purification or liberation from evil, n. 5506; and by numbering the sons of Israel is signified to ordain and arrange all the truths and goods of the church, n. 10,217. The case herein is this; it was prohibited to number the sons of Israel, inasmuch as by numbering was signified to ordain and to arrange, and by the sons of Israel, and by the tribes into which they were distinguished, were signified all the truths and goods of faith and love in the complex; and since the ordination and arrangement of these was of the Lord alone, and not of man, therefore to number them was prevarication, such as appertains to those who claim to themselves the truths which are of faith and the goods which are of love, together with their ordination and arrangement. What is the quality of such persons, is known in the church, for they are such as justify themselves by the consideration that all things of faith and love promote their merits, and consequently they believe that by virtue of faith and works they of themselves merit heaven. The numbering of the people by David involved this evil, concerning which it is thus written in the Second Book of Samuel, "The anger of Jehovah burnt yet further against Israel; therefore He stirred up David against them, saying, go, number Israel and Judah; he said therefore to Joab, wander through all the tribes of Israel, and number the people, that I may know the number of the people. Joab said to the king, let Jehovah thy God add to the people so many and so many a hundred times; but why doth my lord the king desire this word? Nevertheless the word of the king prevailed against Joab and against the princes of the army, wherefore they went forth to number the people Israel. Afterwards the heart of David smote him, wherefore he said to Jehovah, I have sinned exceedingly in what I have done; nevertheless, O Jehovah, cause I pray the iniquity of thy servant to pass away, because I have done exceeding foolishly. But Gad the prophet was sent to David, that he might choose one evil out of three; and he chose the pestilence, whereof died seventy thousand men," xxiv. 1 and following verses. From this passage it is evident how great a sin it was to number Israel; not that numbering considered in itself was a sin, but because, as was said, the numbering of the sons of Israel by David signified the ordination and arrangement of all things of faith and love from self and not from the Lord, the numbering itself signifying ordination and arrangement, and the sons of Israel all the truths and goods of faith and of love. To the intent therefore that they might be delivered from sin in numbering the sons of Israel, the half of a shekel was given for expiation; for it is said, "*They shall give every one the expiation of his soul to Jehovah in numbering them, lest there be in them a plague in numbering them.*" Hence it is evident that by these words is signified purification or liberation from evil by the acknowledgment that all the truths and goods of faith and love, together with their ordination and arrangement are from the Lord, and nothing from man. That this is the case, namely, that all the goods and truths of faith and love are from the Divine, and nothing from man, is also known in the church; and likewise that it is evil for man to attribute them to himself; and that they are delivered from that evil who acknowledge and believe, that those things are from the Lord, for thus they claim to themselves nothing which is Divine, and which is from the Divine; but see what has been above shown on this subject, namely, that those who believe that they do goods from themselves, and not from the Lord, believe that they merit heaven, n. 9974; that goods from self and not from the Lord are not goods, since those who do good from themselves do them from evil, n. 9975, 9980. That they despise the neighbor; and that they are angry with God Himself if they do not receive a reward, n. 9976. That such persons cannot receive heaven in themselves, n. 9977. That they cannot in any wise fight against the hells; but that the Lord fights for those, who acknowledge and believe that all goods and truths are from the Lord, n. 9978. That the Lord alone is merit and justice, n. 9486, 9715, 9809, 9979 to 9984, 10,019, 10,152.

10,219. "And there be not in them a plague in numbering them"—that hereby is signified lest there be the punishment of evil in doing good as from themselves, appears from the signification of a plague, as denoting the punishment of evil, of which we shall speak presently; and from the signification of numbering the sons of Israel, as denoting to ordain and arrange the truths and goods of faith and love, see above, n. 10,217, thus to do them; it is said as from themselves, since the goods which a man does, he does as from himself, nor does he perceive otherwise until he be in faith derived from love, for goods from the Lord flow in, and are received by man, and those which are received are at first felt no otherwise than as in himself and from himself, nor is it perceived that they are from the Lord, until he comes into knowledge, and afterwards into acknowledgment derived from faith; for before this he cannot reflect that any thing flows in from the

Divine, neither can he at all perceive this, that is, be sensible of it in himself, until he begins to will and to love that it be so. The case herein is, like that of the life itself appertaining to man, and like the two interior faculties of life, which are understanding and will; who does not believe until he be instructed, that life is in himself, and thus that what he thence acts is from himself; in like manner understanding and the will; when yet both life in general, together with understanding and will flow in, the truths of the understanding and the goods of the will out of heaven from the Lord, but the falses of understanding and the evils of will from hell; for unless spirits and angels be attendant on man, to communicate influx, man cannot live even a single moment, consequently neither can he think, nor will, as may be manifest from manifold experience treated of at the close of several chapters, where influx was spoken of; see the passages cited, n. 9223, 9276, 9682. But so long as man believes that he does all things from himself, both goods and evils, so long goods do not affect him, and evils adhere to him; whereas so soon as he acknowledges and believes that goods flow in from the Lord, and not from himself, and that evils are from hell, in this case goods affect him, and evils do not adhere to him; and also in proportion as goods affect him, in the same proportion evils are removed, thus he is purified and liberated from them. But so long as the state of man is such, that he cannot perceive and be sensible of the influx of goods from the Lord, so long he does goods as from himself, nevertheless he ought to acknowledge and believe that they are from the Lord; for when this is the case, he is also liberated from evils; but to the intent that he may be liberated from evils, that acknowledgment must not be the confession of the mouth alone, but the confession of the heart itself. That a plague denotes the punishment of evil, is manifest without explication; there are three plagues, or three punishments which follow those who attribute to themselves the truths of faith and goods of love, or who believe that they merit heaven by their works, for those who attribute to themselves those principles, believe also that of themselves they merit heaven, those three punishments are, 1. That they cannot receive any thing of the good of love and of the truth of faith. 2. That evils and falses continually pursue them. 3. And that the truths and goods received from infancy perish; these three punishments are signified by the three plagues, which were proposed to David by the prophet Gad on account of numbering the people, which were, 1. Seven years of famine; 2. A flight of three months before enemies; 3. And a pestilence of three days; 2 Samuel xxiv. 13; for by a famine is signified the defect and scarcity of the goods and truths which are of faith and love, for these things are signified by bread, food, wheat, barley, oil, and wine, which are deficient during famine; but by flight before enemies in the internal sense is meant persecution by evils and falses; for those who attribute to themselves goods and truths, are not able to fight against the evils and falses which are from hell, n. 9978, which are enemies in the spiritual sense, before whom there is flight, and from whom there is persecution; but by pestilence is signified the vastation and consumption of goods and truths which have been received from infancy, n. 7505. By David's choosing the pestilence, and by seventy thousand men dying of it, was signified that with the Israelitish and Jewish nation every truth and good of faith and love was about to perish, which also came to pass, for they did not acknowledge the Lord, from whom nevertheless are all goods and truths; three days signified to the full, and the same was also signified by the seventy thousand men who died.

10,220. "This they shall give every one that passeth upon the numbered"—that hereby is signified the ascribing of all things which are of faith and love to the Lord, appears from the signification of giving, namely, an expiation of the soul, which was the half of a shekel, as denoting liberation from evils by the acknowledgment that the all of faith and love is from the Lord, and nothing from man, see above, n. 10,211; hence every one that passeth upon the numbered, signifies whatsoever is of truth and good which is ordained and arranged by the Lord; for every one that passeth is every one of the sons of Israel, and by the sons of Israel are signified all spiritual goods and truths, n. 5414, 5801, 5803, 5812, 5817, 5819, 5826, 5833, 5879, 5981, 7956, 8234, 8805; and by the numbered are signified those which are ordained and arranged by the Lord, n. 10,218.

10,221. "The half of a shekel in the shekel of holiness"—that hereby are signified all things of truth derived from good, appears from the signification of half, as denoting all; and from the signification of a shekel, as denoting truth derived from good; the reason why half denotes all is, because the half of a shekel was ten gerahs or oboli, and by ten are signified all, n. 4638, and also remains, n. 576, 1906, 1988, 2284, which are the truths and goods appertaining to man stored up in his interiors from the Lord, n. 5135, 5342, 5897, 5898, 7560, 7564. The reason why a shekel denotes truth derived from good is, because a shekel was a weight of silver and also of gold, and by silver is signified truth, and by gold good; but how much of truth derived from good, and of good by truth, is determined by the number of gerahs or oboli of the shekel; and the shekel considered in itself as a weight, denotes quantity; and when it is called the shekel of holiness, it denotes the quantity of truth and good, for truth and good are what are called holy, since they are from the Lord, who alone is holy. More may be seen concerning the skekel and its signification, in n. 2959.

10,222. "Twenty oboli a shekel"—that hereby are signified all things of good, appears from the signification of twenty, as likewise denoting all, and remains of good, and also what is holy; that it denotes all and hence what is full, see n. 9641; that it denotes remains of good, n. 2280; and what is holy, n. 4759, 7842, 7903; for twenty, when relating to the Lord, signify His proprium, which is the holy [principle] itself, n. 4176; hence it is evident why a shekel was of twenty gerahs or oboli, and why it is called a shekel of holiness, as in this and other passages, as Levit. xxvii. 3; Numb. iii. 47, 50; chap. vii. 13, 19, 25, 31, 37, 49, 55, 61, 67, 73; chap. xviii. 16. That the shekel was a weight both of silver and of gold, see Gen. xxiv. 22; Exod. xxxviii. 24; Ezek. iv. 10; xlv. 12.

10,223. "The half of a shekel an up-lifting to Jehovah"—that hereby is signified that all things of truth derived from good are of the Lord alone, appears from the signification of the half of a shekel, as denoting all things of truth derived from good, see above, n. 10,221; and from the signification of an up-lifting to Jehovah, as denoting what are of the Lord alone, see n. 10,093.

10,224. "Every one that passeth upon the numbered"—that hereby is signified that all truths and goods are to be ascribed to the Lord alone, appears from what was shown above, n. 10,220.

10,225. "From a son of twenty years and upwards"—that hereby is signified a state of intelligence of truth and good, appears from the signification of twenty, when applied to the age of man, as denoting a state of the intelligence of truth and good. The reason why twenty denotes a state of the intelligence of truth and good is, because man when he attains to the age of twenty years, begins to think from himself; for man from first infancy to extreme old age undergoes several states as to his interiors, which are of intelligence and wisdom. The *first* state is from nativity to the fifth year of his age; this state is a state of ignorance, and of innocence in ignorance, and is called infancy; the *second* state is from the fifth year of age even to the twentieth; this state is a state of instruction and of science, and is called boy-hood; the *third* state is from the twentieth year of age to the sixtieth, which state is a state of intelligence, and is called adolescence, youth, and manhood; the *fourth* or last state is from the sixtieth year of age and upwards, which is a state of wisdom, and of innocence in wisdom. These successive states of the life of man are signified by the numbers of the years of age, five, twenty, and sixty, in the following passage in Moses, "When any one shall make a singular vow, the estimation of a male shall be *from a son of twenty years even to a son of sixty years*, fifty shekels of silver, if a female, the estimation shall be thirty shekels. *But from a son of five years even to a son of twenty years*, the estimation shall be, if a male, twenty shekels, if a female, ten shekels. *But from a son of a month even to a son of five years*, the estimation of a male shall be five shekels, of a female three shekels. *But from a son of sixty years and upwards*, the estimation shall be fifteen shekels, but of a female ten shekels," Levit. xxvii. 2 to 7. That the first state is a state of ignorance, and also of innocence in ignorance, is evident; during the continuance of this state, the interiors are forming to use, consequently are not manifested, but only the most external, which are of the sensual man; when these alone are manifested, there is ignorance; for whatsoever man understands and perceives, is from the interiors. Hence also it may be manifest, that the innocence which exists at that time, and is called the innocence of infancy, is innocence the most external. That the second state is a state of instruction and of science is also evident; this state is not yet a state of intelligence, because the child at that time does not form any conclusions from himself, neither does he discern between truths and truths, nor even between truths and falses, from himself, but from others. He only thinks and speaks things of the memory, thus from science alone, nor does he see and perceive whether a thing be so, except on the authority of his master, consequently because another has so said. But the third state is called a state of intelligence, since at this time man thinks from himself and discerns and concludes; and what he then concludes is his own and not another's; at this time faith commences, for faith is not the faith of the man himself until from the ideas of his own proper thought he has confirmed what he believes; previous to this time, faith is not his, but another's in himself, for he believed the person, not the thing. Hence it may be manifest, that a state of intelligence then commences with man, when he no longer thinks from a master, but from himself; which effect has not place until the interiors are open towards heaven. It is to be noted that the exteriors appertaining to man are in the world, and the interiors in heaven; and that in proportion to the quantity of light which flows in from heaven into those things which are from the world, in the same proportion man is intelligent and wise; this is effected in the degree, and according to the quality in which the interiors are opened; and they are so far opened, as man lives for heaven and not for the world. But the last state is a state of wisdom, and of innocence in wisdom; which is when man has no longer any concern about understanding truths and goods, but about willing them and living them; for this it is to be wise.

And man is enabled to will truths and goods and to live them, so far as he is in innocence, that is, so far as he believes that he has nothing of wisdom from himself, but that whatsoever relish he has of wisdom is from the Lord; also so far as he loves it to be so; hence it is that this state also is a state of innocence in wisdom. From the succession of these states the man who is wise may also see the wonderful things of Divine Providence, which are these, that a prior state is the plane of those which continually follow, and that the opening or unfolding of the interiors proceeds from outermost things even to inmost things successively; and at length in such a sort, that what was first, but in things outermost, this also is last, but in things inmost, namely, ignorance and innocence; for he who knows that of himself he is ignorant of all things, and that whatsoever he knows is from the Lord, is in ignorance of wisdom, and also in the innocence of wisdom. From these considerations it may now be manifest what a state of intelligence is, which is signified by twenty, when that number is predicated of the age of man. The like is also meant by that number in other passages of the Word, as in Moses, "Take the sum of all the congregation *from a son of twenty years and upwards*, every one that goeth forth into the army in Israel," Numb. i. 2, 3, 18, and following verses. The subject treated of in this passage is the encampment and journeying of the sons of Israel according to tribes, and thereby is also signified the ordination and arrangement of the truths and goods of faith and love by the Lord; by encampment the ordination and arrangement, n. 4236, 8103, 8130, 8131, 8155; and by the tribes the goods and truths of faith and love in every complex, n. 3858, 3926, 3939, 4060, 6335, 6337, 6397; hence by a son of twenty years and upwards are meant those who are in a state of intelligence, for with them the truths and goods of faith and love from the Lord can be ordained and arranged, for the Lord flows-in into their intellectual and will principle, and ordains and arranges, and also removes and casts down falses and evils; therefore it is said from a son of twenty years and upwards *every one that goeth forth into the army*, for by the army are signified truths arranged in that order, that they are not afraid of falses and evils, but repel them if they assault; that such truths are meant by an army in the internal sense, see n. 3448, 7236, 7988, 8319; but with those who are in a state of infancy and of childhood, thus who are below twenty years, truths and goods are not so ordained as to enable them to go forth into the army and into war, since, as was said above, they do not as yet discern and form any conclusions from themselves, consequently they cannot as yet shake off any thing of what is false or evil by the rational principle, and they who are not able to do this, are not led into combat; wherefore man is not admitted into temptations, which are spiritual combats against falses and evils, until he is in a state of intelligence, that is, until he comes to the exercise of his own judgment, n. 3928, 4248, 4249, 8963. The like is signified by the age of twenty years and upwards in other passages in Moses, "Jehovah said to Moses and Eleazer, "Take ye the sum of the whole assembly of the sons of Israel, *from a son of twenty years and upwards*, every one that goeth forth to war in Israel," Numb. xxvi. 2, 3; by going forth to war in the spiritual sense is signified to go forth into combat against the falses and evils which are from hell. He who does not know that a son of twenty years and upwards signifies a state of intelligence, or those who are in that state, cannot know why it is said, when they murmured against *Jehovah, they should die in the wilderness from a son of twenty years and upwards*, all who came up out of Egypt, Numb. xiv. 29; chap. xxxii. 10, 11; for those who are in that state of intelligence, that they can discern, conclude, and judge from themselves, are blameable for their evil, but not those who are not yet in that state: hence also it is evident that by twenty years, when they are predicated of age, is signified a state of intelligence, or a state of judgment. But the number twenty has another signification, when another subject is treated of, see n. 10,222.

10,226. "Shall give an up-lifting to Jehovah"—that hereby is signified an ascribing to the Lord alone, appears from the signification of an up-lifting to Jehovah, as denoting what is of the Lord alone, see n. 10,093. That this denotes all the truths and goods of faith and love, with their ordination and arrangement, is evident from what precedes.

10,227. "A rich [person] shall not give more, and a poor [person] shall not give less, from the half of a shekel to give an up-lifting to Jehovah"—that hereby is signified that all, of whatsoever faculty they be, ought alike to ascribe to the Lord all things of truth derived from good, appears from the signification of a rich person, as denoting one who abounds in truths and goods and the knowledges thereof, of which we shall speak presently; and from the signification of a poor person, as denoting one who does not abound in those things, of which also we shall speak presently; and from the signification of not giving more and not giving less, as denoting all alike [or equally]; and from the signification of half a shekel, as denoting all things of truth derived from good, see n. 10,221; and from the signification of giving to Jehovah, as denoting to ascribe to the Lord, for by Jehovah in the Word is meant the Lord, see what is cited, n. 9373. From these considerations it is evident, that by a rich person not giving more, and a poor person not giving less, from half a shekel to give to Jehovah, is signified that all, of whatsoever faculty they be, ought alike to ascribe to the Lord all things of truth derived from good. The case herein is this; all have the faculty of understanding and of growing wise, but the reason why one is wiser than another is, because they do not in like manner ascribe to the Lord all things of intelligence and wisdom, which are all things of truth and good. Those who ascribe all things to the Lord are wiser than others, since all things of truth and good which constitute wisdom flow in from heaven, that is from the Lord there; the ascribing of all things to the Lord opens the interiors of man towards heaven, for thereby it is acknowledged that nothing of truth and good is from himself, and in proportion as this is acknowledged, in the same proportion the love of self departs, and with the love of self the thick darkness derived from falses and evils; in the same proportion also man comes into innocence, and into love and faith to the Lord; hence conjunction with the Divine, influx thence, and illustration; from these considerations it is evident, whence it comes that one is more wise and another less, and also why a rich person should not give more and a poor person less, namely, that all have alike the faculty of growing wise; all have not indeed an equal faculty of growing wise, but they have the faculty alike, since both one and the other have the ability of growing wise. By the faculty of growing wise is not meant the faculty of reasoning concerning truths and goods from sciences, thus neither the faculty of confirming whatsoever a man pleases, but of discerning what is true and good, of choosing what is suitable, and applying it to uses of life; those who ascribe all things to the Lord, both discern, choose, and apply; but those who do not ascribe to the Lord, but to themselves, are skilled only in the art of reasoning concerning truths and goods, nor do they see any thing but what they have from others, not from reason, but from the activity of memory; inasmuch as they cannot look within into truths themselves, they stand without, and confirming whatsoever they receive, whether it be true or false; those who have the ability from the sciences to do this more learnedly, are believed by the world to be wiser than others; but the more they attribute all things to themselves, thus the more they love what themselves think from themselves, so much the more they are insane, for they confirm falses more than truths, and evils more than goods; for they derive light from no other source than from the fallacies and appearances which are in the world, and hence from their own lumen, which is called natural lumen, separated from the light of heaven, which lumen, when it is separated, as to the truths and goods which are of heaven, is thick darkness. That riches and wealth denote those things which are of intelligence and wisdom, consequently also the knowledge of truth and good, which are likewise called spiritual wealth and riches, is manifest from the passages in the Word where they are named; as in Isaiah, "I will visit on the fruit of the pride of the king of Ashur, because he hath said, in the virtue of my hand I have done [it], and by my wisdom because I am intelligent; whence I will remove the borders of the people, and *will depopulate their treasures*; my hands shall find as a nest *the wealth of the people*," x. 12, 13, 14; the subject here treated of in the internal sense is those who trust to their own proper intelligence, and do not believe that true wisdom comes from heaven, but from themselves. The king of Ashur denotes ratiocination, in this case from self-intelligence, n. 1186; hence to depopulate the treasures and wealth of the people denotes to destroy those things which are of the truths of intelligence and wisdom. Again, what is prophetic concerning the beasts of the south: "*They carry their wealth on the shoulder of asses, and their treasures on the back of camels, to Egypt*," xxx. 6, 7. The beasts of the south denote those who are within the church, thus in the light of truth from the Word, but still do not read the Word except merely for the sake of science, and not for the sake of uses of life; for the south denotes where the light of truth is, thus where the Word is, n. 3195, 3708, 5672, 9642; an ass denotes science, and likewise a camel, and also Egypt; that an ass has this signification, see n. 5492, 5741, 7024; that a camel, n. 3048, 3071, 3143, 3145, 4516; and that Egypt, see what is cited, n. 9391. That these prophetics are to be understood in a spiritual sense, may be manifest from this consideration, that without that sense no one knows what is meant by the beasts of the south, or what by carrying their wealth on the shoulder of asses, and their treasures on the back of camels, and this to Egypt. Again in the same prophet, "*I will give thee the treasures of darkness, and the hidden wealth of hiding places*, that thou mayest know that I am Jehovah," xlv. 3; where the treasures of darkness and the hidden wealth of hiding places denote such things as relate to heavenly intelligence and wisdom, which are hidden from the natural man. And in Jeremiah, "The sin of Judah is written with a pen of iron; O my mountain in a field, *I will give thy wealth and all thy treasures for a prey*," xvii. 1, 3. Judah is called a mountain in a field, because with Judah there was a representative of a Celestial Church, for a mountain denotes the love of the Celestial Church, n. 6435, and a field denotes the church, n. 2971, 3766, 7502, 9139, 9295; the wealth and the treasures which were to be given for a prey, denote all the truths and goods of the church, which were to be dissipated. Again, "By reason of thy confidence in thy works and *in thy treasures*, thou also shalt be taken," xlviii. 7; treasures also in this passage denote the doctrinals and knowledges of the church. Again, "O sword against his horses, and against his chariots, and against the promiscuous crowd which is in the midst of him; *O sword against his treasures that they may be plundered;* drought is upon the waters that they are dried up," l. 36, 37; these words are against the Chaldeans, by whom are meant those who are in external worship without internal, thus who with the mouth profess the truths of the Word, but in heart deny them; the sword denotes the false principle combating against truths, n. 2799, 4499, 6353, 7102, 8294; horses denote the intellectual principle, n. 2760, 2761, 2762, 3217, 5321; chariots denote those things which are of doctrine, n. 5321, 8215; the treasures which were to be plundered, the truths and goods of the church, which would be perverted and perish by application to the evils of the loves of self and the world; drought upon the waters the deprivation and consumption of the truths of faith: that water denotes the truths of faith, see n. 2702, 3058, 3424, 4976, 8568, 9323. Who cannot see, that the literal sense is not the genuine sense of those words? For what principle of sanctity, or what of the church, or what of heaven, or what sense is there in these expressions—that a sword should be against the horses, against the chariots, against a promiscuous crowd, against treasures, and that drought should be upon the waters that they should be dried up? Wherefore from these and all other passages of the Word it may be manifestly seen that a spiritual sense, which differs from the natural, is in every expression, and that the Word without that sense cannot be called holy, and that in very many passages it cannot even be comprehended. Again, "O Babel, who dwellest upon many waters, *great in treasures,*" li. 13; Babel denotes those who possess the Word, and hence all the goods and truths of the church, but who apply them to the love of self, and thereby profane them, n. 1326; which was also represented by the king of Babel, taking *all the vessels of the temple, which were of gold and silver,* and drinking out of them, and then praising the gods of gold and of silver, Dan. v. 2, 3, 4, and following verses; hence Babel is said to dwell upon many waters, and to be great in treasures. Waters denote truths, and in the opposite sense falses, n. 2702, 3058, 4976, 8568, 9323. This is further described in the Apocalypse, where the riches of Babylon, which are there called merchandise, are enumerated, chap. xviii. And in Ezekiel, "I will bring Nebuchadnezzar against Tyre, by the hoofs of his horses he shall tread down all thy streets; *they shall plunder thy wealth and shall make a prey of thy merchandise,*" xxvi. 7, 12. By Tyre is meant the church as to the knowledges of good and truth, n. 1201; by Nebuchadnezzar king of Babel, the profane principle which vastates, n. 1327, which is the case when the truths and goods of the church serve for means to favor the evils of the loves of self and the world, by wrong application; for in such case the evils of those loves are inwardly in the heart, and the holy things of the church are in the mouth; the hoofs of the horses denote the outermost natural principles which are scientifics merely sensual, n. 7729, and streets the truths of faith, n. 2336; wealth and merchandise denote the knowledges of good and truth. Inasmuch as by Tyre are signified the knowledges of good and truth, n. 1201, therefore where Tyre is treated of in the Word, various kinds of merchandise and riches are also treated of, as in the same prophet, "Tarshish is thy trader, *by the multitude of all wealth in silver, iron, tin, and lead.* Damascus is thy trader, *above the multitude of thy wealth and thy merchandise,* thou hast enriched all the kings of the earth," xxvii. 1 to the end. Again, "In thy wisdom and in thine intelligence *thou hast made to thyself wealth, gold and silver in thy treasures: by the multitude of thy wisdom thou hast multiplied to thyself wealth,*" chap. xxviii., speaking also of Tyre; by which it is very manifest, that by wealth and riches, in the Word, are meant spiritual wealth and riches, which are the knowledges of good and truth, thus which are the means of wisdom. So likewise in Zechariah, "*Tyre hath collectea silver as dust, and gold* as the mire of the streets; behold the Lord will make her poor, and *will shake off her wealth into the sea,*" x. 3, 4. And in David, "*The daughter of Tyre will offer to thee a gift,* O daughter of the king; *the rich of the people* shall deprecate thy faces," Psalm xlv. 13. In this passage is described the church as to the affection of truth, and she is called the daughter of a king, for daughter denotes the church as to affection, n. 3262, 3963, 6729, 9059, and king denotes truth, n. 1672, 2015, 2069, 3670, 4575, 4581, 4966, 6148; wherefore it is said that the daughter of Tyre shall offer a gift, and that the rich of the people shall deprecate faces, where the rich of the people denote those who abound in truths and goods. And in Hosea, "Ephraim said, *truly I am enriched, I have found to myself wealth,*" xii. 8; where by being enriched and finding wealth is not meant that he was enriched with worldly riches and wealth, but with heavenly; for by Ephraim is meant the intellectual principle of the church, which is illustrated when the Word is read, n. 5554, 6212, 6238, 6267. And in the Apocalypse, "To the angel of the church of the Laodiceans, *because thou sayest that I am rich, and am enriched, and want no wealth,* when thou knowest not that thou art wretched, and miserable, and needy, and blind, and naked; I counsel thee to buy of Me *gold purified in the fire, that thou mayest be rich,* and white raiment, that thou mayest be clothed," iii. 17, 18; the subject there treated of is the church which makes every thing of the church to consist in bare knowledges, and hence lifts up itself above others, when yet knowledges are nothing else than means to amend and perfect the life; wherefore he who possesses them without a life according to them is wretched, miserable, needy, blind, and naked; to buy gold purified in the fire denotes to procure to themselves from the Lord genuine good; and white raiment denotes to procure to themselves from the Lord genuine truths derived from that good; that gold denotes the good of love, see what is cited, n. 9874; and that raiment denotes the truths of faith, n. 4545, 5248, 5319, 5954, 9212, 9216, 9814, 9952. And in Jeremiah, "I Jehovah give to every one according to his ways, according to the fruits of his works, *as a partridge he gathereth*, but doth not bring forth, *he maketh riches but not with judgment;* in the midst of his days he shall forsake them; in the latter end of days he shall become foolish," xvii. 10, 11. The subject treated of in this passage is those who procure to themselves knowledges without an end of any other use than that they may grow rich, that is, that they may know, when yet it is the life which they ought to serve; this is meant by gathering as a partridge, and yet not bringing forth, and by making riches, but not with judgment. And in Luke, "Whosoever he be of you *who denieth not all his faculties*, he cannot be My disciple," xiv. 33. He who does not know that faculties, in the internal sense, denote spiritual riches and wealth, which are knowledges from the Word, cannot in any wise conceive otherwise, than that he must deprive himself of all wealth in order that he may be saved; when yet this is not the sense of those words, for by faculties are there meant all things which are from man's own intelligence; for no one can be wise from himself but from the Lord. Wherefore to deny all faculties denotes to attribute nothing of intelligence and wisdom to himself; and he who does not know this cannot be instructed by the Lord, that is, be His disciple. Inasmuch as by faculties, riches, wealth, silver, and gold, are signified those things which are of intelligence and wisdom, therefore also the kingdom of the heavens is compared by the Lord *to treasure hid in a field*, Matt. xiii. 44; and it is said, that they "*should make to themselves treasures in the heavens which doth not fail; since where the treasure is there is the heart*," Matt. vi. 19, 20, 21; Luke xii. 33, 34. They who do not know that by the rich are meant those who possess the knowledges of truth and good, thus who have the Word, and that by the poor are meant those who do not possess those knowledges, but who still desire them, cannot know otherwise than that by the rich man, who was clothed in purple and fine linen, and by the poor man, who was cast at his gate-way, Luke xvi., are meant a rich and poor man according to the common meaning of those expressions, when yet by the rich man is there meant the Jewish nation, which had the Word; by the purple, with which he was clothed, genuine good, n. 9467; and by the fine linen, genuine truth, n. 5319, 9469, 9596, 9744; and by the poor person cast at the gate-way, are meant those who are out of the church and have not the Word, and yet desire the truths and good of heaven and of the church. Hence also it is evident that by the rich are meant those who have the Word, consequently Divine Truths; as also in the prophetic [enunciation] of Mary in Luke, "God hath filled the hungry with good things, *and the rich He hath sent away empty*," i. 53. The hungry in this passage denote those who are in other places called the poor, thus who have not bread and water, and consequently who are in hunger and thirst, that is, who do not know what is good and true, and still desire those things; by bread and water, in the Word, are signified good and truth, n. 9323; and by hungering and thirsting, thus by hunger and thirst, is signified a desire to those things. Such are also meant by the poor in other places, as in Luke, "*Blessed are the poor*, because theirs is the kingdom of the heavens; *blessed are ye that are hungry*, for ye shall be filled," vi. 20, 21. Again, "The father of the family said to the servant, that he should go out into the streets and lanes of the city, and *should bring in the poor*, the maimed, the lame, and the blind," xiv. 21. Again, "*To the poor the gospel shall be preached*," vii. 22. And in Matthew, "*The poor hear the gospel*," xi. 5. And in Isaiah, "Then shall the *first-begotten of the poor* feed, and *the needy* shall lie down confidently," xiv. 30. Again, "*The needy of men* shall exult in the Holy One of Israel," xxix. 19. And in Zephaniah, "I will leave in the midst of thee *a people miserable and poor*, who *shall hope in the name of Jehovah*, they *shall feed* and rest, neither shall any terrify them," iii. 12, 13. And in Isaiah, "*The poor and needy seek water*, but there is none; their tongue fainteth with thirst; I, Jehovah, will hear them, I will open rivers on the hills, and in the midst of the valleys I will set fountains," xli. 17, 18. The poor and needy seeking water denote those who desire the knowledges of good and truth; water denotes truth; the desire is described by their tongue fainting with thirst; and the abundance which they were about to have by rivers being opened upon the hills and fountains in the midst of the valleys. From these considerations it is further evident, that heavenly things, which are the truths of faith and of the good of love, are meant by earthly things, which are waters, rivers on hills, fountains in valleys, and that the latter is the literal sense of the Word, but the former the spiritual, and that the Word by this sense is Divine, and that without it, it is not Divine. The signification of wealth and riches, as denoting such things as relate to intelligence and wisdom, is also grounded in correspondence; for in heaven amongst the angels all things appear glittering as with gold, silver, and precious stones, and this because they are in the intelligence of truth and in the wisdom of good; for the interiors of the angels are presented thus to view from correspondence. Also with the spirits who are below the heavens, there are riches in appearance according to the state of reception of truth and good from the Lord.

10,228. "To expiate on your soul"—that hereby is signified that evils may be removed, appears from the signification of expiating on their souls, as denoting to be purified or liberated from evils by the truth of faith, see above, n. 10,218; and whereas purification or liberation from evils is nothing else but their removal, therefore this is also signified by the same words. That man is not liberated from evils and thereby purified, but that he is withheld from them, when he is held in good by the Lord, and thus that evils are removed, see what is cited, n. 10,057.

10,229. "And thou shalt take the silver of expiations from [being] with the sons of Israel"—that hereby are signified purifying truths derived from good, which are of the church, appears from the signification of silver, as denoting truth derived from good, see n. 1551, 2954, 5658, 6112, 6914, 6917, 8932; and from the signification of expiations, as denoting purification from evils, see above, n. 10,218; thus the silver of expiations denotes purifying truth; and from the representation of the sons of Israel as denoting the church, see what is cited, n. 9340. It is called purifying truth, because all purification from evils is effected by truths, see n. 2791, 5954, 7044, 7918, 9089. The case herein is this; man of himself thinks nothing but evil, for of himself he does not think about God, nor about what is good and just towards his neighbor, except for the sake of himself; yea, neither about heaven, and about eternal life, but about the world and about life in the world. So long as man is in such a state, he thinks from those things which are beneath him, and not from those which are above him, thus from hell, and not from heaven; to the intent therefore that man may think what is good, he ought to think from heaven, consequently, his mind ought to be elevated thither; this is effected solely by truths, such as are in the church derived from the Word; for those truths teach what God is, what the neighbor, that there is a heaven, that there is eternal life, and specifically what evil is, and what good; when these truths enter, then the interiors are elevated above self, and are thus withdrawn from those things which are beneath self, thus from evils. Hence it may be manifest that all purification or removal from evils is effected by truths, which are hence called purifying truths.

10,230. "And thou shalt give it for the work of the tent of the congregation"—that hereby is signified conjunction with heaven by the acknowledgment that all truths and goods are from the Lord, appears from the signification of the work of the tent of the congregation, as denoting what operates and makes heaven, for work denotes what operates and makes, and the tent of the congregation denotes heaven where the Lord is. That the tent of the congregation denotes heaven where the Lord is, see n. 9457, 9481, 9485, 9784, 9963; thus also what conjoins man with heaven, for what operates and makes heaven with man, this also conjoins him with heaven. The reason why conjunction is signified by the acknowledgment that all goods and truths are from the Lord is, because what was given for the work of the tent of the congregation, was half of a shekel, which is called the silver of expiations on account of the numbering of the people, and by giving half of a shekel is signified the ascribing of all things which are of faith and love to the Lord, n. 10,220, 10,221; and by numbering is signified the ordination and arrangement of all things from the Lord, n. 10,218.

10,231. "And it shall be to the sons of Israel for remembrance before Jehovah"—that hereby is signified thus the conservation of the church and of all things of the church by the Lord, appears from the representation of the sons of Israel, as denoting the church, see what is cited, n. 9340; and from the signification of remembrance, when by Jehovah, as denoting conservation, see n. 9849: and from the signification of before Jehovah, as denoting by the Lord, see n. 10,146.

10,232. "To expiate on your souls"—that hereby is signified since thus evils are removed, appears from the signification of expiating on their souls, as denoting to remove evils by truths, see above, n. 10,228. The reason why by expiating on your souls is here signified since evils are removed, and not to remove evils, is, because these things so follow from those which precede; for the internal sense does not respect the sense of the words as it coheres in the letter, but as it coheres in its own sense, which is, that the conservation of the church and of all things of the church is from the Lord, since evils are removed; for the reason why the church is preserved with man is, because evils do not hinder; for the Lord flows in continually with His mercy, and provides that the truths and goods which are of the church, are not only preserved with man, but are also multiplied and grow; but so long as evils reign, the truths and goods of the church flowing in from the Lord are either rejected by man, or are suffocated, or perverted; whereas on the removal of evils they are accepted and acknowledged.

10,233. Verses 17 to 21. *And Jehovah spake to Moses, saying. And thou shalt make a laver of brass, and its base of brass to wash; and thou shalt give it between the tent of the congregation and between the altar; and thou shalt give waters there. And Aaron and his sons shall wash out of it their hands and their feet. In their entering-in into the tent of the congregation, they shall wash with waters lest they die; or in their coming near to the altar to minister, to cause to burn an offering made by fire to Jehovah. And they shall wash their hands and their feet, lest they die; and it shall be to them the statute of an age, to him and to his seed, to their generations.* And Jehovah spake to Moses, saying, signifies what is perceptive from illustration by the Word from the Lord. And thou shalt make a laver of brass, signifies the good of the natural principle of man, in which is purification. And its base of brass, signifies the good of the ultimate of the natural principle which is of the sensual principle. To wash, signifies purification from evils and falses. And thou shalt give it between the tent of the congregation and between the altar, signifies that there may be conjunction of truth and of good. And thou shalt give waters there, signifies the truths of faith, by which there is purification in the natural principle. And Aaron and his sons shall wash out of it, signifies a representative of the purification and regeneration of man, by the Lord. Their hands and their feet signifies the interior and exterior principles of man. In their entering-in to the tent of the congregation, signifies worship from the good of faith. They shall wash with waters, signifies purification by the truths of faith. Lest they die, signifies lest the representative perish. Or in coming near to the altar to minister, to cause to burn an offering by fire to Jehovah, signifies worship from the good of love. And they shall wash their hands and their feet, signifies purification of the exteriors and interiors of man. Lest they die, signifies lest the representative perish. And it shall be to them the statute of an age, signifies the eternal law of order. To him and to his seed, to their generations, signifies all who receive those things which proceed from the Lord, thus who are regenerated by Him.

10,234. "And Jehovah spake to Moses, saying"—that hereby is signified what is perceptive from illustration by the Word from the Lord, appears from the signification of Jehovah speaking to Moses, as denoting illustration by the Word from the Lord, see n. 10,215; and from the signification of saying, as denoting perception, see n. 2862, 3509, 5743, 8660. It is to be noted, that when any thing new, distinct from what goes before, is to be expounded, it is said that *Jehovah spake to Moses*, as in this chapter, verses 11, 17, 22, 34; and also in other passages; the new thing which is now expounded is concerning purification from evils and falses.

10,235. "And thou shalt make a laver of brass"—that hereby is signified the good of the natural principle of man, in which is purification, appears from the signification of a laver, wherein is water for washing, as denoting the natural principle of man, of which we shall speak presently; and from the signification of brass, as denoting its good, see n. 425, 1551. The subject treated of in what now follows is concerning washing, and it is said that Aaron and his sons should wash their hands and their feet when they entered-in to the tent of the congregation, or came near to the altar to minister; and in other places it is said that they who were made unclean should wash themselves and their garments, and thus that they would be clean; from which considerations it may be manifest that washing represented purification from evils; thus the washing of the body and of the garments represented the purification of the heart and mind. Every one who thinks from any illustration, may see that by washing, the evils of the heart and mind were not wiped away, but only the filth of the body and of the garments, and that after this was wiped away, the evils still remained; and that evils cannot in any wise be washed away by waters, but by repentance. From these considerations it is further evident that those things which were instituted with the Israelitish nation, were things external which represented things internal, and that the internal things were the holy things themselves of the church appertaining to them, and not the external things without them; but that that nation still made every thing holy to consist in things external, and not at all in things internal, is manifest from the Lord's words in Matthew, "Woe to you scribes and pharisees, hypocrites, ye purge the outside of the cup and platter, but the interiors are full of rapine and intemperance; thou blind pharisee, purge first the inside of the cup and platter, and the outside will also become clean. Ye make yourselves like to whitened sepulchres, which outwardly indeed appear beautiful, but inwardly are full of the bones of the dead and of all uncleanness," xxiii. 25, 26, 27; also Mark vii. 2 to 8; and Luke xi. 39. The reason why a laver signifies the natural principle is, because by washing therein is signified purification from evils, and purification from evils is effected in the natural principle; and moreover by vessels in general are signified those things which are of the natural principle of man, n. 3068, 3079, 9394, inasmuch as the natural principle is the recipient of the spiritual things which are of the internal man. By the natural principle is meant the external principle of man, that is, what is called the external man. It may seem as a strange thing that by the laver is signified the natural principle of man; but it is to be noted that the subject here treated of in the internal sense is concerning purification from evils, and man is [the being] who is purified. Hence it follows, that somewhat of man is signified by that in which washing was effected, by which washing is signified purification. The reason why this is the natural principle is, because in that principle, as was said, purification is effected. Moreover all things, which were established for the sake of worship with the Israelitish and Jewish nation, signified those things which are of heaven and of the church, consequently such things as appertain to man; for unless they had signified something appertaining to man, they would not have represented any thing. Inasmuch as by the laver is signified the natural principle of man, by the waters in the laver the truths which are of faith, and by washing purification from evils, it may hence be known, what was signified by the brazen sea near the temple, and also what by the twelve oxen which carried it; in like manner what by the ten other lavers placed also near the temple, and by the lions, the oxen and the cherubs engraven on them, also by the wheels as of a chariot under them. The signification of all these things is evident, when it is known what is signified by a laver, by water, and by washing, and when it is known how the case is with purification from the evils appertaining to man, for all and singular things were representative of things celestial and spiritual. The brazen sea made by Solomon, and set near the temple, is thus described, "He made a molten sea, ten cubits from laver to laver, round as to its circumference; five cubits the height; and a line of thirty cubits encompassed it round about. Wild gourds beneath the laver encompassing it, of ten cubits, surrounding the sea round about. It stood on twelve oxen, three looking to the north, and three looking to the west, and three looking to the south, and three looking to the east; but the sea was upon them above, and all their hinder parts were inwards. Its thickness was a hand breadth, its brim according to the work of the laver of a cup, the flower of a lily. It contained two thousand baths; and the sea was set from the right shoulder of the house towards the east over against the south," 1 Kings vii. 23, 24, 25, 26, 39. This vessel or this laver is called a sea, because by the sea is signified the scientific principle in general; and all the scientific principle is of man's natural principle; that the sea denotes the scientific principle in general, see n. 28, 2850, 8184; and that the scientific principle is of man's natural principle, n. 1486, 3019, 3020, 3309, 3310, 5373, 6004, 6023, 6071, 9918. The reason why this laver was according to the work of the laver of a cup was, because by a cup, a bowl, or drinking pot, is also signified the scientific principle which is of the natural or sensual principle of man, n. 9557, 9996. By the twelve oxen were signified all the goods of the natural or sensual principle of man in the complex, since they were instead of a basis, and by a basis is signified what is ultimate, and what supports; that twelve denotes all in the complex, see n. 3272, 3858, 3913; and that an ox denotes the good of the natural principle of man, n. 2781, 9135. The reason why they looked to all the quarters of the world was, because the good of the natural principle of man is the receptacle of all things which flow in from the world, both those which have relation to goods and which have relation to truths. The diameter of ten cubits signified what is full, n. 3107; and the circumference thirty cubits signified a plenary complex, n. 9082. The two thousand of baths signified the conjunction of good and of truth, thus purification and regeneration, for regeneration is nothing else but the conjunction of good and of truth; two thousand signifies the same as two, for the multiplied numbers signify the like with the simple ones from which they are multiplied, n. 5292, 5335, 5708, 7973; that two denotes conjunction, see n. 5194, 8423. The brazen sea being set on the right shoulder of the house towards the east over against the south, signified that it looked to the Lord, for the Lord is the east, n. 101, 9668. The house or temple denotes heaven and the church where the Lord is, n. 5720. From these considerations it may now be manifest what was signified by the brazen sea, consequently what by a laver, namely, the natural principle of man, in which is purification.

10,236. "And the base of brass"—that hereby is signified the good of the ultimate natural principle, which is the good of the sensual principle, appears from the signification of the base of the laver wherein was water for washing, as denoting the ultimate of the natural principle, which is called the sensual principle; and from the signification of brass, as denoting good, see above, n. 10,235. The reason why the base denotes the ultimate of the natural principle, which is called the external sensual principle, is, because by the laver, which is above, is signified the natural principle in which is purification; hence by that which is beneath is signified what is in the lowest place, that is, in the ultimate, thus the external sensual principle of man. The natural principle of man is external, is middle, and is internal; the external of the natural principle communicates with the world, and is called the external sensual principle; the internal natural principle is what communicates with the internal man, who is in heaven; the middle natural principle is the principle conjoining each, for where there is an external and an internal principle, there must be a conjoining middle principle. That man has an external, a middle, and an internal natural principle, see n. 4009, 4570, 5118, 5120, 5649, 9216. By the sensual principle, which is the ultimate of the natural principle, is properly meant that which is called the flesh, and perishes when man dies, thus what served man for his functions in the world, as the sensual principle of sight, of hearing, of the smell, of the taste, and of the touch. That this sensual principle is the ultimate plane, in which the life of man terminates, and on which as on a basis, it reposes itself, may be manifest, for it is immediately extant in the world, and by it as an outermost principle the world enters, and heaven makes its exit; but this sensual principle is common to man with the brute animals; whereas the external sensual principle which man has not so in common with other animals, and which still is an external sensual principle, is what man has in the memory from the world, and is constituted of mere worldly, corporeal, and terrestrial things there. The man who thinks and reasons from those things alone, and not from interior things, is called a sensual man. This sensual principle remains with man after death, but is quiescent; this external sensual principle is what is properly signified by the basis. What its quality is, was represented by the ten lavers, which were set near the temple; those bases are thus described: "Solomon made ten bases of brass, four cubits the length of every basis, and four cubits the breadth; three cubits the height. On the inclosures which were between the ledges, were lions, oxen and cherubs; and on the ledges in like manner above. Moreover each base had four wheels and plates of brass; but there were shoulders to its four corners; the shoulders were molten under the laver; the work of the wheels was as the work of a chariot wheel; their hands, and their backs, and their felloes, and their spokes were all graven. Near this he made ten bases; they had all one casting, one measure, one proportion. Hence he made ten lavers of brass; each laver contained forty baths; each laver was four cubits;" 1 Kings vii. 27 to 39. The quality of the external sensual principle appertaining to man is here described by representatives, and especially the protection of the Lord, to prevent man from entering into those things which are of heaven or the church from his sensual principle, thus from the world; for this is contrary to Divine order; for the world cannot enter into heaven, but heaven into the world, as is the case when the Lord by [or through] heaven flows in with man, illustrates him, teaches him, and leads him, by the Word. That to enter from the world into those things which are of heaven is contrary to Divine order, may be manifest from those who enter from their sensual principle, thus from the scientifics which are from the world, in that they believe nothing at all. The protection to prevent this is signified by the lions, the oxen, and the cherubs; for by the lion is signified protection to prevent truths entering, for lions denote truths in their power, n. 6367, 6369; by oxen is signified protection to prevent goods entering, for oxen denote goods in their power, n. 2781; that by cherubs is signified the protection of the Lord to prevent that being done, n. 308, 9509; that the shoulders, of which also mention is made, denote power and resistance, see n. 1085, 4931 to 4937, 9836. By the wheels of a chariot is signified the faculty of growing wise when all things enter from heaven, for thus all things proceed according to order, for the wheels of a chariot denote the faculty of proceeding, thus of learning, n. 9212, 9216; and chariots denote those things which are of the doctrine of heaven and of the church, n. 5321, 8215.

What the sensual man is, it may be expedient further briefly to explain. He is called a sensual man, who thinks only from such things as are in the memory from the world, and who cannot be elevated towards interior things; such especially are they who believe nothing of heaven and of what is Divine, because they do not see those things, for they trust only to the senses, and what does not appear before the senses, they believe to be nothing. People of this description approach near to the genius of brute animals, which also are led solely by the external senses; nevertheless they are cunning and skilful in acting and reasoning, but they do not see truth from the light of truth: such were formerly called serpents of the tree of science; the infernal crew is mostly of this description. But what the sensual man is, and what the sensual principle, see in the passages cited, n. 9331, 9726, 9730, 9731, 9922, 9996; and what it is to be elevated above sensual things, or to be withdrawn from them, see the passages cited, n. 9922. The good of the sensual principle, which is signified by the basis of brass, is what is called the pleasurable and delightful principle affecting the imaginative thought, which thought is derived merely from such things as are terrestrial, corporeal, and worldly, and is distinguished from other delights by this, that it has respect to no other uses than what relate to self or for the sake of self; for the sensual man is in the love of self, and of the world, and his delights are the delights of those loves. And whereas the loves of the sensual man are of this description, it is evident that he is more skilful than others in reasoning and in acting for the sake of gain and honour; for his body burns with the fire of that love, and this fire kindles a lumen, which is called natural lumen; and when this is enkindled even to brightness, then the light of heaven, which is of the interior man, is altogether obscured; hence the things which are of this latter light, inasmuch as they are in thick darkness, are said to be nothing. It is otherwise with those who act from the fire of heaven, and think from the light thence derived. From these considerations it may be manifest what is meant by the good of the sensual principle, which is signified by the base of the laver.

10,237. "To wash"—that hereby is signified purification from evils and falses, appears from the signification of washing, as denoting purification from evils and falses, see n. 3147, 5854. Since the subject treated of in what now follows in the internal sense is concerning purification from evils and falses by the truths of faith, it may be expedient briefly to say how the case is; for by washing is signified purification, by waters are signified the truths of faith, and by the laver containing the water is signified the natural principle, for all spiritual purification is effected in the natural principle. Man has an external and an internal, the external is called natural and also the natural man, and the internal is called spiritual, and also the spiritual man, by reason that the internal of man is in the spiritual world, where spirits and angels are, and his external is in the natural world, where men are; both the internal and the external is purified; the internal in heaven, and the external whilst man lives in the world, thus in the natural principle which is in the world. The reason why purification is performed in the natural principle at that time is, because the truths of faith in the natural principle come to manifest perception; for they are in that principle amongst scientifics, or amongst things of the memory, which, when they are thought of are manifestly perceived; but not so those things which are thought in the internal man, these do not come to manifest perception whilst man is in the world, because the ideas in that man are spiritual. Hence it is, that purification is effected in the natural principle. That it is effected by the truths of faith, may be manifest from this consideration, that those who are purified ought not only to know what is evil and false, but also to acknowledge them, and next to hold them in aversion, and to shun them; when this is the case, then first man is purified from them; and evils and falses cannot be known, thus neither acknowledged, except in the natural principle by the truths of faith; for these truths teach what is evil and false, thus make them manifest. He who believes that he is purified from evils, before he sees and acknowledges them in himself, is greatly deceived, see n. 8388, 8390. It was said that man knows his own evils and falses by the truths of faith in the natural, that is, in the external man, but not in the internal; the reason is, because the ideas of thought in the internal man are spiritual, and spiritual ideas cannot be comprehended in the natural principle, for they are intellectual ideas which are without objects of a quality like those in the material world: nevertheless those ideas, namely, spiritual ideas, which are proper to the internal man, flow-in into the natural ideas which are of the external man, and produce and make them, which is effected by correspondences. But concerning spiritual ideas, which are of the internal man, by the Divine mercy of the Lord, an account will be given, when we come to treat of heaven, and of spirits and angels, for they think by spiritual ideas, and also discourse one with another by them.

10,237½. "And thou shalt give it between the tent of the congregation and between the altar"—that hereby is signified that there may be conjunction of truth and of good, appears from the signification of between the tent of the congregation and the altar, as denoting conjunction of truth and of good, see n. 10,001, 10,025. The reason why the laver was set between the tent of the congregation and the altar, and why Aaron and his sons there washed their hands and their feet, was, that purification of heart might be represented, and regeneration, which in its essence is the conjunction of truth and of good; for the conjunction of truth and of good is heaven itself with man; wherefore also heaven is compared in the Word to a marriage; this conjunction is effected by the truths of faith, since these teach how man ought to live; wherefore when the life is formed according to the truths of faith, the conjunction of truth and of good is effected, for truth in such case is made good by life The life of truth is good. This also is meant by man's being regenerated by water and spirit; water denotes the truth of faith, and spirit denotes its life. That regeneration is conjunction of truth and of good, see n. 2063, 3155, 3158, 3607, 4353, 5365, 5376, 8516, 8517, 8772, 10,067.

10,238. "And thou shalt give waters there"—that hereby are signified the truths of faith by which purification is effected in the natural principle, appears from the signification of waters, as denoting the truths of faith, see n. 28, 739, 2702, 3058, 3424, 4976, 5668, 8568, 9323; and from the signification of the laver, as denoting the natural principle, see above, n. 10,235. He who does not know that waters signify the truths of faith, will be unable to apprehend very many passages in the Word, as what is signified by this, that *unless a man be born of water and of the spirit, he cannot enter into the kingdom of God*, John iii. 5. They who by water in this passage understand nothing else but water, believe that the water of baptism is that by which man is regenerated, when yet water contributes nothing to regeneration, but the truth of faith and the good of love, for water only washes away the filth of the body, and in no wise the evils of the heart. He who does not know that waters signify the truth of faith, is incapable also of knowing what *baptism* signifies; for he believes that that external [rite] saves man, when yet what is external is of no effect, but the internal thing which is signified, which is regeneration by the truths of faith; for those who are of the church, are distinguished from all others in the world by baptism, since they can be regenerated by the truths of faith, but not those who are out of the church, for within the church is the Word, in which are the truths of faith. He who does know that waters signify the truths of faith, cannot know also what is meant *by the waters above the expanse and by the waters below the expanse*, Gen. i. 6, 7, 8, 9, 10; when yet by the waters above the expanse are signified the truths of faith in the internal man, and by the waters below the expanse the truths of faith in the external man; for the subject treated of in that chapter is concerning the new creation of the man of the most ancient church, thus concerning his regeneration. He who does not know that waters signify the truths of faith also cannot know what is signified by waters in John, "*He who drinketh of the water which I shall give, shall never thirst; but the water which I shall give, shall be in him a fountain of water springing up into eternal life,*" iv. 13. And in Isaiah, "*The poor and needy seeking water, but there is none; their tongue fainteth with thirst; I will open rivers upon the hills, and in the midst of the valleys I will set fountains; I will make the wilderness into a pool of waters, and the dry land into springs of waters,*" xli. 17, 18. Again, "*They shall not thirst, he shall make waters to flow forth for them from the rock; and shall cleave the rock that the waters may flow forth,*" xlviii. 20, 21; and in several other passages elsewhere. But see what has been before said and shown on this subject, as that purification from evils and falses is effected by the truths of faith, n. 2799, 5954, 7044, 7918, 9089, 10,229. That also regeneration, see what is cited, n. 9859. That baptism signifies regeneration by the truths of faith, n. 4255, 5120, 9089. That purification is effected in the natural principle, n. 3147, 9572; and also regeneration, may be seen in what is cited, n. 9325.

10,239. "And Aaron and his sons shall wash out of it"—that hereby is signified a representative of the purification and regeneration of man by the Lord, appears from the signification of washing, as denoting purification, see above, n. 10,237; and from the representation of Aaron, as denoting the Lord as to Divine Good celestial, see n. 9806, 10,068; and from the representation of the sons of Aaron, as denoting the Lord as to Divine Good spiritual, see n. 9807, 10,068; from which considerations it is evident, that by Aaron and his sons washing out of it, is signified a representative of the purification of man by the Lord. The reason why it is also a representative of regeneration is, because regeneration was also represented by washing, but by the washing of the whole body, which washing was called baptizing; that baptizing or baptism signifies regeneration, see n. 4255, 9089. But regeneration differs from purification in this, that regeneration precedes and purification follows; for no one can be purified from evils and falses but he who is regenerating, and after that he is regenerated; for he who is not regenerated, is indeed withdrawn from evils so far as he suffers it, but he is not purified from them, for he is always impure; it is otherwise with the regenerate man, he is every day purifying, which is meant by the Lord's words to Peter, "He who is washed hath no need but to be washed as to the feet, thus he is wholly clean," John xiii. 10. He who is washed signifies he who is regenerated. That total washing was called baptizing, is manifest from Mark, chap. vii. 4; and that the washing of the whole was so called, is manifest from Matthew, chap. iii. 13 to 16; Mark i. 9; and also 2 Kings v. 10, 14. Jordan, in which washings were effected, which were baptizings, Matt. iii. 6, 13; Mark i. 3; 2 Kings v. 10, 14, signified the natural principle, n. 1585, 4255. That by the washing of baptism is also signified temptation, Matt. xx. 21, 22, 23, is because all regeneration is effected by temptations, n. 5036, 5773, 8351, 8958, 9859. It may be expedient here briefly to say why the Lord, when He was in the world, Himself also was willing to be baptized, when yet by baptizing is signified the regeneration of man by the Lord; the reason was, because the baptizing of the Lord Himself signified the glorification of His Human [principle]; for what in the Word signifies the regeneration of man, this also signifies the glorification of the Human [principle] in the Lord, for the regeneration of man is an image of the glorification of the Lord, see n. 3138, 3212, 3296, 3490, 4402, 5688. Therefore when the Lord permitted John to baptize Him, He said, *thus it becometh us to fulfil all the justice of God*, Matt. iii. 15. To fulfil all the justice of God denotes to subdue the hells, and to reduce them and the heavens into order, from his own proper power; and at the same time to glorify His Human [principle]; which things were effected by temptations admitted into Himself; thus by continual combats with the hells, even to the last on the cross. That this is the justice which the Lord fulfilled, see n. 9486, 9715, 9809, 10,019, 10,152. Like things are also signified by all things being fulfilled which were written concerning the Lord in the law and the prophets, Luke xviii. 31; chap. xxii. 37; chap. xxiv. 44; and by the Lord coming to fulfil all things of the law, Matthew v. 17, 18. He who does not know the arcana of the Word, believes that the Lord was made justice by fulfilling all things of the law, and that by that fulfillment He delivered the human race from the yoke of the law, thus from damnation; whereas this is not the sense of those words, but that He was made justice by the subjugation of the hells, the reduction of the heavens into order, and by the glorification of His Human [principle]; for by this latter He let Himself into the power, that from His Divine Human [principle] He might to eternity subjugate the hells and keep the heavens in order, and thereby regenerate man, that is, deliver him from hell and save him.

10,240. Inasmuch as by washing is also signified regeneration, it may be expedient to say something further on that subject. He who does not know that the Lord, both in the writings of the prophets and the evangelists, spake by correspondences, consequently that in the Word there is an internal sense, cannot in any wise know what is meant by the Lord's words in John, "*Verily, verily, I say unto thee, unless a man be born of water and spirit, he cannot enter into the kingdom of God. That which is born of the flesh, is flesh; but that which is born of the spirit, is spirit. The spirit breatheth where it wills, and thou hearest the voice thereof, but dost not know whence it cometh and whither it goeth; so is every one who is born of the spirit*," iii. 5, 6, 8. If these words be unfolded by correspondences, it is evident what their sense is, for they are arcana of heaven. From correspondence water denotes the truth of faith, which in the natural man comes to manifest perception. Spirit denotes the Divine Truth which flows in from the Lord through the internal principle of man into his external or natural principle, whence the man who is regenerating has the life of faith. The flesh is the proprium of man, which is nothing but evil. By the spirit breathing where it willeth, is signified that the Lord, by Divine Truth, out of mercy gives new life. By hearing the voice thereof, is signified that those things come to perception in the external or natural man; voice denotes what is announced from the Word. By not knowing whence it comes and whither it goes, is signified that man does not know how regeneration is effected, for it is effected by innumerable and ineffable arcana from the Lord. That from correspondence waters denote the truths of faith, see n. 28, 739, 2702, 3058, 3424, 4976, 5668, 8568, 9323, 10,238. That spirit denotes the Divine Truth, from which comes the life of faith, n. 9228, 9818. That flesh denotes the proprium of man, which is nothing but evil, n. 8409. That breathing denotes a state of the life of faith, n. 9281. That voice denotes what is announced from the Word, thus the truth thence derived, n. 9926. That hearing denotes perception, n. 9311, 9926. That to come and to go, or to enter in and go out, denotes the state of a thing from beginning to end, n. 9927. That the arcana of regeneration are innumerable and ineffable, n. 3917, 3573, 5398, 9334, 9336. And that it is not perceived what is transacting in the internal man, when man is in the world, but what in the external or natural man, n. 10,236 above.

10,241. "His hands and his feet"—that hereby is signified the interiors and exteriors of man, appears from the signification of hands, as denoting the interiors of man, of which we shall speak presently; and from the signification of feet, as denoting the exteriors of man, thus his natural things, for these are exterior. That the feet denote things natural, thus those which are of the exterior principle of man, see n. 2162, 3761, 3986, 4280, 4938 to 4952, 9406. But the reason why the hands denote interior things is, because the superior things of the body extend themselves into the hands, and there terminate; hence by the hands is signified whatsoever appertains to the man, and also his power, see the passages cited, n. 10,019. But when mention is made of both the hands and the feet, in this case is signified whatsoever is in the internal and also in the external man, or things spiritual and things natural; hence it is, that by lifting up the hand is signified power in what is spiritual, and by lifting up the foot, power in what is natural, n. 5327, 5328. Moreover by the extreme parts of man are signified all things appertaining to him, n. 10,044, and the extremes are the hands and the feet. From these considerations it may be manifest whence it is, that Aaron and his sons were to wash the hands and the feet, when they entered-in to the tent of the congregation, or came near to the altar to minister.

10,242. "In their entering-in to the tent of the congregation"—that hereby is signified worship from the good of faith, appears from the signification of entering-in to the tent of the congregation, when concerning Aaron and his sons, as denoting to represent all things of worship from the good of faith. The reason why these things were represented by entering-in to the tent of the congregation is, because by coming near to the altar were represented all things of worship from the good of love. There are two essentials of Divine Worship, the good of faith and the good of love: worship is Divine, whether it be from the former good or from the latter. The good of faith is the good of charity towards the neighbor; and the good of love is the good of love to the Lord; these goods differ from each other like what is spiritual and what is celestial, the quality of which difference may be seen in the passages cited, n. 9277. Worship from the good of faith, or from the good of charity towards the neighbor, was represented by the ministration of Aaron and of his sons in the tent of the congregation, wherein ministration was performed every day, since by that tent was represented the heaven where spiritual good reigns; but worship from celestial good, which is the good of love to the Lord, was represented by the ministration of Aaron and of his sons at the altar, see n. 9963, 9964, 10,001, 10,025.

10,243. "They shall wash with waters"—that hereby is signified purification by the truths of faith, appears from the signification of washing, as denoting purification from evils and falses, see above, n. 10,237; and from the signification of waters, as denoting the truths of faith, see also above, n. 10,238. He who does not know what is signified by washing, and what by feet and hands, cannot in any wise know what these words involve in John, "*Jesus put water into a basin, and began to wash the feet of the disciples, and to wipe them with a linen cloth with which He was girded. And He came to Simon Peter, who said to Him, dost Thou wash my feet? Jesus replied, what I do thou knowest not yet, but thou shalt know afterwards. Peter said to Him, Thou shalt never wash my feet; Jesus answered him, If I wash thee not, thou hast no part with Me. Peter said to Him, Lord, not my feet only, but also the hands and the head. Jesus said to him, he who is washed hath no need to be washed except as to the feet, but is wholly clean; now ye are clean,*" xiii. 5 to 10. Who can know what is involved in what the Lord said, "What I do thou knowest not yet, but thou shalt know afterwards." Also, "If I wash thee not, thou hast no part with Me." And likewise, "He who is washed, hath no need to be washed except as to the feet, and is wholly clean." That the subject here treated of is concerning purification from evils and falses, cannot be known but from the internal sense; from which it is evident, that by washing is meant purification from evils and falses; by the water in the basin, the truth of faith in the natural principle; by the linen cloth, with which the Lord was girded, and with which He wiped, the Divine Truth proceeding from Him; by the feet, the natural principle of man; by washing the head, the hands, and the feet, regeneration; in like manner by him who is washed. Thus by washing the feet is meant to purify the natural principle of man, for unless this principle appertaining to man, when he lives in the world, is purified and cleansed, it cannot afterwards be purified to eternity; for such as the natural principle of man is when he dies, such it remains, for it is not afterwards amended, inasmuch as it is that plane into which interior things, which are spiritual, flow in, it being their receptacle; wherefore when it is perverted, interior things, when they flow in, are perverted like it. The case herein is as when the eye is injured, or any other organ of sense, or member of the body, on which occasion interior things feel and act by them no otherwise than according to reception there. That therefore man cannot be purified to eternity, if he be not purified as to his natural principle in the world, is meant by the Lord's words, *what I do, thou knowest not yet, but thou shalt know afterwards.* That he who is regenerated is not to be purified except as to the natural principle, is meant by these words, *he who is washed hath no need to be washed except as to the feet, and is wholly clean.* And that all purification is effected by the Lord alone, by these words, *if I wash thee not, thou hast no part with Me.* And that this is effected by the Divine Truth which proceeds from the Lord, is signified by His *wiping with a linen cloth, with which He was girded.* That a linen cloth denotes truth from the Divine [being or principle], see n. 7601; thus the linen cloth, with which the Lord was girded, denotes the Divine Truth from Him. That water denotes the truth of faith, see n. 10,238. That a basin, or laver, in which is water, denotes the natural principle, n. 10,235. That the washing of the head, of the hands and feet, or of the whole body, denotes regeneration, n. 10,239. And that the feet denote the natural principle of man, n. 10,241. From these considerations it may again be manifest that the Lord spake by correspondences, thus from the internal sense, inasmuch as from heaven, in which that sense is; wherefore unless the Word of the Lord be understood as to that sense, it is little understood.

10,244. "Lest they die"—that hereby is signified lest the representative perish, appears from the signification of dying, when concerning the ministration of Aaron and of his sons, as denoting the cessation of representatives, and hence of conjunction with heaven, see n. 9928. The case herein is this; conjunction with heaven, and by [or through] heaven with the Lord, in the church established with that nation, was solely by representatives, that is, by things external which represented things internal; wherefore so soon as they did not minister according to the prescribed rituals, the representative perished, and with it conjunction with heaven; and when conjunction with heaven perished, they had not any protection against hell; hence the death of the sons of Aaron, Nadab and Abihu, for they gave incense upon strange fire, Levit. x. 1, 2; by which was represented worship grounded in other love than that of the Lord, hence their separation from heaven and extinction. The like would have happened if Aaron or his sons had come near to minister without washing; for thus they would have represented worship not from heaven, but profane which is from hell. From which considerations it is evident, that by dying, when concerning the ministration of Aaron and of his sons, is signified the extinction of representatives, and hence conjunction with the heavens.

10,245. "Or in coming near to the altar to minister, to cause to burn an offering by fire to Jehovah"—that hereby is signified worship from the good of love, appears from the signification of coming near to the altar to minister, as denoting to represent the Lord as to the good of love, see n. 9164; and from the signification of causing to burn an offering by fire to Jehovah, as denoting worship from the love of the Lord; for by causing to burn, or sacrificing, is signified worship, n. 6905, 8936, and by an offering by fire to Jehovah is signified what is from the Divine Love of the Lord, n. 10,055. Moreover how the case herein is, see just above, n. 10,241.

10,246. "And they shall wash their hands and their feet"—that hereby is signified the purification of the interiors and exteriors of man, appears from what was shown above, n. 10,239, 10,240, where like words occur.

10,247. "Lest they die"—that hereby is signified lest the representative perish, see above, n. 10,243.

10,248. "And it shall be to them the statute of an age"—that hereby is signified an eternal law of order, appears from the signification of a statute, as denoting a law of order, see n. 7884, 7995, 8537; and from the signification of an age, as denoting what is eternal. The reason why an age denotes what is eternal is, because by an age is meant duration even to the end; and by that duration, in the internal sense, is signified what is eternal; the term also by which an age is here expressed, in the original tongue, signifies eternity. The reason why an age denotes what is eternal is, because an age in the Word, when it is spoken of the church, signifies its duration even to the end; hence when it is spoken of heaven, where there is no end, and when concerning the Lord, it signifies what is eternal. It is predicated in general of every church, but specifically of the Celestial Church. Moreover also an age signifies the world, and the life there, and likewise the life after it to eternity. As to what concerns the FIRST, namely, *that an age, when it is spoken of the church, signifies its duration even to the end*, it is manifest from the following passages, "The disciples said to Jesus, tell us what is the sign of Thy coming, and of the *consummation of the age*," Matt. xxiv. 3; by the consummation of the age, is signified the last time of the church, thus its end, when there is no longer any faith because there is no charity. That this is the consummation of the age, consequently that an age is the duration of the church, even to its end, may be manifest from all those things which were said by the Lord in that chapter, which may be seen explained before the chapters of Genesis, from chap. xxvi. to chap. xl. The like is signified elsewhere by an age and its consummation, in the same evangelist, "The harvest is the *consummation of the age*," xiii. 39, 40, 49; also, "Lo, I am with you all days, *even to the consummation of the age*," xxviii. 20; by age also is there meant the duration of the church from beginning to end. And in Ezekiel, "They shall dwell on the land, they and their sons, and their sons sons, *even to an age; David* shall be a prince to them *for an age*. My sanctuary shall be in the midst of them *for an age*," xxxvii. 25, 28; these things are said of Israel, by whom, in the internal sense, is meant the Spiritual Church; by the land [or earth] on which they shall dwell, is also signified the church; by sanctuary, every thing of the church; and by David, the Lord. Hence it is evident, that by to an age is signified even to the end. That Israel in the Word denotes the Spiritual Church, see the passages cited, n. 9340. That land [or earth] denotes the church, see the passages cited, n. 9325. That sanctuary denotes the all of the church, and that it is predicated of the good and truth of the Spiritual Church, n. 8330, 9479. And that David denotes the Lord, n. 1888, 9954. And in David, "Before the mountains were born, and the earth was formed, and the orb, *from age even to age*, Thou art God," Psalm xc. 2. By the mountains born, and by the earth formed, and by the orb, is not meant the creation of the world, but the establishment of the church; for mountains in the Word signify celestial love, thus the church in which that love is; the earth also and the orb signify the church, hence from age to age signifies from the establishment of churches to their ends; for churches succeed one after another, since when one is finished or vastated, another is established; that a mountain denotes celestial love, consequently the church which is in that love, see n. 795, 796, 4210, 6435, 8758; and that earth denotes the church specifically, but orb generally, see the passages cited, n. 9325. SECONDLY, *that an age, when it is spoken of heaven, where there is no end, and of the Lord, signifies what is eternal*, is manifest from the following passages, "*Jehovah is king for an age and for ever*," Psalm x. 16. Also Exod. xv. 18. Again, "Thy kingdom is *the kingdom of all ages;* and thy dominion is to every generation and generation," Psalm cxlv. 13. And in Jeremiah, "*The living God is the king of an age*," x. 10. And in Daniel, "His dominion is *the dominion of an age* which shall not pass away; afterwards the saints of the Most High shall receive the kingdom, and shall confirm the kingdom *even to an age, and even into ages of ages*," vii. 14, 18, 27. And in Matthew, "Thine is the kingdom, the power and the glory *into ages*," vi. 13. And in Luke, "God shall give to him the throne of David, that he may reign over the house of Jacob *for ages*," i. 32, 33. And in the Apocalypse, "To Jesus Christ be glory and strength *into ages of ages*," i. 6. And again, "Behold I live into *ages of ages*," i. 18. And again, "To the Lamb be blessing, and honor, and glory, and strength, *into ages of ages*. The twenty-four elders adored *Him that liveth into ages of ages*," v. 13, 14; chap. x. 6; chap. xi. 15. And in Isaiah, "My salvation shall be *for an age*, and My justice for generation of generation," li. 6, 8. "The angel of faces carried them *all the days of an age*," lxiii. 9. And in Daniel, "Many of those who sleep shall awake *to the life of an age*," xii. 2. And in John, "If any one shall eat of this bread, he shall live *for an age*," vi. 51, 58. Again, "I give them eternal life, and *they shall not perish for an age*," x. 28. And in David, "Lead me *in the way of an age*," Psalm cxxxix. 24. Again, "He hath set them for ever, and *for an age;* He hath given a statute which shall not pass away," Psalm cxlviii. 6. In these passages an age signifies what is eternal, since it is said of the Lord, and of His kingdom, and of heaven, and of the life there, whereof there is no end. Ages of ages are not eternities of eternities, but denote what is eternal; howbeit it is so said, in respect to churches in the earths, of which one succeeds another. From the Word it is evident that the church on this earth has been four times established, of which the first was the most ancient which was before the flood, the second the ancient which was after the flood, the third the Israelitish and Judaic, and lastly the Christian; the period of each from beginning to end is an age; after this latter also a new one will commence; these successions of churches are meant by ages of ages; that an age is the duration of a church even to the end, was shown above. THIRDLY; *That an age is predicated in general of every church, but specifically of the Celestial Church*, is manifest from the following passages, "I will set up the tent of

David that is fallen, and will build *according to the days of an age*," Amos ix. 11. By the days of an age is meant the time when the most ancient church was, which was celestial. And in Micah, "Bethlehem-Ephratah, out of thee shall come forth to Me He who is ruler in Israel, and whose going forth is from antiquity, *from the days of an age*," v. 2; where the sense is the same. And in Moses, "Remember thou *the days of an age*, understand ye the years of generation and generation," Deut. xxxii. 7. The days of an age denote the time of the most ancient church, which was a celestial church; and the years of generation and generation denote the time of the ancient church, which was a spiritual church. And in Isaiah, "Awake, awake, put on strength, the arm of Jehovah; awake according to the days of antiquity, *of the generation of ages*," li. 8, 9; according to the days of a generation of ages, denotes according to the states of love and of faith in the ancient churches derived from the most ancient. And in David, "I have considered the days of old, *the years of ages*," Psalm lxxvii. 5; where the sense is the same. And in Isaiah, "Remember the former things *from an age*," xlvi. 9. And in Malachi, "Then shall the meat-offering of Judah and of Jerusalem be sweet to Jehovah, *according to the days of an age*, and according to the ancient years," iii. 4. And in Joel, "*Judah shall sit for an age*, and Jerusalem to generation and generation," iii. 20; by Judah is there signified the Celestial Church, concerning which it is therefore said according to the days of an age, and for an age; and by Jerusalem is signified the Spiritual Church, of which it is said according to the ancient days and to generation and generation; that Judah denotes the Celestial Church, seen n. 3654, 3881, 6363, 8770; and Jerusalem the Spiritual Church, n. 402, 3654. FOURTHLY, *That an age signifies the world, and the life there*, is manifest from Matthew, "That which is sown amongst thorns is he, who hears the Word, *but the care of this age*, and the deceitfulness of riches, suffocates the Word," xiii. 22. And in Luke, "*The sons of this age* are more prudent than the sons of light," xvi. 8. Again, "*The sons of this age* marry and are given in marriage," xx. 34. And in David, "The wicked and *the secure ones of the age* multiply wealth," Psalm lxxiii. 12. FIFTHLY, *That an age signifies the life after death to eternity*, is manifest from Luke, "He shall receive a hundred-fold now in this time, *and in the age to come eternal life*," xviii. 30. And in Ezekiel, "When I will cause thee to descend with those that go down to the pit, *to the people of an age*," xxvi. 20. And in other passages, as Luke, chap. xx. 35; Isaiah xxxiv. 10, 17; Apoc. xiv. 11; chap. xx. 10; chap. xxii. 5.

10,249. "To him and to his seed, to their generations"—that hereby are signified all who receive those things which proceed from the Lord, thus who are regenerated by Him, appears from the representation of Aaron, as denoting the Lord as to Divine Good, see n. 9806, 9966; and from the signification of seed, as denoting those who are born of the Lord, thus who are regenerated, for they who are regenerated are said to be born of God, and are also called sons; but in the sense abstracted from persons by the seed of Aaron are signified those things which proceed from the Lord, thus by which man is regenerated, which are the goods of love and the truths of faith; and from the signification of generations, as denoting the goods and truths which proceed from the former as from their parents, and their derivations; for by generations in the Word, in the internal sense, are meant spiritual generations, which are of love and of faith, see what is cited, n. 10,197. Inasmuch as the Lord is meant by Aaron in the representative sense, therefore by the seed of Aaron are specifically meant those who are in the Lord's celestial kingdom, and by generations those who are in His spiritual kingdom; for the goods and truths of love and of faith in the heavens are born and proceed thus from the Lord. That by seed, those that are born, and generations, are meant those who are in love and faith to the Lord, and in the abstract sense the goods of love and the truths of faith, is manifest from several passages in the Word, of which it is allowed to adduce only the following: "From the east *I will bring thy seed*, and from the west I will gather thee," Isaiah xliii. 5; these things are said of Jacob and Israel, by whom, in the internal sense, is meant the church external and internal, the seed of which is the truth of faith and the good of charity. Again, "I will pour forth My spirit *upon thy seed*, and My blessing upon those that are born of thee," xliv. 3; upon seed and upon those that are born denotes upon those who are of the church, thus upon those things which are of the church, which are goods and truths, or charity and faith, for these constitute the church with man. Again, "In Jehovah shall *all the seed of Israel* glory," xlv. 25; where the sense is the same. Again, "If He shall make His soul guilt, *He shall see seed*," liii. 10, speaking of the Lord, Whose seed they are called who are born of Him, thus who are regenerated. Again, "To the right hand and to the left thou shalt break forth, and *thy seed shall inherit the nations*," liv. 3; where the sense is the same. And in Jeremiah, "Behold the days are coming, in which I will sow the house of Israel and the house of Judah *with the seed of man, and with the seed of beast*," xxxi. 27; these words are not intelligible, unless it be known what is signified by the house of Israel, and the house of Judah, also what by the seed of man and the seed of beast; they who do not think beyond the sense of the letter, will believe the sense to be this, that man and beast were to be multiplied in Israel and in Judah, but this sense involves nothing of the holy principle of the church. But by the house of Israel is there meant the Spiritual Church, and by the house of Judah the Celestial Church, the seed of man is the internal good of those churches, and the seed of the beast is their external good; that beast denotes the affection of good, see the passages cited, n. 9280; and that when mention is made of man and beast it denotes what is internal and what is external, n. 7523. And in Jeremiah, "As the army of the heavens shall not be numbered, and the sand of the sea is not measured, *so will I multiply the seed of David*," xxxiii. 22. And in David, "I have made a covenant with My chosen, I have sworn to David, *for an age I will strengthen thy seed*, and will build thy throne to generation and generation," Psalm lxxxix. 3, 4. By the seed of David is not meant the posterity from David as a father, for this was not so much multiplied, nor of so much importance that it should be multiplied as the army of the heavens, and as the sand of the sea; but by David in this passage, and also in other places, is meant the Lord as to Divine Truth, thus by his seed those who are regenerated or born of the Lord, and, in the abstract sense, those things which appertain to them from the Lord, which are the truths of faith and the goods of charity. That David denotes the Lord, see n. 1888, 9954. And in David, "*The seed which shall serve Jehovah, shall be numbered to the Lord*, for a generation," Psalm xxii. 30. And in Isaiah, "*Their seed shall be made known in the nations*, and they that are born of them in the midst of the people," lxi. 9; where seed denotes those who are regenerated, thus those who are of the church in whom the church is, thus in the sense abstracted from persons, those things which make a regenerate person, or which make the church with man, which are faith and charity from the Lord. And in the Apocalypse, "The dragon was angry against the woman, and went away to make war *with the remnant of her seed*, who kept the commandments of God, and have the testimony of Jesus Christ," xii. 17. By the dragon are meant those who are about to attempt to destroy the church of the Lord hereafter to be established; by the woman is meant that church; and by those who are of her seed are meant those who are in love and faith to the Lord from the Lord. But seed in the opposite sense, signifies those who are against the things of the church, thus who are in evils and the falses thence derived, and, in the abstract sense, evils and falses; as in Isaiah, "Woe to the sinful nation, *a seed of evils*," i. 4. Again, "Sons of the sorceress, *seed of the adulterer*, are not ye born of prevarication, the seed of a lie?" lvii. 3, 4. And again, "*The seed of evil doers* shall not be named for ever," xiv. 20.

10,250. Verses 22 to 33. *And Jehovah spake to Moses, saying, And do thou take to thyself chief spices, the best myrrh five hundred, and aromatic cinnamon the half thereof, fifty and two hundred, and aromatic calamus fifty and two hundred. And cassia five hundred, in the shekel of holiness; and oil of olive, a hin. And thou shalt make it oil of anointing of holiness, an ointment of ointment, the work of an ointment dealer, it shall be the oil of anointing of holiness. And thou shalt anoint with it the tent of the congregation, and the ark of the testimony. And the table and all its vessels, and the candlestick and its vessels, and the altar of incense. And the altar of burnt-offering and all its vessels, and the laver and its base. And thou shalt sanctify them, and they shall be the holy of holies; every one that toucheth them shall be sanctified. And Aaron and his sons thou shalt anoint, and shalt sanctify them to perform the office of the priesthood to Me. And to the sons of Israel speak, saying, this shall be to Me the oil of anointing of holiness to your generations. Upon the flesh of man it shall not be poured; and in its quality ye shall not make like it, it is holy, it shall be holy to you. The man who shall make ointment like it, and who shall give of it upon a stranger, shall be cut off from his people.* And Jehovah spake to Moses, saying, signifies another perceptivity from illustration by the Word from the Lord. And do thou take to thyself chief spices, signifies from the Word truths with goods, which are gratefully perceived. The best myrrh, signifies the perception of sensual truth. Five hundred, signifies what is full. And aromatic cinnamon, signifies the perception and affection of natural truth. The half thereof, fifty and two hundred, signifies as much as is correspondent. And aromatic calamus, signifies the perception and affection of interior truth. Fifty and two hundred, signifies corresponding quantity and quality. And cassia, signifies truth still more interior derived from good. Five hundred, signifies what is full. In the shekel of holiness, signifies the estimation of truth and of good. And oil of olive, signifies Divine Celestial Good of the Lord. A hin, signifies the quantity of conjunction. And thou shalt make it oil of anointing, signifies a representative of the Divine Good of the Divine Love of the Lord. An ointment of ointment, signifies in all and singular things of His Human [principle]. The work of an ointment dealer, signifies from the influx and operation of the Divine [principle] itself which was in the Lord from conception. It shall be the oil of anointing of holiness, signifies a representative of the Lord as to the Divine Human [principle]. And thou shalt anoint with it the tent of the congregation, signifies to represent the Divine [principle] of the Lord in the heavens. And the ark of the testimony, signifies in the celestial good which is of the inmost heaven. And the table and all its vessels, signifies in the spiritual good derived from the celestial which is of the second heaven, and in the ministering goods and truths. And the candlestick and its vessels, signifies in spiritual truth, which is of the second heaven, and in ministering truths. And the altar of incense, signifies in all things of worship from those goods and truths. And the altar of burnt-offering, signifies to represent the Divine Human [principle] of the Lord, and the worship of Him, in general. And all its vessels, signifies Divine Goods and Divine Truths. And the laver, and its base, signifies all things which are of purification from evils and falses, and of regeneration from the Lord. And thou shalt sanctify them, and they shall be the holy of holies, signifies thereby the influx and presence of the Lord in the worship of the representative church. Every one that toucheth them shall be sanctified, signifies communicative with all who receive in love and faith. And Aaron and his sons thou shalt anoint, signifies inauguration to represent the Lord in each kingdom. And thou shalt sanctify them to perform the office of the priesthood to Me, signifies to represent the Lord as to all the work of salvation. And to the sons of Israel thou shalt speak saying, signifies instruction to those who are of the church. This shall be the oil of anointing of holiness to Me, signifies a representative of the Lord as to the Divine Human [principle]. To your generations, signifies in all things of the church. Upon the flesh of man it shall not be poured, signifies non-communicative with the proprium of man. And in its quality ye shall not make like it, signifies non-imitation from the study [or application] of man. This is holy, it shall be holy to you, signifies because it is the Divine [principle] of the Lord. The man who shall make ointment like it, signifies the imitation of things Divine from art. And who shall give of it upon a stranger, signifies conjunction with those who do not acknowledge the Lord, thus who are in evils and the falses of evils. Shall be cut off from his people, signifies separation and spiritual death.

10,250. " And Jehovah spake to Moses, saying"—that hereby is signified another perceptivity from illustration by the Word from the Lord, appears from what was explained above, n. 10,215, where like words occur. The reason why it denotes another perceptivity is, because when any thing anew is revealed and commanded, it is so said, see n. 10,234.

10,251. " And do thou take to thyself chief spices "—that hereby are signified from the Word truths with goods which are gratefully perceived, appears from the signification of spices, as denoting truths conjoined to goods, which are grateful, see n. 10,199. The reason why it denotes which are gratefully perceived is, because odor signifies the perceptive principle, and hence an aromatic odor what is gratefully perceptive; that odor signifies the perceptive principle, see n. 3577, 4624 to 4634, 4748, 10,054; that they denote truths conjoined to goods derived from the Word is, because this is said to Moses, for it is said, do *thou* take to *thyself* spices, and by Moses is represented the Lord as to the Word, n. 9372. Moreover it is the Word from which all the truths of the church are derived, for the Word is the Divine Truth itself sent down from heaven by the Lord.

10,252. "The best myrrh"—that hereby is signified the perception of sensual truth, appears from the signification of odoriferous myrrh, as denoting the perception of sensual truth; for its odor denotes the perceptive principle, as just above, and myrrh denotes sensual truth. The subject treated of in what now follows is concerning the oil of anointing, by which is signified celestial good, which is the Divine good of the Divine Love of the Lord in the inmost heaven; its quality is described by the fragrant [or sweet-smelling] things, of which it was composed, which were the best myrrh, aromatic cinnamon, aromatic calamus, cassia, and oil of olive, by which are signified celestial truths and goods in their order, namely, from last to first, or from outermost to inmost; the last or outermost are signified by myrrh. The reason why celestial good, or good of the inmost heaven, is thus described is, because that good exists by those truths which are signified, and also subsists by them. But whereas this is a subject of deeper investigation than common, it is allowed further to explain how the case herein is; that celestial good, which is inmost good, may be born with man, which is effected by regeneration from the Lord, truths must be acquired from the Word, or from the doctrine of the church which is from the Word; these truths first have their seat in the memory of the natural or external man; hence they are called forth into the internal man by the Lord, as is the case when man lives according to them; and so far as man is affected by them, or loves them, so far they are elevated still higher, or more interiorly, by the Lord, and become there celestial good. Celestial good is the good of the love of doing truths from the Word for the sake of good, thus for the sake of the Lord, for the Lord is the source of good, thus is good; this is the generation of that good; from which it is evident that that good exists by truths from the Word, first in the most external or sensual man, next by their elevation into the internal, and lastly into the very inmost, where they become celestial good; and whereas thus that good exists by truths in their order, so afterwards it subsists in a like order by the same truths, for subsistence is perpetual existence. And when it so subsists, as it had existed, it is complete, for then superior things subsist, rest, and repose themselves, in order, upon inferior things, as upon their planes, and upon things outermost or ultimate, which are scientific sensual truths, as upon their foundation. These truths are described in the Apocalypse by the precious stones, forming the foundation of the wall of the holy Jerusalem descending out of heaven, chap. xxi. 19, 20; by the precious stones are signified Divine Truths received in good, see n. 9476, 9863, 9873, 9905. That odoriferous myrrh denotes sensual truth, is manifest also from David, "Thou hast loved justice, therefore God hath anointed thee, thy God, with the oil of gladness above thy companions; with myrrh, aloes, and cassia, all thy garments," Psalm xlv. 8, 9; these things are said of the Lord, who alone is the anointed of Jehovah, since the Divine Good of the Divine Love, which is signified by the oil of anointing, was in Him, n. 9954; by His garments, which are said to be anointed with myrrh, aloes, and cassia, are signified Divine Truths from His Divine Good in the natural principle, n. 5954, 9212, 9216, 9814; thus by myrrh, Divine Truth in the sensual principle, because it is named in the first place. And in Matthew, "The wise men from the east opening their treasures offered to the Lord, who was born, gifts, *gold, frankincense, and myrrh*," ii. 11; gold in this passage denotes good, frankincense denotes internal truth, and myrrh denotes external truth, each derived from good; the reason why gold is there named in the first place is, because gold signifies good which is inmost; in the second place frankincense, because it signifies internal truth derived from good; and the reason why myrrh is named in the third or last place is, because it signifies external truth derived from good; that gold denotes good, see the passages cited, n. 9874, 9881; and that frankincense denotes internal truth derived from good, will be seen in what follows at verse 34 of this chapter. The reason why the wise men from the east offered those things to the Lord then born was, that they might signify His Divine [principle] in the Human; for they knew what gold signified, what frankincense, and what myrrh, inasmuch as they were in the science of correspondences and representations; this was the principal science of those times amongst the Arabians, Ethiopians, and amongst others in the east, wherefore also in the Word by Arabia, Ethiopia, and by the sons of the east, in the internal sense are meant those who are in the knowledges of things celestial, n. 1171, 3240, 3242, 3762. But that science in time perished, since, when the good of life ceased, it was turned into magic; and it was first obliterated with the Israelitish nation, and afterwards with the rest: and at this day to such a degree, that it is not even known to have any existence; in the Christian orb, so much so, that if it be said that all and singular the things of the Word in the sense of the letter from correspondence signify celestial things, and that hence is its internal sense, it is not known what this means. Inasmuch as myrrh signified truth the most external, which is sensual truth, and its perception, therefore the bodies of the dead were formerly anointed with *myrrh and aloes*, by which anointing was signified the preservation of all truths and goods with man, and also their resurrection; wherefore also such [a thing or substance] was applied, as signified the ultimate principle of life appertaining to man, which ultimate principle is called sensual life. That the body of the Lord was anointed with such [things or substances], and encompassed together with a linen cloth, and that this was the custom with the Jews, see John, chap. xix. 39, 40; also Luke, chap. xxiii. 53, 56. But it is to be noted, that the things which are said of the Lord Himself in the Word, are to be understood in a super-eminent sense, wherefore those things there signify His Divine Life in the sensual [principle], which is the life proper to the body, and also the resurrection of this latter. That the Lord rose again with the whole body which he had in the world, otherwise than other men, is a known thing, for he left nothing in the sepulchre; wherefore also He said to the disciples, who supposed that they saw a spirit, when they saw the Lord, "Why are ye troubled? Behold My hands and My feet, handle Me and see, *for a spirit hath not flesh and bones, as ye see Me have.*"

10,253. "Five hundred"—that hereby is signified what is full, appears from the signification of the number five hundred, as denoting what is full. The reason why five hundred denotes what is full is, because this number is compounded of five and ten twice multiplied together, or of five times a hundred; and by five is signified much, in like manner by ten, and by a hundred, hence by five hundred is signified what is full; that five denotes much, see n. 5708, 5956, 9102; in like manner ten, n. 3107, 4638; also hundred, n. 4400, 6582, 6594; that all numbers in the Word signify things, see the passages cited, n. 9488; and that the compound numbers signify the like with the simple, from which they exist by multiplication, see n. 5291, 5335, 5708, 7973. That numbers signify things, is very manifest from Ezekiel, where the house of God, with all things within and without it, and also the new earth, are measured, and described by the numbers of a measure, from chap. xl. to xlviii.; and by the new earth is there meant the church, and by the house of God its holy [principle]. In like manner in the Apocalypse, where also the New Jerusalem is described by the numbers of measure, by which also is meant a New Church. Unless numbers had signified things, all those mensurations would have been of no account. That five hundred signifies the whole from one end to the other, thus what is full, is manifest from the above chapters in Ezekiel, "He measured out of the house, or the temple, to the quarter of the east *five hundred reeds round about;* to the quarter of the north *five hundred reeds round about;* to the quarter of the south *five hundred reeds;* and the quarter of the sea *five hundred reeds:* its walls round about, the length *five hundred reeds*, and the breadth *five hundred reeds*, to distinguish between what is holy and profane," xlii. 15 to 20. From which words it is evident, that five hundred denotes the whole in the complex, or every thing holy from one end to the other, thus what is full, for it is said, that the wall, which was of that length and breadth in a square, distinguished between what is holy and what is profane. That five hundred signifies much, and its tenth part, or fifty, somewhat respectively, is manifest from the Lord's words to Simon in Luke, "Jesus said, a certain creditor had two debtors, *one owed five hundred pence*, but the other *fifty;* when they had nothing to pay, he forgave them both; which of them loveth him most? Simon answered, he to whom he forgave most. Jesus said, therefore *many sins* are remitted to the woman, because she loved *much;* but to whom *little* is remitted, the same loveth *little*," vii. 41, to the end. The reason why the Lord applied those numbers was, because they signified much and somewhat; for He spake from the Divine [being or principle], thus by significatives according to correspondences; in like manner in other places throughout, as when He spake of the virgins, whom He called *ten*, and of whom *five* were prudent, and *five* foolish. He called them ten, because by that number are signified all, namely, who are of the church; and five, because by that number is signified some part, see n. 4637, 4638.

10,254. "And aromatic cinnamon"—that hereby is signified the perception and affection of natural truth, appears from the signification of aromatic cinnamon, as denoting the perception and affection of natural truth, which truth is the interior truth of the external principle of man, for with man there is sensual life and natural life, each of the external man, but the sensual life is exterior, deriving its truths from the objects which are in the earths, and in the body, and the natural life is interior, deriving its truths from the causes of those objects. The life of the internal man in like manner is exterior and interior, the exterior derives its truths from those things which are in the ultimates of heaven, but the interior from those which are in the interiors of heaven; these latter truths are signified by the fragrant things which follow. The reason why by aromatic cinnamon is signified the perception and affection of truth is, because by what is aromatic is signified grateful perception; grateful perception is from affection which is of the love, for what is grateful in perception is from no other source. That all odors signify perception, see n. 3577, 4626, 4748; and that grateful odors signify the perception of truth derived from good, n. 1514, 1517, 1518, 1519, 4628, 10,054; thus from the affection which is of love; and that the spheres of perceptions are turned into odors with spirits and angels, n. 4626. Moreover it is to be noted, that all those aromatics from which the oil of anointing was prepared, belong to the celestial class, that is, to those things which are of the celestial kingdom; whereas the aromatics of which the incense was compounded, belonged to the spiritual class, that is, to those things which are of the spiritual kingdom; wherefore also, in the original tongue, the aromatics from which the oil of anointing was composed, are from another term and derivation than the aromatics from which the incense was composed; for there are in the Word peculiar terms, by which are expressed those things which are of the celestial kingdom, and peculiar terms by which are expressed those things which are of the spiritual kingdom; and others, which are common to both. But in order that it may be known what those terms are, it must be first known that heaven is divided into two kingdoms, in like manner the church; and that in the celestial kingdom the essential principle is the good of love to the Lord, but in the spiritual kingdom the good of charity towards the neighbor: what the difference between them is, see the numbers cited, n. 9277. That the aromatic which is here named, signifies the perception and affection of celestial truth, is manifest from Isaiah, "*In the place of an aromatic shall be infection*, and in the place of a girdle, a rent, and in the place of entwisted work, baldness," iii. 24. The subject here treated of is concerning the daughters of Zion, by whom is signified the celestial church, in this case perverted; wherefore aromatic is expressed by the same term as in this verse; and by infection in the place of an aromatic, is signified that in the place of the perception and affection of truth from good, and life thence derived, shall be the perception and affection of what is false grounded in evil, in which is nothing of life. And in Ezekiel, "The traders of Sheba and Raamah were thy traders *by the chief of every aromatic*, and by precious stone, and gold," xxvii. 22. These thing were said of Tyre, by which are signified the knowledges of good and truth in the church; and by Sheba and Raamah are signified those who are in the knowledges of things celestial. In like manner where the Queen of Sheba is treated of in the first book of the Kings, "The Queen of Sheba gave to Solomon a hundred and twenty talents of gold, *and aromatics exceedingly many*, and precious stone: there came not *as this aromatic* any more for multitude," x. 10; that Sheba principally denotes those who are in the knowledges of things celestial, see n. 1171, 3240. From which considerations it is evident that these spices, from which the oil of anointing was prepared, signify the perception and affection of truth, such as they have who are in the Lord's celestial kingdom. The reason why the aromatics, by which the oil of anointing was prepared, which were noble myrrh, aromatic cinnamon, aromatic calamus, and cassia, belong to the celestial class, that is, to those things which are of the Lord's celestial kingdom, is, because the oil of anointing signified the Divine Good of the Divine Love in the Lord, which in heaven is His Divine Celestial [principle]. That the oil of anointing has this signification, see n. 9954, 10,019.

10,255. "Half thereof fifty and two hundred"—that hereby is signified as much as is correspondent, appears from the signification of a number, the half of a foregoing number, as denoting somewhat, and as much as is sufficient, or as much as is for uses, thus also as much as is correspondent. Hence it is that fifty and two hundred, inasmuch as they are half of the former number, namely, the half of five hundred, denote as much as is correspondent. How the case herein is, may be manifest from examples. Let the number ten be for an example; when this number signifies all, then the half of it, or five, signifies some; when ten signifies what is full, then five signifies as much as is sufficient; but when ten signifies much, five signifies somewhat, and so forth; the case is similar with other numbers when they are halved. That five signifies some, also somewhat, and likewise as much as is sufficient and as much as is for uses, see n. 4638, 5708, 5956, 9102, 9689, thus with a variety in respect to the number ten when this signifies all, what is full, or much. Similar things are signified by fifty in respect to a hundred, and similar things by fifty and two hundred in respect to five hundred. It is of no concern whether a number be greater, or lesser, since the greater numbers have a like signification with the lesser from which they are composed, see n. 5335, 5708, 7973; and that numbers in the Word signify things, see the passages cited, n. 9488, 10,127. From these considerations it may be manifest that this number, which is the half of the foregoing, does not signify the half of the perception of interior truth in respect to the perception of exterior truth, but as much as is correspondent. For things in the heavens are not measured and numbered as things in the earths, since in the heavens there are not spaces, nor times, but instead thereof states, which are perceived as to quality and quantity, without respect to any numeration; for numeration and mensuration involve such things as are of space and time, thus which are proper to nature in ultimates.

10,256. "And aromatic calamus"—that hereby is signified the perception and affection of interior truth, appears from the signification of aromatic calamus, as denoting the perception and affection of interior truth, for calamus denotes that truth, and aromatic denotes the perception and affection thereof; that calamus denotes truth, will be seen beneath, and that aromatic denotes perception and affection thereof, see just above, n. 10,254. By interior truth is here meant the truth of the internal man which is exterior there, according to what was said above, n. 10,254, namely, that in the external man there is an interior and exterior principle, in like manner in the internal. Hence it is that four aromatics were applied to prepare the oil of anointing, namely, noble myrrh, aromatic cinnamon, aromatic calamus, and cassia; and by noble myrrh is signified the perception of exterior truth in the external man, which is sensual truth; by aromatic cinnamon interior truth there, which is natural truth; by aromatic calamus exterior truth in the internal man, and by cassia interior truth there, and by oil of olive the good itself, from which are the affections and perceptions of those truths. That calamus denotes interior truth, may be manifest from the passages in the Word where it is mentioned; yet in those passages it is not called aromatic calamus, but only calamus, and good calamus, as in Isaiah, "Thou hast not called Me, O Jacob; and thou hast been weary of Me, O Israel; *thou hast not bought for Me calamus for silver*, and with the fat of thy sacrifices thou hast not filled Me," xliii. 22, 24. And in Ezekiel, "Dan and Javan have given thread in thy tradings; smooth iron, cassia, and *calamus* was in thy trading," xxvii. 19. And in Jeremiah, "To what purpose doth frankincense come to Me from Sheba, and *good calamus* from a land afar off?" vi. 20. That in these passages by calamus is meant something of the church, and of worship there, is evident; for otherwise to what purpose would it be that they should buy for Jehovah calamus with silver; and that good calamus should come to Him from a land afar off; and whereas something of the church and of its worship is signified, it follows that it is truth or good, since all things of the church and of its worship have reference to those principles. But what truth or good is signified, celestial or spiritual, of the external or the internal man, is manifest from the internal sense of the above passages examined in its series; that it is interior truth, is evident.

10,257. "Fifty and two hundred"—that hereby is signified corresponding quantity and quality, is manifest from what was shown just above, n. 10,255.

10,258. "And cassia"—that hereby is signified interior truth derived from good, appears from the signification of cassia, as denoting interior truth of the internal man; that cassia has this signification, is evident from what has been said and shown above; for celestial things follow in that order from outermost to inmost; wherefore it is inmost truth, which is signified by cassia, for it is fourth in order. The reason why cassia denotes truth derived from good is, because inmost truth proceeds immediately from good, and conjointly acts with good in inferior [things or principles]; which is the case when the intellectual principle acts altogether in unity with the will, so that it is not known whether the agency be from the latter or from the former; celestial things also, the more interior they are, so much the more perfect they are, for all perfection increases towards the interiors, and all perfection is from good, that is, by good from the

Lord. Cassia is mentioned amongst those things which signify things celestial in Ezekiel, "Dan and Javan gave thread in their tradings; smooth iron, *cassia and calamus* was in thy trading," xxvii. 19; the subject here treated of is concerning Tyre, by which are signified the knowledges of truth and of good in the church, see n. 1201; and by Dan and Javan those who are in the knowledges of things celestial: smooth iron denotes ultimate celestial truth, and cassia denotes inmost truth. Cassia is not mentioned in other passages of the Word, but kessia in David, which is also a species of cassia, "God, thy God, hath anointed thee with the oil of gladness, with myrrh, aloes, kessia, all thy garments," Psalm xlv. 8, 9; the subject treated of in that Psalm throughout is concerning the Lord, and indeed concerning the glorification of His Human [principle]. He who is unacquainted with the internal sense of the Word, cannot in any wise know what is signified by anointing all garments with myrrh, aloes, and kessia, where the Lord is treated of; that garments are not meant, is evident, neither myrrh, aloes, and kessia, with which they were anointed, but Divine Truths derived from Divine Good, which the Lord put on as to His Human [principle]; for anointing was nothing else but a representative of the Divine Good in the Divine Human [principle] of the Lord, hence by myrrh, aloes and kessia, are signified Divine Truths in their order proceeding from the Divine Good which was in Himself; hence by garments is signified His Divine Human [principle]; for whether we speak of the Divine Human [principle] of the Lord, or of the Divine Truth, it is the same thing, inasmuch as the Lord, when He was in the world, was the Divine Truth itself, and when He went forth out of the world, He made Himself Divine Good, from which is the Divine Truth, see the numbers cited, n. 9199, 9315. That principle also in the Word is called garment, which invests another, whatsoever it be. The like is signified by the Lord's garments in Isaiah, chap. lxiii. 2, 3, and also in other places; that garments signify truth investing good, see n. 2576, 4545, 4763, 5248, 5319, 5954, 9093, 9212, 9216, 9952. Hence now it is evident that by kessia in the above passage, which is a species of cassia, is signified the Divine Truth, which immediately proceeds from the Divine Good, which truth is inmost truth.

10,259. "Five hundred"—that hereby is signified what is full, appears from what was shown above, n. 10,253. The reason why five hundred in the shekel of holiness were taken of myrrh, and five hundred of cassia, but only fifty and two hundred of aromatic cinnamon and aromatic calamus, was, because myrrh signifies sensual truth which is ultimate in order, and cassia the truth which immediately proceeds from good, which is inmost truth; whereas aromatic cinnamon and aromatic calamus signified interior truths, which are middle; and of the last and inmost there must be what is full, but of the middle as much as is correspondent; for middle principles ought to be in correspondence to what is first and last.

10,260. "In the shekel of holiness"—that hereby is signified the estimation of truth and of good, appears from the signification of the shekel of holiness, as denoting the price and estimation of truth and of good, as to its quality and quantity, see n. 2959, 10,221.

10,261. "And oil of olive"—that hereby is signified the Divine Celestial Good of the Lord, appears from the signification of oil, as denoting good both celestial and spiritual, see n. 886, 4582, 9780; and from the signification of olive, as denoting celestial love, of which we shall speak presently; hence by oil of olive is signified the good of celestial love, or, what is the same thing, celestial good. It is called the Divine Celestial Good of the Lord, because all good, which is essentially good in the heavens, is from the Divine [principle] of the Lord. But it is to be noted, that the Divine Good of the Lord in itself is simply one [*unicum*], for it is infinite, and contains infinite things in itself; what is infinite, this is simply one, since the infinite things which it contains make one. But the reason why it is distinguished into celestial and spiritual, is owing to its reception by angels in the heavens and by men in the earths; being received by angels and men, who are of the Lord's celestial kingdom, it is called Divine Good Celestial, but received by angels and men, who are of the Lord's spiritual kingdom, it is called Divine Good Spiritual; for all angels and men variously or dissimilarly receive the one only good of the Lord. This is comparatively like the heat and light of the sun of the world, which, although considered in themselves they are simply one, still vary according to the times of the year, and according to the times of the day, and also dissimilarly in every region of the earth; which variation of heat and of light is not effected by the sun, but by the various turning of the earth, according to the varieties of its circuit and volution, thus also by reception; the same light also varies in singular objects according to reception, whence come colors. From these considerations it may be manifest from what ground it is that the Divine Good of the Lord, which is simply one, because infinite, is called celestial and spiritual. That oil denotes good, both celestial and spiritual, is manifest from the passages above cited; but that olive denotes celestial love, and oil the perception and affection of that love, is manifest from the passages in the Word where oil and olive are named, as from the following; "The prophet saw a candlestick wholly of gold, its seven lamps were upon it, *two olives were near it*, one on the right hand of the bowl, and one near its left hand. He said to the angel, *what are these two olive-trees, and what are these two olive-berries*, which are in the hand of the two pipes of gold? He said, *these are the two sons of olives standing near the Lord of the whole earth*," Zech. iv. 2, 3, 11, 12, 14. What these prophetics involve, cannot be known to any one, unless he knows from the internal sense what is signified by a candlestick, and what by an olive-tree. That a candlestick signifies the spiritual heaven, and its lamps the holy truths there, see n. 9548, 9551, 9555, 9558, 9561, 9684. Hence it is manifest that an olive-tree signifies the celestial kingdom from the perception and affection of good, and the olive berries signify holy goods there, the truths of which are signified by sons of olives; two signifies the internal and external of that kingdom, and conjunction. Like things are signified by oil and candlestick in the Apocalypse, "I will give to my two witnesses to prophecy a thousand two hundred and sixty days, clothed in sackcloth; *these are the two olives, and the two candlesticks standing before the God of the earth*," xi. 3, 4. And in Isaiah, "I will give in the wilderness the cedar, the shittim-tree, and the myrtle, and *wood of oil*," xli. 19. Mention is made of the cedar and the wood of oil, because the cedar signifies spiritual good, and the wood of oil celestial good. Spiritual good is charity towards the neighbor, and celestial good is love to the Lord; to give them in the wilderness denotes in the lands out of the church, thus amongst the nations. And in Hosea, "His branches shall go forth; *and his honor shall be as of the olive*, and his odor like Lebanon," xiv. 6: by olive is here also signified celestial good, and by Lebanon spiritual good, thus by Lebanon the like as by cedar, since Lebanon was a forest of cedars. And in Isaiah, "So shall it be in the midst of the land, in the midst of the people, *as the beating off of the olive*, as the gleanings when the vintage is finished," xxiv. 13; also chap. xvii. 6. It is called the beating of the olive and the gleanings of the finished vintage, since the olive signifies the church which is in celestial good, and the vine the church which is in spiritual good; for in the Word where good is treated of, truth is also treated of, by reason of their marriage; in like manner where the celestial principle is treated of, the spiritual principle is also treated of; the celestial principle is also predicated of good and the spiritual of truth, see in the passages cited, n. 9263, 9314, therefore of the vine and of the olive. That a vine denotes the spiritual church, and its good and truth, see n. 1069, 5113, 6376, 9277. On this account also the vine and the olive are named together in other places, as in David, "Thy wife as the *fruitful vine* in the sides of thy house; thy sons as *olive plants* round about thy table," Psalm cxxviii. 3. And in Habakkuk, "The fig-tree shall not flourish, neither shall there be *produce in the vines, the work of the olive shall lie*," iii. 17 And in Amos, "The palmer-worm hath devoured most of your gardens, and *your vineyards*, and your fig-trees, and *your olives*," iv. 9. The fig-tree is also mentioned, because the fig-tree signifies the good of the external church, n. 5113; but the vine, the good of the internal spiritual church; and the olive, the good of the internal celestial church. In like manner in other places. Inasmuch as the wood of olive signified the good of celestial love, therefore the two cherubs, which were in the secret place of the temple, were made of the wood of oil, in like manner the doors, the threshold, and the posts, 1 Kings vi. 23, 31, 32; for by the secret place of the temple was represented the inmost heaven, where celestial good is, therefore all things which were therein signified celestial things; that the ark which was there, and for the sake of which the secret place was constructed, signified the inmost heaven where the Lord is, see n. 9485. The like also was signified by the Mount of Olives, which was over against the temple, as by the olive, in like manner as the like was signified by Lebanon, as by the cedar; on which account, that all things in the heavens might be represented, which the Lord performed when He was in the world, and especially Divine Celestial things, the Lord was very often in the Mount of Olives, when He was in Jerusalem, as is manifest from Luke, "Jesus was in the days teaching in the temple, *but in the nights going forth he passed the night in the mountain which is called the Mount of Olives*," xxi. 37. And in another place, "*Jesus going forth went according to custom into the Mount of Olives*," xvii. 39. That that mountain was over against the temple, see Mark xiii. 3; Matt. xxiv. 3. That the Mount of Olives signified Divine Celestial Good is manifest from Zechariah, where it is said, "*that the feet of Jehovah shall stand upon the Mount of Olives*, which is before the faces of Jerusalem, and He shall there fight against the nations; and that *that mountain shall be divided asunder*, part towards the east, and towards the sea, with a great valley; and part thereof shall recede towards the north, and part towards the south," xiv. 4. In this passage is described the state of heaven and the church when the Lord was in the world, and fought against the hells, and overcame them, and at the same time reduced the heavens into order; the nations there, against which he fought, denote evils from the hells; the Mount of Olives, on which His feet stood, denotes the Divine Good of the Divine Love, for from this He fought and conquered. The rending asunder of the mountain towards the east and towards the sea, with a great valley, signifies the separation of heaven and hell; in like manner its receding towards the north and the south; for they are said to be in the south who are in the light of truth, in the east who are in the love of good, but to the sea who are in evils, and to the north who are in falses.

10,262. "A hin"—that hereby is signified the quantity of

conjunction, appears from the signification of a hin, which was a measure of liquids, in this case, as denoting the quantity of conjunction; for by oil is signified the Divine Celestial Good of the Lord, which is the conjunctive principle itself of all things in the heavens, hence by its measure is signified the quantity of conjunction, and the all of conjunction. The reason why the Divine Celestial Good of the Lord is the conjunctive principle itself of all things is, because it is the esse itself of the life of all things; for it vivifies all things by the Divine Truth proceeding from that Divine Good, and it vivifies according to the quality of reception; angels are receptions, and also men; the truths and goods appertaining to them give the quality, for according to that quality is effected reception, thus conjunction. Two measures, which were in holy use, are mentioned in the Word, one for liquids, which was called the hin, the other for dry [substances], which was called the ephah; by the hin was measured oil and wine, and by the ephah meal and fine flour; the measure hin, which was for oil and wine, was divided into four, but the measure ephah was divided into ten. The reason why the measure hin was divided into four was, that it might signify what is conjunctive, for four denotes conjunction; but the reason why the measure ephah was divided into ten was, that it might signify what is receptive, the quality whereof was marked by numbers, for ten signifies much, all, and what is full; that four denotes conjunction, see n. 8877, 9601, 9674, 10,136, 10,137; and that ten denotes much, all, and what is full, alike with a hundred, n. 1988, 3107, 4400, 4638, 8468, 8540, 9745, 10,253. That the measure hin was for oil and wine in the sacrifices, and that it was divided into four, but the measure ephah for meal and fine flour, which were for the meat-offering in the sacrifices, and that it was divided into ten, may be manifest from Exod. chap. xxix. 40; Levit. chap. v. 11; chap. xxiii. 13; Numb. xv. 3 to 10; chap. xxviii. 5, 7, 14. From these considerations it is evident, that by a hin is signified the quantity of conjunction, and by an ephah the quantity of reception; oil also conjoined the fine flour, and this latter received, for in the meat-offering there was oil and fine flour. There were besides other measures, which were in common use both for dry [substances] and for liquids; the measures for dry [substances] were called homer and omer, and the measures for liquids the cor and the bath; the homer contained ten ephahs, and the ephah ten omers; but the cor contained ten baths, and the bath ten lesser parts, concerning which, see Exod. xvi. 36; Ezek. xlv. 11, 13, 24. But in Ezekiel, where the new temple is treated of, there is extant another division of the ephah and the bath, the ephah and the bath being there not divided into ten, but into six; and the hin there corresponds to the ephah, as is evident in that prophet, chap. xlv. 13, 14, 24; chap. xlvi. 5, 7, 11, 14. The reason is, because the subject there treated of is not concerning celestial good and its conjunction, but spiritual good and the conjunction of this latter, and in the spiritual kingdom the correspondent numbers are twelve, six, and three, since by those numbers are signified all things, and when they are predicated of truths and goods, all things of truth and good in the complex. That those things are signified by twelve, see n. 3272, 3858, 3913, 7973. That also by six, n. 3960, 7973, 8148, 10,217; in like manner by three, by which is signified from beginning to end, thus what is full, and as to things, all, n. 2788, 4495, 5159, 7715, 9825, 10,127. The reason why these numbers involve similar things is, because the greater numbers have a like signification with the simple ones, from which by multiplication they exist, n. 5291, 5335, 5708, 7973. Inasmuch as by the hin is signified the quantity of conjunction also with spiritual truth, therefore likewise for the meat-offering in the sacrifices made from the ram a third part of a hin of oil was taken, and for a libation a third part of wine, Numb. xv. 6, 7; for by the ram is signified spiritual good, n. 2830, 9991. From these considerations it is now further evident that by numbers in the Word are signified things; otherwise to what purpose would have been the designation of quantity and of measure by numbers so often in Moses, in Ezekiel, and elsewhere?

10,263. "And thou shalt make it oil of anointing"—that hereby is signified a representative of the Divine Good of the Divine Love of the Lord, appears from what was shown above concerning the oil of anointing, n. 9954, 10,011, 10,019.

10,264. "Ointment of ointment"—that hereby is signified in all and singular things of His Human [principle], appears from the signification of ointment, when concerning the oil of anointing, by which is signified a representative of the Divine Good of the Divine Human [principle] of the Lord, as denoting what is Divine in all and singular things of His Human [principle]. The reason why this is signified by ointment of an ointment is, because all the aromatics mentioned above, which were the best myrrh, aromatic cinnamon, aromatic calamus, and cassia, are meant by the ointment of ointment; in the original tongue also an aromatic in general is signified by that term; but interpreters call it ointment from anointing. The reason why an aromatic of an aromatic signifies in all and singular things of the Lord's Human [principle] is because the truths of the whole Human [principle] with their perceptions and affections are signified, namely, ultimate truth which is of the sensual principle, with its perception, by myrrh, n. 10,252; interior truth of the natural or external man, with its perception and affection, by aromatic cinnamon, n. 10,254; truth still more interior, which is of the internal man, with its perception and affection, by aromatic calamus, n. 10,256 ; and inmost truth with its perception and affection, by cassia, n. 10,258 ; thus by those things the whole human [principle], for all and singular things appertaining to man have reference to truths and their perceptions and affections, for they constitute his life. For it may be known that man, without the perception and affection of truth and good, is not a man, for all and singular the things which he thinks, have reference to truths and their perceptions, and to goods and their affections; the thoughts and affections of man are nothing else; for man has an intellectual principle, and has a will principle; the intellectual principle is constituted from the perception of truth, and the will principle from the affection of good. That the whole man from the head to the heel, both interiorly and exteriorly, is nothing but his own truth or false, and his own good or evil, and that the body is their external form, is an arcanum which has not been yet known in the world. From these considerations it may now be manifest, that by an aromatic of an aromatic, or ointment of ointment, by which are meant all truths from what is ultimate to what is inmost, thus truths in their whole complex, are signified all and singular the things appertaining to man, or by virtue of which he is a man. Consequently when that aromatic is predicated of the Lord, that it signifies all and singular the things of His Human [principle]. It is said, "Thou shalt make it oil of anointing, and aromatic of an aromatic, the work of the dealer in aromatics," since the oil of anointing signifies the Divine Good Itself of the Divine Love, which was in the Lord from conception, n. 9954, 10,011, 10,019 ; an aromatic of an aromatic signifies that good in all and singular the things of His Human [principle] ; and the work of a dealer in aromatics, or of a dealer in ointment, signifies from the influx and operation of His Divine [principle]; for the Lord alone as to His Human [principle] was the anointed of Jehovah, see n. 9954.

10,265. "The work of the dealer in ointment"—that hereby is signified from the influx and operation of His Divine[principle] which was in the Lord from conception, appears from the signification of a dealer in ointment, or a dealer in aromatics, as denoting him who makes it, wherefore when it is said of the Lord, the Divine [principle] Itself is signified, and by work its operation. Whatsoever is said in the Word, is to be understood in respect to that of which it is said, wherefore when it is said of the Divine [being or principle], it is to be understood of the Divine [being or principle], and of His operation, influx, and attributes, howsoever it sounds in the sense of the letter. In the inmost heaven all things of the Word are applied to the Divine Human of the Lord, for the angels there think immediately from the Lord, and perceive the Word in its inmost sense, which is the celestial sense. Wherefore there by ointment of ointment the work of a dealer in ointment, they perceive nothing else but what is of the Divine Itself which was in the Lord from conception, and its influx and operation into all and singular the things of His Human; for the Human of the Lord is the Divine Itself appertaining to them; they know that the Divine Good of the Divine Love, which is called the Father, is in the Divine Human of the Lord, which is the Son, reciprocally, according to the Lord's words, *that the Father is in Him, and He in the Father*, John xiv. 10, 11, *and that they are one*, John x. 30. Wonder not that by a dealer in ointment or in aromatics is signified the Divine Itself, when Jehovah in the Word throughout calls Himself the Former, and the Workman, yea even the Potter, as in Isaiah, "O Jehovah, Thou art our Father; we are the clay, and *Thou art our Potter*, and we are all the work of Thy hands," lxiv. 8; and also in other passages in the same prophet, and in Jeremiah chap. xviii. 2, 3, 4, 6.

10,266. In what has been said just above is described, by the preparation of the oil of anointing, the Divine Good of the Divine Love of the Lord in His Divine Human, and in the respective sense the good of love appertaining to man from the Lord; for what is said in the Word in the supreme sense concerning the Lord, in the respective sense is also said concerning man, since the regeneration of man is an image of the glorification of the Lord's Human, n. 3138, 3212, 3296, 3490, 4402, 5688. Hence it is evident that the preparation of the oil of anointing involves also the generation and formation of the good of love appertaining to man from the Lord; consequently that the good of love is formed by the truths of the church which are from the Word, first the external truths, next those which are more and more interior, according to the description given just above, and that thus the external man is first imbued with them, and next the interior man successively. It is to be noted, that in the order in which that good has been formed by truths from the Lord, or in the order in which it has existed, in the same also it is preserved by the Lord, and subsists, for preservation is perpetual formation, as subsistence is perpetual existence. Hence it follows, that according to the quality of the perception and affection, and according to the order with which man has imbued truths, such is the good of love appertaining to him; if the affection of truth has been for the sake of truth and for the sake of good, without affection for the sake of self and the world, and if the order has been from outermost truths to interior by degrees, in this case the good of love is genuine; if otherwise, it is spurious, or not good. It is of no consequence if in the beginning when the man begins to be formed, the affection of truth be also for the sake of himself and the world; but this must be put off as good increases by truths; and also the man afterwards is purified from those things continually, as the belly from things that are useless. He who believes that man can be gifted with the good of love without the truths of faith, and without a life according to them, is greatly deceived.

10,267. "It shall be the oil of anointing of holiness"—that hereby is signified a representative of the Lord as to the Divine Human, appears from the signification of the oil of anointing, as being a representative of the Divine Good of the Divine Love of the Lord, see n. 9954, 10,011, 10,019; this is here called the oil of anointing of holiness, that the Lord may be understood as to the Divine Human principle, for this is the Very Holy [principle] Itself in the heavens; for the angels in the heavens know and acknowledge no other Divine than the Divine Human of the Lord, for of this they can think, and this they can love; but of the Divine which is called the Father, they cannot think, thus neither love it, since it is incomprehensible, according to the Lord's words, "*Ye have neither heard His voice at any time, nor seen His shape,*" John v. 37; what cannot be seen, and cannot be heard, cannot enter into any idea of thought, nor into any affection of love; what is presented as an object to be comprehended by faith and love, must be in a state of accommodation. That the incomprehensible Divine, which is called the Father, is together worshiped, when the Lord as to the Divine Human is worshiped, is also manifest from the words of the Lord Himself, where He says, "*That He is the way, and that no one cometh to the Father but by Him,*" John xiv. 6: "*And that no one knoweth the Father but the Son, and he to whom the Son shall be willing to reveal Him,*" Matt. xi. 27: "*And that no one hath seen the Father at any time, except the only begotten Son, Who is in the bosom of the Father, and he will bring Him forth to view,*" John i. 18; wherefore the Lord saith, "*Come ye all to Me, and I will refresh you,*" Matt. xi. 28. That the Divine Human of the Lord is the All in All of heaven and that it is the Holy [principle] Itself there, see n. 9933, 9972, 10,067, 10,159; that the Lord alone is holy, and that every thing holy is from Him, n. 9229, 9479, 9680, 9818, 9820, 9956.

10,268. "And thou shalt anoint with it the tent of the congregation"—that hereby is signified to represent the Divine [principle] of the Lord in the heavens, appears from the signification of anointing with the oil of holiness, as denoting to induce a representation of the Divine Good of the Divine Love of the Lord as to the Divine Human; for to anoint signifies to induce a representation, for the things which were anointed were called holy, not from the oil but from the representation of the Divine which is signified by oil, for oil signifies the Divine Good of the Divine Love, and holiness signifies the Divine Human, since this alone is holy, as may be manifest from what has been shown above, n. 9954, 10,011, 10,019, 10,264, 10,265, 10,266, 10,267. And from the signification of the tent of the congregation, as denoting heaven in the whole complex, the inmost or third where the ark of the testimony was, the middle or second where the table was on which were the breads of faces, where also was the candlestick and the altar of incense, and the ultimate or first where the court was, n. 9457, 9481, 9485, 9784, 9963, 10,230, 10,242, 10,245. Hence it is evident that by anointing the tent of the congregation is signified to induce a representation of the Divine Good of the Divine Love of the Lord as to His Divine Human; and whereas this is signified by anointing the tent of the congregation, it is also signified to represent the Divine of the Lord in the heavens; for heaven is not heaven from the angels, viewed in their own proprium, but from the Divine of the Lord appertaining to them, see n. 9408, 10,125, 10,151, 10,157, 10,159.

10,269. "And the ark of the testimony"—that hereby is signified in celestial good which is of the inmost heaven, appears from the signification of anointing the ark of the testimony, as denoting to induce a representation of the Divine in celestial good which is of the inmost heaven; for by anointing is signified to induce a representation of the Divine of the Lord, as just above, n. 10,268; and by the ark of the testimony is signified the good of the inmost heaven; that the ark denotes the inmost heaven, and that the testimony denotes the Lord there, n. 9485; and whereas the good, which reigns in that heaven, is the good of love to the Lord, which good is called celestial good, therefore by anointing the ark of the testimony, is signified to induce a representation of the Divine of the Lord in celestial good, which is of the inmost heaven. How the case herein is, may be manifest from what has been every where shown above, namely, that anointing represented the Lord as to the Divine Human; for the Lord as to His Divine Human was alone the anointed of Jehovah, for in Him was the Divine of the Father from conception, and hence in His Human. That the human body is what proceeds from the esse of the Father which is called His soul, may be known; for the likeness of the Father as to the various affections which are of the love, is extant with the children even in their faces; hence every family has something peculiar to itself by which it is distinguished from another; what then must have been the case with the Lord, in whom the Divine Itself was His esse, which is called the soul. Hence it is that the Lord says, "*He who hath seen Me, hath seen the Father; believe Me, that I am in the Father, and the Father in Me*," John xiv. 9, 11.

10,270. "And the table and all its vessels"—that hereby is signified in spiritual good derived from celestial, which is of the second heaven, and in ministering goods and truths, appears from the signification of the tent of the congregation, out of the vail, where that table was, as denoting the second heaven, see n. 9457, 9481, 9485 ; and from the signification of the table, on which were the breads of faces, as denoting spiritual good derived from celestial ; for the breads signify celestial good, n. 9545, and the table on which they were spiritual good, n. 9684, 9685 ; and from the signification of its vessels, as denoting the knowledges of celestial good and truth, see n. 9545, thus ministering goods and truths, for knowledges minister. The reason why it is spiritual good from celestial, which is signified by the table on which were the breads of faces, is because by the tent of the congregation out of the vail was represented the second heaven, in which the good of charity towards the neighbor reigns, which good is called spiritual good, and this good is so far good, as there is in it celestial good, which is the good of love to the Lord. For there are three kinds of goods, which make the three heavens. There is the good of love to the Lord which is called celestial good, this makes the inmost heaven ; there is the good of charity toward the neighbor, which is called spiritual good, and makes the second heaven ; and there is the good of faith, which is called natural spiritual good, this makes the ultimate heaven ; into celestial good, which is of the inmost heaven, the Lord flows in from the Divine Human immediately ; into spiritual good which is of the second heaven the Lord flows in from the Divine Human, also mediately by [or through] celestial good ; and into natural spiritual good, which is of the ultimate heaven, the Lord flows in from the Divine Human, again also mediately ; it is said *also mediately*, since the Lord not only flows-in into the goods of these heavens mediately, but also immediately, as may be manifest from what was shown concerning Divine Influx immediate and mediate, in the numbers cited, n. 9682.

10,271. "And the candlestick and its vessels"—that hereby is signified in spiritual truth, which is of the second heaven, and in the ministering truths, appears from the signification of the candlestick, as being a representative of the Lord as to spiritual truth, which is of the second heaven, see n. 9548, 9551, 9555, 9558, 9561, 9684 ; and from the signification of its vessels, as denoting scientific truths, which are ministering, see n. 3068, 3079, 9572, 9724.

10,272. "And the altar of incense"—that hereby is signified in all things of worship from those goods and truths, appears from the signification of the altar of incense, as being a representative of all things of worship, which are grounded in love and charity from the Lord, see n. 10,177, 10,198. It is called a representative of the Lord in goods and truths, and in the things which minister, and in all things of worship, by reason that the goods and truths, which are represented, are so far goods and truths, as there is in them the Divine ; for all goods and truths which appertain to man and angel, are from the

Lord; without life from the Lord in them they are dead things, yea even evils, for if they are not from the Lord, but from man, they respect man and the world, and those things which have man and the world for an end, are in themselves evil, for the end regarded is the inmost principle of man, since it is the soul of all things which are in him. From these considerations it may be manifest, what is meant by a representative of the Lord in goods and truths, and in their ministering [goods and truths]. By ministering goods and truths are meant goods and truths which are in the natural or external man, which are called knowledges and scientifics; for these are the things into which the internal man looks, and from which he chooses such things as confirm, which are in agreement with the life of his affections or his love; and whereas those things are thus subordinate, therefore they are called ministering things. There are also goods and truths again ministering to these latter, which are called scientific sensual [goods and truths]. For the goods and truths appertaining to man are as families, or as houses, where there is the father of the family, and where there are sons, daughters, sons-in-law and daughters-in-law, and men servants and maid servants; in the lowest place of the house or family are what are meant by sensual scientifics, although at this day with the generality they are in the highest place.

10,273. "And the altar of burnt-offering"—that hereby is signified to represent the Divine Human of the Lord, and His worship in general, appears from the representation of the altar of burnt-offering, as being a principal representative of the Divine Human of the Lord, and of the worship of Him, see n. 2777, 2811, 8935, 8940, 9388, 9389, 9714, 9964, 10,123, 10,151.

10,274. "And all its vessels"—that hereby is signified Divine Goods and Divine Truths, appears from the signification of vessels, as denoting knowledges and scientifics, see n. 3068, 3079, 9394, 9544, 9724; but when they are predicated of the Divine Human of the Lord, they denote Divine Goods and Divine Truths ministering.

10,275. "And the laver and its base"—that hereby are signified all things relating to purification from evils and falses, and to regeneration by the Lord, appears from the signification of the laver, in which washing was performed, as denoting what is purificatory from evils and falses, and also what is regeneratory, see n. 10,235; and from the signification of its base, as denoting the sensual principle sustaining and ministering, see n. 10,236.

10,276. "And shalt sanctify them, and they shall be the holy of holies"—that hereby is signified thus the influx and presence of the Lord in the worship of the representative church, appears from the signification of being sanctified, as denoting to represent the Lord as to the Divine Human and the reception of Divine Good and Divine Truth from Him ; for the Lord alone is holy, and hence that only is holy which proceeds from Him. Hence it is evident, that by being sanctified is also signified the influx and presence of the Lord in the worship of the representative church. That to be sanctified denotes to represent the Lord as to the Divine Human, see n. 9956, 9988, 10,069 ; and likewise the reception of Divine Good and Divine Truth from Him, n. 8806, 9820, 10,128. That the Lord alone is holy, and that that only is holy which proceeds from Him, n. 9229, 9479, 9680, 9818. Thus that the holy things appertaining to the Israelitish and Jewish nation were representatively holy, n. 10,149 ; and from the signification of the holy of holies, as denoting Divine Celestial Good, see n. 10,129. Hence it is evident that all those things which were anointed, were called the holy of holies from the influx and presence of the Divine Human of the Lord ; and all influx and presence of the Lord is effected immediately, and also in the inferior heavens mediately by [or through] celestial good, which is the good of the inmost heaven ; therefore so far as the goods of the inferior heavens contain and store up in them celestial good, which is the good of love to the Lord, so far they are goods. From this ground it is, that those things which were anointed were called the holy of holies ; concerning the immediate and mediate influx of the Lord, see the passages cited, n. 9682, and n. 9683. But to the intent that it may be known how the case herein is, it is to be noted what representation is, and what a representative church ; what they are, has been abundantly shown in the passages cited, n. 9229, 9280, 10,033. But whereas few at this day know what they are, it is allowed to illustrate the subject further in some respects. In the inmost heavens the affections of good and truth, from the Lord, appertaining to the angels, are what constitute their life, and their happiness ; these in the ultimate heaven are presented in external forms, which are innumerable, with infinite variety ; whatsoever they see there with their eyes is from this source. These things are representatives of interior things, which are the affections of good and of truth, and are called celestial and spiritual things ; the good spirits, who perceive in those things, as in subjects, the holy things of heaven, are interiorly affected. As for example, they see paradises with trees and fruits of innumerable species, in like manner beds of roses, grass-plats, fields with sown corn, houses and palaces, and several other things besides, all which correspond to the affections of good and of truth, which are from the Lord in the superior heavens ; there are also in these heavens representatives, but which immensely exceed in perfection, in delight, and in happiness, those things which are in the ultimate heaven ; these representatives are the things of which it is said, that no eye has ever seen such things; if any thing also was to be said concerning them, it would exceed human belief. From these considerations it may be manifest what representatives are; all things, which were instituted with the Israelitish nation, were similar to those which are in the ultimate heaven, but in less perfection, because in the nature of the world; as the tent with the ark, with the table on which were the breads of faces, with the candlestick and its lamps, with the altar of incense, the garments of Aaron and his sons, and afterwards the temple, with the secret place there containing the ark on which were the propitiatory and the cherubs; also the brazen sea, the lavers, and the like; nevertheless innumerable more things appear in the ultimate heaven, but in greater excellency and perfection. From that heaven the things which were to be instituted amongst the Israelitish nation were shown to Moses by the Lord in Mount Sinai, as is evident in Exod. chap. xxv. 40; chap. xxvi. 30; chap. xxvii. 8; howbeit they were not seen by Moses there with the eyes of his body, but with the eyes of his spirit. The nature and quality of representatives may be further manifest from the things which were seen by the prophets, as by Daniel, by John in the Apocalypse, and by the rest, all which things contain stored up in them Divine Spiritual and Celestial things; that these things are not intelligible without interpretation from the internal sense, may be manifest to every one. From these considerations it is now further evident what the representative church is. This church was established in the land of Canaan principally for the sake of the Word, that this might be written by representatives and significatives, thus by such things as appertained to that nation, being in their church, and in their land; for all places in the land of Canaan, all mountains and rivers there, from the most ancient times represented such things as are in the heavens, see n. 3686, 4240, 4447, 4454, 5136, 6516; and afterwards the inheritances, the tribes, and other things. The literal sense of the Word of the Old Testament was from such things, that there might be some ultimate into which interior things might close, and on which they might stand, as a building on its foundation, see n. 9360, 9824, 10,044. He who is intelligent may know from these considerations, that the Word is most holy, and that its literal sense is holy from its internal sense, but that separated from it, it is not holy; for the literal sense, separate from the internal, is as the external of man separate from his internal, which is an image of no life, and is as the rind of a tree, of a flower, of a fruit, or of a seed, without their interior principles, and as a foundation without a house; wherefore they who lay stress on the sense of the letter of the Word alone, neither have doctrine, or procure to themselves from the Word a doctrine suitable to its internal sense, may be drawn into any heresies whatsoever. Hence it is, that the Word is called by such a book of heresies; doctrine itself, derived from the Word, ought altogether to give previous light, and to guide. This doctrine is taught by the internal sense, and he who is acquainted with this doctrine has the internal sense of the Word. The Jewish nation, inasmuch as they did not acknowledge any holy principle in the Word, except in the mere sense of its letter, which they separated altogether from the internal sense, fell on this account into such darkness, that they did not know the Lord when he came into the world; such is also the quality of that nation at this day, wherefore although they live amongst Christians, still they do not yet acknowledge the Lord from the Word. That that nation was in external things without internal from the earliest time, see what has been shown in the passages cited, n. 9320, 9380. Wherefore unless the Lord had come into the world, and had opened the interiors of the Word, communication with the heavens by the Word would have been broken; and if this had been broken, the human race would have perished, for man can think nothing of truth, and do nothing of good, except from heaven, that is, by [or through] heaven from the Lord; the Word is what opens heaven.

10,277. "Every one that toucheth them shall be sanctified"—that hereby is signified communicative with all who receive in love and faith, appears from the signification of touching, as denoting communication, see n. 10,130; and from the signification of being sanctified, as denoting the influx and presence of the Lord, see just above, n. 10,273; and whereas the influx and presence of the Lord is in love and faith, thus with those who receive Him with love and faith, hence they are such as are here called sanctified; but it is the Divine appertaining to them which alone is holy, and not at all their proprium.

10,278. "And Aaron and his sons thou shalt anoint"—that hereby is signified inauguration to represent the Lord in both kingdoms, appears from the signification of anointing, as denoting to induce representation, as above; and from the representation of Aaron, as denoting the Lord as to Divine Celestial Good, thus in the celestial kingdom; and from the representation of the sons of Aaron, as denoting the Lord as to spiritual good, thus in the spiritual kingdom, see n. 9807, 10,017, 10,068.

10,279. "And shalt sanctify them to perform the office of the priesthood to Me"—that hereby is signified to represent the Lord as to all the work of salvation, appears from the signification of sanctifying, as denoting to represent the Lord as to the Divine Human, see above, n. 10,273; and from the representation of the priesthood of Aaron and of his sons, as denoting the work of the salvation of the Lord in successive order, see n. 9809, 10,017.

10,280. "And thou shalt speak to the sons of Israel, saying"—that hereby is signified instruction for those who are of the church, appears from the signification of the sons of Israel, as denoting the church, see the passages cited, n. 9340; and from the signification of speaking and saying when from Jehovah, as denoting instruction, see n. 6879, 6881, 6889, 6891, 7186, 7226, 7241, 7267, 7304, 7380, 7517, 8127.

10,281. "This shall be to Me the oil of anointing of holiness"—that hereby is signified a representative of the Lord as to the Divine Human, appears from what was shown above, n. 10,266.

10,282. "To your generations"—that hereby is signified in all things of the church, appears from the signification of generations, when concerning the sons of Israel, by whom is signified the church, as denoting those who are of the church, see n. 10,212; thus abstractedly from persons, the things which are of the church. It is said abstractedly from persons, because the Divine things which proceed from the Lord, make the church, and nothing at all of man; they flow in indeed with man, nevertheless they are not man's, but are of the Lord with man. This being the case, the angels, in discoursing one amongst another, discourse abstractedly from persons. Therefore neither does the name of any person, of whom mention is made in the Word, enter heaven, but the thing which is there signified by the person. That all names of persons and of places in the Word signify things, see n. 1888, 4442, 5905, 5225; and that names do not enter heaven, n. 1876, 6516, 10,216.

10,283. "On the flesh of man it shall not be poured"—that hereby is signified non-communicative with the proprium of man, appears from the signification of the flesh of man, as denoting his proprium, of which we shall speak presently; and from the signification of pouring, as denoting to communicate; for the like is signified by pouring as by touching, but to pour is predicated of liquids, as of oil, wine and water, and to pour forth of things Divine, celestial, and spiritual; whereas to touch is predicated of things dry and corporeal; that the touch denotes to communicate, see n. 10,130. Hence it follows, that by the oil of anointing not being to be poured on the flesh of man, is signified that the Divine Good of the Divine Love of the Lord is not communicative with the proprium of man; the reason is, because the proprium of man is nothing but evil, and the Divine Good of the Lord cannot be communicated with evil. That the proprium of man is nothing but evil, see n. 210, 215, 731, 874, 875, 876, 987, 1023, 1024, 1047, 5660, 5786, 8480. There is appertaining to man the voluntary proprium, and the intellectual proprium; his voluntary proprium is evil, and his intellectual proprium is the false principle thence derived; the former, namely, the voluntary proprium, is signified by the flesh of man, and the intellectual proprium by the blood of that flesh. That this is the case, is manifest from the following passages, "Jesus said, blessed art thou, Simon, *because flesh and blood hath not revealed it to thee*, but My Father Who is in the heavens," Matt. xvi. 17. That flesh here denotes the proprium of man, and also blood, is very evident. And in John, "As many as received, to them gave He power that they should be the sons of God, who were born, *not of bloods, nor of the will of the flesh*, but of God," i. 12, 13. By bloods are there signified the falses which proceed from the intellectual proprium of man, and by the will of the flesh, the evils which are from the voluntary proprium. That blood denotes what is false derived from evil, thus the intellectual proprium derived from the voluntary proprium, see n. 4735, 9127. And in Isaiah, "I will feed thine oppressors *with their flesh, and they shall be* drunken *with their blood* as with new wine," xlix. 26; where to feed them with their flesh, and to make them drunken with their blood, denotes to fill them full of evil and the falses of evil, thus of the proprium, for each, as well what is evil as what is false, is from the proprium. And in Jeremiah, "Cursed is the man who confideth in man, and *maketh flesh his arm*," xvii. 5. To confide in man, and to make flesh his arm, denotes to trust to himself and to his proprium. And in Isaiah, "The people is become as the food of fire; if he fall off to the right hand he shall hunger, and if he eat to the left hand they shall not be satisfied; *a man shall devour the flesh of his arm;* Manasseh Ephraim, and Ephraim Manasseh," ix. 19, 20; by the food of fire is signified the appropriation of evils or of the lust of the love of self and of the world; by being hungry and not being satisfied is signified not to receive the good and truth of faith; by the flesh of the arm each proprium of man; by Manasseh, evil of the will, by Ephraim, the false of the understanding; and by devouring, appropriation. That fires denote evils or the lusts of the love of self and of the world, see n. 5071, 5215, 6314, 6832, 7324, 7575, 9041. The reason why being hungry and not being satisfied denotes not to receive the good and truth of faith is, because by hunger and by thirst is signified the desolation of good and of truth, n. 5360, 5376, 6110, 7102, 8568; that the right hand denotes good from which truth is derived, and the left hand truth productive of good, see n. 10,061; hence to hunger if he fall off to the right hand, and not to be satisfied if he devour to the left hand, signifies that howsoever they are instructed concerning good and truth, still they would not receive. That Manasseh denotes the good of the will, see n. 5351, 5353, 6222, 6234, 6238, 6267, and Ephraim the truth of the understanding, n. 3969, 5354, 6222, 6234, 6238, 6267; hence in the opposite sense Manasseh denotes evil of the will, and Ephraim the false of the understanding, for almost all things in the Word have also an opposite sense. That to devour [or eat] denotes to appropriate, see n. 3168, 3513, 3596, 4745. Hence it is evident what is meant by devouring the flesh of his arm, namely, that it denotes to appropriate to themselves what is evil and false derived from their own proprium. It is said the flesh of the arm, because by the arm, in like manner as by the hand, is signified that which appertains to man, and on which he confides, see the passages cited, n. 10,019. And in Zechariah, "I said, I will not feed you, dying let him die, *let the rest eat every one the flesh of another*," xi. 9; not to feed denotes not to instruct and reform; to die denotes to perish as to spiritual life; to eat the flesh of another denotes to appropriate to themselves the evils which are from the proprium of another. And in Ezekiel, "Jerusalem hath committed whoredom with the sons of Egypt her neighbors *great in flesh*," xvi. 26; Jerusalem denotes the perverse church; to commit whoredom with the sons of Egypt great in flesh denotes to falsify the truths of the church by scientifics which are from the natural man alone, thus by sensual scientifics; that Jerusalem denotes the church, see n. 402, 2117, 3654, in this case the perverse church; that to commit whoredom denotes to falsify truths, n. 2466, 2729, 8904; that sons denote truths and also falses, n. 1147, 3373, 4257, 9807; that Egypt denotes the scientific principle in both senses, see the passages cited, n. 9340; and that it denotes the natural principle, see the passages cited, n. 9391; hence they are called great in flesh, who reason and conclude from sensual things concerning the truths of the church; they who do this, seize upon falses instead of truths, for to reason and conclude from sensual things is to reason and conclude from the fallacies of the bodily senses; wherefore they are sensual men who are meant by great in flesh, since they think from the corporeal proprium. And in Isaiah, "Egypt is man, not God; *and his horses are flesh, not spirit*," xxxi. 3; Egypt also in this passage denotes the scientific principle, his horses the intellectual principle thence derived; this is called flesh not spirit, when they form conclusions from the proprium and not from the Divine. That horses denote the intellectual principle, see n. 2761, 2762, 3217, 5321, 6534; and that the horses of Egypt denote the scientifics grounded in a perverse intellectual principle, n. 6125, 8146, 8148. That by flesh is signified the proprium of man, or what is the same thing, his voluntary evil, is manifest from Moses, where the subject treated of is the desire of the Israelitish people to eat flesh, of which it is thus written, "The rabble which was in the midst of the people, *lusted concupiscence*, and said, *who will feed us with flesh:* Jehovah said, to-morrow *ye shall eat flesh;* ye shall not eat it one day, nor two days, nor five days, nor ten days, nor twenty days, even to a month of days. And a wind went forth from Jehovah and brought *quails from the sea*, and let them down upon the camp, as it were of two cubits on the faces of the earth. The people arose the whole day and the whole night, and the whole morrow, and gathered and spread them round about the camp. The flesh was yet between their teeth before it was swallowed, and the anger of Jehovah burned into the people, and smote in the people an exceeding great plague; whence he called the name of the place the *sepulchres of concupiscence*," Num. xi. 4, 18, 19, 20, 31, 32, 33. That flesh signified the proprium of that nation, may be manifest from all things in the above passage; for unless this had been the case, what evil could there have been in desiring flesh, when also flesh was before promised them, Exod. xvi. 12; but whereas it signified the proprium, thus the voluntary evil, in which that nation was principled more than other nations, therefore it is said, when they desired flesh, that they lusted concupiscence; and on this account they were smitten with a great plague; and therefore the name of the place where they were buried, was called the sepulchres of concupiscences; whether we speak of voluntary evil, or of concupiscence, it is the same thing, for voluntary evil is concupiscence, since the proprium of man desires nothing but its own, and not any thing of the neighbor, or any thing of God, except for the sake of itself. Inasmuch as that nation was of such a character, therefore it is said that they should eat flesh, not one day, nor two, nor five, nor ten, nor twenty, but a month of days, by which is signified that that nation is of such a character for ever, for a month of days denotes for ever, and therefore it is said, that the flesh being yet between their teeth, before it was swallowed, they were smitten with a great plague, for by the teeth is signified the corporeal proprium, which is the lowest principle of man, n. 442, 4424, 5565 to 5568, 9062. That that nation was of such a character, see in the passages cited, n. 9380; and in the song of Moses, Deut. xxxii. 20 to 28, 32 to 34. In the Word, the spirit is opposed to the flesh, since by the spirit is signified life from the Lord, and by the flesh life from man; as in John, "*It is the spirit which vivifies, the flesh profiteth nothing;* the words which I speak to you *are spirit and are life*," vi. 63. Hence it is manifest, that spirit denotes life from the Lord, which is the life of love and faith to Him from Him, and that flesh denotes life from man, thus his proprium. Hence it is said, the flesh profiteth nothing, in like manner in another passage in John, "*That which is born of the flesh, is flesh*, but that *which is generated from the spirit, is spirit*," iii. 6. And in David, "God remembered *that they were flesh; the spirit which went away would not return*," Psalm lxxviii. 39. Since by flesh, when predicated of man, is signified the proprium, which is the evil of the love of self and the world, it is evident what is signified by flesh, when predicated of the Lord, namely, His proprium, which is the Divine Good of the Divine Love; this is signified by the flesh of the Lord in John, "The bread which I shall give, *is my flesh. Unless ye shall eat the flesh of the Son of Man, and shall drink His blood*, ye shall not have life in you. *He who eateth My flesh, and drinketh My blood*, hath eternal life; *for My flesh is truly meat, and My blood is truly drink*," v. 51, 53, 54, 55. That by the flesh of the Lord is signified the Divine Good of His Divine Love, and by blood the Divine Truth proceeding from that Divine Good, thus similar things as by the bread and wine in the holy supper, and that those things are the propriums in His Divine Human, see n. 1001, 3813, 4735, 4978, 7317, 7326, 7850, 9127, 9393, 10,026, 10,032, 10,152. And that the sacrifices represented the good things which are from the Lord, and that on this account their flesh signified good things, see n. 10,040, 10,079. Moreover, in the Word throughout mention is made of all flesh, and by it is meant every man, as Gen. vi. 12, 13, 17, 19; Isaiah xl. 5, 6; chap. xlix. 26; chap. lxvi. 16, 23, 24; Jer. xxv. 31; chap. xxxii. 27; chap. xlv. 5; Ezek. xx. 48; chap. xxi. 4, 5; and elsewhere.

10,284. "And in its quality ye shall not make like it"—that hereby is signified non-imitation from the study of man, appears from the signification of making in quality like it, or of making like oil by like aromatics, as denoting to procure for imitation from the study of man; that these things are signified by those words follows from the series of things in the internal sense; for it is said first, that it should not be poured upon the flesh of man, by which is signified that it is non-communicative with the proprium of man; and next that it shall be holy to you; whereas that which is made from man, and from his study, is made from his proprium, and is not holy, because study from the proprium of man is nothing but what is false derived from what is evil, for it respects itself and the world for an end, and not the neighbor and God; therefore it is called imitation. The case herein is this; all that is good and true, which is from the Lord; but the good and truth made in imitation thereof by man, is not good and true; the reason is, because every thing good and true has life in it from an end; an end from man is only for the sake of himself; but what is good and true from the Lord is for the sake of good itself and truth as ends, thus for the sake of the Lord, since from the Lord is all good and truth. The end appertaining to man is the man himself, for it is his will, and his love; for what a man loves and what he wills, this he regards as an end; all love appertaining to man from man is the love of self, and the love of the world for the sake of self; but the love appertaining to man from the Lord is love towards the neighbor and love to God. The difference between those loves is as great as between hell and heaven; and likewise the love of self, and the love of the world for the sake of self, reign in hell, and are hell; whereas love towards the neighbor, and love to the Lord reign in heaven, and are heaven; man also is such, and remains such to eternity, as his love is; for love is the all of man's will, and hence of his understanding, since the love which makes the will, continually flows-in into the understanding, enkindling it, and illustrating it; hence it is that they who love evil think what is false in conformity with that love, and derived from it, when they think with themselves, although they speak otherwise before men from hypocrisy, and some from persuasive faith, the quality of which may be seen n. 9360, 9369. It is to be noted that man can from study imitate Divine things themselves, and present himself before men as an angel of light; but before the Lord, and before the angels, the external form does not appear, but the internal, which, when it is from the proprium, is filthy; inwardly appertaining to such persons is a mere natural principle, and nothing spiritual: they see only from natural light, and not at all from the light of heaven, yea, neither do they know what the light of heaven is, and what a spiritual principle is, for all their interiors are turned outwards and almost like the interiors of animals, nor do they suffer themselves to be elevated upwards by the Lord; when yet man has this peculiar privilege above the beasts, that he is capable of being elevated to heaven, and to the Lord from the Lord, and of thus being led; all those are so elevated, who love what is good and true for the sake of what is good and true, which is the same thing as loving the neighbor and God; for the neighbor in the general sense is what is good and true, and in an inferior sense is what is just and right; and likewise God is what is good and true, and what is just and right, since those principles are from God. From these considerations it may be manifest what it is to imitate Divine things from the study of man. What is the quality of such persons, is described in the Word throughout by Egypt and Pharaoh, for by Egypt and Pharaoh are signified the scientifics which are of the natural man; it is likewise described by Ashur, by whom is signified reasoning from scientifics. Concerning Egypt, see the passages cited, n. 9340, 9391; and concerning Ashur, n. 1186. Amongst spirits there are great numbers who imitate Divine things by study and art; for they pretend things sincere, upright, and pious, insomuch that the good spirits would be seduced, unless the Lord enlightened them, and made them see their interiors, at the appearance of which the good are seized with horror, and fly away; but spirits of this description are stripped of their externals, and let into their interiors, which are diabolical, and thus of themselves they sink down into hell. More may be seen concerning these spirits in the following article, n. 10,286.

10,285. "It shall be holy to you"—that hereby is signified because the Divine of the Lord, appears from the signification of holy, when concerning the oil of anointing, as denoting the Divine of the Lord; for the oil of anointing was representative of the Divine Good of the Divine Love in the Divine Human of the Lord, thus is representative of His Divine Human principle; for whether we speak of the Divine Good of the Divine Love, or of the Divine Human, it is the same thing. Inasmuch as this was signified by the oil of anointing, and was represented by anointing, and this alone is holy, and hence what proceeds from Him is holy, because it is of Him, therefore it is so often said, that it is holy, see also above, n. 10,266.

10,286. "The man who shall make ointment like it"—that hereby is signified the imitation of Divine things from art, appears from the signification of making like it, as denoting imitation; and from the signification of ointment, as denoting Divine Truths which are of the Lord alone, and from the Lord alone, see above, n. 10,264. The reason why imitation from art is signified, is, because all imitation of things Divine by man is effected from art. How the case herein is, may be manifest from what was said and shown above, n. 10,284. But these things may be further illustrated by those which have place amongst spirits; such of them as attribute all things to fortune, and to their own prudence, and nothing to the Divine, as they have done in the world, have the skill to imitate Divine things by various methods; for they present to view palaces almost like those in the heavens, also groves and rural objects nearly resembling those presented by the Lord amongst good spirits; they adorn themselves with shining garments, yea, the syrens also induce a beauty almost angelical; but all these things are the effect of art by phantasies; nevertheless, howsoever like they appear in the external form, still in the internal they are filthy; which also is instantly made manifest to good spirits by the Lord, for unless it was manifested, they would be seduced; for what is external is taken away, and when this is the case, the diabolical principle within is extant. It is taken away by light let in upon it from heaven, by virtue whereof the delusive lumen, which is of phantasies, by which they produce such effects, is dispersed. Hence it may be manifest what is the nature of imitation of Divine things from art. But those things which are from the Lord are inwardly celestial, and the more interior, so much the more celestial, for Divine things increase in perfection towards interiors, until at length they are of ineffable perfection and beauty. The case is similar with the imitation of what is good and true amongst those who live evilly. Such of them as have the skill to assume a semblance of good affections, and of somewhat of charity towards the neighbor, and of love to God, and together with those affections speak and preach the truths of faith as from the heart, are in a like delusive and fantastic lumen; wherefore when the external principle is taken away from them, which make a pretence or what is internal, the infernal principle appears, which lay inwardly concealed, which is mere evil, and the false of evil; and in this case it is in like manner presented to view, that that evil is their love, and the false of that evil their faith. From these considerations it is further evident what the imitation of things Divine from the study of man is, treated of above, n. 10,281.

10,287. "And he who shall give of it upon a stranger"—that hereby is signified conjunction with those who do not acknowledge the Lord, thus who are in evils, and in the falses of evil, appears from the signification of giving upon any one, when concerning Divine Truths, which are signified by the aromatic ointment, as denoting to conjoin; and from the signification of a stranger, as denoting one who is not of the church, thus who does not acknowledge the Lord, and hence who is in evils and falses; for he who does not acknowledge the Lord, is not of the church; and he who denies the Lord, is in evils and falses, for what is good and true comes from no other source than from Him. That strangers signify such, will be manifest from the passages in the Word which will follow; but it may be expedient first to say something concerning the conjunction of Divine Truth with those who do not acknowledge the Lord. This conjunction is profanation, for profanation is the conjunction of Divine Truth with falses derived from evil; and this conjunction, which is profanation, is not given with any others but those who have first acknowledged those things which are of the church, and especially the Lord, and afterwards deny the same; for by the acknowledgment of the truths of the church and of the Lord, communication is effected with the heavens, and hence the opening of the interiors of man towards heaven; and by denial afterwards is effected the conjunction of the same with falses derived from evil; for all things which man acknowledges remain implanted, since nothing perishes with man which has entered by acknowledgment. The state of the man who is a subject of profanation, is, that he has communication with the heavens, and at the same time with the hells, by truths with the heavens, and by the falses of evil with the hells; hence in the other life is effected their dilaceration, whereby every thing of interior life perishes. They appear after dilaceration scarce as men any longer, but as burnt bones, in which is little of life, see what has been before said and shown concerning profanation, namely, that they profane who have first acknowledged Divine Truths, and afterwards deny them, n. 1001, 1010, 1059, 2051, 3398, 4289, 4601, 6348,

6960, 6963, 6971, 8394. That they who have denied those things from infancy, as the Jews and others, do not profane, n. 593, 1001, 1010, 1059, 3398, 3489, 6963. And that the greatest heed is taken by the Lord to prevent profanation being effected by man, n. 301, 302, 303, 1327, 1328, 2426, 3398, 3402, 3499, 6955. But it is to be noted, that there are very many genera of profanations, and very many species of those genera; for there are those who profane the goods of the church, and there are those who profane its truth; there are those who profane much, and there are those who profane little; there are those who profane interiorly, and there are those who profane more exteriorly; there are those who profane by faith against the truths and goods of the church, there are who profane by life, and there are who profane by worship. Hence are given several hells of profaners, which are distinct from each other according to the diversities of profanations. The hells of the profanations of good are to the back; but the hells of the profanations of truth are under the feet and to the sides; they are deeper than the hells of all other evils, and are seldom opened. That strangers denote those who do not acknowledge the Lord, and are unwilling to acknowledge, whether they be out of the church, or within it, thus who are in evils, and in the falses of evil, and in the sense abstracted from persons, that they denote evils and the falses of evil, is manifest from several passages in the Word. It is said, who do not acknowledge the Lord, thus who are in evils and the falses of evil, since they who do not acknowledge the Lord, must needs be in evils and the falses of evil, for from the Lord is every good and truth of good; wherefore they, who deny the Lord, are in evils and the falses of evil, according to the Lord's words in John, "*Unless ye believe that I am, ye shall die in your sins,*" viii. 24. That these are strangers, is manifest from the following passages in Isaiah, "Your land is a desert, your cities are burned with fire; *your ground before you strangers shall devour;* and the desert shall be *as the overthrow of strangers,*" i. 7; by land in this passage is not meant land nor by cities and by ground cities and ground; but by land is meant the church, in like manner by ground, and by cities the truths of the church, which are called doctrinals, and which are said to be burned with fire, when they are consumed by the evils of the loves of self and the world; hence it is evident what is signified by strangers devouring the ground, namely, evils and the falses of evil the church; and by the land being a desert. That land [or earth] denotes the church, see the passages cited, n. 9325; and that ground in like manner, n. 566, 1068; that cities denote the doctrinals of the church, thus its truths, n. 2268, 2450, 2712, 2943, 3126, 4492, 4493, and fire the evils of the loves of self and the world, n. 1297, 1861, 2446, 5071, 5215, 6314, 6832, 7575, 9041. And in Jeremiah, "He covered our faces with ignominy, *when strangers came against the sanctuaries of the house of Jehovah*," li. 51. Strangers against the sanctuaries of the house of Jehovah, denote evils and the falses of evil against the truths and goods of the church; those of the nations were called strangers who served in the Jewish Church, and by the nations of that land are also signified evils and falses, n. 9320. Again, in the same prophet, "Thou sayest there is no hope, none; but *I will love strangers, and will go after them*," ii. 25; to love strangers and to go after them, denotes to love evils and the falses of evil, and to worship them. And in Ezekiel, "I will bring the sword upon you, and *will give you into the hand of strangers*," xi. 8, 9; where to bring a sword denotes falses from evil fighting against truths derived from good; to give into the hand of strangers denotes that they should believe and serve those falses. That a sword denotes truth combating against falses, and in the opposite sense the falses combating against truths, see n. 2799, 6353, 7102, 8294. Again, "By the deaths of the uncircumcised thou shalt die, *in the hand of strangers*," xxviii. 10; the uncircumcised denote those who are in filthy loves and their lusts as to life, howsoever they may be in doctrinals, n. 2049, 3412, 3413, 4462, 7045, 7225, whose death is spiritual death; in the hand of strangers denotes in evils themselves and the falses of evils. Again, "Jerusalem is an adulterous woman, under her man [*vir*], *she receiveth strangers*," xvi. 32; Jerusalem an adulterous woman denotes the church wherein good is adulterated; to receive strangers denotes to acknowledge evils and the falses of evil in life and doctrine. And in Joel, "Jerusalem shall be holiness, *neither shall strangers pass through it any more*," iii. 17; Jerusalem also in this passage denotes the church, but in which the Lord is acknowledged: the life is formed by the good, and faith by the truths which are from the Lord; strangers not passing through it any more denote evils and the falses of evil which are from hell, that they shall not enter. And in David, "*Strangers have risen against me*, and the violent have sought my soul," Psalm liv. 3; strangers also here denote evils and the falses of evil; the violent denote the same offering violence to goods and truths; they who look at the sense of the letter of the Word alone, understand nothing else by strangers but those who are out of the church, and that they rose up against David; nevertheless there does not any thing of person enter into the heavens, but the things which are signified, n. 8343, 8985, 9007; thus not strangers, but instead of them, strange things, which are those that are alienated from the church, thus evils and the falses of evil, which destroy the church; by David also, against whom they arose, is perceived the Lord, n. 1888, 9954. And in Moses, "He hath forsaken the God who made him, and made light of the rock of his salvation; *they provoked him to zeal by strangers*,"

Deut. xxxii. 15, 16; to forsake God, and to make light of the rock of salvation, denotes to deny the Lord; to provoke by strangers, denotes by evils and the falses of evil. That a rock denotes the Lord as to the truths of faith, see n. 8581. Moreover also in other places strangers denote evils and falses, as Isaiah xxv. 2, 5; Jer. xxx. 8; Ezek. xxxi. 11, 12. Since strangers signified those who are in evils and the falses of evil, therefore it was forbidden *that a stranger should eat the holy things*, Levit. xxii. 10; that *a stranger shall approach to the office of the priesthood*, or to *the guard of the sanctuary;* and if he came near, that he should be slain, Numb. i. 51; chap. iii. 10, 38; chap. xviii. 7. It was also forbidden *to burn incense from strange fire*, on which account Nadab and Abihu, the sons of Aaron, were consumed by fire from heaven, Levit. x. 1, 2; for by the holy fire which was from the altar, was signified Divine Love, but by strange fire, infernal love, and hence also evils and their lusts, see n. 1297, 1861, 2446, 5071, 5215, 6314, 6832, 7575, 9041. Mention is also made of strangers [*alienigenae*], expressed in the original tongue by another term than strangers [*alieni*], and by them are signified falses themselves, as in the Lamentations, "O Jehovah, have respect to our ignominy; our inheritance is *turned away to strangers* [alienos], and our houses to *strangers* [alienigenae]," v. 1, 2. And in Obadiah, "*Strangers* [alieni] have led captive his strength, and *strangers* [alienigenae] have entered his gates, and upon Jerusalem they shall cast a lot," verse 11. To cast a lot upon Jerusalem denotes to destroy the church, and to dissipate its truths. And in Zephaniah, "I will visit upon the princes and upon the sons of the king, *and upon all that are clothed in the clothing of a stranger* [alienigenae,]" i. 8. Clothed in the clothing of a stranger denote those who are in falses; for princes and the sons of a king, upon whom was visitation, denote primary truths, and, in the opposite sense, primary falses. That princes have this signification, see n. 1482, 2089, 5044. That kings denote truths themselves, and, in the opposite sense, falses themselves, n. 2015, 2069, 3009, 4581, 4966, 5044, 5068, 6148. Hence the sons of a king denote the things thence derived. And in David, "Deliver me, and snatch me *from the hands of the son of a stranger* [alienigenae]; whose mouth speaketh vanity, and their right hand is the right hand of a lie," Psalm cxliv. 7, 8, 11. That the sons of a stranger [*alienigenae*] denote those who are in falses, thus falses, is very manifest, for it is said, whose mouth speaketh vanity, and their right hand is the right hand of a lie; for vanity is falsity of doctrine, and a lie is the false [principle] of life, n. 9248.

10,288. "Shall be cut off from his people"—that hereby is signified separation and spiritual death, appears from the signification of being cut off and slain, as denoting to be separated from those who are in good and the truths thence derived, and to perish as to spiritual life, see n. 6767, 8902; and from the signification of people, as denoting those of the church who are in the truths and goods of faith, see n. 3581, 4619, 6451, 6464, 7207; thus to be cut off from the people, denotes to be separated from them and to perish. They who are of the church, are called in the Word sometimes a people, sometimes a nation, as the Israelitish people, and the Judaic nation; by people are there signified those who are of the spiritual church, and by nation those who are of the celestial church; hence it is that people signify the truths and goods of faith, but nations the goods of love, see the passages just now cited.

10,289. Verses 34, 35, 36, 37, 38. *And Jehovah said to Moses, take to thee fragrant spices, stacte, and onycha, and galbanum [which are] fragrant, and pure frankincense; so much shall be in so much. And thou shalt make it incense, an ointment the work of an ointment-dealer, salted, pure, holy. And thou shalt bruise of it into small pieces, and shall give of it before the testimony in the tent of the congregation, where I will meet thee there, the holy of holies it shall be to you. And the incense which thou makest in its quality, ye shall not make to yourselves; it shall be holy to thee to Jehovah. The man* [vir] *who shall make like it, to make an odor with it, shall be cut off from his people.* And Jehovah said to Moses, signifies illustration and perception again by the Word from the Lord. Take to thee fragrant spices, signifies the affections of truth derived from good which shall be in Divine Worship. Stacte, signifies the affection of sensual truth; and onycha, the affection of interior natural truth; and galbanum, the affection of truth still more interior. Fragrant, signifies affections derived from spiritual good; and pure frankincense, inmost truth, which is spiritual good. So much shall be in so much, signifies all manner of correspondence. And thou shalt make it incense, signifies worship from those principles. An ointment, the work of an ointment-dealer, signifies from the influx and operation of the Divine of the Lord into all and singular things. Salted, signifies the desire of truth to good. Pure, signifies without evil. Holy, signifies without the false of evil. And thou shalt bruise of into small pieces, signifies the arrangement of truths into their series. And thou shalt give of it before the testimony in the tent of the congregation, signifies the worship of the Lord in heaven and the church. Where I will meet thee there, signifies from the influx of the Lord. The holy of holies it shall be to you, signifies since from the Lord. And the incense which thou makest, in its quality ye shall not make to yourselves, signifies that worship derived from the holy truths of the church ought not to be applied to the loves of man. It shall be holy to thee to Jehovah, signifies that worship ought to be applied to Divine Love. The man who shall make like it to make odor with it, signifies imitation of Divine Worship by the affections of truth and good derived from the proprium. Shall be cut off from his people, signifies separation from heaven and the church, and spiritual death.

10,290. "And Jehovah said to Moses"—that hereby is signified illustration and perception again by the Word from the Lord, appears from the signification of saying, when concerning Jehovah, as denoting illustration and perception; that it denotes illustration, see n. 7019, 10,215, 10,234; and that it denotes perception, n. 1791, 1815, 1819, 1822, 1898, 1919, 2080, 2862, 3509, 5877; and from the representation of Moses, as denoting the Word, see n. 6752, 7014, 7089; and that Jehovah in the Word denotes the Lord, see the passages cited, n. 9373. Hence it is evident that by Jehovah said to Moses is signified illustration and perception by the Word from the Lord. The reason why these things are signified is, because the Lord speaks with the man of the church no otherwise than by the Word, for on such occasion He illustrates man, so as to enable him to see the truth, and He also gives perception that man may perceive that it is so; but this is effected according to the quality of the desire of truth with man, and the desire of truth with man is according to the love of it; they who love truth for the sake of truth are in illustration, and they who love truth for the sake of good are in perception. What perception is, may be seen, n. 483, 495, 521, 536, 597, 607, 784, 1121, 1387, 1919, 2144, 2145, 2171, 2515, 2831, 5227, 5920, 7680, 7977, 8780. But the Lord spake with Moses and the prophets by a living voice, to the intent that the Word might be promulgated, that it was of such a quality as to contain an internal sense in all and singular things; hence also these words, *Jehovah said to Moses*. The angels, who are in the internal sense, do not know what Moses is, since the names of persons do not enter heaven, n. 10,282, but instead of Moses they perceive the Word, and the expression *to say* is turned with them into what is congruous, thus in the present instance, into being illustrated and perceiving; saying and speaking also, when from the Lord by the Word, in the angelic idea, have no other meaning.

10,291. "Take to thee fragrant spices"—that hereby are signified the affections of truth derived from good, which ought to be in Divine Worship, appears from the signification of spices, as denoting the perceptions and affections of truth and good, see n. 10,254. The reason why it denotes which ought to be in Divine Worship is, because by the incense, which was prepared from them, is signified Divine Worship, of which we shall speak presently. The spices which are now mentioned, are altogether of another kind than the spices from which the oil of anointing was prepared, spoken of above, in verses 23,

24; those are also called spices, but in the original tongue they are expressed by another term. Those spices, from which the oil of anointing was prepared, signify in like manner the perceptions and affections of truth and good like these spices, but with this difference, that the former truths belong to the celestial class, but the latter to the spiritual class; that the former truths belong to the celestial class, see n. 10,254; that the latter truths belong to the spiritual class, will be seen in what follows. It may be expedient to say briefly what is meant by belonging to the celestial class, and to the spiritual class; it has been often said that heaven is distinguished into the celestial kingdom and into the spiritual kingdom; in each kingdom there is a difference of truths as of goods; the good of the celestial kingdom is the good of love to the Lord; and the good of the spiritual kingdom is the good of charity towards the neighbor; every good has its own truths, celestial good its own, and spiritual good its own, which are altogether different from each other; what the quality of the difference is, may be manifest from what was shown concerning each kingdom in the passages cited, n. 9277. The reason why every good has its own truths is, because good is formed by truths, see n. 10,252, 10,266, and also manifests itself by truths. Those principles are like the voluntary and intellectual principles appertaining to man; his voluntary principle is formed by the intellectual and also manifests itself by it. What is of the will is called good, and what is of the understanding is called truth.

10,292. "Stacte"—that hereby is signified the affection of sensual truth, appears from the signification of stacte, as denoting sensual truth; that it denotes the affection of that truth, is owing to its fragrance; for odor signifies what is perceptive, a fragrant odor what is gratefully perceptive, and a disagreeble stinking odor what is ungratefully perceptive; and all that is grateful and ungrateful of perception is from the affection which is of love, and according to it, see n. 925, 1514, 1517, 1518, 1519, 3577, 4624 to 4634, 4748, 5621, 10,054. In general it is to be noted, that all things whatsoever in the vegetable kingdom, whether they be the productions of forests, or of gardens, fields, plains, as trees, sown corn, flowers, grasses, and pulse, both generally and specifically, signify things spiritual and celestial; the reason of this is, because universal nature is a theatre representative of the Lord's kingdom, see the passages cited, n. 9280. The reason why stacte denotes the affection of sensual truth is, because it is named in the first place; for there are four spices from which the incense was prepared, as there were also four spices from which the oil of anointing was prepared; and that which was named in the first place, is the most external; as what was named in the first place for the preparation of the oil of anointing, which was the best myrrh. That this denotes the perception of sensual truth, see above, n. 10,252. The reason why four spices were taken for the preparation both of the oil and of the incense was, because they signified truths in their order from what is external to what is internal; and with man they also have such a succession; for man has an external principle which is called the external man, and an internal principle which is called the internal man, and in each there is what is exterior and interior; the most external principle is called sensual; this therefore is what is signified by stacte. What the sensual principle is, and what is its quality, see n. 9996, 10,236. That stacte denotes the affection of sensual truth, cannot be confirmed from other passages in the Word, because it is no where else mentioned; but stacte of another kind, which is also expressed by another term in the original tongue, is mentioned amongst those spices which were brought down into Egypt, Gen. chap. xxxvii. 25; chap. xliii. 11. And those things which were brought down into Egypt involve such as are in the external or natural man, since by Egypt is signified the scientific principle, which is of the natural man, see the passages cited, n. 9391.

10,293. "And onycha"—that hereby is signified the affection of interior natural truth, appears from the signification of fragrant onycha, as denoting the affection of natural truth; by onycha is signified that truth, and by fragrant the perceptivity of what is grateful, which is from the affection of truth, thus the affection itself. It is called fragrant onycha, because it is said above and after the enumeration of these spices, in these words, take to thee *fragrant spices*, stacte and onycha, and galbanum, *that are fragrant*. The reason why it is the affection of truth in the natural principle, which is signified by onycha, is, because it is named in the second place; for the spices are named in order according to the truths appertaining to man from the most external to the inmost. Hence it is that by stacte is signified the affection of sensual truth, which is truth the most external, by onycha the affection of natural truth, which is interior truth in the natural man, by galbanum the affection of truth still more interior, which truth is interior truth in the spiritual or internal man, and by frankincense inmost truth in the internal man, which is spiritual good; in like manner as was signified by the spices from which the oil of anointing was prepared, which was the best myrrh, aromatic cinnamon, aromatic calamus and cassia; that those spices signified truths in such an order, see n. 10,252, 10,254, 10,256, 10,258; but that the difference is, that those truths which are signified by the spices of the oil of anointing, belong to the celestial class, whereas these truths which are signified by the spices of the incense, belong to the spiritual class, on which subject see above, n. 10,254, 10,290.

10,294. "And galbanum"—that hereby is signified the affection of truth still more interior, appears from what was said just above, n. 10,293. That onycha and galbanum denote truths successively interior, cannot otherwise be confirmed than from order, since they do not occur in the Word elsewhere.

10,295. "That are fragrant"—that hereby are signified affections from spiritual good, appears from the signification of fragrant spices, as denoting the affections of truth derived from good, see above, n. 10,291: that it is from spiritual good, see n. 10,254, 10,290, 10,293. The reason why the incense was wrought from spices, which signified truths derived from spiritual good, or what is the same thing, why the truths which are signified by those spices belong to the spiritual class, is, because by incense is signified Divine Worship which is effected by truths derived from that good, for confessions, adorations, prayers, and the like, are what are specifically signified by incense, see n. 9475. Such things come forth from the heart by the thoughts and by the speech; that this worship is effected by spiritual truths, may be manifest from the ideas which influence man when in that worship, for the ideas, in which man is on such occasions, are from his memory and thence from the intellectual principle, and the things which thence proceed are called spiritual. But as to what concerns Divine Worship from celestial good, such as prevails with those who are in the Lord's celestial kingdom, it is not effected by confessions, adorations, and prayers, of the same quality with those who are in the spiritual kingdom, thus not by truths from the memory, but by truths from the heart, which act in unity with the love itself in which they are principled; for the truths appertaining to them are inscribed on their love, wherefore when they do from love what is prescribed, they do it at the same time from truths, without any thought concerning them from what is doctrinal, thus without calling them forth from the memory. That such is the state of those who are in the Lord's celestial kingdom, may be manifest from what was shown concerning that kingdom and concerning the spiritual kingdom in the passages cited, n. 9277. That incense signifies confessions, adorations, prayers, which through the mouth proceed from the thought, see n. 9475, 10,177, 10,198.

10,296. "Pure frankincense"—that hereby is signified inmost truth, which is spiritual good, appears from the signification of frankincense, as denoting what is defecated from the false of evil. The reason why inmost truth, which is signified by frankincense, is spiritual good, is, because the good appertaining to those who are in the Lord's spiritual kingdom, is nothing but truth, which is called good, when man wills and does it from conscience and from affection; for with the spiritual all the will principle is destroyed, but the intellectual principle is preserved entire by the Lord, and in it is implanted a new will principle by regeneration from the Lord, which will principle is the conscience appertaining to them, which is the conscience of truth; for whatsoever is implanted in the intellectual principle, and proceeds from the intellectual principle, is truth, for the intellectual principle of man is dedicated to the reception of the truths which are of faith, but the will principle is dedicated to the reception of the goods which are of love. Hence it is evident that spiritual good in its essence is truth. That a new will principle with the spiritual is implanted in their intellectual part, and that hence the good appertaining to them in its essence is truth, may be seen in the passages cited, n. 9277, 9596, 9684. It is said of inmost truth that it is good, by reason that the more interior things are, so much the more perfect, and because the inmost principle of man is his will principle, and what is of the will principle, this is called good. That frankincense denotes inmost truth, thus spiritual good, may be manifest from the passages above adduced from the Word, n. 10,177. Inasmuch as frankincense denotes spiritual good, and good is what reigns in all truths, arranges them, conjoins them, and gives affection for them, therefore frankincense is mentioned in the last place, and on this account vessels of fuming were from it called censers; for the denomination is made from the essential principle, which is good; in like manner as the oil of anointing is denominated from the oil of olive, and not from the spices from which it was together prepared, for a similar reason, namely, because oil signified good, and spices truths. It is called pure frankincense because pure signifies what is defecated from the falses of evil; and in the original tongue, by that expression is signified what is interiorly pure, but by another expression what is exteriorly pure or clean. That what is interiorly pure is signified by that expression, is manifest from Isaiah, "*Wash ye, render yourselves pure*, remove the evil of your works from before mine eyes," i. 16. And in David, "*In vain have I rendered my heart pure*, and washed my hands in innocence," Psalm lxxiii. 13; to render the heart pure is to be purified interiorly, and to wash the hands in innocence is exteriorly. And again, "*Be pure in thy judging*," Psalm li. 4. That by another expression is signified what is exteriorly pure or clean, see Levit. xi. 32; chap. xii. 7, 8; chap. xiii. 6, 13, 17, 23, 28, 34, 37, 58; chap. xiv. 6, 8, 9, 20, 48, 53; chap. xv. 13; 28; chap. xvi. 30; chap. xxii. 7; Jer. xiii. 27; Ezek. xxiv. 13; chap. xxix. 12; and elsewhere.

10,297. "So much shall be in so much"—that hereby is signified all manner of correspondence, appears from the signification of the expression so much in so much, by which is meant as much alike from one and from the other, or as much from the frankincense as from the spices, and by the quantity both of measure and of weight is signified correspondence, in this case all manner of correspondence.

10,298. "And thou shalt make it incense"—that hereby is signified worship grounded therein, appears from the signification of incense, as denoting confessions, adorations, prayers, and such things of worship which come forth from the heart into the thought and speech, see n. 9475; for by the smoke of incense is signified elevation, n. 10,177, 10,198; and by fragrant odor, grateful perception and reception, see the passages cited, n. 10,292. Inasmuch as Divine worship, which is signified by the incense of spices is here described, and by the spices from which that incense was prepared, are signified truths in their order, it may be expedient to say briefly how the case is with that worship; but this is an arcanum which cannot be revealed, unless it be known what is the nature and quality of man. Man is not a man from the face, nor even from speech, but from understanding and will; such as his understanding and his will is, such is the man. That he has nothing of understanding at his birth, and also nothing of will, is a known thing; also that his understanding and his will is formed by degrees from infancy; hence man is made a man, and of a quality according to the quality of the formation of both those principles with him. The understanding is formed by truths, and the will by goods, insomuch that his understanding is nothing else but the composition of such things as are referred to truths, and the will nothing else than the affection of such things as are called goods; hence it follows, that man is nothing else but the truth and the good, from which both his faculties are formed. All and singular the things of his body correspond to those faculties, which may be manifest from this consideration, that the body in an instant acts what the understanding thinks, and the will wills; for the mouth speaks according to the things thought of, the face changes itself according to the affections, and the body exercises gesture according to the pleasure of both; hence it is evident that the quality of the whole man throughout is according to the quality of his intellectual principle and his will principle, thus according to his quality as to truths and as to goods; for, as was said, truths constitute his intellectual principle, and goods his will principle; or, what is the same thing, man is his own truth and his own good. That this is the case, appears manifestly amongst spirits; these are nothing else but their own truths and their own good, which they have put on during their lives in the world as men; and still they are human forms; hence from their face shines forth the quality of the truths and goods in which they are principled, and also from the sound and affection of their discourse, and from the gestures, especially from the expressions of their speech; for the expressions of their speech are not such as prevail amongst men in the world, but are altogether consonant to the truths and goods which appertain to them, so that they proceed from them naturally; in this speech spirits and angels are principled when they discourse together. Man is in like speech as to his spirit, when he lives in the world, although at that time he is ignorant of it; for he thinks from similar ideas, as has also been observed by some of the learned, who have called those ideas immaterial and intellectual; those ideas become expressions after death, when man becomes a spirit. From these considerations it is further evident, that man is nothing but his own truth and his own good: hence it is that man after death remains as he has been made truth and good. It is said as he has been made truth and good, and thereby is also meant as he has been made what is false and evil; for evil men call what is false truth, and what is evil good. This is the arcanum which ought altogether to be known, to the intent that it may be known how the case is with Divine worship. But besides this, there is one arcanum more, namely, that in every idea of thought proceeding from the will of man, there is the whole man; this latter also follows from the former, for man thinks from his own truth, and wills from his own good, which are himself. That this is the case, may be manifest from this experience, that when the angels perceive one idea of a man, or one idea of a spirit, they instantly know what is the quality of the man, or what is the quality of the spirit. These observations are made to the intent that it may be known how the case is with Divine worship, which is signified by the incense of spices, namely, that the whole man is in all and singular the things of his worship, inasmuch as truth and good are therein, which are himself: this is the reason why four spices are mentioned, by which are signified all truths in the complex. From these considerations it also follows, that it is the same thing whether we say that Divine worship consists of these truths and goods, or say that man consists of them, since the whole man is in all the ideas of thought which are of worship, as was said.

10,299. "Ointment, the work of a dealer in ointment"—that hereby is signified from the influx and operation of the Divine of the Lord into all and singular things, appears from the signification of ointment or what is aromatic, as denoting truths in all and singular the things of worship, see n. 10,264; and from the signification of the work of a dealer in ointment or a dealer in spices, as denoting the influx and operation of the Divine itself, see n. 10,265. How it is to be understood that influx and operation must be into all and singular the things of worship, it may be expedient also briefly to say. It is believed by those who are not acquainted with the arcana of heaven, that worship is from man, because it proceeds from thought and from affection, which are principles appertaining to him; but the worship which is from man is not worship, consequently the confessions, adorations, and prayers, which are from man, are not confessions, adorations, and prayers, which are heard and received by the Lord; but they must be from the Lord Himself with man. That this is the case, is known to the church, for she teaches that from man there does not any good proceed, but that all good is from heaven, that is from the Divine there; hence also all good in worship, and worship without good is not worship; from this ground the church prays, when she is in a holy principle, that God may be present, and lead her thoughts and discourse. The case herein is this; when man is in genuine worship, on such occasion the Lord flows-in into the goods and truths which appertain to the man and elevates them to Himself, and with them the man, so far and in such quality as he is in them. This elevation does not appear to the man if he be not in the genuine affection of truth and good, and in the knowledge, acknowledgment, and faith, that all good comes from above from the Lord. That the case is so, may be apprehended even by those who are worldly wise, for they know from their erudition, that natural influx, which is called by them physical influx, is not given, but spiritual influx; that is, that nothing can flow in from the natural world into heaven, but *vice versa*. From these considerations it may be manifest how it is to be understood, that the influx and operation of the Divine of the Lord is into all and singular the things of worship. That the case is so, it has also been given frequently to experience, for it has been given to perceive the influx itself, the calling forth of the truths which appertained to me, the application to the objects of prayer, the affection of good adjoined, and the elevation itself. But although this is the case, still man ought not to let down his hands and expect influx, for this would be to act the part of an image without life; he ought still to think, to will, and to act, as from himself, and yet to ascribe to the Lord the All of the thought of truth, and of the endeavor of good; by so doing the faculty is implanted from the Lord of receiving Himself and influx from Himself. For man was created to no other intent, than to be a receptacle of the Divine, and the faculty of receiving the Divine is no otherwise formed; the faculty being formed, he has then no other will than that it should be so; for he loves influx from the Lord, and holds in aversion operation from himself, inasmuch as influx from the Lord is the influx of good, but operation from himself is the operation of evil. In such a state are all the angels of heaven; wherefore by them in the Word are signified truths and goods which are from the Lord, inasmuch as they are receptions of them, see n. 1925, 3039, 4085, 4295.

10,300. "Salted"—that hereby is signified the desire of truth to good, appears from the signification of salt, as denoting the desire which is of the love of truth to good, of which we shall speak presently; hence salted denotes [the thing or principle] in which that desire is. The reason why there ought to be a desire of truth to good is, because that desire is conjunctive of both; for so far as truth desires good, so far it is conjoined to it. The conjunction of truth and good is what is called the heavenly marriage, which is heaven itself with man; wherefore when in Divine worship and in all and singular the things thereof, there is the desire of that conjunction, heaven is in all and singular the things there, thus the Lord; this is signified by the requirement that the incense should be salted. That salt has this signification, is from its conjunctive nature; for it conjoins all things, and hence gives them relish; yea, it conjoins water and oil, which otherwise are not conjoinable. When it is known that by salt is signified the desire of the conjunction of truth and good, it may be known what is signified by the Lord's words in Mark, "*Every one shall be salted with fire;* and every sacrifice *shall be salted with salt; salt is good, but if the salt be without saltness,* wherewith will ye season it. *Have salt in yourselves,*" ix. 49, 50. Every one shall be salted with fire, denotes that every one from genuine love will desire; every sacrifice shall be salted with salt, denotes that the desire derived from genuine love must be in all worship; salt without saltness signifies desire from some other love than what is genuine; to have salt in themselves denotes the desire of truth to good. That fire denotes love, see n. 4906, 5071, 5215, 6314, 6832, 10,055; and that sacrifice denotes worship in general, n. 922, 6905, 8680, 8936. Who can know what is meant by being salted with fire, and why the sacrifice should be salted, and what by having salt in themselves, unless it be known what fire means, what salt, and being salted? In like manner in Luke, "Every one of you, who doth not deny all his faculties, cannot be My disciple. *Salt is good, but if the salt be infatuated,* by what shall it be seasoned; it is neither fit for the earth, nor for the dunghill, they shall cast it forth abroad," xiv. 34, 35. To deny all his faculties denotes to love the Lord above all things, faculties denote the things which are proper to man; salt infatuated denotes desire grounded in the proprium, thus in the love of self and the world; such desire is salt infatuated, not fit for any thing; as also in Matthew, "*Ye are the salt of the earth, but if the salt be infatuated, by what shall it be salted;* it is no longer fit for any thing but to be cast forth abroad, and to be trodden under foot of men," v

13, 14. That in all worship there must be a desire of truth to good, is also signified by the law, "*That every offering of a cake should be salted; and that upon every offering there should be the salt of the covenant of Jehovah,*" Levit. ii. 13. By a cake and an offering, which is sacrifice, is signified worship, as above; and salt is there called the salt of the covenant of Jehovah, since by covenant is signified conjunction, see n. 665, 666, 1023, 1038, 1864, 1996, 2003, 2021, 6804, 8767, 8778, 9396, 9416. Desire also is the very ardor of love, thus what is continuous of it, and love is spiritual conjunction. As the desire of truth to good conjoins, so the desire of what is false to what is evil disjoins, and what disjoins, this also destroys, hence by salt in the opposite sense is signified the destruction and devastation of truth and good; as in Jeremiah, "Cursed be the man who maketh flesh his arm; he shall not see when good shall come, but *shall dwell in parched places, in a salt land*, which is not inhabited," xvii. 5, 6. To make flesh his arm denotes to trust in self, thus in his own proprium, and not in the Divine, see n. 10,283; and whereas the proprium consists in loving self above God and the neighbor, it is the love of self which is thus described. Hence it is said that he shall not see when good shall come, and that he shall dwell in parched places and in a salt land, that is in filthy loves and their desires, which have destroyed the good and truth of the church. And in Zephaniah, "*It shall be as Gomorrah, a place left to the nettle, and a pit of salt*, and a waste to eternity," ii. 9; a place left to the nettle denotes the ardor and burning of the life of man from the love of self; a pit of salt denotes the desire of what is false, which, inasmuch as it destroys truth and good, is called a waste to eternity; it is said that it shall be as Gomorrah, since by Gomorrah and Sodom is signified the love of self, n. 220. That the wife of Lot was turned *into a statue of salt*, because she turned her faces to those cities, Gen. xix. 26, signified the vastation of truth and good, for to turn the faces to any thing in the internal sense denotes to love, n. 10,189. Hence it is that the Lord says, let him not return to the things behind him, *remember Lot's wife*, Luke xvii. 31, 32. And in Moses, "*The whole land thereof is sulphur and salt and burning*, according to the overthrow of Sodom and Gomorrah," Deut. xxix. 22; by [land or earth] in this passage, as also in other passages in the Word, is meant the church, see the passages cited, n. 9325. Hence now it was that the cities which were no longer to be inhabited, *were to be sown with salt*, Judges ix. 45. From these considerations it is evident that by salt, in the genuine sense, is signified the desire of truth to good, thus what is conjunctive, and in the opposite sense the desire of the false to evil, thus what is destructive. He therefore who knows that salt denotes the desire of truth to good, and their conjunctive principle, may also know what is signified by *the waters of Jericho being healed by Elisha through the casting-in of salt into their going forth*, 2 Kings ii. 19, 20, 21, 22 ; for by Elisha as by Elias was represented the Lord as to the Word, n. 2762, 8029 ; and by waters are signified the truths of the Word, by the waters of Jericho the truths of the Word in the sense of the letter, in like manner by the going forth of the waters; and by salt is signified the desire of truth to good, and the conjunction of both, whence comes healing.

10,301. "Pure"—that hereby is signified without evil, appears from the signification of pure, as denoting without evil. Inasmuch as all evil is impure, and all good is pure, therefore mention is made of being purified from sins and from iniquities, and it is predicated of the heart, that is of the will, for the heart in the Word signifies the will, n. 2930, 7542, 8910, 9300, 9494, because the love, n. 3883 to 3896, 9050.

10,302. "Holy"—that hereby is signified without the false of evil, appears from the signification of holy, as denoting the Divine Truth proceeding from the Lord, see n. 6788, 7499, 8302, 8330, 9229, 9818, 9820 ; hence that is called holy, which is without the false of evil. It is called the false of evil, since there is given what is false without evil, as in the case of some upright ones amongst the nations out of the church, and also with some amongst Christians within the church ; but what is false defiled from what is evil, is evil itself, for it is from that source; whereas what is false with those who are principled in good is not defiled by evil, but is purified from it; whence also such a false principle is accepted of the Lord almost as truth, and is also easily turned into truth, for they who are in good are inclinable to receive truth. Concerning each false principle, both that which is from evil, and that which is not from evil, see the passages cited, n. 9304, 10,109.

10,303. "And thou shalt bruise of it into small pieces"—that hereby is signified the arrangement of truths into their series, appears from the signification of bruising, when applied to frankincense and to spices, by which are signified truths, as denoting the arrangement of truths into their series ; for bruising has a like signification with grinding, but grinding is predicated of wheat, barley, fitches, whereas bruising is predicated of oil, frankincense, and spices. What is specifically signified by bruising and grinding, cannot be known, unless it be known how the case is with man in respect to the goods and truths which are signified by wheat, barley, meal, fine flour, oil, frankincense and spices, when they are arranged for uses ; for grinding and bruising denote arranging them for use. When grinding is predicated of the goods, which are signified by wheat or barley, then by grinding is signified the arrangement and production of good into truths, and thereby application to uses. Good also, in no case, puts itself forth into uses except by truths; it is arranged into truths and is thereby qualified; for good, unless it can be arranged into truths, has not any quality, and when it is arranged into truths, it is then arranged into series in application to things according to uses, into which things good enters as the affection of love, whence comes what is grateful, pleasant, delightful. The like is here signified by bruising into small pieces, for pure frankincense denotes spiritual good, n. 10,296; and the truths, which are arranged from that good, are the spices, stacte, onycha, and galbanum, n. 10,292, 10,293, 10,294. What is meant by arrangement into series, it may also be expedient briefly to explain; truths are said to be arranged into series, when they are arranged according to the form of heaven, in which form the angelic societies are; what the quality of that form is, is manifest from the correspondence of all the members, viscera, and organs of man with the GRAND MAN, which is heaven, concerning which correspondence, see the passages cited, n. 10,030; in those members, viscera, and organs, all and singular things are arranged into series, and series of series; fibres and vessels form them, as is known to those who are acquainted with the textures and contextures of the interiors of the body from anatomy; into similar series the truths derived from good are arranged with man. Hence it is that a regenerate man is a heaven in the least form, corresponding to the GRAND MAN; and that man throughout is altogether his own truth and good. That a regenerate man is heaven in the least form, see the passages cited, n. 9279; and that man is his own truth and good, see above, n. 10,298; and that truths with man are arranged into series according to angelic societies with the regenerate, n. 5339, 5343, 5530. The series into which truths are arranged with the good, and the series into which falses are arranged with the evil, are signified in the Word, by sheaves and bundles, as Levit. xxiii. 9 to 15; Psalm cxxvi. 6; Psalm cxxix. 7; Amos ii. 13; Micah iv. 12; Jer. ix. 22; Zech. xii. 6; Matt. viii. 30. When therefore it is evident what is signified by bruising and grinding, it may be known what is signified in the internal sense by *the sons of Israel grinding the manna in mills, or bruising it in a mortar*, and baking it into cakes, Numb. xi. 8; for by the manna was signified celestial and spiritual good, n. 8464; and by grinding and bruising, arrangements to serve for use; for whatsoever is said in the Word is significative of such things as are in heaven and in the church, for all things have an internal sense. Also what is signified by *not taking for a pledge a mill or a mill-stone*, since he receives the soul for a pledge, Deut. xxiv. 6; for by a mill and a mill-stone is signified that which prepares good that it may be applied to uses; by barley also and by wheat is signified good, and by meal and fine flour truths, and good by its truths is applied to use, as was said above. Hence it may be manifest what is signified by a mill, by a mill-stone, and by sitting at mills in the following passages, "*Then two shall be grinding at the mill*, the one shall be taken, the other shall be left," Matt. xxiv. 41. Again, " He who shall scandalize one of these little ones that believe in Me, it is expedient for him that an *ass-millstone* be hanged about his neck, and he be sunk into the depths of the sea," Matt. xviii. 6; Mark ix. 42. And in the Apocalypse, " A strong angel lifted up *a stone as a great mill-stone*, and cast it into the sea, saying, thus with violence shall Babylon be cast down; *no voice of a mill shall any longer be heard in her*," xviii. 22. And in Jeremiah, " I will take from them the voice of joy, *the voice of mills* and the light of a lamp," xxv. 10. And in Isaiah, " O daughter of Babel sit in the earth, there is no throne O daughter of the Chaldeans; *take a mill and grind meal*," xlvii. 1, 2; as a mill and grinding in a good sense signifies application to good uses, so in the opposite sense it signifies application to evil uses; hence when it relates to Babel and Chaldea it signifies application in favor of their loves, which are the loves of self and the world; for by barley and wheat with them is signified good adulterated, and by meal thence derived truth falsified. The profanation of good and truth by application to those loves is also signified by Moses *breaking into pieces the golden calf*, and sprinkling it upon the waters that came down from Mount Sinai, and making the sons of Israel to drink, Exod. xxxii. 20; Deut. ix. 21.

10,304. " And thou shalt give of it before the testimony in the tent of the congregation"—that hereby is signified the worship of the Lord in heaven and the church, appears from the signification of the incense, which was to be given before the testimony, as denoting worship, see above, n. 10,298; and from the signification of the testimony, as denoting the Lord as to Divine Truth, see n. 9503; and from the representation of the tent of the congregation, as denoting heaven, see n. 9457, 9481, 9485; and since it denotes heaven it denotes also the church, for the church is heaven in the earth.

10,305. " Where I will meet thee there"—that hereby is signified from the influx of the Lord, appears from the signification of meeting, when concerning the Lord, as denoting his presence and influx, see n. 10,147, 10,148, 10,197; in this case from the influx of the Lord, since the subject treated of is worship, which is signified by incense; for the all of worship, which is truly worship, flows-in from the Lord, as may be manifest from what was shown above, n. 10,299.

10,306. " It shall be to you the holy of holies"—that hereby is signified since from the Lord, appears from the signification of holy, as denoting all that and only that which proceeds from the Lord, see n. 6788, 7499, 8302, 8330, 9229, 9818, 9820,

10,307. "And the incense which thou makest in its quality, ye shall not make to yourselves"—that hereby is signified that worship grounded in the holy truths of the church ought not to be applied to the loves of man, appears from the signification of incense, as denoting worship, see above, n. 10,298; and from the signification of making in its quality, as denoting from the holy truths of the church, for to make in its quality is to make from the same spices, and by the spices which were stacte, onycha, and galbanum, are signified the holy truths of the church in their order, n. 10,292, 10,293, 10,294; and from the signification of not making to yourselves, as denoting to apply to man's own proper uses, thus to his loves, for what a man does for the sake of himself, he does for the sake of his loves. Application is here understood, because it is said to make to themselves. It may be expedient also to say how the case herein is; all the truths of the church have respect to two loves, namely, love to God, and love towards the neighbor; that the whole Word, which is the Divine Truth itself, from which all the truths of the Word are derived, hangs on those two loves, is manifest from Matthew, chap. xxii. 37; and from Mark, chap. xii. 30, 31; and from Luke, chap. x. 27; it is there said that all the law and the prophets hang on those loves, and by the law and the prophets, is signified the whole Word. But it is the contrary to apply the Divine Truth or the truths of the church to the loves of man; hence man turns himself from the Lord to himself, which is from heaven to hell, and becomes as one of them there; for in hell they have the Lord to the back, and their own loves in front; yea, when they are inspected by the angels, they appear inverted with the head downwards and the feet upwards. When Divine Truths are applied to the loves of man, they are no longer truths, since by application evil enters them which perverts them, and induces the face of what is false. If in this case it is said to them, that they are not so to be understood but otherwise, they are not willing to apprehend, and some do not apprehend; for to say what is contrary to principles confirmed by his loves, is to say what is contrary to the man himself, because contrary to his intellectual principle derived from his will-principle. Concerning those who by application to their own loves falsify truths, and adulterate goods, much is said in the Word where Babel is treated of, especially in the Apocalypse.

10,308. "It shall be holy to thee to Jehovah"—that hereby is signified that worship ought to be applied to Divine Love, appears from the signification of holy, as denoting all that proceeds from the Lord, as above, n. 10,306; and from the signification of incense, of which it is said that it shall be holy to thee to Jehovah, as denoting worship, see also above, n. 10,298; that it denotes that it ought to be applied to Divine Love, follows from what immediately precedes, where it is said that they should not make such incense to themselves, by which is signified that worship grounded in the holy truths of the church ought not to be applied to the loves of man, n. 10,307. By Divine Love is meant love to the Lord, and love towards the neighbor; the reason why the latter love is also Divine is, because it likewise proceeds from the Lord; for no one can love the neighbor from himself, for in such case he loves the neighbor and confers benefits upon him for the sake of himself, which is to love himself. That the whole Word which is the Divine Truth Itself, from which all the truths of the church are derived, has respect to those two loves as ends, see just above, n. 10,307; hence also Divine worship ought to respect the same, since all worship, which is truly worship, is from truths, as may be manifest from what was shown above concerning the spices of the incense, by which are signified the truths of worship; and the truths of worship are then applied to Divine Love, when it is made to appertain to man from the Lord, according to what was said above, n. 10,299.

10,309. "The man who shall make like it to make an odor with it"—that hereby is signified the imitation of Divine worship by the affections of truth and good from the proprium, appears from the signification of making like it, as denoting the imitation of Divine worship, for by making is signified to imitate, and by the incense of which it is said, is signified Divine worship, as above; and from the signification of making an odor, as denoting to please, which, since it is effected by the affections of truth and good, these are what are signified by pleasing, for odor denotes the perceptivity of what is grateful, thus what pleases, n. 10,292. That it denotes from the proprium, is evident, for it is said, whosoever shall make it shall be cut off from his people; for from the proprium denotes what is not from the affection of truth and good for the sake of truth and good, but for the sake of self, and to do any thing for the sake of self, is for the sake of gain, honors, and reputation, as ends, and not for the sake of the salvation of the neighbor and the glory of the Lord; hence it is from evil and not from good, or what is the same thing, from hell and not from the Lord; this therefore is what is meant by the imitation of Divine worship by the affections of truth and good from the proprium, which is signified by making incense like it to make an odor with it. Those who do so, are those who love the world above heaven, and themselves above God; such persons also, when they think inwardly, or with themselves, believe nothing about heaven, and about the Lord, but when they think out of themselves, as is the case when they speak before men, they then speak of heaven and of the Lord from a greater affection and faith than others, and this in proportion as they are inflamed by gain, by honor and reputation. Their state on such occasions is, that they are interiorly black, and exteriorly white, that is, they are devils in the form of angels of light; for the interiors are closed, which should be exposed to heaven, and the exteriors are open, which are exposed to the world; and if on such occasions from an affection as of love they elevate the eyes and the hands to heaven, they are yet as images made so by art; they appear also as such before the angels. And if you are disposed to believe it, there are several of this character in hell, who are present with and inspire men of a like character, especially preachers, who imitate Divine worship by the affections of truth and good from the proprium. Which also is permitted of the Lord, since they thus also perform uses; for good men still receive the Word from them well, since the Word from whatsoever mouth it comes forth is received by man according to the quality of his good. But such external things, inasmuch as they are pretences, are stripped off from them in the other life; and in this case their spirit appears black as it had been in the body.

10,310. "He shall be cut off from his people"—that hereby is signified separation from heaven and the church, and spiritual death, appears from the signification of being cut off from people, as denoting separation and spiritual death, see n. 10,289; that it denotes separation from heaven, is manifest from what was said just above, n. 10,309. The reason why it denotes also from the church is, because they alone are of the church, in whom the church is; and the church is in those who are in the affection of truth for the sake of truth, and in the affection of good for the sake of good, thus who are in love towards the neighbor, and in love to God; for the neighbor is good and truth, and also is God, since good and truth are of God, thus are God with them. They who are not such, are not of the church, howsoever they may be in the church.

CONCERNING THE THIRD EARTH IN THE STARRY HEAVEN.

10,311. *THERE appeared some spirits from afar, who were not willing to approach; the reason was, because they could not be together with the spirits of our earth who were then about me; hence I perceived that they were from another earth, and I was afterwards told that they were from a certain earth in the universe; but where that earth is, I was not informed.*

10,312. *They were unwilling to think at all about their body, or even about any thing corporeal and material, contrary to the spirits from our earth; hence it was that they were not willing to approach, for spirits consociate and dissociate ac cording to affections and the thoughts thence derived; nevertheless after the removal of several spirits from our earth, they came nearer and discoursed with me. But on this occasion there was felt an anxiety arising from the collision of spheres; for spiritual spheres encompass all spirits and societies of spirits, flowing forth from the life of the affections and of the thoughts thence derived; wherefore if the affections be contrary, collision takes place, whence comes anxiety.*

10,313. *They told the spirits of our earth, that they durst not approach to them, since in approaching they were not only seized with anxiety, but also appeared to themselves from a phantasy as if they were bound as to the hands and feet with serpents, from which they could not be loosed until they retired; such phantasy is from correspondence; for the sensual corporeal principle of man is represented, in the other life, by serpents; wherefore by serpents in the Word is also signified the sensual principle, which is the ultimate of the life of man.*

10,314. *Inasmuch as the spirits of that earth are of such a quality, therefore they do not appear as other spirits in a perspicuous human form, but as a cloud; the better of them as a dusky cloud with whitish tints, resembling what is human. They said, that inwardly they are white, and that when they become angels, that duskiness is changed into a beautiful blue, which also was shown me.*

10,315. *I asked them whether they entertained such an idea concerning their bodies during their abode in the world as men; they replied, that the men of their earth make no account of their bodies, but only of the spirit in the body, because they know that the spirit is to live for ever, but that the body must perish. The face however they do not call body, by reason that the affections of their spirits appear from the face, and the thoughts grounded in affections from the eyes. They said also, that several in their earth believe that the spirits of their bodies have been from eternity, being infused into the body when they were conceived; but they added, that now they know that it is not so, and that they repent for having entertained so false an opinion.*

10,316. *When I asked them whether they were willing to see any objects in our earth, informing them that it was possible to do so through my eyes, they replied first that they could not, and next that they would not, since they should see nothing but terrestrial and material things, from which they remove their thoughts as far as possible.*

10,317. *A continuation of the subject concerning this third earth in the universe will be given at the close of the following chapter.*

EXODUS.

CHAPTER THE THIRTY-FIRST.

THE DOCTRINE OF CHARITY AND FAITH.

10,318. MAN, without a revelation from the Divine, cannot know any thing about eternal life, nor even any thing about God, and still less about love and faith to Him; for man is born into mere ignorance, and must after birth learn every thing from worldly things, from which he must form his understanding; he is also born hereditarily into all evil, which is of self-love and the love of the world; the delights thence derived are perpetually prevalent, and suggest such things as are diametrically opposite to the Divine. Hence now it is that man of himself knows nothing about eternal life; therefore there must necessarily be a revelation to communicate such knowledge.

10,319. That the evils of the love of self and the world induce such ignorance concerning those things which relate to eternal life, is very manifest from those within the church, who, although they know from revelation that there is a God, that there is a heaven and a hell, that there is eternal life, and that that life is to be acquired by the good of love and faith, still fall into denial concerning those subjects, as well the learned as the unlearned. Hence it is further evident what great ignorance would prevail, if there were no revelation.

10,320. Since therefore man lives after death, and moreover to eternity, and a life awaits him according to his love and faith, it follows that the Divine, out of love towards the human race, revealed such things as may lead to that life, and conduce to man's salvation. What the Divine has revealed, with us, is the Word.

10,321. The Word, inasmuch as it is a revelation from the Divine, is Divine in all and singular things; for what is from the Divine cannot be otherwise.

10,322. What is from the Divine descends through the heavens even to man; wherefore in the heavens it is accommodated to the wisdom of the angels who are there, and in the earths it is accommodated to the apprehension of the men who are there. Wherefore in the Word there is an internal sense, which is spiritual, for the angels, and an external sense, which is natural, for men. Hence it is that conjunction of heaven with man is effected by the Word.

10,323. The genuine sense of the Word is apprehended by

none but those who are illustrated; and they only are illustrated, who are in love and faith to the Lord, for the interiors of such are elevated by the Lord even into the light of heaven.

10,324. The Word in the letter cannot be apprehended except by doctrine derived from the Word by one who is illustrated; for the sense of its letter is accommodated to the apprehension of men, even the simple; wherefore doctrine derived from the Word must be to them for a lamp.

10,325. The books of the Word are all those which have an internal sense; but those which have not, are not the Word. The books of the Word in the Old Testament are, the five books of Moses, the book of Joshua, the book of Judges, the two books of Samuel, the two books of the Kings, the Psalms of David; the Prophets Isaiah, Jeremiah, the Lamentations, Ezekiel, Daniel, Hosea, Joel, Amos, Obadiah, Jonah, Micah, Nahum, Habakkuk, Zephaniah, Haggai, Zechariah, Malachi; and in the New Testament, the four Evangelists, Matthew, Mark, Luke, John, and the Apocalypse.

CHAPTER XXXI.

1. AND JEHOVAH spake to Moses, saying,

2. See, I have called by name, Bezaleel the son of Uri, the son of Hur, of the tribe of Judah.

3. And I have filled him with the spirit of God, in wisdom, and in intelligence, and in science, and in every work.

4. To contrive contrivances, to make in gold, and in silver, and in brass.

5. And in the engraving of a stone for filling, and in the engraving of wood, to make in every work.

6. And I, behold, I have given with him Aholiab, the son of Ahisamach, of the tribe of Dan; and in the heart of every wise one in heart I have given wisdom; and they shall make all things which I have commanded thee.

7. The tent of the congregation, and the ark for the testimony, and the propitiatory which is above it, and all the vessels of the tent.

8. And the table and its vessels; and the pure candlestick and all its vessels, and the altar of incense.

9. And the altar of burnt-offering and all its vessels, and the laver and its base.

10. And the garments of ministry, and the garments of holiness for Aaron the priest, and the garments of his sons, to perform the office of the priesthood.

11. And the oil of anointing, and the incense of spices for

what is holy; according to all things which I have commanded thee, they shall do.

12. And JEHOVAH spake to Moses, saying,

13. Also speak thou to the sons of Israel, saying; altogether My sabbaths ye shall keep, because it is a sign between Me and between you to your generations, to know that I JEHOVAH sanctify you.

14. And ye shall keep the sabbath, because this is holy to you; he that profaneth it, dying shall die; because every one that doeth work in it, that soul shall be cut off from the midst of his people.

15. Six days shall work be done, and on the seventh day is the sabbath of a sabbath, holy to JEHOVAH; every one that doeth work on the day of the sabbath, dying shall die.

16. And the sons of Israel shall keep the sabbath, to make the sabbath to their generations the covenant of an age.

17. Between Me and between the sons of Israel this sign is for an age; because in six days JEHOVAH made the heaven and the earth, and on the seventh day rested and respired.

18. And he gave to Moses, in his finishing to speak with him on Mount Sinai, the two tables of the testimony, tables of stone, written with the finger of God.

THE CONTENTS.

10,326. THE subject here treated of in the internal sense is, *first*, a representative church about to be established with those who are in the good of love and in the good of faith to the Lord; this is signified by those things which are in a sum recounted to be done by Bezaleel of the tribe of Judah, and Aholiab of the tribe of Dan. The subject *next* treated of is the conjunction of the Lord with that church by representatives, which is signified by the sabbath, which was to be kept holy.

THE INTERNAL SENSE.

10,327. VERSES 1 to 11. *And Jehovah spake to Moses, saying, See, I have called by name, Bezaleel the son of Uri, the son of Hur, of the tribe of Judah. And I have filled him with the spirit of God, in wisdom, and in intelligence, and in science, and in every work. To contrive contrivances, to make in gold, and in silver, and in brass. And in the engraving of a stone for filling, and in the engraving of wood, to make in every work. And I, behold, I have given with him Aholiab, the son of Ahisamach, of the tribe of Dan. And in the heart of every wise one in heart I have given wisdom; and they shall make all things which I have commanded thee. The tent of the congregation, and the ark for the testimony; and the propitiatory which is above it, and all the vessels of the tent. And the table and its vessels; and the pure candlestick and all its vessels; and the altar of incense. And the altar of burnt-offering and all its vessels; and the laver and its base, and the garments of ministry, and the garments of holiness for Aaron the priest, and the garments of his sons, to perform the office of the priesthood. And the oil of anointing; and the incense of spices, for what is holy; according to all things which I have commanded thee, they shall do.* And Jehovah spake to Moses, saying, signifies illustration and perception by the Word from the Lord. See I have called by name, Bezaleel the son of Uri, the son of Hur, of the tribe of Judah, signifies those who are in the good of love, with whom the church was to be established. And I have filled him with the spirit of God, signifies influx and illustration from Divine Truth which is from Divine Good. In wisdom, and in intelligence, and in science, and in every work, signifies as to those things which are of the will, and of the understanding, in the internal and in the external man. To contrive contrivances, to make in gold, and in silver, and in brass, signifies to represent goods and truths interior and exterior, which are of the understanding from the will, thus which are of faith from love. And in the engraving of a stone for filling, signifies to represent all things of faith serviceable to the good of love. And in the engraving of wood to make in all work, signifies to represent all good whatsoever. And I, behold, I have given with him Aholiab, the son of Ahisamach of the tribe of Dan, signifies those who are in the good and truth of faith with whom the church is to be established. And in the heart of every wise one in heart I have given wisdom, signifies all who will and do what is good and true for the sake of what is good and true. And they shall make all things which I have commanded thee, signifies Divine Truths which are from the Word, which were to be represented in things external. The tent of the congregation and the ark for the testimony, signifies a representative of heaven in general where the Lord is. And the propitiatory which is above them, signifies a representative of the hearing and reception of all things which are from the good of love. And all the vessels of the tent, signifies a representative of ministering goods and truths. And the table and its vessels, signifies a representative of spiritual good derived from celestial. And the pure candlestick and all its vessels, signifies a representative of truth from that good. And the altar of incense, signifies a representative of worship derived from them. And the altar of burnt-offering and all its vessels, signifies a representative of worship from the good of love and its truths. And the laver and its base, signifies a representative of purification and regeneration, and the natural principle. And the garments of ministry, and the garments of holiness for Aaron the priest, signifies a representative of the Lord's spiritual kingdom, adjoined to His celestial kingdom. And the garments of his sons, signifies a representative of inferior spiritual things. To perform the office o. the priesthood, signifies a representative of the Lord's salvation. And the oil of anointing, signifies a representative of the Lord as to the Divine Good of the Divine Love in His Divine Human. And the incense of spices, signifies a representative of worship from truths. For what is holy, signifies for the representative church. According to all things which I have commanded thee they shall do [or make], signifies according to Divine Truths which are from the Word, which were to be represented in things external.

10,328. "And Jehovah spake to Moses, saying"—that hereby is signified illustration and perception by the Word from the Lord, appears from what was shown above, n. 10,290.

10,329. "See, I have called by name Bezaleel the son of Uri, the son of Hur, of the tribe of Judah"—that hereby are signified those who are in the good of love, with whom the church is about to be established, appears from the signification of calling by name, as denoting to elect such, namely, who are meet, of which we shall speak presently; and from the representation of Bezaleel, as denoting those who are in the good of love. The reason why those are here represented by Bezaleel is, because he was of the tribe of Judah, and by that tribe are signified those who are in celestial good, which is the good of love to the Lord, and, in the sense abstracted from persons, the good of celestial love. That this is signified by Judah and his tribe, see n. 3654, 3881, 6363, 6364, 8770. But what is represented by Uri, the father of Bezaleel, and by Hur, his grandfather, is manifest from the generation of celestial good; it is generated from the doctrine of celestial truth and good, hence by them are signified those doctrines. That by Hur is represented the doctrine of truth, see n. 9424. They who keep the mind [*animus*] in the sense of the letter of the Word, as is done in the historicals more intensely than the propheticals, may be surprised at its being said that by the names of those men such things are signified; but they who know what the quality of the Word is, will not be surprised; for there is a spiritual principle in all and singular things; in the names themselves which occur in the Word, there is nothing spiritual, unless they signify the things of the church and heaven, for these things are spiritual; hence it follows, that by these names also are signified things. That names in the Word signify things, see n. 1224, 1264, 1888, 4442, 5905, 5225, 6516; and that names do not enter heaven, but the things which are signified, n. 1876, 10,216, 10,282. The reason why calling by name, in the spiritual sense, denotes to elect such as are meet, is, because by name without person is signified quality, as may be manifest from the passages in the Word where mention is made of name. That by name is signified quality, see n. 144, 145, 1754, 1896, 2009, 2724, 3004 to 3011, 3421, 6674, 6887, 8274, 8882, 9310; and also by calling without a name, n. 3421, 3659; and that to call by name denotes to elect, n. 8773. There are two who are here named, who were called by Jehovah to make the works which were commanded by Moses on Mount Sinai, Bezaleel of the tribe of Judah, and Aholiab of the tribe of Dan; by Bezaleel are signified those who are in the good of celestial love, and by Aholiab those who are in the good and truth of faith. They who are in the good of celestial love, are in the inmost principle of heaven and of the church, but they who are in the good and truth of faith, are in its ultimate principle; thus by these two are signified all in the complex with whom the church can be established, for by first and last, or by what is inmost and outermost, are signified all and all things, see n. 10,044; and that by Aholiab of the tribe of Dan are signified those who are in the good of faith, will be seen in what follows. From these considerations it is now evident, that by the words, "I have called by name Bezaleel the son of Uri, the son of Hur, of the tribe of Judah," are signified those who are in the good of love, with whom the church was about to be established.

10,330. "And I have filled him with the spirit of God"—that hereby is signified influx and illustration from Divine Truth which is from the Divine Good of the Lord, appears from the signification of filling with the spirit of God, as denoting influx and illustration from the Divine Truth; for filling, when it relates to Jehovah, denotes influx, and with man, illustration; and the spirit of God is the Divine Truth which is from the Divine Good of the Lord. The reason why filling, when concerning Jehovah or the Lord, denotes influx, and with man illustration, is, because influx is predicated of all good and all truth which comes out of heaven from the Lord; and since this influx illustrates man, illustration is predicated of man. That that Divine Truth proceeding from the Divine Good of the Lord is the Spirit of God, see n. 9818. Inasmuch as few know how the case is with the influx of Divine Truth, and with illustration thence with man, it is here allowed to make a few observations on those subjects. That all the good of love and the truth of faith is not from man, but out of heaven from the Divine there with man, is a thing known in the church; also that they are in illustration who receive that good and truth. But the influx and illustration is effected in this manner; man is of such a quality, that as to his interiors, which are of the thought and will, he can look downwards, and can look upwards; to look downwards is to look outwards into the world and to himself, and to look upwards is to look inwards to heaven and to God; man looks outwards from himself, which is called looking downwards, since when he looks from himself, he looks to hell; but man looks inwards not from himself, but from the Lord, which is called upwards, because he is elevated in such case as to his interiors, which are of the will and understanding, by the Lord to heaven, thus to the Lord. The interiors also are actually elevated, and in this case are actually withdrawn from the body and from the world; when this is effected, the interiors of man come actually into heaven, and into its light and heat; hence he has influx and illustration; the light of heaven illuminates the understanding, for that light is the Divine Truth which proceeds from the Lord as a sun, and the heat of heaven enkindles the will, for that heat is the good of love which together proceeds from the Lord as a sun. Since man in such case is amongst the angels, there is communicated to him from them, that is, by [or through] them from the Lord, the intelligence of truth and the affection of good. This communication is what is called influx and illustration; but it is to be noted, that influx and illustration are effected according to the faculty of reception with man, and the faculty of reception is according to the love of truth and good; wherefore they who are in the love of truth and good, for the sake of truth and good as ends, are elevated; but they who are not in the love of truth and good for the sake of truth and good, but for the sake of self and the world, inasmuch as they continually look and gravitate downwards, cannot be elevated, thus cannot receive Divine influx out of heaven, and be illustrated. The intelligence, which with these latter appears as the intelligence of truth, is from the infatuated lumen which shines before their eyes from principles of confirmation and thence of persuasion; but it shines in like manner whether it be false or true; nevertheless this brightness is mere thick darkness, when light flows in out of heaven. That this is the case, has been shown me to the life. From these considerations it may be manifest whence it comes to pass, that so many heresies exist in the world, namely, because the rulers and guides have looked to themselves, and have regarded their own glory as an end, and in such case have considered the things of the Lord and of heaven as means conducive to an end.

10,331. "In wisdom, and in intelligence, and in science, and in every work"—that hereby is signified as to those things which are of the will and of the understanding in the internal and in the external man, appears from the signification of wisdom, as denoting those things which are of the will in the internal man; and from the signification of intelligence, as denoting the things of the understanding also in the internal man; and from the signification of science, as denoting the things of the understanding and of the speech thence derived in the external man; and from the signification of works, as denoting the things of the will and of the effect thence derived in the external man; hence by those words are signified all things of the man who is in the good of celestial love, both his interior and exterior things, which receive the influx of Divine Truth from the Lord, and are thence in illustration, as treated of just above. But it may be expedient briefly to say, what is meant by wisdom, intelligence, science, and work. They who do not know what the internal man is, and what the external, also what the understanding and will are, cannot comprehend how wisdom, intelligence, science, and work, are distinct from each other; the reason is, because they cannot form a distinct idea concerning the one and the other; wherefore they who have not that knowledge, call him wise, who is only intelligent, yea, who is only scientific; but he is wise, who from love does truths; intelligent, who does them from faith; scientific, who does them scientifically; and work is what is effected from those principles, thus work is their effect in which they conjoin themselves: wherefore no one can be called wise, nor intelligent, nor scientific, in a genuine sense, who does not do; for both wisdom, and intelligence, and science, are of the life, and not of doctrine without life; for life is the end for the sake of which [those principles exist]; such therefore as the end is, such is the wisdom, the intelligence, and the science; if the end be genuine good, which is the good of love to the Lord, and of charity towards the neighbor, then there is wisdom, intelligence, and science, in their proper sense; for in such case they appertain to man from the Lord; but if the end be for the sake of the good of the love of self and the world, they are not wisdom, intelligence, and science, since in such case they appertain to man from himself, for the good of the love of self and the world as an end is evil, and of evil as an end it is not possible to predicate in any wise any thing of wisdom and intelligence, nor even of science, unless there be in it the intelligence of truth, and the wisdom of good; for in any other case man is led to think from it that evil is good, and that what is false is true. With those who are in the good of love to the Lord, wisdom, intelligence, science, and work, follow together in order, from what is inmost to what is ultimate; wisdom with them is inmost, consisting in willing well from love; intelligence is another principle, for it consists in understanding well from willing well, these two are of the internal man; science consists in knowing well, and work in doing well, each grounded in willing well; these two are of the external man; hence it is evident that wisdom must be in intelligence, intelligence in science, and science in work; thus work includes and concludes all interior things, for it is the ultimate into which they close. From these considerations it may be manifest what is meant by works and deeds, which are so often mentioned, as in the following passages, "The Son of Man *shall render to every one according to his deeds*," Matt. xvi. 27. And in Jeremiah, "I will recompense them *according to their work, and according to the deed of their hands*," xxv. 14. Again, "Jehovah, whose eyes are open upon all the ways of man, to give to every one according to his ways, *and according to the fruit of his work*," xxii. 19. Again, "Return ye every one from his evil way, and *render good your works*," xxxv. 15. And in Hosea, "I will visit upon their ways, and *their works will I recompense to them*," iv. 9. And in Zechariah, "Jehovah doeth with us according to our ways, and *according to our works*," i. 6. And in the Apocalypse, "*I will give to every one according to his works*," ii. 23. Again, "*They were judged every one according to his works*," Apoc. xx. 13, 15. Again, "Behold I come, and my reward is with Me, *that I may give to every one according to his works*," Apoc. xxii. 12. By works in the above passages are meant all things appertaining to man, since all things of man, which are in his will and understanding, are in his works, for from those principles man does works; hence works have their life; for works without those principles are as a shell without a kernel, or as a body without a soul; what proceeds from man proceeds from his interiors, hence works are the manifestations of the interiors, and are the effects by which they appear. It is a common law, that such as the man is, such is all his work; hence it is that by the works, according to which there will be reward and retribution, is meant the quality of man as to love and as to faith; for works are of the love and of the faith appertaining to man; that man is nothing but his own love and his own faith, or what is the same thing, his own good and his own truth, see n. 10,076, 10,177, 10,265, 10,284, 10,298. Moreover the very will-faculty is nothing but work, since what any one wills this he does, if not prevented by some unmoveable obstacle; hence by being judged according to the deeds, is meant to be judged according to the will. They who do good from the principle of willing good, in the Word are called just, as is evident in Matt. chap. xxv. 37, 46; of such it is said, "that they shall shine as the sun in heaven," Matt. xiii. 43. And in Daniel, "The intelligent shall shine as the splendor of the expanse, and they who justify many as the stars," xii. 3; they who justify denote those who do good from a principle of willing well.

10,332. "To contrive contrivances to make in gold, and in

silver and in brass"—that hereby is signified to represent goods and truths interior and exterior, which are of the understanding derived from the will, thus which are of faith derived from love, appears from the signification of contriving contrivances, or of inventing inventions, as denoting what proceeds from the understanding, see n. 9598, 9688; and from the signification of making [or doing], as denoting what proceeds from the will, see n. 9282, for what a man makes [or does], this proceeds from his will-faculty, in this case from the will-faculty by [or through] the understanding, for it is said, to contrive contrivances to make [or do]; and from the signification of gold, as denoting good, and of silver, as denoting truth, see n. 1551, 1552, 5658, 6914, 6917, 8932, 9490, 9881, 9974; and from the signification of brass, as denoting the good of the natural or external man, see n. 425, 1551; hence by gold, silver and brass, are signified goods and truths interior and exterior; by gold interior good, by silver interior and exterior truth, and by brass external good. The reason why it is a representative of these goods and truths which is signified is, because the subject treated of is concerning a representative church, and all the things which Bezaleel was about to make, were representative. From these considerations it is evident, that by contriving contrivances, to make in gold, in silver, and in brass, is signified to represent goods and truths interior and exterior which are of the understanding derived from the will. The reason why the things of faith derived from love are also denoted is, because truths are of faith, and truths have reference to the understanding, and goods are of love, and goods have reference to the will. The understanding is said to be from the will, and faith from love, because the understanding is not any thing unless it be from the will, for what a man understands, and does not will, is not of the man's understanding, but is of the understanding of another in himself, wherefore this understanding perishes; it is otherwise with the understanding derived from the will, for this understanding is of the man himself, since the will is the man himself. The case is similar with faith and love, for as was said, the truths of faith have reference to the understanding, and the goods of love to the will.

10,333. "And in the engraving of a stone for filling"—that hereby is signified to represent all things of faith serviceable to the good of love, appears from the signification of the engraving of a stone, as being a representative of all things of faith derived from love; for by the engraving of a stone is meant the engraving of the stones in the breast-plate, which were the Urim and Thummim; that by those stones were represented all things of faith and of love, see n. 3858, 6335, 6640, 9823, 9863, 9865, 9868, 9873, 9905; and from the signification of filling, as denoting to be serviceable to the good of love, from which they are derived; for fillings were wrought in gold therein, and by gold is signified the good of love, n. 1551, 1552, 5658, 6914, 6917, 8932, 9490, 9881, 9884.

10,334. "And in the engraving of wood to make in all work"—that hereby is signified to represent every good whatsoever, appears from the signification of the engraving of wood, as being representative of good; that wood denotes good, see n. 643, 2784, 2812, 3720, 8354, 9474; and from the signification of every work, as denoting whatsoever. It is said all good whatsoever, because there are several genera and species of goods; there is celestial good and spiritual good; there is good interior and exterior, the exterior is natural and sensual; there is the good of innocence, the good of love, the good of faith; good must be in every truth to the intent that it may be truth; and also the good appertaining to man is formed by truths, hence good varies, and becomes manifold, and so manifold that no angel, no spirit, and no man, is in like good with that of another; the universal heaven consists in variety as to good, and by that variety one is distinguished from another; for if several had the same good, there would be no distinction; but those various goods are so arranged by the Lord, as to constitute together one common good. It is to be noted that the Divine Good is one, because infinite, n. 10,261; but it varies with angels, spirits, and men, as to quality and quantity, from receptions in truths, for truths qualify good, that is, give to good its quality, and truths are manifold.

10,335. "And I, behold, I have given with him Aholiab, the son of Ahisamach, of the tribe of Dan"—that hereby are signified those who are in the good and truth of faith, with whom the church was to be established, appears from the representation of Aholiab, as denoting those who are in the good and truth of faith; the reason why those are represented by Aholiab is, because he was of the tribe of Dan, and by that tribe are signified those who are in the good and truth of faith, see n. 3923, 6396. The reason why these two, namely, Bezaleel of the tribe of Judah, and Aholiab of the tribe of Dan, were chosen to make the works by which were to be represented Divine celestial and spiritual things, was, because by Bezaleel are meant all who are in the good of love, and by Aholiab all who are in the good and truth of faith, thus by Bezaleel those who are in the inmost things of heaven and of the church, and by Aholiab those who are in their ultimates; and when the inmost and ultimates are named, thereby are meant all who are in the universal heaven and in the universal church; on which subject see above, n. 10,329, and that when mention is made of first and last, all things are meant, n. 10,044. The tribe of Judah also was actually the first of the tribes, and the tribe of Dan was the last of them; that the tribe of Judah was actually the first of the tribes, appears from the blessing of the sons of Israel, their father, Gen. xlix., where Reuben, Simeon, and Levi, who were the first-born, are cursed, and Judah is blessed; see concerning Reuben, verses 3, 4, of that chapter; concerning Simeon and Levi, verses 5, 6, 7; and concerning Judah, verses 8, 9, 10, 11, 12; and that Dan is the last of the tribes, see n. 1710, 3922, 6396. In the inmost heaven also are those who are in the good of love to the Lord, and in the ultimate heaven those who are in the truth of faith derived from good. It is said in the truth ot faith derived from good, since the truth of faith is not the truth of faith with any one, unless it be from good, for truth is born from good; wherefore unless good be in truth, there is no soul in it, thus no life. They who are in the truths of faith derived from good, are in the ultimates of heaven, but not they who are in the truths of faith without good; these are not in heaven. Since the truth of faith ministers to the good of love, as the last to the first, therefore it is said of Aholiab, that Jehovah gave him with Bezaleel, which is to serve him; and it is said of Bezaleel, that Jehovah filled him with the spirit of God in wisdom, and in intelligence, and in science, and in every work, verse 3.

10,336. "And in the heart of every wise one in heart I have given wisdom"—that hereby are signified all who will and do what is good and true for the sake of what is good and true, appears from the signification of heart, as denoting the inmost principle of man, which is called his will; and since what is of the will of man is also of his love, therefore by the heart is likewise signified the love; that the heart denotes the love, see n. 3635, 3883 to 3896, 9050; and that it denotes the will, n. 2930, 3888, 7542, 8910, 9113, 9300, 9494; and from the signification of a wise one in heart, as denoting one who wills and loves what is good and true for the sake of what is good and true, for it is the part of a wise one and it is wisdom, to do truths from love, n. 10,331; and it is the part of a wise one in heart, and is wisdom of the heart, to do good from love. And from the signification of giving wisdom in the heart, as denoting to do those things from the Lord, thus from the good of love, for the good of love is from the Lord; for all such will and do what is good and true for the sake of what is good and true, since good and the truth of good are the Lord with them; for the things which are from Him, thus which are of Him, are also Himself; from this ground it is said, that the Lord is good itself, and truth itself; that the Lord is good itself, is manifest from the Lord's words, "*Why callest thou Me good? none is good but one, God,*" Matt. xix. 16, 17; Luke xviii. 18, 19; and where the good of love and charity are recounted, "*So much as ye have done to one of the least of these My brethren ye have done to Me,*" Matt. xxv. 40, 45; that they are called brethren who are in good, thus that goods are so called, see n. 2360, 3803, 3815, 4121, 5419; they are the brethren of the Lord, who are in good from Him, n. 4191, 5686, 5692, 6756. And that the Lord is truth itself, "*Jesus saith, I am the way, the truth, and the life*," John xiv. 6. And in another place, "*When the Spirit of Truth shall come, He shall lead you into all truth; He shall not speak from Himself; He shall take of Mine, and shall announce it to you*," John xvi. 13, 14, 15 Hence it is evident what is meant by giving wisdom in the heart. The like is also meant by writing a law on the heart in Jeremiah, "I will give My law in the midst of them, and *upon their heart I will write it*; neither shall they teach any more a man his companion, or a man his brother, saying, know ye Jehovah, for they shall all know Me," xxxi. 34. To write the law on the heart denotes to impress Divine Truth on the will, thus on the love; when this is the case, Divine Truth is no longer called forth from the memory, but is perceived from the good of love itself; wherefore it is said, they shall not teach any longer a man his companion, or a man his brother, saying, know ye Jehovah, for they shall all know Me. That such are the celestial angels, who are in the inmost heaven, see the passages cited, n. 9277. What is meant by willing and doing what is good and true, for the sake of what is good and true, which is signified by giving wisdom in heart in the heart of every wise one, it may be expedient briefly to say. All who love the Lord above all things, and the neighbor as themselves, do what is good and true for the sake of what is good and true; for good and truth are the Lord Himself, as was said above; wherefore when they love good and truth, that is, when they will and do them from love, they love the Lord; this is the case also with those who love the neighbor as themselves, since the neighbor in the universal sense is good and truth; for the neighbor is a fellow-citizen, a society, a man's country, the church, and the Lord's kingdom; and to love the neighbor is to will well to those [connections] or to will their good; wherefore it is their good which is to be loved; and when this is loved, the Lord is loved, because this good is from Him. Hence it is evident that love towards the neighbor, which is called charity, has in it love to the Lord. If this love be not in it, then a fellow-citizen, a society, a man's country, the church, and the Lord's kingdom, are loved for the sake of self, and thus are not loved from good but from evil; for whatsoever is from man, for the sake of himself as an end, is from evil; to love the neighbor for the sake of self is to love him for the sake of gain and honor as ends; the end is what determines whether it be from good or from evil, for the end is the love, since what a man loves, this he regards as an end; the end also is the will, for what a man wills, this he loves, hence the end regarded, or the intention, is the man himself; for man is such as his will is, and as his love is.

10,337. "And they shall make [or do] all things which I have commanded thee"—that hereby are signified Divine Truths from the Word, which were to be represented in things external, appears from the signification of making [or doing] all things which I have commanded, when relating to the Lord, as denoting according to Divine Truths, for Divine Truths are called the precepts of the Lord, n. 9417; and from the representation of Moses, as denoting the Word, see n. 9372. The reason why it denotes which were to be represented in external things was, because the things they were about to make were representative, and things representative are external, in which, as in types, internal things are presented. The representatives which they were to make are recounted in verses 7, 8, 9, 10, 11, which follow. What representatives are, see the passages cited, n. 9280; also n. 9457, 9481, 9576, 9577, 10,149, 10,252, 10,276.

10,338. "The tent of the congregation, and the ark for the testimony"—that hereby is signified a representative of heaven in general, where the Lord is, appears from the signification of the tent of the congregation and of the ark, as being a representative of heaven, see n. 9457, 9481, 9485, 9784. The reason why it denotes a representative of heaven in general is, because by the tent of the congregation within the vail, where the ark was, was represented the inmost or third heaven, n. 9485; by the tent of the congregation out of the vail, the middle or second heaven; and by the court the ultimate heaven, n. 9741; and from the signification of the testimony, as denoting the Lord as to Divine Truth, see n. 8535, 9503.

10,339. "And the propitiatory which is above it"—that hereby is signified a representative of the hearing and reception of all things of worship grounded in the good of love, appears from the signification of the propitiatory which was above the ark, as being a representative of all things of worship which are grounded in the good of love, see n. 9506.

10,340. "And all the vessels of the tent"—that hereby is signified a representative of all ministering goods and truths, appears from the signification of the vessels of the tent of the congregation, as denoting the goods and truths which are serviceable to the heavens, thus which minister; ministering goods and truths are knowledges and scientifics; that these are signified by vessels in general, see n. 3068, 3079, 9724.

10,341. "And the table and its vessels"—that hereby is signified a representative of spiritual good derived from celestial, appears from the signification of the table on which were the breads of faces, as being a representative of celestial and spiritual good, see n. 9527, 9545, 9684, 9685; and from the signification of its vessels, as denoting things ministering; that these are the knowledges of good and truth, see n. 9544.

10,342. "And the pure candlestick, and all its vessels"—that hereby is signified a representative of truth derived from that good, and things ministering, appears from the signification of the candlestick with the lamps and pipes, as being a representative of the spiritual heaven, and of faith and intelligence from the Lord there, thus of truth derived from good, see n. 9548, 9551, 9555, 9558, 9561; and from the signification of the vessels of the candlestick, as denoting things for purification and for snuffing, see n. 9572, thus things ministering.

10,343. "And the altar of incense"—that hereby is signified a representative of worship from those things, appears from the signification of the altar of incense, as being a representative of all things of worship which are from the good of love and faith, see n. 10,177.

10,344. "And the altar of burnt-offering, and all its vessels"—that hereby is signified a representative of worship from the good of love and its truths, appears from the signification of the altar of burnt-offering, as being a representative of the Lord, and of the worship of Him from the good of love, see n. 9714, 9964, 10,123, 10,151, 10,242, 10,245; and from the signification of its vessels, as denoting truth serving good, see n. 9723, 9724.

10,345. "And the laver and its base"—that hereby is signified a representative of purification and of regeneration, and the natural principle, appears from the signification of washing, which was effected by water in the laver, as being a representative of purification and regeneration, see n. 10,237, 10,239; and from the signification of the laver, as denoting the natural principle of man, see n. 10,235. And from the signification of its base, as denoting the sensual principle, which is the ultimate of the natural, see n. 10,236.

10,346. "And the garments of ministry, and the garments of holiness for Aaron the priest"—that hereby is signified a representative of the Lord's spiritual kingdom adjoined to His celestial kingdom, appears from the signification of the garments of Aaron, as being a representative of the Lord's spiritual kingdom adjoined to His celestial kingdom, see n. 9814.

10,347. "And the garments of his sons"—that hereby is signified a representative of inferior spiritual things, appears from the representation of the sons of Aaron and of their garments, as being a representative of inferior spiritual things, see n. 10,068.

10,348. "To perform the office of the priesthood"—that hereby is signified a representative of the work of the Lord's salvation, appears from the signification of the priesthood of Aaron and of his sons, as being a representative of the work of the Lord's salvation, see n. 9809, 10,017.

10,349. "And the oil of anointing"—that hereby is signified a representative of the Lord as to the Divine Good of the Divine Love in His Divine Human, appears from what was said concerning anointing and the oil of anointing, n. 9954, 10,011, 10,019, 10,261.

10,350. "And the incense of spices"—that hereby is signified a representative of the worship from truths, appears from the signification of incense, as being a representative of worship, see n. 9475, 10,198, 10,298; and from the signification of its spices, as denoting truths and their affections, see n. 10,291, 10,295.

10,351. "For what is holy"—that hereby is signified for the representative church, appears from the signification of what is holy in that church, as being a representative of the Lord and of the Divine things which are from Him, see n. 9229, 9956, 10,069, 10,149; thus which are in the worship of the Lord, in the representative church, for it is said of the incense, by which is signified worship, as above, n. 10,350.

10,352. "According to all things which I have commanded thee they shall do [or make]"—that hereby is signified according to Divine Truths which are from the Word, which were to be represented in things external, see above, n. 10,337. All these things, which were commanded to be made [or done] by Bezaleel and Aholiab, are such as have already been explained as to their signification, therefore they are not further explained here, but solely recounted.

10,353. Verses 12 to 18. *And Jehovah said to Moses, saying, Also speak thou to the sons of Israel, saying; altogether My sabbaths ye shall keep, because it is a sign between Me and between you to your generations, to know that I Jehovah sanctify you. And ye shall keep the sabbath, because this is holy to you, he that profaneth it, dying shall die, because every one that doeth work in it, that soul shall be cut off from the midst of his people. Six days shall work be done, and on the seventh day is the sabbath of a sabbath, holy to Jehovah. Every one doing work on the day of the sabbath, dying shall die. And the sons of Israel shall keep the sabbath, to make the sabbath to their generations, the covenant of an age. Between Me and between the sons of Israel this sign shall be for an age; because in six days Jehovah made the heaven and the earth, and on the seventh day rested and respired. And he gave to Moses, in His finishing to speak with him on Mount Sinai, the two tables of the testimony, tables of stone, written with the finger of God.* And Jehovah said to Moses, saying, signifies illustration and perception by the Word from the Lord. And speak thou to the sons of Israel, saying, signifies information of those who are of the church by the Word. Altogether My sabbaths ye shall keep, signifies holy thought continually concerning the union of the Divine with the Human of the Lord. Because this is a sign between Me and between you, signifies that this is the principal thing by which they who are of the church are known in heaven. To your generations, signifies in all and singular the things of the church. To know that I Jehovah sanctify you, signifies the Lord as to the Divine Human, that all things of heaven and of the church respect Him as their only source. And ye shall keep the sabbath, signifies that the Divine Human of the Lord ought to be worshiped. Because this is holy to you, signifies hence all the good and truth which make the church. He who profaneth it, signifies to be led of themselves and their loves, and not of the Lord. Dying shall die, signifies separation from heaven and spiritual death. Every one doing work on that day, signifies who turns himself from heavenly loves to corporeal and worldly loves. That soul shall be cut off from the midst of his people, signifies that heaven and the church is not with him, but hell. Six days shall work be done, signifies the state which precedes, and prepares for the heavenly marriage. And on the seventh day is the sabbath of a sabbath, signifies the state of good which is the end regarded, thus when man becomes a church and enters heaven. Holy to Jehovah, signifies Divine. Every one doing work on the day of the sabbath dying shall die, signifies to be led of self and of its love, and not of the Lord. And the sons of Israel shall keep the sabbath to make [or do] the sabbath to their generations, signifies that the very essential principle of the church is the acknowledgment of the union of the Divine itself in the Human of the Lord, and that this should be in all and singular the things of worship. The covenant of an age, signifies conjunction with the Lord to eternity. Between Me and between the sons of Israel this is a sign for an age, signifies that by it they who are of the church are distinguished from those who are not of the church. Because in six days Jehovah made the heaven and the earth, signifies a state of combat and of labor whilst the church is establishing. And on the seventh day rested and respired, signifies a state of good when the church is established, or when man is regenerated. And He gave to Moses in His finishing to speak with him on Mount Sinai two tables of the testimony, signifies conjunction with the Lord by the Word with man. Tables of stone written with the finger of God, signifies Divine Truth therein from the Lord Himself.

10,354. "And Jehovah said to Moses, saying"—that hereby is signified illustration and perception by the Word from the Lord, appears from what was shown above, n. 10,234, 10,290.

10,355. "Also speak thou to the sons of Israel, saying"—

that hereby is signified the information of those who are of the church by the Word, appears from the representation of Moses, to whom it is said that he should speak to the sons of Israel, as denoting the Word, see the passages cited, n. 9372; and from the signification of speaking and saying, as denoting instruction or information, see passages cited, n. 10,277; and from the representation of the sons of Israel, as denoting the church, see the passages cited, n. 9340; hence it is evident that by "speak thou to the sons of Israel, saying," is signified the information of those who are of the church by the Word. Concerning information by the Word it may here be expedient to make some observations: in the most ancient times men were informed concerning heavenly things, or those which relate to eternal life, by immediate commerce with the angels of heaven, for heaven at that time acted in unity with the man of the church, inasmuch as it flowed in through the internal man into their external, whence they had not only illustration and perception, but also discourse with the angels. This time was called the golden age, from the circumstance that men were then principled in the good of love to the Lord, for gold signifies that good; those things are also described by paradise in the Word. Afterwards information concerning heavenly things, and concerning those which relate to eternal life, was effected by such things as are called correspondences and representations, the science of which was derived from the most ancient [men] who had immediate commerce with the angels of heaven; into those [correspondences and representations] at that time heaven flowed in with men, and illustrated; for correspondences and representations are the external forms of heavenly things; and in proportion as men at that time were in the good of love and charity, in the same proportion they were illustrated; for all Divine influx out of heaven is into the good appertaining to man, and by good into truths; and whereas the man of the church at that time was in spiritual good, which good in its essence is truth, therefore those times were called the silver age, for silver signifies such good. But when the science of correspondences and of representations was turned into magic, that church perished, and a third succeeded, in which indeed all worship was effected almost by similar things, but still it was unknown what they signified. This church was instituted with the Israelitish and Jewish nation. But whereas information concerning heavenly things, or concerning those things which relate to eternal life, could not be effected with the man of that church by influx into their interiors, and thus by illustration, therefore angels from heaven spake by a living voice with some of them, and instructed them concerning external things, and little concerning internal things, because the latter they could not comprehend. They who were in natural good, received those things holily; whence those times were called brazen, for brass signifies such good. But when not even natural good remained with the man of the church, the Lord came into the world, and reduced all things in the heavens and in the hells into order, to the end that man may receive influx from Him out of heaven, and be illustrated, and that the hells might not be any hindrance, and let in thick darkness, on which occasion a fourth church commenced, which is called Christian. In this church information concerning heavenly things, or concerning the things which relate to eternal life, is effected solely by the Word, whereby man has influx and illustration, for the Word was written both by mere correspondences and by mere representatives, which signify heavenly things; into which heavenly things the angels of heaven come, when man reads the Word. Hence by the Word is effected the conjunction of heaven with the church, or of the angels of heaven with the men of the church, but only with those there who are in the good of love and charity. But whereas the man of this church has extinguished also this good, therefore neither can he be informed by any influx and by illustration thence, only concerning some truths, which yet do not cohere with good. Hence these times are what are called iron, for iron denotes truth in the ultimate of order; but when truth is of such a quality, then it is such as is described in Daniel, "Thou sawest iron mixed with the clay of mud, they shall mix themselves together by the seed of man, but they shall not cohere the one with the other, as iron is not mixed together with clay," ii. 43. From these considerations it may be manifest in what manner revelations have succeeded from the most ancient ages to the present; and that at this day revelation is only given by the Word, but genuine revelation with those who are in the love of truth for the sake of truth, and not with those who are in the love of truth for the sake of honors and gains, as ends. For if you are willing to believe it, the Lord is the Word Itself, since the Word is Divine Truth, and Divine Truth is the Lord in heaven, because from the Lord; wherefore they who love Divine Truth for the sake of Divine Truth, love the Lord; and with those who love the Lord, heaven flows in and illustrates; whereas they who love Divine Truth for the sake of honors and gains as ends, avert themselves from the Lord to themselves and to the world, wherefore with them influx and illustration cannot be given; these also, since in the sense of the letter they keep the mind fixed in themselves, and in their own fame and glory, apply that sense to such things as favor their own loves.

10,356. "Altogether My sabbaths ye shall keep"—that hereby is signified holy thought continually concerning the union of the Divine itself with the Human of the Lord, appears from the signification of sabbaths, as denoting, in the supreme sense, the union of the Divine itself with the Divine Human in the Lord, and, in the respective sense, the conjunction of the Lord as to the Divine Human with heaven; also the conjunction of heaven with the church; and in general the conjunction of good and truth with those who are the church, or with whom the church is. That the former union and the latter conjunctions are signified by sabbaths, see n. 8495, 8510, 8890, 8893, 9274. And from the signification of nevertheless or altogether keeping, as denoting to have in the thought holily and continually; for when keeping is said of those things which were represented in that church, it signifies to have in thought and mind the things which were represented, and to worship them holily; for representatives were external things in which were internal, and which thus gave a handle of thinking about internal things. Hence by keeping the sabbaths of Jehovah, is signified to think holily and continually concerning the Lord, the union of the Divine itself with His Divine Human, concerning the conjunction of the Lord as to the Divine Human with heaven, and concerning the conjunction of heaven with the church, also concerning the conjunction of good and truth in the man of the church. Inasmuch as these are the very essentials of the church, for without their acknowledgment and faith the church is not the church, therefore the sabbath, by which those things are signified, is lastly spoken of, and also again and again to the end of the chapter.

10,357. "Because it is a sign between Me and between you"—that hereby is signified that it is the principal thing by which they who are of the church are known in heaven, appears from the signification of a sign between Jehovah and between the sons of Israel, as denoting that which indicates and testifies that they are of the church, thus by which they are known in heaven, and also by which they are conjoined to the Lord; for they who are of the church, in whom the church is, must acknowledge the Lord and the Divine in Him, and must acknowledge the conjunction of the Lord with heaven, and also the conjunction of heaven with the man of the church, and in general the conjunction of good and truth appertaining to him, since this conjunction makes the church with him. Whether we speak of the church with man, or of heaven with him, or of the kingdom of God with him, or of the Lord with him, it is the same thing; for the church is the heaven of the Lord in the earths, and the kingdom of God is heaven and the church together, and the Lord is their source, yea, is them.

10,358. "To your generations"—that hereby is signified in all and singular the things of the church, appears from the signification of generations, when relating to the sons of Israel, as denoting all and singular the things of the church see n. 10,282.

10,359. "To know that I Jehovah sanctify you"—that hereby is signified the Lord as to the Divine Human, that all things of heaven and of the church should respect Him as their only source, appears from the signification of what is holy [*sanctum*], as denoting the Divine in heaven and in the church, for this alone is holy; and the Divine in heaven and the church proceeds from the Divine Human of the Lord, thus it is the Divine Human of the Lord which alone is holy, consequently which sanctifies [or makes holy]. Hence it is evident, that it is what all things of heaven and of the church respect as their only source. For heaven is heaven, not from the proprium of the angels, but from the Divine of the Lord appertaining to them; in like manner the church with men. It is said, "I, Jehovah, sanctify you," and by Jehovah is meant the Lord. But whereas these subjects have been frequently treated of before, see what has been above said and shown concerning them; as that the Lord alone is holy, and that every thing holy proceeds from Him, n. 9229, 9680, 9820. That sanctification is the reception of the Divine of the Lord, n. 9820, 10,128, 10,276. That the angels acknowledge no other Divine but the Divine Human of the Lord, n. 10,159, 9267. Thus that the Lord as to the Divine Human is heaven and the church, because He dwells in His own there, and not in the proprium of others, n. 10,125, 10,151, 10,157. And that Jehovah in the Word is the Lord, see the passages cited, n. 9373.

10,360. "And ye shall keep the sabbath"—that hereby is signified that the Divine Human of the Lord is to be worshiped, appears from the signification of keeping, when it is said of the Divine, as denoting to worship; and from the signification of the sabbath, as denoting, in the supreme sense, the union of the Divine which is called the Father, and of the Divine Human which is the Son, thus the Divine Human which is the subject of that union. The reason why that union is signified by the sabbath is, because by the six days of labor, which precede the seventh, is signified every state of combat, for labor, in the spiritual sense, is not labor such as is in the world, but such as they who are in the church endure, before they enter into the church and become a church, which labor is combat against evils and the falses of evil. In the spiritual sense, the Lord endured similar labor when He was in the world, for He then fought against the hells, and reduced them and likewise the heavens into order; and on the same occasion He glorified His Human, that is, united it to the Divine itself which He had from conception, see n. 9715, 9809. The time and state, when the Lord was in combats, is signified by the six days of labor, but the state, when the union was effected, is signified by the seventh day, which is called the sabbath from rest, because the Lord then had rest. Hence by the sabbath is also signified the conjunction of the Lord with heaven, with the church, with an angel of heaven, and with a man of the church. The reason is, because all who are about to come into heaven, must first be in combats against evils and the falses of evil, and when these are separated they enter heaven, and are conjoined to the Lord, and then they have rest; in like manner men in the world. That these latter must be in combats, or that they must undergo temptations, before good and truth, which constitute the church, are implanted in them, is a known thing; thus before they are conjoined to the Lord, consequently before they have rest. Hence it is evident from what ground it is, that a state of combat is signified by six days of labor, whilst rest and also conjunction is signified by the seventh day or the sabbath. The reason why the conjunction of good and truth is signified by the sabbath is, because when man is in combats, he is then in truths, but when truths are conjoined to good, thus when man is in good, he then has rest. In like manner as the Lord, when He was in the world and fought with the hells, then, as to His Human, He was Divine Truth, and when He united His Human to the Divine itself, then He was made even as to His Human Divine Good, or Jehovah. That the six days which precede the sabbath, denote the combats which precede and prepare for the heavenly marriage, which is the conjunction of good and truth, see n. 8510, 8888, 9431. Concerning the former state, when man is in truths, and is then in combats against evils and the falses of evil, which state is signified by the six days of labor, and concerning the latter state, when he is in good, and is led of the Lord, which is signified by the sabbath, see n. 7923, 7992, 8505, 8506, 8510, 8512, 8516, 8539, 8643, 8648, 8658, 8685, 8690, 8701, 8772, 9139, 9832, 9224, 9227, 9230, 9274. That the Lord when He was in the world, made His Human first Divine Truth and next Divine Good, see the passages cited, n. 9199, 9315. And that He did this by the combats of temptations, see the passages cited, n. 9528. He therefore who knows that by the sabbath, in the supreme sense, is meant the union of the Divine itself in the Divine Human of the Lord, may know what those things signify which are so often said in the Word concerning the sabbath, as in Isaiah, "*If thou turn away thy foot from the sabbath, and doest not thine own wills in the day of My holiness, but shalt call the sabbath delights, honorable to the Holy One of Jehovah, and shalt honor it, so as not to do thine own ways, nor find thine own desire, or speak a word, then shalt thou delight on Jehovah, and I will exalt thee into the heights of the earth, and will feed thee with the inheritance of Jacob thy father*," lviii. 13, 14. He who is acquainted with the internal sense of the Word, may see manifestly, that in this passage by sabbath is signified a state of the conjunction of man with the Lord, thus a state when man is led of the Lord, and not of himself, which state is when he is in good. For to be led of the Lord, and not of self, is to turn away the foot from the sabbath not to do his own wills, not to do his own ways, not to find his own desire, and not to speak a word. That in this case the church is in him and heaven, is signified by being exalted into the heights of the earth, and being fed with the inheritance of Jacob. And that the sabbath is the Divine Human in which is union, is signified by the sabbath being called a day of holiness, and delights to the Holy One of Jehovah. And in Jeremiah, "*If ye sanctify the day of the sabbath, there shall enter through the gates of this city kings and princes, sitting on the throne of David, riding in a chariot and on horses*," xvii. 24, 25. He who is unacquainted with the internal sense of the Word, may be led to suppose that these things are to be understood according to the sense of the letter, namely, that if they would sanctify the sabbath, kings and princes would enter through the gates of the city Jerusalem, and would ride in a chariot and on horses; this however is not the sense of the above words, but that they who worship holily the Divine Human of the Lord, shall be in the Divine Truths of heaven and of the church, for by Jerusalem is meant the church, by kings and princes its Divine Truths, by the throne of David heaven, where the Lord is, by chariot the doctrine of good and truth, and by horses an enlightened intellectual principle. That Jerusalem denotes the church, see n. 2117, 3654. That kings denote Divine Truths, n. 1672, 2015, 2069, 3009, 4575, 4581, 4966, 5044, 5068, 6148. That princes denote primary truths, n. 1482, 2089, 9954. That a throne denotes heaven, n. 5313. That a chariot denotes the doctrine of good and truth, n. 5321, 8215. And that horses denote the intellectual principle which is enlightened, n. 2760, 2761, 2762, 3217, 5321, 6534. Inasmuch as by the sabbath was signified the Lord as to the Divine Human in which is union, therefore it was commanded that *the breads of faces should be arranged on the table every sabbath*, Levit. xxiv. 8. That the Lord as to the Divine Human is meant by bread, is a thing known in the church. On this account also the Lord, when He was in the world, *called Himself the Lord of the sabbath*, Matt. xii. 8; Mark ii. 27, 28; Luke vi. 1 to 5. And therefore the Lord, when He was in the world, and united His Human to the Divine itself, abrogated the sabbath as to representative worship, or as to the worship which prevailed amongst the Israelitish people, and made the sabbath day a day of instruction in the doctrine of faith and love. This is involved in what is written in John, "Jesus healing a certain person on the sabbath day, said to him, take up thy bed and walk; and he took up his bed and walked." The Jews said, that it was not allowed to carry a bed on the sabbath day, and they sought to kill the Lord, *because He broke the sabbath*, v. 8, 9, 10, 11, 18; by healing a sick person is signified the purification of man from evils and the falses of evil; by a bed is signified doctrine; and by walking is signified life. That all the healings of diseases, which were performed by the Lord, involve purifications from evils and falses, or restorations of spiritual life, see n. 8364, 9031, 9086. That walking denotes life, n. 519, 1744, 8417, 8420. That a bed denotes doctrine, is manifest from the passages in the Word where a bed is named, and also from the representatives in the other life, where, when a bed appears and a person lying in it, is signified the doctrine in which the person is principled; hence beds appear there most exquisitely adorned for those who are in truths derived from good; but that such things are signified by the above words of the Lord, it is impossible for any one to know but by the internal sense; for the Lord spake by correspondences, thus by significatives, because from the Divine.

10,361. "Because this is holy to you"—that hereby is signified hence every good and truth which make the church, appears from the signification of what is holy, as denoting all that and only that which proceeds from the Lord, see n. 9479, 9680, 9820, thus the good of love and the truth of faith, for these are what proceed from the Lord. That these constitute the church with men, and heaven with angels, may be manifest from this consideration, that love and faith are essentials of the church, because they conjoin men and angels to the Lord, the good of love their will principle, and the truth of faith their intellectual principle, thus all things appertaining to them.

10,362. "He that profaneth it"—that hereby is signified to be led of themselves and their own loves, and not of the Lord, appears from the signification of profaning the sabbath, or of doing work on the day of the sabbath, as denoting to be led of themselves and not of the Lord, thus of their own loves. That this is signified by profaning the sabbath, is manifest from Isaiah, "*If thou turnest away thy foot from the sabbath, so as not to do thine own wills on the day of My holiness, and not to do thine own ways, neither findest thine own desire, and speakest a word*," lviii. 13; where to turn away the foot from the sabbath denotes such things as are of the natural man; to do his own wills is to do those things which favor the lusts and evils of the loves of self and the world; to do his own ways is to favor the falses of evil; to find his own desire is to live according to the delights of those loves, and to speak a word denotes to think such things; hence it is evident that by profaning the sabbath is signified to be led of themselves and of their own loves, and not of the Lord, who in the supreme sense is the sabbath, as was shown just above. Similar things are signified by works on the sabbath day, as by cutting wood, kindling a fire, preparing food at that time, gathering-in the harvest, and several other things which were forbidden to be done on the sabbath day; by which also like things are signified. By cutting wood, the operating good from themselves; by kindling a fire, the doing it from their own loves; and by preparing food, the teaching themselves from their own proper intelligence. That such things are involved in the above prohibitions, no one can know but from the internal sense. It is further to be noted, that to be led of self and to be led of the Lord are two opposites, for he who is led of himself is led of his own loves, thus of hell, for the proper loves of man are from that source; and he who is led of the Lord, is led of the loves of heaven, which are love to the Lord and love towards the neighbor. He who is led by these loves, is withdrawn from his own proper loves; and he who is led of his own proper loves, is withdrawn from the loves of heaven, for they in no wise agree together; for the life of man is either in heaven or in hell, nor is it granted to be at the same time in one and in the other. This is meant by the Lord's words in Matthew, "No one can serve two lords, for either he will hate the one, and love the other, or he will adhere to the one, and neglect the other," vi. 24. From these considerations it is evident what is signified by doing work on the sabbath day.

10,363. "Dying shall die"—that hereby is signified separation from heaven and spiritual death, appears from the signification of dying, when concerning the sabbath, by which is signified the Lord and the acknowledgment of Him, as denoting no conjunction with heaven, see n. 9928, 10,224, thus separation from heaven; and separation from heaven is spiritual death.

10,364. "Every one doing work on that day"—that hereby is signified who turns himself from heavenly loves to corporeal and worldly loves, appears from what was shown just above, n. 10,362.

10,365. "That soul shall be cut off from the midst of his people"—that hereby is signified that heaven and the church is not with him, but hell, appears from the signification of being cut off from the midst of his people, as denoting separation from the church, and spiritual death, see n. 10,288; thus that the church is not with him, but hell; and since when the church is not with man, neither is heaven with him, for the church and heaven act in unity; for with the man in whom the church is, heaven flows in, that is, the Lord through heaven, and makes the church there; hence it is that when the church is not with man, hell is with him. This therefore is signified by being cut off from the midst of his people.

10,366. "Six days shall work be done"—that hereby is signified the state which precedes and prepares for the heavenly marriage, appears from the signification of the six days which precede the sabbath, as denoting the state which precedes and prepares for the heavenly marriage, see n. 8510, 8888, 9431. The heavenly marriage is the conjunction of good and truth with a man of the church and an angel of heaven, and in the supreme sense is the union of the Divine Itself in the Human of the Lord, see n. 10,356; and that the work of six days denotes the preceding state, see n. 10,360.

10,367. "And on the seventh day is the sabbath of a sabbath"—that hereby is signified a state of good, which is the end intended, thus when man becomes a church and enters heaven, appears from the signification of the seventh day, as denoting a state of good, which is the end intended; for when the six days which precede signify the state of man which precedes and prepares for the heavenly marriage, hence the seventh day denotes when man is in that marriage. That marriage is the conjunction of truth and good with man, thus when man becomes a church and enters heaven. The ground and reason why man enters heaven, and becomes a church, when he is in good, is, because the Lord flows-in into the good appertaining to man, and by good into its truth; the influx is effected into the internal man, where his heaven is, and through the internal into the external, where his world is; wherefore unless man be in good, his internal man is not opened, but remains shut, howsoever he be in truths as to doctrine; and since heaven is in the internal man, therefore when this is opened, man is in heaven, for heaven is not in place, but in the interiors of man. That man is created to the image both of heaven and the world, his internal man to the image of heaven, and the external to the image of the world, see the passages cited, n. 9279, 9706. The man is throughout such as he is as to good, and not as to truth without good, every one who reflects may know, for by his good, and according to it, he deals with another, is affected towards another, conjoins himself to another, suffers himself to be led by another, but not by truth and according to it, unless this be in accord with his good. When mention is made of good, its delight is meant, its pleasure, or its love, for all things appertaining to those principles are to the man goods, and so far as he is left to himself, so as to think from himself, truths are what favor those goods. Hence it may be manifest that man by good is conjoined to the Lord, and in no wise by truth without good. Conjunction by good with the Lord has indeed been often treated of above, in speaking of the regeneration of man; but whereas the man of the church at this day studies much the truths which are of faith, and but little the good which is of love, and hence is in ignorance about good, it is allowed to make some further observations concerning the conjunction of good and truth, which is called the heavenly marriage. Man is born into evils of every kind, and hence into falses of every kind, thus of himself he is damned to hell; to the intent therefore that he may be snatched out of hell, he must be altogether re-born by the Lord; this re-birth is what is called regeneration. With a view to be thus re-born, he must first learn truths, if he be of the church, from the Word, or from doctrine derived from the Word. The Word, and doctrine from the Word, teach what is true and good, and what is true and good teaches what is false and evil; unless man be acquainted with those principles, he cannot in any wise be regenerated, for he remains in his evils and the falses thence derived, calling the former goods, and the latter truths. Hence it is that the knowledges of truth and good must precede, and enlighten the understanding of man; for the understanding was given to man, that by the knowledges of good and truth it may be enlightened, to the intent that they may be received by his will, and become good; for truths then become good, when man wills them, and from willing does them. Hence it is evident in what manner good is formed witl man, and that unless he be in good, he is not born anew or re generated. When therefore man is in good as to the will, he ' then in the truths of that good as to the understanding; for the understanding with man actually acts in unity with his wi. since what a man wills, this he thinks when he is left to himsel this now is what is called the conjunction of truth and good or the heavenly marriage. Whether we speak of willing good, or of loving good, it is the same thing, for what a man loves, this he wills; and in this case whether we speak of understanding the truth which is of good, or of believing it, it is also the same thing; hence it follows that with the regenerate man love and faith act in unity. This conjunction, or this marriage is what is called the church, and heaven, and also the kingdom of the Lord; yea, in the supreme sense, the Lord with man. But they who love their own evils, which they have either received hereditarily, and from infancy have confirmed with themselves, or which they have superadded of themselves, and have imbued anew, are capable indeed of apprehending, and in some measure understanding, truths derived from the Word or from doctrine, but still they cannot be regenerated; for every man is kept by the Lord in that state as to the understanding, to the intent that he may be regenerated; but when he loves his own evils, in this case the intellectual principle of his internal man is not imbued with those truths, but only the intellectual principle of his external man, which intellectual principle is merely scientific. Such men do not know what good is, nor do they care to know that it is, but only what truth is, hence it is that they make the church and heaven to consist in truths which are called the truths of faith, and not in goods which are also of the life; in favor of their principle they explain the Word by various methods; hence it is that with persons of such a character, who are not at the same time in truths as to life, there is not a conjunction of truth and good, thus neither the church and heaven; the truths also, which they have called the truths of faith, are separated from them in the other life, for evil of the will ejects them, and in their place succeed falses conformable to the evils in which they are principled. From these considerations it may now be manifest what the conjunction of good and truth is, which is signified by the sabbath. This conjunction is called the sabbath from rest, for sabbath denotes rest; for when man is in the first state, that is, when by truths he is leading to good, in this case he is in combats against the evils and falses which appertain to him; for by combats, which are temptations, evils and their falses are shaken off and separated, nor is there rest from them, until good and truth are conjoined; in this case man has rest, and the Lord has rest, for man does not fight against evils and falses, but the Lord with him. The reason why the sabbath, in the supreme sense, signifies the Divine Human of the Lord is, because the Lord, when He was in the world, fought from His Human against all the hells, and subdued them, and at the same time reduced the heavens into order, and after this labor united His Human to the Divine, and also made it Divine Good, hence on this occasion He had rest, for the hells do not snarl against the Divine. Hence now it is that by the sabbath, in the supreme sense, is meant the Divine Human of the Lord; but on these subjects see what has been before shown, as that the Lord, when He was in the world, first made His Human Divine Truth, to the end that He might fight with the hells, and subdue them; and that afterwards He glorified His Human, and made it the Divine Good of the Divine Love, see the passages cited, n. 9199, 9315; also n. 9715, 9809. That the Lord, when He was in the world, underwent the most grievous temptations, see the passages cited, n. 9528. That hence He has Divine power to save man, by removing from him the hells, and thus regenerating him, n. 10,019, 10,152. Concerning the two-fold state of the man who is regenerating by the Lord, see the passages cited, n. 9274. And that man does not come into heaven, until conjunction is effected of truth and good with him, n. 8516, 8539, 8722, 8772, 9139, 9832. That the regeneration of man is an image of the glorification of the Lord, n. 3138, 3212, 3296, 3490, 4402, 5688.

10,368. "Holy to Jehovah"—that hereby is signified the Divine, appears from the signification of holy to Jehovah, as denoting the Divine Human of the Lord, and all that and only that which proceeds from Him, see n. 9479, 9680, 9820.

10,369. "Every one doing work on the sabbath day, dying

shall die"—that hereby is signified to be led of themselves and their own loves, and not of the Lord, and hence spiritual death, appears from what was shown above, n. 10,362.

10,370. "And the sons of Israel shall keep the sabbath to make [or do] the sabbath to their generations"—that hereby is signified that the very essential principle of the church is the acknowledgment of the union of the Divine itself in the Human of the Lord, and that this must be in all and singular the things of worship, appears from the signification of keeping the sabbath, as denoting holy thought continually concerning the union of the Divine itself with the Human of the Lord, see above, n. 10,356, thus also acknowledgment, for thought without acknowledgment and faith is not spiritual thought; and from the representation of the sons of Israel, as denoting the church, see the passages cited, n. 9340; and from the signification of doing [or making] the sabbath, as denoting to worship that union holily, thus to worship the Lord as to the Divine Human, for in that principle is that union; and from the signification of the generations of the sons of Israel, as denoting in all and singular the things of the church, see n. 10,282. From these considerations it is evident, that by the sons of Israel keeping the sabbath to do [or make] the sabbaths to their generations, is signified the acknowledgment of the Divine itself in the Human of the Lord in all and singular the things of worship. The reason why this is an essential of the church, and hence an essential of its worship, is, because the salvation of the human race depends solely on that union. For the sake of effecting that union also the Lord came into the world; therefore also the whole Word, in the inmost sense, treats of it, and the rituals of the church established amongst the sons of Israel, represented and signified it. That the salvation of the human race is from that source, consequently that that acknowledgment is an essential of the church and of its worship, the Lord teaches in several passages, as in John, "He that believeth on the Son hath eternal life; but he who doth not believe the Son, shall not see life," iii. 36; also verses 15, 16, of the same chapter; likewise chap. vi. 40; chap. xi. 25, 26; chap. xx. 31. The Son is the Divine Human of the Lord. The reason why they who do not from faith acknowledge the Lord, have not eternal life is, because the whole heaven is in that acknowledgment; for the Lord is the Lord of heaven and of earth, as Himself teaches in Matthew, "All power is given unto Me in heaven and in earth," xxviii. 18; wherefore to those who do not acknowledge Him, heaven is closed; and he who does not acknowledge in the world, that is, who is within the church, does not acknowledge in the other life; such is the state of man after death.

10,371. "The covenant of an age"—that hereby is signified

conjunction with the Lord to eternity, appears from the signification of a covenant, as denoting conjunction, see n. 665, 666, 1023, 1038, 1864, 1996, 2003, 2021, 6804, 8767, 8775, 9396, 9416; and from the signification of an age, as denoting what is eternal, see n. 10,248.

10,372. "Between Me and between the sons of Israel this shall be a sign for an age"—that hereby is signified that by it are distinguished those who are of the church, from those who are not of the church, appears from the signification of a sign, as denoting that by which they are known, see above, n. 10,357; thus also by which they are distinguished; and from the representation of the sons of Israel, as denoting the church, see the passages cited, n. 9340; hence by a sign between Jehovah and between the sons of Israel, is signified that it is that by which they who are of the church are distinguished from those who are not of the church, namely, by the acknowledgment of the union of the Divine in the Human of the Lord, see above, n. 10,370. That the church is not where the Lord is not acknowledged, the church itself also teaches; and also that in His Human is the Divine itself, the Lord Himself teaches in John, "*The Father and I are One; believe ye that the Father is in Me and I in the Father,*" x. 30, 38. Again, "*Believest thou not that I am in the Father, and the Father in Me?*" xiv. 6 to 11. Again, "*Jesus said, the hour is come, Father glorify thy Son, and let Thy Son glorify Thee. All Mine are Thine, and all Thine are Mine,*" xvii. 1, 10. Again, "*Now is the Son of Man glorified, and God is glorified in Him, and God shall glorify Him in Himself,*" xiii. 31, 32. And again, "*If ye have known Me, ye have also known My Father, and henceforth ye have known Him and have seen; he who seeth Me, seeth the Father,*" xiv. 6 to 11.

10,373. "Because in six days Jehovah made the heaven and the earth"—that hereby is signified a state of combat and of labor when the church is establishing, appears from the signification of six days, when the establishment of the church and the regeneration of man are treated of, as denoting states of combat against evils and falses, thus the state which precedes and prepares for the conjunction of good and truth, see above, n. 10,366, 10,367; and from the signification of heaven and earth, as denoting the church. By making heaven and earth in the Word is not meant the first creation itself of the visible heaven and earth, but the establishment of the church, and the regeneration of man therein; by heaven is meant its internal, and by earth its external; that this creation is meant, is manifest from the passages in the Word, where mention is made of creating, as in David, "*The people who shall be created shall praise Jah,*" Psalm cii. 18. Again, "*Thou sendest forth the spirit, they are created, and Thou renewest the faces of the earth*," Psalm civ. 30. And in Isaiah, "Thus saith Jehovah, *thy Creator*, *Jacob thy Former*, *Israel;* for I have redeemed thee, I have called by thy name, thou art Mine ; *every one called by My name, and to My glory I have created, I have formed him*, and I have also *made him*," xliii. 1, 2, and in other places. Mention is made of creating, of forming and making, and in other places of a creator, a former, and a maker ; and by creating is signified what is new which was not before, by forming is signified quality, and by making, effect. That to create and make a new heaven and a new earth denotes to establish a new church, its internal and external, as in Isaiah, chap. lxv. 17 ; chap. lxvi. 22 ; Apoc. xxi. 1, see n. 1733, 1850, 2117, 2118, 3355, 4535 ; and that earth in the Word denotes the church, n. 9325 ; also that the creation of the heaven and the earth in the first chapter of Genesis denotes the establishment of the most Ancient Church, n. 8891, 9942.

10,374. "And on the seventh day rested and respired"—that hereby is signified a state of good when the church is established, or when man is regenerated, appears from the signification of the seventh day, as denoting a holy state, which is that of the church when it is in good, thus when it is established ; or when the man of the church is in good, thus when regenerated. In the supreme sense by the seventh day, and by the rest and respiration of Jehovah on the occasion, is signified the union of the Divine itself which is called Father, and of the Divine Human which is called Son in the Lord, thus when the Lord, even as to His Human, was made the Divine Good of the Divine Love, or Jehovah ; hence it is that seven in the Word denotes what is holy, see n. 395, 433, 716, 881, 5265, 5268. The reason why Jehovah is said on this occasion to have rested and respired, is, because the Lord as to His Human was then above all infestations from the hells, and at the same time heaven and earth were under His government, Matt. xxviii. 18. There was at that same time also a rest and respiration of heaven, because all things in heaven were then reduced by the Lord into order, and the hells were subdued. In like manner in the earths, since when heaven is in order, and the hells subdued, man may be saved. Hence it is evident that the rest of Jehovah denotes peace and salvation to the angels in the heavens, and to men in the earths ; to the latter when they are in good, and by good in the Lord.

10,375. "And He gave to Moses, in His finishing to speak with him from Mount Sinai the two tables of the testimony"—that hereby is signified the conjunction of the Lord by the Word with man, appears from the representation of Moses, as denoting the Word, see the passages cited, n. 9372 ; and from the signification of in finishing to speak with him, as denoting when all things were instituted, for the things which Jehovah spake with Moses on Mount Sinai, were those which were to be instituted amongst the sons of Israel, thus which were of the church; and from the signification of Mount Sinai, as denoting heaven, whence comes Divine Truth, see n. 8805, 9420; and from the signification of the two tables, as denoting the law in every complex, thus the Word, see n. 9416; and from the signification of the testimony, as denoting the Lord as to Divine Truth, see n. 8535, 9503. Conjunction thereby with man is signified by the tables being two, and joined together in esemblance of a covenant, see n. 9416; by two also is signified conjunction, n. 5194, 8423. Hence it is evident that by Jehovah giving to Moses in His finishing to speak with him from Mount Sinai the two tables of the testimony, is signified that when the church is established, there is conjunction of the Lord with man by the Word, which is sent down from Him out of heaven. That it is the Word by which the Lord flows in with man, speaks with him, and is conjoined, see n. 1775, 2310, 2899, 3476, 3735, 3982, 4217, 9212, 9216, 9357, 9380, 9396, 9400, 9401, 10,290.

10,376. "Tables of stone written with the finger of God"—that hereby is signified Divine Truth therein from the Lord Himself, appears from the signification of the tables, as denoting the law in every complex, thus the Word, see n. 9416; and from the signification of stone, as denoting Divine Truth in ultimates, of which we shall speak presently; and from the signification of being written with the finger of God, as denoting from the Lord Himself, for what is written by the finger of any one is from him. The reason why those tables were of stone, and the words of the law were written on stone, was, because stone signifies truth in ultimates, and Divine Truth in ultimates is the sense of the letter of the Word, in which is the internal sense. That stone denotes truth, see n. 643, 1298, 3720, 6426, 9476. And that it denotes truth in ultimates, n. 8609.

CONTINUATION OF THE SUBJECT CONCERNING THE THIRD EARTH IN THE STARRY HEAVEN.

10,377. *THEY acknowledge, as in every earth, God under a human form, thus our Lord; for whosoever acknowledge a God under a human form, are accepted by our Lord and are led. No others can be led, for they think without determination to a form, thus they think of nature.*

10,378. *The spirits who are from that earth are well-disposed; the reason is, because they are withheld from evils by their not loving to think of things terrestrial and corporeal; for these things withdraw the mind from heaven, since in proportion as any one is immersed in them, in the same proportion he is removed from heaven, thus from the Lord, consequently in the same proportion he is in evils, and ill-disposed.*

10,379. *The spirits of that earth appear above in the plane of the head towards the right; for all spirits are distinguished from their situation in respect to the human body, by reason that the universal heaven corresponds to all things of man. These spirits keep themselves at a distance, because their correspondence is not with the externals appertaining to man, but with the interiors. Their action is into the left knee, a little above and below, with a certain vibration of undulation very sensible, which is a sign that they correspond to the conjunction of things natural and of things celestial; for the feet correspond to natural things, the thighs to celestial, thus the knee to their conjunction.*

10,380. *I have been informed that the inhabitants of their earth are instructed concerning the things of heaven by some immediate commerce with angels and spirits, which they can be more easily led into than others, because they reject corporeal things from their thought and affection. But concerning that commerce, it is only allowed to relate what has been told me.*

10,381. *A certain spirit of their number came to me, who was perceived above the head near a bubbling fountain, which is called Fontanella, whence he discoursed with me. He was able to explore dexterously all the things of my thought, and to keep them together in order, and to manifest them to me. But he brought forth only such as he could reprehend; the reason was, because spirits from our earth were around me, to whom he was not willing to approach freely, because they think of things corporeal. When he reprehended me, it was given to say, that what he reprehended was not mine, but belonged to the spirits who were around me, since what I think, I do not think from myself, but from them by influx. He wondered at this, but still perceived that it was so. It was given to add, that it is not angelical to inquire into the evils appertaining to man, unless the goods are inquired into at the same time. On hearing this he departed, perceiving that he had done it from the indignation pointed at above.*

10,382. *I afterwards discoursed with those spirits at a distance, and asked what became of those amongst them who are evil. They replied, that on their earth it is not allowed for any to be ill-disposed; but if he thinks evil and does evil, he is chided by a certain spirit who threatens him with death if he persists in so doing; and also if he persists, that he dies by a swoon; and that by this means the men of that earth are preserved from the contagions of evils. A certain spirit of this kind was sent to me, speaking with me as with them; and moreover he induced some what of pain in the region of the abdomen, saying, that this is the method he uses with those who give into evil thoughts and evil actions, and to whom he threatens death. But this spirit was a chiding spirit. He stood at the occiput, and thence discoursed uith me in a way of undulation [undulatorie].*

10,383. *They said, that they who profane holy things are grievously punished, and that before the punishing spirit comes, there appears to them a lion's jaw wide open, of a livid color, which seems as if he would swallow the head, and tear it asunder from the body, whence they are seized with horror. The punishing spirit they call the devil.*

10,384. *Inasmuch as they were desirous to know how we are circumstanced on our earth in regard to revelation, I told them that it is effected by writing and preaching from the Word, and not by immediate commerce as in other earths; and that what is written may be printed and published, and be read and comprehended by whole companies of people, and thus the life be amended. They were much surprised that such an art, so utterly unknown in other places, could be given; but they comprehended that on this earth, where corporeal and terrestrial things are so much loved, divine things from heaven cannot otherwise be received; and that it would be dangerous in such circumstances to discourse with angels.*

10,385. *The subject concerning this earth in the starry heaven will be continued at the close of the following chapter.*

EXODUS.

CHAPTER THE THIRTY-SECOND.

THE DOCTRINE OF CHARITY AND FAITH.

10,386. BAPTISM was instituted for a sign that man is of the church, and for a memorial that he is to be regenerated. For the washing of baptism is nothing else than spiritual washing, which is regeneration.

10,387. All regeneration is effected from the Lord by the truths of faith, and by a life according to them; therefore baptism testifies that man is of the church, and that he can be regenerated, for in the church the Lord is acknowledged, Who regenerates, and in the church is the Word, containing the truths of faith by which regeneration is effected.

10,388. This the Lord teaches in John, "*Except a man be*

generated of water and the spirit, he cannot enter into the kingdom of God," iii. 5 ; water in the spiritual sense is the truth of faith derived from the Word ; spirit is a life according to that truth ; and to be generated of them is to be regenerated.

10,389. Inasmuch as every one who is regenerated also undergoes temptations, which are spiritual combats against evils and falses, therefore by the waters of baptism those temptations are also signified.

10,390. Since baptism is for a sign and for a memorial of those things, therefore man may be baptized when an infant, and if not at that time, when an adult.

10,391. Let it be known therefore to those who are baptized, that baptism itself does not give faith, nor salvation, but that it testifies that men receive faith, and that they are saved if they are regenerated.

10,392. Hence it may be manifest what is meant by the Lord's words in Mark, "*He who believeth and is baptized, shall be saved ; but he who believeth not, shall be condemned,*" xvi. 16 ; he who believeth denotes who acknowledgeth the Lord, and receives Divine Truths from Him by the Word ; he who is baptized denotes who is regenerated by those truths from the Lord.

CHAPTER XXXII.

1. AND the people saw that Moses delayed to come down from the mountain ; and the people gathered together unto Aaron, and they said unto him, Arise, make for us gods, who may go before us, because this Moses, that man who made us to come up out of the land of Egypt, we know not what is become of him.

2. And Aaron said to them, pluck away the ear-rings of gold, which are in the ears of your women, of your sons, and of your daughters, and bring [them] to me.

3. And all the people plucked away the ear-rings of gold, which were in their ears, and brought them to Aaron.

4. And he took them from their hand, and formed it with a graving tool, and made it a calf of what is molten ; and they said, These are thy gods, O Israel, who made thee to ascend out of the land of Egypt.

5. And Aaron saw, and built an altar before it, and Aaron proclaimed, and said, A festival to Jehovah to-morrow.

6. And they arose in the morning the day following, and offered burnt-offerings, and brought peace-making offerings ; and the people sat down to eat and drink, and rose up to play.

7. And JEHOVAH spake to Moses, Go, descend, because

thy people have corrupted themselves, whom thou hast made to come up out of the land of Egypt.

8. They have receded suddenly from the way which I commanded them, they have made to themselves a calf of what is molten, and have adored it, and have sacrificed to it, and have said, These are thy gods, O Israel, who made thee to come up out of the land of Egypt.

9. And JEHOVAH said to Moses, I have seen this people, and behold the people, they are hard necked.

10. And thou, suffer Me, and let Mine anger burn into them, and I will consume them, and make thee into a great nation.

11. And Moses deprecated the faces of JEHOVAH his God, and said, Wherefore, O JEHOVAH, should Thine anger burn into this people, whom Thou hast brought forth out of the land of Egypt, with great virtue and a strong hand?

12. Wherefore should the Egyptians say, saying, For evil hath He brought them forth to slay them in the mountains, and to consume them from upon the faces of the earth? Return from the wrath of Thine anger, and let it repent Thee on evil to thy people.

13. Remember Abraham, Isaac and Israel, Thy servants, to whom thou hast sworn in Thyself, and hast spoken to them, I will multiply your seed, as the stars of the heavens; and all this land, which I said, I will give to your seed, and they shall inherit it for an age.

14. And JEHOVAH repented on the evil, which He said He would do to His people.

15. And Moses looked back, and descended from the mountain, and the two tables of the testimony were in his hand, tables written from two transits, from hence and from hence they were written.

16. And the tables they were the work of God, and the writing it was the writing of God, cut on the tables.

17. And Joshua heard the voice of the people in their vociferation, and he said to Moses, The voice of war is in the camp.

18. And he said, it is not the voice of the shout victory, and it is not the voice of the shout of a thing that is lost, the voice of a miserable shout I hear.

19. And it came to pass as he approached to the camp, and saw the calf, and the dancing, the anger of Moses was kindled, and he cast the tables out of his hand, and broke them beneath the mountain.

20. And he took the calf which they made, and burned it with fire, and ground it even into powder, and sprinkled it on the faces of the waters, and made the sons of Israel to drink.

21. And Moses said to Aaron, what hath this people done to thee, that thou hast brought upon them so great sin?

22. And Aaron said, let not anger burn, my lord; thou knowest the people that they are in evil.

23. And they said to me, Make for us gods, who may go before us, because this Moses, that man, who made us come up out of the land of Egypt, we know not what is become of him.
24. And I said to them, He that hath gold, pluck ye it away; and they gave it to me, and I cast it into the fire, and this calf came forth.
25. And Moses saw the people, that they were dissolute, because Aaron made them dissolute for annihilation to their insurgents.
26. And Moses stood in the gate of the camp, and said, Who is for JEHOVAH [let him come] to me; and all the sons of Levi were gathered together to him.
27. And he said to them, Thus saith JEHOVAH GOD of Israel, put ye every one his sword upon his thigh, pass ye and return from gate to gate in the camp, and slay ye a man his brother, and a man his companion, and a man his neighbor.
28. And the sons of Levi did according to the word of Moses: and there fell of the people that day to three thousand men.
29. And Moses said, Fill ye your hand to-day to JEHOVAH, because a man is for his son, and for his brother, and to give upon you to-day a blessing.
30. And it came to pass on the day following, and Moses said to the people, ye have sinned a great sin; and now I will go up to JEHOVAH, peradventure I shall expiate for your sin.
31. And Moses returned to JEHOVAH, and said, I beseech, this people hath sinned a great sin, and they have made to themselves gods of gold.
32. And now if Thou remittest their sin; and if not, blot me, I pray, out of Thy book which Thou hast written.
33. And JEHOVAH said to Moses, Whosoever hath sinned against me, him will I blot out of My book.
34. And now go, lead the people to what I said to thee, behold Mine angel shall go before thee, and in the day of My visitation I will visit upon them their sin.
35. And JEHOVAH smote the people, because they made the calf, which Aaron made.

THE CONTENTS.

10,393. IN the internal sense in this chapter is described that a church could not be established with the Israelitish people, since they were altogether in externals without any internal principle; and to prevent their profaning the holy things of heaven and the church, interior things with them were absolutely closed. That that people was altogether in externals without any internal principle, is signified by the golden calf, which they worshiped instead of Jehovah; and that interior things with them were absolutely closed, lest they should profane the holy things of heaven and of the church, is signified by the tables of the law being broken by Moses; and by Moses grinding the golden calf, and sprinkling the dust into the waters, and giving them to drink; also by their being slain by the sons of Levi in the camp to three thousand men.

10,394. In the internal sense is further described, that although a church could not be established amongst them, still there were with them representatives, which are the ultimates of a church, to the end that the Word might be written, which might close in those ultimates; these things are signified by Jehovah being entreated of Moses.

THE INTERNAL SENSE.

10,395. VERSES 1 to 6. *And the people saw that Moses delayed to come down from the mountain; and the people gathered together unto Aaron, and they said unto him, Arise, make for us gods, who may go before us, because this Moses, that man, who made us to come up out of the land of Egypt, we know not what is become of him. And Aaron said to them, Pluck ye away the ear-rings of gold, which are in the ears of your women, of your sons, and of your daughters, and bring them to me. And all the people plucked away the ear-rings of gold, which were in their ears, and brought them to Aaron. And he took from their hand, and formed it with a graving tool, and made it a calf of what is molten; and they said, These are thy gods, O Israel, who made thee to come up out of the land of Egypt. And Aaron saw, and built an altar before it, and Aaron proclaimed, and said, A festival to Jehovah to-morrow. And they arose in the morning the day following, and offered burnt-offerings, and brought peace-making-offerings; and the people sat down to eat and to drink; and arose to play.* And the people saw that Moses delayed to come down from the mountain, signifies the Israelitish nation when they did not perceive in the Word any thing from heaven. And the people gathered together to Aaron, signifies that they betook themselves to the externals of the Word, of the church, and of worship, separate from what is internal. And they said to him, signifies exhortation. Arise, make us gods, who may go before us, signifies falses of doctrine and of worship, thus things idolatrous. Because this Moses, that man, who made us to come up out of the land of Egypt, we know not what is become of him, signifies that it is altogether un known what other Divine Truth is in the Word, which elevates man from what is external to what is internal. And Aaron said to them, signifies the external of the Word, of the church, and of worship, without an internal principle. Pluck ye away the ear-rings of gold from the ears of your women, of your sons, and of your daughters, signifies the extraction of such things from the sense of the letter of the Word as favor external loves and the principles thence derived. And bring them to me, signifies the bringing together into one. And all the people plucked away the ear-rings of gold, which were in their ears, and brought them to Aaron, signifies the effect. And he took from their hand, signifies things favoring their proprium. And formed it with a graving tool, signifies from their own proper intelligence. And made it a calf of what is molten, signifies according to the delight of the loves of that nation. And they said, these are thy gods, O Israel, signifies that it was to be worshiped above all things. Who made thee to come up out of the land of Egypt, signifies which led. And Aaron saw, signifies approbation. And built an altar before it, signifies worship. And Aaron proclaimed, and said, a festival to Jehovah to-morrow, signifies that this is the very principle of the church which was to be celebrated, and the Divine itself which was to be adored perpetually. And they arose in the morning the day following, signifies excitation from their loves. And offered burnt-offerings, and brought peace-making-offerings, signifies the worship of their loves, thus their delights, and hence of falses. And the people sat down to eat and to drink, signifies their appropriation. And arose to play, signifies the festivity of their interiors thence derived, and agreement.

10,396. "And the people saw that Moses delayed to come down from the mountain"—that hereby is signified the Israelitish nation when they did not perceive in the Word any thing from heaven, appears from the signification of seeing, when concerning the understanding of the Word, as denoting perception, see n. 2150, 3764, 3863, 4567, 4723, 5400; and from the representation of Moses, as denoting the Word, see the passages cited, n. 9372; and from the signification of delaying to come down, when concerning the perception of Divine Truth from the Word, as denoting not to flow in, for the Divine Truth which flows in with man, is said to descend from heaven; and from the signification of Mount Sinai, as denoting heaven as to Divine Truth, see n. 9420. By the people is here meant the Israelitish nation in a proper sense, since in this chapter that nation is treated of, such as it was as to the perception of Divine Truth from the Word, and as to the perception of the interior things which were represented in those which were commanded of Jehovah by Moses to the sons of Israel from Mount Sinai, treated of in the preceding chapters, from xxv. to xxxi. inclusively. From these considerations it is manifest, that by the people seeing that Moses delayed to come down from the mountain, is signified the Israelitish nation when they did not perceive in the Word any thing from heaven; thus neither any thing which was represented in those things which were commanded from Mount Sinai, which are interior things. The case herein is this: the subject treated of in the preceding chapters is the statutes, the judgments, and the laws, which were commanded of Jehovah to the sons of Israel, amongst whom a church was to be instituted. All and singular, those commands were external things which represented internal, as has been shown in the explications upon those chapters: but the Israelitish nation was of such a quality, that they were not willing to know any thing at all concerning the internal things which were represented, but only concerning the external which represented. The cause why they were of such a quality was, because they were altogether in corporeal and terrestrial loves; and with those who are in those loves, the interiors are closed, which would otherwise open into heaven; for with man there is an internal and an external, his internal is for heaven, and his external for the world; when the external rules, then worldly, corporeal, and terrestrial things rule, but when the internal, then heavenly things; but man was so created, that the external may be subordinate to the internal, thus the world to heaven, for, as was said, the external is for the world, and the internal for heaven; when therefore the external rules, the internal is closed, by reason that man in such case turns himself from heaven and from the Lord to the world and to himself, and his heart is there where he turns himself, consequently his love, and with his love the all of his life, for the life of man is his love. These observations are made to the intent that it may be known how the case is with those who are in corporeal and terrestrial loves, namely, that the interiors appertaining to them are closed; and they with whom the interiors are closed, do not acknowledge any thing internal, saying, that those things which they see with their eyes, and touch with their hands, alone are, and that other things are not, which they do not see with their eyes, and touch with their hands; hence also they have not any faith that there is a heaven, that there is a life after death, and that the interior things, which the church teaches, are any thing. Of such a quality was the Israelitish nation. That they were of such a quality, is described in this chapter. He who does not know that interior things constitute the church with man, and not exterior things without them, cannot know otherwise than that that nation was chosen, and also loved by Jehovah, above all other nations; but the case is altogether otherwise; they were received because they pressed to be received, but not that any church might pertain to them, but only the representative of a church, to the end that the Word might be written, which might ultimately close in such things. The reason why that people is called in the Word, the people of Jehovah, the chosen and beloved nation is, because by Judah is there meant the celestial church, by Israel the spiritual church, and by all the sons of Jacob, somewhat of the church; also by Abraham, Isaac, and Jacob, the Lord Himself, as likewise by Moses, Aaron, and David. But whereas that nation is treated of in this chapter throughout that a church could not be instituted amongst them, but only the representative of a church, therefore before it is allowed to proceed further, see what has been before said and shown concerning that nation, namely, that a church did not appertain to them, but only the representative of a church, n. 4281, 4288, 4311, 4500, 4899, 4912, 6304, 7048, 9320. Thus that they were not chosen, but received, because they were urgent to be received, n. 4290, 4293, 7051, 7439. That they were altogether in externals without any internal principle, n. 4293, 4311, 4459, 4834, 4844, 4847, 4865, 4868, 4874, 4903, 4913, 9373, 9380, 9381. That their worship was merely external, n. 3147, 3479, 8871. That neither were they willing to know the internal things of worship and of the Word, n. 3479, 4429, 4433, 4680. That on this account it was not given them to know those things, n. 301, 302, 304, 2520, 3769. If they had known, that they would have profaned, n. 3398, 3489, 4289. That nevertheless by the externals of worship appertaining to them, which were representative of things interior, there was communication with heaven, and in what manner, n. 4311, 4444, 6304, 8588, 8788, 8806. That when they were in worship, their interiors which were filthy, were closed, n. 3480, 9962. That this could be effected with that nation, and that on this account they were preserved even to this day, n. 3479, 4281, 6588, 9377. That they worshiped Jehovah only as to name, n. 3732, 4299, 6877. That in heart they were idolaters, n. 4208, 4281, 4820, 5998, 6877, 7401, 8301, 8882. In general that they were the worst of nations, n. 4314, 4316, 4317, 4444, 4503, 4750, 4751, 4815, 4820, 4832, 5057, 7248, 8819, 9320.

10,397. "And the people gathered together to Aaron"—that hereby is signified that they betook themselves to the externals of the Word, of the church, and of worship, separate from an internal principle, appears from the signification of gathering together, as denoting to betake themselves; and from the representation of Aaron, as here denoting the external of the Word, of the church, and of worship, separate from what is internal. The reason why this is here represented by Aaron is, because he was the head of that nation during the absence of Moses, and by Moses, who was absent, is represented the Word, from which the church and worship are derived, both in the internal sense and external, see the passages cited, n. 9372. That such is represented by Aaron, is evident also from all and singular the things which are related of Aaron in what follows, namely, that it was he who made the calf, and proclaimed a feast, and made the people dissolute; all which things coincide with the external of the Word, of the church, and of worship, separate from the internal. He who separates the internal of the Word, of the church, and of worship, separates from it the holy Divine; for the internal of those things is their spirit, but the external is the body of that spirit; and the body without the spirit is dead; to worship therefore what is dead is to worship an idol, in this case to worship a golden calf, and to proclaim a feast to it, and thereby to make the people dissolute. From these considerations it may be manifest what is signified by Aaron in this chapter. What the internal of the Word, of the church, and of worship, is, and what their external, has been shown in what goes before.

10,398. "And they said to him"—that hereby is signified exhortation, appears from the signification of saying, when concerning the religious principle to which the people inclined, as denoting exhortation. That saying also denotes exhortation, see n. 5012, 7098, 8178, 7215. The religious principle, to which the people inclined, was to worship what is external without an internal principle.

10,399. "Arise, make for us gods who may go before us"—that hereby are signified falses of doctrine and of worship, thus things idolatrous, appears from the signification of gods, as denoting truths, see n. 4295, 4402, 7010, 7268, 7873, 8301; and in the opposite sense falses, n. 4402, 4544, 7873; hence to make gods denotes falses of doctrine, or doctrine derived from falses; and from the signification of going before us, as denoting what they may follow, thus according to which they may institute worship. That to make gods who may go before us denotes things idolatrous, is evident; what is idolatrous also consists in worshiping external things without internal, see n. 4825, 9429. Concerning this kind of idolatry it may be expedient here to make a few observations. The externals of the church about to be established with the Israelitish nation, were all those things which were commanded by the Lord to Moses on Mount Sinai, which were the tent of the congregation with the ark there, the propitiatory upon it, the table on which were the breads of faces, the candlestick, the altar of incense, likewise the altar of burnt-offering, the garments of Aaron and of his sons, especially the ephod on which was the breast-plate; moreover also the oil of anointing, the incense, the blood of the burnt-offering and sacrifice, the wine for a libation, the fire on the altar, with several other things besides. The Israelitish and Jewish nation worshiped all those things as holy, without the noly principle which they represented, and thought nothing at all of the Lord, of heaven, of love, of faith, of regeneration, thus of those things which were signified; when their worship was of such a quality, then there was the worship of wood, of bread, of wine, of blood, of oil, of fire, of garments, but not of the Lord in them; that such worship, in respect to them, is not Divine worship, but idolatrous, is evident.

10,400. "Because this Moses, that man, who made us to come up out of the land of Egypt, we know not what is become of him"—that hereby is signified that it is altogether unknown what other Divine Truth is in the Word, which elevates man from what is external into what is internal, and makes the church, appears from the representation of Moses, as denoting the Word, thus Divine Truth, see the passages cited, n. 9372; hence a doubtful and negative principle that the Divine Truth is any thing else than what is extant in the sense of the letter, is signified by this Moses, that man, we know not what is become of him. The reason why he is here called man is, because by man [*vir*] in the Word is signified truth, see n. 3134, 3309, 3459, 7716, 9007; and from the signification of making the sons of Israel to come up out of the land of Egypt, as denoting elevation of the natural or external man to the internal or spiritual, to be made a church; for by the land of Egypt is signified the natural or external principle of the church, by making to come up, elevation, and by the sons of Israel, the church. That the land of Egypt denotes the natural or external principle of the church, see the passages cited, n. 9391; that to make to come up denotes to elevate from what is external to what is internal, n. 3084, 4539, 4969, 5406, 5917, 6007, thus from the natural man to the spiritual; and that the sons of Israel denote the church, see the passages cited, n. 9340. From these considerations it is evident, that by this Moses, that man, who made us to come up out of the land of Egypt, we know not what is become of him, is signified that it is altogether unknown what other Divine Truth is in the Word, which elevates man from what is external to what is internal, and makes the church, than what is extant in the sense of the letter. So likewise all those think and speak, who are in external things without internal; and all those who are in external things without internal, who are in the loves of self and the world; for with them, the internal man is closed, and only the external open; and what the external man, when he reads the Word, sees without the internal, he sees in thick darkness, for natural lumen without light from heaven is mere thick darkness in things spiritual; and light from heaven enters through the internal man into the external, and illuminates the latter. Hence it is that so many heresies have existed, and that the Word is called by some a book of heresies, and that it is altogether unknown that there is any internal principle in the Word; and that they who think that there is such a principle, are still ignorant where it is. That such are they, who are meant in the Apocalypse, chap. xii. by the dragon which drew with his tail a third part of the stars from heaven, and cast them to the ground, will be shown elsewhere by the Divine Mercy of the Lord. Let such as are so disposed observe, whether any one at this day knows any other than that the sense of the letter is the Divine itself of the Word; but let them consider also whether any one can know the Divine Truths of the Word in that sense, except by doctrine thence derived; and if he has not doctrine for a lamp, that he is carried away into errors, whithersoever the obscurity of his understanding and the delight of his will leads and draws him. The doctrine, which should be for a lamp, is what the internal sense teaches, thus it is the internal sense itself, which in some measure is evident to every one, although he is ignorant what the internal sense is, who is in the external from the internal, that is, to whom the internal man is open; for heaven, which is in the internal sense of the Word, flows in with that man when he reads the Word, enlightens him, and gives him perception, and thereby teaches him: yea, if ye are willing to believe, the internal man appertaining to man is of itself in the internal sense of the Word, since it is heaven in the least effigy, and hence is with angels in heaven when it is open, wherefore also it is in like perception with them; which also may be manifest from this consideration, that the interior intellectual ideas of man are not such as his natural ideas are, to which nevertheless they correspond; but of what quality they are, man is ignorant so long as he lives in the body, yet he comes into them spontaneously when he comes into the other life, because they are ingrafted, and by them he is instantly in consort with the angels. Hence it is evident that man whose internal is open, is in the internal sense of the Word, although he is ignorant of it; hence he has illustration when he reads the Word, but according to the light which he is capable of having by means of the knowledges appertaining to him: but who they are, see n. 9025, 9382, 9409, 9410, 9424, 9430, 10,105, 10,324.

10,401. "And Aaron said to them"—that hereby is signified the external of the Word, of the church, and of worship, without the internal, appears from the representation of Aaron in this passage, as denoting the external of the Word, of the Church, and of worship, without the internal, see above, n. 10,397. That with the Israelitish and Judaic nation there was not a church, but only the representative of a church, thus what is external without an internal principle, appears manifest from Aaron, who, although of such a quality, was still made the high priest, to whom the most holy things of the church were committed, and who was hence accounted holy above all others; for it is said of him, that he made a golden calf, built an altar for it, proclaimed a feast to Jehovah for it, that he brought that sin upon the people, and that he made them dissolure, verses 2, 4, 5, 21, 25, 35. And in another place, "That Jehovah was moved with anger against Aaron exceedingly, to destroy him, and that Moses prayed for him," Deut. ix. 20; which things involve that Aaron was like the people, who in heart were idolaters, n. 4208, 4281, 4820, 5998, 6877, 7401, 8301, 8882. But whereas the external of the church only was with that nation, without the internal, and by it there was still communication with heaven, therefore it was the same thing of what quality the man of the church was, if so be, when he was in externals, he only acted according to the statutes, and worshiped them. That representatives did not respect the person, but the thing which was represented, see n. 665, 1097, 3670, 4208, 4281, 4288, 4444, 8588.

10,402. "Pluck away the ear-rings of gold from the ears of your women, of your sons, and of your daughters"—that hereby is signified the extraction of such things from the sense of the letter of the Word as favor external loves, and the principles thence derived, appears from the signification of plucking away, as denoting to extract, in this case from the sense of the letter of the Word, since this is the subject treated of; and from the signification of ear-rings of gold which were in the ears, as denoting representative tokens of the obedience and perception of the delights which are of the external loves, for by the ears is signified obedience and perception, by gold the good of love, in this case the delight of external loves, hence ear-rings of gold denote representative tokens of those loves. That by the ears is signified obedience and perception, see n. 2542, 4652 to 4660, 8990, 9397, 10,061; that by gold the good of love, n. 1551, 1552, 5658, 6914, 6917, 9510, 9874, 9881, hence when it is predicated of external loves, which are the loves of self and the world, by gold is signified their delight, thus evil, n. 8932; and that hence ear-rings are representative tokens of obedience and perception, n. 4551; and from the signification of women, as denoting the goods of the church, see n. 3160, 4823, 6014, 7022, 7337, hence in the opposite sense its evils, n. 409; and from the signification of sons, as denoting truths, and in the opposite sense falses, see n. 489, 491, 533, 1147, 2623, 2803, 2813, 3373, 3704, 4257, 6583, 6584, 9807; and from the signification of daughters, as denoting the affections of truth and good, and hence in the opposite sense the affections of what is false and evil, see n. 2362, 3963, 6729. Hence it is evident that by plucking away the ear-rings of gold from the ears of your women, of your sons, and of your daughters, is signified the extraction from the sense of the letter of the Word of such things as are perceived to obey or favor the delights of external loves, and the principles thence derived. That ear-rings are tokens of obedience and perception, is manifest from Hosea, "Contend ye with your mother, since she is not my wife, that she may remove her whoredoms from her faces, lest peradventure I strip her naked, and set her as a wilderness, and be not merciful to her sons; because she hath said, I will go after my lovers, that give my bread, and my waters, my wool, and my flax. And she hath not known that I have given her corn, and new wine, and oil, and have multiplied silver to her; and they have made gold for Baal. And I will make waste her vine, and her fig-tree; and I will visit upon her the days of Baalim, to whom she hath burned incense, and *hath put on her ear-ring* and her ornament; and she hath gone after her lovers, and hath forgotten Me," ii. 1 to 14. To burn incense, and to put on an ear-ring to Baalim, denotes to worship Baalim gods, and to obey them. The preceding verses in that chapter are also adduced, to the end that it may hence be known what is the quality of the external sense of the Word without the internal, and what is its quality together with the internal; thus what is the quality according to which they perceive the Word, who are in externals without an internal, and what is the quality with those who are in externals from the internal; they who are in externals separate from what is internal, cannot otherwise apprehend the above words than according to the letter, which is, that they should contend with the mother of the sons of Israel, that she was no longer loved by Jehovah as a wife; and if she does not remove whoredoms from her, that she would be stripped naked, and be set as a wilderness; and Jehovah would not have mercy on her sons, because she said that she would go after her lovers, who gave her bread, waters, wool, and flax; and that she did not know that Jehovah gave her corn, new wine, and oil, and multipled silver; that they made gold for Baal; and that on this account her vine was laid waste, and her fig-tree, and that it will be visited upon her, because she burned incense to Baalim, and put on them an ear-ring and ornament, and went after her lovers, her adulterers, forgetting Jehovah. This is the sense of the letter, and thus the Word is understood by those who are in externals without an internal principle, for thus it is understood by the Jews at this day, and also by some Christians; but that that is not the sense of the Word, may be seen by all those who are in some degree of illustration; since these by the mother, of whom all those things are said, do not understand mother, but the church, such as it was with that nation; they instantly comprehend that something of the church is signified by all the things which are said of her, for they are such as follow in order from the first position, or from the first subject; as by whoredoms, by lovers, by sons, and by bread, waters, wool, flax, corn, new wine, oil, silver, gold, and by vine and fig-tree, and likewise by incense and by ear-ring. What each of these things signifies, cannot be known from any other source than from the internal sense, in which by mother and wife is signified the church, by setting her naked and as a wilderness, is signified without the goods of love and the truths of faith. The truths of faith and the goods of love, of which she shall be widowed, are signified by sons, by bread and waters, by wool and flax, by corn, new wine, oil, silver, gold, and finally by vine and fig-tree; the worship itself grounded in obedience to falses and evils, which will succeed in the place of truths and goods, is signified by burning incense, and putting on an ear-ring and an ornament to Baalim. That mother denotes the church, see n. 289, 2691, 2717, 4257, 5580. That the same is true of a wife, n. 252, 409, 749, 770, 7022. That to set naked denotes to be deprived of the goods of love and the truths of faith, n. 9960. That a wilderness denotes a state without the truths and goods of the church, n. 2708, 3900, 4736, 7055. That whoredoms denote falsifications of truth, n. 2466, 2729, 4865, 8904; hence lovers denote those who falsify. That sons denote truths, and in the opposite sense falses, n. 489, 491, 533, 1147, 2623, 2803, 2813, 3373, 3704, 4257, 6583, 6584, 9807. That bread and water denote the good of love and the truth of faith, n. 9323. The wool denotes good in the external man, n. 9470. That flax denotes truth there, n. 7601, 9959. That corn denote good from which truth is derived, n. 5295, 5410, 5959. That new wine denotes the truth thence derived, n. 3580. That oil denotes celestial good, n. 9780, 10,261. That silver denotes truth, and gold good in general, n. 1551, 1552, 5658, 6914, 6917, 9881. That vine denotes the internal spiritual church, n. 1069, 3676, 9277, and that fig-tree denotes the external good of that church, n. 217, 4231, 5113. That to burn incense denotes worship, n. 10,177, 10,298. And that an ear-ring is a representative token of obedience, n. 4551, hence to put it on denotes to obey. When these things are understood in the place of the above words, or together with them, it then appears what the quality of the Word is, when it is spiritually perceived, thus what its quality is as to its spirit. In this sense all are kept by the Lord who read the Word, but it is not received by any others except those with whom the interiors are open, and since it is received in knowledges, therefore according to their intellectual principle, [it is received] in the degree and according to the quality that this principle can be enlightened by the knowledges appertaining to them; moreover in general they are affected with a holy principle thence derived.

10,403. "And bring them to me"—that hereby is signified a bringing together into one, appears from the signification of bringing to Aaron, as denoting to bring into one such things from the sense of the letter of the Word, as favor external loves, and the principles thence derived. That this is signified by bringing to Aaron the ear-rings of gold which were in the ears of the women, of the sons, and of the daughters, is manifest from what was shown just above, n. 10,402.

10,404. "And all the people plucked away the ear-rings of gold which were in their ears, and brought them to Aaron" —that hereby is signified the effect, appears without explication.

10,405. "And he took them out of their hand"—that hereby are signified things favoring their proprium, appears from the signification of taking out of the hand of any one, as denoting to take such things as are his, thus which are of the proprium, or which favor the proprium; for by the hand is signified the power or ability of man, and hence whatsoever is of him, see the passages cited, n. 10,019; and n. 10,082, 10,241.

10,406. "And formed it with a graving tool"—that hereby is signified from their own proper intelligence, appears from the signification of forming with a graving tool, when concerning an idol, as denoting to trim out a false doctrinal from their own proper intelligence, which is effected by the application of the sense of the letter of the Word in favor of the loves of self and of the world; for when these loves reign, then man is not in any illustration from heaven, but takes all things from his own intelligence, and confirms them from the sense of the letter of the Word, which he falsifies by wrong application and perverse interpretation, and afterwards favors those things because from himself. In the Word throughout mention is made of things graven, and things molten; they who apprehend the Word only according to the letter, suppose that idols alone are meant by those things; nevertheless idols are not meant, but false doctrinals of the church, such as are formed by man himself, under the guidance of some love of his. The formation of those falses that they may cohere, and appear as if they were truths, is signified by a graven thing; their conjunction in favor of external loves, that evils may appear as goods, is signified by a molten thing. Since each is meant by the golden calf, therefore it is here said, that Aaron formed it with a graving tool, by which is meant the formation of falses that they may appear as truths; and by his making gold the calf of what is molten, and afterwards casting it into the fire, and the calf coming forth, verse 24, is meant conjunction in favor of external loves, that evils may appear as goods. Such also is the case with every doctrinal which is made from man, and not from the Lord; and it is then made from man, when he regards his own glory, or his own gain, for an end; but from the Lord, when the good of the neighbor and the good of the Lord's kingdom is regarded for an end. Such things are signified by things graven and molten in the following passages, "Ye shall judge unclean *the covering of the graven things of thy silver, and the clothing of thy molten gold*," Isaiah xxx. 22. The covering of the graven things of silver denotes the appearance of falses as if they were truths; the clothing of molten gold denotes the appearance of evils as if they were goods; for covering and clothing are external appearances, which are induced, or with which they are invested; silver denotes truth, therefore graven things are said to be of silver; and gold, good, see n. 1551, 1552, 5658, 6914, 6917, 9874, 9881. Again, "*The artificer fuseth a graven thing*, and the founder covereth it over with gold, and melteth chains of silver, *he seeketh to himself a wise artificer, to prepare a graven thing*, which is not moved," xl. 19, 20. In this passage is described the formation of falses that they may cohere, and appear as if they were truths; a graven thing is that false principle; an artificer is the man who forms it from his own proper intelligence; a founder covering it over with gold denotes his making it to appear as good; melting chains of silver denotes by coherence; not being moved denotes which on that account cannot be weakened and destroyed. Again, "*The formers of a graven thing* are vanity, and their most desirable things do not profit. Who hath *formed a god, and molten a molten thing*, that it doth not profit. All his companions shall be ashamed, and the fabricators themselves; he fabricates iron with a forceps, and worketh with coal, and formeth it with sharp hammers, thus he worketh by the arm of his strength, he fabricates wood, he stretcheth out a thread and describeth it with a line, he maketh it into its angles, and defineth it with a circle, and maketh it into the form of a man [*vir*], according to the beauty of a man [*homo*], to dwell in the house," xliv. 9 to 14. In this passage also is described in what manner false doctrinals are formed, that they may cohere, and appear as truths and goods; by all the expressions is described how this is effected, when from man's own proper intelligence, under the guidance of pleasure, of lust, and of love. That this is the case, may be seen by those who know that all things in the Word have an internal sense, by which they are spiritually understood; otherwise to what purpose would be such a description of the formation of a graven thing. That it may appear as truth and good, is signified by making it in the form of a man [*vir*] according to the beauty of a man [*homo*]; for man [*vir*] in the internal sense denotes truth, and man [*homo*] the good of that truth. And in Jeremiah, "Every man [*homo*] is made foolish by science, *every founder is ashamed of a graven thing, because his molten thing* is a lie, neither is spirit in them," x. 14; chap. li. 17. That a graven thing in this passage denotes what is from man's own proper intelligence, and a molten thing what is according to love, is very manifest; for it is said, every man is made foolish by science, and every founder is ashamed of a graven thing, and that the molten thing is a lie; science in this passage denotes man's own proper intelligence, and a lie denotes the false of evil; inasmuch as no Divine is in them, it is said, neither is there spirit in them. Again, "O sword against his horses, and against his chariots, against his treasures, that they may be spoiled; drought is upon her waters, that they are dried up, *because it is a land of graven things*," l. 37, 38. That a land of graven things denotes the church where falses reign, is also very manifest from all the expressions in the passage understood in the spiritual sense, without which sense what would a sword be against horses, against chariots, against treasures, and drought upon the waters, but sounding words without any spirit in them; yet from all the things understood in the internal sense it is evident that the destruction of the church as to truths is there described, and thus that falses would reign therein, which are the land of graven things; for a sword denotes the false combating and destroying truths; horses denote the intellectual principle which is enlightened; chariots denote doctrinals; treasures, the knowledges of truth and good; waters on which is drought denote truths that they are no longer truths; and land, the church. That a sword denotes truth combating against the false, and in the opposite sense the false combating against truths, and destroying them, see n. 2799, 6353, 7102, 8294; that horses denote the intellectual principle which is enlightened, n. 2760, 2761, 2762, 3217, 6534; that chariots denote doctrinals, n. 5321, 8146, 8148, 8215; that treasures denote the knowledges of truth and good, n. 10,227; that waters denote truths, n. 2702, 3058, 3424, 4976, 5668, 8137, 8138, 8568, 9323, 10,238; and that earth [or land] denotes the church, see the passages cited, n. 9325. Hence it is evident what is meant by drought upon the waters that they are dried up, and what by a land of graven things. And in Habakkuk, "What *profiteth a graven thing*, because the fabricator hath engraven it, and a molten thing, and the teacher of a lie; because the fabricator of his contrivance confideth upon it," ii. 18; from these words it is also evident, that by a graven thing and a molten thing are not meant what is graven and molten, but the false which is devised, and the evil which the false favors; for it is said the fabricator of his contrivance, and the teacher of a lie. Like things are signified by what is graven and molten in the following passages: "Babel is fallen, and all *the graven things of her gods* he hath cast to the earth," Isaiah xxi. 9. Again, "All *that trust in a graven thing* shall be ashamed with shame, saying to the *molten thing*, ye are our gods," xlii. 17.

Again, I have told thee, and have made thee to hear, lest thou shouldest say, *mine idol* hath done this; *my graven thing and my molten thing* hath commanded them," xlviii. 5. And in Hosea, "They have called themselves, and have gone from their faces, they have sacrificed to Baalim, and have *fumed incense to graven things*," xi. 2. And in Micah, "*All the graven things of Samaria* shall be beaten in pieces, and all her meretricious hires shall be burned with fire; *and all her idols* I will make a waste," i. 7. Inasmuch as the falses and evils of doctrines, which are signified by graven and molten things, are fabricated by man's own proper intelligence under the guidance of his love, therefore also in the Word they are called the work of the hands of man, the work of the hands of the artificer, and the work of the hands of the smith, as in the following passages; "They add to sin, *they make to themselves a molten thing* of their silver, *idols in their intelligence, the whole work of artificers*," Hosea xiii. 2. And in Moses, "Cursed is the man *who shall make a graven thing or a molten thing*, an abomination to Jehovah, *the work of the hands of the artificer*," Deut. xxvii. 15. And in David, "*Their idols*, silver and gold, *the work of the hands of man*," Psalm cxv. 4; Psalm cxxxv. 15. And in Jeremiah, "They have fumed incense to other gods, and have bowed themselves to the *works of their own hands*," l. 16. Again, "He cutteth wood from the forest, *the work of the hands of the workman by an axe;* they adorn it with silver and gold, with nails and hammers they secure it," x. 3, 4. The work of the hand denotes what is from the proprium of man, thus what is from his own proper understanding, and from his own proper will, and those things are from the proprium of each, which are of self-love, hence the origin of all falses in the church. Since all falses ore from the proprium of man, and by the work of the hands is signified what is thence derived, therefore it was forbidden to move iron, an axe, or a graving tool, upon the stones of which the altar was formed, and also the temple, as is evident from Moses, "If thou makest for Me an altar of stones, *thou shalt not build them hewn*, because *if thou movest thy tool upon it*, thou shalt profane it," xx. 25. Also in another place, "If thou shalt build to Jehovah an altar of stones, *thou shalt not move iron upon them*," Deut. xxvii. 5. And in the 1st book of the Kings, "The house was built of entire stone, as it was brought, *for a hammer and an axe, any instruments of iron*, were not heard in the house, when it was building," vi. 7. These things are adduced, to the intent that it may be known what is meant by Aaron forming the gold with a graving tool, and making it a calf of what is molten.

10,407. "And made it a calf of what is molten"—that hereby is signified according to the delight of the loves of that nation, appears from the signification of a calf, as denoting external or natural good, of which we shall speak presently; and from the signification of what is molten, as denoting worship made to favor external loves, see just above, n. 10,406. And whereas the subject treated of in this chapter is concerning the Israelitish nation, and it was in externals without an internal principle, thus in external loves, therefore it is said, according to the delight of the loves of that nation; for by a calf, as an idol, is signified that delight. The ancients, who were in representative worship, knew what was signified by the various kinds of animals, for every animal has its signification, according to which also they appear in heaven, consequetly according to which they are named in the Word, and also according to which they were applied in the burnt-offerings and sacrifices. By a calf is signified the good of innocence and charity in the external or natural man, see n. 9391, 9990, 10,132; but when there is no good of innocence and charity, as with those who are in externals without an internal principle, then by a calf is signified natural and sensual delight, which delight is the delight of pleasures, of lusts, and of the loves of self and the world. This delight is what they are principled in who are in externals without an internal principle, and which they worship, for what a man loves above all things, this he worships: they say indeed, that they worship the God of the universe, but they say this with the mouth and not with the heart. Persons of this description are meant by those who worship a calf of what is graven. The Egyptians were of this character above all others, and being principled in the science of correspondences and representations above other nations, on this account they made to themselves various idols, as is evident from the Egyptian idols which are still extant; but their chief idol was a calf, by which they were willing to signify their external good in worship; but when the science of correspondences and representations, in which they were versed above others, was turned amongst them into magic, then a calf put on a contrary signification, which is that of the delight of external loves; and when a calf was placed in the temples, and worshiped for a god, it signified such a delight in worship. Inasmuch as the Israelitish nation brought along with them from Egypt that idolatrous principle, therefore in application to that nation, by a calf when it was worshiped by them for a god, is signified the delight of the loves of that nation in worship. Of what quality those loves were, may be manifest from what was shown in the passages cited above, n. 10,396. For they were at that time, as at this day, in the love of self and in the love of the world above all others. That at this day they are in a love most terrestrial, is a known thing, for they love silver and gold not for the sake of any use, but for the sake of silver and gold itself, which love is of all others the most terrestrial, for it is sordid avarice; the love of self is not extant with them, so as to appear, but it lies concealed inwardly in their heart, as is usual with all who are sordidly avaricious. That no love of the neighbor prevails amongst them, is also a known thing, and in proportion as no love of the neighbor prevails with any one, in the same proportion he is in self-love. From these considerations it may now be manifest, what is signified by a calf of what is molten made by Aaron for that nation. The like is signified by a calf in the following passages, "*A most beautiful calf is Egypt*, destruction cometh from the north, and her hirelings are in the midst of her *as fatted calves*," Jer. xlvi. 20, 21. And in David, "*They made a calf in Horeb, and bowed themselves to what is molten*, and changed glory into the effigy *of an ox* that eateth herbs," Psalm cvi. 19, 20. And in Hosea, "They add to sin, and make to themselves *a molten thing* of their silver, *idols* in their intelligence, the whole work of artificers, saying to them, they sacrifice a man, *they kiss calves*," xiii. 2. And in Isaiah, "The unicorns shall come down with them, and *the calves with the strong*, and their land shall be made drunken with blood, and their dust shall be made fat with fatness," xxxiv. 7. Again, "The fortified city shall be solitary, a habitation let down and forsaken, there *the calf shall feed, and there shall he lie down* and shall consume the branches thereof, and the harvest thereof shall wither," xxvii. 20. And in David, "Rebuke the wild beast of the reed, the congregation of the strong, *amongst the calves of the people*, treading down the payments of silver, he hath dispersed the people," Psalm lxviii. 30. And in Jeremiah, "I will give the men that have transgressed my covenant, who have not established the words of the covenant which they made before Me, *of the calf which they have cut into two*, that they might pass between the parts thereof, the princes of Judah, and the princes of Jerusalem, the royal ministers, and the priests, and all the people of the land *passing between the parts of the calf;* and I will give them in the hand of their enemies, that their carcase may be for food to the fowl of the heavens and the beast of the earth," xxxiv. 18, 19, 20. And in Hosea, "They have made a king, and not from Me, they have made princes, and I have not known; their silver and gold they have made *idols*, that it may be cut off; *thy calf hath forsaken*, O Samaria, for it also was from Israel, the smith hath made it, and he is not a god, *because the calf of Samaria shall be made into pieces*," viii. 4, 5, 6. All these passages may be seen explained, n. 9391.

10,408. "And they said, these are thy gods, O Israel"—that hereby is signified what is to be worshiped above all things, appears from the signification of gods, as denoting the things which are worshiped; by strange gods in the genuine sense are signified falses, in this case both falses and evils, since by the graven thing, which is meant by Aaron forming gold with a graving tool, is signified the false, and by a molten thing the evil of that false. That strange gods denote falses and the evils thence derived in worship, see n. 4402, 4544, 7873, 8867, 8941.

10,409. "Who made thee to come up out of the land of Egypt"—that hereby are signified which led, appears from the signification of making to come up out of the land of Egypt, when it relates to those who are in externals without an internal principle, as denoting to lead themselves, for by the land of Egypt, when it relates to such, is signified servitude, and by making to come up, is signified hence to lead themselves; for in this case the contrary is signified by the same words, than when they are spoken of those who are in what is internal, and at the same time in externals; for in relation to these latter, by those words is signified to be led of the Lord, thus to be elevated from the natural man to the spiritual, or from the world into heaven, consequently from servitude into liberty; but when the words relate to those who are in externals without internals, they signify to be led of self, which is not to be elevated to heaven, but to cast themselves down to hell, consequently from liberty into servitude; that servitude consists in being led of self, and liberty in being led of the Lord, see n. 2892, 9096, 9586, 9589, 9590, 9591. But whereas these latter believe that the Divine operates nothing with man, and that man leads himself, and also that this is freedom, it may be expedient to make a few observations on the subject; all those are in this opinion, and also persuasion, who love themselves and the world above all things; for what they love above all things, this they worship for a god; of this character are very many at this day in the Christian world; but of what quality they are, it has been given principally to know from such in the other life, for man after life in the world, when he becomes a spirit, is then altogether like to himself as to the affections which are of the love, and as to thoughts and persuasions, as he had been when he lived in the body; they said, that they confirmed themselves in that faith, from the consideration that man comes to dignities and to opulence not from any Divine aid of Providence, but from his own proper intelligence and prudence; and sometimes from fortune, and still in such cases from causes which they see to proceed from men; saying that common experience testifies this, since the wicked, the cunning, and the impious, are often raised to dignities and made rich in preference to the good, which would not be the case if the Divine ruled. But it was given to say to them, that confirmation from such things is reasoning from man's own proper intelligence and from his own proper love, which reasoning is from mere fallacies, and in thick darkness concerning causes; for they believe that to be exalted to dignities, and to gain wealth in greater abundance than others, is the very essential good which the Divine gives to man, and thus that the Divine benediction, as they also call those things, consists in them alone ; yet still such things are rather a curse to those who love themselves and the world above all things, for in proportion as they are exalted to honors and gain wealth by their own study and their own art, in the same proportion also they are lifted up into the love of self and the world, till at length they place their whole heart in those things, and regard them as the only goods, thus as the only satisfactions and happinesses of man ; when yet those things have an end with the life of man, in the world: whereas the goods, the satisfactions and happinesses, which are given and provided for man from the Divine, are eternal, and have no end, thus they are true benedictions ; what is temporary bears no proportion to what is eternal, as what is finite of time bears no proportion to its infinite; what endures to eternity, this is, but what has an end, respectively is not; the former, which is, the Divine provides, but not what is not, except so far as this latter conduces to the former ; for Jehovah, which is the Divine itself, is, and what is from Him, also is; hence it is evident what is the quality of that, which is given and provided for man from the Divine, and what is the quality of what man procures for himself. Moreover every man is led of the Divine by his intellectual principle, otherwise no man could be saved. Hence it is that the Divine leaves that intellectual principle appertaining to man in its freedom, nor restrains it; from this cause it comes to pass, that the evil succeed in the machinations and cunnings which are from their understanding, but the satisfactions which they obtain thereby have an end with their life in the world, and become unsatisfactory; whereas the things which are provided for the good from the Divine, have no end, and become satisfactions and happinesses to eternity. Thus I have discoursed with those who have been of such a character in the world, who replied, that they then thought nothing of what is good, satisfactory, and happy to eternity, and that when they were in their own loves, they altogether denied the life of man after death ; and that in proportion as they have attained to honors and riches, in the same proportion they believed that no other goods were given, yea, neither heaven, nor the Divine; consequently that they knew not what it is to be led by the Divine. They who have confirmed themselves in these ideas by doctrine and life in the world, remain also such in the other life; interior things are closed to them, and thus they have no communication with heaven; and exterior things alone are open, by which they then have communication only with the hells. Such of them as by machinations, arts, and cunning, have attained to honors or to riches, become magicians there; they appear beneath the buttocks, sitting at a table with a hat depressed even to the eye-brows; and thus, as if about to meditate, they collect such things as serve the magic art, supposing that they can lead themselves by those things; their speech falls between the teeth with a kind of hissing; and afterwards when they are devastated, they are cast into a pit of a broad bottom, where there is thick darkness; the lumen of their understanding is there obscured even to infatuation. I have seen some cast thither, who have been esteemed in the world the most ingenious.

10,410. "And Aaron saw"—that hereby is signified approbation, appears from the signification of seeing, as denoting approbation; that seeing here denotes approbation is evident from what now follows, namely, that he built an altar, and proclaimed a festival for it; for by Aaron is represented the external of the Word, of the church, and of worship, separate from what is internal, n. 10,397. And this principle approves all that which is done from man's own proper intelligence and from his own proper love, which is signified by the calf of what is graven formed from gold with a graving tool by Aaron, as described in what goes before.

10,411. "And built an altar before it"—that hereby is signified worship, appears from the signification of an altar, as being a principal representative of Divine Worship, see n. 4541, 8935, 8940, 9714, 10,242, 10,245; but of diabolical worship in this case, since those who are in externals, without what is internal, communicate with the hells, and not with the heavens; for the internal of man is his heaven, and his external is his world; also his internal is formed to the image of heaven, thus to the reception of such things as are there, and the external to the image of the world, thus to the reception of such things as are there, see the passages cited, n. 9279, 10,156. Hence when the internal is closed, heaven is also closed, and in this case the external is no longer ruled from heaven, but from hell; wherefore their worship is not Divine but diabolical. They make mention indeed of what is Divine, and also worship it, but in the external form, and not in the internal, which is from the mouth and not from the heart; and they who do otherwise do not worship what is Divine for the sake of what is Divine, but for the sake of themselves and the world; where the heart is, there is worship. Hence it is evident, that by building an altar before the golden calf, is signified the worship of the devil.

10,412. "And Aaron proclaimed, and said, a festival to Jehovah to-morrow"—that hereby is signified that this is the very essential thing of the church which is to be celebrated, and the Divine Thing itself which is to be perpetually adored, appears from the signification of a feast, as denoting the worship of the church as to celebration, for on feast days celebration was effected; thus by proclaiming a feast is signified the very essential thing of the church which was to be celebrated. That it denotes the Divine Thing itself which was to be adored, is signified by that feast being called a feast to Jehovah; and from the signification of to-morrow, as denoting what is eternal and perpetual, see n. 3998, 7140, 9939: they also who are in externals without an internal principle, are willing to be worshiped as a god, and their own to be adored as what is Divine, so far as they dare on account of the vulgar. From this consideration it may be concluded, that in their heart they deny what is Divine, and that themselves are continually aspiring to things higher, and so far as obstacles are not presented, to things highest, thus at length to the throne of God, as appears evident from those who in the Word are meant by Babel, who derogate from the Lord all power in the heavens and in the earths, and claim it to themselves; for they open heaven, and shut it at pleasure. That they are of such a character, is manifest from Isaiah, "Thou shalt utter this parable concerning the king of Babel; the lower hell is moved for the sake of thee; how hast thou fallen from heaven, O Lucifer, thou art cut down to the earth, thou art weakened beneath the nations: *and thou hast said in thine heart, I will ascend the heavens, I will exalt my throne above the stars, and I will sit in the mount of assembly, I will ascend above the heights of a cloud, I will become like to the Most High:* nevertheless thou art let down to hell," xiv. 4, 9, 12, 13, 14, 15. That the king of Babel also commanded that he should be worshiped for a god, is manifest in Daniel, chap. vi. By Babel are meant those who are holy in externals, but profane in internals; thus those who use the holy things of the church as means that themselves may be worshiped for gods; which likewise all they do, who, by the holy things of the church as means, are eager to emerge to dignities above others and to opulence above others, as ends. With such the case is similar in the other life: there also in heart they deny what is Divine, and by wicked arts labor to make themselves gods; they set themselves aloft upon mountains, and proclaim some one in the midst of them for a god, and also adore him; but when they are in that profane worship, the mountain opens itself into a gap, and they are swallowed down, and are thus cast down into hell. That this is the case, it has been given occasionally to see.

10,413. "And they rose in the morning the day following"—that hereby is signified excitation from their loves, appears from the signification of rising in a morning, as denoting excitation from their loves; for by the morning is signified a state of love, and by rising, elevation to it. That morning denotes a state of love, see n. 5962, 8426, 8812, 10,114, 10,134; and that rising denotes elevation, n. 2401, 2785, 2912, 2927, 3171,

4103. But when rising in the morning is said of those who are in externals without an internal principle, thus of the evil, then by rising is not signified elevation, but excitation, and by morning, not a state of heavenly love, but a state of infernal love; for when the evil are in that state, they are in their morning; since in such case they are in the delight of their life, because in their own loves. The distinction between elevation to a state of loves with the good and with the evil, is this, that the good ascend on the occasion, and that the evil descend; for the loves appertaining to the good are heavenly loves, which elevate them and increase according to ascent to heaven; but the loves appertaining to the evil are infernal loves which depress them and increase according to descent to hell; hence it is evident, that rising in the morning has a contrary signification, when it is said of the evil from what it has when it is said of the good. Also in the other life the states of spirits and of angels vary as to love and faith, as the times of days and of years vary in respect to heat and light; when it is morning to those who are in the heavens, they are then in a state of celestial loves, and thence in their joy; whereas in the hells on such occasion they are in a state of infernal loves, and thence in their torment; for every one in such case is willing to be greatest, and to possess all things belonging to another, whence come intestine hatreds, savageness, and cruelties, which are the things signified by infernal fires.

10,414. "And they offered burnt-offerings and brought peace-making offerings"—that hereby is signified the worship of their loves, thus of their delights and of the falses thence derived, appears from the signification of burnt-offerings and sacrifices, as denoting all worship in general, see n. 6905, 8936, 10,042; and that burnt-offerings denote worship from the good of love, sacrifices from the truths of faith, see n. 8680, 10,053. Hence, in the opposite sense, by burnt-offerings is signified worship from their own proper loves, which worship is from their delights, which are evil; and by sacrifices is signified worship from the falses thence derived. It is called the worship of loves, because that is worshiped which is loved, and love worships.

10.415. "And the people sat to eat and to drink"—that hereby is signified their appropriation, appears from the signification of eating and drinking, as denoting appropriation, eating the appropriation of evil, and drinking the appropriation of the false; that eating denotes the appropriation of good, see n. 3168, 3513, 3596, 3832, 9142; hence in the opposite sense, it denotes the appropriation of evil, n. 4745; and that drinking denotes the appropriation of truth, and hence in the opposite sense the appropriation of the false, n. 3069, 3168, 3832, 8562, 9412.

10,416. "And rose to play"—that hereby is signified the festivity of their interiors thence derived, and consent, appears from the signification of playing, as denoting festivity of the interiors, for play [or sport] is thence derived, since it is the activity of body which comes forth as an effect from gladness of mind, and all festivity and gladness is from the delights of the loves in which man is principled. The reason why consent is also signified, is, because all interior festivity has in it consent [or agreement], for if any thing dissents and reproaches, the festivity perishes; interior festivity is in man's freedom, and all freedom is from the love, to which nothing is contrary. Inasmuch as in the Word internal things are described by external, so also the joys and gladnesses, which are in the interiors of man, by plays [or sports] and dances, as in the following passages, "The city shall be built upon its own heap, then shall confession go forth from them, and *the voice of them that play*," Jer. xxx. 18, 19. And in the same prophet, "Again, I will build thee, that thou shalt be built, O virgin Israel; thou shalt again adorn thy tabrets and *go forth into the chair of those who play:* their soul shall become as a watered garden, neither shall they add to grieve any longer; and *the virgin shall be glad in the dance*, and the young men and the old together; I will turn their mourning *into joy*," xxxi. 4, 12, 13. And in Zechariah, "The streets of the city shall be filled *with boys and girls playing*," viii. 5. And in David, "Praise ye the name of Jehovah *with the timbrel and dance*," cxlix. 2, 3; Psalm cl. 5. Again, "Thou hast turned my mourning *into a dance* for me," Psalm xxx. 11. And in Jeremiah, "The joy of our heart hath ceased, *our dance* is turned into mourning," Lam. v. 15. Inasmuch as plays and dances signified the joys and gladness of the interiors which are from love, therefore, when the Egyptians were overwhelmed in the sea Suph, Miriam with the women came forth *with timbrels into the dances*," Exod. xv. 30; and on this account David, when the ark was brought down from the house of Obed-Edom into the city of David, *danced and leaped before Jehovah*," 2 Samuel vi. 12, 16. That interior things are expounded and described in the Word by exterior, is manifest from these words in David, "Thou hast made the sea great and wide in spaces, there go the ships, *Leviathan whom thou hast formed to play therein*," Psalm civ. 25, 26. He who does not know that there is a spiritual sense in all the things of the Word, knows no otherwise than that by the sea and by ships in this passage are meant the sea and ships, and by Leviathan the whales which are therein, and by playing those courses and consociations; but the Word, which as to every iota is Divine, does not consist in such things; but when the spiritual things, which are signified, are understood for them, then it becomes Divine; sea, in the internal sense, denotes the congregation of scientific truths, thus what is external with man and in the church; ships denote knowledges and doctrinals from the Word; Leviathan denotes the scientific principle in general, and playing denotes the delight thence derived; that sea denotes the congregation [or gathering together] of scientific truths, see n. 2850, 8184, 9340; that ships denote knowledges and doctrinals from the Word, n. 1977, 6385; and the Leviathan denotes the scientific principle in general, n. 7293; thus playing denotes the delight and festivity derived from those things, which is effected when scientifics confirm spiritual things and consent [or agree] with them.

10,417. Verses 7 to 14. *And Jehovah spake to Moses, go descend, because thy people have corrupted themselves, whom thou hast made to come up out of the land of Egypt. They have receded suddenly from the way which I commanded them, they have made to themselves a calf of what is molten, and have adored it, and have sacrificed to it, and have said, these are thy gods O Israel, who have made thee to come up out of the land of Egypt. And Jehovah said to Moses, I have seen this people, and behold the people they are hard of neck. And thou, suffer me, and let mine anger burn into them, and I will consume them, and will make thee into a great nation. And Moses deprecated the faces of Jehovah his God, and said, wherefore Jehovah doth thine anger burn into this people, whom Thou hast brought forth out of the land of Egypt, with great virtue and a strong hand. Wherefore shall the Egyptians say, saying, for evil He hath brought them forth to slay them in the mountains, and to consume them from upon the faces of the earth; return from the wrath of Thine anger, and repent Thou upon evil to this people. Remember Abraham, Isaac, and Israel, thy servants, to whom thou hast sworn in Thyself, and hast spoken to them, I will multiply your seed as the stars of the heaven; and all this land, which I have said, I will give to your seed, and they shall inherit it for an age. And Jehovah repented on the evil, which He said He would do to His people.* And Jehovah spake to Moses, signifies perception and instruction concerning the Israelitish nation, what its quality was within. Go, descend, signifies intuition into their externals. Because thy people have corrupted themselves, signifies that they have altogether averted themselves from the Divine. Whom thou madest to come up out of the land of Egypt, signifies whom thou believedst that thou wast leading to the Divine. They have receded suddenly from the way which I commanded them, signifies that they have removed themselves from the Divine Truth. And have made to themselves a calf of what is molten, signifies worship according to the delight of the loves of that nation. And have adored it, and have sacrificed to it, signifies that they worship it as essential good and as essential truth.

And have said, these are thy gods, O Israel, signifies that it is to be worshiped above all things. Who made thee to come up out of the land of Egypt, signifies which have led. And Jehovah said to Moses, signifies further instruction. I have seen the people, signifies what is foreseen. And behold the people they are hard of neck, signifies that they do not receive influx from the Lord. And thou, suffer Me, signifies that it ought not so obstinately to be insisted. And let Mine anger burn into them, and I will consume them, signifies that thus they avert themselves from things internal, thus from things Divine, so that they must needs perish. And I will make thee into a great nation, signifies the Word elsewhere that it is good and excellent. And Moses deprecated the faces of Jehovah, signifies that the Lord out of mercy remembered. And said, wherefore, Jehovah, doth Thine anger burn, signifies the aversion of that nation. Into the people whom thou hast brought up out of the land of Egypt, signifies elevation even from it. By great virtue and a strong hand, signifies from the Divine Power. Wherefore shall the Egyptians say, saying, signifies those who are in mere externals. For evil hath He brought them forth to slay them in the mountains, signifies that they are about to perish who are in good. To consume them from upon the faces of the earth, signifies that they are about to perish who are of the church. Return from the wrath of Thine anger, signifies thereby the aversion of that nation that it would not be hurtful. And repent Thou upon Thy people, signifies mercy for them. Remember Abraham, Isaac, and Israel, thy servants, signifies for the sake of heaven and of the church. To whom Thou hast sworn in Thyself, signifies confirmation from the Divine. And hast spoken to them, signifies foresight and providence. I will multiply your seed as the stars of the heavens, signifies goods and truths and their knowledges. And all this land, which I have said, I will give to your seed, signifies from which is heaven and the church. And they shall inherit it for an age, signifies eternal life. And Jehovah repented upon the evil which He said He would do to His people, signifies mercy for them.

10,418. "And Jehovah spake to Moses"—that hereby is signified perception and instruction concerning the Israelitish nation, what its quality was within, appears from the signification of speaking, when from Jehovah, as denoting perception and instruction, see the passages cited, n. 10,277, 10,290. That it denotes concerning the Israelitish nation what its quality was within, is manifest from what follows, for that nation is there treated of, and its quality as to worship.

10,419. "Go, descend"—that hereby is signified intuition into their externals, appears from the signification of descending from Mount Sinai, as denoting to look in, to survey, and to examine, for by Mount Sinai is signified heaven, from which comes the Divine Truth, n. 9420; hence to descend, in the spiritual sense, does not denote to descend with body, but with mind, thus it denotes to look in and to survey.

10,420. "Because thy people have corrupted themselves" —that hereby is signified that they have altogether averted themselves from the Divine, appears from the signification of corrupting themselves, when concerning worship, as denoting to avert themselves from the Divine; for all corruption and prevarication in worship is a recession and aversion from the Divine. Since mention is made of aversion, it may be expedient briefly to explain how the case herein is; they who are in externals separate from an internal principle, all of them avert themselves from the Divine, for they look outwards and downwards, and not inwards and upwards; for man looks inwards or upwards, when the internal is open, thus when it is in heaven; but he looks outwards or downwards, when his internal is closed and only the external open, for this latter is in the world; wherefore when the external is separated from the internal, man cannot be elevated upwards; for that principle into which heaven should operate, is not present, because it is closed; hence it is that all things of heaven and of the church are to them thick darkness; wherefore also they are not believed by them, but are denied in heart, by some also with the mouth. When heaven operates with man, as is the case when the internal is open, it withdraws him from the loves of self and the world, and from the falses therein originating, for when the internal is elevated, the external is also elevated, since the latter is then kept in a similar direction of its views with the former, because it is in subordination; but when the internal cannot be elevated, because it is closed, then the external looks in no other direction than to itself and the world, for the loves of self and the world reign; this also is called looking downwards, because to hell, for those loves reign there, and the man who is in them is in consort with those who dwell there, although he is ignorant of it; as to his interiors also he actually averts himself from the Lord, for he turns the back to Him, and the face to hell; this cannot be seen in man, whilst he lives in the body; but whereas his thought and will produce this effect, it is his spirit which thus turns itself, for the spirit is what thinks and wills in man. That this is the case, is manifestly apparent in the other life, where spirits turn themselves according to their loves; they who love the Lord and the neighbor, look continually to the Lord, yea, what is wonderful, they have Him before the face in every turning of their body; for in the spiritual world, there are not quarters, as in the natural world, but the quarter is there determined by the love of every one, which turns him: but they who love themselves and the world above all things, turn away the face from the Lord, and turn themselves to hell, and every one to those there who are in a similar love with himself, and this also in every turning of their body. Hence it may be manifest what is meant by averting themselves from the Divine: also what is properly signified by averting themselves in the Word, as in Isaiah, "*They avert themselves backwards*, confiding in a graven thing," xlii. 17. And in David, "The heart *hath averted itself backwards*," Psalm xliv. 18. And in Jeremiah, "Their prevarications are multiplied, and *their aversions are made strong*," v. 6. Again, "*They avert themselves*, that they do not return; this people *have averted themselves*; Jerusalem perpetuates *things averted*, they refuse to return," viii. 4, 5. Again, "*They have averted themselves*, they have let themselves down into the deep to dwell," xlix. 8; and in several other passages.

10,421. "Whom thou hast made to come up out of the land of Egypt"—that hereby is signified whom thou didst believe thou wast leading to the Divine, appears from the signification of making to come up out of the land of Egypt, as denoting to elevate from what is external to what is internal, thus to lead to the Divine, for by making to ascend is signified to elevate from what is external to what is internal, and by Egypt is signified the natural or external man, from which is elevation. That to make to come up denotes to elevate from what is external to what is internal, see n. 3084, 4539, 4969, 5406, 5817; and that Egypt denotes the natural or external principle, see the passages cited, n. 9391.

10,422. "They have receded suddenly from the way which I commanded them"—that hereby is signified that they have removed themselves from the Divine Truth, appears from the signification of receding from the way, as denoting to remove themselves from truth; for to recede is to remove themselves, since they who are in externals, separate from what is internal, remove themselves; and way denotes truth, of which we shall speak presently. The reason why it is the Divine Truth, from which they remove themselves, is, because it is said, from the way which Jehovah commanded them. That way denotes truth, is grounded in appearance in the spiritual world, where also ways and paths, and in the cities, streets and rows of houses appear; and spirits go in no other direction than to those with whom they are consociated by love; hence it is that the quality of the spirits there, in regard to truth, is known from the way which they go, for all truth leads to its love, inasmuch as that is called truth which confirms what is loved. Hence it is that way also in common human discourse denotes truth, for the speech of man has derived this, like several other expressions, from the spiritual world. From this ground now it is that in the Word, by way, path, by-path, orbit, street, and rows of houses, are signified truths, and in the opposite sense falses, as is evident from the following passages: "*Stand ye near the ways* and see, inquire *concerning the ways of an age*, which way is the best," Jer. vi. 16. Again, "*Make good your ways*, and your works; confide not in yourselves *on the words of a lie*," vii. 3, 4, 5. Again, "Learn not *the way of the nations*," x. 2. Again, "I will give to every one *according to his ways*, according to the fruit of his works," xvii. 10. "They have made them to stumble *in their ways*, the by-paths of an age, that they might go away into *paths, a way not paved*," xviii. 15. Again, "I will give them one heart, and *one way*," xxxii. 39. And in David, "*Thy ways O Jehovah make known to Me, Thy paths* teach me; lead me *in Thy truth*," Psalm xxv. 4, 5. And in the book of Judges, "In the days of Jael *the ways ceased*, and they that went in *paths*, went *winding-ways*," v. 6. And in Isaiah, "Re cede *from the way*, make to decline *from the path;* let thine ears hear a word from behind thee, *this is the way*, go ye in it," xxx. 11, 21. Again, "The paths are devastated, he that passeth *the way* ceaseth," xxxiii. 8. Again, "*A path and a way* shall also be there, which shall be called *the way of holiness;* the unclean shall not pass it, but this is for them; *he that walketh in the way*, and fools shall not err," xxxv. 8. Again, "The voice of one crying in the wilderness, *prepare ye the way* for Jehovah; make smooth in the desert *a path* for our God; with whom hath He deliberated, that He might teach him *the way of judgment*, and show him the *way of intelligence*," xl. 3, 14. Again, "To say to those who are in darkness, be ye revealed, they shall feed *on the ways;* I will set all My mountains *for a way; My paths* shall be exalted," xlix. 9, 10. Again, "*The way of peace* they have not known, neither is there judgment *in their orbits; their paths* they have perverted to themselves, he who *treadeth it* shall not know peace," lix. 9. Again, "*Prepare ye a way* for the people, pave ye, *pave ye a path*, say ye to the daughter of Zion, behold thy salvation cometh," lxii. 10, 11. Again, "I have given *a way* in the sea, in the strong waters *a path;* I will set *a way* in the wilderness," xliii. 16, 19. And in Moses, "Cursed is he who maketh the blind to err *in the way*," Deut. xxvii. 18. And in Matthew, "Go ye *to the cross-ways of the ways*, and whomsoever ye shall find, call to the marriage," xxii. 16. And in John, "Jesus said, I am *the way*, the truth, and the life," xiv. 6. In these passages, and in several others, by a way is signified truth, and in the opposite sense the false.

10,423. "And they have made to themselves a calf of what is molten"—that hereby is signified worship, according to the delight of the loves of that nation, appears from what was shown above, n. 10,407, where similar words occur.

10,424. "And have adored it, and sacrificed to it"—that hereby is signified that they worship it as essential good, and as essential truth, appears from the signification of adoring, as denoting to worship as essential good; and from the signification of sacrificing, as denoting to worship as essential truth. The reason why adoring is predicated of the good which is of love, and sacrificing of the truth which is of faith, is, because in the Word, where mention is made of good, it is also made of truth, on account of the heavenly marriage in all its expressions, see the passages cited, n. 9263, 9314. That sacrificing is predicated of truth, see n. 8680, 10,053, and that adoring is predicated of good, is evident from the passages in the Word where the expression occurs.

10,425. "And have said, these are thy gods, O Israel"—that hereby is signified which is to be worshiped above all things, appears from what was shown above, n. 10,148, where like words occur.

10,426. "Who made thee to come up out of Egypt"—that hereby is signified which have led, see above, n. 10,409.

40,427. "And Jehovah said to Moses"—that hereby is signified further instruction, appears from the signification of saying, when from Jehovah, as denoting perception and instruction, see the passages cited, n. 10,277, 10,2[illegible].

10,428. "I have seen the people"—that hereby is signified what is foreseen, appears from the signification of seeing, when relating to Jehovah, as denoting foresight, see n. 2807, 2837, 2839, 3686, 3863, for what Jehovah sees, he sees from eternity, and to see from eternity is foresight and providence.

10,429. "And behold the people they are hard of neck"—that hereby is signified that they do not receive influx from the Lord, appears from the signification of hard of neck, as denoting not to receive influx; for by the neck [*cervix*] and by the neck [*collum*] is signified the conjunction and communication of things superior and inferior, thus influx, see n. 3542, 3603, 3695, 3725, 5320, 5328, 5926, 6033, 8079, 9913, 9914. And by hard is signified what resists and refuses, thus what does not receive. This people is so called, because they were in externals without an internal principle; and they who are of such a quality, refuse all influx out of heaven or from the Lord; for influx is effected through the internal into the external, therefore when the internal is closed, there is not any reception of what is Divine in the external; for nothing is received but what flows in from the world, thus nothing but what is worldly, corporeal, and terrestrial. Such also in the other life, when they are seen in the light of heaven, appear like grates of teeth or like somewhat hairy, or as a bony substance without life, instead of a head and face; for the face corresponds to those things which are of the internal man, and the body to those which are of the external, and the neck to their conjunction. It may be expedient here briefly to explain what is meant by being in externals without an internal principle, as is said of that nation. Every man has an internal and an external, for the internal is his thought and his will, and the external is his speech and his action; but the internal appertaining to the good, differs exceedingly from the internal appertaining to the evil; for each has an internal, which is called the internal man, and an external, which is called the external man; the internal man is formed to the image of heaven, but the external to the image of the world, n. 9279. With those who are in the good of love and the truths of faith, the internal man is open, and by it they are in heaven; but with those who are in evils and the falses thence derived, the internal man is closed, and by the external they are only in the world; these are they of whom it is said that they are in externals without an internal. These indeed have also interiors, but the interiors appertaining to them are the interiors of their external man, which is in the world, but not the interiors of the internal man which is in heaven; those interiors, namely, which are of the external man, when the internal is closed, are evil, yea, filthy, for they think only of the world and of themselves, and will only those things which are of the world and which are of self, and think nothing at all about heaven and about the Lord, yea, neither do they will these latter things. Hence it may be manifest what is meant by being in externals without an internal. Inasmuch as the Israelitish nation was of such a character, therefore when they were in a holy external principle, their interiors were closed, because they were filthy and defiled, namely, full of the love of self and the world, thus of contempt of others in comparison with themselves, of hatred against all who offended them, of savageness towards them, and of cruelty, avarice, rapine, and the like. That that nation was of such a character, is very manifest from the Song of Moses, Deut. xxxii. verses 15 to 43; where they are described by the command of Jehovah; and also from Jeremiah throughout; and lastly from the Lord Himself in the evangelists.

10,430. "And thou, suffer Me"—that hereby is signified that it ought not so obstinately to be insisted upon, appears from the signification of suffering [or allowing], when from Jehovah concerning that nation, as denoting that it ought not so obstinately to be insisted upon; for that nation was not chosen by the Lord, but received, because they had obstinately insisted, see n. 4290, 4293, 7051, 7439; for that nation, above all other nations in the universal orb of the earths, could exercise fasting, lie on the earth, roll themselves in ashes, and be in mourning for whole days together, nor desist until they obtained what they wanted; but this obstinacy was only for the sake of themselves, namely, grounded in the most ardent love of themselves and the world, and not for the sake of the Divine;

they who are of such a quality, are indeed heard, but still they do not receive any thing of heaven and of the church in themselves, but only such things as are of the world, if they continue in statutes and laws in the external form. Hence it is that in the other life they are amongst infernals, except some who have been principled in good, and except their infants. Hence it is evident, that by "thou, suffer Me," is signified that it ought not so obstinately to be insisted upon them.

10,431. "And let Mine anger burn into them, and I will consume them"—that hereby is signified that in so doing they avert themselves from internal things, thus from Divine things, so that they must needs perish, appears from the signification of anger burning, when concerning Jehovah, as denoting aversion on the part of man, of which we shall speak presently; and from the signification of consuming, when also concerning Jehovah, as denoting to perish in consequence of their own evil. In the Word, in many passages, it is said of Jehovah, that He burns with anger, and is wroth, and also that He consumes and destroys; but it is so expressed because it so appears to man, who turns himself away from the Lord, as is the case when he does evil; and whereas on such occasion he is not heard, and is also punished, he believes that the Lord is in anger against him; when yet the Lord is in no case angry, and in no case consumes, for He is mercy itself, and good itself. Hence it is evident what the quality of the Word is as to the letter, namely, that it is according to appearance with man. In like manner when it is said that Jehovah repents, as in what follows, when yet Jehovah in no case repents, for He foresees all things from eternity. Hence also it may be manifest, into how many errors they fall who do not think beyond the sense of the letter when they read the Word, thus who read it without doctrine from the Word, which doctrine teaches how the case is. For they who read the Word from doctrine, know that Jehovah is mercy itself and good itself, and that it cannot in any wise be said of infinite mercy and of infinite good, that it burns with anger and consumes; wherefore from that doctrine they know and see that it is so said according to the appearance presented to man. That anger and evil are from man, and not from the Lord, and that still they are attributed to the Lord, see the passages cited, n. 9306; and that anger, when it is predicated of the Lord, denotes the aversion of man from the Lord, n. 5034, 5798, 8483, 8875.

10,432. "And I will make thee into a great nation"—that hereby is signified the Word elsewhere, which is good and excellent, appears from the representation of Moses, as denoting the Word, see the passages cited, n. 9372; and from the signification of nation, as denoting those who are in good, thus abstractedly from person, good, see n. 1259, 1260, 1416, 1849,

6005, 8771. Mention is made in the Word throughout of nation and people, and by nation there are signified those who are in good, and by people those who are in truth, or abstractedly from persons, by nation is signified good, and by people truth, n. 10,288. When therefore by Moses is signified the Word, then by the nation derived from him, is signified good thence derived. The case herein is this; the sons of Israel were received, because amongst them the Word could be written; the external or literal sense of which consists of mere external things, to which internal things correspond; such were all the representatives which appertained to the Israelitish nation; and since that nation was of such a quality in externals, therefore the Word could be written amongst them. Hence it is evident, when by Moses is meant the Word, and when it is said of the Israelitish nation that they should be consumed or perish, that in this case by Jehovah making Moses into a great nation, is signified that the Word elsewhere should be written, which is good and excellent. That this is the sense of these words, does not appear in the letter, nevertheless it may be known from this consideration, that the names of persons do not enter heaven, but that they are turned there into the things which they signify; as when the names of Abraham, of Isaac, of Jacob, of Moses, of Aaron, of David, and of others, are mentioned, in this case it is altogether unknown there that those persons are meant by man; they vanish away instantly there, and put on a spiritual sense, which is the sense of the things signified by those persons. Hence it is evident what is the sense of these words in heaven concerning Moses, that he should be made into a great nation.

10,433. "And Moses deprecated the faces of Jehovah"—that hereby is signified that the Lord out of mercy remembered, appears from the representation of Moses, as denoting the Word, see just above, n. 10,432; and from the signification of faces, when concerning Jehovah, as denoting mercy and all good, see n. 222, 223, 5585, 7599, 9306, 9546; and from the signification of deprecating, as denoting to remember, for when by Moses is meant the Word, then to deprecate does not signify to deprecate, but what is in concord with that of which it is predicated, in this case with the Word; that Jehovah is the Lord in the Word, see the passages cited, n. 9373.

10,434. "And said, wherefore O Jehovah doth thine anger burn"—that hereby is signified the aversion [turning away] of that nation, appears from the signification of anger burning when concerning Jehovah, as denoting the aversion [turning away] of the man who is in evil, see above, n. 10,431.

10,435. "Into the people whom thou hast brought forth from the land of Egypt"—that hereby is signified elevation even from it, appears from the signification of bringing forth from the land of Egypt, as denoting to be elevated from external things to internal, see above, n. 10,421.

10,436. "With great virtue and a strong hand"—that hereby is signified by Divine Power, appears from the signification of great virtue and of a strong hand when concerning Jehovah, as denoting Divine Power, see n. 7188, 7189, 8050, 8069, 8153. How the case herein is, may be manifest from the series of things in the internal sense, which is, that although the Israelitish nation were in things external without an internal principle, so that they could not at all be elevated towards interior things, still the representative of a church could be instituted amongst them and the Word be there written, by reason that, through the Divine Power, communication could still be given with heaven by external things without an internal principle, and thus a similar effect be produced as if they were at the same time in an internal principle; on which subject see what was shown concerning that nation in the passages cited above, n. 10,396; as that by the externals appertaining to them, which were representative of interior things, there was communication with heaven from the Divine Power of the Lord, n. 4311, 4444, 6304, 8588, 8788, 8806. It is to be noted that the church is not the church from external worship, but from internal worship; for external worship is of the body, whereas internal is of the soul, hence external worship without internal is only a gesture, thus worship without life from the Divine. The man of the church, by the interior things of worship, communicates with the heavens, to which heavens what is external serves for a plane, upon which interior things may subsist, as a house upon its foundation; and when it so subsists, it is complete and firm, and the whole man is ruled from the Divine. Such was the man of the Ancient Church, which was also a representative church, wherefore that church was accepted of the Lord, as is manifest from several passages in the Word; it is described in the Song of Moses, Deut. xxxii. verse 3 to 15. But such a church could not be established with the Israelitish and Judaic nation, by reason that, as was above said, their interiors were filthy, thus altogether contrary to the good of celestial love and the good of faith, which are the interior things of worship; therefore, when they so obstinately insisted that they would come into the land of Canaan, which was the same thing with representing a church, it was provided by the Lord that still communication with heaven should be given by their merely external worship; for the end of all worship is communication with heaven, and thereby the conjunction of the Lord with man. These are the things which are now treated of in the internal sense.

10,437. "Wherefore shall the Egyptians say, saying"—that hereby are signified those who are in mere externals concerning those who are elevated into internals, appears from the representation of the Egyptians, as denoting those who are in mere externals; and from the signification of saying, saying, as denoting concerning those who are elevated into internals, for these are treated of in the internal sense in what now follows. The reason why by the Egyptians are represented those who are in mere externals, is, because the Egyptians in ancient times were amongst those with whom also there was a representative church; for this church was extended through several regions of Asia, and at that time the Egyptians were principled, more than others, in the science of correspondences and representations which were of that church, for they were acquainted with the internal things which were represented and thence signified by things external. But in process of time the like befel them as others, amongst whom the church was instituted, that from internal men they became external, and at length had no concern about things internal, placing all worship in externals. When this came to pass also with the Egyptians, then the science of correspondences and representations, in which they excelled all the rest of the nations in Asia, was turned into magic, as is the case when the internal things of worship, relating to love and faith, are obliterated, the external representative worship still remaining, together with the knowledge of the interior things which are represented. It was in consequence of the Egyptians becoming of such a quality, that by them in the Word is signified the science of such, and also the external or natural principle; and whereas this principle without an internal one is either magical or idolatrous, each of which is infernal, therefore by Egypt is also signified hell. Hence it is evident, from what ground it is that by "wherefore shall the Egyptians say, saying," are signified those who are in mere externals. That in Egypt also there was a representative church, see n. 7097, 7296, 9391. That Egypt is the science of such in both senses, n. 1164, 1165, 1186, 1462, 2588, 4749, 4964, 4966, 5700, 5702, 6004, 6015, 6125, 6651, 6672, 6679, 6683, 6750, 7926. That Egypt denotes the natural or external principle, n. 4967, 5079, 5080, 5095, 5460, 5276, 5278, 5380, 5288, 5301, 5799, 6004, 6015, 6147, 6252, 7353, 7355, 7648. And that Egypt denotes hell, n. 7039, 7097, 7017, 7110, 7126, 7142, 7220, 7228, 7240, 7278, 7307, 7317, 8049, 8132, 8135, 8138, 8146, 8148, 8866, 9197.

10,438. "For evil he hath brought them forth to slay them in the mountains"—that hereby is signified that they would perish who are principled in good, appears from the signification of bringing forth to slay, as denoting to destroy, but when concerning Jehovah, who never destroys any one, it denotes to perish by their own evil; and from the signification of mountain as denoting heaven, hence the good of love, which signification is from representatives in the other life, for in that life, as on earth, there appear mountains, hills, rocks, valleys, and several other things; and on the mountains are those who are in celestial love, on the hills those who are in spiritual love, on the rocks those who are in faith, and in the valleys those who have not yet been raised up to the good of love and of faith. Hence it is that by mountains are signified those who are in the good of celestial love, thus who are in the inmost heaven, and in the abstract sense the goods of celestial love, thus the heaven which is in that love; and that by hills are signified those who are in the good of spiritual love, thus who are in the middle heaven, and in the abstract sense the good of that love, and the heaven which is in it; and that by rocks are signified those who are in the good of faith, and hence who are in the ultimate heaven, and in the abstract sense that good and that heaven; also that by valleys are signified those who have not yet been raised up to those goods, thus to heaven. Inasmuch as such things appear in the other life, and hence such things are signified by them, therefore like things are signified by them in the Word; and like things by the mountains, the hills, the rocks, and the valleys, in the land of Canaan, by which land on this account was represented heaven in its complex. That mountains signify heaven, where the good of celestial love prevails, is evident from several passages in the Word, as from the following, "In the latter end of days the *mountain of Jehovah* shall be for *the head of the mountains*, and shall be exalted *above the hills*," Isaiah ii. 2; Micah iv. 1. And in David, "The *mountains* shall bring peace, and the *hills* in justice," Psalm lxii. 3. Again, "Praise Jehovah, *ye mountains*, and all *hills*," Psalm cxlviii. 9. Again, "The *mountain* of God, the *mountain* of Bashan; the *mountain* of hills, the *mountain* of Bashan. Why leap ye, ye *mountains*, ye hills of *mountains*; *God desireth to inhabit it*, even Jehovah shall inhabit it for ever," Psalm lxviii. 15, 16. And in Moses, "Of the first-fruits of *the mountains of the earth*, and of *the precious things of the hills of an age*, let them come to the head of Joseph," Deut. xxxiii. 15, 16; besides in other passages, see n. 795, 6435, 8327, 8658, 8758, 9422, 9434. Hence it is that the Lord descended upon Mount Sinai; and hence it is that the city of David was built on a mountain, and that that mountain, which was called Mount Zion, signifies the inmost heaven; and hence also it is, that the ancients performed holy worship on mountains and hills, see n. 2722.

10,439. "To consume them from upon the faces of the earth"—that hereby is signified that they should perish who were of the church, appears from the signification of consuming, as denoting to destroy, but when it is said of Jehovah, who does not destroy any one, it denotes to perish by their own evil, as above, and from the signification of the earth, as denoting the church, see the passages cited, n. 9325, 10,373.

10,440. "Return from the wrath of thine anger"—that hereby is signified that thus the aversion of that nation would not be hurtful, appears from the signification of the wrath of anger when relating to Jehovah, as denoting aversion on the part of man, see above, n. 10,431; thus to return from the wrath of anger denotes that aversion would not be hurtful. How the case herein is, is evident from what was said and shown in what goes before.

10,441. "And repent Thou upon Thy people"—that hereby is signified mercy for them, appears from the signification of repenting, when concerning Jehovah, as denoting to be merciful. The reason why repenting denotes to be merciful, is, because Jehovah never repents, for he foresees and provides all things from eternity. Repentance belongs only to him who does not know what is to come, and who then observes that he has erred, when it comes to pass. Nevertheless it is so said in the Word concerning Jehovah, because the sense of the letter is grounded in such things as appear to man, for it is for the most simple, and for infants, who at first do not go beyond it; both the latter and the former are also in things most external from which they commence, and into which afterwards their interiors close: wherefore the Word in the letter is to be understood otherwise by those who are become wiser. The Word in this respect resembles man, whose interiors close into flesh and bones, the latter containing the former, so that man could not subsist, unless they were in the place of a basis or fulcrum, for he would have no ultimate into which interior things might close, and on which they might rest. The case is similar with the Word; it must have an ultimate, into which interior things may close, which ultimate is the sense of the letter, and the interior things are the celestial things which are of the internal sense. Hence now it is evident why, from the appearance presented to man, it is said that Jehovah repents, when yet he does not repent. That repenting is predicated of Jehovah, is manifest from several passages in the Word, as from the following: "If he shall do evil in Mine eyes, so as not to obey My voice, *I will repent on the good*, wherewith I had said that I would benefit him," Jer. xviii. 10. Again, "Peradventure they will hear, and return a man [*vir*] from his wickedness, and *I will repent of the evil*, which I thought to do to them on account of the wickedness of their works," xxvi. 3. And in Ezekiel, "When Mine anger is consummated, and I make My wrath to rest in them, *I will repent*," v. 13. And in Amos, "*Jehovah repented*, and said, it shall not be done," vii. 3, 6. And in Moses, "Jehovah shall judge His people, and *He shall repent upon His servants*," Deut. xxxii. 36. And in Jonah,

"The king of Nineveh said, who knoweth, let him return, and *let God be led by repentance*, that He may return from the burning of His anger, lest we perish; and they returned from their evil way, *therefore God repented on the evil* which He had said He would do to them, that He did it not," iii. 9, 10. And in the book of Genesis, "*Jehovah repented*, that he had made man in the earth, and He was grieved at His heart," vi. 6. And in the 1st book of Samuel, "*It repenteth Me*, that I have made Saul king, because he turneth himself back from following Me," xv. 11, 35. In these passages, Jehovah is said to have repented, when yet He cannot repent, since He knows all things before He does [them]; from which consideration it is evident, that by repenting is signified mercy. That Jehovah never repents, is manifest also from the Word, as in Moses, "Jehovah is not a man [*vir*] that He should lie, *or the son of man that He should repent*; hath He said, and shall He not do? or hath He spoken, and shall He not establish it?" Numb. xxiii. 19. And in the 1st book of Samuel, "The invincible One of Israel doth not lie, *neither doth He repent, because He is not a man that He should repent*," xv. 29. That repenting, when it relates to Jehovah, denotes mercy, is plain from Joel, "Jehovah is gracious and *merciful, suffering long and great in compassion, who is wont to repent of evil*," ii. 13. And in Jonah, "God is *gracious and merciful, and great in benignity, and who repenteth upon evil*," iv. 2.

10,442. "Remember Abraham, Isaac, and Israel, thy servants"—that hereby is signified for the sake of heaven and the church, appears from the signification of Abraham, of Isaac, and of Israel, as denoting the Lord as to the Divine Human, thus as to His Divine in heaven and in the church; and whereas the Divine of the Lord makes heaven and the church, hence by the same [namely, Abraham, Isaac, and Israel], is signified heaven and the church. That such things are signified in the Word by Abraham, Isaac, and Jacob, see n. 1965, 3305, 4615, 6098, 6185, 6276, 6589, 6804, 6848; and also by Israel, n. 4286, 4570; and in the passages cited, n. 8805, 9340. That such things are signified by Abraham, Isaac, and Jacob, is manifest from the Lord's words in Matthew, "I say unto you, that many shall come from the east and the west, and shall lie down *with Abraham, Isaac, and Jacob*, in the kingdom of the heavens," viii. 11; where to lie down with them denotes to be in heaven where the Lord is; and also from this consideration, that names do not enter heaven, but the Celestial and Divine things which are signified by them, 10,216, 10,282.

10,443. "To whom Thou hast sworn in Thyself"—that hereby is signified confirmation from the Divine, appears from the signification of swearing, when concerning the Lord, as denoting irrevocable confirmation from the Divine, see n. 2842.

10,444. "And spakest to them"—that hereby is signified foresight and providence, appears from the signification of saying and speaking, when concerning confirmation from the Divine, as denoting foresight and providence, see n. 5361, 6946, 6951, 8095.

10,445. "I will multiply your seed as the stars of the heavens"—that hereby are signified goods and truths, and their knowledges, appears from the signification of seed, when relating to heaven and the church, as denoting good and truth therein, see n. 1940, 3038, 3310, 3373, 3671, 6158, 10,249, and from the signification of stars, as denoting the knowledges of good and truth, see n. 2495, 2849, 4697. In the sense of the letter, by multiplying the seed of Abraham, of Isaac, and of Israel, as the stars of the heavens, is meant to multiply innumerably the Israelitish and Judaic nation; but whereas by names in the Word are signified things spiritual and celestial, and by the above names, heaven and the church, therefore by their seed are signified the goods and truths which are in heaven and in the church. It is said, as the stars of the heavens, by reason that comparisons in the Word are also derived from significatives, see n. 3579, 8989, in this case comparison with the stars of the heavens, because by them are signified goods and truths as to knowledges.

10,446. "And all this land, which I said, I will give to your seed"—that hereby is signified from which are heaven and the church, appears from the signification of land [or earth], as denoting the church, see the passages cited, n. 9325; and whereas the church is signified by land [or earth], heaven is also signified, for the church is the Lord's heaven in the earths; and the church also acts in unity with heaven, for one exists and subsists from the other; and from the signification of seed, as denoting good and truth there, see just above, n. 10,445.

10,447. "And they shall inherit it for an age" that hereby is signified eternal life, appears from the signification of inheriting, when concerning heaven, as denoting to have the life of the Lord, thus the life of heaven, see n. 2658, 2851, 3672, 7211, 9338; and from the signification of an age, as denoting what is eternal, see n. 10,248.

10,448. "And Jehovah repented on the evil which He said He would do to His people"—that hereby is signified mercy for them, see above, n. 10,441.

10,449. Verses 15 to 20. *And Moses looked back and went down from the mountain; and the two tables of the testimony were in his hand; tables written from two transits, from hence and from hence they were written. And the tables they were the work of God, and the writing it was the writing of God, cut upon the tables. And Joshua heard the voice of the people in their vocife-*

ration, and said to Moses, the voice of war is in the camp. And he said, it is not the voice of the shout of victory, and not the voice of a shout the thing is lost, the voice of a miserable shout I hear. And it came to pass as he approached to the camp, and saw the calf, and the dances, Moses burned with anger, and he cast the tables out of his hand, and brake them beneath the mountain. And he took the calf which they made, and burned it with fire, and ground it even to powder, and sprinkled it on the faces of the waters, and made the sons of Israel to drink. And Moses looked back, and descended from the mountain, signifies the Word let down from heaven. And the two tables of the testimony were in his hand, signifies the Word of the Lord specifically and generally. Tables written from the two transits, from hence and from hence they were written, signifies by which there is conjunction of the Lord with the human race, or of heaven with the world. And the tables they were the work of God, and the writing it was the writing of God, cut on the tables, signifies the external and internal sense of the Word from the Divine, and the Divine Truth. And Joshua heard the voice of the people in their vociferation, signifies survey and apprehension as to the quality of the interiors of that nation. And he said to Moses, the voice of war is in the camp, signifies the assault of truth and good, which are of heaven and the church, by the falses and evils which are from hell. And he said, it is not the voice of the shout of victory, and not the voice of the shout the thing is lost, signifies that heaven acts on one part, hell on the other, thus what is false against what is true, and what is true against what is false. The voice of a miserable shout I hear, signifies the lamentable state of their interiors. And it came to pass as he approached to the camp, signifies hell in which that nation was at that time. And saw the calf and the dances, signifies infernal worship, which was according to the delights of the external loves of that nation, and their interior festivity thence derived. And Moses burned with anger, signifies the aversion of that nation from the internal of the Word, of the church and of worship. And he cast the tables out of his hand and brake them beneath the mountain, signifies the external sense of the Word changed, and another for the sake of that nation. And he took the calf which they made, signifies the delight of the idolatrous worship of that nation. And burned it with fire, signifies derived altogether from the loves of self and the world, which are damned to hell. And ground it even to powder, signifies the infernal false thence derived. And made the sons of Israel to drink, signifies conjoined and appropriated to that nation.

10,450. "And Moses looked back and descended from the mountain"—that hereby is signified the Word let down from heaven, appears from the signification of looking back and descending, when concerning the Word, as denoting to be let down; and from the representation of Moses, as denoting the Word, see the passages cited, n. 9372; and from the signification of Mount Sinai, as denoting heaven, from which is Divine Truth, see n. 9420.

10,451. "And the two tables of the testimony were in his hand"—that hereby is signified the Word of the Lord specifically and generally, appears from the signification of the tables, on which the ten precepts were inscribed, as denoting the Word in every complex, see n. 9416; and from the signification of the testimony, as denoting the Lord as to Divine Truth, see n. 9503. The reason why by those tables is signified the Word in every complex, thus specifically and generally, is, because on them was inscribed the law of life, and by the law in a confined sense are meant the ten precepts; in a less confined sense is meant the Word written by Moses; in a more extended sense the historical Word; and in the most extended sense the whole Word, see n. 6752. Also because Mount Sinai, where the law was written on those tables, signified heaven, from which is the Divine Truth; and Moses represented the Word which is Divine Truth itself from the Lord, therefore in his hand were the tables, as a badge of that representation.

10,452. "The tables were written from the two transits, from hence and from hence they were written"—that hereby is signified by which there is conjunction of the Lord with the human race, or of heaven with the world, appears from the signification of the tables on which the law was inscribed, as denoting the Word in every complex, see just above, n. 10,451. That the writing from the two transits, from hence and from hence, signifies conjunction of the Lord with the human race, see explained, n. 9416, 10,375; on this account also those tables were called tables of the covenant, for covenant denotes conjunction, n. 665, 666, 1023, 1864, 1996, 2003, 2021, 6804, 8767, 8778, 9396. Since mention is here made of conjunction of the Lord with the human race, or of heaven with the world, by the Word, it may be expedient to say how the case herein is. They who do not know what the quality of the Word is, cannot at all believe that by it there is conjunction of the Lord with the human race, and of heaven with the world; and still less they who despise the Word, or make no account of it; but let them know, that the heavens subsist by the Divine Truth, and that without it the heavens would not be, and that the human race subsists by heaven; for unless heaven flowed in with man, man would not be able to think at all, thus neither to will any thing rationally. To the intent therefore that heaven may subsist, and the human race from conjunction with it, the Word was provided by the Lord, in which is Divine Truth for angels and for men.

For such is the Word in its spiritual and celestial sense, that therein is angelic wisdom itself, in so super-eminent a degree, that man can scarce form any conception as to the quality of its eminence, although in the letter it appears very simple and rude. Hence it is evident, that heaven is in its wisdom from the Word, when it is read by man, and at the same time man is in conjunction with heaven. For this end such a Word was given to man. Hence it follows, that if this medium of conjunction was not in the world, conjunction with heaven would perish, and with that conjunction every good of the will and every truth of the understanding appertaining to man; and with these that human principle itself, which consociates man with man; hence evil and the false would occupy all things, whereby one society would perish after another; for it would be as when man goes in thick darkness, and stumbles wheresoever he goes; and it would be as when the head is in a delirium, in consequence of which the body is carried madly and insanely even to its own destruction; and it would be as when the heart is faint, in consequence whereof the viscera and members cease to perform their uses, until the whole [body] dies. Such would be the state of man unless heaven was conjoined to him, and heaven would not be conjoined to him unless there was the Word, or unless Divine Truth was communicated immediately by the angels, as in ancient times. When it is said heaven, the Divine is also meant, for the Divine of the Lord makes heaven; thus to be conjoined with heaven is to be conjoined with the Lord, and to be disjoined from heaven is to be disjoined from the Lord, and to be disjoined from the Lord is to perish; for arrangement into good, which is called providence, is from that source, and when that arrangement is removed, all things rush into evil, and thereby into devastation. From these considerations it may be manifest for what use the Word is; but that the Word is of such and so important use, few will believe.

10,453. "And the tables they were the work of God, and the writing it was the writing of God cut upon the tables"—that hereby is signified the external and internal sense of the Word from the Divine and the Divine Truth, appears from the signification of the tables, as denoting the Word in the whole complex, see just above, n. 10,452; but in this case the external of the Word, of which we shall speak presently; and from the signification of the work of God, as denoting from the Divine; and from the signification of writing, as denoting the internal of the Word, of which also we shall speak presently; hence the writing of God denotes the internal of the Word from the Divine; and from the signification of being cut on the tables, as denoting the internal upon the external, thus in it. The reason why the tables here signify the external of the Word is, because they are here distinguished from the writing, which is its internal; but when they are not distinguished from the writing, then by them is signified the internal and external of the Word together, thus the Word in the whole complex, as above, n. 10,452. The reason why they are here distinguished is, because the tables were broken, and still the same words were afterwards inscribed by Jehovah on other tables, which were hewn out by Moses. The external of the Word is the sense of its letter; this sense, namely, the sense of the letter, is signified by the tables, because this sense is as a table, or as a plane, on which the internal of the sense is inscribed. That the tables, which were the work of God, were broken by Moses, when he saw the calf and the dances, and that at the command of Jehovah other tables were hewn out by Moses, and on them were afterwards inscribed the same words, and thus that the tables were no longer the work of God, but the work of Moses, whereas the writing was still the writing of God, involves an arcanum which as yet is unknown. The arcanum is, that the sense of the letter of the Word would have been another, if the Word had been written amongst another people, or if this people had not been of such a quality; for the sense of the letter of the Word treats of that people, because the Word was written amongst them, as is evident both from the historicals and the propheticals of the Word, and that people were in evil, because in heart they were idolaters, and yet, that the internal and external sense might agree together, this people was to be commended, and to be called the people of God, a holy nation, a peculiar property; hence the simple, who were to be instructed by the external sense of the Word, were about to believe, that that nation was of such a character, as also that nation itself believes, and likewise the generality of the Christian world at this day; and moreover several things were permitted them on account of the hardness of their heart, which things are extant in the external sense of the Word, and constitute it, as those mentioned in Matt. xix. 8, and also other things which are here passed by. Since, therefore, the sense of the letter of the Word was made such for the sake of that people, therefore those tables, which were the work of God, were broken, and at the command of Jehovah, others were hewn out by Moses. But whereas the same Holy Divine was still within, therefore the same words, which had been inscribed on the former tables, were inscribed by Jehovah on the latter, as is evident from these words in Moses, "Jehovah said to Moses, hew thee out two tables of stones, like the former, that I may write upon the tables the words which were on the former tables, which thou hast broken; and Jehovah wrote on those tables the words of the covenant ten words," Exod. xxxiv. 1, 4, 28. And in another place, "At that time Jehovah said to me, Hew thee out two tables of stone, like unto the former, and I will write upon the tables the words which were on the former tables, which thou hast broken; and Jehovah wrote on the tables according to the former writing, ten words; after wards Jehovah gave them to me," Deut. x. 1 to 4. That Jehovah did not acknowledge that people for His people, although it was so said on account of the agreement of the internal sense with the external, but for the people of Moses, is manifest in this chapter, "*Thy people* have corrupted themselves, *whom thou madest to come up* out of the land of Egypt; go thou, *lead the people*, to what I said to thee," verses 7, 34. And again, "Jehovah spake to Moses, Go up, *thou and the people whom thou madest to come up* out of the land of Egypt, into the land which I have sworn to Abraham, to Isaac, and to Jacob, and I will send an angel before thee, *since I will not go up in the midst of thee*, because the people they are hard of neck," Exod. xxxiii. 1, 2, 3. The like is signified by *Moses being placed in the hole of a rock*, and not being allowed to see the faces of Jehovah, *but only the hinder parts*, Exod. xxxiii. 22, 23. And in like manner by Moses, when the skin of his face shone, *putting a veil over his face when he spake to the sons of Israel*, Exod. xxxiv. 30 to 35. What the quality of that people was about to be, is predicated by Jehovah to Abraham, when he was willing that his seed should inherit the land of Canaan, where it is said, "After that Abraham had divided the she-calf of three years old, the she-goat of three years old, and the ram of three years old in the midst, which were for entering into a covenant, that on this occasion sleep fell upon Abraham, *and behold the terror of great darkness falling upon him;* and when the sun was set, *it became thick darkness, and lo, a furnace of smoke, and a torch of fire passed between those segments*," Gen xv. 8, 9, 12, 17.

10,454. "And Joshua heard the voice of the people in their vociferation"—that hereby is signified survey and perception as to the quality of the interiors of that nation, appears from the signification of hearing, as denoting survey and perception; for the subject now treated of is concerning that nation, what its quality was interiorly, thus what was the quality of its interiors; and from the representation of Joshua, as denoting the truth of the Word surveying and perceiving; for he was the minister of Moses, and by Moses was represented the Word, as was shown above, hence by minister is represented truth, for all truth is of the Word, in this case truth surveying, exploring and perceiving; and from the signification of the voice of the people in their vociferation, as denoting what the quality of that nation was interiorly, thus what was the quality of its interiors; for by voice in the Word is signified interior voice, which is thought, hence interior quality as to what is true or false, for thought is from the latter or the former, see n. 219, 220, 3563, 7573, 8813, 9926 ; but by vociferation is signified the articulation of sound, whether it be speech, or singing, or shouting, which proceeds from the thought, which is the interior voice ; hence by hearing a voice in vociferation, is signified perception as to the quality of the interiors, from its tone as an index. For the tone [or sound], whether it be of speech, or of singing, or of shouting, proceeds from interior affection and thought, the latter and the former being in the tone, and also being perceived by those who attend and reflect ; as for example, if it be angry, if menacing, if friendly, if mild, if glad, if mournful, and so forth ; in the other life so exquisitely, that from the sound of one expression it is perceived by the angels what the quality of any one is as to his interiors. These now are the things which are signified by hearing the voice of the people in their vociferation.

10,455. " And he said to Moses, the voice of war is in the camp "—that hereby is signified the assault of truth and good, which are of heaven and the church, by falses and evils which are from hell, appears from the signification of a voice, as denoting thought and affection, which are the interiors of a voice, thus the quality of interiors, as above, n. 10,454 ; and from the signification of war, as denoting the combat of truth grounded in good, with the false grounded in evil, and, in the opposite sense, the combat of the false grounded in evil against truth grounded in good, of which we shall speak presently ; and from the signification of the camp, as denoting the church and heaven ; for by the camp of the sons of Israel those things were represented, see n. 10,038. Hence it is evident that by the voice of war in the camp, is signified the assault of truth and good, which are of the church and of heaven, by the falses and evils which are from hell. It is said from hell, because all falses and evils are from thence, and because here by the camp, when the golden calf was worshiped there, is signified hell, see beneath, n. 10,458. The reason why these things are signified by the voice of war in the camp, is, because the subject now treated of, in the internal sense, is concerning the interiors of the Israelitish nation, whose interiors were against the truths and goods of the church and of heaven, so as altogether to reject them ; for the interiors of that nation were occupied by the loves of self and the world, and where those loves reign, the truths and goods of the church are continually assaulted, howsoever the externals in worship appear to be holy ; the holy principle of worship with such is a medium, and eminence and opulence are the ends ; thus those things which are of heaven and of the church, are mediums, and those which are of the world and of self, are ends ; and the end regarded has rule with man, whilst the medium serves ; hence it follows that with persons of such a character heaven serves, and the world rules, consequently that the world is in the highest place, thus in the place of the head, and heaven in a lower place, thus in the place of the foot; wherefore if heaven does not favor their loves, it is then cast down beneath the feet and is trod and trampled upon; such inversion has place with those amongst whom the loves of self and the world reign; hence also it is that when such are inspected by the angels, they appear inverted with the head downwards and the feet upwards. The reason why war denotes the combat of truth with the false, and in the opposite sense of the false against truth, is because war in the spiritual sense is nothing else. Such combats are also signified by wars in the historicals of the Word in the internal sense, also by wars in the propheticals, as may be manifest from the passages adduced from the Word, n. 1664, 8273. He who does not know that by wars in the Word are signified wars in a spiritual sense, cannot know what is involved in the things related concerning wars in Daniel, chap. vii. viii. xi.; and in the Apocalypse throughout, and in the Evangelists, where the last times of the church are treated of, Matt. xxiv. 5, 6, 7; Mark xiii. 7, 8; and in other places. Hence also it is that all the instruments of war, as swords, spears, shields, bows, arrows, and several others, signify such things as relate to spiritual combat, as may be seen in the above explications throughout.

10,456. "And he said, it is not the voice of the shout victory, and not the voice of the shout the thing is lost"—that hereby is signified that on the one part heaven acts, on the other hell, thus the false against truth, and truth against the false, appears from the signification of the voice of a shout, or of the voice in vociferation, as denoting the quality of the interiors of that nation, see above, n. 10,454; and from the signification of not victory and not the thing lost, as denoting the suspense of combat between what is false and what is true, and non-decision; and whereas every thing false is from hell, and every thing true from heaven, by the same words is signified that heaven acts on one part, and hell on the other. That a shout denotes what is false, see n. 2240; that it denotes thought with the full intention of doing, n. 7119; and that it denotes interior lamentation, n. 7782. By these words is described the state of the interiors of that nation, in which state they are when hell acts with them against heaven, and heaven acts against hell, thus when they are kept between both, which was the case when they were in external worship, whilst the internal was closed; which was closed to the intent that still by external things, which were representative of interior things, there might be communication with heaven; which subject has been treated of above.

10,457. "The voice of a miserable shout I hear"—that

hereby is signified the lamentable state of their interiors, appears from the signification of the voice of a miserable shout, as denoting what is lamentable; for this in the original tongue is expressed by a term which signifies both shout, and affection, and misery, thus which signifies a miserable shout; and when voice signifies the quality of the interiors, n. 10,454, hence the voice of a miserable shout signifies the lamentable state of the interiors.

10,458. "And it came to pass, as he approached to the camp"—that hereby is signified to hell, in which that nation was at the time, appears from the signification of the camp of the sons of Israel, as denoting heaven and the church, see n. 4236, 10,338; hence when they were in idolatrous worship, adoring a calf for Jehovah, by their camp is signified hell, for the representative of heaven and of the church is turned into the representative of hell, when the people turn themselves from Divine worship to diabolical worship, which was the worship of a calf. The like is signified by a camp in Amos, "I have sent into you the pestilence in the way of Egypt, I have slain your young men with the sword, with the captivity of your horses, so that I have made *the stench of your camp* to come up even into your nose," iv. 10. The subject treated of in this passage is concerning the vastation of truth, which being vastated, a camp signifies hell. That the vastation of truth is treated of, is evident from all the expressions in the passage viewed in the internal sense; for pestilence denotes vastation, n. 7102, 7505; way denotes truth, and in the opposite sense the false, n. 10,422; Egypt denotes what is external, and also hell; see the passages cited, n. 10,437; sword denotes the false combating against truth, n. 2799, 4499, 6353, 7102, 8294; young men denotes the truths of the church, n. 7668; to be slain, denotes spiritually to perish, n. 6767, 8902; captivity denotes the privation of truth, n. 7990; horses denote the intellectual principle, which is enlightened, n. 2760, 2761, 2762, 3217, 5321, 6125, 6534; stench denotes what is abominable, which exhales from hell, n. 7161; hence it is evident that camp in that sense denotes hell. Hell also is signified by the camp of the enemies who were against Jerusalem, and in general who were against the sons of Israel, in the historicals of the Word.

10,459. "And he saw the calf and the dances"—that hereby is signified infernal worship, which is according to the delight of the external loves of that nation, and hence its interior festivity, appears from the signification of a calf, as denoting the delight of the external loves of that nation, see above, n. 10,407. The reason why it here denotes worship according to that delight is, because when Moses approached to the camp, that nation was in that worship, which worship, that it is from hell, is manifest from what was shown above; and from the signification of dances, as denoting interior festivity, see also above, n. 10,416.

10,460. "And the anger of Moses burned"—that hereby is signified the aversion of that nation from the internal of the Word, of the church, and of worship, appears from the signification of burning with anger, when concerning the Lord, as denoting the aversion of man from things internal, thus from things Divine, see above, n. 10,431; the like is signified by burning with anger, when it is predicated of Moses, because by Moses is represented the Word or Divine Truth which is from the Lord, or, what is the same thing, the Lord as to Divine Truth, concerning which representation, see the passages cited, n. 9372. It is said from the internal of the Word, of the church, and of worship, for he who averts himself from the internal of the Word, averts himself also from the internal of the church, and likewise from the internal of worship, since the internal of the church and the internal of worship are from the internal of the Word; for the Word teaches what ought to be the quality of the man of the church, or what ought to be the quality of the church with man, and likewise what ought to be the quality of worship with the man of the church; for the goods and truths of love and faith are what constitute the internal church, and also internal worship; the Word teaches those goods and truths, and they are the internal things of the Word.

10,461. "And he cast the tables out of his hand, and brake them beneath the mountain"—that hereby is signified the external sense of the Word changed, and another on account of that nation, appears from the signification of the tables, on which the same was written, as denoting the external sense of the Word, or the sense of its letter, see above, n. 10,453; and from the signification of casting them out of the hand and breaking them, as denoting to destroy the genuine and external sense, thus also to change and make it another. That the external sense of the Word was changed and made another on account of the Israelitish nation, see above, n. 10,453; and from the signification of Mount Sinai, as denoting heaven, from which is Divine Truth, see n. 9420; it is said beneath the mountain, since the external sense of the Word is beneath heaven, but the internal in heaven.

10,462. "And he took the calf which they made"—that hereby is signified the delight of the idolatrous worship of that nation, appears from the signification of the calf, as denoting the delight of the external loves of the Israelitish nation, from which and according to which was their worship, which was idolatrous, see above, n. 10,407, 10,459.

10,463. "And burned it with fire"—that hereby is signified

grounded altogether in the loves of self and the world which are damned to hell, appears from the signification of fire, as denoting heavenly love, which is love to the Lord, and love towards the neighbor, and, in the opposite sense, infernal love, which is the love of self and the love of the world, see n. 4906, 5071, 5215, 6314, 6832, 6834, 6849, 7324, 7575, 10,055. Hence to be burned with fire denotes to be filled altogether with the loves of self and the world, thus to be damned to hell; for those loves, when they reign, are hell with man; from which consideration it is evident what is signified by the infernal fire, spoken of in the Word throughout.

10,464. "And ground it even to powder"—that hereby is signified the infernal false thence derived, appears from the signification of grinding to powder, or, what is most minute, as denoting to form what is false from infernal delight, thus the infernal false. That this is signified by grinding, when concerning evil, may be manifest from what was shown, n. 4335, 9995, 10,303.

10,465. "And sprinkled it on the faces of the waters"—that hereby is signified commixture with truths, appears from the signification of waters, as denoting truths, see the passages cited, n. 10,238; and whereas it is said that the powder into which the calf was ground was sprinkled on the waters, therefore it is signified that the false derived from infernal delights was mixed with the truths which are from heaven. The reason why by these waters are signified truths which are from heaven, is, because those waters descended from Mount Sinai, and by Mount Sinai is signified heaven, from which is Divine Truth, n. 9420. That those waters were from thence, is manifest from another passage in Moses, "I took your sin, the calf which ye made, and burned it with fire, and bruised it by grinding it well, until it was made small into dust, *and I cast the dust thereof into the stream descending from the mountain*," Deut. ix. 21.

10,466. "And he made the sons of Israel to drink"—that hereby is signified conjoined and appropriated to that nation, appears from the signification of drinking, as denoting to conjoin and appropriate to themselves truths, and in the opposite sense, the false, see n. 3089, 3168, 8562; in this case the false of evil. By the sons of Israel is meant that nation without any other sense, since the subject here treated of is concerning its proprium. From these considerations it may now be manifest what was the quality of that nation as to their interiors, for those interiors are described in this chapter.

10,467. Verses 21, 22, 23, 24, 25. *And Moses said to Aaron, what hath this people done to thee, that thou hast brought upon them so great a sin? And Aaron said, let not anger burn, my lord, thou knowest the people that they are in evil. And they said to me, make us gods, who may go before us, because this Moses, that man, who made us to come up out of the land of Egypt, we know not what is become of him. And I said to them, he that hath gold, pluck ye it away; and they gave to me, and I cast it into the fire, and this calf came forth. And Moses saw the people that they were dissolute, because Aaron made them dissolute, for annihilation to their insurgents.* And Moses said to Aaron, signifies perception from the internal concerning such an external. What hath this people done to thee, that thou hast brought upon them so great a sin, signifies whence is this that that nation have averted themselves from the Divine. And Aaron said, signifies what was perceived. Let not anger burn, my lord, signifies let not the internal avert itself on that account. Thou knowest the people that they are in evil, signifies that that nation is in an external separate from a holy internal. And they said to me, signifies exhortation. Make us gods, who may go before us, signifies the falses of doctrine and of worship, thus things idolatrous. Because this Moses, that man, who made us to come up out of the land of Egypt, we know not what is become of him, signifies that it is altogether unknown what other Divine Truth is in the Word, which elevates man from what is external to what is internal, and constitutes the church. And I said to them, he who hath gold, pluck ye it away, signifies the extraction of such things from the sense of the letter as favor the delight of external loves, and the principles thence derived. And they gave to me, signifies the bringing together into one, and the effect. And I cast it into the fire, and this calf came forth, signifies the loves of self and the world, from which and according to which is that worship. And Moses saw the people, that they were dissolute, signifies that it was perceived by the internal principle, that that nation was averse from what is internal, thus from what is Divine. Because Aaron made them dissolute, signifies that this was from the external things which they loved. For annihilation to their insurgents, signifies without all power of resisting the evils and falses which are from hell.

10,468. "And Moses said to Aaron"—that hereby is signified perception from the internal concerning such an external, appears from the signification of saying, as denoting perception, see the passages cited, n. 10,290; and from the representation of Moses, as denoting the Word, see the passages cited, n. 9372, in this case its internal; and from the representation of Aaron, as denoting the external of the Word, of the church, and of worship, see above, n. 10,397. The reason why Moses here denotes what is internal, is, because he speaks to Aaron, by whom is represented what is external. Whether we speak of the internal and external of the Word, or simply of what is internal and external, it is in this case the same thing, for the

Word is the Divine Truth, from which man has perception, in this case perception concerning such an external with the Israelitish nation, as well in worship as in every thing of the church, and in every thing of the Word. It is to be noted, that all perception concerning what is external is from what is internal; for from what is internal may be seen the things which are in what is external, but not from what is external the things which are in itself, and still less the things which are in what is internal. Hence it is that they who are in externals without an internal, do not acknowledge internal things, because they do not feel and see them, also that some deny those things, and with them things Celestial and Divine.

10,469. "What hath this people done to thee that thou hast brought upon them so great a sin"—that hereby is signified whence is this that that nation has averted itself from the Divine, appears from the signification of what hath this people done to thee, as signifying whence is it that that nation is of such a quality, for by doing is not here signified doing, since by Aaron is not signified Aaron, but the external principle which, as to its quality, is surveyed by the internal; wherefore when the meaning is abstracted from persons, by what have they done to thee, is signified whence is this; and from the signification of sin, as denoting aversion from the Divine, see n. 5841, 9346.

10,470. "And Aaron said"—that hereby is signified what was perceived, appears from the signification of saying, when concerning the internal surveying and exploring what is in the external, as denoting to perceive, hence on the other hand when concerning the external, it denotes what is perceived.

10,471. "Let not anger burn, my lord"—that hereby is signified let not on that account the internal avert itself, appears from the signification of burning with anger, when concerning Moses, by whom is signified what is internal, as denoting to avert itself, in this case let it not avert itself; and from the representation of Moses, who in this case is my lord, as denoting what is internal, see above, n. 10,468; Moses is here called my lord by Aaron, because what is internal is a lord, and what is external is respectively a servant, for what is internal with man is in heaven, and hence when it is open is his heaven, and what is external with him is in the world, thus is his world, and the world was made to serve heaven as a servant his lord. The case is similar with the external of worship, and likewise with the external of the church, and also of the Word, in respect to their internal.

10,472. "Thou knowest the people that they are in evil"—that hereby is signified that that nation is in an external separate from a holy internal, appears from the signification of evil and of sin, as denoting seclusion, separation, and aversion from the Divine, see n. 4997, 5746, 5841, 9346. It is said separate from a holy internal, since what is external separate from what is internal is also separate from what is holy, for the holy principle of man is in his internal. That is called holy, which flows in with man out of heaven, that is, through heaven from the Lord; heaven flows-in into the internal of man, and through it into his external, since the internal of man is formed to the image of heaven, thus to the reception of the spiritual things which are there, and the external to the image of the world, thus to the reception of the natural things which are there, n. 9277, 10,156. Hence it is evident what is the quality of the man with whom the external is separate from the internal, namely, that he is in worldly, terrestrial, and corporeal things alone. They who are such do not comprehend what is meant by an internal principle, thus neither what it is to be in things celestial and Divine; they suppose that when they are in those things which relate to the external worship of the church, they are also in things Divine; nevertheless it is not so; for on such occasions they are either in corporeal delight in consequence of what they have been accustomed to from infancy, or for the sake of the world that they may appear, or from obligation of duty for the sake of gain or honor; thus also they are in worldly, terrestrial, and corporeal things, and not in celestial and Divine. It is otherwise with those who are in externals from internal principles.

10,473. "And they said to me"—that hereby is signified exhortation, appears from the signification of saying, when concerning those who are in things external separate from what is internal, as denoting exhortation, as above, n. 10,398.

10,474. "Make for us gods who may go before us"—that hereby are signified falses of doctrine and of worship, thus things idolatrous, see above, n. 10,399.

10,475. "Because this Moses, that man, who made us to come up out of the land of Egypt, we know not what is become of him"—that hereby is signified that it is altogether unknown what other Divine Truth is in the Word, which elevates man from what is external to what is internal, and constitutes the church, see also above, n. 10,400.

10,476. "And I said to them, he that hath gold, pluck ye it away"—that hereby is signified the extraction of such things from the sense of the letter of the Word as favor the delight of external loves, and the principles thence derived, appears from what was explained and shown above, n. 10,402.

10,477. "And they gave to me"—that hereby is signified the bringing together into one, and the effect, see above, n. 10,403, 10,404.

10,478. "And I cast it into the fire and this calf came forth"—that hereby are signified the loves of self and the world from which and according to which that worship is, appears from the signification of fire, as denoting love in each sense, see n. 4906, 5071, 5215, 6314, 6832, 6834, 6849, 7324, 7575, 10,055; in this case the love of self and the love of the world, because that nation was in those loves, since it was in things external, separate from what is internal. Hence to cast into the fire denotes into those loves, and to extract such things from the sense of the letter of the Word as favor them, and thence to make what is doctrinal; and from the signification of a calf, as denoting worship from those loves, and according to them, which is infernal, see n. 10,459.

10,479. "And Moses saw the people that they were dissolute"—that hereby is signified that it was perceived by the internal principle, that that nation was averted from what is internal, thus from the Divine, appears from the signification of seeing, as denoting to perceive; and from the representation of Moses, as denoting what is internal, see above, n. 10,468; and from the signification of being dissolute, as denoting to be averted, in this case from what is internal, thus from the Divine, according to what was explained above, n. 10,472; by that expression in the original tongue is also signified to be averted, and to go back, also to be made naked, and by being made naked is signified to be deprived of the good of love and the truths of faith, which are the internal things of the church and of its worship, n. 9960.

10,480. "Because Aaron made them dissolute"—that hereby is signified that this was from the external things which they loved, appears from the signification of making dissolute, as denoting to be averted from what is internal, thus from the Divine, as just above, n. 10,479; and from the representation of Aaron, as denoting what is external, see also above, n. 10,468. The reason why it denotes which they loved, is, because they who are in external things separate from what is internal, love external things alone. The reason why in this case by making dissolute is signified to be averted and not to make averse, is, because by Aaron in the internal sense is not meant Aaron, but what is external, thus abstractedly from person, according to what was said above, n. 10,469.

10,481. "For annihilation to their insurgents"—that hereby is signified without all power of resisting the evils which are from hell, appears from the signification of annihilation, as denoting without all power of resisting evils and falses, for this in the spiritual world is to have no power; and from the signification of insurgents or enemies, as denoting evils and the falses thence derived, for these are the enemies who are insurgent in the spiritual sense; wherefore also those things are signified by enemies and insurgents in the Word, as in David, "O Jehovah, *how much are mine enemies multiplied, many are the insurgents against me*, saying of my soul, he hath no salvation in God," Psalm iii. 1, 2. Again, "Make wonderful Thy mercy, the Saviour of them who are confident *from the insurgents against me*, by Thy right hand; *guard me against the wicked*, who encompass me in opposition to my soul," Psalm xvii. 7, 8, 9. Again, "Deliver me not to the desire *of mine enemies*, because *the witnesses of a lie have risen against me*, and such as breathe out violence; lest I should believe that I should see good in the land of life," Psalm xxvii. 12, 13. Again, O God, command the salvations of Jacob, by Thee we will strike *our enemies*, in Thy name we will tread under foot the *insurgents* against us," Psalm xliv. 4, 5. Again, "Strangers *have risen* against me, and the violent have sought my soul; they have not set God before them; the Lord is amongst them that sustain my soul," Psalm liv. 3, 4. Again, "*Deliver me from mine enemies*, O my God, lift me up from them that are *insurgent* against me; deliver me from the workers of iniquity, lo! they wait for my soul," Psalm lix. 1, 2, 3; in these and several other passages, by enemies and insurgents are signified the evils and falses which are from hell. They are called insurgents, because evils and falses are insurgent against goods and truths, but not *vice versa*. The reason why they who are in things external separate from what is internal, have nothing of power to resist the evils and falses which are from hell, is, because all power of resisting those things is from the Divine, wherefore they, who are separated from what is internal, who are also separated from what is Divine, have no power; hence they are tossed to and fro by evils and falses, whithersoever hell carries them, like a flake of snow and chaff by the wind, as is very manifest from the evil ones who come from the world into another life. This also is represented by that nation, that they conquered their enemies, so long as they remained in the worship which was commanded them, and that they were conquered as often as they receded from that worship, thus as often as they were in evil, according to these words in Moses, "*If ye reprobate My statutes, the sound of a driven leaf shall pursue you, and ye shall fly the flight of the sword, and ye shall fall without a persecutor; they shall stumble a man on his brother, as before the sword, when none pursueth*," Levit. xxvi. 15, 36, 37. And in another place, "*One shall pursue a thousand, and two a myriad, because their rock hath sold them, and Jehovah hath shut them up*," Deut. xxxii. 30. From these considerations it is evident what is signified by being for annihilation to their insurgents.

10,482. Verses 26, 27, 28, 29. *And Moses stood in the gate of the camp, and said, who is for Jehovah [let him come] to me; and all the sons of Levi were gathered together to him. And he said to them, thus saith Jehovah God of Israel, put ye every one his sword upon his thigh, pass ye and return from gate to gate in the camp, and slay ye a man his brother, and a man his companion, and a man his neighbor. And the sons of Levi did according to the word of Moses; and there fell of the people in that day to three thousand men. And Moses said, fill ye your hand to-day to Jehovah, because a man is for his son, and for his brother, and to give upon you to-day a blessing.* And Moses stood in the gate of the camp, signifies where the opening into hell is. And said, who is for Jehovah to me, signifies those who are in externals from what is internal. And all the sons of Levi were gathered together to him, signifies those who are in truths derived from good. And he said to them, signifies exhortation. Thus saith Jehovah God of Israel, signifies from the Lord. Pass ye and return from gate to gate in the camp, signifies wheresoever any thing is open from what is internal into what is external. And slay ye a man his brother, and a man his companion, and a man his neighbor, signifies a closing-up as to the influx of good and truth, and of what is in affinity therewith, lest there be any reception and communication. And the sons of Levi did according to the word of Moses, signifies effect from those who are in truths derived from good. And there fell of the people in that day to three thousand men, signifies the plenary closing-up of what is internal. And Moses said, fill ye your hand to-day to Jehovah, signifies what is communicative and receptive of Divine Truth in the heavens. Because a man is for his son, and for his brother, signifies when what is internal is closed up, lest truth and good from heaven enter into what is external. To give upon you to-day a blessing, signifies the reception of Divine Truth from the Word, and by it conjunction with the Lord.

10,483. "And Moses stood in the gate of the camp"—that hereby is signified where the opening into hell is, appears from the representation of Moses, as denoting what is internal, see above, n. 10,468; and from the signification of in the gate, as denoting where there is an opening, of which we shall speak presently; and from the signification of the camp, as denoting hell, see also above, n. 10,458. The reason why Moses stood in the gate of the camp, and did not enter into the camp itself, was, that it might be represented that what is internal cannot enter into hell; for by Moses was represented what is internal, and by the camp hell; for all who are in hell are in things external separate from what is internal, since they are in the loves of self and the world; wherefore what is internal cannot enter thither, for it is not received, but with some is rejected immediately, with some is suffocated and extinguished, and with some is perverted; whether we speak of what is internal, or of heaven, it is the same thing, for heaven is in what is internal, both in the internal of the Word, and the internal of the church, and of worship, consequently in the internal of man, who is in celestial and spiritual love, that is in love to the Lord and in charity towards the neighbor. It may be expedient briefly to say what the opening of hell is, which is signified by the gate of this camp. Every hell is closed round about, but is opened above, according to necessity and need; this opening is into the world of spirits, which world is the middle one between heaven and hell, for there the hells terminate from above, and the heavens from beneath, n. 5852. It is said that they are opened according to necessity and need, since every man has attendant upon him spirits from hell, and angels from heaven; the spirits from hell are in his corporeal and worldly loves, and the angels from heaven in celestial and spiritual loves; for man without spirits cannot in any wise live; if they were taken away from him, he would fall down dead as a stone. Hence that man may have life according to his loves, the hells are opened from necessity and according to need, when such spirits come forth to him as are in similar loves. This opening is what is meant by the gate of hell; such opening it has been granted me occasionally to see. Those gates are guarded of the Lord by angels, to prevent more spirits coming forth thence than are needful. Hence it is evident what is signified in the Word by the gates of hell, and by the gates of enemies; as in Matthew, Jesus said to Peter, "On this rock I will build My church, *and the gates of hell shall not prevail over it*," xvi. 18; the gates of hell not prevailing, denotes that the hells durst not go forth and destroy the truths of faith; the rock on which the church is built, denotes faith from the Lord to the Lord, which faith is the faith of charity, because in this and with this it is so one; that a rock denotes that faith, see preface to chap. xxii. Gen. and n. 8581, 10,438. And that faith itself is charity, see n. 654, 1162, 1176, 1608, 2228, 2340, 2349, 2419, 2839, 3324, 4368, 6348, 7039, 7623 to 7627, 7752 to 7762, 8530, 9154, 9224, 9783. The like also is signified by the words, "*Thy seed shall inherit the gates of thine enemies*," Gen. xxii. 17; chap. xxiv. 60; to inherit the gates of enemies, denotes to destroy the evils and falses which are from hell; which also was represented by the expulsion and destruction of the nations in the land of Canaan; for the nations there represented the evils and falses which are from hell, see n. 1573, 1574, 1868, 4818, 6306, 8054, 8317, 9320, 9327. Also in David, "*The inhabitants of the gate* contrive against me, they that drink strong drink make songs," Psalm lxix. 12. Again, "Blessed is the man who hath filled his quiver, they shall not be ashamed, *because they shall speak with the enemies in the gate*," Psalm cxxvii. 5. But gates in the good sense denote an opening into heaven, in David, "*Lift up your heads, O ye gates*, and be ye lift up, *ye eternal doors*, and the King of Glory shall enter," Psalm xxiv. 7, 8, 9, 10. Moreover by gates in the Word is signified an entrance into heaven and into the church by truth and good, and also the influx of truth and good with man.

10,484. "And he said, who is for Jehovah, to me"—that hereby are signified those who are in things external from what is internal, appears from the representation of Moses, as denoting what is internal, see n. 10,468; and whereas the internal of man is in heaven, and his external in the world, and heaven enters through the internal into the external with man, it is evident that by those who are for Jehovah, are meant those who are in things external from what is internal; when it is said that heaven enters, it is meant that the Lord enters, since the Divine of the Lord makes heaven. That those are signified, is evident also from this consideration, that they are opposed to those who are in things external separate from what is internal; and also that by the sons of Levi, who were gathered together to Moses, are represented those who are in truths derived from good; and those who are in truths derived from good are in things external from what is internal.

10,485. "And all the sons of Levi were gathered together to him"—that hereby are signified those who are in truths derived from good, appears from the signification of the sons of Levi, as denoting those who are in spiritual love, or in charity towards the neighbor, see n. 3875, 4497, 4502, 4503. Whether we speak of charity towards the neighbor, or of truth derived from good, it is the same thing, since they who are in charity are in the life of truth, that is, a life according to Divine Truths is charity.

10,486. "And he said to them"—that hereby is signified exhortation, appears from the signification of saying, when the subject treated of is concerning combat to which they are excited, which is the case in this instance, as denoting exhortation.

10,487. "Thus saith Jehovah God of Israel"—that hereby is signified from the Lord, appears from this consideration, that Jehovah and the God of Israel in the Word is the Lord; that Jehovah is the Lord, see the passages cited, n. 9373, and that God and the Holy One of Israel is the Lord, see n. 7091.

10,488. "Put ye every one his sword upon his thigh"—that hereby is signified truth derived from good combating against the false derived from evil, appears from the signification of sword, as denoting truth combating against the false, see n. 2799, 8294; and from the signification of the thigh, as denoting the good of love, see n. 3021, 4277, 4280, 5050 to 5062, 9961. It is said the sword upon the thigh, because truth combating against the false and evil, and conquering, must be derived from good; all the power of truth is from that source; truth without good is not indeed truth, for it is only a scientific principle without life, hence truth without good has no power; by truth derived from good is meant a life according to truth, for good is of the life. Hence it is evident why mention is made of putting the sword upon the thigh, as also in David, where the Lord is treated of, "*Gird thy sword upon the thigh,* O hero, in Thy gracefulness and Thine honor," Psalm xlv. 3.

10,489. "Pass ye and return from gate to gate in the camp"—that hereby is signified wheresoever any thing is open from what is internal into what is external, appears from the signification of passing and returning, as denoting to survey and look around from one end to the other; and from the signification of gate, as denoting an opening, see above, n. 10,483, thus from gate to gate denotes wheresoever any thing is open; and from the signification of the camp, as denoting hell, see also above, n.10,483, thus also what is external, for what is external separate from what is internal is hell with man. Hence it is evident that by pass ye and return from gate to gate in the camp, is signified, that they ought to survey and look around wheresoever there is any thing open from what is internal into what is external. How the case herein is, will be shown in the following article. The reason why what is external separate from what is internal is hell with man, is, because what is internal with man is heaven, as was shown above, n. 10,472; hence what is external, when it is separate from heaven, is hell; which may be further manifest from this consideration, that with those who are in things external separate from things internal, infernal loves reign, which are the loves of self and the world; the man also, who has an external separate from what is internal, is actually in hell, al though he is ignorant of this whilst he lives in the world.

10,490. "And slay ye a man his brother, and a man his companion, and a man his neighbor"—that hereby is signified the closing up as to the influx of good and truth, and of things in affinity with them, lest there be any reception and communication, appears from the signification of slaying, as denoting to take away spiritual life, thus the good of love and the truth of faith; in this case therefore to close up, lest there be any reception and communication of those principles, which being taken away, spiritual life is also taken away, whilst natural life only remains; that to slay denotes to take away spiritual life, see n. 3387, 3395, 3607, 6767, 7043, 8902; and from the signification of brother, as denoting the good of love and of charity; see n. 3815, 4121, 4191, 5409, 5686, 5692, 6756; and from the signification of a companion, as denoting the truths of that good, and from the signification of a neighbor, as denoting what is conjoined to them, see n. 5911, 9378, thus what is in affinity, for they who are in affinity are neighbors. Hence it is evident that by slay ye a man his brother, and a man his companion, and a man his neighbor, is signified the closing of what is internal with that nation, as to the influx of good, of truth, and of things in affinity with them, lest there be any reception of them and communication with them. The case herein is this: inasmuch as that nation was in heart idolatrous, and absolutely in the loves in which hell is, and still a worship representative of things celestial was to be instituted amongst them, therefore internal things appertaining to them were altogether closed up. There were two causes of this closure, one that there might be conjunction with heaven by their externals without an internal principle; the other, lest the holy things of the church and of heaven should be profaned; for if that nation had acknowledged the internal things of worship, which are the holy things of the church and of heaven that were represented, they would have defiled and profaned them; hence it is that so little was revealed to that nation in the light concerning heaven and concerning the life after death; and hence it is that they were altogether ignorant that the kingdom of the Messiah was in heaven; that that nation is also of such a character at this day, is a known thing; but see what has been shown concerning that nation in the passages cited above, n. 10,396; as that they were altogether in external things without any internal principle, n. 4293, 4311, 4459, 4834, 4844, 4847, 4865, 4868, 4874, 4903, 4913, 9320, 9373, 9380, 9381. That hence their worship was merely external, n. 3147, 3479, 8871. That neither were they willing to know the internal things of worship and of the Word, n. 3479, 4429, 4433, 4680. That if they had known holy internal things they would have profaned them, n. 3398, 3489, 4289. That on this account it was not given to know them, n. 301, 302, 304, 2520, 3769. That still by the externals of worship, which were representative of heavenly things amongst them, there was communication with heaven, n. 4311, 4444, 6304, 8588, 8788, 8806. These now are the things which are meant and signified by the above words, that they should slay a man his brother, a man his companion, and a man his neighbor. He who does not know that by brethren, companions, neighbors, and by several other names of relationship, are signified the goods and truths of the church and of heaven, and their opposites, which are evils and falses, cannot know what is involved in several passages in the Word, where those names occur, as in the following, "Think not that I am come to send peace upon earth, I came not to send peace, but a sword; for I am come *to set a man at variance against his father, and the daughter against her mother, and the daughter-in-law against her mother-in-law:* and a man's enemies shall be those of his own house. Whoso loveth *father or mother* above Me, is not worthy of Me: and whoso loveth *son or daughter* above Me, is not worthy of Me; and whoso doth not take up his cross and follow after Me, is not worthy of Me," Matt. x. 34, 35, 36, 37, 38; the subject treated of in this passage is spiritual combats, which are temptations to be undergone by those who are to be regenerated, thus concerning the disagreements attendant on man, in such case between the evils and falses which influence him from hell, and between the goods and truths which influence him from the Lord; inasmuch as those combats are here described, therefore it is said, whoso doth not take up *his cross*, and follow after Me, is not worthy of Me; by the cross is meant the state of man in temptation. He who does not know that such things are signified by man and father, by daughter and mother, by daughter-in-law and mother-in-law, will believe that the Lord came into the world that He might take away peace in houses and families, and that He might induce disagreement, when yet He came to give peace, and to take away disagreements, according to His own words in John, chap. xiv. 27, and elsewhere. That the disagreement of the internal and external man is described in the above passage, is manifest from the signification of man [*homo*], and father, of daughter and mother, of daughter-in-law and mother-in-law, in the internal sense, in which sense man denotes the good which is from the Lord, father denotes the evil which is from the proprium of man, daughter denotes the affection of good and truth, mother denotes the affection of what is evil and false, daughter-in-law denotes the truth of the church adjoined to its good, and mother-in-law denotes the false adjoined to its evil. And inasmuch as the combat between goods and evils, and between falses and truths appertaining to man is thus described, therefore also it is said, that a man's enemies shall be those of his own house, for by those of his own house are signified those which appertain to the man, thus which are proper to him, and enemies, in the spiritual sense, are the evils and falses which assault goods and truths. That such things are signified by man [*homo*], father, daughter, mother, daughter-in-law, and mother-in-law, has been shown in the explications throughout. In like manner by these words in Matthew, "The *brother* shall deliver the *brother* to death, *and the father the son, and children* shall rise up against *parents*, and shall put them to death," x. 21. Also by these words in Luke, "If any one cometh to Me, *and hate not his father and mother, and wife and children, and brethren, and sisters*, yea, and his own soul also, he cannot be My disciple; and whosoever doth not carry his cross, and come after Me, cannot be My disciple. So then every one of you who doth not deny all his faculties, cannot be My disciple," xiv. 26, 27, 33. Who does not see that these words are to be understood otherwise than according to the letter? especially from this consideration, that it is said without restriction, that a father, a mother, a wife, children, brethren, sisters, are to be hated, before any one can be a disciple of the Lord; when yet it is a precept of the Lord's, that no one is to be hated, not even an enemy, Matt. v. 43, 44. That things proper to man, which are evils and falses in their order, are meant by the above names, is evident, for it is said also that he shall hate his own soul, and that he shall deny all his faculties, which things are things proper to him [or his proprium]. A state of temptation or of spiritual combat is also here described, for it is said, whosoever doth not carry his cross, and come after Me, cannot be My disciple. To be a disciple of the Lord, is to be led by Him, and not by self, thus by goods and truths which are from the Lord, and not by evils and falses which are from man. In like manner the Word is to be understood elsewhere, where the above names are mentioned, as in Jeremiah, "To My words they do not attend, and My law, they rejected it; wherefore thus saith Jehovah, behold I give before this people things of offence, that the *fathers and the sons* together, *a neighbor and his companion*, shall offend in them, and perish," vi. 19, 21. And again, "I will disperse them, *a man with his brother*, and *the sons* together; I will not spare, neither will I remit, neither will I pity, that I should not destroy them," xiii. 14. Again, "Jehovah hath multiplied them that stumbled, a *man* also hath fallen *upon his companion*," xlvi. 16. And in Isaiah, "I will mix Egypt with Egypt, that *a man shall fight against a brother, and a man against his companion*," xix. 2. In these passages also similar things are meant by fathers, sons, brethren, and companions.

10,491. "And the sons of Levi did according to the word of Moses"—that hereby is signified the effect from those who were in truths derived from good, appears from the representation of the sons of Levi, as denoting those who are in truths derived from good, and, in the abstract sense, truths derived from good, see above, n. 10,485; and from the signification of doing according to the word of Moses, as denoting effect.

10,492. "And there fell of the people in that day to three thousand men"—that hereby is signified the plenary closing up of what is internal, appears from the signification of falling or of being slain, as denoting to be closed up, see above n. 10,490; and from the signification of three thousand, as denoting what is plenary; for by three is signified what is full and complete, see n. 2788, 4495, 7715, 8347, 9198, 9488, 9489; in like manner by three thousand, since the greater numbers signify the like with the lesser, from which they exist by multiplication, n. 5291, 5335, 6708, 7973. That all numbers in the Word signify things, see the passages cited, n. 9488, and n. 10,127, 10,217, 10,253. Inasmuch as the subject here now treated of is concerning the closing up of what is internal with the Israelitish and Judaic nation, it is allowed to make some further observations concerning the closing up of what is internal. Evils and falses are what close up the internal man, or, what is the same thing, worldly, terrestrial and corporeal loves, when they prevail, for thence are all evils and falses. The reason why the internal is closed up by those loves is, because they are opposite to heavenly loves, or, what is the same thing, evils and falses are opposite to goods and truths; when therefore opposites act against each other, that which is hurt contracts itself, in like manner as a fibre when it is pricked, and in other cases the all of man from pain. That his face knits its brows from the hurt and mournful state of the mind, and that the abdomen of man with the lungs and their respiration contract themselves, is a known thing; so also it is with the internal man, when evils and falses enter into the thought and into the will. That aversion is excited on such occasion, and from it contraction is perceived, and is also apparent; this is the general cause why the internal is closed; but the special cause is, lest goods and truths should enter from heaven through the internal man into the external man, and should there be defiled and profaned; to prevent this therefore being the case with the Israelitish nation, with whom was the Word and the holy things of the church, the internal with them was plenarily closed up. That it was plenarily closed up, is very manifest from this consideration, that although they live amongst Christians, and although the Lord is manifestly treated of in the propheticals of the Word, still they do not at all acknowledge him; yea, they are of such a quality, that through interior repugnance and aversion they cannot even think any thing which confirms faith in the Lord. Moreover it is to be noted, that in the Christian world also the internal is closed with those who know the truths of faith from the Word, and do not live according to them, for the life itself according to them opens the internal man, otherwise the truths reside only in the memory of the external man; but with those who deny them, the internal is altogether closed; and what may seem wonderful, the internal is closed in more instances with the intelligent than with the simple. The reason is, because the intelligent are in the lusts of eminence and gain, and thence in the loves of self and the world, more than the simple; and also in the faculty of confirming evils and falses which are from those loves, by scientifics, in which the intelligent excel the simple. Add to this, that most of them think of the soul from some hypothesis established in the learned world, from which they conceive no other idea of the soul than as of breath or of wind, in which possibly there is a living principle; when on the other hand the simple good do not think from such an idea, but only from the idea that the soul is a man who lives after death; hence it is that to the latter the internal is opened, but to the former is closed. Whether we speak of the internal being opened or closed, or speak of heaven, it is the same thing.

10,493. "And Moses said, fill ye your hand to-day to Jehovah"—that hereby is signified what is communicative and receptive of Divine Truth in the heavens, appears from the signification of filling the hand to Jehovah, as being representative of the Divine Power of the Lord in the heavens by the Divine Truth proceeding from His Divine Good, and what is communicative and receptive thereof there, see n. 10,076; in this case what is communicative of Divine Truth with the heavens by representatives, which were the external things of worship with that nation, after the internal was closed to them. That by the external things of worship, which were representative of things celestial with that nation, when the internal was closed, there was communication with heaven by virtue of the Divine Power of the Lord, see n. 4311, 4444, 6304, 8588, 8788, 8806.

10,494. "Because a man is for his son, and for his brother"—that hereby is signified when the internal is closed, lest truth and good from heaven should enter into the external, appears from the signification of a man being for a son and for a brother, or after they have slain them, as denoting the closing-up of the internal as to the influx of truth and good, see above, n. 10,490, 10,492. That a son denotes truth, see n. 489, 491, 533, 1147, 2623, 2628, 2803, 2813, 3373, 3704, 4257, 9807; and that a brother denotes good, n. 3815, 4121, 4191, 5409, 5686, 5692.

10,495. "To give upon you to-day a blessing"—that hereby is signified the reception of Divine Truth from the Word, and by it conjunction with the Lord, appears from the signification of a blessing, as denoting in general what man is gifted with from the Lord; and whereas every thing of that description has relation to the good of love and the truth of faith, this, and every thing which is thence derived, is what is signified by blessing; in the present case therefore is signified the reception of Divine Truth from the Word, and by it conjunction with the Lord, see n. 1096, 2846, 3017, 3408, 4216, 4981, 6298, 8674, 8939; and that blessing denotes conjunction with the Lord, n. 3504, 3514, 3530, 3565, 3584, 6091, 6099. How the case herein is, has been shown in what goes before; and that by the Word there is conjunction of the Lord with man, and of heaven with the world, see n. 10,452.

10,496. Verses 30, 31, 32, 33, 34, 35. *And it came to pass on the day following, and Moses said to the people, ye have sinned a great sin, and now will I go up to Jehovah; peradventure I shall expiate for your sin. And Moses returned to Jehovah, and said, I beseech, this people hath sinned a great sin, and they have made to themselves gods of gold. And now if Thou remittest their sin, and if not, blot me, I pray, out of Thy book which Thou hast written. And Jehovah said to Moses, whosoever hath sinned against Me, him will I blot out of My book. And now go, lead the people to what I said to thee; behold Mine angel shall go before you, and in the day of My visitation I will visit upon them their sin. And Jehovah smote the people because they made the calf which Aaron made.* And it came to pass the day following, signifies the duration of such worship even to the end of the church. And Moses said to the people, ye have sinned a great sin, signifies aversion and total alienation. And now I will go up to Jehovah, signifies the elevation of the interiors to the Lord. Peradventure I shall expiate for your sin, signifies possibility from the Divine Power of the Lord with those who have altogether so averted themselves. And Moses returned to Jehovah, signifies conjunction. And said, I beseech, this people hath sinned a great sin, signifies that although that nation has altogether averted and removed itself from the Divine. And they have made to themselves gods of gold, signifies and worship infernal delight. And now if thou remittest their sin, signifies that still that aversion from the Divine would not oppose. And if not, blot me I pray out of Thy book, which Thou hast written, signifies the internal of the Word, of the church, and of worship, that it would not perish. And Jehovah said, whosoever hath sinned against Me, him will I blot out of My book, signifies a reply that they will perish who avert themselves from the Divine. And now go, lead the people to what I said to thee, signifies that nation to represent a church, and not that a church should be established among them. Behold Mine angel shall go before you, signifies that still Divine Truth will lead. And in the day of my visitation I will visit upon them their sin, signifies their last state in particular and in general when there is judgment. And Jehovah smote the people, signifies the devastation of truth and good with the Israelitish nation. Because they made the calf, signifies on account of worship from infernal love. Which Aaron made, signifies this from the external things which alone they loved.

10,497. "And it came to pass the day following"—that hereby is signified the duration of such worship, even to the end of the church, appears from the signification of the day following, as denoting what is perpetual and eternal, but when concerning the Jewish nation, as denoting even to the end of the church. The reason why the day following denotes what is perpetual and eternal, is, because by the morrow, when it is said of such things as signify Divine celestial and spiritual things, is signified what is perpetual and eternal, see n. 3998, 9939; but the reason why it denotes duration even to the end of the church, is, because it is said of the Jewish nation and its worship, which had an end when the Lord came into the world, according to the prediction in Daniel, "Seventy weeks are decided upon thy people, and upon thy city of holiness, to consume prevarication, and to seal up sins, and to expiate iniquity, and to bring the justice of ages, and to seal up the vision and the prophet, and to anoint the holy of holies: in the middle of the week, he shall cause to cease the sacrifice and oblation, at length upon the bird of abominations shall be desolation, and even to the consummation and decision, it shall drop upon the devastation," ix. 24, 27; and that the residue of the worship of that nation is to have an end with the end of the church at this day in Europe, the Lord predicts in Matthew, "Verily I say unto you, this generation shall not pass away, until all these things are done," xxiv. 34. The subject treated of in that chapter is concerning the consummation of the age, which is the end of this church, as may be seen shown in the introductions to the chapters xxvi. to xl. of Genesis.

10,498. "And Moses said to the people, ye have sinned a great sin"—that hereby is signified total alienation and aversion, appears from the signification of sin, as denoting aversion and alienation from the Divine, see n. 5229, 5474, 5841, 7589, 9346, in this case total aversion and alienation, because it is called a great sin. Aversion and alienation from the Divine is total, when there is no longer any thing of truth and good from heaven received, for truth and good from heaven is the Divine with man. That there was no reception of truth and good from heaven, consequently that there was a total aversion from the Divine with that nation, is described in these words in Isaiah, "Say to this people, hearing hear ye, but do not understand, and seeing see ye, but do not know: make fat the heart of this people, and make their ears heavy, and bedaub their eyes, lest possibly they should see with their eyes, and hear with their ears, and their heart should understand, and they should be converted, so as to be healed," vi. 9, 10; John xii. 37, 38, 39, 40; it is said lest they should be converted so as to be healed, by which is signified, that if they were to understand the internal things of the Word, of the church, and of worship, they would profane them, according to what was said above, n. 10,490.

10,499. "And now I will go up to Jehovah"—that hereby is signified elevation of the interiors to the Lord, appears from the representation of Moses, as denoting what is internal, see above, n. 10,468; and from the signification of going up, as denoting elevation towards interior things, see n. 3084, 4539, 4969, 5406, 5817, 6007; in this case elevation to the Lord, because it is said, I will go up to Jehovah, and by Jehovah, in the Word, is meant the Lord, see the passages cited, n. 9373. How the case herein is, may be manifest from what was shown concerning the elevation of the internal things of the Word, of the church, and of worship, into heaven, or to the Lord, from the external things appertaining to the Israelitish nation, n. 4311, 4444, 6304, 8588, 8788, 8806.

10,500. "Peradventure I shall expiate for your sin"—that hereby is signified possibility derived from the Divine Power of the Lord with those who have so altogether averted themselves, appears from the signification of expiating, as denoting to effect that it be no longer reflected upon, thus that their worship is nevertheless accepted and heard; that expiation also denotes the hearing and reception of all things which are of worship, see n. 9506; in this case therefore the possibility that it can be effected with those who have thus averted themselves; and from the signification of sin, as denoting total aversion from the Divine, as above, n. 10,498. The reason why these things are signified by those words, is, because the subject treated of in this chapter throughout is concerning the aversion of the Israelitish nation from the Divine, and concerning the possibility still, that by the external things in which alone they were principled, communication might be effected with heaven. In order to show how the case herein is, it may be expedient to say a few words more on the subject; the church on earth is instituted solely for the end, that there may be communication of the world, that is, of the human race with heaven, that is, by [or through] heaven with the Lord; for without a church there would be no communication, and without communication the human race would perish, n. 10,452; but the communication of man with heaven is effected by the spiritual and celestial things appertaining to man, but not by worldly and corporeal things without them; or what is the same thing, it is effected by internal things, but not by external things without them. When therefore the Israelitish nation were in external things without internal, and yet somewhat of a church was to be instituted amongst them, it was on this account provided by the Lord, that still communication with heaven might be effected by representatives, which were the external things of worship with that nation; but this communication was miraculously effected, on which subject see the passages adduced above, n. 10,499. But two things were requisite that this might be effected; first, that the internal principle appertaining to them should be altogether closed up; and secondly, that they might be in a holy external principle when in worship; for when the internal principle is altogether closed up, in this case the internal of the church and of worship is neither denied nor acknowledged, being as it were none; and in this case a holy external principle may be given, and also be elevated, because nothing opposes and hinders. On this account also that nation was in plenary ignorance concerning things internal, which are the things of love and faith in the Lord, and of life eternal by them: but as soon as the Lord came into the world, and revealed Himself, and taught love and faith in Himself, then that nation, inasmuch as they heard those things, began to deny them, and thus could no longer be kept in such ignorance as before; therefore they were then driven out of the land of Canaan, lest they should defile and profane internal things by denial in that land, where all places, from the most ancient times, were made representative of such things as relate to heaven and the church, see n. 1585, 3686, 4447, 5136, 6516. On this account, so far as at this day they are acquainted with things internal, and confirm themselves intellectually against them, and deny them, so far they can no longer be in a holy external principle, since what is negative not only closes up what is internal, but also takes away what is holy from what is external, thus every thing communicative with heaven. The case is similar with Christians, who from the Word, or from the doctrine of the church, are acquainted with things internal, and still deny them in heart, as is the case when they live evilly, and think evilly with themselves, howsoever they may seem to be in external devotion and piety when in worship.

10,501. "And Moses returned to Jehovah"—that hereby is signified conjunction, appears from the signification of returning to Jehovah. The reason why conjunction is here signified by returning to Jehovah, is, because by going up to Jehovah, n. 10,499, is signified elevation of the internal to the Lord.

10,502. "And said, I beseech, this people have sinned a great sin"—that hereby is signified that although that nation have altogether averted and removed themselves from the Divine, appears from the signification of sinning a great sin, as denoting altogether to avert and alienate themselves from the Divine, see above, n. 10,498. It is said *although* they have averted themselves, on account of the series of the thing, in the internal sense; for they who are in that sense, do not attend to the letter, but to the sense of the things in their order.

10,503. "And have made to themselves gods of gold"—that hereby is signified and worship infernal delight, appears from the signification of making to themselves gods, as denoting worship; and from the signification of gold, as denoting the delight of external loves, thus infernal delights, see above, n. 10,402. Mention is made in the Word of four kinds of idols, namely, of stone, of wood, of silver, and of gold. The idols which were of stone, signify worship from falses of doctrine; those which were of wood, worship from evils of doctrine; those which were of silver, the worship of what is false both in doctrine and life; and those which were of gold, the worship of evil both in doctrine and life; hence the idols of gold signified worship the worst of all. They who were in this worship, not only falsified truths, but also adulterated goods; for evils they called goods, and the falses thence derived they called truths. All they are in that worship, who are in the love of self, and still believe the Word; for they apply the sense of the letter of the Word in favor of all things which they think and which they do, thus to the worship of self.

10,504. "And now if Thou remittest their sin"—that hereby is signified that still that aversion from the Divine would not oppose, appears from the signification of sin, as denoting aversion from the Divine, as above, n. 10,498, 10,502; and from the signification of remitting it, as denoting not to oppose, but that still the internal things of the Word, of the church, and of worship, can be elevated from their external things, and thus communication be effected with the heavens; for when this communication is nevertheless effected, then the aversion is not attended to, and what is not attended to, this is said to be remitted.

10,505. "And if not, blot me I pray out of Thy book which Thou hast written"—that hereby is signified the internal of the Word, of the church, and of worship, that it was not about to perish, appears from the representation of Moses, who says these things, as denoting the internal of the Word, of the church, and of worship, see n. 10,468; and from the signification of which Thou hast written, as denoting what is therein from the Lord; for by the book is signified what is in the internal principle, and by writing, when concerning Jehovah, that is, the Lord, is signified what is therein from the Lord; and from the signification of blotting out of it, as denoting to perish, but in this case not to perish, because it is answered, "Him who hath sinned against Me I will blot out of My book," by which is signified that the internal of the Word, of the church, and of worship, would not perish, but that they would perish who avert themselves from the Divine, thus who are in things external without an internal principle. The reason why the book which Jehovah wrote, which in the following verse is called My book, or the book of Jehovah, and in other places the book of life, denotes the internal principle, is, because the internal principle of man is in heaven, thus where the Lord is, and hence those things which are in his internal principle are from heaven from the Lord, all which things are Divine Celestial and spiritual things; these can be received by the internal of man, but not by his external separate from the internal, since the external is in the world, and formed to receive the natural things which are in the world, which without influx through internal things have not heavenly life, and hence are said to be dead. From these considerations it may be manifest what is meant in the Word by the book of life, and who they are who are said to be written in that book, namely, they who are in the life of truth and good, thus who do Divine precepts from love and faith; for a life according to those precepts opens the internal man, and forms him, and what is there inscribed, is inscribed by the Lord, and remains to eternity. These are they who are meant by the written in the book of life in the following passages, "In this time Thy people shall be snatched away, *every one who is found written in the book*," Dan. xii. 1. And in the Apocalypse, "He that overcometh, shall be clothed in white raiment, and *I will not blot his name out of the book of life*," iii. 5. Again, "None enter into the New Jerusalem, *except they who are written in the Lamb's book of life*," Apoc. xxi. 26. Again, "I saw *that the books were opened; and another book was opened which is of life;* and the dead were judged according to those things *which were written in the book* according to their works; and if *any one was not found written in the book of life*, he was cast out into the lake of fire," Apoc. xx. 12, 13, 15. Again, "All shall adore the beast, *whose names are not written in the Lamb's book of life*," Apoc. xiii. 8; and chap. xvii. 8; besides also in other places. It is to be noted, that all things which are inscribed in the internal man, are inscribed by the Lord; and that the things there inscribed constitute the spiritual and celestial life itself of man; also that all and singular the things which are there inscribed, are inscribed on the love. See likewise, n. 2474, 8620, 9386.

10,506. "And Jehovah said, him who hath sinned against Me, I will blot out of My book"—that hereby is signified the reply, that they would perish who avert themselves from the Divine, appears from the signification of Jehovah saying to Moses, as denoting a reply; and from the signification of sinning against Jehovah, as denoting to avert himself from the Divine, see above, n. 10,498; and from the signification of being blotted out of the book of Jehovah, as denoting not to appear in heaven; thus to perish as to spiritual life. The reason why this is signified by being blotted out of the book of Jehovah, is, because those who are in things external, separate from what is internal, cannot receive any thing from heaven; for it is the internal principle which thence receives; and the external without it does not receive any thing from any other source than from hell. That heaven is with man in his internal, and that the internal is the book of life, and that the things which are in the internal are from heaven from the Lord, see just above, n. 10,505.

10,507. "And now go, lead the people to what I said to thee"—that hereby is signified that nation to represent a church, and not that a church should be with that nation, appears from the signification of leading the people to the land of Canaan, as denoting to cause them to become a church, for by the land of Canaan is signified the church, and by leading the people to it, in the spiritual sense, is signified to establish the church amongst them; for that nation was led into that land for this purpose, that it might become a church;

but in this case only to represent a church, since it is said, lead the people *to what*, and not to the land. That with the Israelitish and Judaic nation there was not a church, but only the representative of a church, see n. 4281, 4288, 4311, 4500, 4899, 4912, 6304, 7048, 9320; and that the land of Canaan denotes the church, n. 3705, 4447, 5736, 6516; and that hence land [or earth] in the Word denotes the church, see the passages cited, n. 9325.

10,508. "Behold Mine angel shall go before thee"—that hereby is signified that still the Divine Truth will lead, appears from the signification of the angel of Jehovah, as denoting, in the supreme sense, the Lord as to the Divine Human, and, in the respective sense, the Divine which is of the Lord with the angels in the heavens, see n. 1925, 2821, 4085, 6831, 9303, and that hence it signifies the Divine Truth, n. 8192; and from the signification of going before thee, as denoting to lead.

10,509. "And in the day of My visitation I will visit upon them their sin"—that hereby is signified their last state in particular and in general, when there is judgment, appears from the signification of the day of visitation, as denoting the last state of the church in particular and in general, see n. 2242, 6588; and from the signification of visiting sin, as denoting to be judged, and to be damned. It is said in particular and in general, because the day of visitation to every one, thus in particular, is when he comes into the other life, as is the case when he dies; and also it is of the church in general, when the church ceases to be. On this occasion all are explored as to their quality, and are separated, those who are in evils are cast down into hell, and those who are in goods are elevated into heaven; this however is not effected on earth, but in the other life. But in what manner exploration is accomplished there, and in what manner separation; also in what manner damnation and casting down into hell, and elevation into heaven, by the Divine Mercy of the Lord will be shown elsewhere.

10,510. "And Jehovah smote the people"—that hereby is signified the devastation of truth and good with the Israelitish nation, appears from the signification of smiting, as denoting to destroy, as n. 6761; and to destroy, in the spiritual sense, is to deprive any one of the truths and goods of faith and love, which in the Word is called desolation and vastation. The reason why devastation is here signified by smiting, is, because the subject treated of in this chapter is concerning the closing of the internal principle with the Israelitish nation, and the closing of the internal principle is devastation as to truth and good.

10,511. "Because they made the calf"—that hereby is signified on account of worship grounded in infernal love, appears from the signification of the calf, as denoting the delight of the love of self, see above, n. 10,407, hence to make a calf denotes worship grounded in the delight of that love, or what is the same thing, worship derived from that love; which love, that it is infernal love, has been frequently shown. The reason why by making the calf is signified worship, is, because the making it involves all those things which are said concerning the adoration and worship of it in verses 4, 5, 6, of this chapter.

10,512. "Which Aaron made"—that hereby is signified this from the external things which alone they loved, appears from the representation of Aaron, as denoting the external of the Word, of the church, and of worship, see n. 10,397, 10,468, 10,480. And when the external alone is loved, then the external is said to do it· but the nation is meant, which loves external things alone.

CONTINUATION OF THE SUBJECT CONCERNING THE THIRD EARTH IN THE STARRY HEAVEN.

10,513. *BEFORE the spirits of that earth were represented magnificent palaces, resembling those in which kings and princes dwell on our earth; for such things may be represented before spirits, and when they are represented, they appear exactly as if they existed; but the spirits from that earth held those things in no estimation, calling them marble images; and then related, that they have more magnificent objects with them, which are their sacred temples, not built of stone, but of wood. When it was objected, that these were still terrestrial objects, they replied, that they were not terrestrial, but celestial, because in beholding them, they conceive not a terrestrial idea but a celestial one; believing that they shall see like objects in heaven after death.*

10,514. *They represented also their sacred temples before the spirits of our earth, who said that they never saw any thing more magnificent; they were also represented to me, whence the manner of their construction was seen. They are constructed of trees not cut down, but growing in their native soil; it was declared that on that earth there are trees of an extraordinary size and height; these they set in rows when young, that they may serve for porticos and for galleries; in the meanwhile, by cutting and pruning the tender shoots, they fit and prepare them to entwine one with another, and join together, s' as to form together the groundwork and floor of the temple to be constructed, whilst some branches by a side-elevation serve as walls, and others being bended into an arch above, constitute the roof; in this manner they construct the temple with admirable art, elevated high above the ground; they prepare also an ascent into it by continuous branches of the trees, extended from the trunk and firmly connected together. Moreover they adorn the temple without and within in various ways, by disposing the leaves into particular forms; thus they build an entire grove. But it was not given to see the nature of the construction of these temples within, only that the light of their sun is let in through apertures between the branches, and is every where transmitted through crystals, whereby the light falling on the walls is refracted into divers colors like those of the rainbow, especially the colors of blue and orange, which they are most fond of. Such is the nature of their architecture, which they prefer to the most magnificent palaces of our earth. The spirits of our earth held it in like esteem and preference.*

10,515. *They said further, that the inhabitants do not dwell in high places, but on the earth in low cottages, since high places are for the Lord who is in heaven, and low places for men who are on earth. Their cottages were also shown me, they were oblong, having within along the walls a continued couch, in which they lie one behind another. On the side opposite to the entrance, where there is a kind of alcove, there is a table, and behind it a fire-place from which the whole chamber is illuminated. In the fire-place there is not burning fire but luminous wood, which emits from itself as much light as that of a common fire. They said that in an evening this wood appears as if it contained in it lighted charcoal.*

10,516. *They informed me further, that they do not live in societies, but in houses apart by themselves, and that they are joined in societies when they meet for worship; and that on these occasions, they who are teachers walk beneath the temple in porticos, and the rest at the sides; and that in their meetings they experience interior joys, arising from the sight of the temple, and from the worship therein celebrated.*

10,517. *Moreover they are well disposed, so that they may be called good dispositions; they suffer patiently the injuries which are done them without any inclination to revenge. They become anxious when they first approach to those who think about corporeal and terrestrial things, but glad and cheerful in approaching those who think about heavenly things. Their anxiety was also perceived arising from the spirits of our earth who were about me, because they were of a contrary disposition; for the spirits of our earth think little about heavenly things and much about corporeal and terrestrial things; and when they think about heavenly things, they think about truths, and not about good, but the spirits from that earth think about good, and little about truths. Hence it is that the inhabitants of that earth love plantations of trees, and their sacred edifice made of trees, and hold in aversion works of stone and houses of stone; for trees and wood from correspondence signify goods, whereas stones and houses built of them signify truths, n.* 3720; *man also is such, that he loves those things which correspond to his interior affections, although during his life in the world he is ignorant of it.*

10,518. *A fourth earth in the starry heaven, together with its spirits and inhabitants, will be described at the close of the following chapter.*

EXODUS.

CHAPTER THE THIRTY-THIRD.

THE DOCTRINE OF CHARITY AND FAITH.

10,519. THE Holy Supper was instituted by the Lord, that by it there may be conjunction of the church with heaven, thus with the Lord. On this account it is the most holy thing of the church.

10,520. But in what manner conjunction is effected by it, is not apprehended by those who do not know any thing concerning the internal or spiritual sense of the Word, for they do not think beyond its external sense, which is the sense of the letter. From the internal or spiritual sense of the Word it is known what is signified by body and blood, and what by bread and wine, also what by chewing [or eating].

10,521. In that sense the body or flesh of the Lord is the good of love, in like manner the bread; and the blood of the Lord is the good of faith, in like manner the wine; and chewing [or eating] is appropriation and conjunction. The angels who are attendant on man during the ceremony of the sacrament of the Supper, have no other perception of those terms, for they apprehend all things spiritually; hence it is that the holy principle of love, and the holy principle of faith, flows-in on the occasion from the angels to men, thus by or through heaven from the Lord. Hence comes conjunction.

10,522. From these considerations it is evident that man, when he takes the bread, which is the body, is conjoined to the Lord by the good of love to Him from Him; and when he takes the wine, which is the blood, he is conjoined to the Lord by the good of faith to Him from Him. But it is to be noted, that conjunction with the Lord by the sacrament of the Supper is effected solely with those who are in the good of love and faith to the Lord from the Lord. The Holy Supper is the seal of that conjunction.

CHAPTER XXXIII.

1. AND JEHOVAH spake to Moses, go, ascend from hence, thou and the people, whom thou hast made to ascend out of the land of Egypt, to the land which I have sworn to Abraham, to Isaac, and to Jacob, saying, to thy seed I will give it.

2. And I will send before thee an angel, and will drive out the Canaanite, the Amorite, and the Hittite, and the Perizite, the Hivite, and the Jebusite.

3. To a land flowing with milk and honey, because I will not go up in the midst of thee, because thou art a people hard of neck, peradventure I shall consume thee in the way.

4. And the people heard this evil word, and they mourned, and they set not any one his ornament upon him.

5. And JEHOVAH said to Moses, say to the sons of Israel, ye are a people hard of neck, in one moment I should ascend in the midst of thee, and should consume thee; and now cause thine ornament to descend from upon thee, and I shall know what I shall do to thee.

6. And the sons of Israel snatched away their ornament, from Mount Horeb.

7. And Moses took the tent, and stretched [it] for himself out of the camp, by removing it at a distance from the camp, and he called it the tent of the congregation: and it came to pass, every one that asked JEHOVAH went forth to the tent of the congregation, which was out of the camp.

8. And it came to pass, when Moses went forth to the tent, all the people arose, and they stood every one at the door of his tent, and they looked after Moses even to his entering into the tent.

9. And it came to pass, when Moses entered the tent, the pillar of the cloud descended, and stood at the door of the tent, and spake with Moses.

10. And all the people saw the pillar of the cloud standing at the door of the tent, and all the people arose, and they bowed themselves every one at the door of his tent.

11. And JEHOVAH spake to Moses faces to faces, as a man speaketh to his neighbor; and he returned to the camp; and his minister Joshua the son of Nun, a boy, did not move himself from the midst of the tent.

12. And Moses said to JEHOVAH, see; Thou sayest to me, cause this people to ascend, and Thou hast not made known to me whom Thou wilt send with me, and Thou hast said, I know thee by name, and also thou hast found favor in mine eyes.

13. And now if I pray I have found favor [or grace] in Thine eyes, make known to me I pray Thy way, and I shall

know thee, since I have found favor [or grace] in Thine eyes, and see that this nation is Thy people.

14. And He said, My faces shall go, and I will cause thee to rest.

15. And he said to Him, if Thy faces go not, cause us not to go up from hence.

16. And wherein shall it be made known at any time, that I have found favor [or grace] in Thine eyes, I and Thy people, is it not in Thy going with us; and we shall be rendered excellent, I and Thy people above every people which is on the faces of the ground.

17. And JEHOVAH said to Moses, also this word which thou hast spoken, I will do, because thou hast found favor [or grace] in Mine eyes, and I know thee by name.

18. And he said, cause me I pray to see Thy glory.

19. And He said, I will cause all My good to pass above thy faces, and I will call upon the name of JEHOVAH before thee, and I will do favor [or grace] to whom I do favor [or grace], and I will do mercy to whom I do mercy.

20. And He said, thou canst not see My faces; because no man seeth Me and liveth.

21. And JEHOVAH said, behold a place with Me, and thou shalt stand upon a rock.

22. And it shall come to pass, in My glory passing by, I will set thee in a cleft of the rock, and will cover the palm of My hand over thee, until I shall pass by.

23. And I will remove the palm of My hand, and thou shalt see My posteriors; and My faces shall not be seen.

THE CONTENTS.

10,523. IN this chapter in the internal sense the subject is further continued concerning the Israelitish nation, but here concerning its quality as to worship, thus concerning its quality as to those things which are of the church. The contents from verse 1 to 6 are, that although they could be in representatives, which are the external things of worship and of the church, still there did not appertain to them any thing Divine, because not any thing internal. The contents from verse 7 to 17 are, that in worship itself viewed in itself, thus separated from them, the Divine might be therein. The contents from verse 18 to 23 are, that nevertheless this was not seen nor perceived by them.

THE INTERNAL SENSE.

10,524. VERSES 1, 2, 3. *And Jehovah spake to Moses, go, ascend from hence, thou and the people whom thou hast made to ascend from the land of Egypt, to the land which I sware to Abraham, to Isaac, and to Jacob, saying, to thy seed I will give it. And I will send before thee an angel, and I will drive out the Canaanite, the Amorite, and the Hittite, and the Perizite, the Hivite, and the Jebusite. To a land flowing with milk and honey, because I will not ascend in the midst of thee, because thou art a people hard of neck; peradventure I shall consume thee in the way.* And Jehovah spake to Moses, signifies instruction concerning the quality of worship and of the church with the Israelitish nation. Go, ascend from hence, thou and the people whom thou hast made to ascend out of the land of Egypt, to the land, signifies that that nation was to represent the church, but the church was not to be with it, because it cannot be elevated from things external. Which I sware to Abraham, to Isaac, and to Jacob, to thy seed will I give it, signifies promised to those who from the Lord are in the good of love and the truths of faith. And I will send before thee an angel, signifies the Divine of the Lord, from which is the external of the church and its worship. And I will drive out the Canaanite, the Amorite, and the Hittite, and the Perizite, the Hivite, and the Jebusite, signifies the ejection thence of all evils and falses. To a land flowing with milk and honey, signifies what is pleasant and delightful from the good of faith and love. Because I will not ascend in the midst of thee, signifies that nevertheless the Divine was not with the nation itself. Because thou art a people hard of neck, signifies that it does not receive any influx from the Divine. Peradventure I shall consume thee in the way, signifies that that nation, if the Divine flowed-in with them, would perish.

10,525. "And Jehovah spake to Moses"—that hereby is signified instruction concerning the quality of worship and of the church with the Israelitish nation, appears from the signification of speaking, when by Jehovah, as denoting instruction, see the passages cited, n. 10,277. The reason why it denotes instruction concerning the quality of worship and of the church with the Israelitish nation, is, because that is the subject treated of in this chapter, as may be manifest from its contents, see above, n. 10,523.

10,526. "Go, ascend from hence, thou and the people whom thou hast made to ascend out of the land of Egypt, to the land"—that hereby is signified that that nation was to represent a church, but that a church was not to be with it, because it cannot be elevated from things external, appears from the signification of ascending into the land, as denoting to institute a church, for by land [or earth] in the Word is signified the church, see the passages cited, n. 9375; and by ascending to it, is signified to institute the church, since on that account they were led thither, or ascended; but in this case it is not signified to institute it, but only to represent it, since that nation was in things external without an internal principle, and the church with man is in his internal principle. Inasmuch as here it is not signified to institute a church, but only to represent those things which are of the church, therefore it is said "*go*, ascend *from hence*, and also thou and the people whom *thou hast made* to ascend out of the land of Egypt," thus whom Moses made to ascend, and not Jehovah; and in the subsequent verse, "I will not ascend in the midst of thee, because thou art a people hard of neck;" by which is signified that the Divine is not with them, and where the Divine is not received in the internal, there the church is not, but only an external representative of the church; and from the signification of making to ascend out of the land of Egypt, as denoting to be elevated from things external to what is internal; but in this case not to be elevated, because it is said, that Moses made them to ascend, and not that Jehovah; that this is signified by making to ascend out of the land of Egypt, see n. 10,421. That there was no church with the Israelitish nation, but only the representative of a church, see n. 4281, 4288, 4311, 4500, 4899, 4912, 6304, 6704, 9320; and throughout in the preceding chapter.

10,527. "Which I have sworn to Abraham, to Isaac, and to Jacob, to thy seed will I give it"—that hereby is signified promised to those who from the Lord are in the good of love and the truths of faith, appears from the signification of swearing, when by Jehovah, as denoting confirmation from the Divine in the internal man, see n. 2842, 3375, 9166, thus also promised from the Divine, for what is promised from the Divine, this is also confirmed; and from the representation of Abraham, of Isaac, and of Jacob, as denoting in the supreme sense the Lord as to the Divine itself and the Divine Human, and in the respective sense heaven and the church, see n. 3245, 3251, 3305, 4615, 6098, 6185, 6276, 6804, 10,445; and from the signification of their seed, as denoting those who are in the good of love and the truths of faith from the Lord, thus in the abstract sense the good of love and the truth of faith, see n. 3373, 10,445.

10,528. "And I will send before thee an angel"—that hereby is signified the Divine of the Lord, from which is the church and its worship, appears from the signification of an angel, as denoting in the supreme sense the Lord as to the Divine Human, and in the respective sense the Divine of the Lord in heaven with angels, also in the church with men, of which we shall speak presently; and from the signification of sending before thee, as denoting to prepare. That an angel in the supreme sense denotes the Lord as to the Divine Human, see n. 1925, 3039, 6280, 6831, 9303, and that in the respective sense it denotes the Divine of the Lord in heaven with angels, see n. 1925, 2821, 4085, 6831, 8192; hence it follows that an angel also denotes the Divine of the Lord with men who receive it; for men, who are in the good of love and in the truths of faith to the Lord from the Lord, become angels after death, and they who become angels also are angels as to their interiors whilst they live in the world; hence it is that John the Baptist is called an angel in the Word, as in Luke, "*He it is of whom it is written, behold I send Mine angel before Thy face*, who shall prepare Thy way before Thee," vii. 27. And that angel in this passage denotes the Divine of the Lord appertaining to Him, is plain from Malachi, "*Behold I send Mine angel*, who shall prepare the way before Me; and suddenly shall come to His temple the Lord whom ye seek, and *the angel of the covenant* whom ye desire," iii. 1; the reason why the Divine of the Lord is there meant by angel, is, because John the Baptist represented the Lord as to the Word, like Elias, and the Word is the Divine Truth which is from the Lord; that Elias represented the Word, see preface to chap. xviii. Gen. and n. 2762, 5247; and that John the Baptist, n. 9372. And whereas in the supreme sense the Lord as to the Divine Human is an angel, therefore it is said, "There shall come to His temple the Lord and the angel of the covenant," where temple denotes His Divine Human, as is evident in John, chap. ii. v. 18 to 23. The reason why mention is made both of the Lord and of an angel, is, because He is called Lord from the Divine Good, and angel from Divine Truth. Inasmuch as Jehovah in the Word is the Lord Himself, therefore it is said, "I send Mine angel who shall prepare the way *before Me*," this is said by Jehovah.

10,529. "And I will drive out the Canaanite, the Amorite, and the Hittite, and the Perizite, the Hivite, and the Jebusite"—that hereby is signified the ejection thence of all evils and falses, appears from the representation of the nations in the land of Canaan, as denoting the evils and falses of the church and of worship, see n. 9320, and the passages cited, n. 9327; but what particular evil and false principle is signified by each nation, see the explications where they are treated of, as concerning the Canaanite, n. 1573, 1574, 4818; concerning the Amorite, n. 1857, 6306, 6854; concerning the Hittite, n. 2913, 6858; concerning the Perizite, n. 1573, 1574, 6859; concerning the Hivite and concerning the Jebusite, n. 6860.

10,530. "To a land flowing with milk and honey"—that hereby is signified what is pleasant and delightful from the good of faith and of love, appears from the signification of land [or earth] as denoting the church, see the passages cited, n. 9375; and from the signification of milk, as denoting spiritual good, which is the good of faith, see n. 2184 ; and from the signification of honey, as denoting celestial good, which is the good of love ; and from the signification of flowing, as denoting to be full ; and since these things are signified by a land flowing with milk and honey, what is pleasant and delightful from the good of faith and of love is also signified, see n. 5620. It is said what is pleasant and delightful from those principles, since in the good of faith and of love is pleasantness itself and celestial delight ; for all good has its delight, inasmuch as that is called good which is loved, and all delight is of the love : the delight which is meant by heavenly joy and eternal happiness is from no other source than from the love of truth and good ; that this delight is above every delight of every love in the world, is altogether unknown to those who place all delight in things worldly, corporeal and terrestrial.

10,531. "Because I will not ascend in the midst of thee"—that hereby is signified that nevertheless the Divine is not with the nation itself, appears from the signification of not ascending in the midst of the people, when this is said by Jehovah, as denoting that the Divine is not in the nation itself, thus not the church ; for with whomsoever the church is, there is the Divine ; for to ascend to the land, denotes to constitute a church, as above, n. 10,526 ; and in the midst of thee, denotes in its internal.

10,532. "Because thou art a people hard of neck"—that hereby is signified that they do not receive any influx from the Divine, appears from what was shown, n. 10,429, where like words occur.

10,533. "Peradventure I shall consume thee in the way"—that hereby is signified that that nation, if the Divine flowed-in with them, would perish, appears from the signification of consuming, as denoting to perish. That that nation would perish if the Divine flowed-in with them, is evident, for it is said, I will not ascend in the midst of thee, peradventure I shall consume thee in the way. The case herein is this ; they who are in things external without an internal principle, thus in the loves of self and the world, are absolutely incapable of receiving any Divine ; wherefore the internal with them is kept closed. If the internal was opened with them, and the Divine flowed-in, they would altogether perish ; for their life is derived from the loves of self and the world, and there is a perpetual opposition and contrariety between those loves and heavenly loves, and heavenly loves are the Divine ; wherefore from the influx of the Divine their life would be extinguished. That the Israelitish nation were in things external without an internal principle, thus in those loves, has been often shown above.

10,534. Verses 4, 5, 6. *And the people heard this evil word, and they mourned, and they placed not any one his orna-*

ment upon him. And Jehovah said to Moses, say to the sons of Israel, ye are a people hard of neck, in one moment I will ascend in the midst of thee, and will consume thee; and now cause thine ornament to descend from upon thee, and I shall know what I will do to thee. And the sons of Israel snatched away their ornament from Mount Horeb. And the people heard this evil word, and they mourned, signifies their grief on account of non-eminence over others. And they placed not any one his ornament upon him, signifies the quality of their external principle, that it was without the Divine. And Jehovah said to Moses, signifies instruction. Say to the sons of Israel, ye are a people hard of neck, signifies that that nation would not receive influx from the Divine. In one moment I will ascend in the midst of thee, and will consume thee, signifies that they would perish, if the Divine flowed in with them. And now cause thine ornament to descend from upon thee, signifies the quality of their external principle that it was without the Divine. And I shall know what I shall do to thee, signifies that thus something may exist with them. And the sons of Israel snatched away their ornament, signifies the deprivation of Divine Truth in the external things appertaining to them. From Mount Horeb, signifies in the external things of worship, of the church, and of the Word.

10,535. "And the people heard this evil word, and they mourned"—that hereby is signified their grief on account of non-eminence over others, appears from the signification of hearing this evil word and mourning. That it denotes grief on account of non-eminence over others, is evident from what has been above shown concerning that nation, namely, that they were urgent that a church might be instituted amongst them, but this for no other end than to be distinguished above all nations in the universal world of the earths, for they were principled in self-love more than them, and they could not be lifted to eminence over them by any thing else, than by Jehovah being amongst them, thus also by the church being amongst them, for where Jehovah is, that is, the Lord, there the church, is. That this was the end, is manifest from several passages in the Word, as also from these words in this chapter, "Moses said, wherein shall it be made known at any time, that I have found favor [or grace] in thine eyes, I and thy people, *is it not in Thy going with us, and our being rendered excellent, I and Thy people, above every people which is on the faces of the ground*," verse 16. That there was no election, but permission that a church should be instituted amongst them, but that still in the nation itself there was not a church, but only the representative of a church, see the passages cited, n. 10,396, at the end

10,536. "And they placed not any one his ornament upon

him"—that hereby is signified the quality of their external principle, that it was without the Divine, appears from the signification of ornament, as denoting what is Divine in things external, thus not placing ornament upon him denotes to be without the Divine in things external. The reason why this is signified by ornament, is, because ornament has reference to garments, and by garments in general are signified Divine Truths; this signification of garments in general has its ground in representatives in the other life, where all, both angels and spirits, appear clothed in garments, and every one according to his truths; they who are in genuine Divine Truths appear clothed in white shining garments, and others in others. Some spirits do not know whence garments come to them, but they are put on whilst they are ignorant of it; and also their garments vary according to the changes of their state as to truths. In a word, their intellectual principle is what is exhibited and represented by garments; for the intellectual principle of every one is formed by truths, and becomes of a quality such as the truths from which it is formed. The intellectual principle appertaining to the angels of heaven is in their internal, hence they have white shining garments; the shining is from the Divine Good, and the whiteness is from the light of heaven, which is the Divine Truth. But the garments of those who are in things external without an internal principle, are dirty and tattered, like those of beggars in the streets and of robbers in forests. Hence it may be manifest what is signified by ornament, namely, the holy truths of the church; and hence by not putting on ornament, is denoted to be without the holy truths of the church; and in application to the Israelitish nation, which was in things external without an internal principle, it denotes the quality of what is external without truths from the Divine. That garments denote truths, see n. 2132, 2576, 4545, 4763, 5248, 5319, 5954, 6378, 6914, 6917, 6918, 9093, 9158, 9212, 9216, 9814, 9827, 9952. What is signified by the garments of Aaron and of his sons, see n. 9814, 10,068. That ornament in the Word signifies the holy truths of the church, will be seen in the following articles, see n. 10,540.

10,537. "And Jehovah said to Moses"—that hereby is signified instruction, appears from the signification of saying, when from Jehovah, as denoting instruction, see the passages cited, n. 10,277; in this case instruction that Divine Truth was not with the nation itself, which is signified by causing his ornament to descend from upon him, which is presently treated of.

10,538. "Say to the sons of Israel, ye are a people hard of neck"—that hereby is signified that that nation would not receive influx from the Divine, appears from what was shown, n. 10,429, where like words occur.

10,539. "In one moment I will ascend in the midst of thee, and will consume thee"—that hereby is signified that they would perish if the Divine flowed in with them, appears from what was shown above, n. 10,531, 10,532; where also like words occur.

10,540. "And now cause thine ornament to descend from upon thee"—that hereby is signified the quality of their external principle, that it was without the Divine, appears from the signification of ornament, when the church is treated of, as denoting holy truth, or what is Divine in externals, see above, n. 10,536; and from the signification of causing it to descend from upon them, as denoting to put it off, thus to be without it. That the Divine in things external, or that holy truth is signified by ornament, is manifest from the following passages, "*I clothed* thee with needle-work, and *shod* thee with yew-tree, and *girded* thee with fine linen, and *covered* thee with silk, and *adorned thee with ornament*, and gave bracelets upon thine hands, and a necklace upon thy throat, and I gave a jewel upon thy nose, and ear-rings upon thine ears, and a *crown of gracefulness* upon thine head. *Thus wast thou adorned with gold and silver;* and thy garments were fine linen and silk, and needle-work. Whence thou becamest very exceedingly beautiful, and didst prosper even to a kingdom; wherefore thy name went forth into the nations concerning thy beauty, *for this was perfect in my ornament, which I had set upon thee*," Ezek. xvi. 10 to 14. The subject here treated of is concerning Jerusalem, by which is signified the church which was established by the Lord after the flood, to which the Israelitish and Judaic Church succeeded; what the quality of this latter church was, is also described in the same chapter; but what the quality of that Ancient Church was, is described in the above passage, and its holy truths by the above ornaments. Every one may see that such things as relate to the church are signified by all the things in the above passage, and that somewhat peculiar is signified by each; otherwise to what purpose would be such a description of Jerusalem? But what principle of the church each thing signifies, cannot be made manifest from any other source than from the internal sense; for this sense teaches what thing in the spiritual world corresponds to every expression; from which it may be manifest that needle-work denotes scientific truth, n. 9688; fine linen intellectual truth which is from the Divine, n. 5319, 6469, 9596, 9744; bracelets, truths as to power, n. 3103, 3105. A necklace, truth derived from good as to influx, and thence the conjunction of things interior and exterior, n. 5320. A jewel, truth as to perception, and ear-rings truths as to obedience, n. 4551, 10,402. A crown of gracefulness, spiritual good, which is the good of truth, a crown good, n. 9930, gracefulness, what is spiritual, n. 9815; gold and silver, good and truth in general, n. 113, 1551, 1552, 5658, 6914, 6917, 9874; fine flour, honey, and oil, denote truth external and internal; fine flour, truth derived from good, n. 9995, honey, external good, n. 10,530; oil, internal good, n. 886, 4582, 4638, 9474, 9780, 10,254, 10,261; beauty is the form of truth derived from good, n. 3080, 3821, 4985, 5199. That Jerusalem, of which those things are said, denotes the church, see n. 402, 2117, 3654. Hence it is evident what is meant by ornament, namely, Holy Truth in every complex. Like things are signified by the ornaments of the daughters of Zion, which are recounted in Isaiah, "In that day *the Lord will remove the ornaments of the feet-knots*, and of the net-work, and of the little moons; and of the repositories of ointments, and of the little chains, and of the bracelets, and the turbans, and the garters, and the knots and houses of the soul, and incantations; the rings, and *ornaments of the nose*, the changeable garments, and the upper garments, and the loose garments, and the crisping-pins, the looking-glasses, and the fine linen and hoods, and the vails: and it shall come to pass, instead of an aromatic there shall be consumption, and instead of a girdle a rent, and instead of entwined work baldness, and instead of a robe a girding of sackcloth, burning instead of beauty; thy men shall fall by the sword, and thy strength in war," iii. 18 to 23. They who do not think beyond the sense of the letter, know no other than that all those things, with which the daughters of Zion are said to be adorned, are to be understood according to the letter; and that on account of their ornament, and the loftiness and pride thence derived, the men of that kingdom would perish, for it is said, that *the men shall fall by the sword, and strength in war*; but that such things are not meant, may be known to those who elevate the mind in some degree above the letter; these know from various passages in the Word, that by the daughters of Zion, are not meant the daughters of Zion, but such things as are of the church, as also by the daughters of Jerusalem, the daughters of Israel, the daughters of Judah, and several others; that by them are signified the church, and those things which are of the church, see n. 6729, 9055; when therefore the church, and those things which are of the church, are signified by the daughters of Zion, it follows that by their ornaments recounted in the above passage are signified the truths and goods of the church, and that each ornament denotes some specific truth and good; for in the Word nothing is said without a meaning, not even one expression; and whereas that church was to be deprived of its truths and goods, which are signified by those ornaments, therefore it is said, that *instead of an aromatic shall be consumption, instead of a girdle a rent, instead of entwined work baldness, instead of a robe a girding of sack-*

cloth, burning instead of beauty, and also that the men should fall by the sword, and strength in war, for by an aromatic, is signified Divine Truth as to its preceptive principle, n. 10,199, 10,291; by a consumption, its privation; by a girdle, is signified the bond containing truths and goods in their connection, n. 9341, 9828, 9837; a rent instead of it, denotes their dissolution and dissipation; by entwined work, scientific truth, n. 2831; by baldness, the deprivation of the intelligence of truth and of the wisdom of good, n. 9960; by burning, their consumption by the evils of self-love, n. 1297, 2446, 7852, 9055, 9041; by beauty, the form of truth derived from good in the church, thus its perfection, n. 3080, 3821, 4985, 5199; and by a sword, whereby men shall fall, the false principle destroying truth and good, n. 2799, 4499, 6353, 7102, 8294; by no strength in war, is signified not any resistance against evil and the false; for war denotes spiritual combat and temptation, n. 1659, 1664, 2686, 8273, 8295, 10,455. From these considerations it is now evident, that by ornament in general is signified the Divine Truth of the church. The like is signified by ornament in the second book of Samuel, "Ye daughters of Israel weep over Saul, who clothed you with double-dyed [scarlet], with things pleasant, *who set an ornament of gold upon your garment*," i. 24. These words occur in the lamentation of David over Saul, which he wrote to teach the sons of Judah the bow, verse 18 of the same chapter, where by bow is signified the doctrine of truth combating against the falses of evil, 2686, 2709, 6402; hence by the daughters of Israel are signified the affections of truth which are of the church, n. 2362, 3963, 6729, 6775, 6788, 8994; to be clothed with double-dyed [scarlet], denotes with the interior truths of the church, which are from good, n. 4922, 9468; to set an ornament of gold upon the garment, denotes to make truths beautiful from good. That gold denotes good, see the passages cited, n. 9874; and that garment denotes truth in general, see the passages cited above, n. 10,536 at the end. The reason why the lamentation of David over Saul treats of the doctrine of truth combating against the false of evil, which doctrine is signified by bow, was, because by a king, or by the royalty which Saul had, is signified Divine Truth as to protection and as to judgment, n. 1672, 2009, 2015, 3009, 4575, 4581, 4966, 5044, 5068, 6148. The like is signified by ornament elsewhere in David, "Give to Jehovah the glory of His name, bow your selves to Jehovah *in the ornament of holiness*," Psalm xxix. 2; in the ornament of holiness, denotes in the genuine truths of the church. In like manner in Isaiah, "Thy sons shall make haste: lift up thine eyes round about, and see they are all gathered together: I live, saith Jehovah, *thou shalt put them all on as an ornament, and bind them about as a bride*," xlix.

17, 18; speaking also of Zion, by which is signified the celestial church; by the sons who shall hasten, are signified the truths of that church. That sons denote truths, see n. 489, 491, 2623, 2803, 2813, 3373, 3704, 4257, 9807; hence it is that it is said, that she shall put them all on as an ornament, and bind them about as a bride, which may be said of the truths of the church, but not of the sons of Zion. Since almost all things in the Word have also an opposite sense, so likewise have those which relate to ornament, by which things are signified truths falsified, as in Jeremiah, "When thou art vastated, what wilt thou do, if thou clothest thyself with what is double-dyed, *if thou adornest thyself with ornament of gold*, if thou rendest thine eyes with vermillion, in vain wilt thou render thyself beautiful," iv. 30. And in Hosea, "I will visit upon her the days of Baalim, to whom she hath burnt incense, and hath put on her ear-ring, and *her ornament*, and hath gone after her lovers, and hath forgotten Me," ii. 13; and in other places.

10,541. "And I shall know what I shall do to thee"—that hereby is signified that thus something may exist amongst them, appears from the series of things in the internal sense, for that nation could be in a holy external principle, and not at the same time in a holy internal principle; and since thus the external of the church could appertain to that nation, although not the internal, therefore by I shall know what I shall do, is signified that thus something may exist amongst them.

10,542. "And the sons of Israel snatched away their ornament"—that hereby is signified the deprivation of Divine Truth, in the external things appertaining to them, appears from the signification of snatching away, as denoting to be bereft and deprived; and from the signification of ornament, as denoting holy truth, or what is Divine, see n. 10,536, 10,540.

10,543. "From Mount Horeb"—that hereby is signified in the external things of worship, of the church, and of the Word, appears from the signification of Mount Horeb, as denoting Divine Truth in externals; for Horeb was a mountainous [country] around Mount Sinai, and by Mount Sinai is signified Divine Truth; hence by Mount Horeb, which was mountainous round about, is signified Divine Truth in externals; for what is in the midst, and what is high above things circumjacent, signifies what is internal, and hence by what is around and beneath, is signified what is external. That Mount Sinai signifies Divine Truth, see n. 8805, 9420. That the midst denotes what is internal, see n. 1074, 2940, 2973, 5897, 6084, 6103, 9164; in like manner height, n. 2148, 4210, 4599, 9489, 9773, 10,181. That round about denotes what is external, n. 2973; in like manner beneath. Inasmuch as the people were in externals and not in what was internal, therefore when the law was promulgated from Mount Sinai, they stood in Horeb beneath the mountain, and the mountain was fenced about, lest it should be touched by the people, Exod. xix. 12, 13, 21, 23, 24; chap. xx. 18; Deut. iv. 10, 11, 12. It is said the external of worship, of the church, and of the Word, because the external of one is the internal of the other, for worship is of the church, and the truths and goods of the church and its worship are from the Word; wherefore they who are in the externals of worship and the church, are in the externals of the Word.

10,544. Verses 7 to 12. *And Moses took the tent, and stretched it for himself out of the camp, by removing far from the camp, and he called it the tent of the congregation; and it came to pass, every one that asked Jehovah went forth to the tent of the congregation which was out of the camp. And it came to pass, when Moses went forth to the tent, all the people arose, and they stood every one at the door of his tent, and they looked after Moses even to his entering into the tent. And it came to pass, when Moses entered the tent, the pillar of the cloud descended, and stood at the door of the tent, and spake with Moses. And all the people saw the pillar of the cloud standing at the door of the tent, and all the people arose, and they bowed themselves every one at the door of his tent. And Jehovah spake to Moses, faces to faces, as a man speaketh to his neighbor; and he returned to the camp, and his minister Joshua, the son of Nun, a boy, removed not himself from the midst of the tent.* And Moses took the tent, signifies the holy principle of worship, of the church, and of the Word. And stretched it for himself out of the camp, by removing far from the camp, signifies remote from the external things, in which the nation itself was. And he called it the tent of the congregation, signifies the external of worship, of the church, and of the Word. And it came to pass every one that asked Jehovah went forth to the tent of the congregation which was out of the camp, signifies that all instructions concerning the truths and goods of the church and worship, were given to every one by [or through] the external of the Word, remotely from the external things in which that nation was. And it came to pass, when Moses went forth to the tent, all the people arose, and they stood every one at the door of his tent, signifies that that nation was not in the external of the Word, of the church, and of worship, but out of it. And they looked after Moses, even to his entering into the tent, signifies that they see the external of the Word, of the church, and of worship, but that it vanishes from their apprehension. And it came to pass, when Moses entered into the tent, the pillar of the cloud descended, and stood at the door of the tent, and spake with Moses, signifies after that the Word vanished from their apprehension, an obscure density seized them without, and yet was clearly perceived from within. And all the people saw the pillar of the cloud standing at the door of the tent, signifies an obscure density seizing them without. And all the people arose, and bowed themselves, every one at the door of his tent, signifies that that nation holily adored their external. And Jehovah spake to Moses faces to faces, signifies Divine things in the Word conjoined. As a man speaketh to his neighbor, signifies the conjunction of truth and good. And he returned to the camp, signifies to the external in which that nation was. And his minister Joshua, the son of Nun, a boy, removed not himself from the midst of the tent, signifies Divine Truth ministering in the holy things of the church and of worship in the place of Moses in the mean time.

10,545. "And Moses took the tent"—that hereby is signified the holy principle of worship, of the church, and of the Word, appears from the signification of the tent, as denoting in the supreme sense the Lord, and also heaven and the church, and in the respective sense, every holy thing of heaven and of the church, hence also the holy principle of worship and the holy principle of the Word, for these are of the church, and are of the Lord, because from Him. The reason why a tent has these significations, is, because the most ancient dwelt in tents, and also performed therein their holy worship; amongst the most ancient was the Celestial Church, which was the most holy of all following churches, for they adored the Lord, He being to them Jehovah; and because He led them, they had commerce with the angels of heaven, and hence were from the Lord in celestial wisdom. The establishment of that church is what is described by the creation of heaven and of earth in the first chapter of Genesis, and their wisdom by paradise; for by heaven and earth in the Word is signified the church, by paradise intelligence and wisdom, and by man [*homo*] the church itself, in like manner by ground, from which he was named Adam; that heaven and earth in the Word denote the church, heaven the internal church, and earth the external church, see n. 1733, 1850, 2117, 2118, 3355, 4535, 10,373; that intelligence and wisdom is described by paradises and gardens, n. 100, 108, 2702, 3220. That man [*homo*] denotes the church, n. 478, 768, 4287, 9176; and also the ground, n. 566, 1068. And that to create man denotes to establish the church, n. 16, 88, 10,373; see besides, n. 8891, 9942. In consequence of that church being loved above the rest, and the Lord dwelling with them in tents (for the Lord is said to dwell with man who is principled in love to Him, John xiv. 24,) therefore in memory thereof the tabernacle or tent of the congregation was constructed with the Jewish nation, wherein was exercised the holy principle of worship; and that on the same account the feast of tabernacles or of tents was instituted. That by tent are signified those holy things, and specifically the holy principle of worship, is manifest from the following passages, "Sing thou barren that hath not borne;

enlarge the place of thy tent, let them stretch out the curtains of thy habitations," Isaiah liv. 1, 2; to enlarge the place of a tent denotes those things which are of the church, and thence which are of worship; to stretch out the curtains of habitations denotes to multiply truths; that curtains denote the truths of the church, see n. 9595, 9596, 9606, 9756; barren denotes one who was not before in the truths and goods of the church, n. 3908, 8325. And in Jeremiah, "The whole land is devastated, *suddenly my tents are devastated*, my curtains in a moment," iv. 20; that land [or earth] denotes the church, see the passages cited, n. 9325; and whereas the church is the church from the goods of love and the truths of faith, therefore it is said the tents and curtains are devastated, tents denoting the goods of the church, and curtains denoting its truths. Again, "*My tent is devastated* and my cords are plucked away, my sons have departed from me, and they are not, *there is none that stretcheth out any longer my tent*, or that setteth up my curtains, because the shepherds are become foolish," x. 20, 21; like things are here signified by tent and by curtains; the cords plucked away denote that there is no longer conjunction of good and of truth, and of truths one with another; therefore also it is said, my sons have departed, because by sons are signified truths; that cords denote conjunction, see n. 9777, 9880: and that sons denote truths, n. 489, 491, 533, 2623, 2803, 2813, 3373, 3704, 4257, 9807. And in David, "*Jehovah, who shall tarry in Thy tent;* who shall dwell in the mountain of Thy holiness? He who walketh entire, and who doeth justice, and speaketh the truth in his heart," Psalm xv. 1, 2; where to tarry in the tent of Jehovah denotes in heaven, and in the good of love there. Again, "*I will abide in Thy tent to eternities*," Psalm lxi. 4; where the sense is the same. And in Amos, "*In that day I will set up the tent of David that was fallen down*, and hedge up the breaches, and restore her ruins," ix. 11; the tent of David denotes the church of the Lord and the holy principle of the worship of Him; to hedge up the breaches and to restore the ruins denotes to restore those things, by removing falses. That David in the Word denotes the Lord, see n. 1888, 9954; hence it is that the tent of David denotes the church of the Lord, and the holy principle of worship. And in Jeremiah, "Behold, I bring back *the captivity of the tents of Jacob*, and will have mercy on his habitations," xxx. 18; where the tents of Jacob and his habitations denote the goods and truths of the church. Since by tents are signified the goods of the church and of worship, therefore by tents in the opposite sense are signified the evils of worship and of the church, as may be manifest from the following passages: "I will liken the daughter of Zion to a beautiful [woman], to her shall come shepherds and their flocks, *and they shall pitch against her tents* round about," vi. 2, 3. Again, "Go up against Arabia, and lay waste the sons of the east, let them take *their tents* and their flock, their curtains and all their vessels," xlix. 28, 29. And in Hosea, "What will ye do in the day of solemnity, and in the day of the feast of Jehovah, for lo, they are gone away because of devastation, the desirable things of their silver, the thistles shall possess them, *the thorn in their tents*," ix. 5, 6. And in David, "He smote all the first-born of Egypt, the beginning of mights *in the tents of Ham*," Psalm lxxviii. 51.

10,546. "And stretched it for himself out of the camp, by removing far from the camp"—that hereby is signified remote from the external things in which the nation itself was, appears from the signification of stretching a tent, as denoting to provide, to dispose, and to arrange those things which are of the church and of worship; for by a tent is signified the holy principle of the church, of worship, and of the Word, see just above, n. 10,545, hence by stretching it is signified to provide, to dispose, and to arrange those things; and from the signification of camp, as denoting the heavenly order, from which and according to which is heaven and the church; and whereas all the truths and goods of heaven and the church are of that order, hence also is signified the continent of those truths and goods. The reason why these things are signified by the camp is, because by the sons of Israel, who formed the camp, are signified all goods and truths in the complex; but when the sons of Israel worshiped a calf instead of Jehovah, then by their camp was signified the contrary, thus infernal order, and also the continent of what is false and evil, which make hell. Whether we speak of the external of worship and the church without the internal, or of hell, it is the same thing; for they who are in the external of worship without the internal, are in the loves of self and the world, and the loves of self and the world are from hell; hence it is evident why Moses took his tent, and stretched it out of the camp, by removing far from the camp, for by the tent, as was said above, was signified the holy principle of worship, of the church, and of the Word; and why by those words is signified what is remote from things external, in which the Israelitish nation was. That by the camp is signified heavenly order, and by the encampment the arrangement of good and truth according to heavenly order, see n. 4236, 8103, 8130, 8131, 8155, 8193, 8196; and that hence by the camp is signified heaven and the church so far as they are continent, n. 10,038; and in the opposite sense hell, n. 10,458. That the external of worship and the church separate from what is internal is also hell, see n. 10,483, 10,489; by reason that they who are in things external separate from what is internal, in no case receive any Divine Influx, n. 10,429; and hence can have nothing of faith and love to the Lord, n. 10,396, 10,400, 10,401. That they look only to their own loves, thus to hell, n. 10,422; and hence that they worship themselves for a god, n. 10,407, 10,412. That the Israelitish nation was in things external, separate from what is internal, see the passages cited, n. 9380; and n. 9373, 9381, 10,396, 10,401, 10,407, 10,492, 10,498, 10,500, 10,533.

10,547. "And he called it the tent of the congregation"—that hereby is signified the external of worship, of the church, and of the Word, in which are internal things, appears from the signification of the tent of the congregation, as denoting the external of worship, of the church, and of the Word, in which are things internal; for by the tent is signified the holy principle of worship, of the church, and of the Word, n. 10,545, and by congregation is signified where internal things are, for all internal things are together in things external, see n. 6451, 9216, 9828, 9836. By congregation, in the sense of the letter, is meant the congregation of the sons of Israel, but in the internal is signified the congregation of the goods and truths of the church, since by the sons of Israel, in the good sense, are signified the truths and goods of the church in the complex, see n. 5414, 5879, 5951, 7956; in like manner by the congregation and company of the sons of Israel, n. 7830, 7843. And the truths and goods of the Word, of the church, and of worship, are in this internal, for in the internal of the Word, of the church, and of worship, are celestial and spiritual things, but in the external are natural and worldly things, and all celestial and spiritual things flow-in into natural and worldly things, and close in them, and form and constitute them; hence it is that what is external is signified by congregation. This is the case with the external sense of the Word, which is called the sense of its letter; and likewise with the externals of the church and of worship, for those things are from the Word.

10,548. "And it came to pass every one that asked Jehovah went forth to the tent of the congregation which was out of the camp"—that hereby is signified that all instructions concerning the truths and goods of the church and of worship were given to every one by [or through] the external of the Word, remotely from the external things in which that nation was, appears from the signification of asking Jehovah, as denoting to be instructed concerning the truths and goods of the church and of worship, for all asking of Jehovah is for the sake of instruction on those subjects; and from the signification of the tent of the congregation, as denoting the external of the church and of worship, see just above, n. 10,547; and from the signification of out of the camp, as denoting what is remote from the external things in which that nation was, see also above, n. 10,546. Hence it is evident that by every one that asked Jehovah going forth to the tent of the congregation which was out of the camp, is signified that all instruction concerning the truths and goods of the church and of worship was given by the external of the Word, remotely from the external things in which that nation was. It is said by the external of the Word, because all instruction concerning the truths and goods of faith and love, which make the church, and enter worship, is from that source; and because to ask the Lord is to consnlt the Word, for in the Word the Lord is present, the Word being the Divine Truth which is from Him, and He is with the angels in His own Divine Truth, and also with the men of the church who receive Him. It is said by the external of the Word, because in the external of the Word all internal things are together, thus all the truths and goods of heaven and the church, according to what was shown, n. 10,547; hence it is that answers and revelations were made in ultimates, n. 9905. All the doctrinals also of the church serviceable for worship are given by the external of the Word; but they are given only to those who are in illustration from the Lord when they read the Word; for in such case light flows in from heaven into them by [or through] the internal sense, see n. 9382, 9409, 9424, 9430, 10,105, 10,324, 10,401, 10,431. The reason why it denotes remotely from the external things in which the Israelitish nation was, is, because the external of the Word with that nation appears altogether otherwise, and hence is otherwise explained, as may be manifest from this consideration, that they see nothing therein concerning faith and love to the Lord, nor indeed concerning the Lord, and concerning heaven from Him; but the things which they see, relate only to worldly and terrestrial things, and especially to their own eminence over others; the reason is, because they are in externals without an internal; and they who are such, are incapable of seeing any thing from the internal; to see from the internal is to see out of heaven from the Lord. From these considerations it is evident that the external of the Word, and hence of the church and of worship, with that nation, is remote from the external of the Word, of the church, and of worship, viewed in itself. The external worship of that nation is now described in the internal sense even to verse 11.

10,549. "And it came to pass when Moses went forth to the tent all the people arose, and they stood every one at the door of his tent"—that hereby is signified that that nation was not in the external of the Word, of the church, and of worship, but out of it, appears from the representation of Moses, as denoting the Word, see the passages cited, n. 9372; and from the signification of the tent, as denoting the holy principle of worship, of the church, and of the Word, see above, n. 10,545; and from the signification of rising and standing before the door of the tent, as denoting out of it; for the door is the entrance, the introduction and communication, n. 2145, 2162, 8989, hence to stand before it denotes not to enter, be introduced and be communicated.

10,550. "And they looked after Moses until he entered into the tent"—that hereby is signified that they see the external of the Word, of the church, and of worship, but that it vanishes from their apprehension, appears from the signification of looking after Moses, as denoting to see the external of the Word, for by Moses is signified the Word, as above, n. 10,549; and by looking after him is signified to see its external; for what is before signifies what is within, and what is after [or behind] signifies what is without; hence to see the posteriors of Jehovah, and not the faces, is to see what is external and not what is internal, which subject is treated of at the last verse of this chapter; and from the signification of until he entered into the tent, as denoting that it vanishes from their apprehension, for when he entered, he was no longer seen.

10,551. "And it came to pass, when Moses entered into the tent the pillar of the cloud descended, and stood at the door of the tent, and spake with Moses"—that hereby is signified after that the Word vanished from their apprehension, an obscure density occupied them without, and yet was clearly perceived from within, appears from the signification of when Moses entered into the tent, as denoting after that the Word vanished from their apprehension, see just above, n. 10,550; and from the signification of the pillar of the cloud, as denoting obscure density in respect to that nation; for by cloud is signified the external of the Word, see preface to chap. xviii. Gen and n. 4060, 4391, 5922, 6343, 6752, 8443, 8781; and also the obscurity of the Word to those who are not in illustration, and obscure density [or dense obscurity] to those who are in the external of the Word separate from the internal, n. 8106, 8632, 8814, 8819, 9430; and from the signification of standing at the door, as denoting without, see above, n. 10,549; and from the signification of speaking with Moses, as denoting to perceive clearly from within; for by Moses is signified the Word viewed in itself, see n. 9372; and by speaking is signified to perceive, see the passages cited, n. 10,290. The reason why it denotes from within, is, because Moses, with whom the pillar of the cloud spake, was within in the tent. It may be expedient to say what it is to see from without, and what to perceive from within; they who are in illustration, when they read the Word, see it from within, for their internal is open, and the internal, when open, is in the light of heaven; this light flows in and enlightens, although man is ignorant of it. The reason why he is ignorant of it, is, because that light flows-in into the knowledges which are in man's memory, and those knowledges are in natural light; and whereas man thinks from those knowledges as from himself, he cannot perceive the influx, nevertheless he may know from various proofs, that he was in illustration. Howbeit, every one is deceived, who believes himself to be in illustration, if he does not love to know truth for the sake of truth, and for the sake of the good of life, thus who does not love Divine Truth for the sake of life, since to live according to Divine Truths from the Word is to love the Lord; and from the Lord, when he is loved, comes all illustration. But they who have not for an end a life according to Divine Truths from the Word, but regard honor, gain, and reputation, as ends, and thus the Divine Truths of the Word as means, cannot in any wise be in any illustration, for this latter end is worldly and corporeal, and not spiritual and celestial; and on this account it closes the internal man, in which case no light can flow in from heaven and illustrate. If these believe that they are in illustration when they read the Word, they are altogether deceived; for they do not think from heaven, but from the world, thus not from the Lord, but from themselves, and so far as they think from themselves and from the world, so far they think from natural light, separate from heavenly light, and natural light separate from heavenly light is mere thick darkness in things spiritual. In case these persuade themselves that they have seen any thing from illustration, it is a fallacy, for they perceive whether a thing be true from no other source than from others by confirmations, which is to see truth from without, and not from within, or to see it from persuasive faith, the quality of which may be seen, n. 9363 to 9369. Persons of such a character may see what is false as what is true, and what is true as what is false, also what is evil as what is good, and what is good as what is evil. From these considerations it is manifest what it is to see the Word from without, and to perceive it from within. To see it from without is what is signified by the people standing at the door of the tent, and looking after Moses; also by their seeing the pillar of the cloud standing at the door of the tent, and by their bowing themselves at the door of the tent. But to perceive the Word from within is what is signified by Moses entering into the tent, and by the pillar of the cloud which was at the door of the tent speaking with Moses. It may be expedient also briefly to say in what manner influx is effected, by which is illustration; the angels, alike with men, perceive the Word when it is read, but the angels spiritually, and men naturally. The man whose internal is open, also perceives the Word spiritually, but this he is ignorant of whilst he lives in the world; because his spiritual thought flows-in into the natural in the external man, and there presents itself to be seen; nevertheless that interior thought is what illustrates, and by which is effected influx from the Lord. Some of the learned, by looking into their own thoughts, and by reflection on the occasion, have also observed, that there is given with man interior thought, which does not appear, wherefore the ideas of that thought they have called immaterial and intellectual, which they have distinguished from the ideas of exterior thought which appear, calling these latter natural and material; but they knew not that the ideas of interior thought are spiritual, and that when they flow-down, they are turned into natural, and appear under another species and under another habit. From these considerations it may in some measure be manifest in what manner influx is effected, by which is illustration.

10,552. "And all the people saw the pillar of the cloud standing at the door of the tent"—that hereby is signified the obscure density [or dense obscurity] occupying them without, appears from what was explained just above, n. 10,551.

10,553. "And all the people arose, and bowed themselves every one at the door of the tent"—that hereby is signified that that nation holily adored its external principle, appears from the signification of rising and bowing themselves, as denoting to adore holily; and from the signification of at the door of the tent, as denoting the external of the Word, of the church, and of worship, see above, n. 10,549. In these words is described the genius of that nation, that although they are out of the genuine sense of the Word, and in obscure density [or dense obscurity] concerning it, they still holily adore it; but that holy principle is an idolatrous holy principle arising from the love of self, altogether separate from the holy Divine. That that nation was in such a holy idolatrous principle, when in worship, see n. 3479, 4281, 6588, 9377, 10,430, 10,500.

10,554. "And Jehovah spake to Moses faces to faces"—that hereby are signified Divine Things in the Word conjoined, appears from the signification of speaking faces to faces, as denoting to be conjoined, for by faces are signified the interiors, and when the interiors mutually look at each other, and see what is like, they then conjoin themselves; this is signified by speaking faces to faces, when concerning Jehovah to Moses, by whom is meant the Word, for by speaking is signified perception, and by faces to faces is signified mutually, hence the mutual perception of one in that of the other, which is conjunction. This is meant concerning the Word, that it is of such a quality, since Moses here denotes the Word. For the Word is of such a quality in its internal, and in its external. In the internal all and singular things are conjoined, and likewise in the external; and also the things which are in the internal are conjoined with those which are in the external by correspondences. Those conjunctions cannot be described, and if they were described, they could not be apprehended by any idea of thought; things celestial and spiritual are what are there thus conjoined together with each other, and these by correspondences with things natural and worldly, which make the sense of the letter. What the quality of those conjunctions is, may be presented to the idea in some measure by the conjunctions of the angelic societies in the heavens, which taken together are one, just as the members, the viscera, and the organs appertaining to man, which, although they are various, and each of them inwardly consists of innumerable various things, still make one; such also is the Word as to its truths and goods. That the Word is of such a quality, is altogether unknown to man; but the angels know it, for they perceive the connection of the interior things of the Word. From these considerations it may be manifest, that by Jehovah speaking to Moses faces to faces are signified Divine Things in the Word conjoined. That one thing is signified by speaking faces to faces, and another by seeing Jehovah face to face, is evident from what follows in this chapter, where Jehovah says to Moses, "*Thou canst not see My faces*, because *no man seeth Me and liveth;* but I will set thee in a cleft of the rock, and will cover the palm of My hand over thee, until I shall pass by, and I will remove the palm of My hand, and *thou shalt see My posteriors, and My faces shall not be seen*," verses 20, 22, 23; that Moses denotes the Word, see the passages cited, n. 10,549; and that faces denote the interiors, see the passages cited n. 9546; and that speaking denotes perception, see the passages cited, n. 10,290.

10,555. "As a man speaketh to his neighbor"—that hereby is signified the conjunction of truth and good, appears from the signification of speaking, as denoting mutual perception, and thence conjunction, as just above, n. 10,554; and from the signification of a man [*vir*], as denoting truth, see n. 3134, 3459, 4823, 7716, 9007; and from the signification of a neighbor, as denoting the good with which truth is conjoined. In the Word throughout mention is made of a man and a neighbor, of a man and a companion, and thereby is signified mutually, as also by a man and a brother; and when mutually is signified, then is meant mutual conjunction, such as has place between truth and good; for truth mutually conjoins itself with good, by reason that truth has its esse from good, and good has its quality in truth; in heaven, there is not given any truth which is not conjoined with good, by reason that truth is not any thing without good, neither is good any thing without truth; for truth without good is an existence without an esse, and good without truth is an esse without an existere; or truth without good is as a body without life, and good without truth is as life without a body, wherefore unless they be conjoined together they are not any thing, from which any thing is effected, or they are not any thing of which any thing of heaven and of the church can be predicated. The case herein is like that of the understanding of man without the will principle, and of the will principle without the understanding; one indeed is given separate from the other, as to understand truth and good, and not to will it; but in this case, to understand has its will from another source than from good, namely, from self-will, or for the sake of self, to which the understanding of truth and good serves for a medium. He who reflects well, may know that the understanding appertaining to man has its life from the will principle, and that without the will principle it is not any thing; also that the understanding and the will principle mutually respect each other, and are conjoined. The case is the same with truth and good, consequently with faith and love; unless truth be conjoined to good, or faith to love, it is not truth or good, neither faith or love. These observations are made to the intent that it may be known what is meant by mutual conjunction, which is signified in the spiritual sense by a man and a companion, or by a man and a neighbor, and also by a man and a brother.

10,556. "And he returned to the camp"—that hereby is signified to the external in which that nation was, appears from the signification of the camp, as denoting the external of the Word, of the church, and of worship, in which the Israelitish nation was, see n. 10,506. On this occasion, when Moses returned to the camp, he no longer represents the Word, but the head of the Israelitish nation, for to be in the camp with those who were in things external separate from what is internal, denotes to be in a similar state; it was otherwise when he was out of that camp, and stretched a tent there by removing afar off from the camp. In what manner therefore Moses represents the head of that nation may be manifest from what follows of this chapter even to the end in the internal sense. Since Moses puts on this representation, it is on that account said, that his minister Joshua the son of Nun, a boy, removed not himself from the midst of the tent, by which is signified that the representative still continues in the tent which was out of the camp.

10,557. "And his minister Joshua the son of Nun, a boy, removed not himself from the midst of the tent"—that hereby is signified Divine Truth ministering in the holy things of the church and of worship in the place of Moses in the mean time, appears from the representation of Joshua the minister of Moses, as denoting the Divine Truth ministering instead of Moses, who is called the son of Nun from truth, and boy from good; and from the signification of not removing himself out of the midst of the tent, as denoting in the mean time not ceasing in the holy things of the church and of worship; by not removing himself is signified not to cease in the mean time, and by the tent is signified the holy principle of the Word, of the church, and of worship, see above, n. 10,545. In the article just above, n. 10,556, it was said that Moses now begins to represent the head of the

Israelitish nation, wherefore lest the series of things in the internal sense should be broken, it came to pass that Joshua remained in the tent when Moses was absent; for by Joshua is represented Divine Truth as to any function, as Divine Truth combating, n. 8595; Divine Truth surveying and perceiving, n. 10,454; but in this case Divine Truth ministering in the absence of Moses; therefore it is said the minister of Moses.

10,558. Verses 12 to 17. *And Moses said to Jehovah, see, Thou sayest to me, cause this people to ascend, and Thou hast not made known to me whom Thou wilt send with me; and Thou hast said I know thee by name, and also thou hast found favor in Mine eyes. And now I pray if I have found favor in Thine eyes, make known to me I pray Thy way, and I shall know Thee, since I have found favor in Thine eyes, and see that this nation is Thy people. And He said, My faces shall go, and I will cause thee to rest. And he said to Him, if Thy faces go not, cause us not to go up from hence. And wherein shall it be made known at any time that I have found favor in Thine eyes, I and Thy people? Is it not in Thy going with us; and we shall be rendered excellent, I and Thy people, above every people which is on the faces of the ground? And Jehovah said to Moses, also this word which thou hast spoken I will do, because thou hast found favor in Mine eyes and I know thee by name.* Moses said to Jehovah, signifies indignation that the Divine, thus the church itself, was not with them. See Thou sayest to me, cause this people to ascend, signifies the betrothing of the church with that nation. And Thou hast not made known to me whom Thou wilt send with me, signifies that it cannot be effected without Divine auspices. And Thou hast said I know thee by name, signifies his quality. And also thou hast found favor in Mine eyes, signifies that he was accepted because he could preside over that nation. And now I pray if I have found favor in Thine eyes, signifies if he was accepted on that account. Make known to me I pray Thy way, and I shall know Thee, signifies instruction concerning the Divine as to its quality with them. Since I have found favor in Thine eyes, signifies because he was received to preside over the people. And see that this nation is Thy people, signifies that they alone in the world have the Divine which is over all things. And He said, My faces shall go, and I will cause thee to rest, signifies that the Divine of the church, of worship, and of the Word, shall be there, but with the nation itself an external principle without it. And he said to Him, if Thy faces go not, cause us not to go up from hence, signifies if the Divine be not there, there will not be any thing of the church. And wherein shall it be known at any time that I have found favor in Thine eyes I and Thy people, is it not in Thy going with us, signifies reception in preference to others, if the Divine be manifested among them. And we shall be rendered more excellent I and Thy people above all people who are on the faces of the ground, signifies pre-eminence over all in the universal world. And Jehovah said to Moses, also this word which thou hast spoken I will do, signifies that the Divine will be in the external of the church, of worship, and of the Word, which is amongst them. Because thou hast found favor in Mine eyes, and I know thee by name, signifies that he is accepted on account of his quality.

10,559. "And Moses said to Jehovah"—that hereby is signified indignation that the Divine was not with them, thus not the church itself, appears from the signification of saying, as here denoting indignation, for saying involves the things which follow, these being the things which he said, and the things which follow are things of indignation on this account, that the Divine was not willing to be with them, thus that the church was not with them, whereby they might be rendered more excellent than all who are on the faces of the earth, as is evident from verse 16 which follows. The reason why the words of Moses to Jehovah were words of indignation on that account, was because Moses here has reference to the head of the Israelitish nation, see above, n. 10,566; wherefore he speaks for himself, and that nation, for he says, I and the people, verse 16; and whereas he here has reference to that nation as the head, therefore by Moses said to Jehovah is signified indignation; for man, who is of such a quality as that nation, is indignant against God if he does not enjoy his desires; this is the case with all those who are in things external without an internal principle, for if they venerate and adore God, and as it were love Him, it is not for the sake of Him, but for the sake of themselves, for they will nothing else but pre-eminence above others, and superior opulence, this being the fire which excites their veneration and adoration, and as it were their love; but if they do not obtain what they desire, they leave God. That that nation was of such a quality, is very manifest from the historicals of the Word. The like is signified by these words of Jacob, "Jacob vowed a vow, saying, if God shall be with me, and shall keep me in this way in which I walk, and shall give me bread to eat and raiment to put on, and I shall return in peace to the house of my father, and *Jehovah shall be to me for a God*," Gen. xxviii. 20, 21; which words involve, that if he received those things, he would acknowledge Jehovah for his God; but if he did not receive, he would not acknowledge. Such also was the nation which was from him. Hence it is that that nation so often fell away and worshiped other gods, until at length they were ejected on that account from the land of Canaan, first the Israelitish nation, and afterwards the Judaic. That the cause of indignation above spoken of was, that they were not to be made more excellent than all in the universal orb of earths, if Jehovah went not with them, is evident; that it was also a cause of indignation that the church itself was not with them, follows from this consideration, that to be introduced by Jehovah into the land of Canaan denotes to be made a church; the reason of this is, because the church had been in the land of Canaan from the most ancient time, and because the Word could not be written in any other land but that, thus amongst the nation which possessed that land, and where the Word is, there is the church. The reason why the Word could not be written elsewhere, was, because all the places which were in the whole of that land, and which were round about it, as the mountains, the valleys, the rivers, the forests, and the rest, had been made representative of things celestial and spiritual, and the sense of the letter of the Word, both in the historicals and in the propheticals, must necessarily consist of such things, since the interiors of the Word, which are celestial and spiritual things, close in such representatives, and as it were stand upon them as a house upon its foundation; for unless the Word as to the sense of the letter, which is its ultimate, stood upon such things, it would be as a house without a foundation. That this is the case is evident from the Word, where mention is so often made of the places of that land, all which, inasmuch as they were made representative, signify the things of heaven and the church. Hence it is that to be introduced into the land of Canaan signifies the establishment of the church, and that the indignation of Moses involves this also, although he did not think of it. That the church was in the land of Canaan from the most ancient times, and that hence all the places there were made representative, see n. 3086, 4447, 4454, 4516, 4517, 5136, 5364, 6306, 6516, 8317, 9320, 9325. And that hence the land of Canaan in the Word signifies the church, see the passages cited, n. 9325.

10,560. "See Thou sayest to me, cause this people to ascend"—that hereby is signified the betrothing of the church with that nation, appears from the signification of Thou sayest to Me, when from Jehovah, as denoting betrothing; and from the signification of causing this people to ascend, as denoting that the church may be established with that nation; these are the things which are signified by those words in the internal sense; but in the proximate sense, that they should be introduced into the land of Canaan, and should possess it; that to be introduced into the land of Canaan, and to possess it, denotes to establish the church, see above, n. 10,559. How the case herein is, has been shown in what goes before, namely, that with that nation no church could be instituted, but only the representative of a church, since they were in things external separate from what is internal; and they who are such cannot receive any influx from the Divine; and still the church appertaining to man is in his internal, but not in the external separate from the internal. Persons of such a character may indeed represent the church, but not be the church. To represent the church, and not to be the church, is to worship things external, and to call them holy and Divine, but not to acknowledge and perceive them by faith and love from heaven. See what was said above concerning the signification of causing the people to ascend into the land, n. 10,526.

10,561. "And Thou hast not made known to me whom Thou wilt send with me"—that hereby is signified that it cannot be effected without Divine auspices, appears from the signification of sending with Moses and that nation, when from Jehovah, as denoting the Divine, which will lead, of which we shall speak presently; and because Moses knew that he could indeed introduce the people into the land of Canaan, but if that was effected without Divine leading and auspices, that they would not come into possession of it; which involves and signifies, that the church was not instituted with that nation, according to what was adduced above, n. 10,559, 10,560; hence it is evident that, by cause this people to ascend, but Thou hast not made known to me whom Thou wilt send with me, is signified that the church with that nation could not be instituted without Divine auspices; so the angels perceive these words, whatsoever may be the perceptions of men, for the angels perceive all things of the Word according to its internal sense, but men according to the external sense, in which nevertheless is the internal. The reason why sending with them, when from Jehovah, denotes the Divine which shall lead, is, because by being sent of Jehovah is signified the Divine leading, and also the Divine proceeding; therefore angels in the original tongue are so called from being sent; and therefore the Lord so frequently called Himself The Sent of the Father, by which is signified the Divine proceeding, see n. 4710, 6834. From these considerations it is evident what is meant by whom Thou wilt send with me, in the internal sense.

10,562. "And Thou hast said, I know thee by name"—that hereby is signified his quality, appears from the signification of knowing, when concerning Jehovah, as denoting to know and foresee from eternity, see n. 5308; and from the signification of a name, as denoting the quality of a state, of a thing, or of a man, see n. 144, 145, 1754, 1896, 2009, 2724, 3004 to 3011, 3421, 6674, 6887, 8274, 8882, 9310; the quality of Moses is involved in the things which follow. Hence it is evident that by I know thee by name, when from Jehovah, is signified to know and foresee from eternity what is his quality.

10,563. "And also thou hast found favor in Mine eyes"—that hereby is signified that he was received because he could preside over that nation, appears from the signification of finding favor [or grace] in the eyes of Jehovah, as denoting to be received, in this case for the sake of quality, which is signified by I know thee by name; the quality was that he could preside over that nation; for Moses was foreseen of the Lord that he might preside over the Israelitish people; that this was foreseen, is evident from this consideration, that he was educated in the palace of king Pharaoh where dominion was exercised, whence his mind was tinctured with pre-eminence over others; on this account also he was received, that he might preside over his own people. His quality likewise was, that he could receive discourse from the Divine better than others of that nation, for he was not so principled in what is external separate from what is internal, as that nation was. These therefore are the things which are signified by I know thee by name, and also thou hast found favor in Mine eyes.

10,564. "And now if I pray I have found favor in Thine eyes"—that hereby is signified if he was accepted, appears from what was said just above, n. 10,562, 10,563.

10,565. "Make known to me I pray Thy way, and I shall know Thee"—that hereby is signified instruction concerning the Divine as to its quality with them, appears from the signification of making known the way of Jehovah, as denoting instruction concerning the Divine, for by making known is signified instruction, and by the way of Jehovah is signified the Divine Truth leading; and from the signification of knowing Jehovah, as denoting to know what is the quality of the Divine with them. That way denotes truth, see n. 627, 2333, 10,422, in this case Divine Truth leading. "Since I have found favor in Thine eyes"—that hereby is signified because he was received to preside over the people, and to lead them, see above, n. 10,563, 10,564.

10,566. "And see that this nation is Thy people"—that hereby is signified that they only in the world are those with whom is the Divine which is above all things, appears from the signification of the nation of Jehovah, as denoting where the Divine itself dwells, and in the spiritual sense where the church of the Lord is, for all they who acknowledge the Lord by faith and love, taken together, are the nation of Jehovah; but the sons of Israel at that time thought nothing of the church, but only of the possession of the land of Canaan, and of eminence over others; and whereas it was told Moses, that the name of their God was Jehovah, which yet before they knew not, Exod. iii. 13, 14, and whereas they saw so great miracles wrought by him in Egypt, and at the sea Suph, and in the wilderness, therefore they acknowledged Jehovah for their God; nevertheless in their heart they did not believe in Him, for they believed that there were more gods; as may sufficiently appear from the golden calf, which, whilst Moses tarried in the mountain, they adored for their god, yea for Jehovah; and afterwards from the gods, to whom they so often turned aside, as is evident from the historicals of the Word. From which considerations it may be manifest, that they worshiped Jehovah merely for the sake of miracles, and not because He was the only God; and he who worships God for the sake of miracles alone, only worships the name of God, and not God, and falls away from it as often as he does not enjoy what he desires. That the Israelitish nation worshiped Jehovah only as to name, see n. 3732, 4299, 6877, and that in heart they were idolaters, n. 4208, 4281, 4820, 5998, 6877, 7401, 8301, 8882; and that they were the worst of all nations, n. 4314, 4316, 4317, 4444, 4503, 4750, 4751, 4815, 4820, 4832, 5057, 7248, 8819, 9320; and besides, 10,396. From these considerations now it may be manifest what is signified by the words, this nation is Thy people, namely, that they were the only people amongst whom was Jehovah, and that thus they were to become more eminent than all other nations. But although these things are signified by those words in the proximate sense, still by the same words in the internal sense is signified that the Divine was with them, consequently the church.

10,567. "And he said, My faces shall go, and I will cause thee to rest"—that hereby is signified that the Divine of the church, of worship, and of the Word, will be there, but with the nation itself what is external without it, appears from the signification of faces, as denoting the interiors, see the passages cited, n. 9546; and when concerning Jehovah, as denoting things Divine, in this case the Divine things of the church, of worship, and of the Word; and from the signification of going, as denoting to live, see n. 3335, 4882, 5493, 5606, 8417, 8420, 9440; but when concerning Jehovah, it denotes to give life, to be present, and to lead; for hence man has the faculty of life; and from the signification of causing Moses to rest, as denoting the external of the church, of worship, and of the Word, into which interior Divine things close; for by Moses is represented that external, as above n. 10,563, and by resting is signified to be still and to close, thus wherein interior Divine things are still, or into which they close; by that expression also in the original tongue is signified to be still and to close. That the interiors of the church, of worship, and of the Word, close into their external, and that they rest upon it as on their plane, or as a house upon its foundation, see n. 9216. That these things are signified by causing Moses to rest, appears from what follows of this chapter in the internal sense, in which the interiors of the Word, of the church, and of worship, are treated of; and in which the external is treated of into which they close; this external is what is represented by Moses.

10,568. "And he said to Him, if Thy faces go not, cause us not to ascend from hence"—that hereby is signified if the Divine be not there, there will not be any thing of the church there, appears from the signification of the faces of Jehovah, as denoting the interior Divine things of the church, of worship, and of the Word, see just above, n. 10,567; and from the signification of cause us not to ascend from hence, as denoting that there will not be any thing of the church; the reason why this is signified by those words is, because by being introduced into the land of Canaan, is signified the establishment of the church, hence by not causing us to ascend from hence is signified that thus there will not be any thing of the church; that by being introduced into the land of Canaan is signified the establishment of the church, see above, n. 10,560, 10,561. The reason why by being introduced into the land of Canaan is signified the establishment of the church, is, because by the land of Canaan in the Word nothing else is meant in heaven but the church; for in heaven all things of the Word are spiritually perceived, wherefore when mention is made of any land [or earth], then they think of such things there, as relate to the church in that land [or earth], or as appertain to the nation which inhabits it; the angels of heaven cannot keep the mind in the idea of land [or earth], since the idea of land [or earth], is material, nor in the idea of any nation, for this idea also is material, wherefore a spiritual idea instantly occurs to them, which idea is concerning the church; a spiritual idea in general is concerning the Lord, concerning his kingdom, concerning heaven, concerning the church, concerning love and faith in the Lord, and concerning innumerable things which relate to faith and love, thus which relate to the church; and if you are willing to believe it, it is impossible that any material idea should enter heaven, it being put off at the very threshold. This is the case with all and singular the things of the Word. Hence now it is that by being introduced into the land of Canaan is signified the establishment of the church, and by not being introduced, as in the present case, no establishment.

10,569. "And wherein shall it be made known at any time that I have found favor in Thine eyes; I and Thy people; is it not in Thy going with us?"—that hereby is signified reception above others if the Divine be manifested amongst them, appears from the signification of being made known, when concerning the Divine amongst them, as denoting to be revealed; and from the signification of finding favor in the eyes of Jehovah, as denoting to be received, see above, n. 10,563, in this case above others, since it follows, so shall we be rendered more excellent, I and Thy people, above every people on the faces of the ground; and from the signification of going with us, when concerning Jehovah, as denoting the Divine eading, in this case into the land of Canaan, see above, n. 10,567. Hence it is evident that by the words, "Wherein shall it be made known at any time that I have found favor in Thine eyes, I and Thy people, is it not in Thy going with us?" is signified reception above others if the Divine be manifested amongst them. It is said in the eyes of Jehovah, and thereby is signified the Divine presence of the Lord in the truths and goods of faith and of love, with men in the earths, and with angels in the heavens; the reason why the presence of the Lord is in the truths and goods of faith and of love, is because these things are from the Lord Himself; and when the Lord is present with men and with angels in those things He is then present in His own [principles] with them, and not in their proprium, for this is evil. Hence also it is that by eyes in the Word, where men are treated of who receive the Divine things of the Lord, is signified faith, and also the receiving intellect, for the intellect is the internal eye, and faith is the truth which is seen and perceived; that the eyes, when men are treated of, in the Word signify faith, and also understanding, see n. 2701, 4403 to 4421, 4523 to 4534, 9051. It may be expedient also to say whence that sight [or vision] comes; it is real light which illuminates the understanding, altogether distinct from the light which illuminates the sight of the body; the light which illuminates the understanding is from heaven, but that which illuminates the sight of the body is in the world; the light of heaven is from the Lord as a sun there, and is in its essence the Divine Truth proceeding from the Divine Good of the Lord. Hence it is evident whence it is that by eyes, when relating to Jehovah, is signified the Divine presence of the Lord, and that by eyes, when relating to men who receive the Divine Truth of the Lord, or His light, is signified faith and an enlightened understanding. That it is real light, which illuminates minds, and constitutes understanding with men, is not known in the world, although sight and light are attributed by men to the understanding, and although the Lord in the Word is very frequently called light, and thereby is meant that He is seen by faith and its light. That it is real light which illuminates minds, and that the Divine Truth proceeding from the Lord as a sun is that light, and that it gives the understanding of truth where it is received, see the passages cited, n. 9548, 9684; also n. 9570, 9571, 9574. From these considerations it may be manifest what is signified in the Word by the eyes of Jehovah, as in Isaiah, "Incline, O Jehovah, Thine ear, and hear, and *open, O Jehovah, Thine eyes, and see*," xxxvii. 17. And in Jeremiah, "*I will set Mine eye upon them for good*, and will bring them back upon their own land, and will build them," xxxiv. 6. And in David, "*Behold the eye of Jehovah is upon them that fear Him*," Psalm xxxiii. 18. And again, "Jehovah is in the temple of His Holi ness, the throne of Jehovah is in heaven; *His eyes see, and His eye-lids prove the sons of men,*" Psalm xi. 4, and elsewhere.

10,570. "And we shall be rendered more excellent, I and Thy people, above all people who are on the faces of the ground"—that hereby is signified hence eminence over all in the universal world where the church is, appears from the signification of being rendered more excellent than all people who are on the faces of the ground, as denoting eminence over all in the universal world. The reason why it denotes also where the church is, is, because by ground is signified the church, of which we shall speak presently. That this end, that they might be rendered more excellent than all in the universal world was the end for which the Israelitish nation worshiped Jehovah, and for the sake of which they could be in a holy external principle, is manifest from what has been above shown concerning that nation. That such can be in a holy external principle, and appear to others as worshipers of God, is manifest from the idolaters spoken of in the historicals of the Word, who in like manner could be in things external, but that they had no holy internal principle, every one may know and conclude from this consideration, that the Divine Truths, which are revealed in the Word, cause worship to be internal, if men know them, and live according to them; for if man without them could worship God holily, there would be no need of any doctrine of the church, nor of any preaching. Inasmuch as that nation was of such a quality, that for the sake of eminence over others as an end, they could be in a holy external principle, and inasmuch as with persons of such a character, the representatives of celestial and spiritual things, which were the externals of worship, can be communicated with the angels, and thereby conjunction be effected with heaven, therefore that nation was received. But he who believes that they were thereby worshipers of God, is very greatly deceived, for they were worshipers of self and of the world, and in heart idolaters; and whereas they were of such a quality, the interior things of worship, which are the things of faith and love to the Lord, were not revealed to them, as is evident from the books of the Old Testament; and also from this consideration, that they did not acknowledge the Lord when He came into the world, yea, neither do they yet acknowledge; and if they are taught from the prophetical books concerning the Lord, still they do not receive it; they wish for a Messiah who may exalt them above all in the universal world of the earths, and not a Messiah whose kingdom is in the heavens, and who thence provides for the salvation of all even in the earths. From these considerations it may be manifest what was the quality of that nation from the earliest ages, and from what ground it is here said, that by Jehovah going with them they should be rendered more excellent than all people who are on the faces of the ground. It is said on the faces of the ground, and thereby is meant wheresoever the church is, for by ground, in like manner as by land [or earth], is signified the church; that this is signified by land or earth, see the passages cited, n. 9325; but ground signifies the church from a similar cause that field does, thus from the reception of various seeds, with their growth and produce, by which are signified the truths and goods of faith and love, for man is a receptacle of the latter, as the ground is of the former; but the church is called land [or earth] from the people who inhabit it, with whom the church is; but whereas ground involves extension as to space, alike with land [or earth], therefore interpreters call it land [or earth] instead of ground, as in the present case they say on the faces of the earth, instead of on the faces of the ground, and also in other passages, and still in the original tongue the expression, which signifies ground, is altogether from another origin than the expression which signifies earth. That ground signifies the church alike with land [or earth], is manifest from various passages in the Word, of which it is allowed to adduce only some; as in Jeremiah, "The great ones sent the lesser ones for water, they came to the pits, nor did they find waters, their vessels returned empty, *because the ground was broken*, inasmuch as there was no rain *on the earth*," xiv. 3, 4. In this passage ground denotes the church, and also earth; for the subject there treated of in the internal sense is concerning a defect of truth, and thence the vastation of the church; waters denote truths; pits denote where they are, thus doctrine; vessels denote recipients; rain denotes influx from heaven; earth denotes where the church is, and ground denotes the church itself, which is said to be broken from drought, thus from the defect of truth from heaven. And in Isaiah, "It shall come to pass at the end of seventy years, Jehovah will visit Tyre, and she shall return to meretricious hire, and shall commit whoredom with all the kingdoms *of the earth on the faces of the ground;* at length her merchandise and meretricious hire shall be holy to Jehovah," xxiii. 17, 18; by Tyre is signified the church as to the knowledges of truth and good, thus in the abstract sense those knowledges which are called meretricious hire, when they are taught for the sake of gain, of honor, and of reputation, and are thus, as it were sold, and are not taught for the sake of truth itself; this is called meretriciousness and whoredom in the Word; to commit whoredom with all the kingdoms of the earth, is to do so with all the truths of the church; on the faces of the ground denotes wheresoever the church is; inasmuch as the knowledges of truth and good still remain knowledges of truth and good in themselves, thus Divine, although they are for gain, and hence meretricious hire, to the man who teaches and sells, therefore it is said that her merchandise and her meretricious hire shall be holy to Jehovah; that meretricious hire is not there meant, neither whoredoms with all the kingdoms of the earth, nor that such a thing shall be holy to Jehovah, may be seen by every one, who thinks beyond the sense of the letter. And in David, *Thou sendest forth Thy Spirit, they are created, and Thou renewest the faces of the ground*," Psalm civ. 30. The Spirit of Jehovah is the Divine Truth proceeding from the Lord, n. 9228; to be created denotes to be created anew, that is, to be regenerated, n. 10,373; to renew the faces of the ground is to reform and establish the church; the faces of the ground denote wheresoever any thing of the church can be received; in like manner as in other places where the faces of the ground are mentioned, as Gen. vii. 4; chap. viii. 8, 13; Exod. xxxii. 12; Numb. xii. 3; Deut. vi. 15; chap. vii. 6; 1st Samuel xx. 15; 2nd Samuel xiv. 7.

10,571. "And Jehovah said to Moses, also this word which thou hast spoken I will do"—that hereby is signified that the Divine will be in the external of the church, of worship, and of the Word, which is with them, appears from the representation of Moses, as denoting, in character, as the head of that nation, the external of the church, of worship, and of the Word, not so separate from the internal, as their external with the nation itself, see above, n. 10,557, 10,563; and from the signification of doing the word which Moses spake when from Jehovah, as denoting that the Divine will be in what is external; for by doing the word is meant to go with them, and introduce them into the land of Canaan; and by going with them and introducing into the land of Canaan, is signified that the Divine will be manifested amongst them, see above, n. 10,569. The arcanum which lies concealed in these and in the following verses, can hardly be described, unless an idea be had of the external of the church, of worship, and of the Word, which Moses represents, and of the external of the church, of worship, and of the Word, in which the nation itself was. The one is distinguished from the other in this, that the external which Moses represents is an external not so separate from what is internal, as the external in which the nation itself was. Hence it is that one time mention is made of Moses and the people, at another time of Moses without the people, and at another of the people without Moses; and that when Moses speaks to Jehovah, he says I and Thy people, and when Jehovah speaks to Moses, He speaks of Moses alone, as in verses 12, 14, 18, 19, 20, 21, 22, 23, or of the people separately from him, as in verse 2 of the following chapter, and elsewhere.

10,572. "Because thou hast found grace in Mine eyes and I know thee by name"—that hereby is signified that he was received on account of his quality, appears from what was said and shown above, n. 10,562, 10,563, where like words occur.

10,573. Verses 18, 19, 20, 21, 22, 23. *And he said, cause me I pray to see Thy glory. And He said, I will cause all My good to pass by upon thy faces, and I will call upon the name of Jehovah before thee; and I will do favor to whom I do favor, and I will do mercy to whom I do mercy. And He said, Thou canst not see My faces, because no man seeth Me and liveth. And Jehovah said, Behold a place with Me and thou shalt stand upon a rock. And it shall come to pass, in My glory passing by I will set thee in a cleft of the rock, and will cover the palm of My hand over thee, until I shall pass by. And I will remove the palm of My hand, and thou shalt see My posteriors; and My faces shall not be seen.* And he said, Cause me I pray to see Thy glory, signifies the perception of internal Divine Truth in what is external. And He said I will cause all My good to pass by upon thy faces, signifies every thing Divine of heaven and of the church upon what is external. And I will call upon the name of Jehovah before thee, signifies the holy principle of Divine worship there. And I will do favor to whom I do favor, and I will do mercy to whom I do mercy, signifies that Divine Truth and Good will be revealed to those who receive. And He said thou canst not see My faces, signifies that the interior Divine things of the church, of worship, and of the Word, cannot appear to the Israelitish nation. Because no man seeth Me and liveth, signifies that the Divine Itself cannot be seen such as it is in Itself, but such as it is by [or through] the Lord in heaven. And Jehovah said, Behold a place with Me, and thou shalt stand upon a rock, signifies a state of faith in God. And it shall come to pass in My glory passing by, signifies the interiors of the Word, of the church, and of worship. And I will set thee in a cleft of the rock, signifies the obscure and false principles of faith, such as appertain to those who are in externals without an internal principle. And I will cover the palm of My hand over thee, until I pass by, signifies the closing of what is internal. And I will remove the palm of My hand, and thou shalt see My posteriors, and My faces shall not be seen, signifies that they should see the externals of the Word, of the church, and of worship, but not the internals.

10,574. "And he said, cause me I pray to see Thy glory"—that hereby is signified the perception of internal Divine Truth in what is external, appears from the representation of Moses on this occasion, as denoting the external of the church, of worship, and of the Word, not so separate from the internal as with the nation itself, see n. 10,563, 10,571; and from the signification of causing to see, as denoting to perceive, see n. 2150, 3764, 4567, 4723, 5400; and from the signification of the glory of Jehovah, as denoting the internal of the Word, see the preface to chap. xviii. Gen. and n. 5922, 9429. Hence it is evident that by Moses saying, Cause me, I pray, to see Thy glory, is signified the perception of the internal in the external of the Word, of the church, and of worship. That these things are signified by the above words, may also be manifest from the preceding parts of this chapter, for in the internal sense the Israelitish nation is there treated of, and that the church could not be established amongst them by reason that they could not receive any thing internal; to receive the internal of the church is to receive Divine Truth from heaven and thereby heavenly love. Inasmuch as this is the subject treated of in the internal sense, and Moses was still urgent that Jehovah would introduce them into the land of Canaan, by which is signified the establishment of the church, therefore now Moses saith, Cause me to see Thy glory, by which is therefore signified the perception of internal Divine Truth in what is external. That by the glory of Jehovah is meant such a Divine which could not be perceived by Moses, appears manifest from what follows of this chapter, where it is said, that he could not see the faces of Jehovah, (for so glory is there called,) but after that he had passed by, he should see the posteriors, and this from a cleft of the rock, by which things is signified, that he would perceive only the externals of the church, of worship, and of the Word, but not the internals. That such is the signification of the glory of Jehovah, is evident from this consideration, that it is sometimes said that they saw the glory of Jehovah, but it was a cloud which was so called, as on Mount Sinai, and on the tents, and in it, see Exod. xvi. 10; chap. xxiv. 16, 17; chap. xl. 34, 35; Numb. xiv. 22, and elsewhere; by the cloud in those passages, which was called the glory of Jehovah, is signified the external of the church, of worship, and of the Word, or the sense of the letter of the Word, see preface to chap. xviii. Gen. and n. 4060, 4061, 5922, 6343, 6752, 8106, 8781, 9430, 10,551. The reason why the glory of Jehovah signifies the internal of the Word, of the church, and of worship, is, because the Divine Truth proceeding from the Lord, such as is in heaven, is the glory of Jehovah; for the Divine Truth proceeding from the Lord appears there as light, and the appearance of the Lord in that light is what is meant in the genuine sense by the glory of Jehovah; by the appearance of the Lord are meant all things therein which are from the Lord, which are innumerable, and are called by a general term celestial and spiritual. The reason why the internal of the Word, of the church, and of worship, is signified by the glory of Jehovah, is, because such internal is in that light, but the external in the light of the world, wherefore this latter in the Word is signified by cloud; hence it is evident that the internal sense of the Word is glory. From these considerations it may now be manifest what is signified by the glory of Jehovah, and by His light, in the following passages, as in Isaiah, "Arise, *illuminate, because thy light is come, and the glory of Jehovah is risen upon Thee;* behold darkness covers the earth, and thick darkness the people, but upon thee shall Jehovah arise, and *His glory shall be seen upon thee; nations shall walk to the light, and kings to the brightness of thy rising;* thy sun shall no more set, and thy moon shall not be gathered, because Jehovah will be to thee *for the light of eternity,*" lx. 1, 2, 3, 20. The subject treated of in this passage is concerning the coming of the Lord; the light there spoken of is the Divine Truth proceeding from the Lord; and His glory and the brightness of His rising denote all that which appears in that light respecting the Lord, and respecting faith and love to Him; darkness and thick darkness which cover the earth and the people, denote the obscure things of faith and love; for the passage relates to the establishment of the church amongst the gentiles; hence it follows, that by the light and glory which were to arise, and which were to be seen, and to which they were to walk, are denoted Divine Truths concerning the Lord, and concerning faith and love to Him from Him. Again, "I Jehovah have called thee in justice, and have given thee for a covenant to the people, *for a light of the nations:* I am Jehovah, this is My name, *My glory* I will not give to another," xlii. 6, 8; in this passage also the Lord is treated of, who is called a light of the nations, because from Him is all Divine Truth; and who is called the glory of Jehovah, because to Him is directed every thing of faith and love. Again, "*Thy light shall break forth as the day dawn,* My justice shall walk before thee, the *glory of Jehovah shall gather thee,*" lviii. 8, where the sense is the same. Again, "Rejoice with Jerusalem, be delighted *at the brightness of His glory,*" lxvi. 10. Jerusalem in this passage, as in others, denotes the church; and the brightness of glory is the love of truth from the Lord. And in Zechariah, "I will be to them a wall of fire round about, and *I will be for glory in the midst thereof,*" ii. 5, speaking also of Jerusalem which is the church; glory in the midst thereof is the Lord Himself as to all things of truth and good, which are of faith and love. That by glory in the above passages are meant those things which are of Divine light, is evident. In like manner as in the Apocalypse, "The Holy Jerusalem *having the glory of God, and her luminary* like to most precious stone; *the glory of God shall enlighten her, and the Lamb is the lamp thereof;* the nations which are saved *shall walk in her light;* and the kings of the earth shall bring their glory and honor into her. Her gates shall not be shut in the day-time; for night shall not be there," xxi. 11, 23, 24, 25. The Holy Jerusalem in the above passage denotes the church which is to succeed to the present; those things which are of the church, relating to faith and love to the Lord from the Lord, are described by a luminary, by light, and by glory. Inasmuch as by glory are meant those things which are of light, therefore it is said, *the glory of God shall enlighten it.* Every considerate person, who takes a view of things themselves, and does not abide in the words alone, may see that by all the above things are signified such things as relate to the church, but the internal sense teaches what is signified by each, for in the Word nothing is said in vain, not even the slightest expression. And in Luke, "Mine eyes have seen Thy salvation, which Thou hast prepared before the face of all people, *a light for the revelation of the nations, and the glory of Thy people Israel,*" ii. 30, 31, 32, which words are prophetically spoken by Simeon concerning the Lord who was born; a light for the revelation of the nations is the Divine Truth proceeding from the Lord; and the glory of the people Israel is all that which was revealed by the Lord concerning Himself, and concerning faith and love to Him with those who receive; all this is called glory, because it appears in heaven in the light there, which light is the Divine Truth; by the sons of Israel are meant those who are in faith and love to the Lord. That light denotes the Lord as to Divine Truth, and also glory the things which are of light, is evident from the words of the Lord Himself in John, "They loved the glory of man more than *the glory of God; I am come a light into the world,* that whosoever believeth may not abide in darkness," xii. 43, 46. And again, "In the beginning was the Word, and the Word was with God, and God was the Word: *this was the true light, which illuminates every man that cometh into the world:* and the Word was made flesh, and dwelt amongst us, and *we saw His glory, the glory as of the Only-begotten of the Father,*" i. 9, 14. The Word is the Divine Truth, and also light; and glory denotes all that appears concerning the Lord in that light. These passages are quoted from the Word, because in them glory and light are named together, and they are quoted to the intent that it may be known, that light is Divine Truth from the Lord, thus the Lord Himself, as to Divine Truth, and that glory is every thing which is of the light, consequently every thing which is from the Divine Truth, which makes intelligence and wisdom with the angels, and with the men who receive the Lord in faith and love. The like is signified by glory in other passages, as in John, "I will that where I am, they also may be with Me, *that they may see My glory,*" xvii. 20. And in Luke, "Ought not Christ to suffer these things, and *to enter into His glory,*" xxiv. 26. And in Matthew, "Then shall appear the sign of the Son of Man, and then shall all the tribes of the earth lament, and they shall see *the Son of Man coming in the clouds of heaven with virtue and glory,*" xxiv. 30. By clouds in this passage is meant Divine Truth such as is in the light of the world, thus such as is with men; and by glory is meant Divine Truth such as is in the light of heaven, thus such as is with angels; and whereas Divine Truth is meant by a cloud and by glory, therefore the Word is meant as to the external sense and as to the internal sense, as to the external sense by a cloud, and as to the internal sense by glory; also what appears in the light of the world is a cloud in respect to what appears in the light of heaven; that a cloud has this signification, see preface to chap. xviii. Gen. and n. 4060, 4301, 5922, 6343, 6752, 8106, 8443, 8781, 9430, 10,551. Hence it is that a cloud also in the Word is called glory, as in Exodus, "*The glory of Jehovah appeared in the cloud*," xvi. 10. Again, "*The glory of Jehovah* dwelt on Mount Sinai; and *a cloud covered it* six days; but *the appearance of the glory of Jehovah* was as devouring fire in the head of the mountain before the eyes of the sons of Israel," xxiv. 16, 17. And again in Exodus, "*A cloud covered the tent of assembly, and the glory of Jehovah covered the habitation;* nor could Moses enter, because *the cloud dwelt upon it, and the glory of Jehovah filled the habitation*," xl. 34, 35. And in Numbers, "When the assembly gathered together against Moses and against Aaron, and looked to the tent of the congregation, *behold a cloud covered it, and the glory of Jehovah appeared*," xvi. 42. And in the first book of the Kings, "A cloud filled the house of Jehovah, so that the priests could not stand to minister *by reason of the cloud*, inasmuch as *the glory of Jehovah filled the house of Jehovah*," viii. 10, 11. And in the Apocalypse, "The temple was filled with *smoke and the glory of God*," xv. 8; inasmuch as the Divine appeared as a cloud, therefore by a cloud is signified the Divine presence, and where the Divine presence is, there the Divine Truth is, for the Divine without it does not appear, since it is in it and is it; hence it is that cloud in these passages is called glory; nor could it otherwise appear to the Israelitish nation, since they were in externals without an internal principle, see n. 6832, 8814, 8819, 10,551; nevertheless cloud and glory are distinguished like the light of the world and the light of heaven, or like the sense of the letter of the Word and its internal sense; and like human wisdom and angelic wisdom. From these considerations it may now be manifest that by Moses said, cause me I pray to see Thy glory, is signified that the internal Divine may be shown to him; and whereas Moses represented the external of the church, of worship, and of the Word, therefore the perception of internal Divine Truth in external is signified.

10,575. "And he said, I will cause all my good to pass by upon thy faces"—that hereby is signified every thing Divine of heaven and of the church, upon the external separate from the internal, in which Moses was and the nation over which he presided, appears from the signification of causing to pass by over his faces, as denoting over the external separate from the internal in which Moses was, and the nation over which he presided, for by thy faces is signified the external of worship, of the church, and of the Word, in which is an internal, and by causing to pass is signified upon it; and from the signification of all the good of Jehovah, as denoting every thing Divine of heaven and of the church. How the case herein is, may be manifest from what was said and shown above concerning Moses and concerning the nation over which he presided, namely, that they were in external things separate from what is internal, by which is meant, that they were in holy externals without an internal principle when in worship; and whereas a holy internal principle was still present, but did not enter into their holy external, it is hence evident what is signified by Jehovah causing all good to pass by upon his faces. That nation indeed had an internal principle, but this was filthy, full of uncleanness arising from the love of self and the world, nevertheless this was closed when they were in worship, lest the internal Divine of heaven, of the church, and of the Word, should be defiled; for if that principle had been defiled by their internal, there would have been no communication at all of their external with heaven, when they were employed in worship and in reading the Word, on which subject see what was said and shown above, n. 10,454 to 10,457, 10,462 to 10,466, 10,492, 10,498, 10,500, 10,533, 10,549, 10,550, 10,551, 10,570, where these things have been more fully explained.

10,576. "And I will call upon the name of Jehovah before thee"—that hereby is signified the holy principle of Divine worship there, appears from the signification of calling upon the name of Jehovah, as denoting the holy principle of worship, see n. 440, 2724; and from the signification of before thee, as denoting before the external, which Moses now represents, see above, n. 10,563, 10,571. How the case herein is, may be manifest from what was said above, n. 10,566, and in the passages there adduced.

10,577. "And I will do favor to whom I do favor, and I will do mercy to whom I do mercy"—that hereby is signified that Divine Truth and good will be revealed to those who receive, appears from the signification of doing favor [or grace], as denoting to gift with spiritual truth and good, in this case to reveal it, because the subject treated of is the internal and external of the church, of worship, and of the Word; and from the signification of doing mercy, as denoting to gift with celestial truth and good, in this case to reveal it. The reason why it denotes with those who receive, is, because the internal things of the Word, of the church, and of worship, are revealed to no others but those who receive. The reason why doing favor [or grace] denotes to gift with spiritual truth and good, and doing mercy denotes to gift with celestial truth and good, is, because favor [or grace] is predicated of faith, and mercy of love; and the good of faith is spiritual good, and the good of love is celestial good; what spiritual good is, and celestial good, and what is the difference, see the passages cited, n. 9277; and that they who are in the Lord's spiritual kingdom speak of favor [or grace], and they who are in the Lord's celestial kingdom speak of mercy, n. 598, 981, 5929. Unless such were the difference between favor and mercy, no mention would have been made of doing favor and doing mercy. Hence also it is that Jehovah is called Favorable [or gracious] and merciful, Exod. xxiv. 6; Joel ii. 13; Psalm ciii. 8; cxlv. 8. And in Isaiah, "Therefore will Jehovah remain to *show favor* [or grace] to *you*, and therefore will He lift Himself up *to be merciful to you*," xxx. 18. Inasmuch as there are two principles to which all things of the church have reference, namely, love and faith, and whereas mercy is of love and favor [or grace], and also truth is of faith, therefore in the Word it is called mercy and favor [or grace] when the Lord is implored, and it is called mercy and truth when the Lord is described, as in the following passages: "*Thy mercy* is before mine eyes, and I walk *in Thy truth*," Psalm xxvi. 3. Again, "O Jehovah, *Thy mercy* is in the heavens, and *Thy truth* is even to the ethers," Ps. xxxvi. 5. Again, "God shall send from the heavens *His mercy and His truth: Thy mercy* is great even to the heavens, and *Thy truth* even to the ethers," Psalm lvii. 3, 10. Again, "*Mercy and truth* shall meet; and justice and peace shall kiss," Psalm lxxxv. 10. And again, "I will sing the *mercy of Jehovah* to eternity, to generation and generation *Thy truth* with my mouth: since I have said, *mercy* shall be built for ever, in the heavens themselves Thou shalt confirm *Thy truth:* justice and judgment are the support of Thy throne, *mercy and truth* shall stand together before Thy faces," Psalm lxxxix. 1, 2, 14. Mercy in the above passages is love, and truth is faith.

10,578. "And he said, thou canst not see my faces"—that hereby is signified that the interior Divine things of the church, of worship, and of the Word, cannot appear to the Israelitish nation, is manifest from the signification of the faces of Jehovah, as denoting the interior Divine things of the church, of worship, and of the Word, see above, n. 10,567, 10,568; and from the signification of seeing them, as denoting to appear. That those things cannot appear to the Israelitish nation, is manifest from the consideration that this is said to Moses, and Moses here represents the head of the Israelitish nation, n. 10,556. That the faces of Jehovah are the interior Divine things of the Word, of the church, and of worship, is evident also from this consideration, that the like is signified by the faces of Jehovah, as by the glory of Jehovah; for Moses said, cause me I pray to see Thy glory; and Jehovah said, thou canst not see My faces;

and by the glory of Jehovah are signified the interior Divine things of the Word, of the church, and of worship, see above, n. 10,574. How the case herein is, may be manifest from what has been frequently said before, namely, that the Israelitish nation could in no wise see the interior things of worship, of the church, and of the Word, because they were in externals separate from what is internal, thus neither could they see the faces of Jehovah: but they who are in externals not separate from what is internal, can all of them see the interior things of the Word, of the church, and of worship, thus the faces of Jehovah; hence it follows, that they who are in love to the Lord, and also they who are in charity towards the neighbor, all of them see; for love to the Lord and charity towards the neighbor open the internal man, and when this is open, man as to his interiors is in heaven amongst angels where the Lord is. But it may be expedient here briefly to say what love to the Lord is, or what it is to love the Lord; he who believes that he loves the Lord, and does not live according to His precepts, is very much deceived: for to live according to his precepts, is to love the Lord; those precepts are the truths which are from the Lord, thus in which the Lord is, wherefore so far as they are loved, that is, so far as the life is formed according to them from love, so far the Lord is loved; the reason is, because the Lord loves man, and from love wills that he may be happy to eternity, and man cannot be made happy but by a life according to His precepts; for by them man is regenerated, and is made spiritual, and thus can be elevated into heaven; but to love the Lord without a life according to His precepts is not to love Him, for in such case there is not any thing appertaining to man, into which the Lord may flow-in, and elevate him to Himself; for he is an empty vessel; since there is not any thing of life in his faith, nor any thing of life in his love. The life of heaven, which is called eternal life, is not infused into any one immediately, but mediately. From these considerations it may be manifest what it is to love the Lord, and also what it is to see the Lord, or His faces, namely, that He is seen from such faith and love. To live according to the precepts of the Lord is to live according to the doctrine of charity and faith, which you may see in what is prefixed to each chapter at the book of Exodus. That this is the case, the Lord also teaches in John, "*He that hath My precepts, and doeth them, he it is who loveth Me; but he who loveth Me, shall be loved by My Father, and I will love him, and will manifest Myself to him: If any one loveth Me, he will keep My Word, and My Father will love him, and We will come to him, and make abode with him: he who loveth Me not, keepeth not My words*," xiv. 21, 23, 24. What is further signified by the faces of Jehovah, will be shown in the article which now follows.

10,579. "Because no man seeth Me and liveth"—that hereby is signified that the Divine itself cannot be seen, such as it is in itself, but such as it is [by or through] the Lord in heaven, may be manifest from this consideration, that no one has seen at any time Jehovah the Father, but when He is seen it is the Lord who is seen; for the Lord is the very face of Jehovah. *That no one has seen at any time Jehovah the Father*, is manifest from the words of the Lord Himself in John, "No one hath seen God at any time, the Only-Begotten Son, who is in the bosom of the Father, He hath brought Him forth," i. 18. Again, "Ye have never heard at any time the voice of the Father, nor seen His shape," v. 37. And in Matthew, "No one knoweth the Father but the Son, and he to whom the Son hath willed to reveal Him," xi. 27. *That when Jehovah the Father is seen, it is the Lord who is seen*, the Lord also teaches in John, "Jesus said, if ye have known Me, ye have also known My Father, and henceforth ye have known Him, and have seen Him. Philip said, Lord, show us the Father. Jesus saith to him, have I been so long time with you, and hast thou not known Me, Philip? he who hath seen Me, hath seen the Father; how then sayest thou, show us the Father?" xiv. 7, 8, 9. Again, "Your father Abraham exulted, that he might see My day, and he saw, and rejoiced; verily, verily, I say unto you, before Abraham was, I Am," viii. 56, 58. Hence it may be manifest that the Lord as to the Divine Human, is Jehovah who is seen, and thus that He is the face of Jehovah. *That the Lord is the face of Jehovah*, is also manifest from the Word, as in Isaiah, "He was made into a Saviour for them, *the Angel of the faces of Jehovah* liberated them, on account of His love and His indulgence; He redeemed them, and took them, and carried them all the days of eternity," lxiii. 8, 9. In like manner in Exodus, "Behold I send an Angel before thee, to keep thee in the way, and to bring thee to the place which I have prepared; beware of *His face*, lest thou embitter him, because he will not bear your prevarication, because My name is in the midst of Him," xxiii. 20. For Jehovah, before the coming of the Lord into the world, when He appeared, appeared in the form of an angel, for when he passed through heaven, He clothed Himself with that form, which was the human form; for the universal heaven, by virtue of the Divine there, is as one man, as has been abundantly shown in treating of the GRAND MAN, which is heaven; hence then is the Divine Human; and whereas Jehovah appeared in a human form as an angel, it is evident that still it was Jehovah Himself, and that very form also was His, because it was His Divine in heaven; this was the Lord from eternity. But inasmuch as that human form was assumed by transition through heaven, and yet to save the human race, it was necessary to be really and essentially a man, therefore He was pleased to be born, and thereby actually to assume the human form, in which was Jehovah Himself. That this is the case, the Lord teaches in John, "Believe Me, that I am in the Father, and the Father in Me," xiv. 11. And in another place, "I and the Father are One," x. 30. That the Lord was from eternity, He also teaches in John, "In the beginning was the Word, and the Word was with God, and God was the Word. All things were made by Him, and without Him was not any thing made which was made. And the Word was made flesh, and dwelt amongst us," i. 1, 2, 3, 14. Again, "I came forth from the Father, and am come into the world; again I leave the world, and go to the Father," xvi. 28. Again, "Jesus said, O Father, glorify Me with Thine own self, with the glory which I had with Thee before the world was," xvii. 5. Again, "Verily, verily, I say unto you, before Abraham was, I Am," viii. 58. From these passages it may be manifestly known, that the Lord even as to His Human is Jehovah, thus that His Human is Divine; on this account it is said in John, "*God was the Word, and the Word was made flesh;* and also before Abraham was, *I Am*, and not I was, for I Am is Jehovah, Exod. iii. 14. From these considerations it may now be manifest, that by no man seeth Me and liveth, is signified that the Divine cannot be seen such as it is in Itself, but such as it is by [or through] the Lord in heaven. It is said by [or through] the Lord in heaven, because the Lord is above the heavens, for He is the Sun of heaven, but still He is present in the heavens, being the Divine Truth there, and the Divine Truth proceeding from the Lord as a Sun is the Lord in heaven, on which account the Divine Truth therein is His face. It was said above, that by the faces of Jehovah are signified the interior Divine things of the Word, of the church, and of worship, n. 10,567, 10,568; the reason is, because the interior Divine things of the Word, of the church, and of worship, are the Divine Truth proceeding from the Lord, thus the Lord in heaven. This is signified by the face of Jehovah, where it is named in the Word, as in Matthew, "See that ye despise not any of these little ones; for I say unto you that their angels in the heavens always *see the face of the Father who is in the heavens*," xviii. 10. And in the Apocalypse, "The throne of God and of the Lamb shall be in the holy Jerusalem, and His servants shall minister to Him, *and they shall see His faces*," xxii. 3, 4. And in Moses, "*Jehovah shall cause His faces to shine upon you*, and shall be merciful to thee; *Jehovah shall lift up His faces upon thee*, and shall appoint peace for thee," Numb. vi. 25, 26. And in David, "Many say, who will show us good; *O Jehovah, lift up the light of Thy faces upon us*," Psalm iv. 6. Again, "How long, *O Jehovah, hidest Thou thy faces from me*," Psalm xiii. 1. Again, "My heart hath said to Thee, *seek ye My faces, Thy faces, O Jehovah*, I seek," Psalm xxvii. 8. Again, "God will be merciful to us, and bless us, *He will cause his faces to shine upon us*," Psalm lxvii. 1. Again, "O God bring us back, *and cause Thy faces to shine*, that we may be saved," Psalm lxxx. 3, 7, 19. Again, "Blessed are Thy people, *who walk in the light of Thy faces*," Psalm lxxxix. 15. Again, "O Jehovah, *hide not Thy faces from me*," Psalm cii. 1, 2. Again, "*Thou hidest Thy faces*, they are disturbed," Psalm civ. 29. What is here meant by the faces of Jehovah, every one may comprehend, namely, the Divine, and whatsoever is of the Divine, thus mercy, peace, and all good, but in the universal sense, the Divine Truth, since in the Divine Truth is all good; and with man and with angel there is Divine Good in Divine Truth, and without the latter there is not the former; for truth is the recipient of good, thus also of mercy and peace. Hence now it follows, that where Divine Good is not in Divine Truth, there the faces of Jehovah are not; and it also follows, that where evil is in what is false, the Divine does not appear. This is meant by Jehovah hiding and turning away His faces in the following passages, "*Your sins have hid the faces of Jehovah from you*," Isaiah lix. 2. And in Jeremiah, "*By reason of their wickedness I have hid My faces from this city*," xxxiii. 5. And in Ezekiel, "*I turn away My faces from them*, and they profane My secret," vii. 22. And in Micah, "*Jehovah will hide His faces from them*, as they have rendered their works evil," iii. 4. But it is to be noted, that Jehovah, that is, the Lord, never turns away His faces from man, but that man, who is in evil, turns away his face from the Lord; and whereas in such case the Divine is to his back, therefore it appears as if it hid or turned itself away. The case also is actually so, infernal spirits all turn the back to the Lord as the sun, but the angels always the face to Him; in like manner man as to his spirit whilst he lives in the world.

10,580. "And Jehovah said, behold, a place with Me, and thou shalt stand upon a rock"—that hereby is signified a state of faith in God, appears from the signification of a place, as denoting state, see n. 2625, 2837, 3356, 3387, 4321, 4882, 5604, 7381, 9440, 9967, 10,146; and from the signification of a rock, as denoting faith, see n. 8581, 10,438. The reason why it denotes a state of faith in God, is, because it is called a place with Me. That this is signified by these words, no one can know but from the internal sense, thus unless he knows what is meant in that sense by a place, and what by a rock; for without that sense, of what consequence would it be, that there was a place with Jehovah upon a rock? in such case it could only mean that Jehovah dwelt there, and gave Moses a place with Him, when yet Jehovah dwells in heaven with the angels, and in the church with men. The signification of a rock, as denoting faith, is grounded in appearances in the other life; they who are principled in faith dwell there upon rocks; but they who are principled in love dwell upon mountains; the rocks there appear stony, but the mountains not stony, because they are elevations of the earth. Hence it is that a rock signifies faith.

10,581. "And it shall come to pass in My glory passing by"—that hereby are signified the interiors of the Word, of the church, and of worship, appears from the signification of the glory of Jehovah, as denoting the interior Divine things of the Word, of the church, and of worship, see above, n. 10,574.

10,582. "And I will set thee in a cleft of the rock"—that hereby is signified an obscure and false principle of faith, such as appertains to those who are in things external without what is internal, appears from the signification of a cleft of the rock, as denoting an obscure and false principle of faith; for by a rock is signified faith, as just above, n. 10,578, and by a cleft, its obscurity and also false principle, of which we shall speak presently. It is said, such as appertains to those who are in things external without what is internal, because with them all truth which is of faith is in obscurity, and also mixed with what is false; for such of them who believe the Word, believe it according to the letter throughout, and not according to its interior sense; and they who so believe, cannot be in any light, for light from heaven flows-in through what is internal into what is external; and also what they believe without light from heaven, appears as true, but still with them it is false, for concerning truth they have a material and terrestrial idea, and not at the same time a spiritual and celestial one, and every material and terrestrial idea, if light from heaven be not in it, abounds in fallacies. As for example, James and John, inasmuch as they had a terrestrial idea concerning the Lord's kingdom, "asked that they might sit one on His right hand, and the other on the left in His kingdom; but Jesus said, ye know not what ye ask, ye know that the princes of the nations domineer over them; it shall not be so amongst you, but whosoever will become great amongst you, ought to be your minister, and whosoever will be first, ought to be your servant," Matt. xx. 21, 22, 25, 26, 27. They who are of such a character, like those at that time, do not know what the heavenly kingdom is, nor what the glory there, nor what love is, yea, nor what faith, in general not what good is, for they judge from things corporeal and earthy, and every delight of the body and its senses they call good, and pre-eminence over others they call glory, the love of the world and the love of self they call heavenly love, and the scientific principle rendered persuasive they call faith; when they think about God, they think materially, and therefore either deny God, and hold nature instead of God, or worship idols, or dead men. Hence it is evident how obscure the principle of faith is with those who are in mere external things, and also that it is false. In such an obscure and false principle of faith are they who believe the Word as to the sense of its letter only, without doctrine thence derived by one who is enlightened: they who read the Word without doctrine are like those who walk in the dark without a lantern; such are all mere sensual men. That the Jewish nation is of such a character, is evident, for they explain all things of the Word according to the sense of the letter, by reason that they are in things external separate from what is internal. Persons of this description, in the other life, do not even dwell upon rocks, but either in caves there or in clefts. That a cleft of the rock denotes an obscure and false principle of faith, is manifest also from other passages in the Word: as in Isaiah, "In that day Jehovah will hiss at the fly which is in the extremity of the rivers of Egypt, and at the bee which is in the land of Ashur, which shall come and rest all of them in the rivers of desolations, and *in the clefts of the rocks*," vii. 18, 19. The subject treated of in this passage is the coming of the Lord, and the state of the church at that time, that there would be a desolation of all things which are of spiritual truth and good; for by those words is signified that the man of the church receded at that time from things internal, and was made altogether external, thus merely sensual; to be made sensual is not to apprehend or believe any thing but what the external senses dictate; the fly in the extremity of the rivers of Egypt, denotes the false principle altogether of the external or merely sensual man; the bee in the land of Ashur denotes the false principle of reasoning thence derived; the rivers of desolations are the truths of doctrine altogether desolated; and the clefts of the rocks are the falses of faith thence derived. Who could conceive that those words signify such things? and what things they signify would be altogether concealed unless they were discovered by the internal sense. Again, "In that day a man shall cast away the idols, which they have made for themselves to bow themselves to moles and bats, *to enter into the rents of the rocks, and into the clefts of the ragged rocks*," ii. 20, 21. To bow himself to moles and bats is to worship such things as are in thick darkness and in the shade of night, which is to worship external things without an internal principle; to enter into the rents of the rocks, and into the clefts of the ragged rocks, denotes into the obscure and dark things of faith, thus into falses. And in Jeremiah "I will bring back the sons of Israel upon their land, and send to many fishers, who shall fish them, and to hunters who shall hunt them from upon every mountain, upon every hill, and *from the holes of the rocks*," xvi.

15, 16. The subject treated of in this passage is the restoration of the church, which is signified by bringing back the sons of Israel upon their land; to fish them denotes to instruct in the externals of the church; to hunt them denotes to instruct in the internals; they who are on the mountain and on the hill denote those who are in love and charity; they in the holes of the rocks denote those who are in faith, not being yet enlightened, thus who are in an obscure principle of faith. Again, "I have given thee the least among the nations; *the pride of thy heart dwelling in the holes of a rock* holdeth the height of a hill," xlix. 15, 16. And in Obadiah, "The pride of thine heart hath deceived thee, *who dwellest in the rents of a rock* the height of thine habitation; who saith in his heart, who shall draw me down to the earth; if thou shalt exalt thyself as an eagle, and if thou shalt set thy nest amongst the stars, thence will I draw thee down," verses 3, 4: to dwell in the holes of a rock denotes in the falses of faith. The subject treated of is those who exalt themselves above others, believing that they are more learned than the rest of mankind, when yet they are in falses, and cannot even see truths; these in the other life dwell in the holes of rocks; and sometimes they project themselves upon the rocks, nevertheless they are thence cast down into their holes, and into caves, which are beneath the rocks; this is meant by holding the height of a hill, and exalting himself as an eagle, and setting his nest among the stars, and still being drawn down. From these considerations it may now be manifest, that by setting Moses in a cleft of the rock is signified the obscure and false principle of faith, such as appertains to those who are in things external without an internal principle; for by Moses is here meant the people, because he here represents their head, see n. 10,556.

10,583. "And I will cover the palm of My hand upon thee, until I pass by"—that hereby is signified the closing of what is internal, appears from the signification of covering the palm of the hand over Moses, as denoting to close the internal of the church, of worship, and of the Word, which is upon their external. The reason why it is their internal principle which is signified, is, because covering the palm of the hand involves in it the preventing them seeing the glory and faces of Jehovah, and by the glory of Jehovah is signified the internal of the Word, of the church, and of worship, see n. 10,574; in like manner by the faces of Jehovah, n. 10,567, 10,568, 10,576.

10,584. "And I will remove the palm of My hand, and thou shalt see My posteriors, and My faces shall not be seen"—that hereby is signified that they should see the externals of the Word, of the church, and of worship, but not the internals, appears from the signification of the posteriors of Jehovah, as denoting the external things of the Word, of the church, and of worship, of which we shall speak presently; and from the signification of the faces of Jehovah, as denoting their internals, see above n. 10,576; hence by seeing the posteriors and not the faces of Jehovah, is signified to see the externals of the Word, of the church, and of worship, and not the internals. That the Israelitish and Judaic nation was of such a quality and also is at this day, has been shown in all that goes before of this and the former chapter. The reason why the posteriors of Jehovah signify the externals of the Word, of the church, and of worship, is, because the faces signify the internals, n. 10,576; and they are said to see the posteriors of Jehovah and not the faces, who believe and adore the Word, but only its external, which is the sense of the letter, and do not go more interiorly, like those who are enlightened, and make to themselves doctrine from the Word, by which they may see its genuine sense, thus its interior sense; that the Word without doctrine cannot be comprehended, and that doctrine derived from the Word by one who is enlightened ought to be as a lantern to the understanding, see n. 9382, 9409, 9412, 9424, 9430, 10,105, 10,324, 10,401, 10,431; and that the internal sense of the Word teaches that doctrine, n. 9430. From these considerations it may be manifest what it is to see the posteriors of Jehovah, and not His faces. But they who do not believe the Word, do not even see the posteriors of Jehovah, but turn themselves back from Jehovah, and see only themselves and the world. These are they who are meant by those in the Word, who are said to turn their posteriors to the temple, and to adore the sun, of whom it is written in Ezekiel, "I was introduced into the court of the house of Jehovah, and to twenty and five men, *whose posteriors were towards the temple of Jehovah, and their faces towards the east;* and the same bowed themselves *towards the rising of the sun,*" viii. 16. By the sun and its rising is meant the sun of the world and its rising, and thereby is signified the love of self, which love is altogether opposite to love to the Lord; hence it is that the sun of the world is presented in the idea of the angels as somewhat on the back altogether obscure, but the Lord, who is the sun of heaven, on the face, see n. 7078; of those men it is said, that they turn the posteriors to the temple; and also that they go backwards, as in Jeremiah. "Thou hast forsaken Jehovah, *thou hast gone backwards,*" xv. 6; and in another place in the same prophet, "They have gone away in the stubbornness of their evil heart, and *are become backward, but not forward,*" vii. 24.

CONCERNING THE FOURTH EARTH IN THE STARRY HEAVEN.

10,585. *TO this earth, which is treated of in what now follows, I was not conveyed as to the others; but the spirits themselves, who were from that earth, were brought to me; and when they were at a distance, they were seen as a volume extended in length, not continuous, but discrete; for there were several of them and in companies. They were carried first towards inferior things; and it was perceived that they attempted to ascend thence and thus come to me, but that they could not; wherefore they proceeded a little to the left in front even to the earth Mars, and there they attempted to immerge, which also was effected, but with difficulty. The reason of this was, because they were altogether of another genius than the spirits of our earth; and they who are of another genius are conveyed by various ways, that spirits may be associated to them by whom conjunction may be effected; for affections and thoughts are what conjoin and disjoin spirits and angels; in proportion as they differ with respect to affections and thoughts, in the same proportion they appear separated from each other, but still they are conjoined by intermediates, when yet it so pleases the Lord. This was the reason why they were brought even to the earth Mars.*

10,586. *After that they were conjoined to them, they immediately appeared above the head, thus near me; for by conjunction with them consociation was effected, as to the affections and thoughts thence derived, with the spirits of our earth, who were about me, and according to consociation as to affections and thoughts, presence appears, as may be manifest from what has been said above. They spake with me on this occasion, and said that they had there found consociate spirits.*

10,587. *The discourse was first concerning the speech of those in their earth; they said that they hold discourse with each other by an internal way, and not as others by an external, and this by means of the atmosphere and by means of sight; which is effected in this manner; they think within themselves, and the ideas of thought are communicated to another by a kind of sliding into the interiors of the ears, by a way unknown in this earth, but still known to learned anatomists; for there is a certain channel within the mouth, which is called the eustachian tube, which is open in the mouth, and terminates in the chamber of the ear, and is encompassed with a thin membrane; through that channel respiratory air slides in under a gentle sound and thus speaking thought is communicated;* this is effected by means of the atmosphere, *as was said. Moreover when they so discourse one amongst another, they also move the lips both in general and particular; and those little motions advance toward the eyes, especially toward the left eye, and their interior thought and its vital principle there manifests itself;* this is effected by means of sight, *as was said. Hence it was evident that their faces act in unity with their thoughts. For the face is altogether formed to effigy and represent those things which man thinks and loves; hence also the face is called the index of the mind; this is the case with the sincere, but it is otherwise with the insincere, with pretenders, and with hypocrites. To confirm me in the truth of this, it was given them in like manner to move my lips, and my face, and on this occasion by agreement to perceive the objects of their thought. They were asked, whether any speak there by sonorous expressions, or articulate sounds? They said, that they know not what is meant by the articulation of sound, but that they know what sound is. On hearing these things, I perceived the reason why they were led away to the spirits of the earth Mars, and consociated with them before they came to me; for a similar speech prevails amongst them, on which subject see what was said concerning the inhabitants and spirits of that earth, n.* 7359, 7360, 7361, 7362.

10,588. *From hearing their discourse, a doubt occurred concerning their respiration, whether it was similar to the respiration of the men of our earth, and it was said that it was indeed similar, but that it does not articulate in the way when it goes forth into sound, as is the case with us in the trachea and the larynx; also that their lips are moved not only by the influx of ideas into their fibres, but also by a breathing of the lungs from within.*

10,589. *Some of the spirits of our earth suggested a doubt, whether they were from the starry heaven; wherefore it was given to the angels to explore whence they were, and it was found that they were from a star, which is their sun, considerably distant from the sun of our world, and that its situation was beneath near the milky way; and that that star is amongst the lesser stars.*

10,590. *The continuation of the subject concerning this fourth earth in the starry heaven will be given at the close of the following chapter.*

EXODUS.

CHAPTER THE THIRTY-FOURTH.

THE DOCTRINE OF CHARITY AND FAITH.

10,591. MAN is so created, that as to his internal he cannot die; for he can believe in God, and also love God, and thus be conjoined with God by faith and love; and to be conjoined with God is to live for ever.

10,592. This internal appertains to every man who is born; his external is that by which he brings into effect the things which are of faith and love, thus which are of the internal. The internal is what is called soul, and the external what is called body.

10,593. The external which man carries about with him in the world, is accommodated to uses in the world; this external is what is rejected when man dies; but the external which is accommodated to uses in the other life, does not die; this latter external together with the internal is called a spirit; a good spirit and an angel, if man in the world had been good, and an evil spirit, if man in the world had been evil.

10,594. The spirit of man appears in the other life in a human form altogether as in the world; he enjoys also the faculty of seeing, of hearing, of speaking, and of feeling, as in the world; and he is endowed with every faculty of thinking, of willing, and of doing, as in the world; in a word, he is a man as to all and singular things, except that he is not encompassed with that gross body which he had in the world; this he leaves when he dies, nor does he ever resume it.

10,595. This continuation of life is what is meant by the resurrection. The reason why men believe that they are not to rise again until the last judgment, when also every visible object of the world is to perish, is, because they have not understood the Word; and because sensual men make most essential life to consist in the body, and believe that unless the body was to live again, every thing of man would perish.

10,596. The life of man after death is the life of his love and of his faith; hence such as his love had been, and such as his faith, when he lived in the world, such a life remains with him to eternity. The life of hell appertains to those who have loved themselves and the world above all things; and the life of heaven to those who have loved God above all things, and the neighbor as themselves; these latter are they who have faith, but the former are they who have not faith. The life of heaven is what is called life eternal; and the life of hell is what is called spiritual death.

10,597. That man lives after death, the Word teaches; as where it is said, that God is not the God of the dead but of the living, Matt. xxii. 31. That Lazarus after death was taken up into heaven; but the rich man cast into hell, Luke xvi. 22, 23. That Abraham, Isaac, and Jacob, are in heaven, Matt. viii. 11; chap. xxii. 31; Luke xvi. 23, 24, 25, 29. That Jesus said to the thief, to-day shalt thou be with Me in paradise, Luke xxiii. 43; and in other places.

CHAPTER XXXIV.

1. AND JEHOVAH said to Moses, hew for thyself two tables of stones, according to the former, and I will write on the tables the words which were on the former tables, which thou hast broken.

2. And be prepared for the morning, and thou shalt come up in the morning to Mount Sinai, and shalt stand for Me there upon the head of the mountain.

3. And there shall not any one ascend with thee, and also there shall not any one be seen in the whole mountain, also the flock and the herd shall not feed over against this mountain.

4. And he hewed two tables of stones according to the former, and Moses arose in the morning early, and ascended to Mount Sinai, as JEHOVAH commanded him, and took in his hand the two tables of stones.

5. And JEHOVAH descended in a cloud, and stood with him there, and called on the name of JEHOVAH.

6. And JEHOVAH passed on His faces, and invoked, JEHOVAH, JEHOVAH, GOD merciful and gracious, long-suffering to angers, and great in goodness and truth;

7. Keeping goodness to thousands, bearing iniquity, and prevarication, and sin, and in absolving absolveth not; visiting the iniquity of the fathers upon the sons, and upon the sons of sons, upon the thirds and upon the fourths.

8. And Moses hastened, and bended himself to the earth, and adored;

9. And said, If I pray I have found grace in Thine eyes, O LORD, let the LORD go I pray in the midst of us, because the people they are hard of neck; and be propitious to our iniquity, and to our sin, and make us Thine inheritance.

10. And He said, behold I establish a covenant, before all thy people I will do wonderful things, which have not been created in all the earth, and in all nations, and all the people shall see, in the midst of whom thou art, the work of JEHOVAH, that this is the wonderful thing which I do with thee.

11. Keep to thyself that which I command thee to-day, behold I drive out from thy faces the Amorite, and the Canaanite, and the Hittite, and the Perizite, and the Hivite, and the Jebusite.

12. Take heed to thyself, lest peradventure thou establish a covenant with the inhabitant of the land, upon which thou comest, lest peradventure it become a snare in the midst of thee.

13. Wherefore their altars ye shall overturn, and their statues ye shall break, and his groves ye shall cut off.

14. Wherefore thou shalt not bow thyself to another god, for JEHOVAH His name is zealous, a zealous God is He.

15. Lest peradventure thou establish a covenant with the

inhabitant of the land, and they commit whoredom after their gods, and sacrifice to their gods, and he call thee, and thou eatest of his sacrifice.

16. And thou takest of his daughters for thy sons, and his daughters commit whoredom after their gods, and make thy sons to commit whoredom after their gods.

17. Gods of what is molten thou shalt not make to thyself.

18. The feast of unleavened things thou shalt keep; seven days thou shalt eat unleavened things, which I commanded thee, at the stated time of the month Abib, because in the month Abib thou wentest forth out of Egypt.

19. Every opening of the womb is for Me, out of all thy cattle thou shalt give a male, the opening of an ox and of cattle.

20. And the opening of an ass thou shalt redeem in cattle, and if thou shalt not redeem, thou shalt neck it. Every first-begotten of thy sons thou shalt redeem: and My faces shall not be seen empty.

21. Six days thou shalt work, and in the seventh day thou shalt rest, in plowing and in reaping thou shalt rest.

22. And the feast of weeks thou shalt make to thyself of the first-fruits of the harvest of wheat, and the feast of gathering of the revolution of the year.

23. Three times in the year shall every male of thine be seen at the faces of the LORD JEHOVAH GOD of Israel.

24. Because I drive out nations from thy faces, and I will make thy border to be dilated, and there shall not any one covet thy land in thy going up to see the faces of JEHOVAH thy God three times in the year.

25. Thou shalt not slay upon what is leavened the blood of My sacrifice, and the sacrifice of the feast of the passover shall not remain all night to the morning.

26. The first-fruit of the first things of thy ground thou shalt bring into the house of JEHOVAH thy GOD. Thou shalt not seethe a kid in the milk of its mother.

27. And JEHOVAH said to Moses, write for thyself those words, because on the mouth of those words I establish with thee a covenant, and with Israel.

28. And he was there with JEHOVAH forty days and forty nights, he did not eat bread, and he did not drink water; and he wrote on the tables the words of the covenant, ten words.

29. And it came to pass as Moses descended from Mount Sinai, and the two tables of the testimony were in the hand of Moses in his descending from the mountain, and Moses knew not that the skin of his faces shone in his speaking with Him.

30. And Aaron and all the sons of Israel saw Moses, and behold the skin of his faces shone, and they were afraid of approaching to him.

31. And Moses called to them, and there returned to him

Aaron and all the princes in the assembly, and Moses spake to them.

32. And afterwards came near all the sons of Israel, and he commanded them all things which JEHOVAH spake with him in Mount Sinai.

33. And Moses left off speaking with them, and gave a vail over his faces.

34. And in Moses entering-in before JEHOVAH to speak with Him, he removed the vail even to his going out; and he went out and spake to the sons of Israel that which was commanded.

35. And the sons of Israel saw the faces of Moses, that the skin of the faces of Moses shone, and Moses drew back the vail over his faces even to his entering-in to speak with Him.

THE CONTENTS.

10,598. THE subject treated of in this chapter in the internal sense is the church about to be established with the Israelitish nation; but whereas that nation was of such a quality that they could not receive the Divine from within, they were received that the representative of a church, and not a church, might be amongst them; which subject is treated of from verses 1 to 9.

10,599. The subject afterwards treated of in the internal sense is the principal things of the church, which were altogether to be observed that they might represent a church, from verses 10 to 28.

10,600. The subject lastly treated of is the transparency of the Divine Internal of the Word, of the church, and of worship by [or through] their external, but not before that nation. This is signified by the shining of the skin of the face of Moses, and the interposition of a vail when he spake with the people, treated of from verse 29 to the end.

THE INTERNAL SENSE.

10,601. VERSES 1 to 9. *And Jehovah said to Moses, hew for thyself two tables of stones according to the former, and I will write upon the tables the words which were on the former tables, which thou hast broken. And be prepared for the morning, and thou shalt ascend in the morning to Mount Sinai, and shall stand for Me there on the head of the mountain. And there shall not any one ascend with thee, and also there shall not any one be seen in the whole mountain; also the flock and the herd shall not feed over against this mountain. And he hewed two tables of stones according to the former, and Moses rose in the morning early, and ascended to Mount Sinai, as Jehovah commanded him, and took in his hand the two tables of stones. And Jehovah descended in a cloud, and stood with him there, and called on the name of Jehovah. And Jehovah passed upon his faces, and invoked, Jehovah, Jehovah, God merciful and gracious, long-suffering to angers, and great in goodness and truth; keeping goodness to thousands, bearing iniquity, and prevarication, and sin, and absolving absolveth not; visiting the iniquity of the fathers upon the sons and sons of sons, upon the thirds and upon the fourths. And Moses hastened, and bended himself to the earth, and adored. And said, if, I pray, I have found favor* [*or grace*] *in Thine eyes, O Lord, let the Lord go I pray in the midst of us, because the people they are hard of neck, and be propitious to our iniquity and to our sin; and make us thine inheritance.* And Jehovah said to Moses, signifies what was concluded concerning the Israelitish nation. Hew for thyself two tables of stones according to the former, signifies the external of the Word, of the church, and of worship, such as it was for the sake of that nation. And I will write on the tables the words which were on the former tables, which thou hast broken, signifies their interior Divine celestial and spiritual things also in those externals. And be prepared for the morning, and thou shalt ascend to Mount Sinai, signifies a new rising of the revelation of Divine Truth. And thou shalt stand for Me there on the head of the mountain, signifies from the inmost heaven where the Divine Love is. And there shall not any one ascend with thee, signifies that the Israelitish nation cannot be in Divine Truth. And also there shall not any one be seen in the whole mountain, signifies that they are altogether removed from it, thus out of it. Also the flock and the herd shall not feed over against this mountain, signifies that neither could they be instructed concerning the interior and exterior good of the church, of worship, and of the Word. And he hewed two tables of stones according to the former, signifies the external of the Word, of the church, and of worship, such as was for the sake of the Israelitish nation. And Moses rose in the morning early, and ascended to Mount Sinai, signifies a new rising of the revelation of the Divine Truth. As Jehovah commanded him, signifies that it was done because they were urgent. And he took in his hand the two tables, signifies the external of the Word, of the church, and of worship, such as was for the sake of the Israelitish nation. And Jehovah descended in a cloud, and stood with him there, signifies the external of the Word in which is the Divine. And called on the name of Jehovah, signifies the worship of the Lord from the truths and goods of faith and love. And Jehovah passed upon His faces, signifies internal Divine things in external.

And invoked, Jehovah, Jehovah, God merciful and gracious, signifies the Divine itself, the Divine Human and the Divine Proceeding, from whom is all good. Long suffering to angers, signifies the Divine clemency. And great in goodness and truth, signifies that He is good itself and truth itself. Keeping goodness to thousands, signifies to eternity. Bearing iniquity, prevarication, and sin, signifies the removal of evil and its false that it does not appear. And absolving absolveth not, signifies endurance even to consummation. Visiting the iniquity of the fathers upon the sons and upon the sons of sons, signifies the rejection and damnation of evils and the falses thence derived in a long series. On the thirds and on the fourths, signifies of falses and the evils thence derived. And Moses hastened, and bended himself to the earth, and adored, signifies reception on the occasion from influx into the external, and worship grounded in humiliation. And said, if, I pray, I have found favor in Thine eyes, O Lord, signifies because such an external was received. Let the Lord, I pray, go in the midst of us, signifies that the Divine may be within in it. Because the people they are hard of neck, signifies although the Israelitish nation does not receive the Divine from within. And be propitious to our iniquity, and to our sin, signifies that their interiors may be removed which abound with falses and evils. And make us Thine inheritance, signifies that still the church may be there.

10,602. "And Jehovah said to Moses"—that hereby is signified what was concluded concerning the Israelitish nation, appears from the signification of saying, when from Jehovah to Moses, as denoting a reply, but in this case what is concluded, since said involves the things which follow, because those are the things which He said, or which are said; here therefore by said is signified what was concluded concerning the Israelitish nation, which was treated of in the two preceding chapters; it was concluded, that a church indeed might be instituted amongst them, and the Word might be written amongst them, but that they were only in things external, and not at all in what is internal. To be in things external and not in what is internal, is to worship external things as holy, without acknowledgment of the Lord, and without love to God for the sake of God, but for the sake of self, which is to love self and not God; yea it is to avert themselves from God, and not to convert themselves to God; but whereas they could be in a holy external for the sake of themselves, and this could be miraculously converted into a holy external for the sake of God by the spirits attendant upon them, and be received from these by the angels, and thus be elevated into a holy internal, therefore that nation was still received, on which subject see n. 10,500,

10,570. This conclusion is what is contained in this chapter, thus what is signified by Jehovah said to Moses.

10,603. "Hew for thyself two tables of stones according to the former"—that hereby is signified the external of the Word, of the church, and of worship, such as it was for the sake of that nation, appears from the signification of tables of stones, as denoting the external of the Word, see n. 10,453, 10,461. The external of the Word is the sense of its letter; the reason why it is also the external of the church and of worship, is, because the church is from the Word, and also worship, for all the truth which is of faith, and the good which is of love, which constitute the church, and also worship, must be from the Word; hence, inasmuch as in the Word there is an external and an internal, there is also an external and an internal in the church and in worship; and from the signification of hewing them, when by Moses, as denoting to make such an external for the sake of that nation, of which we shall speak presently; and from the signification of according to the former, as denoting in imitation, for the former were made by Jehovah; that the former, which were made by Jehovah, were broken by Moses, when he saw the worship of the golden calf instead of Jehovah by that nation, was of providence; inasmuch as the external of the Word, which is signified by the two tables of stones, could not be written such with that nation, which in heart was merely idolatrous; hence it is, that the former tables were broken, and it was now said to Moses, that he should hew others in imitation of the former. It is said in imitation, because the internal sense remained and the external sense was changed; the internal sense is signified by Jehovah writing on these tables the same words which were on the former. That this subject may be rendered more evident, it is allowed here to explain in what manner the external sense or sense of the letter was changed for the sake of that nation. For the sake of that nation altars, burnt-offerings, sacrifices, meat-offerings, and libations, were commanded, and on this account, both in the historical and prophetical Word, those things are mentioned as the most holy things of worship, when yet they were allowed of, because they were first instituted by Eber, and were altogether unknown in the ancient representative church, on which subject, see n. 1128, 2180, 2818. For the sake of that nation also it came to pass, that Divine worship was performed in Jerusalem alone, and that on this account that city was esteemed holy, and was also called holy, both in the historical and prophetical Word; the reason was, because that nation was in heart idolatrous, and therefore unless they had all met together at that city on each festival, every one in his own place would have worshiped some god of the gentiles, or a graven and molten thing. For the sake of that nation also it was forbidden to celebrate holy worship on mountains and in groves, as the ancients, the reason of which prohibition was, lest they should set idols there, and should worship the very trees. For the sake of that nation also it was permitted to marry several wives, which was a thing altogether unknown in ancient times, and likewise to put away their wives for various causes; hence laws were enacted concerning such marriages and divorces, which otherwise would not have entered the external of the Word, on which account this external is called by the Lord [the external] of Moses, and said to be granted for the hardness of their heart, Matt. xix. 8. For the sake of that nation mention is so often made of Jacob, and likewise of the twelve sons of Israel, as being the only elect and heirs, as in the Apocalypse vii. 4 to 8, and in other places, although they were such as they are described in the song of Moses, Deut. xxxii. 15 to 43, and also in the prophets throughout, and by the Lord Himself. Besides other things, which form the external of the Word for the sake of that nation. This external is what is signified by the two tables hewed by Moses. That still in that external there is a Divine internal not changed, is signified by Jehovah writing on these tables the same words which were on the former tables.

10,604. "And I will write on the tables the words which were on the former tables, which thou hast broken"—that hereby are signified their interior Divine celestial and spiritual things also in those externals, appears from the signification of these tables, as denoting the externals of the Word, of the church, and of worship, see above, n. 10,603; and from the signification of the words which Jehovah wrote upon them, as denoting interior Divine things, thus the things which are of the internal sense, see n. 10,413, 10,461; which things, since they appear in heaven before the angels, and in the light there, are called celestial and spiritual things; the celestial things are those which are of love, and the spiritual things those which are of faith derived from love. From which considerations it is evident, that by I will write on the tables the words which were on the former tables which thou hast broken, is signified that the interior Divine celestial and spiritual things of the Word, ot the church, and of worship, are also in these externals. How the case herein is, may be seen in the article immediately preceding. Inasmuch as at this day it is altogether unknown that in the Word there is an internal sense, yea, what the internal sense of the Word is, it may be expedient to say a few words further concerning it. The ideas of the thought of angels are not natural, such as are the ideas of the thought of men, but they are spiritual; nevertheless the quality of their spiritual ideas can hardly be comprehended by man, except by interior thought and reflection on the first rudiments of their thoughts, which, that they are without expressions of speech, is known from this circumstance, that they are such that man can in a moment comprehend more things than he is able to express by speech in any given time; these ideas of thought appertain to his spirit; but the ideas of thought which man comprehends, and which fall into expressions, are natural: and by the learned are called material; whereas the former or interior ideas are called spiritual, and by the learned immaterial; into these ideas man comes after death, when he becomes a spirit, and by these ideas he consociates in discourse with other spirits. There is a correspondence between these ideas and the former, and by correspondence the former are turned into these, or spiritual ideas into natural, when man speaks. This is not known to man, because he does not reflect upon it, and no others are capable of reflecting upon it, but those who think interiorly, that is, who think in their spirit abstractedly from the body; sensual men are utterly unable to do this. Now since there is correspondence between spiritual thought and natural, and since the angels are in spiritual thought, hence the angels perceive spiritually what man perceives naturally, and this in an instant without any reflection on the difference; this is effected principally when man reads the Word, or when he thinks from the Word, for the Word is so written, that there is correspondence in all and singular things. As for example, when man reads these words of the Lord in Matthew, "*After the affliction of those days the sun shall be obscured, and the moon shall not give her light, and the stars shall fall from heaven, and the virtues of the heavens shall be moved; then shall appear the sign of the Son of Man, and then shall all the tribes of the earth mourn; and they shall see the Son of Man coming in the clouds of heaven with virtue and glory,*" xxiv. 29, 30. These words the angels perceive altogether otherwise than man; by the sun which shall be obscured they do not perceive the sun, but love to the Lord; by the moon they do not perceive the moon, but faith in the Lord; nor by stars, stars, but the knowledges of good and truth; by the Son of Man, they perceive the Lord as to Divine Truth; by the tribes of the earth, all the truths of the church; by the clouds of heaven, they perceive the Word in the sense of the letter; and by virtue and glory, the Word in the internal sense. Into this understanding of those words the angels come in an instant from correspondence, when man reads them; nor do they know that man thinks of the sun, of the moon, of the stars, of the clouds of heaven, &c. the reason is, because the angels are in a spiritual idea, and a spiritual idea is such, that the things which are of nature are turned into things of heavenly light, which is the Divine Truth from the Lord. Another reason why the angels so perceive the Word, when man reads it, is, because angels are attendant on men, and dwell in their affections; and because man as to his spirit is in society with spirits, and as to interior thought, which is spiritual, with the angels of heaven. Hence also man has the faculty of thinking. These observations are intended to show what the internal sense of the Word is, or what the interior things of the Word, of the church, and of worship are, which are called celestial and spiritual things.

10,605. "And be prepared for the morning, and thou shalt come up to Mount Sinai"—that hereby is signified a new rising of the revelation of Divine Truth, appears from the signification of morning, as denoting a rising state, or a rising, in this case a new rising, of which we shall speak presently; and from the signification of Mount Sinai, as denoting heaven whence comes the Divine Truth, thus whence comes revelation, see n. 8805, 8931, 9420. The reason why morning denotes a rising state or rising, is, because all times signify states, inasmuch as in heaven time is not thought of, but only changes of state as to affections, and the thoughts thence derived; and because changes of state there are as the times of the day, which are morning, mid-day, evening and night, and morning is that from which they commence. It may seem strange that in heaven there are not times, when yet the inhabitants live there one amongst another like men in the world, yet with a difference as to intelligence, wisdom and happiness; but the reason is, because the light there which is from the sun, which is the Lord, does not undergo diurnal vicissitudes like light from the sun in the world, but varies according to states of love and faith with the angels, which states undergo vicissitudes like states of heat, of light, and of shade, every day in the earth. The reason of this is, because the light from the sun there, which [sun] is the Lord, is Divine Truth, and the heat from that sun is love, with which the angels are affected as men are with the state of light and heat in the world. That light in heaven is from the Lord, as a sun there, see the passages cited, n. 9548, 9684. That that light is Divine Truth, from which angels and men derive intelligence and wisdom, see the passages cited, n. 9548, 9684, 9571, 10,569. That times signify states, see the passages cited, n. 10,133. That in heaven states vary like the times of the day and the year in the world, n. 5962, 8426. That morning is the beginning of those states, thus a new rising, n. 8427, 10,114. That in heaven there is a state of evening and twilight, but not a state of night, n. 6110.

10,606. "And thou shalt stand for Me there on the head of the mountain"—that hereby is signified from the inmost heaven where the Divine Love is, appears from the signification of Mount Sinai, as denoting heaven, whence comes revelation, see n. 8805, 8931, 9420; and from the signification of its head or top, as denoting the inmost heaven, see n. 9422, 9434. The reason why it denotes where the Divine Love is, is because in the inmost heaven celestial love reigns, which is love to the Lord from the Lord; but in the inferior heavens, spiritual love reigns, which is charity towards the neighbor, see n. 10,438. Hence it is evident that by be prepared for the morning, and thou shalt come up to Mount Sinai, and shalt stand for Me there on the head of the mountain, is signified a new rising of the revelation of Divine Truth from the inmost heaven where the Divine Love is, thus from the Divine Love; hence also the Word descends, which is Divine Revelation.

10,607. "And there shall not any one ascend with thee"—that hereby is signified that the Israelitish nation could not be in Divine Truth, appears from the signification of not ascending, in this case into Mount Sinai with Moses, as denoting not into heaven whence the revelation of Divine Truth is, thus not to be able to be in Divine Truth, for by Mount Sinai is signified heaven, whence comes the revelation of Divine Truth, see n. 8805, 8931, 9420, 10,605; and by Moses is represented the external of the church, of worship, and of the Word, which receives Divine Truth. That the Israelitish nation is meant, is evident, for it is said concerning it, that there shall not any one ascend with thee, and that neither shall any one be seen in the whole mountain. That Moses here represents the external of the Word, of the church, and of worship, which receives Divine Truth, is manifest from all the things contained in this chapter; as that Moses ascended into Mount Sinai, and stood there in its head; and that the people was to be removed thence; in what follows also Jehovah speaks to Moses, as to him, and not to the people, as in verse 10, "And the people shall see, *in the midst of whom thou art*, that this is a wonderful thing which I do *with thee*;" and in verse 11, "Keep *to thyself* that which I command *thee* to-day; behold I drive out *from thy faces*;" verse 12, "*Take heed to thyself*, lest peradventure *thou establish* a covenant with the inhabitant of the earth, upon which *thou comest*;" verse 14, "*Thou shalt not bow thyself* to another god;" verse 15, "Lest peradventure *thou establish* a covenant, and *he call thee*, *and thou eat* of his sacrifice;" verse 16, "*Thou shalt not take* of his daughters for *thy sons*," and so forth. And afterwards that the skin of the face of Moses shone, and that the people were afraid to come to him; and that on this account he put a vail on his face when he spake with the people. From which considerations it is evident, that Moses in this chapter represents the external of the Word, of the church, and of worship, which receives Divine Truth, thus by [or through] which internal Divine Truth is translucent. That Moses represents that external, and not the internal, is also evident from all the things in this chapter; as that Jehovah descended in a cloud, and stood with him; for by a cloud is signified the external of the Word; and then that Jehovah commanded the externals of the church and of worship, which were to be observed by him, and not the internals. The like external was represented by Moses in the preceding chapter, as is evident from verses 7 to 11, and from verses 17 to 23, see n. 10,563, 10,571; but the external, which did not receive the internal, appertained to the Israelitish nation.

10,608. "And also there shall not any one be seen in the whole mountain"—that hereby is signified that they are altogether removed from it, thus out of it, appears from the signification of mountain, in this case the mountain of Horeb, as denoting heaven in the whole complex, thus also Divine Truth; for whether we speak of heaven or Divine Truth, it is the same thing, since the angels, of whom heaven consists, are receptions of Divine Truth; the whole extent of that mountain was called Horeb, and the more elevated part in the midst of it was Mount Sinai, hence by Horeb is signified heaven, or what is the same thing, Divine Truth in the whole complex; its internal by Mount Sinai, and its external by the mountainous country round about; hence it is that by Horeb, when the mountainous country round about is also meant, is signified what is external, see n. 10,543. The Israelitish nation, inasmuch as they were in an external which did not receive the internal, thus in an external separate from the internal, or what is the same thing, out of that principle in which the internal was, were on that account commanded not to be seen any of them in the whole mountain. The like is signified by that nation standing at the door of the tent in which Moses was, and bowing themselves to it, chap. the foregoing, verses 8, 9, 10; see n. 10,545 to 10,555. It may be expedient here briefly to say from what ground it is that Mount Horeb and Sinai signify heaven and the Divine Truth. It is believed in the world that angels are in a region above that of the atmosphere, and subsist there as aerial beings, and that they have no plane to stand upon. The reason why such an opinion prevails in the minds of the generality of mankind, is, because they do not comprehend that angels and spirits are in a like form with men on earth; thus that they have faces, that they have arms and hands, that they have feet, in a word that they have body; and still less that they have habitations or abodes; when yet angels and spirits dwell amongst one another altogether like men here below, the celestial angels on mountains, and the spiritual angels on rocks, and they who are not yet made angels, on plains between the mountains and rocks; but the infernal spirits beneath the mountains and rocks. These observations are made, to the intent that it may be known from what ground it is, that mountains in the Word signify heaven, and specifically

Mount Horeb and Mount Sinai. The interior angels also dwell higher upon the mountains, and the higher they dwell, so much the more interior and perfect they are. Hence it is evident why Jehovah descended on the top of Mount Sinai, when the law was promulgated, and why Moses was ordered to stand with Him on the head of the mountain. Mountains in the earths are not heaven, but represent the mountains on which the angels in heaven dwell.

10,609. "Also the flock and the herd shall not feed over against this mountain"—that hereby is signified that neither could they be instructed concerning the interior and exterior good of the church, of worship, and of the Word, appears from the signification of the flock, as denoting interior good, and from the signification of the herd, as denoting exterior good, see n. 5913, 6048, 8937; and from the signification of feeding, as denoting to be instructed, see n. 5201, 6277; and from the signification of mountain, in this case Mount Horeb, as denoting the external of the church, of worship, and of the Word, see n. 10,543. Hence it is evident, that by those words is signified, that neither could that nation be instructed concerning the interior and exterior good of the church, of worship, and of the Word, since they were out of that external, and not in any manner within. The reason why they could not be instructed concerning that good, was, because they were in the loves of self and of the world, and they who are in those loves, cannot in any wise know what celestial and spiritual good is, thus what the good of the church is, for this good is spiritual and celestial, because Divine; if that good was described to them, they would not at all comprehend it, inasmuch as the internal, where the preception of that good is, is closed with them. That such things are signified by the flock and herd not feeding over against the mountain, may seem strange to those, who keep the mind fixed in the historical sense of the Word only, and do not think further, that any thing is signified respecting the nation itself; nor do they know [that any thing is signified], who are not acquainted with the internal sense of the Word, in which sense flock and herd do not signify flock and herd, but interior and exterior good appertaining to man; for what has the Word, which is Divine, in common with flock and herd, or with beast, which only relates to men, their worship, love, and faith, thus to such things as constitute the church; in this respect the Word is Divine. That flock and herd signify such things, and not flock and herd, is manifest from the passages in the Word where they are named, as in David, "Thou hast made Him to have dominion over the works of Thy hands, and hast put all things under his feet, *all flocks and herds*, and also the *beasts of the fields*," Psalm viii. 6, 7. The subject here treated of is the

Lord and His power over all things in heaven and in earth; and by flocks and herds are signified the interior and exterior goods appertaining to men, and by beasts, the affections appertaining to them. According to any other sense of the words, of what consequence would it be to describe the power of the Lord, which is Divine, over flocks, herds, and beasts? That beasts denote the affections appertaining to man, see the passages cited, n. 9280. And in Joel, "The day of Jehovah is nigh, as a devastation from Schaddai it shall come; *the beast sighs, the companies of the herd are perplexed*, because they have no pasture, also *the companies of the flock are desolate*," i. 18. In this passage also beasts denote the affections appertaining to man, companies of the herd and of the flock denote interior and exterior goods; for the subject there treated of is the coming of the Lord, which is signified by the day of Jehovah; and concerning the church at that time that it was vastated, that is, that there was no longer at that time any good of love, or good of faith, these goods being the things which are signified by beasts, herds, and flocks; according to any other meaning of the words, what sense could there be in the beasts sighing, the companies of the herd being perplexed, and the companies of the flock being desolate, for what has this to do with the church? by the pasture which at that time they had not, is signified that there is no truth by which they may be instructed. And in Jeremiah, "Shame hath devoured the labor of our fathers from our childhood, *their flocks and their herds*, and their sons and their daughters," iii. 24. In this passage also by flocks and herds are signified the goods of the church, which are the goods of love and faith, interior and exterior. And in Isaiah, "I will bring forth a seed out of Jacob, and out of Judah an inheritor of My mountains, then Sharon shall be *for the habitation of a flock*, and the valley of Achor *for the herd to lie down in*, for My people who have sought Me," lxv. 10. By Jacob and Judah in this passage is not meant the people of Jacob and of Judah, but the celestial church external and internal, by Jacob the external, by Judah the internal; the internal good of that church by the habitation of a flock, and the external by a place for the herd to lie down in; Sharon is the internal principle where that good is, and the valley of Achor is the external; that Sharon denotes the internal principle of the celestial church, is manifest from the passages where Sharon is mentioned, as in Isaiah, chap. xxxiii. 9, and chap. xxxv. 2; and that the valley of Achor denotes the external of that church, see Hosea, chap. ii. 15. And in Hosea, "Israel, Ephraim, and Judah, *with their flocks and with their herds*, shall go to seek Jehovah and shall not find," v. 6. In this passage also flocks and herds signify the interiors and exteriors appertaining to those who are meant by Israel, Ephraim, and Judah; otherwise to what purpose would it be that they should go with flocks and herds to seek Jehovah.

10,611. "And Moses arose in the morning early, and went up to Mount Sinai"—that hereby is signified a new rising of the revelation of Divine Truth, appears from what was shown above, n. 10,605, where like words occur.

10,612. "As Jehovah commanded him"—that hereby is signified that it was so done because they were urgent, appears from the signification of Jehovah commanding, when concerning such an external of the Word, for the sake of the Israelitish nation, which is signified by the two tables of stones hewed by Moses, as denoting that it was so done because they were urgent; in the Word throughout, where the Israelitish nation is treated of, and the representative worship instituted amongst them, it is said that Jehovah commanded, and thereby is not signified what was well-pleasing, but permission that it might so be done because they were urgent; for they were urgent to be introduced into the land of Canaan, and that Jehovah might be with them, consequently that a church might be instituted amongst them; that they were urgent, see n. 10,430, 10,335. To illustrate this by an example; they were to offer on the altars burnt-offerings, sacrifices, meat-offerings, and libations, concerning which several laws were enacted, and concerning which it is also said that Jehovah commanded, when yet those things were not commanded but permitted, as may be manifest from the passages adduced from the Word, n. 2180. In like manner they were allowed to marry several wives and to give a bill of divorce for any cause whatsoever, when yet Jehovah did not command this, although it is so said, but only permitted it on account of the hardness of their hearts, Matt. xix. 7, 8; and so in several other cases.

10,613. "And he took in his hand the two tables"—that hereby is signified the external of the Word, of the church, and of worship, such as it was for the sake of the Israelitish nation, appears from what was shown above, n. 10,603, concerning the signification of the two tables which were hewed by Moses.

10,614. "And Jehovah descended in a cloud, and stood with him there"—that hereby is signified the external of the Word wherein is the Divine, appears from the signification of a cloud, as denoting the sense of the letter of the Word, thus its external, see preface to chap. xviii. Gen. and n. 4060, 4391, 5922, 6343, 6752, 8106, 8781, 9430, 10,574; and from the signification of standing with Moses there, when concerning Jehovah, as denoting the Divine therein. The rea son why Jehovah appeared to Moses in a cloud, is, because by Moses in this chapter is represented the external of the

Word, which receives the internal, see above, n. 10,607; for the Lord appears to every one according to his quality, n. 6832, 8814, 8819, 9434, 10,551. It may be expedient here briefly to say what the external is, which receives the internal, and what the external which does not receive. In the Word there is an external sense, there is an internal sense, and there is an inmost sense. The Word in the external sense is such as it appears in the letter; this sense is natural, because it is accommodated to the apprehension of men, for men think naturally; but the Word in the internal sense is spiritual, which sense is accommodated to the understanding of the angels in the spiritual kingdom of the Lord; for those angels think spiritually; but the Word in the inmost sense is celestial, this sense being accommodated to the perception of the angels in the celestial kingdom of the Lord, for the angels in that kingdom think super-spiritually. Inasmuch as the Word is such, it follows that one is in another in a like order, the inmost in the internal, and the internal in the external; hence the connection of all, and influx according to connection, and hence the subsistence of one from another; from which considerations it is evident, that interior things in order are in what is external, in like manner as what is prior is in what is posterior successively, or as the end is in the cause, and the cause in the effect; or as with man, the will is in the thought, and the thought in the speech. When therefore man is such, that in the externals of the Word, of the church, and of worship, he perceives a holy principle inwardly in himself, there appertains to him an external in which is the internal, for that holy principle is from the internal, because from heaven; this external is what Moses represents. But when man is such, that in the external of the Word, of the church, and of worship, he does not perceive an internal holy principle, then there appertains to him an external separate from the internal; in this external was the Israelitish nation, see n. 10,396.

10,615. "And called on the name of Jehovah"—that hereby is signified the worship of the Lord, from the truths and goods of faith and love, and thus preparation for reception, appears from the signification of calling on the name of Jehovah, as denoting the worship of the Lord from the truths and goods of faith and love, for by calling on is signified worship, see n. 440, 2724; and by the name of Jehovah, every thing in one complex by which the Lord is worshiped, thus every thing of faith and love, n. 2724, 6774, 9310; and that the name of Jehovah is the Lord as to the Divine Human, see n. 2628, 6887; and that Jehovah in the Word is the Lord, see the passages cited, n. 9373. Hence it is evident that by calling on the name of Jehovah, is signified the worship of the Lord from the truths and goods of faith and love; the reason why it also denotes preparation for reception, is, because the subject treated of in what now follows is the Israelitish nation about to be received, for which Moses intercedes.

10,616. "And Jehovah passed upon his faces"—that hereby are signified internal Divine things upon external, appears from the representation of Moses, as denoting the external which receives the internal, see above, n. 10,607, 10,614; hence by Jehovah passing upon his faces is signified the internal Divine upon the external.

10,617. "And invoked Jehovah, Jehovah, God merciful and gracious"—that hereby is signified the Divine Itself, the Divine Human, and the Divine proceeding, from which is all good, appears from the signification of invoking Jehovah, as denoting the worship of the Lord, see n. 440, 2724; and whereas the Divine of the Lord is three-fold, namely, the Divine Itself which is called the Father, the Divine Human which is called the Son, and the Divine Proceeding which is called the Holy Spirit; on this account it is here said Jehovah, Jehovah, God The reason why the Divine Itself which is the Father, and the Divine Human which is the Son is called Jehovah, Jehovah, and the Divine Proceeding is called God, is, because the Lord, as to the Divine Itself and as to the Divine Human, is Divine Good, and as to the Divine Proceeding is Divine Truth; wherefore in the Word, where the Divine Good is treated of, the Lord is called Jehovah, and where the Divine Truth is treated of, He is called God, see n. 2769, 2807, 2822, 3921, 4402, 9167, 10,158; and from the signification of Merciful and Gracious, as denoting that from Him is all good; for by doing mercy is signified to gift with celestial good, and by doing grace [or favor] is signified to gift with spiritual good, see n. 10,577. What celestial good is, and what spiritual good, see also in the same article.

10,618. "Long-suffering to angers"—that hereby is signified the Divine clemency, appears from the signification of long-suffering to angers, when concerning Jehovah, as denoting that he long sustains the evils of man, for long-suffering denotes to sustain and bear for a long time, and angers denote the evils appertaining to man. The reason why angers, when they are predicated of Jehovah, denote the evils appertaining to man, is, because evil is angry, and in no case good, and evil appertains to man, and in no case to the Lord, for the Lord is good itself: nevertheless it is attributed to the Lord, because it so appears to man, when he does not obtain what he desires, and when he is punished on account of evil. Since then long-suffering to angers, when concerning Jehovah, denotes to sustain for a long time the evils appertaining to man, it hence follows that by it is signified the Divine clemency. As to what concerns anger, it is further to be noted, that evil is angry, and in no case good, for to be angry is to will evil to another, which good cannot do, for good consists in willing good to another; all evil has in it enmity, hatred, revenge, and cruelty; in these things and from these evil has its delight; and moreover evil hates good, because good is opposite to its delights, hence when evil cannot hurt good, which it is ever attempting to do, in this case it is first indignant, afterwards it is angry: whether we speak of evil, or of an evil man, it is the same thing, for evil is in man, as in its subjects: and since such evil is against good, therefore such is against the Divine, for all good is the Divine appertaining to man, because it is from the Divine; hence it is that an evil man is always angry against the Divine, although he externally speaks otherwise before men; this speaking otherwise is either from hypocrisy, or from this consideration, that he is willing that the Divine should favor him in all things, by giving whatsoever he desires, that he may also on his own account take vengeance on all against whom he bears hatred; but as soon as he sees that this is not done, and especially if he himself is punished on account of his evil, he is then angry against God, even to deny Him, and also in heart to blaspheme Him: that this is the case, is manifested clearly in the other life, for in that life man acts according to his interiors, and not according to exteriors as in the world; and punishment in that life adheres to its evil, and as it were inheres. See what has been shown above, as that anger is evil, n. 6358, 6359: that anger and evil are attributed to God, when yet they appertain to man, and nothing of evil is from God, see the passages cited, n. 9306, 10,431; and that evil has punishment along with it, n. 1857, 8214, 8223, 8226, 9049.

10,619. "And great in goodness and truth"—that hereby is signified that He is good itself and truth itself, appears from this consideration, that the Divine is infinite, and concerning infinite nothing can be said but that it is It Itself, or It Is, thus good itself, and because it is good itself, it is also truth itself, since all truth is of good; but this Itself is expressed in the sense of the letter by great in goodness and truth, thus finitely on account of the state of finite perception appertaining to man. That the Divine is good itself, is manifest in Matthew, "Jesus said to the young man, *Why callest thou Me good? there is none good but one God,*" xix. 17, by which is meant that it is the Lord who alone is good, thus good itself: and that He is truth itself is manifest in John, "Jesus said, I am the way, and the *truth*, and the life," xiv. 6.

10,620. "Keeping goodness to thousands"—that hereby is signified to eternity, appears from the signification of goodness, when concerning Jehovah, as denoting good itself, as just above, n. 10,619; and from the signification of to thousands, as denoting for ever and to eternity, see n. 2575, 8715.

10,621. "Bearing iniquity, prevarication, and sin"—that hereby is signified the removal of evil and its false that it may not appear, is manifest from the signification of bearing or taking away, as denoting to remove that it may not appear, of which we shall speak presently; and from the signification of iniquity, of prevarication, and of sin, as denoting evils, and because they are evils, they are also their falses, for every evil is conjoined to its false; but what evil is signified by iniquity, what by preva rication, and what by sin, see n. 9156. The reason why bearing and taking away evil denotes to remove it that it may not appear, is, because the evils appertaining to man cannot be taken away, but only be removed so as not to appear, and when they do not appear, it is believed that they are taken away; therefore in the sense of the letter of the Word it is said that they are taken away and altogether rejected; that the evils appertaining to man are not taken away, but only removed so as not to appear, see the passages cited, n. 10,057.

10,622. "And absolving He will not absolve"—that hereby is signified endurance even to consummation, appears from the signification of absolving, as denoting to remit sin, but when it is added [He will not absolve], it denotes to endure [or tolerate]; the reason why it denotes even to consummation, is, because evil is tolerated by the Lord until it is consummated or fulfilled. In the Word throughout mention is made of the consummation of the age, and it is said of evil that it is consummated, or not consummated; and when it is consummated, that then is visitation. Inasmuch as this is signified by the above words, absolving He will not absolve, it may be expedient briefly to say what is meant thereby. In *general* by consummation is meant the end of the church, and the end of the church then is, when there is no longer any charity and any faith, because then the church averts itself altogether from the Lord, and is no longer in any good, but in evil; then is said to be its consummation, and then is effected visitation; when visitation is effected all they are rejected who are in evil, and all are received who are in good. Visitation is effected in the other life, where all are together who have been of the church from its beginning even to its end. The rejection of the evil into hell, and the salvation of the good on the occasion, is what is called the last judgment. Consummation in *particular* is effected with every man nearly in like manner; every one, when he comes into the other life, which is the case immediately after death, is tolerated amongst the good, although he be evil. But in process of time his interiors are opened, and if these be evil, he is then brought by degrees into his own evil, until he becomes his own evil as to will, and the false of his evil as to understanding; when this is effected, evil is said to be consummated with him, and he is then cast into hell; these are the things which are meant by absolving He will not absolve. The like is meant by what Jehovah said to Moses, "Now go lead the people to what

I said to thee; behold, My angel shall go before thee; and *in the day of My visitation I will visit upon them their sin*," Exod. xxxii. 34. That consummation is the end of the church is manifest from the following passages, "*With Israel and with Judah I will not make consummation*, neither rendering will I render thee innocent, because thy breach is desperate, thy wound is incurable, thou hast no medicines of restoration," Jer. xxx. 11, 12, 13; chap. xlvi. 28. Again, "*Thine iniquity is consummated*, O daughter of Zion; *He will visit thine iniquity*, O daughter of Edom, he will manifest thy sins," Lam. iv. 22. And in Daniel, "Seventy weeks are decided upon thy people, *to consummate prevarication*, and to seal up sins, and to expiate iniquity. At length on the bird of abominations shall be desolation, and *even to the consummation*," ix. 24, 27. And in Matthew, "*The harvest is the consummation of the age*, as the tares are gathered together and burned with fire, *so shall it be in the consummation of the age*," xiii. 39, 40. Again, "The disciples said to Jesus, tell us, what is the sign of Thy coming, and of *the consummation of the age*," xxiv. 3. Again, "Jesus said, "Lo! I am with you all days, *even to the consummation of the age*," xxviii. 20.

10,623. "Visiting the iniquity of the fathers on the sons and on the sons of sons"—that hereby is signified the rejection and damnation of evils and of the falses thence derived in a long series, appears from the signification of visiting, as denoting the ejection and damnation of evils, of which we shall speak presently; and from the signification of fathers, as denoting goods, and in the opposite sense evils, see n. 3703, 5902, 6050, 10,490; and from the signification of sons, as denoting truths, and in the opposite sense falses, see n. 1147, 10,490; hence the sons of sons denote falses derived from evils in a long series. By the ejection and damnation of evils and the falses thence derived is meant the ejection and damnation of those who are in evils, and consequent falses, for evils and falses are not given except in subjects, which are men. It is to be noted, that the falses of evil are meant by sons, because the fathers from whom they spring denote evils. What the falses of evil are, and the falses not of evil, see the passages cited, n. 10,109. He who is not acquainted with the internal sense of the Word, may easily be led to believe that Jehovah visits the iniquity of the fathers upon the sons and upon the sons of sons, consequently that the sons are to suffer punishment for the evils of their fathers, but that this is not meant, is very manifest from the Divine law, that fathers are not to die for the sons, nor the sons for the fathers, but every one for his own evil, Deut. xxiv. 16; hence it is evident that those words are to be understood otherwise than according to the letter. That they who are in evils, and thence in falses in a long series, are those who are signified by fathers and their sons and sons of sons, is manifest from the internal sense, in which fathers and sons signify evils and falses. Nothing else is here understood by fathers and by sons in the apprehension of the angels, by whom the Word read by man is also perceived, for in heaven, where the angels are, it is not known what a father is, and what a son, as with men, for no one there acknowledges any one for his father, nor any one for his son, since there are no births there as in the world; therefore when mention is made of father and son in the Word, the angels perceive the terms according to spiritual nativities, which are of good and truth, or of evil and the false, and therefore by fathers they perceive goods or evils, and by sons truths or falses, since good is the father of truth, and evil is the father of the false. The reason why visitation signifies ejection and damnation, is, because it follows the consummation of evils, and precedes damnation itself, which in the Word is meant by the last judgment; for visitation is the exploration of man as to his quality; but this is effected in the other life, in particular with every one who comes thither from the world, and in general with all at the end of the church, as was said just above, n. 10,622. Concerning visitation, see what was said and shown, n. 6588, 6895, 10,509.

10,624. "On the thirds and on the fourths [sons]"—that hereby is signified the damnation of falses, and of the evils thence derived, appears from the signification of sons, as denoting the falses of evil, see above, n. 10,623. The reason why it is said on the thirds and on the fourths, is, because three are predicated of truths or falses, and four of goods or evils; for in the Word all numbers signify things, and some numbers belong to the spiritual class, and some to the celestial class; the numbers three, six and twelve to the spiritual class, and the numbers two, four and eight to the celestial class; the numbers which are of the spiritual class are predicated of truths or falses, and those which are of the celestial class, of goods or evils; by three also is signified all truth in the complex, and by four all good in the complex, hence it is that by sons, thirds and fourths, are signified falses and the evils thence derived; but this sense of those words is the celestial sense, because it arises from this consideration, that they are predicated of those things. What evils and the falses thence derived are, and what falses and the evils thence derived are, see the passages cited, n. 10,109. It may be expedient here also to say something concerning evils and the falses thence derived, and concerning falses and the evils thence derived. Evils are the sources of all falses, inasmuch as falses are what confirm evils, and they act in unity with man like will and understanding, for what man wills to do, this also he wills to understand; for by the understanding he forms his own evil before himself in thought and before others in speech; hence it is evident what evil is and the false thence derived, or what is the false of evil. But the evil of the false is when man has confirmed evil with himself, and has concluded that it is not evil, and hence does it, in this case he does evil from what is false; as he who has confirmed with himself that adulteries are not evils, and hence does them, he is in the evil of what is false, because he does them from a false principle. The evils of what is false are especially given in corrupt religious principles, for from falses of doctrine a man persuades himself that a thing is good, which yet is evil, and sometimes that a thing is evil which yet is good.

10,625. "And Moses hastened, and bended himself to the earth, and adored"—that hereby is signified in this case reception from influx into the external, and worship from humiliation, appears from the signification of hastening, as denoting affection, see n. 7695, 7866, in this case, reception by influx, because all influx from the Divine is into the affection of man, and also reception by man therein; and from the representation of Moses, as denoting the external of the church, of worship, and of the Word, which receives the internal, see n. 10,607, 10,614; and from the signification of bending himself, as denoting exterior humiliation, see n. 5680, 7068; and from the signification of adoring, as denoting worship.

10,626. "And said, if I pray I have found favor in Thine eyes, O Lord"—that hereby is signified because such an external was received, appears from the representation of Moses, as denoting an external which receives the internal, see n. 10,607, 10,614; and from the signification of finding favor in the eyes of Jehovah, when concerning Moses, as denoting that he was received because of such a quality, thus that that external was received, see n. 10,563.

10,627. "Let the Lord go I pray in the midst of us"—that hereby is signified that the Divine may be within in it, appears from the signification of going, as denoting to live, see n. 3335, 4882, 5493, 5606, 8417, 8420; and when concerning the Lord, as denoting to give life, and to be present; and from the signification of in the midst, as denoting inwardly therein, see n. 1074, 5897, 6068, 6084, 6103, 9164. The reason why by Jehovah going in the midst of us is signified that the Divine may be within in the external, is, because by Moses is represented the external of the Word, of the church, and of worship, which receives the internal, and in their external there must be an internal, which is Divine; and a Divine internal is then in the external, when all and singular things have an internal sense, which is for the angels of all the heavens; to effect this, the external sense, which is the sense of the letter, must consist of mere correspondences; and it then consists in mere correspondences, when all the expressions, and all the series of the expressions, in the internal sense, signify things spiritual and celestial; these are internal Divine things in what is external.

10,628. "Because this people is hard of neck"—that hereby is signified although the Israelitish nation does not receive the Divine from within, appears from the signification of a people hard of neck, as denoting which does not receive influx from the Divine, see n. 10,429, thus not the Divine from within, for the Divine flows in from within with man. How the case herein is, is manifest from what was above shown concerning the Israelitish nation, namely, that they were in the external ot worship, of the church, and of the Word, and not at all in the internal, consequently out of the external, and not within. That it denotes to be out of the external and not within, see n. 10,551, 10,608.

10,629. "And be propitious to our iniquity, and to our sin"—that hereby is signified that their interiors may be removed which abound in falses and evils, appears from the signification of being propitious to iniquity and to sin, when concerning the external of worship, of the church, and of the Word, in which the people was, as denoting that their interiors may be removed because they abound in falses and evils. That these things are signified by those words, follows from the series of things in the internal sense, in which sense the church is treated of about to be instituted with that people; and the church cannot be instituted with any people, unless their interiors be open, by which there may be communication with heaven; and the interiors are not open, except with those who are in truths of faith grounded in good of life from the Lord; but with this people the interiors could not be opened, because by the worship of Jehovah they thought of nothing else than obtaining eminence and opulence over others, thus they had in mind nothing else but self and the world; and these are the things which close the interiors towards heaven, and open them towards hell. That these were the interior principles of that nation, which were closed when they were in worship, see n. 10,575. These therefore are the things which are signified.

10,630. "And make us Thine inheritance"—that hereby is signified that still the church may be there, appears from the signification of the inheritance of Jehovah, as denoting the reception of the life of heaven by good from the Lord, see n. 9338; thus also denoting to be made a church, for to be made a church is to receive the life of heaven by the good of love and faith from the Lord.

10,631. Verses 10, 11. *And He said, Behold I establish a covenant, before all thy people I will do wonderful things, which have not been created in all the earth, and in all nations, and all the people shall see in the midst of whom thou art, the work of Jehovah, that this is the wonderful thing which I do with thee.*

Keep to thyself that which I command thee to-day; behold I drive out from thy faces the Amorite, and the Canaanite, and the Hittite, and the Perizite, and the Hivite, and the Jebusite. And He said, Behold I establish a covenant, signifies the primary things whereby there is conjunction of the Lord with the human race by the Word. Before all thy people I will do wonderful things, signifies the Word that it is Divine in all and singular things for the church. Which have not been created in all the earth, and in all nations, signifies that such a Divine never was in the world where the church is and where the church is not. And all the people shall see, in the midst of whom thou art, the work of Jehovah, signifies that all, by whom the Word is received, will acknowledge the Divine therein. That this is the wonderful thing which I do with thee, signifies the quality of the Word in all and singular things. Keep to thyself that which I command thee to-day, signifies if they do these primary things which are of the eternal truth. Behold I expel from thy faces the Amorite, and the Canaanite, and the Hittite, and the Perizite, and the Hivite, and the Jebusite, signifies the removal in such case of evils and of the falses thence derived.

10,632. "And He said, Behold I establish a covenant"—that hereby are signified the primary things whereby there is conjunction of the Lord with the human race by the Word, appears from the signification of a covenant, as denoting conjunction, see n. 665, 666, 1023, 1038, 1864, 1996, 2003, 2021, 6804, 8767, 8778; in this case the conjunction of Jehovah, that is, of the Lord, with the human race by the Word, for this conjunction is treated of in what now follows. That this is the case is also manifest from the series of things in the internal sense. The subject treated of, in what goes before, was concerning the law which was enacted and promulgated from Mount Sinai, by which law in an extended sense is signified the Word, n. 6752, 7462; that law was also the beginning of the Word, for the Word was afterwards promulgated, first by Moses, then by the rest. The subject next treated of was the Israelitish nation, as not being of such a quality that the Word could be written amongst them, such as it otherwise might have been written, since a church could not be instituted amongst them, and where the church is there is the Word, on which subjects see what has been said and shown in chapters xxxii. xxxiii. and hitherto in this chapter; but whereas Moses was urgent for the people, that Jehovah might be in the midst of them, and that they might be accepted as an inheritance, and thus introduced into the land of Canaan, by all which things in the internal sense is signified that the church was to be instituted amongst that people, and thus that the Word was to be written there, and whereas it was now received by reason that Moses was urgent, therefore the subject now treated of is the primary precepts, which were altogether to be observed for the effecting of that purpose; which primary precepts were, that the Lord alone is to be worshiped, and no other, and that it is to be acknowledged that all good and truth is from Him, besides several other things treated of in what presently follows. It is said, that they are treated of in what presently follows, but it is to be noted, that those precepts are contained in the internal sense; but in the external sense, which is the sense of the letter, are contained such things as represent those precepts, thus which signify them, as will be manifest from the explication of what follows. It is said that by this covenant, which Jehovah established with Moses, is signified the conjunction of the Lord with the human race by the Word, wherefore it may be expedient here to say how the case is with that conjunction. In the most ancient times the Word was not, but immediate revelation before the man of the church, and by it conjunction; for when there is immediate revelation, then there is conjunction of heaven with man; the conjunction of heaven with man is the conjunction of the Lord with him, since the Divine of the Lord with the angels constitutes heaven; when this immediate revelation ceased, as was the case when man turned away from the good in which he had been principled, then another revelation succeeded, which was by representatives, whereby the man of the church at that time knew what was true and good, hence that church was called a representative church; in that church also was the Word, but which only served that church: but when this church also was vastated, as was the case in consequence of their beginning to worship idolatrously those representatives, by which the church at that time had conjunction with heaven, and in several lands to turn them into magic, it was then provided by the Lord that the Word should be written, which was Divine in all and singular things, even as to every smallest expression, and which consisted of mere correspondences, and was thereby accommodated to the perception of the angels in all the heavens, and at the same time to men; to the intent that by it there might be conjunction of the Lord with the human race; for without conjunction by such a Word, heaven would have altogether receded from man, and man would thereby have perished. The subject therefore treated of in what follows is concerning that conjunction by the Word, and the primary precepts are opened which ought to be observed by man, that he may be in that conjunction by the Word. That the most ancient people had immediate revelation, see n. 2895, 3432. Concerning the representative church which afterwards succeeded, and concerning its Word, see n. 2686, 2897, 3432, 10,355: and that conjunction of the Lord with the human race is by the Word, see the passages cited, n. 10,375, and n. 10,452.

10,633. "Before all thy people I will do wonderful things"—that hereby is signified the Word which is Divine in all and singular things for the church, appears from the signification of the people of Moses, as denoting where the church is, inasmuch as the church was instituted amongst them; and from the signification of the wonderful things which Jehovah was about to do, as denoting Divine things in all and singular the things of the Word; for the Word is wonderful in this respect, that it is Divine as to every iota, for every expression corresponds to some spiritual thing which may be said to be stored up in it, inasmuch as its spiritual principle is laid open with the angels, when the Word is read by man. The case herein is this: all and singular the things which are in the natural world, have correspondence with those which are in the spiritual world, and this even to every single expression, and the Word is so written, that the expressions therein, in their series, involve a series of spiritual things, which do not appear to man unless he be acquainted with correspondences; herein lies concealed the Divine in the Word; hence the Word is spiritual, as also it is called. This therefore is what is here meant by a wonderful thing, since the subject treated of is the Word, which was about to be written amongst that people.

10,634. "Which have not been created in all the earth, and in all nations"—that hereby is signified that such a Divine was never in the world where the church is and where the church is not, appears from the signification of wonderful things, as denoting the Divine things of the Word, see just above, n. 10,633; which are said to be created, when they are Divine from inmost principles to outermost, or from first principles to last; and from the signification of in all the earth, as denoting wheresoever the church is; for by earth in the Word is signified the church, see the passages cited, n. 9325; and from the signification of in all nations, as denoting where the church is not; for by nations in the Word are signified those who are out of the church, because not in the light of truth from the Word. It is said that Jehovah is about to do [or make] wonderful things, which have not been *created* in all the earth, because by creation is signified that which is Divine from inmost principles to outermost, or from first principles to last; for every thing, which is from the Divine, commences from Himself, and advances according to order even to the ultimate end, thus through the heavens even into the world, and there rests as in its ultimate, for the ultimate of Divine Order is in the nature of the world; what is of such a quality, this is said to be created. In such an order exists, and in such subsists every thing which is created in the world; and in such an order also is the man of the church, who by truths from the Word is regenerated of the Lord; hence the Lord in the

Word is called Creator, and man who is regenerate is said to be created anew, see n. 10,373, 10,545. In such an order also is the Word, and because it is of such a quality, it is on that account said of its wonderful things that they are created. By those same words, namely, before all thy people I will do wonderful things which have not been created in all the earth and in all nations, in the historical sense is signified that Jehovah was about to do miracles amongst the Israelitish people, which have not been heard in all the earth; but in the internal sense are not meant miracles, but wonderful things, which the Lord was about to do or make by being about to give such a Word, whereby there might be conjunction of heaven with the church, and universally whereby there might be conjunction of the Lord with the human race. That the Word is so wonderful, is not apprehended by those who do not know something concerning the correspondence of natural things with spiritual; and who do not know something concerning the spiritual thought in which the angels are principled; such persons do not know that there is given somewhat within in all the things of the Word, in which is heaven, thus in which is Divine life, when nevertheless all the expressions of the Word by correspondence are perceived spiritually by the angels, when naturally by men. Hence and from no other source the Word is Divine, and so wonderful that nothing is more so.

10,635. " And all the people shall see, in the midst of whom thou art, the work of Jehovah "—that hereby is signified that all, by whom the Word is received, acknowledge the Divine in it, appears from the representation of Moses, as denoting the Word, see the passages cited, n. 9372; hence by the people in the midst of whom he is, is signified the church where the Word is, thus all by whom the Word is received, for others do not acknowledge the Divine in it; and from the signification of seeing the work of Jehovah, as denoting to acknowledge the Divine therein. That this is the case is evident, for all within the church, who are in the good of life, acknowledge the Divine in the Word. The reason is, because a holy principle from heaven flows-in with them whilst they read the Word, although they do not know that it is effected by means of correspondences; what also flows-in according to correspondences, is no otherwise perceived than as a general holy principle, in which the mind is held. It is otherwise with those who are not in the good of life, the internal principle appertaining to them, by [or through] which heaven flows-in, being closed.

10,636. "That this is the wonderful thing which I do with thee "—that hereby is signified the quality of the Word in all and singular things, appears from the representation of Moses, as denoting the Word, see the passages cited, n. 9372; hence by the wonderful things which Jehovah was about to do with him, is signified that the Divine is in all and singular things, as above, n. 10,633.

10,637. "Keep to thyself that which I command thee to-day"—that hereby is signified if they do these primary things which are of the eternal truth, appears from the signification of keeping to thyself, as denoting if they do so who acknowledge the Word, for by Moses is represented the Word, as above; and from the signification of what Jehovah commands to-day, as denoting the primary things which are of the eternal truth; for the things which Jehovah commands are Divine Truths; and by to-day is signified what is eternal, n. 2838, 3998, 4304, 6165, 6984, 9939. Those eternal truths are what are contained in the internal sense in what follows from verse 12 to 27; but the things contained in the external sense are not eternal truths, but are things to be observed by the Israelitish nation for the sake of things internal, for they signify these latter things, and thereby involve them; they were also to be kept by that nation before the internal things of the Word were opened by the Lord, and when they were opened, then those external things were abrogated. For when man worships the Lord from faith and from love to Him, which are internal things, he has no need of the external things which signify them; for he is then in them, and not in their types. As that the feast of unleavened bread was to be kept in the month Abib; and that on this occasion unleavened bread was to be eaten seven days; that every opening of the womb was to be given to God; that the opening of an ass was to be redeemed, or to be necked; that the first-born of sons was to be redeemed; that the feast of weeks was to be celebrated, also the feast of gathering together; that three times in the year every male was to be seen before Jehovah; that they were not to sacrifice upon what is leavened; that a kid was not to be seethed in the milk of its mother. But although these things are abrogated, still they are the holy Divine things of the Word, inasmuch as an internal holy principle is in them.

10,638. "Behold I drive out from before thy faces the Amorite, and the Canaanite, and the Hittite, and the Perizite, and the Hivite, and the Jebusite"—that hereby is signified the removal on this occasion of evils and the falses thence derived, appears from the signification of driving out from the faces, as denoting to remove from the interiors, which are of the thought and affection; for to drive out is to remove, and faces denote the interiors, see the passages cited, n. 9546, and the interiors of man are those things which are of the understanding and will, or which are of the thought and affection. Hence to drive out from the faces denotes to remove from those things; and from the representation of the nations in the land of Canaan, as denoting evils and falses, see the passages cited, n. 9327; but what evil and false is represented by each nation, see the explications where they are treated of, as what by the Amorite, n. 6306, 6859; what by the Canaanite, n. 1573, 1574, 4818; by the Hittite, n. 2913, 6858; by the Perizite, n. 1573, 1574, 6859; by the Hivite and Jebusite, n. 6860. But these things are said of the Word, since by Moses, from whose faces those nations were to be driven out, is represented the Word, as may be manifest from what goes before. How the case herein is, it may be expedient briefly to explain. It is said, if he keep to himself what Jehovah commands, that He would drive out those nations from his faces, by which is signified, if they did the primary precepts which are of eternal truth, that evils and falses would be removed. Those precepts are the things which follow in the internal sense, the chief of which are, that they should not acknowledge any other god but the Lord, and that from Him is all good and all truth, also that salvation and eternal life are from Him. With those who believe these things, and love that it be so, all evil and the false are removed, whilst they read the Word, inasmuch as the Lord then enlightens them, and leads them; and in this case they do not think from themselves; neither are they affected with the Word from themselves, but from the Lord, hence no evil and false of evil enters, for the Lord removes them; these are they who understand the Word, and are affected with the truths thence derived, and also love to live according to them. But they who do not acknowledge those chief precepts, which are of eternal truth, are not enlightened when they read the Word, thus they do not see from the Lord truths therein, but what they see they see from self, and to see from self is to see falses for truths, and if they see truths, they still falsify them by principles taken from themselves, or by their own proper loves, to which they turn truths, and to which they thereby inwardly apply them, hence come the falses of evil; these are the things which in the internal sense are signified by those words. The reason why these things are signified, is, because the angels, who perceive the Word in its internal sense when it is read by man, do not know what Moses is, nor what the Amorite, the Canaanite, the Hittite, the Perizite, the Hivite and the Jebusite, for names do not enter heaven, but the things which are signified by them, thus by Moses the Word, and by those nations evils and falses.

10,639. Verses 12 to 17. *Take heed to thyself, lest peradventure thou establish a covenant with the inhabitant of the land, upon which thou comest, lest peradventure it become a snare in the midst of thee. Wherefore their altars ye shall overturn, and their statues ye shall break, and his groves ye shall cut off. Wherefore thou shalt not bow thyself to another god; for Jehovah*

His name is zealous, a zealous God is He. Lest peradventure thou establish a covenant with the inhabitant of the land, and they commit whoredom after their gods, and sacrifice to their gods, and he call thee, and thou eatest of his sacrifice. And thou takest of his daughters for thy sons and his daughters commit whoredom after their gods, and make thy sons to commit whoredom after their gods. Gods of what is graven thou shalt not make to thyself. Take heed to thyself lest peradventure thou establish a covenant with the inhabitant of the land upon which thou comest, signifies that no religious principle whatsoever is to be adhered to in which is evil. Lest peradventure it become a snare in the midst of thee, signifies seduction thence in the Word itself. Wherefore their altars ye shall overturn, signifies that the evil of that religious principle and of the worship thence derived is to be rejected. And their statues ye shall break, signifies that the falses of evil are to be dissipated. And his groves ye shall cut off, signifies that their doctrinals are altogether to be rejected. Wherefore thou shalt not bow thyself to another god, signifies that the Lord alone is to be worshiped from faith and love. For Jehovah His name is zealous, a zealous God is He, signifies if another is worshiped that Divine Good and Divine Truth recede. Lest peradventure thou establish a covenant with the inhabitant of the land, signifies conjunction thereby with the evil of every religious principle. And they commit whoredom after their gods, signifies hence the falses of evil. And sacrifice to their gods, signifies this worship grounded in falses. And he call thee, and thou eat of his sacrifice, signifies enticement, reception, and appropriation of what is false derived from evil. And thou take of his daughters for thy sons, signifies conjunction of the affections of evil with truths. And his daughters commit whoredom after their gods, and make thy sons to commit whoredom after their gods, signifies thereby the profanation of good and truth. Gods of what is graven thou shalt not make to thyself, signifies the worship of self and not of the Lord.

10,640. "Take heed to thyself, lest peradventure thou establish a covenant with the inhabitant of the land upon which thou comest"—that hereby is signified that no religious principle whatsoever is to be adhered to in which is evil, appears from the signification of establishing a covenant, as denoting to be conjoined, see the passages cited, n. 10,632, thus also to adhere; and from the signification of an inhabitant of the land, as denoting a religious principle in which is evil, for by inhabitant is signified good, n. 2268, 2451, 2712, and hence in the opposite sense evil, and by land [or earth] is signified the church and whatsoever is of the church, see the passages cited, n. 9325, thus also a religious principle; and from the signification of upon which thou comest, as denoting wheresoever there is a religious principle in which is evil, for by the nations which were in the land of Canaan, into which they were about to come, are signified evils and the falses thence derived, see just above, n. 10,638. From these considerations it is evident that by the words, "lest thou establish a covenant with the inhabitants of the land upon which thou comest," is signified that no religious principle whatsoever is to be adhered to in which is evil. Inasmuch as this is amongst the primary things, by which the man of the church is enlightened when he reads the Word, and since this is the subject treated of in what now follows, it may be expedient to say how the case herein is; the man who is willing to be enlightened by the Lord, must take especial heed lest he appropriate to himself any doctrinal which patronizes evil; for man in such case appropriates it to himself, when he confirms it with himself, for thereby he makes it a principle of his faith, and still more so if he lives according to it. When this is the case, then evil remains inscribed on his soul and his heart; and when this effect has place, he cannot afterwards in any wise be enlightened by the Word from the Lord; for his whole mind is in the faith and in the love of his principle, and whatsoever is contrary to it, this he either does not see, or rejects, or falsifies: as for example; he who believes that he may be saved by faith alone, whatsoever be the quality of his life, and has confirmed this with himself, and has conjoined it with his other doctrinal tenets, insomuch that he next thinks nothing about life, but only about faith; such a person afterwards, howsoever he reads the Word, sees nothing therein relating to good of life, and at length does not know what good is, what charity, what love, and if they are named, he says that faith alone is every thing of the kind; when yet faith alone, or faith without those things, is as an empty vessel, and as a thing without soul; such spiritual life of man may be compared to the respiration of the lungs, without influx of blood from the heart, which is not life, except like that of an image or an automaton. These observatious are made, in order to show how the case is with man who reads the Word, that he cannot in any wise be thence enlightened if he has adhered to any religious principle which patronizes evil.

10,641. "Lest peradventure it become a snare in the midst of thee"—that hereby is signified seduction thence derived in the Word itself, appears from the signification of being a snare, as denoting to be caught and seduced by his own evil and false principle, see n. 7653, 9348; and from the representation of Moses, as denoting the Word, see the passages cited, n. 9372; hence in the midst of thee denotes in the Word itself. How the case herein is, is manifest from what was said just above, n. 10,640.

10,642. "Wherefore their altars ye shall overturn"—that

hereby is signified that the evil of that religious principle and of the worship thence derived is to be rejected, appears from the signification of an altar, as being the principal representative of the Lord and of the worship of Him from good, see n. 921, 2777, 2811, 4541, 8935, 8940, 9388, 9389, 9714, 9964, 10,242, 10,245, and hence in the opposite sense it is a representative of idolatrous worship, thus from evil, of which we shall speak presently; and from the signification of overturning, as denoting to reject; for it is said of the altars, that they are to be overturned, but of the evils of worship, which are signified by the altars of the nations, it is said that they are to be rejected. Mention is made in this verse of altars, of statues, and of groves, and by those things in general are signified all things of idolatrous worship; by altars worship from evil, by statues worship from the false of evil, and by groves their doctrinals. The reason why those things were to be extirpated, was, because by those representatives the Lord was not worshiped, but gods were worshiped who had been men, as Baals, and several others, which worship was diabolical and infernal, for to worship man instead of God Himself, who is the Lord, is diabolical, for man is conjoined to him who is worshiped. But the case is this; if man is worshiped for a god, then some one from hell is conjoined to him, for faith and love conjoin; the faith of truth and the love of good conjoin man to the Lord, but the faith of what is false and the love of what is evil conjoin man to hell. For there are attendant upon every man spirits from hell, and also angels from heaven, without them man cannot live; if any one is worshiped who had been a man, in this case the spirits from hell suppose that they themselves are worshiped, for every one in hell desires to be a god, and these spirits communicate that worship with the infernal societies from which they are; in proportion therefore as they are worshiped, in the same proportion the angels who are from heaven recede; hence man is carried away into infernal lusts, and at length becomes like unto those spirits as to all his life, amongst whom also he comes after death. But when the Lord is worshiped, who is the God of heaven and earth, then the angels who are attendant on man from heaven, do not claim to themselves any thing of worship, because they attribute all the truth of faith and good of love to the Lord, and nothing to themselves; hence by them is opened a way even to the Lord Himself, who conjoins them to Himself by faith and love. From these considerations it may be manifest of what great concern it is to worship the Lord Himself, who has all power in the heavens and in the earths, as He Himself teaches in Matthew, chap. xxviii. 18.

10,643. "And their statues ye shall break"—that hereby is signified that the falses of evil are to be dissipated, appears from the signification of statues, as being representatives of the worship of the Lord from truths, see n. 4580, 4582, 9388, 9389; and, in the opposite sense, representatives of idolatrous worship from falses. The reason why statues were representative of worship, was, because with the ancients it was usual to set up statues, and anoint them with oil, and thereby sanctify them. The ancients celebrated their worship chiefly on mountains, on hills, and in groves, and there they set up statues; the reason why they celebrated worship on mountains, was, because mountains signified the heaven where celestial love reigns, which is love to the Lord; the reason why on hills, was, because hills signified the heaven where spiritual love reigns, which is love towards the neighbor: and the reason why in groves, was, because groves signified heavenly wisdom and intelligence; all these things are from correspondences. The statues which were set up there, signified Divine Truth, for the statues were stones, and stone signifies truth, on which account the Lord as to Divine Truth in the Word is called the stone of Israel: hence now it is that statues signified the worship of the Lord from truths. But when the representatives of the church, which existed amongst the ancients, began to be turned partly into things idolatrous, and partly into things magical, then such things were abrogated, especially with the Israelitish nation, who in heart were idolaters; hence it is that by statues is signified idolatrous worship from falses. So the case is with all worship, when man becomes external, as is the case when he respects himself and the world as ends, and the Divine things of the church as means; for in such case all those things which are of worship, with those who remain in worship, become idols, since external things are worshiped without internal; hence the truths of worship and doctrine become falses, for they are falsified by ideas of self and the world in them, to which are adjoined several other ideas, which withdraw the Divine from those truths, and transfer them to self and the world. This also may be manifest from the altars of the nations, on which, although they sacrificed in like manner [as the Israelitish nation], still their sacrifices were abominations. That statues were in use amongst the ancients, and signified the holy principle of worship, is manifest from the statue erected by Jacob, concerning which it is thus written in Genesis, "And Jacob took the stone, which he had placed for his pillow, and *set it up for a statue*, and said, if I shall return in peace to the house of my father, *this stone, which I have set up for a statue, shall be the house of God*," xxviii. 18, 19, 22. And from the twelve statues set up by Moses beneath Mount Sinai, concerning which it is thus written in Exodus, "Moses wrote all the words of Jehovah, and arose in the morning early, and *builded an altar under the mountain, and twelve statues for the twelve tribes of Israel*," xxiv. 4, and n. 9389. Also in Isaiah, "In that day there shall be an altar to Jehovah in the midst of the land of Egypt, and *its statue in the border thereof to Jehovah*," xix. 19. And in Hosea, "Many days shall the sons of Israel sit, without a king, and without a prince, and without a sacrifice, and *without a statue*," iii. 4. In those passages by statues is signified worship from truths, by reason, as was said above, because a stone signified Divine Truth, and a statue anointed with oil, Divine Truth from Divine Good. But when those representatives began to be idolatrously worshiped, then it was commanded that such things should be overturned and broken, as in this verse, and also Exod. xxviii. 24; Deut. vii. 5; chap. xii. 3: and whereas the Israelitish nation were in heart idolaters, therefore to prevent their setting up statues on mountains and hills, and in groves, and worshiping them idolatrously, it was forbidden to set up statues, and to plant groves, although such things were to the ancients the holy things of worship. That this prohibition was given to that nation, is manifest in Moses, "*Thou shalt not plant to thyself a grove of any tree whatsoever* near to the altar of thy God which thou shalt make to thyself; *neither shalt thou erect to thyself a statue*, since Jehovah thy God hateth it," Deut. xvi. 21, 22; and that the prohibition was given on this account, because they worshiped those things idolatrously, is plain from the 1st book of the Kings, "Judah did evil in the eyes of Jehovah, they builded to themselves *heights and statues* upon every high hill, and *under every green tree*," xiv. 23. In like manner the sons of Israel, 2nd Kings, xvii. 10. And in Micah, "I will cut off thy graven things, and *thy statues from the midst of thee*, that thou mayest not adore any more the work of thy hands; and *I will extirpate thy groves from the midst of thee*," v. 12, 13. And in Isaiah, "*Ye have enflamed yourselves with gods under every green tree*," lvii. 5. And in Ezekiel, "Nebuchadnezzar by the hoofs of his horses will trample upon all thy streets, he will slay all the people with the sword, and *the statues of thy strength* he will cause to descend to the earth," xxvi. 11; besides in other places; from which passages it is also evident what is signified by statues in the internal sense.

10,644. "And his groves ye shall cut off"—that hereby is signified that their doctrinals are altogether to be rejected, appears from the signification of groves, as denoting the doctrinals of the church, in this case the doctrinals of what is religious amongst idolaters, which are the doctrinals of what is false derived from evil. The reason why groves signify doctrinals, is, because trees signify the perceptions and knowledges of good and truth, perceptions with those who are in the Lord's celestial kingdom, and knowledges with those who are in his spiritual kingdom; and every species of tree, a species of perception and knowledge; hence it is that paradises and gardens signify celestial intelligence and wisdom, and forests the science of the natural man; from these considerations it may be manifest whence it is that groves signify doctrine, and whence it is that the ancients celebrated holy worship in groves; for the church amongst the ancients was representative, all the external things of which represented internal things, such as are in heaven, concerning the Lord, concerning love and faith in Him, and concerning such things as relate to love and faith. This signification of groves, also of forests, of gardens and paradises, and likewise of trees according to their species, originates in representatives in the other life, for such things appear there according to the wisdom and intelligence of the angels, for appearances there are from a celestial and spiritual origin. That groves signify doctrine, and that the ancients performed holy worship in groves, see n. 2722, 4522. That paradises signify celestial intelligence and wisdom, n. 3220, 4528, 4529. That gardens in like manner, n. 100, 108, 1588, 2722. That forests signify science which is of the natural man, n. 9011. That trees signify the perceptions and knowledges of good and truth, n. 103, 2163, 2682, 2972, 7692, 8326. That the ancient church performed worship in groves and in gardens under trees according to their significations, n. 2722, 4522.

10,645. "Wherefore thou shalt not bend thyself to another god"—that hereby is signified that the Lord alone is to be worshiped from faith and love, appears from the signification of bending himself, as denoting to adore and worship. The reason why it is the Lord alone who is to be worshiped, and not another, is, because by Jehovah and by God in the Word is meant the Lord, see the passages, n. 9315, 9373; also because the Lord is God of heaven and earth, and likewise the Only God, see the passages cited, n. 9194. It is said that the Lord is to be worshiped from faith and love, because the worship of the Lord is either from faith or from love; worship from faith is called worship according to truths, for truths are of faith; and worship from love is called worship from good, for good is of love; they who are in the Lord's spiritual kingdom worship Him from faith, but they who are in His celestial kingdom worship Him from love. But it may be expedient here to say something on the subject concerning the worship of the Lord from faith and love. Many suppose that they worship the Lord by faith, when they believe the things appertaining to the doctrine of the church, and that they worship the Lord by love when they love Him; but by merely believing and by merely loving, the Lord is not worshiped, but by living according to His precepts, inasmuch as persons of this character alone believe in the Lord, and love Him; others say that they believe in Him, and still they do not believe, and say that they love Him, and still they do not love Him. The reason why they alone believe in the Lord and love Him, who live according to His precepts, is, because the Lord is not in the understanding of truth without willing it, but is in the understanding of truth and willing it; for truth does not enter into man, and become his, until man wills it, and from willing does it, for the will is the man himself, but the understanding is only so far the man, as it partakes of the will. The Lord also is present with man in his truths which are from good, and the truths which are from good are those which man wills and thence does, but not those which he understands and does without willing them, for to do a thing without willing it is hypocrisy, inasmuch as it is done before men, and not before the Lord. The Lord also does not dwell with an empty man, that is, with a man who does not know His truths and do them; in those truths which are from good, that is, which man wills and does, the Lord is present with man, for the truths which are from good make the church with man, and make heaven with him, in a word they make the Lord Himself to be with him. That this is the case, man may perceive from reason alone, if he weighs the subject well; for he may know that all the intellectual principle of man is formed by truths, and all his will principle by goods; for all things in the universe have relation to truth and good; and the intellectual principle of man is formed to receive truths, and the will principle to receive goods; the truths which are believed are said to be of love; hence it may be manifest that such as the truths of faith are by which the intellectual principle is formed, and such as the goods of love are by which the will principle is formed, such is the man; for man is man by virtue of understanding and will; if therefore his intellectual principle be formed by Divine Truths, and those truths become truths of his faith, and the will principle be formed by goods which become goods of his love, it follows that in such case heaven is in the man, and that the Lord can dwell with him as in His own heaven; for the Divine Truths which make the intellectual principle, and the Divine Goods which make the will principle, are from the Lord, or are the Lord's, and those things which are the Lord's are Himself. Hence it is evident that for a man to believe in the Lord is to imbue his intellectual principle with the truths of faith, and that to love the Lord is to imbue the will principle with the goods of love; and that this cannot be effected but by learning truths from the Lord, by willing them, and by doing them. Whether we speak of willing and doing, or of loving, it is the same thing, for what a man loves, this he wills, and what he actually wills, this he loves. From these considerations it may now be manifest what it is to worship the Lord from faith and love. That this is the case also appears evident from this consideration, that the Lord wills the salvation of all. To will the salvation of man is to will to bring him to Himself into heaven; this cannot be effected unless the Lord be in him, and the Lord cannot in any wise be in him except in such things appertaining to him as are from Himself, which things are truths derived from good, thus His precepts which man does from faith and from love; for no other recipients of the Lord and of heaven are given with man, neither can be given; nor does heaven itself consist of any other. That to believe in the Lord and to love, is to do His precepts, the Lord also teaches in John, "*If ye love Me, keep My commandments. He that hath My precepts, and doeth them, he it is who loveth Me. If any one love Me, he will keep My words, and My Father will love him, and We will come to him, and make our abode with him. He that loveth Me not, keepeth not My words,*" xiv. 15, 21, 23, 24. And again, "*Abide in My love; if ye keep My commandments ye will abide in My love. Ye are My friends, if ye do whatsoever I command you,*" xv. 9, 10, 14. The commandments and the precepts which are to be kept, and according to which man ought to live, are taught in the doctrine of charity and faith.

10,646. "For Jehovah His name is zealous, and a zealous God is He"—that hereby is signified if any other be worshiped that Divine Good and Divine Truth recedes, appears from the signification of zealous [or jealous] as denoting one who does not suffer any other but himself to be loved and worshiped; and from the signification of the name of Jehovah, as denoting every thing by which the Lord is worshiped, se n. 2724, 3006, 6674, 9310; and since that is the Divine Truth proceeding from His Divine Human, it is the Divine Human of the Lord, which, in the supreme sense, is meant by the name of Jehovah, n. 2628, 6887, 8274; for the Divine Truth is the Lord Himself in heaven, inasmuch as what proceeds from Him is Himself; from the Divine nothing else can possibly proceed but what is Divine, and what is Divine is one. Hence it is evident, that by His name being zealous [or jealous] is signified that the Lord does not suffer any other to be worshiped but Himself, since from Himself alone is all truth and all good productive of salvation. The Lord is called zealous [or jealous], because as soon as any other is worshiped, all truth and good recedes; for man, by the good and truth which are from the Lord, is conjoined to Him, wherefore as soon as any other is worshiped, disjunction is effected, and in this case the false succeeds in the place of truth, and evil in the place of good. The reason why He is twice called zealous [or jealous], is, because by Jehovah is meant the Divine Good, and by God the Divine Truth. That in the Word the Lord is called Jehovah where the Divine Good is treated of, but is called God where the Divine Truth is treated of, see n. 2586, 2769, 2921, 6303, 6905, 10,158, 10,617; and because each recedes from man when any other is worshiped but the Lord, therefore He is twice called zealous [or jealous]. It is said that the Lord alone is to be worshiped: he who does not know how the case is with the worship of the Lord, may believe that the Lord loves to be worshiped and wills glory from man, as a man who gives to another what he asks for the sake of honor given to himself; he who so believes, is in total ignorance what love is, and still more what Divine Love is. Divine Love consists in willing worship and willing glory not for the sake of itself, but for the sake of man and his salvation, for he who worships the Lord, and gives glory to the Lord, is in humiliation, and from him who is in humiliation the proprium recedes, and in proportion as the proprium recedes, in the same proportion the Divine is received, for the proprium of man is what alone opposes the Divine, since the proprium of man is evil and false. This is the glory of the Lord, and the worship of Him is for the sake of that end. Glory for the sake of self is grounded in self-love, and heavenly love differs as much from selt love, as heaven from hell, and infinitely more the Divine Love.

10,647. "Lest peradventure thou establish a covenant with the inhabitant of the land"—that hereby is signified thus conjunction with the evil of every religious principle, appears from the signification of a covenant, as denoting conjunction, see n. 665, 666, 1023, 1038, 1864, 1996, 2003, 2021, 6804, 8767, 8778, thus to establish a covenant denotes to be conjoined; and from the signification of the inhabitant of the land, as denoting a religious principle in which is evil, see above, n. 10,640: whether we speak of a religious principle in which is evil, or of the evil of a religious principle, it is the same thing. Its being now again said that a covenant must not be established with the inhabitant of the land, is on account of the series in the internal sense.

10,648. "And they commit whoredom after their gods"—that hereby is signified the falses of evil thence derived, appears from the signification of committing whoredom after the gods of the nations, as denoting to be conjoined to the falses of evil, for by committing whoredom is signified to be illegitimately conjoined, and by the gods of the nations are signified the falses of evil. That gods denote falses, see n. 4402, 4544, 7873, 8867; and that nations denote evils, see above, n. 10,683. It is said that hence are the falses of evil, because from evil exist all falses; but the falses which are not from evil, in the external form indeed are falses, but not in the internal; for there are falses given with those who are in the good of life, but interiorly in those falses there is good, which causes the evil of the false to be removed, hence that false before the angels does not appear as the false, but as a species of truth; for the angels look at the interior things of faith, and not at its exterior; hence it is that every one, of whatsoever religion he be, may be saved, even the Gentiles who have no truths from the Word, if so be they have respected the good of life as an end, see n. 2589 to 2604. In the Word frequent mention is made of committing whoredom, and by it is signified illegitimate conjunction with truth, and by committing adultery, illegitimate conjunction with good; hence by committing whoredom is signified the falsification of truth, and by committing adultery the adulteration of good. The falsification of truth is effected in a three-fold manner. *First*, if man be in evil of life, and acknowledges truths of doctrine; for in this case evil is within in the truths, and evil falsifies truth; for evil dissipates what is celestial and Divine out of truths, and implants what is infernal, hence comes falsification. *Secondly*, if man be first in truths as to doctrine, and afterwards accedes to the false of other doctrine, which is effected only with those who are in evil of life, since evil appetites what is false, and eagerly seizes upon it for truth. *Thirdly*, if man, who is in evil as to life and in falses as to doctrine, seizes upon the truths of other doctrine, he also falsifies truth, inasmuch as he does not acknowledge truths for the sake of truths, but for the sake of something of gain, of honor, or reputation. All these falsifications in the Word are called whoredoms and harlotries, by reason that by marriage is meant legitimate conjunction, which is of good and truth, see n. 2727 to 2759, hence illegitimate conjunctions are meant by whoredoms. That this is the case, may be manifest from several passages in the Word, from which it is allowed to adduce only the two following: "Jerusalem, *thou hast committed whoredom* for the sake of thy name; and *thou hast poured forth thy whoredoms* upon every passenger. Thou hast taken of thy garments, and hast made to thyself variegated lights, and *hast committed whoredom upon them.* Thou hast taken the vessels of thine ornaments of my gold and of my silver, which I had given thee, and hast made to thyself images of a male, and hast *committed whoredom* with them. Thou hast taken thy sons and thy daughters, which thou hast brought forth to me, and hast sacrificed them thereto; *is this a little thing concerning thy whoredoms? Thou hast committed whoredom with the sons of Egypt* thy neighbors, great in flesh, and *hast multiplied thy whoredom* to provoke Me. *Thou hast committed whoredom with the sons of Ashur, and hast committed whoredom with them* and wast not satisfied. *And thou hast multiplied thy whoredom* even to Chaldea, the land of trading," Ezek. xvi. 15, 16, 17, 20, 26, 28, 29, and following verses. And again, " Two women, the daughters of one mother, *committed whoredom in Egypt*, in their youth *they committed whoredom*, Oholah Samaria, and Oholibah Jerusalem. *Oholah committed whoredom* under Me, and *loved her lovers* the neighboring Assyrians, *she gave her whoredoms upon them. Her whoredoms from Egypt*, she forsook not, for *they lay* with her in her youth. Oholibah *corrupted her love* more than her, and *multiplied her whoredoms above the whoredoms* of her sister, *she loved* the sons of Ashur; she added *to her whoredoms*, and saw images of the Chaldeans, *she loved them* to the sight of her eyes; the sons of Babel came to her *to the copulation of loves*," Ezek. xxiii. 2, 3, 4, 7, 8, 11, 12, 14, 16, and following verses; besides in many other passages, which may be seen also explained with these, n. 2466, 8904.

10,649. "And sacrifice to their gods"—that hereby is signified thus worship from falses, appears from the signification of sacrificing, as denoting worship in general, see n. 6905, 8680, 8936; and from the signification of the gods of the nations, as denoting the falses of evil, as above, n. 10,648.

10,650. "And he call thee, and thou eat of his sacrifice"—that hereby is signified the enticement, reception, and appropriation of what is false derived from evil, appears from the signification of calling, as denoting enticement and reception, for he who follows and obeys when he is called, is enticed and receives; and from the signification of eating, as denoting appropriation, see n. 3168, 3596, 4745; and from the signification of sacrifice, as denoting worship from falses, see just above, n. 10,649, thus also the falses which are of worship. The reason why they denote falses of evil, is, because every thing false, which is false, is from evil, see above, n. 10,648.

10,651. "And thou take of his daughters for thy sons"—that hereby is signified the conjunction of the affections of evil with truths, appears from the signification of taking, when concerning marriage, as denoting to be conjoined; and from the signification of daughters, as denoting the affections of good, and in the opposite sense the affections of evil, see n. 2362, 3963; and from the signification of sons, as denoting truths, see n. 489, 491, 533, 1147, 3373, 4257, 9807, 10,490.

10,652. "And his daughters commit whoredom after their gods, and make thy sons to commit whoredom after their gods" —that hereby is signified thus the profanation of good and truth, appears from the signification of committing whoredom, as denoting illegitimate conjunction, see above, n. 10,648; and from the signification of his daughters or the daughters of the inhabitant of the land, as denoting the affections of evil; and from the signification of their gods, as denoting the falses of the affections of evil conjoined to truths, for by their gods are meant the gods of the daughters of the inhabitants of the land conjoined with the sons of the Israelitish nation, see just above, n. 10,651, which conjunction is the profanation of good; and from the signification of making thy sons to commit whoredom after their gods, as denoting the conjunction of truth with falses, which is the profanation of truth; that gods denote falses, see n. 4402, 4544, 7873, 8867; and that sons denote truths, n. 489, 491, 533, 1147, 3373, 4257, 7807, 10,490. These things are so said, because the first conjunction of the affections of evil, which is signified by taking of the daughters of the inhabitant of the land for thy sons, is not as yet profanation; but the other conjunction is profanation, for this is effected when evil is applied to truth and truth to evil, which is done by misinterpretation of truth and application to evil, and thus by the insertion of one into the other; hence truth no longer remains truth, but mortifies and is profaned. This profanation also is signified by the whoredom of the people with the daughters of Moab, concerning which it is thus written in Moses, "Israel sat together in Shittim, where the people began to commit whoredom with the daughters of Moab; and they called the people to the sacrifices of their gods, and the people did eat, and bended themselves to their gods. Therefore Jehovah said to Moses, take all the heads of the people and hang them to Jehovah, before the sun; and the people were smitten, and there died of that plague four and twenty thousand," Numb. xxv. 1, 2, 3, 6, 9. By Moab are signified those who adulterate goods, n. 2468, 8315; and by his daughters the affections of that evil; and by whoredom with them profanation; hence the punishment was the hanging of the heads of the people before the sun, and the death of twenty-four thousand; for the sun of the world denotes self-love, n. 10,584; hanging before it, the total extinction of heavenly good. And twenty-four thousand denote all truths and goods of truth in the complex, in like manner as twelve thousand, n. 2089, 3913, 7973; their death denotes the extinction of all truths; this is the case with those who profane.

10,653. "Gods of what is molten thou shalt not make to thyself"—that hereby is signified the worship of self and not of the Lord, appears from the signification of making gods of what is molten, as denoting to institute worship according to the love of self, see n. 10,406, 10,503; and worship according to the love of self is the worship of self and not of the Lord; for the worship of self is the end, but the worship of the Lord is the medium to that end; what is the end has dominion, and what is the medium serves, nor is the medium otherwise regarded by the end than as a servant by his lord. Such worship prevails with those who regard the holy things of the church as mediums [or means] and dominions as an end.

10,654. Verses 18 to 23. *The feast of things unleavened thou shalt keep; seven days thou shalt eat things unleavened which I commanded thee, to the stated time of the month Abib, because in the month Abib thou wentest forth out of Egypt.*

Every opening of the womb is for Me; and of all thy cattle thou shalt give a male, the opening of a cow and of cattle. And the opening of an ass thou shalt redeem in cattle, and if thou dost not redeem, thou shalt neck it. Every first-born of thy sons thou shalt redeem. And My faces shall not be seen empty. Six days thou shalt work, and in the seventh day thou shalt rest, in plowing and in reaping thou shalt rest. And the feast of weeks thou shalt make to thyself of the first-fruits of the harvest of wheat. And the feast of gathering together of the revolution of the year. Three times in the year shall every male of thine be seen at the faces of the Lord Jehovah the God of Israel. The feast of things unleavened thou shalt keep, signifies the worship of the Lord and thanksgiving on account of liberation from evil and from the falses of evil. Seven days thou shalt eat things unleavened, signifies a holy state on the occasion, and the appropriation of Divine Truth purified from evil and from the falses of evil. Which I commanded thee, signifies according to Divine Order. At the stated time of the month Abib, signifies a new state. Because in the month Abib thou wentest forth out of Egypt, signifies because then was liberation from hell. Every opening of the womb is for Me, signifies that all the good of innocence, of charity, and of faith, is to be ascribed to the Lord. Of all thy cattle thou shalt give a male, signifies which is given by truth. The opening of a cow and of cattle, signifies of the external and internal man. And the opening of an ass thou shalt redeem in cattle, signifies that faith merely natural shall not be ascribed to the Lord. And if thou dost not redeem, thou shalt neck it, signifies if the truth of innocence be not in it, that it is to be separated and rejected. Every first-born of thy sons thou shalt redeem, signifies that the truths of faith which are without good are not to be ascribed to the Lord. And My faces shall not be seen empty, signifies reception from mercy and thanksgiving. Six days thou shalt work, signifies the first state of regeneration, when man is in truths, and in such case in combats. And in the seventh day thou shalt rest, signifies a second state of regeneration when man is in good, and in such case in peace. In plowing and reaping thou shalt rest, signifies as to the implantation of truth in good, and its reception. And the feast of weeks thou shalt make to thyself of the first-fruits of the harvest of wheat, signifies the worship of the Lord and thanksgiving on account of the implantation of truth in good. And the feast of gathering together of the revolution of the year, signifies regeneration, and plenary liberation from damnation. Three times in the year shall every male of thine be seen at the faces of the Lord Jehovah God of Israel, signifies the continual appearance and presence of the Lord also in the truths of faith.

10,655. "The feast of things unleavened thou shalt keep"—

that hereby is signified the worship of the Lord and thanksgiving on account of liberation from evil and from the falses of evil, appears from the signification of a feast, as denoting worship and thanksgiving, see n. 7093, 9286, 9287; and from the signification of things unleavened, as denoting which are purified from evil and from the falses of evil, see n. 9992; hence by the feast of things unleavened is signified worship and thanksgiving on account of liberation from evil and from the falses of evil; that this was signified by this feast, see n. 9286 to 9292. As to what concerns this feast it is to be noted, that it properly signifies the glorification of the Lord's Human, thus the remembrance of it, and thanksgiving on account of it, for by it, and by the subjugation of the hells by the Lord, man has liberation from evils and salvation. For the Lord glorified His Human by combats against the hells, and on such occasion by continual victories over them; the last combat and victory was on the cross, wherefore He then fully glorified Himself, as He also teaches in John, "After that Judas was gone out, Jesus said, *Now is the Son of Man glorified and God is glorified in Him; If God be glorified in Him, God will also glorify Him in Himself and will immediately glorify Him*," xiii. 31, 32. Again, "*Jesus lifted up His eyes into heaven, and said, Father, the hour is come, glorify Thy Son, that Thy Son also may glorify Thee; Now O Thou Father, glorify Me with Thyself, with the glory which I had with Thee before the world was*," xvii. 1, 5. And in Luke, "*Ought not Christ to suffer these things, and to enter into His glory*," xxiv. 26. To glorify the Son of Man is to make the Human Divine; that those things were said concerning the passion of His cross, is evident. That by that last combat, which was the passion of the cross, He fully subdued the hells, the Lord also teaches in John, "*Jesus said, the hour is come that the Son of Man shall be glorified; Now is My soul troubled; and He said, Father, glorify Thy name; and there came forth a voice from heaven, I have both glorified, and will again glorify. And Jesus said, Now is the judgment of this world, now shall the prince of this world be cast out abroad. If I be lifted up from the earth, I will draw all to Myself; this He said, signifying by what death He was about to die*," xii. 23, 27, 28, 31, 32, 33; hell in every complex is what is called the prince of the world and the devil. From which consideration it is evident, that the Lord by the passion of the cross not only conquered and subdued the hells, but also fully glorified His Human; hence the human race have salvation. On this account also the Lord came into the world, as He also teaches in John, chap. xii. 27. For the remembrance of this thing the feast of unleavened things or of the passover was primarily instituted, wherefore on this feast He rose again. The reason why it was also for the sake of liberation from evil and from the falses of evil, is, because by the subjugation of the hells by the Lord, and by the glorification of His Human, all liberation from evil is effected, and none without them; for man is ruled by spirits from hell, and by angels out of heaven from the Lord, wherefore unless the hells had been altogether subjugated, and unless the Human of the Lord had been altogether united to the Divine Itself, and thus also made Divine, it would have been impossible for any man to have been liberated and saved from hell, for the hells would always have prevailed, since man is become such that of himself he thinks nothing but what is of hell. Hence it is evident from what ground it is that by the same feast is signified worship and thanksgiving on account of liberation from evil and from the falses of evil.

10,656. "Seven days thou shalt eat unleavened things"—that hereby is signified a holy state on the occasion, and appropriation of Divine Truth purified from evil and from the falses of evil, appears from the signification of seven days, as denoting a holy state from beginning to end; that days denote states, see n. 23, 487, 488, 493, 893, 2788, 3462, 3785, 4850; and that seven denotes what is holy, n. 395, 433, 716, 881, 5265, 5268; and that seven days denotes a holy state from beginning to end, n. 728, 6508, 9228, 10,127; and from the signification of eating, as denoting appropriation, see n. 3168, 3513, 3596, 4745; and from the signification of what is unleavened, as denoting the Divine Truth purified from evil and from the falses of evil, see n. 9992.

10,657. "Which I commanded thee"—that hereby is signified according to Divine Order, appears from the signification of commanding, when from Jehovah, as denoting according to Divine Order, see n. 10,119.

10,658. "At the stated time of the month Abib"—that hereby is signified a new state, appears from the signification of the month Abib, which was the first month of the year, as denoting the beginning of a new state, see n. 8053, 9291.

10,659. "Because in the month Abib thou wentest forth out of Egypt"—that hereby is signified because then was liberation from hell, appears from the signification of the month Abib, as denoting the beginning of a new state, see just above, 10,958; and from the signification of going forth out of Egypt, as denoting liberation from infestation by falses, thus also from hell, see n. 9292, and the passages adduced, 8866, 9197. From these considerations it may be manifest that the feast of the passover, which was also called the feast of things unleavened, was instituted for a remembrance of the liberation of man from hell by the Lord. That that liberation was effected by the Lord subduing the hells, and glorifying His Human, see just above n. 10,655. It is believed by the generality within the church, that the Lord came into the world that

He might reconcile the Father by the passion of the cross, and that afterwards they were accepted for whom He interceded; also that He exempted man from damnation by this, that He alone fulfilled the law, which otherwise would have damned every one; and thus that all were saved who had that faith with confidence and trust. But they, who are in any illustration from heaven, may see that the case is not so; as that the Divine, which is love itself and mercy itself, could reject from itself and damn to hell the human race; and that it was necessarily reconciled by the passion of the cross of its Son; and that in this manner, and in no other, it was moved with mercy; and afterwards that the life did not damn any one, if so be he had a confident faith concerning that reconciliation; and that all salvation is effected by faith from a principle of mercy. They who so think and believe, can see nothing at all; they speak and understand nothing; they call therefore those things mysteries, which are to be believed and not to be comprehended by any understanding. Hence it follows, that all illustration from the Word that the case is otherwise, is rejected; for light from heaven cannot enter, where such a shade of contradictions reigns; it is called a shade, because it is not at all understood. But to those who are in illustration, the Lord gives to understand what they believe; and they are illustrated when they read the Word, and understand it, who acknowledge the Lord and love to live according to His precepts, but not they who say that they believe, and do not live accordingly; for the Lord flows-in into the life of man, and thence into a faith, but not intc faith separate from life. They therefore who are illustrated from the Lord by the Word, understand that the Lord came into the world, that He might subdue the hells, and reduce all things there and in the heavens into order; and that this could not in any wise be effected, except by the Human, for from this he could fight against the hells, but not from the Divine without the Human; also that he might glorify His Human, to the intent that by it He might to eternity keep all things in the order into which He reduced them; hence the salvation of man; for around every man there are hells, inasmuch as every one is born into evils of every kind, and where evils are, there are the hells, which, unless they were rejected by the Divine Power of the Lord, would render it impossible for any one to be saved. That this is the case the Word teaches, and all those comprehend it, who admit the Lord into their life; and these, as was said above, are they who acknowledge Him, and love to live according to his precepts; see what has been adduced and shown from the Word, n. 9937, 10,019, 10,152, 10,579, and in other places abundantly. To be led away from evils, to be regenerated, and thus to be saved, is mercy, which is not immediate, as is believed, but mediate, that is, to those who recede from evils, and thereby admit the truth of faith and the good of love into their life from the Lord; immediate mercy, namely, that which would extend to every one from the good pleasure alone of God, is contrary to Divine Order, and what is contrary to Divine Order is contrary to God, for order is from God, and His Divine in heaven is order; for any one to receive order in himself is to be saved, which is effected solely by living according to the precepts of the Lord. Man is regenerated to the end that he may receive in himself the order of heaven, and he is regenerated by faith and by the life of faith, which is charity He who has order in himself, is in heaven, and also is heaven in a certain effigy, but he who has not, is in hell, and is hell in a certain effigy; the one cannot in any wise be changed and transcribed into the other from immediate mercy, for they are opposites, inasmuch as evil is opposite to good, and in good is life and is heaven, and in evil is death and is hell. That the one cannot be transcribed into the other, the Lord teaches in Luke, "Abraham said to the rich man in hell, Between us and you there is a great gulf fixed, so that they who would cross over from hence to you cannot, neither can they who are there pass to us," xvi. 26. If also immediate mercy was given, all would be saved, as many as are in the world, neither would there be a hell, for the Lord is mercy itself, because He is love itself, which wills the salvation of all, and the death of none.

10,660. "Every opening of the womb is for Me"—that hereby is signified that every good of innocence, of charity, and of faith, is to be ascribed to the Lord, appears from the signification of the opening of the womb, as denoting what is born of the Lord; for man from his parents is conceived and born naturally, but from the Lord spiritually; this latter nativity is what is meant in the internal sense by the opening of the womb; according to any other views, of what consequence would it be that the first-born of cattle should be for Jehovah, that is, for the Lord. Man also, who is regenerated, is conceived, is born, and is educated anew, and thus is withdrawn from the evils of the natural state which he had from his parents. The subject here treated of is the first-born of cattle, but by cattle are meant the goods and truths appertaining to man, for cattle of every kind correspond to the affections such as belong to man, as may be manifest from the passages cited, n. 9280; from which considerations it may be evident, that by the opening of the womb which is for Jehovah, is signified the good of innocence, of charity, and of faith, which are from the Lord communicated to those who are born anew, that is, who are regenerated. It is said, that those things are to be ascribed to the Lord, that is, it is to be acknowledged that they are from Him; for unless they be acknowledged and believed to be from the Lord, they are not goods, for every good is from Him, and that which is not from Him is from man, and whatsoever is from man, howsoever in the external form it may appear good, is still evil, for the proprium of man is nothing but evil, and from evil it is impossible for good to be produced.

10,661. "Of all thy cattle thou shalt give a male"—that hereby is signified which is given by truth, appears from the signification of a male, as denoting truth, see n. 2046, 4005, 7838. The case herein is this: every good which man has from the Lord, is given him by truth; for man is born into mere ignorance, and when he advances in age, he has of himself mere thick darkness in things spiritual, for he knows nothing concerning God, concerning the Lord, concerning heaven and hell, concerning life after death; what he knows from himself relates to the world and to himself, and he calls that good which in the world is in favor of himself, and he calls that true which confirms it. To the intent therefore that he may have heavenly good which he may love above himself and the world, it is necessary that he learn truths from the Word, or from the doctrine of the church which is from the Word; before he knows those truths, he cannot love them, for no affection is given of what is unknown, hence it is that truth is [the medium] by which man has good. The truth appertaining to man then becomes good, when he loves it, for every thing which is loved is good; to love is to will and to do, for what a man loves, this he wills and does, thus truth becomes good. This now is what is signified by giving a male of all cattle.

10,662. "The opening of a cow and of cattle"—that hereby is signified in the external and internal man, appears from the signification of a cow [or an ox] and of cattle, or of herd and of flock, as denoting the external and internal good appertaining to man, see n. 2566, 5913, 6048, 8937, 9135, 10,609.

10,663. "And the opening of an ass thou shalt redeem in cattle"—that hereby is signified that faith merely natural shall not be ascribed to the Lord, but the truth of innocence which is therein, appears from what was said and shown, n. 8078, where like words occur.

10,664. "And if thou shalt not redeem thou shalt neck it"—that hereby is signified if the truth of innocence be not therein, that it is to be separated and rejected, appears from what was said, n. 8079, where like words occur.

10,665. "Every first-born of thy sons thou shalt redeem"—that hereby is signified that the truths of faith, which are without good, are not to be ascribed to the Lord, appears from what was said and shown, n. 8080, where also like words occur.

10,666. "And My faces shall not be seen empty"—that hereby is signified reception from mercy and the giving of thanks, appears from what was shown, n. 9293. where like words occur.

10,667. "Six days thou shalt work"—that hereby is signified the first state of regeneration, when man is in truths, and in such case in combats, appears from the signification of six days, which are called days of labor or of work, as denoting the first state of regeneration, when man is in truths, and in such case in combats against evils and falses, see n. 8510, 8888, 9431, 10,360.

10,668. "And in the seventh day thou shalt rest"—that hereby is signified the other state of regeneration, when man is in good, and in such case in peace, appears from the signification of the seventh day, which is called a day of rest, or of the sabbath, as denoting the other state of regeneration, when man is in good, and in such case in peace, and in heaven with the Lord, see n. 8494, 8495, 8510, 8890, 8893, 9274, 9431, 10,356, 10,360, 10,367, 10,374.

10,669. "In plowing and in reaping thou shalt rest"—that hereby is signified as to the implantation of truth in good, and its reception, appears from the signification of plowing, as denoting the implantation of truth in good, of which we shall speak presently; and from the signification of reaping, as denoting the reception of truth in good. The reason why reaping has this signification, is, because by standing corn is signified truth in conception, n. 9146, and by the ear truth containing, by wheat and barley in the ear good receiving and also received; but in this case is meant, that the labor of man should cease about it, for it is said in plowing and reaping thou shalt rest; for by rest on the sabbath-day is signified the other state of regeneration, when man is in peace, and in heaven, and is led by the Lord, for in this case, those things are effected without the labor and study of man. That harvest denotes the reception of truth by good, see n. 9295; and that the sabbath denotes a state of peace, when man is led of the Lord, see the passages cited, n. 10,668. The reason why plowing signifies the implantation of truth in good, is, because by a field is signified the church as to good, thus also the good of the church; and by the seed which is inseminated, is signified the truth of faith. That a field denotes the church as to good, see n. 2971, 3196, 3310, 3317, 7502, 9139, 9141, 9295; and that seed is the truth of faith, n. 1940, 3310, 3373, 3671, 6158. In the Word, frequent mention is made of earth, ground, field, seed-time, harvest, standing corn, barn-floor, corn, wheat, barley, all which signify such things as relate to the establishment of the church, and to the regeneration of man who is in the church, thus which have reference to the truth of faith and to the good of love, from which the church derives its existence. That such things are signified, is from correspondence, for all things which are in the earth, also which are in its vegetable kingdom, correspond to the spiritual things which are in heaven, as is very manifest from the appearances there; for in heaven there appear fields, fallow-lands, plains, flower-gardens, ripe corn, shrubberies, and like things, such as are in the earths; and it is there known that the things which are of heaven, thus which are of the church, appear in such manner before their eyes. He who reads the Word, believes that such things, when mentioned therein, are merely comparisons, but let him know that they are real correspondences, as these words in Isaiah, "Hearken and hear My voice, *will the plower plow the whole day to sow, will he open and dung his ground?* When he hath made plain the faces thereof, doth he not scatter abroad the fitches; and disseminate the cummin? thus he stores up the measured wheat, and the appointed barley and its determinate spelt. Thus he instructeth him to judgment, his God teacheth him," xxviii. 23 to 26. These words appear as comparisons, but they are real correspondences, by which is described the reformation and regeneration of the man of the church, wherefore also it is said, "Thus he instructeth him to judgment, his God teacheth him." To instruct to judgment, is to give him intelligence, for by judgment is signified the intelligence of truth, n. 2235, and to teach him, when from God, is to give him wisdom; hence it may be manifest what is meant by plowing, dunging, scattering abroad fitches, sowing cummin, storing up wheat, barley, and spelt, namely, that plowing denotes implanting truth in good, fitches and cummin denote scientifics, since these are the first things which are learnt that man may receive intelligence. That wheat denotes the good of love of the internal man, see n. 7605. That barley denotes the good of love of the external, n. 7602. That spelt denotes its truth, n. 7605. That plowing, not from comparison but from correspondence, signifies the first [thing or principle] of the church in general, and also in particular with every one who is regenerated, or who becomes a church, is evident from these words in Moses, "Thou shalt not sow thy vineyard intermixedly: *thou shalt not plow with an ox and an ass together.* Thou shalt not wear a garment mixed with wool and linen together," Deut. xxii. 9, 10, 11. These words involve that the states of good and truth ought not to be confounded; for a vineyard denotes the church as to truth, but a field the church as to good; to plow with an ox, denotes to prepare by good; to plow with an ass, denotes by truth; wool also denotes good, but linen denotes truth. For the case is this; in a state of good are all they who are in the Lord's celestial kingdom, but in a state of truth are they who are in His spiritual kingdom; he who is in one cannot be in the other. Who cannot see that the above words have a deeper signification than they appear to have? for otherwise what of evil could there have been in sowing a vineyard intermixedly, in plowing with an ox and an ass together, and in wearing a garment mixed with wool and linen together.

10,670. "And the feast of weeks thou shalt make to thyself of the first-fruits of the harvest of wheat"—that hereby is signified the worship of the Lord and thanksgiving on account of the implantation of truth in good, appears from what was explained and shown, n. 9294, 9295, where like words occur.

10,671. "And the feast of gathering together of the revolution of the year"—that hereby is signified worship from a grateful mind on account of the implantation of good thence derived, thus on account of regeneration, and plenary liberation from damnation, appears from what was shown concerning that feast, n. 9296.

10,672. "Three times in the year shall every male of thine be seen at the faces of the Lord Jehovah God of Israel"—that hereby is signified the continual appearance and presence of the Lord also in truths of faith, is manifest from the explication of these words, n. 9297.

10,673. Verses 24, 25, 26, 27. *Because I expel nations from thy faces, and I will cause thy border to be dilated; and there shall not any one covet thy land, in thy going up to see the faces of Jehovah thy God three times in the year. Thou shalt not slay upon what is leavened the blood of My sacrifice; and the sacrifice of the feast of the passover shall not pass the night to the morning. The first-fruits of the primitive things of thy ground thou shalt bring into the house of Jehovah thy God. Thou shalt not seethe a kid in the milk of its mother. And Jehovah said to Moses, write for thyself those words, because on the mouth of those words I establish with thee a covenant, and with Israel.* Because I expel nations from thy faces, signifies the removal of evil and of the falses of evil. And I will cause thy border to be dilated, signifies the multiplication and extension of truth derived from good. And there shall not any one covet thy land, signifies the holding in aversion such things as are of the church with those who are in evils and in the falses of evil. In thy going up to see the faces of Jehovah thy God three times in the year, signifies when the presence of the Lord is also in the truths of faith. Thou shalt not slay upon what is leavened the blood of My sacrifice, signifies that the worship of the Lord from the truths of the church ought not to be commixed with falses derived from evil. And the sacrifice of the passover shall not pass the night to the morning, signifies the good of worship not from the proprium but from the Lord always new. The first-fruit of the primitive things of thy ground thou shalt bring into the house of Jehovah thy God, signifies that all the truths of good and goods of truth are holy, because from the Lord Alone. Thou shalt not seethe a kid in the milk of its mother, signifies that the good of innocence of a latter state ought not to be commixed with the truth of innocence of a former state. And Jehovah said to Moses write for thyself those words, signifies information concerning primary truths which ought to be remembered and done. Because on the mouth of those words I establish with thee a covenant, and with Israel, signifies that by them there is conjunction with those who are in external and internal worship.

10,674. "Because I expel nations from thy faces"—that hereby is signified the removal of evil and of the falses of evil, appears from the signification of expelling, when concerning evils and falses appertaining to man, as denoting to remove, for evils and falses are not expelled from man but are removed, see the passages cited, n. 10,057; and from the signification of the nations which were in the land of Canaan, as denoting evils and the falses of evil, see the passages cited, n. 9327.

10,675. "And I will cause thy border to be dilated"—that hereby is signified the multiplication and extension of truth from good, appears from the signification of dilating a border, as denoting the multiplication and extension of truth derived from good, see n. 8063. The reason why this is signified by dilating a border, is, because so far as evils and the falses of evil are removed, so far the truths which are from good are multiplied, since nothing else but evils and the falses thence derived oppose truths flowing in from the Lord and multiplying themselves with man, wherefore so far as evils and falses are removed, so far truths succeed in their place. This is the case with the intellectual principle of man, whether it consists of truths which are from good, or of falses which are from evil; it cannot consist of both together, for they are opposites; and the intellectual principle of man is what receives truths, and is formed by truths, for whatsoever is in his intellect has relation to truth. Hence it is evident, that so far as falses derived from evil are removed, so far truths derived from good are multiplied. This was represented by the expulsions of the nations from the land of Canaan, for by the nations there were represented evils and falses, see the passages cited, n. 10,057; and by the sons of Israel goods and truths. It is said that the intellectual principle of man is what receives truths, and is formed by truths, since nothing else in the proper sense is to be called intellectual, but what is from truths derived from good; what is from falses derived from evil is not intellectual; for intelligence and wisdom cannot in any wise be predicated of falses derived from evil, for such falses altogether destroy intelligence and wisdom, and introduce in their place insanity and foolishness. Wherefore the intellectual principle is in no case opened, except when man perceives and loves truths, and the perception and love of truth is from good; hence it is that truths from good are what constitute the intellectual principle. He who believes that he has an intellectual principle, who can reason dexterously against the truths of the church, is very greatly deceived; for he sees nothing within himself but without himself; to see within himself is from heaven, to see without himself is from the world; and he who sees only from the world, sees from an infatuated lumen, which lumen becomes mere thick darkness, when light from heaven flows-in into it.

10,676. "And there shall not any one lust after thy land"—that hereby is signified the holding in aversion such things as are of the church, with those who are in evils and the falses of evil, appears from the signification of not lusting after, when concerning those who are in evils and the falses of evil, when they see and perceive goods and the truths of good, as denoting to hold in aversion, for between evils and goods there is perpetual enmity, evils holding goods in aversion, and hating them, and goods holding evils in aversion, and putting them to flight or shunning them; and from the signification of land [or earth], as denoting the church, and whatsoever is of the church, see the passages cited, n. 9325.

10,677. "In thy ascending to see the faces of thy God three times in the year"—that hereby is signified when the presence of the Lord is also in the truths of faith, appears from what was explained, n. 9297.

10,678. "Thou shalt not slay upon what is leavened the blood of My sacrifice"—that hereby is signified that the worship of the Lord from the truths of the church ought not to be commixed with falses derived from evil, appears from the explication of the words, n. 9298.

10,679. "And the sacrifice of the feast of the passover shall not pass the night to the morning"—that hereby is signified the good of worship not from the proprium, but from the Lord always new, appears from what was explained, n. 9299.

10,680. "The first-fruits of the primitive things of thy ground thou shalt bring into the house of Jehovah thy God"—that hereby is signified that all the truths of good and the goods of truth are holy, because from the Lord alone, see n. 9300.

10,681. "Thou shalt not seethe a kid in the milk of its mother"—that hereby is signified that the good of innocence of a latter state ought not to be commixed with the truth of innocence of a former state, appears from what was said and shown, n. 9301, where like words occur.

10,682. "And Jehovah said to Moses, write for thyself those words"—that hereby is signified information concerning the primary truths which are to be remembered and done, appears from the signification of saying, when from Jehovah to Moses, as denoting information, as also in the passages cited, n. 10,277; and from the signification of writing, as denoting for remembrance of what is to be done, see n. 8620; and from the signification of those words, as denoting primary truths, for by words in general are signified things, specifically truths, in this case the primary truths which were to be remembered and done, that with the Israelitish nation representative worship of the church might be instituted and the Word be written, which were the subjects treated of in the preceding verses of this chapter.

10,683. "Because on the mouth of those words I establish with thee a covenant and with Israel"—that hereby is signified that by those [words] is conjunction with those who are in worship external and internal, appears from the signification of upon the mouth of those words, as denoting by those primary truths which are to be observed, see above, n. 10,682; and from the signification of establishing a covenant, as denoting conjunction, see n. 665, 666, 1023, 1038, 1864, 1996, 2003, 2021, 6804, 8767, 8778; and from the representation of Moses, with whom and with Israel it is said that the covenant is established, as denoting the external of the Word, of the church, and of worship, in which is an internal principle, see n. 10,563, 10,571, 10,607, 10,614; and from the signification of Israel, as denoting the internal of the church and of worship, see n. 4286, 4292, 4570, 6426; hence it is that it is said, that a covenant is established with Moses and with Israel and not with the sons of Israel, for by the sons of Israel in this and in the preceding chapter are meant those who are in the external of the church, of worship, and of the Word, without an internal principle, see n. 10,454 to 10,457, 10,461, 10,498, 10,459, 10,550, 10,551, 10,570, 10,575, 10,629. It may be expedient here briefly to say what the internal of the Word, of the church, and of worship, is; what their external in which is an internal; and what the external without the internal. *In the internal of the Word, of the church, and of worship*, are they who love to do truth for the sake of truth from internal affection, thus from spiritual affection: *in their external in which is an internal*, are they who love truth for the sake of truth, but from external affection, thus from natural affection; these latter are men of the external church, but the former of the internal, for in every church there are internal men and there are external; *but they who are in external worship without internal*, love truth not for the sake of truth, but for the sake of gains in the world, thus they do not love to do truths except for the sake of themselves, or that they may be seen; these are not within the church, but out of it. They who love to do truth for the sake of truth from internal or spiritual affection, when they hear truths, rejoice, and think about a life according to them: but they who love truth for the sake of truth from external or natural affections, when they hear truth, also rejoice, but they do not think about a life according to it, nevertheless it flows-in from an internal principle whilst they are ignorant of it. But they who love truth for the sake of gains in the world, think nothing about life, neither does any thing flow in from an internal principle; they only make truths to be things of the memory, to the end that they may speak about them. They who love to do truth for the sake of truth, love the Lord, inasmuch as truth is from the Lord, and the Lord makes it to become good by willing and doing it, so that it becomes [a principle] of the life appertaining to man, for truth does not become [a principle] of the life until it enters the will; that it is in the will, may be known and perceived from this, that the man does it, and still more that he loves to do, for so far as man wills truth, so far he loves it. To love truth for the sake of truth and for the sake of living according to it, is thus described by the Lord in Matthew, "*Whosoever receiveth you, receiveth Me, but he who receiveth Me, receiveth Him who sent Me. Whosoever receiveth a prophet in the name of a prophet, shall receive the reward of a prophet. And whosoever receiveth a just one in the name of a just one, shall receive the reward of a just one. And whosoever shall give to drink to one of these little ones a cup of cold water in the name of a disciple, verily I say unto you, he shall not lose a reward*," x. 40, 41, 42. He who is unacquainted with the internal sense of the Word, cannot know what is signified by receiving a prophet in the name of a prophet, a just one in the name of a just one, and a disciple of the Lord in the name of a disciple; and that they would have a reward according to such reception; for without that sense, who knows what is signified by receiving any one in His name? But they who are principled in the internal sense, do not attend to the person, but to the thing which the person signifies, thus not to a disciple, nor to a prophet, but to the things which a disciple and a prophet signify. Disciple in the internal sense signifies truth of life, but prophet truth of doctrine; in the name of any one, signifies on account of his quality; hence it is evident what is signified by those words of the Lord, namely, that they who love truth for the sake of truth, and who love to do truth for the sake of truth, love the Lord, and that they receive heaven in themselves, for the reward which is from the Lord is the affection of truth for the sake of truth, and in the affection of truth for the sake of truth is heaven. That disciples denote all things of love and faith in the complex, thus specifically those who are led of the Lord, see n. 3488, 3858, 5395; that prophet denotes the truth of doctrine, n. 2534, 7269; that name denotes quality, n. 144, 145, 1896, 2009, 2724, 6674, 9310; that reward denotes the affection of truth and good, n. 3956, 6388; that person is turned into the idea of things in the internal sense, n. 5225, 5287, 5434, 8343, 8985, 9007, 10,282; and that to do truth for the sake of truth is to love the Lord, n. 10,336.

10,684. Verse 28 to the end. *And he was there with Jehovah forty days and forty nights; he did not eat bread, and he did not drink water, and he wrote on tables the words of the covenant ten words. And it came to pass as Moses descended from Mount Sinai, and the two tables of the testimony were in the hand of Moses in his descending from the mountain; and Moses knew not that the skin of his faces shone in his speaking with Him. And Aaron and all the sons of Israel saw Moses, and behold the skin of his faces shone, and they were afraid of approaching to him. And Moses called to them, and there returned to him Aaron, and all the princes in the assembly, and Moses spake to them. And afterwards came near all the sons of Israel, and he commanded them all things which Jehovah spake with him in Mount Sinai. And Moses left off speaking with them, and gave upon his faces a vail. And in Moses's entering in before Jehovah, to speak with Him, he removed the vail until he went out; and he went out and spake to the sons of Israel that which was commanded; and the sons of Israel saw the faces of Moses, that the skin of the faces of Moses shone, and Moses brought back the vail over his faces even to his entering in to speak with Him.* And he was there with Jehovah forty days and forty nights, signifies temptations before the internal of the church, of worship, and of the Word, is given. He did not eat bread, and he did not drink water, signifies in the mean time non-appropriation of the good of love and of the truth of faith. And he wrote on the tables the words of the covenant, signifies the Word by which there is conjunction of heaven with man. Ten words, signify all Divine Truths therein. And it came to pass as Moses descended from Mount Sinai, signifies the influx of the internal into the external of the Word, of the church, and of worship. And the two tables of the testimony were in the hand of Moses, signifies a representative of the Word. And Moses knew not that the skin of his faces shone in his speaking with Him, signifies the internal of the Word giving forth light in its external without the external perceiving it. And Aaron and all the sons of Israel saw Moses, signifies the perception of those who are in the external things of the church, of worship, and of the Word, without the internal. And behold the skin of his faces shone, signifies that the internal shines forth by [or through] the external. And they were afraid of approaching to him, signifies that they did not endure the external of the church, of worship, and of the Word, when it was such. And Moses called to them, signifies the accession of that nation to what is external. And there returned to him Aaron and all the princes in the assembly, signifies the chief of those who are in things external without internal, and still represented things internal. And Moses spake to them, signifies instruction. And afterwards came near all the sons of Israel, signifies all who were in things external without internal, and still represented things internal. And he commanded them all things which Jehovah spake with him in Mount Sinai, signifies command concerning the primary truths which were to be represented, revealed from heaven. And Moses left off speaking with them, signifies after information concerning the primary truths which were to be represented in things external. And gave upon his faces a vail, signifies that the internal of the church, of worship, and of the Word, did not appear to the Israelitish nation, but only the external without the internal. And in Moses's entering in before Jehovah, to speak with him, signifies the state of the external when the internal from the Lord flowed-in, and it received information. He removed the vail until he went out, signifies a state of illustration on the occasion. And he went forth and spake to the sons of Israel that which was commanded, signifies communication with those who are in things external without an internal principle, concerning those things of which he was informed by [or through] the internal. And the sons of Israel saw the faces of Moses, that the skin of the faces of Moses shone, signifies that the Israelitish nation acknowledged indeed that there is given an internal in the Word, but they are not willing to know what is its quality. And Moses brought back the vail over his faces, signifies that on this account internal things were closed with them. Even to his entering-in to speak with Him, signifies howsoever they are informed.

10,685. "And he was with Jehovah forty days and forty nights"—that hereby are signified temptations before the internal of the church, of worship, and of the Word, is given, appears from the signification of forty days and nights, when concerning the church appertaining to man, as denoting states of temptation, see n. 730, 862, 2272, 2273, 8098. The reason why it denotes before the internal of the church, of worship, and of the Word, is given, is, because the internal, which is called the internal man, is opened and given to man by temptations; hence it is that all who are regenerating, undergo temptations. The reason why the internal is opened and given by temptations, is, because when man is in temptations, which are combats against evils and falses, the Lord flows-in from an interior principle, and fights for him; which also man may know from this consideration, that when he is in temptations, he interiorly resists, for unless he interiorly resisted, he would not conquer, but would yield. This interior resistance at the time does not come to the perception of man, because when he is in temptations, he is in obscurity from the evil and falses of evil which assault; but after temptations [it comes to perception] with those who are in the perception of truth; for the things which are brought in by the Lord into the internal of man, are not known to man whilst he lives in the world, since he then thinks in the external or natural man, and not perceptively in the internal, until he comes into the other life; nevertheless he ought to know and acknowledge, when he conquers in temptations, that he did not himself fight, but the Lord for him.

10,686. "He did not eat bread, and he did not drink water"—that hereby is signified in the mean time non-appropriation of the good of love and the truth of faith, appears from the signification of bread, as denoting the good of love, see n. 2165, 2177, 3464, 3478, 3735, 3813, 4211, 4217, 4735, 4976, 8410, 9545; and from the signification of water, as denoting the truth of faith, see the passages cited, n. 10,238; that by bread and water in the Word, are meant in general all goods and truths, see n. 9323; and from the signification of eating, as denoting the conjunction and appropriation of good, see n. 2187, 2343, 3168, 3513, 3596, 4745, 5643, 8001; and from the signification of drinking, as denoting the reception and appropriation of truth, see n. 3069, 3089, 3168, 8562. The case herein is this: when man is in temptations, the goods of love and the truths of faith are not then appropriated to him, but afterwards; for during the continuance of temptations, on one part are excited evils and the falses of evil, on the other goods and the truths of good which appertain to man, hence he is in a turbulent state; in this state the internal is opened; but after temptation he has serenity, and in that state goods and the truths of good are brought in by the Lord into the internal now open. Hence it is evident what is meant by the non-appropriation of the good of love and of the truth of faith during the continuance of temptations, which is signified by Moses not eating bread, and not drinking water, for forty days and forty nights.

10,687. "And he wrote on the tables the words of the covenant"—that hereby is signified the Word, by which there is conjunction of heaven with man, appears from the signification of the tables on which the law was written, as denoting the Word, see n. 9416, 10,375, 10,376, 10,453, 10,461; and from the signification of a covenant, as denoting conjunction, see above in the passages cited, n. 10,632. The reason why it denotes the conjunction of heaven with man, is because the Word is written by mere correspondences, and hence it is of such a quality as to conjoin heaven with man; for heaven is in the internal sense of the Word, and the internal sense corresponds to the external sense, wherefore when the Word is read by man, the angels, who are attendant upon him, perceive it in the spiritual sense, which is the internal sense; hence a holy principle from the angels flows-in, by which there is conjunction; for this end such a Word was given. That there is conjunction of the Lord, thus of heaven, with man by the Word, see the passages cited, n. 10,375. What correspondences are by which the Word is written, has been shown in the explications throughout.

10,688. "Ten words"—that hereby are signified all Divine Truths therein, appears from the signification of ten, as denoting all, see n. 4638; and from the signification of words, as denoting Divine Truths, see n. 9886. Hence it is that the precepts in those tables were ten in number.

10,689. "And it came to pass as Moses descended from Mount Sinai"—that hereby is signified the influx of the internal into the external of the Word, of the church, and of worship, appears from the signification of descending, when concerning Moses, by whom is represented the external of the Word in which is the internal, as denoting the influx of the Lord through the internal of the Word into its external; that this is signified by descending, see n. 5406; and from the representation of Moses, as denoting the external of the Word, of the church, and of worship, in which is the internal, see n. 4286, 4292, 4570; and from the signification of Mount Sinai, as denoting heaven where the Lord is, and whence the law or Word is, see n. 9420.

10,690. "And the two tables of the testimony were in the hand of Moses"—that hereby is signified a representative of the testimony, as denoting the law in every complex, thus the Word, see the passages cited above, n. 10,687; and from the signification of in the hand of Moses, as denoting a representative of it, namely, of the Word. That Moses represented the Word, see the passages cited, n. 9372; on this account the tables, by which was signified the Word, were in his hand, as a badge of representation.

10,691. "And Moses knew not that the skin of his faces did shine in his speaking with Him"—that hereby is signified the internal of the Word giving forth light in its external without the external perceiving it, appears from the representation of Moses, as denoting the external of the Word in which is the internal, see n. 10,563, 10,571, 10,607, 10,614; and from the signification of not knowing, as denoting not to perceive; and from the signification of shining, as denoting to give forth light, for the shining of the skin of the faces of Moses is from the giving forth of light from the internal; and from the signification of skin, as denoting the external of truth and good, see n. 3540, 5554, 8980; and from the signification of faces, as denoting the interiors, see the passages cited, n. 9546. Hence by the shining of the skin of the faces is signified the giving forth of light of the interiors in the external, in this case in the external of the Word, which is the sense of its letter, because by Moses is represented the external of the Word, in which is the internal; and from the signification of speaking, as denoting influx. That to speak, when concerning Jehovah, denotes influx, see n. 2951, 5743, 5797, 8660, 7270, 8128. Hence it is evident that by Moses not knowing that the skin of his faces shone in his speaking with Him, is signified the internal of the Word giving forth light in its external without the external perceiving it. It is to be noted, that by the giving forth light [*elucentia*] of the interiors of the Word in the external, is meant the internal sense in the external; the former sense continually gives forth light and shines in the latter, but it is not perceived by any except those who are in things internal; but by those who are in an external in which is an internal, as they who are called the men of the external church, it is not perceived, nevertheless it is present, whilst they are ignorant of it, and it affects them; who they are who are in the internal of the Word, of the church, and of worship, and who are in the external in which is the internal, see above, n. 10,683. But they who are in the external without the internal, as were the Israelitish nation, do not at all endure the internal, or the light thence derived in the external; wherefore it is said of them below, that they were afraid of coming near to Moses, and that Moses, when he spake with them, gave a vail upon his faces. The reason why the internal sense gives light, is, because in that sense is the Divine Truth such as is in the heavens, and the Divine Truth proceeding from the Lord appears to the angels as light, and also is the light of heaven, see the passages cited, n. 9584, 9684.

10,692. "And Aaron and all the sons of Israel saw Moses"—that hereby is signified the perception of those who are in the externals of worship and of the Word without the internals, appears from the signification of seeing, as denoting perception, see n. 2150, 3764, 4567, 4723, 5400; and from the representation of Aaron, and of the sons of Israel, in this and in the two preceding chapters, as denoting those who are in the externals of the church, of worship, and of the Word, without the internals. That Aaron denotes those, see n. 10,397; and that the sons of Israel do the same, see the passages cited, n. 9380, 10,396; and further, n. 10,397 to 10,457, 10,461 to 10,466, 10,492, 10,498, 10,500, 10,526, 10,531, 10,533, 10,535, 10,549, 10,550, 10,551, 10,566, 10,570, 10,575, 10,603, 10,629, 10,632.

10,693. "And behold the skin of his faces shone"—that hereby is signified that the internal gives forth light by [or through] the external, appears from what was explained just above, n. 10,691.

10,694. "And they were afraid of approaching to him"—that hereby is signified that they did not endure the external of the church, of worship, and of the Word, when it is of such a quality, appears from the signification of being afraid to come near, as denoting not to endure, for they who do not endure interior things, are afraid of coming near; and from the representation of Moses, as denoting the external of the Word, of the church, and of worship, in which is the internal, see n. 10,563, 10,571, 10,607, 10,614. The case herein is this; they who are only in the externals of worship, and of the Word, without the internal, cannot endure interior things; the reason is, because they who are in external things without what is internal, are in the love of self and of the world, and hence in a lumen, which is called natural lumen; but they who are in the externals, and at the same time in the internals of the church, of worship, and of the Word, are in love towards the neighbor and in love to the Lord, and hence in the light of heaven; inasmuch as those loves are opposites, and hence also the lights, therefore the one does not endure the other, for heavenly love, which is love to the Lord, and love towards the neighbor, when it flows-in into earthly loves, which are the loves of self and of the world, induce agonies as of death, and when heavenly light flows-in into the light of the world, it induces thick darkness and thence stupor; hence it is that what is external without what is internal cannot endure an external whilst the internal is in it. Inasmuch as the Judaic nation was of such a quality, therefore they could not endure to hear of the Lord, of love and faith to Him, which are the interior things of the Word, of the church, and of worship. These now are the things which are signified by the sons of Israel being afraid of approaching to Moses, because the skin of his faces shone; what the skin of the faces of Moses is, see above, n. 10,691.

10,695. "And Moses called to them"—that hereby is signified the accession of that nation to what is external, appears from the signification of calling to them, as denoting the accession of that nation, for he who is called accedes; and from the representation of Moses, as denoting the external of the Word in which is the internal, see just above, n. 10,694.

10,696. "And there returned to him Aaron and all the princes in the assembly"—that hereby are signified the chief of those who are in things external and still represented things internal, appears from the representation of Aaron and of the princes in the assembly, as denoting the chief who were in externals without the internal; for Aaron was their head, and the princes were leaders; that Aaron denotes what is external without an internal principle see n. 10,397; and that princes denote the chief, n. 1482, 2089, 5044: that it denotes who represented, see below, n. 10,698.

10,697. "And Moses spake to them"—that hereby is signified instruction, appears from the signification of speaking, as denoting instruction, see the passages cited, n. 10,277.

10,698. "And afterwards came near all the sons of Israel"—that hereby are signified all who are in externals, without an internal, and still represented things internal, appears from the representation of the sons of Israel, as denoting those who are in externals without an internal, see just above, n. 10,692. The reason why it also denotes who represented internal things, is, because Moses obtained that the church might be represented with that nation, although they were of such a quality that no church could be instituted amongst them; for a church cannot be given with those who are in things external without what is internal, inasmuch as the church is in the internal of man, and not in the external without it; for the communication of man with heaven and with the Lord is by [or through] the internal, and when there is no internal, that is, when it is closed, then there is communication with hell; but although the sons of Israel were of such a quality, that by [or through] the internal appertaining to them no communication with heaven could be given, still they could represent such things as are of the church and of heaven, which is effected solely by external things to which internal correspond; on this account they were received. That with that nation there was not a church, but only the representative of a church, see the passages cited, n. 9320, 10,396; and that by external things, which represented internal, there was effected communication with heaven, see the passages cited, also n. 9320, 10,396, also n. 10,492, 10,500, 10,549, 10,550, 10,551, 10,570, 10,575, 10,602, 10,629.

10,699. "And he commanded them all things which Jehovah spake with them in Mount Sinai"—that hereby is signified a command concerning the primary truths which were to be represented, revealed from heaven, appears from the signification of commanding, when from Jehovah to Moses, as denoting a command; that it is a command concerning the primary truths which were to be represented, is manifest from this consideration, that the things which were commanded, and which are contained from verses 12 to 28, were primary truths, which were to be represented that they might be received, see above, n. 10,637; and from the signification of which Jehovah spake with him from Mount Sinai, as denoting which were revealed from heaven, for by Jehovah speaking is signified what was revealed, and by Mount Sinai heaven, from which is Divine Truth, n. 9420.

10,700. "And Moses left off speaking with them"—that hereby is signified after information concerning primary truths, which were to be represented in things external, appears from what was said just above, n. 10,699.

10,701. "And gave the vail upon his faces"—that hereby is signified that the internal of the church, of worship, and of the Word, did not appear to the Israelitish nation, but only the external without the internal, appears from the signification of giving a vail upon his faces, as denoting to close the internal, that only the external without the internal may appear, for by the shining of the skin of the faces of Moses, is signified the giving forth light of the internal of the Word, of the church, and of worship, in things external, see above, n. 10,691. That that nation was in things external without an internal, and likewise at this day is so, see the passages cited above, n. 10,692. From these considerations it is also evident how the external of the Word, of the church, and of worship, with that nation, appears in the heavens, namely, that it is not indeed as the face of a man, but as a vail before the face; for they are in such obscurity concerning the interiors of the Word.

10,702. "And when Moses entered in before Jehovah to speak with Him"—that hereby is signified the state of the external when the internal from the Lord flowed in, and it received information, appears from the representation of Moses, as denoting an external in which is an internal, see n. 10,694; and from the signification of entering in before Jehovah, as denoting its state when the Lord flows in, of which we shall speak presently; and from the signification of speaking, as denoting information, see the passages cited, n. 10,277. With the external, when the internal flows-in into it, which is signified by Moses entering in before Jehovah, the case is this; with men there are two states as to those things which relate to the church, to worship, and the Word; some turn themselves to the Lord, thus to heaven, but some to themselves and to the world; they who turn themselves to the Lord, or to heaven, receive influx thence and are in illustration, and thereby in the perception of truth inwardly in themselves; this influx is effected from the Lord by [or through] the internal into the external; this is here signified by entering in before Jehovah. But they who turn themselves to themselves and to the world, cannot receive any influx from the Lord or from heaven, thus cannot be in any illustration and perception of truth; for the world flows in from the views of self, and altogether extinguishes, or repels, or perverts, whatsoever comes from heaven; hence they are in thick darkness concerning all things of the church, of worship, and of the Word; this is signified by the vail before the faces of Moses. The interiors of man also actually turn themselves according to the loves; with those who love the Lord, the interiors turn themselves to the Lord or heaven, thus inwards, but they who love themselves turn themselves to the world, thus outwards. To turn oneself to the Lord is to be turned by the Lord Himself, for man of himself cannot elevate his interiors; but to turn oneself to oneself is to be turned of hell, and when this is the case, then those things which are of the internal man are closed, lest man should serve two lords.

10,703. "He removed the vail even to his going forth"—that hereby is signified a state of illustration on the occasion, appears from the signification of removing the vail, as denoting the appearance of the internal, for when the vail was removed, the faces were laid open, and the shining of their skin; and by faces are signified the interiors, and by shining, light thence derived in the external. That faces denote the interiors, see the passages cited, n. 9546; and that the shining of the skin of the faces of Moses denotes the giving forth lights, or light derived from the internal in the external of the Word, n. 10,691. It is called light, because the light which illuminates the internal of man is the Divine Truth proceeding from the Lord. That this is the light of heaven, thus the light by which angels and spirits see, and also by which man, who is illustrated, has perception and intelligence, see the passages cited, n. 9548, 9684. It is said, light in the external of the Word from its internal, but thereby is meant light in the external of man from his internal when he reads it, for the Word is not lucent of itself but before man, who is in light from the internal, without which the Word is merely the letter. Hence now it is evident whence was the shining of the skin of the faces of Moses, and what it signifies in the internal sense.

10,704. "And he went forth and spake to the sons of Israel that which was commanded"—that hereby is signified communication with those who are in things external without an internal, concerning those things of which he was informed by [or through] the internal, appears from the signification of going forth and speaking, as denoting communication, for what Moses heard from Jehovah, when he went forth, he communicated with the sons of Israel; and from the representation of the sons of Israel, as denoting those who are in things external without things internal, see the passages cited, n. 10,692; and from the signification of what was commanded by Jehovah, as denoting the things of which Moses was informed by the Lord. That to be commanded denotes to be informed, is evident, and that Jehovah in the Word is the Lord, see the passages cited, n. 9373.

10,705. "And the sons of Israel saw the faces of Moses, that the skin of the faces of Moses shone"—that hereby is signified that the Israelitish nation indeed acknowledged that there is given in the Word an internal, but that they are not willing to know what is its quality, appears from the signification of seeing, as denoting perception, understanding, faith, see n. 2150, 2325, 2807, 3764, 3863, 3869, 4403 to 4421, 4567, 4723, 5118,

5400, 6805, 7650, 9128; hence also acknowledgment, 897 3796; and from the signification of the faces of Moses, as denoting the internal things of the Word, see above, n. 10,703, and from the signification of the shining of the skin of his faces, as denoting the giving forth light of the internal in the external, see also above, n. 10,703. That that nation acknowledges that an internal is given in the Word, is a known thing, for they say that Divine arcana are stored up therein even in every syllable; but when they are told that those arcana are concerning the Lord, concerning His kingdom in the heavens and in the earths, and concerning love and faith in Him, they are not willing to know. This is meant by that nation acknowledging indeed that an internal is given in the Word, but not being willing to know what is its quality; wherefore also it follows, that Moses drew back the vail over his faces, by which is signified that on that account the internal was closed to them.

10,706. "And Moses drew back the vail over his faces"—that hereby is signified that on that account internal things were closed to them, appears from the signification of drawing back the vail over the faces, when concerning Moses, by whom is represented the Word, as denoting to close the internal things of the Word, see above, n. 10,701. How the case herein is, appears from what was said just above, n. 10,705.

10,707. "Even to his entering-in to speak with Him"—that hereby is signified howsoever they are informed, appears from the signification of even to Moses entering-in to speak with Jehovah, as signifying a state of the external when the internal from the Lord flowed-in, and it received information, see above, n. 10,702. The reason why it also here denotes howsoever they are informed, is, because by Moses is represented the external of the Word in which is the internal, n. 10,694, and he entered in before Jehovah and went out, and informed them; for by entering-in and going out is signified communication, n. 5249, 6901, and by speaking information, see the passages cited, n. 10,277. That they are not willing to know any thing concerning the internal things of the Word, of the church, and of worship, which relate to the Lord, to His kingdom, and to love and faith in Him, is very manifest from this consideration, that they were not willing to acknowledge the Lord, howsoever, He, when He was in the world, informed them from the Word, and that neither at this day are they willing to acknowledge, although they live amongst Christians, and know that it is predicted in the Word, that the Messiah, that is, Christ, was to come. The reason why they have not acknowledged, neither do acknowledge, is, because they apply all things of the Word to themselves, and to self-pre-eminence over others, thus in favor of their own loves, which are the loves of self and the world. All who do so, see nothing from heaven their internal being closed, which ought to be opened into heaven, wherefore they have nothing of light from that source; on this account they are in thick darkness and blindness concerning spiritual things, thus concerning the internal of the Word, of the church, and of worship. The internal of the Word is spiritual, its external is natural. When it is said the internal of the Word, it is also meant the internal of the church and of worship, since the church is where the Word is, and from the Word, and worship is from those things which are in the Word; hence such as is man's understanding of the Word, such is the church in him, and such his worship.

CONTINUATION OF THE SUBJECT CONCERNING THE FOURTH EARTH IN THE STARRY HEAVEN.

10,708. *WHEN I inquired further concerning their discourse, they said, that the inhabitants have not articulate speech as with me, but that still it closes into somewhat sonorous with a certain elocution as if it was articulate. The nature of this elocution resembling what is articulate was explained, namely, that it was not by expressions, but by ideas, such as are in the proximate thought in which man is when he speaks; which ideas manifestly differ from the ideas of interior thought, in which man is when he does not speak, and when he judges things. From that sonorous* [expression] *thus modified by ideas, discourse is perceived more fully than discourse by expression, for the general affection, which is in the sound of man's speech, being thus modified by ideas, gives an interior, and thereby a fuller perception.*

10,709. *They said further, that when they discourse with each other they advance generally to the ninth use, and that there are some given in the universe, who in speaking advance to the fifth use, to the seventh use, to the tenth, to the fifteenth, to the twentieth, even to the fiftieth. When I wondered what this meant, it was explained, namely, that it consisted in speaking so remotely from the thing, which was the subject of discourse. The case was illustrated by examples; as when any one is in the temple, and it is asked where he is, they do not say that he is there, but either that he is not with himself, or far from his own house, and so forth; by which they mean that he is with God, thus in the temple, for he who is in the temple is with God; and so far as he is with God, so far he is not with himself, or in his own house, by being in his own house they also mean being with himself To take also another example; when any one binds another by such things as are of his love, they say to him, thou knowest how to do it, or now thou art in it, or now it is in thee, or otherwise if it only be remote; this is called speaking to the fifth, the ninth the fifteenth, the twentieth, even to the fiftieth use. To speak to use, is a form of expression received in heaven, and signifies to what degree from the thing which is the subject; and what is wonderful, when any one speaks so remotely, they know instantly to what degree without counting it. They who are in cogitative speech, in which the inhabitants of that earth are and several others, who in like manner join in discourse by the face and the lips, and by sonorous* [expression] *varied according to the ideas of thought, perceive instantly the thing of which it is so said for thought itself more fully unfolds and publishes itself by such speech, than by the speech of expressions, which is respectively material.*

10,710. *On account of such a mode of thinking and speaking, the spirits of that earth cannot be together with the spirits of our earth, since the spirits of our earth think and speak from the thing itself, and not remotely from it. Neither can they be together with the spirits of the earth Mercury, since these also stop in the proximate use; wherefore they remove themselves from the latter and from the former, as far as they are able.*

10,711. *They wish to be bearded, and to appear old, by reason that they always choose and set over themselves a certain bearded old man, who is as it were their king and high priest; the common people also worship him, and love to live according to his manner of living, insomuch that they believe that his life is communicated with them. But the more intelligent of them worship God. Such a bearded old man, who had been their high priest, was with the rest attendant upon me; he, inasmuch as he received Divine worship from the plebeian spirits, and induced them to believe that his life was communicated with them, was grievously punished, which was done by wrapping up in a sack, and by contortion; and he was afterwards cast into the hell near his own earth.*

10,712. *When it was given them to see the objects of this earth through my eyes, they attended but little to them, by reason that it was familiar to them to think remotely from proximate objects, thus neither to see them except in a shade, for such as the thought of man is, such is his sight, since it is the interior sight, which is of the thought, which sees in the exterior, and by it. They said on this occasion, that their earth is very full of rocks, and that there are only some valleys between the rocks which are cultivated. But it was perceived that it was only of such a quality where they dwelt, and that in other places it was otherwise. They were with me almost during a whole day.*

10,713. *The fifth earth seen in the starry heaven, will be described at the close of the following chapter.*

EXODUS.

CHAPTER THE THIRTY-FIFTH.

THE DOCTRINE OF CHARITY AND FAITH.

10,714. THERE are two [things or principles] which make the life of man, love, and faith; love [makes] the life of his will, and faith the life of his understanding: hence such as the love is, and such as the faith is, such is the life.

10,715. The love of good and the faith of truth thence derived make the life of heaven; and the love of evil and the faith of what is false thence derived make the life of hell.

10,716. The Divine of the Lord makes the heavens, and heaven is with every one according to the reception of love and faith from the Lord.

10,717. With all who receive love and faith from the Lord there is heaven, both with angels and with men; wherefore they who have heaven in themselves, whilst they live in the world, come into heaven after death.

10,718. They who have heaven in themselves, will good to all, and perceive a delight in doing good to others, not for the sake of themselves and the world, but for the sake of good and for the sake of the truth which teaches that so it ought to be done. But they who have hell in themselves, will evil to all, and perceive a delight in doing evil to others; these, if they perceive a delight in doing good, it is not for the sake of good and truth, but for the sake of themselves and the world.

10,719. Heaven is with man in his internal, thus in thinking and willing, and hence in the external, that is, in speaking and doing; but not in the external without the internal; for all hypocrites can speak well and do well, but not think well and will well. By thinking well and willing well is meant what is from the love of good and from the faith of truth.

10,720. When man comes into the other life, as is the case immediately after death, it is evident whether heaven be in him or hell, but not when he lives in the world; for in the world the external only appears, and not the internal, but in the other life the internal is made manifest, since man then lives as to the spirit.

10,721. From these considerations it may be manifest what makes heaven, namely, that it is love to the Lord and love towards the neighbor, and likewise faith, but this latter only so far as it has life from those loves. Hence it is again evident that the Divine of the Lord makes heaven, for both that love and the faith thence derived are from the Lord; and whatsoever is from the Lord is Divine.

10,722. Eternal happiness, which is also called heavenly joy, is imparted to those who are in love and faith to the Lord from the Lord; that love and that faith have in them that joy; man comes into it after death, who has heaven in himself; in the mean time it lies stored up and concealed in his internal.

10,723. In the heavens there is a communion of all goods; the peace, intelligence, wisdom, and happiness of all, are communicated to every one there, and those of every one are communicated to all, nevertheless to each according to the reception of love and of faith from the Lord. Hence it is evident how great peace, intelligence, wisdom, and happiness, is in heaven.

10,724. They with whom the love of self and the love of the world reign, do not know what heaven is, and what the happiness of heaven, and it appears incredible to them, that happiness is given in any other loves than in those; when yet the happiness of heaven only so far enters, as those loves are removed as ends; the happiness which succeeds, on their removal, is so great, that it exceeds every apprehension of man.

CHAPTER XXXV.

1. AND Moses gathered together all the company of the sons of Israel, and said to them, These are the words which JEHOVAH hath commanded to do [or make] them.

2. Six days shall work be done, and in the seventh day shall be holiness to you, the sabbath of a sabbath to JEHOVAH, every one that doeth work in it shall die.

3. Ye shall not kindle a fire in all your habitations on the day of the sabbath.

4. And Moses said to all the company of the sons of Israel, saying, This word hath JEHOVAH commanded, saying,

5. Take from being with you an offering to JEHOVAH, every one spontaneous in his heart shall bring an offering to JEHOVAH, gold, and silver, and brass.

6. And blue and purple, and scarlet double-dyed, and fine linen and she-goats.

7. And the skins of red rams, and the skins of badgers, and the wood of Shittim.

8. And oil for the luminary, and aromatics for the oil of anointing, and for the incense of aromatics.

9. And onyx-stones, and stones of fillings for the ephod and for the breast-plate.

10. And every wise one in heart in you, let them come and do [or make] all things which JEHOVAH hath commanded.

11. The habitation, its tent, and its covering, its little handles, and its planks, its staves, its pillars, and its bases.

12. The ark and its staves, the propitiatory, and the vail of covering.

13. The table and its staves, and all its vessels, and the bread of faces.

14. And the candlestick of the luminary and its vessels, and its lamps, and the oil of the luminary.

15. And the altar of incense, and its staves, and the oil of anointing, and the incense of spices, and the covering of the door for the door of the habitation.

16. The altar of burnt-offering and the grate of brass which is for it, its staves, and all its vessels, the laver and its base.

17. The hangings of the court, its pillars, and its bases, and the covering of the gate of the court.

18. The pegs of the habitation, and the pegs of the court, and their cords.

19. The garments of ministry, to minister in the holy [place], the garments of holiness for Aaron the priest, and the garments of his sons, to perform the office of the priesthood.

20. And they went forth all the company of the sons of Israel from before Moses.

21. And they came every man [*vir*], whom his heart impelled, and every one whom his spirit moved him spontaneously, brought an offering to JEHOVAH for the work of the tent of the congregation, and for all its ministry, and for the garments of holiness.

22. And they came the men with the women, every one spontaneous of heart brought a clasp, and an ear-ring, and a ring, and a girdle, every vessel of gold, and every man who shook a shaking of gold to JEHOVAH.

23. And every man with whom was found blue and purple, and scarlet double-dyed, and fine linen, and she-goats, and skins of red rams, and skins of badgers, brought [them].

24. Every one lifting an offering of silver and of brass, brought an offering to JEHOVAH; and every one with whom was found shittim-wood for all the work of the ministry, brought it.

25. And every woman wise in heart spun with their own hands, and they brought spinning, blue and purple, scarlet double-dyed, and fine linen.

26. And all the women, whose hearts impelled them in wisdom, spun she-goats [hair].

27. And the princes brought onyx-stones, and stones of fillings for the ephod and for the breast-plate.

28. And spice, and oil for the luminary, and for the oil of anointing and for the incense of spices.

29. And every man and woman, whose heart moved them spontaneously to bring for every work, which JEHOVAH had commanded to be done by the hand of Moses, the sons of Israel brought what was spontaneous to JEHOVAH.
30. And Moses said to the sons of Israel, See ye, JEHOVAH hath called by name Bezaleel, the son of Uri, the son of Hur of the tribe of Judah.
31. And hath filled him with the spirit of GOD in wisdom, in intelligence, and in science, and in every work.
32. And to contrive contrivances to do [or make] in gold, and in silver, and in brass.
33. And in the engraving of a stone for filling, and in the engraving of wood to do [or make] in every work of contrivance.
34. And to teach hath given into his heart, him and Aholiab the son of Ahisamach of the tribe of Dan.
35. He hath filled them with wisdom of heart to do [or make] every work of the artificer, and of the contriver, and of the worker with the needle, in blue, and in purple, in scarlet double-dyed, and in fine linen, and of the weaver, doing [or making] every work, and contriving contrivances.

THE CONTENTS.

10,725. THE subject treated of in this chapter, in the internal sense, is in general all kinds of good and truth, which are in the church and in heaven, from which the worship of the Lord is performed. These are the things which are signified by those things which the sons of Israel spontaneously contributed to make the tabernacle with all things therein, also the altar of burnt-offering, and likewise the garments of Aaron and of his sons.

THE INTERNAL SENSE.

10,726. VERSES 1, 2, 3. *And Moses gathered together all the company of the sons of Israel, and said to them, these are the words which Jehovah hath commanded to do them. Six days shall work be done, and in the seventh day, shall be holiness to you, the sabbath of a sabbath to Jehovah; every one that doeth work in that day shall die. Ye shall not kindle a fire in all your habitations on the day of the sabbath.* And Moses gathered together all the company of the sons of Israel, signifies all goods and truths of the church in the complex. And said to them.

these are the words which Jehovah hath commanded to do them, signifies instruction concerning the primary things of the church, to which all things have reference. Six days shall work be done, signifies the first state of the regeneration of man from the Lord, and, in the supreme sense, of the glorification of the Human. And in the seventh day shall be holiness to you, the sabbath of a sabbath to Jehovah, signifies the second state of the regeneration of man when he has conjunction with the Lord, and in the supreme sense, the union of the Human of the Lord with the Divine Itself. Every one that doeth work in that day shall die, signifies spiritual death to those who are led of themselves and their own loves, and not of the Lord. Ye shall not kindle a fire in all your habitations on the day of the sabbath, signifies that nothing of the love of the proprium, which is the love of self and the world, ought to appear in all and singular the things of man which are from the Lord.

10,727. And Moses gathered together all the company of the sons of Israel"—that hereby are signified all truths and goods of the church in the complex, appears from the signification of the company of the sons of Israel, as denoting all truths and goods of the church in the complex, see n. 7830, 7843; thus by gathering together that company is signified the enumeration of all. For in what follows, all the things are enumerated which the sons of Israel contributed to make the tabernacle, with all things therein, also the altar of burnt-offering, and likewise the garments of Aaron and of his sons, and by those things are signified all the kinds of good and truth which constitute the church.

10,728. "And said to them, these are the words which Jehovah commanded to do them"—that hereby is signified instruction concerning the primary [thing or principle] of the church, to which all things have reference, appears from the signification of saying, as denoting instruction, see the passages cited, n. 10,277; and from the signification of the words which Jehovah commanded to do, as denoting the primary truth which was altogether to be observed. The reason why this is signified, is, because those things are said of the sabbath, which was the primary representative of all, thus the primary truth to which all have reference; for the representatives of the church with the Israelitish nation were truths in the ultimate of order. For with representatives the case is this; those things which appear in nature, in her threefold kingdom, are the ultimates of Divine Order, for all things of heaven, which are called spiritual and celestial, terminate in them; hence it is that the representative church was instituted, and such things were commanded as in ultimates altogether represented heaven with all the truths and goods the in, and the things which represented were forms of such things as are in nature, as the tabernacle encompassed with curtains, the table therein on which were the breads of faces, the candlestick with lamps, the altar on which incense was offered, the garments of Aaron with the breast-plate of precious stones, besides other things; what such things represented, has been shown in what goes before.

10,729. "Six days shall work be done"—that hereby is signified the first state of the regeneration of man from the Lord, and in the supreme sense of the glorification of the Human of the Lord, appears from the signification of the six days which precede the seventh or the sabbath, and in which work was to be done, as denoting the first state of the regeneration of man from the Lord, which state is when man is in truths and by truths is leading to good, and then is in combats, see n. 8510, 8888, 9431, 10,360. That it also denotes the state of the glorification of the Human of the Lord, when He was in the world, and from Divine Truth fought against the hells, and reduced all things therein and in the heavens into order, see n. 10,360. For there are two states appertaining to man when he is regenerating from the Lord, the former when he is in truths, and by truths is leading to good, the latter when he is in good, and from good sees and loves truths; man in the former state is led indeed of the Lord, but by his own proprium, for to act from truths is to act from those things which appertain to man, but to act from good is to act from the Lord. Hence it is evident, that so far as man suffers himself by good to be led to truths, so far he is led of the Lord and to the Lord; for there is action and re-action in all things which are conjoined, the active principle is good, and the re-active is truth; but truth in no case re-acts from itself, but from good, hence so far as truth receives good, so far it re-acts, and so far as it re-acts, so far it is conjoined to it. Hence also it follows that the Lord, before man is conjoined to Him, draws him by truths to Himself; and so far as man suffers himself to be drawn, so far he is conjoined; for Divine Truths are such, that they may be adapted to good, since truths exist from good; hence now man has perception which in itself is re-active; to suffer oneself to be acted upon or to be led by truths to good, is to live according to them. These observations are made, that it may in some measure be known how the case is with the first state of the man who is regenerating, which is signified by the six days of labor.

10,730. "And in the seventh day shall be holiness to you, the sabbath of a sabbath to Jehovah"—that hereby is signified a second state of the regeneration of man when he has conjunction with the Lord, and that in the supreme sense it signifies the union of the Human of the Lord with the Divine itself, appears from the representation of the sabbath, as denoting another state of the regeneration of man, when man is in good, and is thereby led of the Lord, see n. 8510, 8890, 8893, 9274; and that in the supreme sense it denotes the union of the Human with the Divine itself in the Lord, see n. 8495, 10,356, 10,367, 10,374; for when the Lord was in the world, He first made His Human Divine Truth, but when He went out of the world, He made His Human Divine Good by union with the Divine itself, which was in Himself; this is represented by the sabbath in the supreme sense, wherefore it is called the sabbath of a sabbath to Jehovah. The Lord does the like with man, whom He regenerates, first imbuing him with truths, and afterwards by truths conjoining him to good, thus to Himself; this is represented by the sabbath in the respective sense, for the regeneration of man is an image of the glorification of the Lord, that is, as the Lord glorified His Human, so He regenerates man. By sabbath in the proper sense is signified rest and peace, because when the Lord united His Human to the Divine itself, He had peace, for on that occasion combats ceased, and all things in the heavens and in the hells were reduced into order; and thus not only Himself had peace, but also the angels in the heavens and men in the earths had peace and salvation. Inasmuch as those two things are the universals themselves, on which all other things of the church depend, therefore the sanctification of the sabbath is alone proposed, by which those two things are signified; for the universal of all is, that the Lord united His Human to the Divine itself; and that hence man has peace and salvation; and it is likewise a universal, that man ought to be conjoined to the Lord, which is effected by regeneration, that he may have peace and salvation; on this account also the sabbath with the Israelitish nation was a principal representative, and a principal sign of the covenant with Jehovah, that is, of conjunction with the Lord, see n. 10,357, 10,372; covenant denotes conjunction.

10,731. "Every one that doeth work in it shall die"—that hereby is signified spiritual death to those who are led of themselves and their own loves, and not of the Lord, appears from the signification of works on the day of the sabbath, as denoting to be led of themselves and their own loves, and not of the Lord, see n. 8495, 10,360, 10,362, 10,365; and from the signification of dying, as denoting damnation or spiritual death, see n. 6119, 9008. They who are led of themselves and of their own loves, do not believe in the Lord, for to believe in the Lord is from Him and not from themselves; hence it is that they also make light of the union of His Human with the Divine itself; and likewise make light of regeneration from the Lord, and thus also make light of the truths of the church; for they say in themselves, what are such things, or of what concern is it whether we know them, yea, whether we think them, and desire them? Do not we still live as others, and what is the difference?

The reason why they so think, is, because they think from the life of the world, and not from the life of heaven; the life of heaven is a thing unknown to them, and no one can think from what is unknown; wherefore they who are of such a character cannot be saved, for they have not heaven in themselves, on which account neither can they be in heaven; their interiors are not in accord, for unless these be arranged by the Lord in the image of heaven, there is no conjunction with heaven. Such are they who deny the above universals. This state of man is what is signified by works on the day of the sabbath, and their spiritual death is signified by their natural death.

10,732. "Ye shall not kindle a fire in all your habitations on the day of the sabbath"—that hereby is signified that nothing of the love of the proprium, which is the love of self and of the world, ought then to appear in all and singular the things of man which are from the Lord, appears from the signification of fire, as denoting love in each sense, see n. 6832, 7324, 7575, 9041, in this case man's own proper love, which is the love of self and of the world, from which comes all concupiscence and every thing evil and false; and from the signification of the habitations of the sons of Israel, as denoting the goods and truths of the church which appertain to man from the Lord; for habitations denote the interior things appertaining to man, thus the things which are of his mind, see n. 7719, 7910, 8269, 8309, 10,513; in this case therefore the goods and truths which are from the Lord; and the sons of Israel denote the church, n. 9340. Inasmuch as such things were signified by fire, therefore it was forbidden to kindle a fire on the day of the sabbath. How the case is in regard to being led of themselves and their own loves, and not of the Lord, see just above, n. 10,724.

10,733. What is said from verse 4 to the end of the chapter is passed by without explication, since all and singular the things therein have been before explained in chapters xxv. xxvi. xxvii. xxviii. xxix. xxx. xxxi. speaking of the tabernacle, and of all things therein, also of the altar of burnt-offering, and of the garments of Aaron and of his sons; for here only such things are enumerated as have been before explained.

CONCERNING A FIFTH EARTH IN THE STARRY HEAVEN.

10,734. *I WAS conducted on another occasion to another earth, which is in the universe out of our solar system, and this was effected by changes of the state of my mind, thus as to the spirit, for, as has been occasionally said above, a spirit is conducted from place to place in no other manner than by changes of the state of his interiors, which changes still appear to him as advancements from place to place, or as journeyings. Those changes were continued for about ten hours, before I came from the state of my life to the state of their life, thus before I was brought thither as to my spirit. To change thus the state of the mind successively so as to accede to the state of another, which is so far distant, can be effected by the Lord alone. I was carried towards the east to the left, and I seemed gradually to be elevated from the plane of the horizon. It was also given clearly to observe progression and promotion from a former place, until at length they, from whom I was departed, no longer appeared; and in the mean time I discoursed on various subjects in the way with the spirits who were together with me.*

10,735. *A certain spirit also was with me, who during his life in the world, had been an exceedingly pathetic preacher and writer; from the idea respecting him in myself the attendant spirits supposed that he was in heart a Christian superior to others; for in the world an idea is conceived and judgment is formed from preachings and from writings, and not from the life, if this is not extant, and if any thing of the life appears to be discordant, it is still excused; for the idea, or thought and perception concerning any one, draws every thing over to its own side.*

10,736. *Afterwards I observed that I was in the starry heaven as to the spirit, far beyond the world of our sun, for this can be observed from the changes of state, and hence the apparent progression continued almost ten hours; at length I heard spirits speaking near some earth, which was afterwards seen by me; to whom when I approached, after some discourse together, they said that occasionally guests visit them from a distance, who speak with them concerning God, and confound the ideas of their thought; they also pointed out the way by which they come, whereby it was perceived that they were spirits from our earth; and when they were questioned concerning the subject of such confusion of idea, they said that it arose from this, that they profess to believe in the Divine distinguished into three persons, which still they call one God; and when the idea of their thought is explored, it is presented as a Trinity* [trinum] *not continuous but discrete, and with some as three persons discoursing together, one to the other; and although they call each person God, and have a separate idea of each, still they say they are one God; they complained exceedingly of this confusion of ideas, in consequence of thinking of three and saying one, when yet they ought to think as they say, and to say as they think. The preacher, who was with me, was then also explored as to the quality of the idea which he had of one God and three persons: he represented three gods, yet one by continuity, but exhibited this threefold-one as invisible because Divine, and when he exhibited this, it was per ceived that he then thought only of the Father and not of the Lord, and that his idea concerning the invisible God was no other than as of nature in her first principles, the result of which was, that the inmost principle of nature was to him his Divine. It is to be noted that the idea of every one's thought on any subject whatsoever in the other life is livingly presented, and that by it every one is explored as to the quality of his faith; and that the idea of thought concerning God is the principal of all, for by that idea, if it be genuine, conjunction is effected with heaven; for the Divine is what makes heaven.*

10,737. *They were next asked what idea they had concerning God; they replied, that they do not conceive God to be invisible, but to be visible under a human form; and that they know this not only from interior perception, but also from this, that He has appeared to them as a man, adding, that if according to the idea of some strangers and of the preacher, they conceived God as invisible, they could not in any wise think of God, since what is invisible does not fall into the idea of thought; I perceived that on this account what is invisible was to them without form, thus without quality, and the idea which is without form and quality, is either dissipated, or falls into nature which is visible. On hearing these things it was given to say to them, that they do well in thinking of God under a human form, and that many from our earth think in like manner, especially when concerning the Lord; and that the ancients thought in no other manner; I then told them of Abraham, of Lot, of Gideon, and of Manoah and his wife, and what is related concerning them in our Word, namely, that they saw God under a human form, and acknowledged Him when seen to be the Creator of the universe, and called Him Jehovah, and this also from interior perception; but that at this day that interior perception has perished in the Christian world, and only remains with the simple who are in faith.*

10,738. *Before these things were said they believed that our company also was of that sort, which was willing to confound them by an idea of three concerning God; wherefore on hearing these things they said that from God, whom they then called the Lord, there were also sent some to teach them concerning Himself, and that they are not willing to admit strangers who disturb them, especially by three persons in the Divinity; inasmuch as they know that God is one, consequently that the Divine is one, and not what is unanimous from three, unless they are willing to think of God as of an angel, in whom the inmost principle of life is what is invisible, from which He thinks and is wise, and the external principle of life is what is visible under a human form, from which he sees and acts; and the proceeding principle of life is what is the sphere of love and of faith around him, for every spirit and angel, from the sphere of life proceeding from him, is perceived at a distance as to his quality respecting love and faith; and in regard to the Lord, that the proceeding principle of life from Him is the Divine itself which fills the heavens and makes them, because it is from the very esse itself of the life of love and of faith. On hearing these things it was given to say, that such an idea concerning what is trine and at the same time one, accords with the angelic idea concerning the Lord, and that it is from the very doctrine of the Lord concerning Himself, for He teaches that the Father and Himself are one; that the Father is in Him and He in the Father; that whoso seeth Him seeth the Father; and whoso believeth in Him believeth in the Father and knoweth Him; also that the Paraclete, whom He calls the Spirit of Truth, and also the Holy Spirit, proceeds from Him, and does not speak from Himself, but from Him, by whom is meant the Divine proceeding; and further, that the idea concerning what is trine and at the same time one, agrees with the esse and existere of the life of the Lord when He was in the world. The esse of His life was the Divine itself, for He was conceived of Jehovah, and the esse of the life of every one is that from which he is conceived; the existere of life from that esse is the Human in form. The esse of the life of every man, which he has from his father, is called soul, and the existere of life thence derived is called body; soul and body constitute one man; the likeness between each is as between that which is an effort* [conatus] *and that which is in act thus derived, for act is effort acting, and thus two are one. Effort in man is called will, and effort acting is called action; the body is the instrumental, by which the will, which is the principal, acts, and the instrumental and the principal in acting together are one; thus soul and body. Such an idea concerning soul and body the angels in heaven have; hence they know that the Lord made His Human Divine from the Divine in Himself, which was to Him a soul from the Father. The faith also received throughout the Christian world does not dissent* [from this idea], *for it teaches,* "As body and soul are one man, so also God and Man in the Lord is one Christ." *Inasmuch as such was the union, or such the one in the Lord, therefore He not only rose again as to the soul, but also as to the body, which He glorified in the world, otherwise than any man; on which subject He also instructed the disciples, saying, "Handle Me and see,* for a spirit hath not flesh and bones, as ye see Me have." *Hence it is that the church acknowledges the omnipresence of His Human in the sacrament of the supper, which could not be acknowledged unless His Human also was Divine. These things were well understood by those spirits, for such things fall into the understanding of angelic spirits, and they said, that the Lord alone has power in the heavens, and that the heavens are His; to which it was given to reply, that the church also knows this from the mouth of the Lord Himself before He ascended into heaven, for He then said,* "All power is given unto Me in heaven and in earth."

10,739. *A continuation of the subject concerning this fifth earth in the starry heaven, will be given at the close of the following chapter.*

EXODUS.

CHAPTER THE THIRTY-SIXTH.

THE DOCTRINE OF CHARITY AND FAITH.

10,740. WHAT any one does from love, remains inscribed on his heart, for love is the fire of life, thus is the life of every one; hence such as the love is, such is the life, and such as the life is, such is the whole man as to soul and as to body.

10,741. As love to the Lord and love towards the neighbor make the life of heaven with man, so the love of self and the love of the world, when they reign, make the life of hell with him; for these latter loves are opposite to the former; wherefore they with whom the loves of the world and of self reign, can receive nothing from heaven, but the things which they receive are from hell. For whatsoever a man thinks, and whatsoever he wills, or whatsoever a man believes, and whatsoever he loves, is either from heaven or from hell.

10,742. Hence it is that they with whom the love of self and the love of the world make the life, will good to themselves alone, and not to others, except for the sake of themselves; and whereas their life is from hell, they despise others in comparison with themselves, they are angry at them if they do not favor themselves, they hate them, burn with revenge against them, yea, are desirous to commit all outrage towards them; these things at length become the delights of their life, thus the loves.

10,743. These are they who have hell in themselves, and who after death come into hell, since their life agrees with the life of those who are in hell; for all in hell are of such a quality; and every one comes to his own.

10,744. They, inasmuch as they receive nothing from heaven, in their heart deny God, and a life after death, and hence also make light of all things of the church. It is of no consequence that they do good to a fellow-citizen, to society, to their country, and to the church, and that they speak well concerning them, for these things they do for the sake of themselves and for the sake of the world, that they may save appearances and may secure reputation, honor, and gain. Those things to them are external bonds, by which they are brought to do good, and are withheld from doing evil. But they have no internal bonds which are those of conscience, that evil ought not to be done because it is sin and contrary to Divine laws.

10,745. Wherefore they, when they come into the other life, as is the case immediately after death, and external things are taken away from them, rush headlong into every wickedness according to their interior principles, which are contempt of others in comparison with themselves, enmity, hatred, revenge, savageness, and cruelty, and moreover hypocrisy, fraud, deceit, and several other things which are of malice. These things are to them in such case the delights of life; wherefore they are separated from the good and are cast into hell.

10,746. That such things are to them the delight of life, is unknown to the generality of the world, since those things hide themselves in the loves of self and of the world, and then all things which favor them are called goods, and which confirm them are called truths; nor do they know and acknowledge any other goods and truths, because they receive nothing from heaven, which they have closed to themselves.

10,747. Inasmuch as love is the fire of life, and every one has life according to his love, it may hence be known what heavenly fire is, and what infernal fire. Heavenly fire is love to the Lord and love towards the neighbor, and infernal fire is the love of self and the love of the world, and hence the concupiscence of all evils, which flow from those loves as from their fountains.

10,748. What is the quality of life appertaining to those who are in hell, may be concluded from the life of such one amongst another in the world, if external bonds were taken away, and there were no internal ones to restrain.

10,749. The life of man cannot be changed after death, it remains then such as it had been; nor can the life of hell be transcribed into the life of heaven, since they are opposite. Hence it is evident that they who come into hell, remain there to eternity; and that they who come into heaven, remain there to eternity.

CHAPTER XXXVI.

1. AND Bezaleel and Aholiab did [or made], and every man wise in heart, in whom JEHOVAH gave wisdom and intelligence to know to do all the work of the ministry, of what is holy, as to every thing which JEHOVAH commanded.

2. And Moses called to Bezaleel and to Aholiab, and to every man wise in heart, to whom JEHOVAH gave wisdom in his heart, every one whom his heart impelled to come near to the work to do it.

3. And they received from before Moses every up-lifting, which the sons of Israel brought for the work of the ministry of what is holy to do [or make] it; and they brought to him further what was spontaneous in the morning, in the morning.

4. And all the wise ones brought, who did all the work of what is holy, a man-man of his work, which they did.

5. And they said to Moses, saying, the people multiply to bring more than sufficient of ministry for the work which JEHOVAH commanded to do [or make] it.

6. And Moses commanded, that they promulgated a voice in the camp, saying, let not a man and a woman do [or make] any longer work for the up-lifting of what is holy, and he restrained the people from bringing.

7. And the work was sufficient for every work to do [or make] it, and there was what was superfluous.

8. And every wise one in heart with those who did [or made] work, made the habitation with ten curtains, with fine linen interwoven, and blue, and purple, and scarlet double-dyed; and cherubs, the work of the contriver he made them.

9. The length of one curtain eight and twenty in a cubit, and the breadth four in a cubit, of one curtain; one measure for all the curtains.

10. And he joined together the five curtains, one to one; and the five curtains he joined together one to one.

11. And he made loops of blue upon the borders of one curtain from the end in the joining together, so he made in the border of the extreme curtain in the other joining together.

12. Fifty loops he made in one curtain, and fifty loops he made in the end of the curtain which was in the other joining, the loops took up each other one to one.

13. And he made fifty little handles of gold, and joined the curtains together one to one in the little handles, and it was one habitation.

14. And he made curtains of she-goats [hair] for the tent over the habitation, eleven curtains he made them.

15. The length of one curtain thirty in a cubit, and four

cubits the breadth of one curtain, one measure for the eleven curtains.

16. And he joined together five curtains only, and six curtains only.

17. And he made fifty loops on the border of the last curtain in the joining together, and fifty loops he made on the border of the curtain of the other joining.

18. And he made fifty little handles of brass to join together the tent to be one.

19. And he made a covering for the tent of the skins of red rams, and a covering of the skins of badgers from above.

20. And he made staves for the habitation of shittim-wood standing.

21. Ten cubits the length of a stave, and a cubit and a half of a cubit the breadth of one stave.

22. Two hands to one stave connected together one to one, thus he made for all the staves of the habitation.

23. And he made staves for the habitation, twenty staves for the corner of the south, southward.

24. And forty bases of silver he made under the twenty staves, two bases under one stave for its two hands, and two bases under one stave for its two hands.

25. And for the other side of the habitation at the corner of the north he made twenty staves.

26. And their forty bases of silver, two bases under one stave, and two bases under one stave.

27. And for the legs of the habitation towards the sea he made six staves.

28. And two staves he made for the corners of the habitation in the legs.

29. And they were twined from beneath and together were entire at the head thereof to one ring, so he made for the two in those two corners.

30. And there were eight staves and their bases of silver, sixteen bases, two bases under one stave.

31. And he made bars of shittim-wood five for the staves of the first side of the habitation.

32. And five bars for the staves of the other side of the habitation, and five bars for the staves of the habitation for the legs towards the sea.

33. And he made the middle bar to pass into the middle of the staves from end to end.

34. And the staves he covered over with gold, and their rings he made of gold, receptacles for the bars, and he covered the bars over with gold.

35. And he made a vail of blue, and purple, and scarlet double-dyed, and fine linen interwoven, the work of the contriver he made it of cherubs.

36. And he made for it four pillars of shittim, and covered them over with gold, their hooks of gold, and he fused four bases of silver.

37. And he made a covering for the door of the tent, of blue, and purple, and scarlet double-dyed, and fine linen interwoven, the work of a worker with a needle.

38. And its five pillars, and their hooks, and he covered their heads and their fillets with gold; and their five bases were of brass.

THE CONTENTS.

10,750. WHAT these things signify in the internal sense, is manifest from what has been explained before at chap. xxvi. for they are the same; wherefore the things which are in this chapter are passed by without further explication.

CONTINUATION OF THE SUBJECT CONCERNING THE FIFTH EARTH IN THE STARRY HEAVEN.

10,751. *IT was afterwards given to discourse with those spirits concerning their own earth; for all spirits have this science when their natural or external memory is opened by the Lord, since they bring this memory along with them from the world, but it is not opened except from the good pleasure of the Lord. On this occasion the spirits said concerning their own earth from which they were, that, when leave is given them, they appear to the inhabitants of their earth, and discourse with them as men; and that this is effected by their being let into their natural or external memory, and thence into the thought in which they were when they lived in the world, and that on this occasion the interior sight, or the sight of their spirit, is opened to the inhabitants, and that thus they appear to them. They added, that the inhabitants know no other than that they are men of their earth, and that they then first perceive that they are not, when they are taken away suddenly from their eyes. I told them, that in ancient times the case was similar in our earth, as with Abraham, Sarah, Lot, the inhabitants of Sodom, Manoah and his wife, Joshua, Mary, Elizabeth, and in general with the prophets, and that the Lord in like manner appeared, and they who saw Him did not know, until he revealed Himself, but that He was a man of the earth; but that at this day this rarely comes to pass, lest men by such things should be compelled to believe, for compelled faith, such as is that which enters by miracles, does not inhere, and also might be prejudicial to those with whom faith might be implanted by* [or through] *the Word in a state not compelled.*

10,752. *The preacher who was with me did not believe at all that any other earths were given but our own, by reason of his having thought in the world, that the Lord was born only on this earth, and without the Lord there is no salvation; wherefore he was reduced into a similar state with that of the spirits spoken of just above, when they appear in their own earth as men, and thus he was let into that earth, so that he not only saw it, but also discoursed with the inhabitants there, which being done, communication was also thence given with me, that I saw the inhabitants in like manner, and also some things on that earth. Spirits and angels can discourse with men of every tongue, for their thought falls into the ideas of men, and thus into the expressions of their speech.*

10,753. *There then appeared four kinds of men, but one kind after another successively; first were seen men clothed; next naked, of a human flesh color; afterwards naked, but with a body enflamed; and lastly, black.*

10,754. *When the preacher was with those who are clothed, there appeared a female of a very beautiful countenance, clothed in simple raiment, with a robe hanging decently behind, and also with gloves on the arms, and a beautiful covering for the head, in the form of a garland of flowers; the preacher, on seeing the virgin, was exceedingly delighted, and discoursed with her, and also took hold of her hand; but whereas she perceived that he was a spirit, and not from that earth, she hurried away from him. Afterwards there appeared to him on the right several other females, who fed sheep and lambs, which they were then leading to a drinking trough, into which water was brought through a little channel from a certain lake; they were clothed in like manner, holding in their hands shepherds' crooks, by which they led the sheep and lambs to drink. They said that the sheep go in the direction in which they point with their crooks. The sheep which were seen were large, with woolly, broad, and stretched out tails. The faces of the women were seen nearer, and were full and beautiful. The men were also seen, their faces were of a human flesh color, as in our earth; but with this difference, that the lower part of their face, instead of being bearded, was black; and the nose was more of the color of snow than of flesh.*

10,755. *Afterwards the preacher was brought on further, but unwillingly, because he had still in his thought the female with whom he was delighted, which was evident from this consideration, that there still appeared something of shade from him in the former place. He then came to those who were naked. These were seen, two and two walking together, they were husband and wife, girded with a covering about the loins, and also with a covering about the head. The preacher, when he was with them, was brought into a state in which he was in the world when he was willing to preach, and he then said, that he was desirous to preach before them the Lord crucified; but they said, that they were not willing to hear of any such thing, because they know not what it means, and that they know that the Lord is alive; he then said that he desired to preach the Lord alive, but this also they refused, saying, that they perceived in his speech what was not celestial, but terrestrial, because much for the sake of himself, his own reputation and honor; and that they hear from the very tone of the speech whether it be from the heart, or only from the mouth; and because he was of such a character, that he could not teach them; wherefore he was silent; when he lived in the world he had been very pathetic, so that he could move the hearers to what is holy; but this pathetic principle had been acquired by art, thus it was from himself and the world, and not from heaven.*

10,756. *They said further that they have a perception whether there be a conjugial principle with those of their own nation who are naked; and it was shown that they perceive this from a spiritual idea concerning marriage, which being communicated with me was such, that a similitude of the interiors was formed by the conjunction of truth and of good, thus of faith and of love, and that from that conjunction descending into the body exists conjugial love; for all things which are of the mind* [animus], *are presented in some species in the body, thus in the species of conjugial love, when the interiors of two mutually love each other and from that love desire to will and to think the one as the other, thus as to the interiors which are of the mind* [mens] *to be together and to be conjoined. Hence the spiritual affection, which is of minds, becomes natural in the body, and clothes itself with the sense of conjugial love. They said also that the conjugial principle is not at all given between one man and a plurality of wives.*

10,757. *Afterwards the preacher came to those who were also naked but of an enflamed body; and lastly to those who were black, of whom some were naked, some clothed; but the latter and the former dwelt in other places in the same earth.*

10,758. *Lastly I discoursed with the spirits of that earth concerning the faith of the inhabitants of our earth respecting the resurrection, that they cannot conceive that men, immediately after death, come into another life, and then appear as men as to face, body, arms feet, and as to all the senses external and internal; and still less, that they are clothed with garments: and that they have mansions and habitations, and this merely by reason that most of them think from the sensual things which are of the body, and on this account believe that to be nothing which they do not see and touch; also because few of them can be withdrawn from external sensual things to interior things, and thereby be elevated into the light of heaven. Hence it is, that they cannot have any idea of a man respecting his soul or spirit, but the idea as of wind, air, or breath of no form, wherein yet there is some vital principle. This is the reason why they do not believe that they are to rise again till the end of the world, which they call the last judgment, and then that the body, although crumbled into dust and dissipated in every direction, is to be brought back and conjoined to its soul or spirit. I added, that they are permitted to believe this, since they cannot otherwise conceive, in consequence of thinking only from things sensual, as was said, than that its soul or spirit cannot live a man and in a human form unless it receives that body which it carried about with it in the world; wherefore unless that body was said to rise again, they would reject in heart the doctrine concerning the resurrection and concerning eternal life, as incomprehensible. Nevertheless this idea concerning the resurrection has this advantage with it, that they believe in a life after death; from which faith it follows, that when they lie sick in bed, and do not think as before from things worldly and corporeal, thus not from things sensual, they then believe that they shall live immediately after decease; they speak also, on this occasion, concerning heaven, and concerning the hope of life there immediately after death, remotely from what they had learned by doctrine concerning the last judgment: I further related that I had been occasionally surprised, that when they who are in faith, speak of a life after death, and of their own* [relatives or friends] *who are dying or have deceased, and on this occasion do not think of the last judgment, they believe that they are about to live or do live as men immediately after their decease; but this idea, as soon as thought flows in concerning the last judgment, is changed into a material idea concerning their terrestrial body, that it is again to be conjoined to its soul: for they know not that every man is a spirit as to his interiors, and that this is what lives in the body, and not the body from itself; and that the spirit of every one is that from which the body has its human form, consequently which principally is a man and in like form, but invisible before the eyes of the body, yet visible before the eyes of spirits; hence also, when the sight of the spirit of man is opened, which is effected by the removal of the sight of the body, angels appear; thus angels appeared as men to the ancients, as it is written in the Word. I have also discoursed occasionally with spirits, whom I was acquainted with whilst they lived as men in the world, asking them whether they are willing to be clothed again with their terrestrial body, as they before thought, on hearing which they fled far away at the mere idea of its conjunction, being struck with amazement that in the world they had so thought from blind faith without any understanding.*

10,759. *The subject will be continued concerning the fifth earth in the starry heaven at the close of the following chapter.*

EXODUS.

CHAPTER THE THIRTY-SEVENTH.

THE DOCTRINE OF CHARITY AND FAITH.

10,760. THAT which makes heaven with man, also makes the church, for the church is the Lord's heaven in the earths; hence from what has been before said concerning heaven, it is evident what the church is.

10,761. That is called the church where the Lord is acknowledged, and where the Word is; for the essentials of the church are love and faith to the Lord from the Lord, and the Word teaches how man ought to live that he may receive love and faith from the Lord.

10,762. The church of the Lord is internal and external, internal with those who from love do the precepts of the Lord, for these are they who love the Lord; external with those who from faith do the precepts of the Lord, for these are they who believe in the Lord.

10,763. To the intent that there may be a church, there must be doctrine from the Word, since without doctrine the Word is not understood; but doctrine alone in man does not make the church in him, but a life according to it; hence it follows that faith alone does not make the church, but the life of faith which is charity.

10,764. The genuine doctrine of the church is the doctrine of charity and of faith together, and not the doctrine of faith without the former; for the doctrine of charity and of faith together is the doctrine of life, but not the doctrine of faith without the doctrine of charity.

10,765. They who are out of the church, and still acknowledge one God, and live according to their religious principles in a certain charity towards the neighbor, are in communion with those who are of the church, since no one who believes in God and lives well, is damned. Hence it is evident that the church of the Lord is every where in the world, although it is specifically where the Lord is acknowledged, and where the Word is.

10,766. Every one with whom the church is, is saved; but every one with whom the church is not, is condemned.

CHAPTER XXXVII.

1. AND Bezaleel made an ark of shittim-wood, two cubits and a half the length thereof, and a cubit and a half the breadth thereof, and a cubit and a half the height thereof.

2. And he covered it over with pure gold from within and from without, and made for it a border of gold round about.

3. And he fused for it four rings of gold upon its four corners; and two rings were upon one rib thereof, and two rings upon the other rib thereof.

4. And he made staves of shittim-wood, and covered them over with gold.

5. And he brought the staves into the rings on the ribs of the ark to carry the ark.

6. And he made the propitiatory of pure gold, two cubits and a half the length thereof, and a cubit and a half the breadth thereof.

7. And he made two cherubs of gold, solid he made them from the two extremities of the propitiatory.

8. One cherub from the extremity on this side, and one cherub from the extremity on that side; of the propitiatory he made cherubs from its two extremities.

9. And the cherubs spread their wings upwards, covering with their wings over the propitiatory, and their faces a man to his brother, to the propitiatory were the faces of the cherubs.

10. And he made a table of shittim-wood, two cubits the length thereof, and a cubit the breadth thereof, and a cubit and a half the height thereof.

11. And he covered it over with pure gold, and made for it a border of gold round about.

12. And he made for it a closure of a span round about, and he made a border of gold for its closure round about.

13. And he fused for it four rings of gold, and he gave the rings upon the four corners, which were for its four feet.

14. Over against the closure were the rings receptacles for the staves to carry the table.
15. And he made staves of shittim-wood, and covered them over with gold to carry the table.
16. And he made the vessels which were on the table, its dishes, and its plates, and its little dishes, and its bowls, with which it was to be covered, of pure gold.
17. And he made the candlestick of pure gold, solid he made the candlestick, its leg, and its pipe, its bowls, its pomegranates, and its flowers, were from it.
18. And six pipes going forth from its sides; three pipes of the candlestick from one side of it, and three pipes of the candlestick from the other side of it.
19. Three bowls like unto almonds in one pipe, a pomegranate and a flower; and three bowls like unto almonds going forth from one pipe, a pomegranate and a flower; so for the six pipes going forth from the candlestick.
20. And in the candlestick four bowls like unto almonds, its pomegranates and its flowers.
21. And a pomegranate under the two pipes from it, and a pomegranate under the two pipes from it, and a pomegranate under the two pipes from it, for the six pipes going forth from it.
22. Their pomegranates and their pipes were from it, the whole of it one solid of pure gold.
23. And he made its seven lamps, and its tongs, and its snuff-dishes of pure gold.
24. With a talent of gold he made it, and all its vessels.
25. And he made the altar of incense of shittim-wood, a cubit the length thereof, and a cubit the breadth thereof, square, and two cubits the height thereof; out of it were its horns.
26. And he covered it over with pure gold, its roof and its walls round about, and its horns, and he made for it a border of gold round about.
27. And two rings of gold he made for it from beneath its border on its two ribs, on its two sides, for receptacles to the staves, to carry it in them.
28. And he made staves of shittim-wood, and covered them over with gold.
29. And he made holy oil of anointing, and pure incense of spices with the work of a dealer in spices.

THE CONTENTS.

10,767. SINCE the subject treated of in this chapter is the ark, the candlestick, and the altar of incense, and the description of those things is here similar to what was before given in chapter xxv. where all and singular things have been explained as to the internal sense, therefore these are passed by without further explication.

CONTINUATION OF THE SUBJECT CONCERNING THE FIFTH EARTH IN THE STARRY HEAVEN.

10,768. *BESIDES those things which have been told, there were some things also seen in that earth itself, which was effected by communication with the angels who were there and appeared as men of the earth, for they, when they are presented as men in the manner above spoken of, see with their eyes the objects there, just as the inhabitants see; but when they are not in that state, they then see nothing of the sort, but only the things which are in heaven.*

10,769. *Their habitations were seen, which were low houses in the form of tents, such as the ancients had, stretched out in length, with windows on the sides according to the number of mansions or chambers into which they were divided; the roof was round, and the door on each side in the extremity; they said that they were constructed out of the ground, and covered with turfs, and that the windows were of threads of grass so woven together that the light was transparent. Infants were also seen there, they said that neighbors come to them, especially for the sake of infants, that they may be in consort with other infants, under the view and management of their parents.*

10,770. *There appeared also fields at the time whitish from the harvest nearly ripe; the seeds or grains of that harvest were shown, which were like to the grains of Chinese wheat; loaves of bread also were shown made from those seeds, which were small in square pieces. Moreover there also appeared plains of grass with flowers there, and also trees with fruits, which were like pomegranates; likewise shrubs, which were not vines, but still bore berries, from which they prepare wine.*

10,771. *The sun there, which is to us a star, appears there of a flaming color, of the magnitude almost of the fourth part of our sun; their year is about two hundred days; and the day fifteen hours in respect to the time of days in our earth. The earth itself is amongst the least in the starry heaven, scarce five hundred German miles in circumference. These things the angels said from comparison made with such things in our earth, which they saw in me, or in my memory. They concluded those things by angelic ideas, whereby the measures of spaces and of times are instantly known in a just ratio in respect to spaces and times elsewhere; angelic ideas, which are spiritual, in such things immensely exceed human ideas, which are natural.*

10,772. *A sixth earth in the starry heaven will be treated of at the close of the following chapter.*

EXODUS.

CHAPTER THE THIRTY-EIGHTH.

THE DOCTRINE OF CHARITY AND FAITH.

10,773. THE government of the Lord in the heavens and in the earths is called providence; and whereas all the good which is of love and all the truth which is of faith is from Him, and nothing at all from man, it is hence evident that the Divine Providence of the Lord is in all and singular the things which conduce to the salvation of the human race. This the Lord thus teaches in John, "*I am the way, the truth, and the life,*" xiv. 6. And in another place, "*As the branch cannot bear fruit from itself, unless it abide in the vine, so neither can ye, unless ye abide in Me. Without Me ye cannot do any thing,*" xv. 4, 5.

10,774. Moreover the Divine Providence of the Lord extends to the most singular things of the life of man, for there is only one fountain of life, which is the Lord, from whom we are, we live, and we act.

10,775. They who think from worldly things concerning the Divine Providence, conclude from them that it is only universal, and that singular things appertain to man; but they do not know the arcana of heaven; for they form their conclusions only from the loves of self and of the world, and their pleasures; wherefore when they see the evil exalted to honors and to gain above the good, and also that they succeed according to their artifices, they say in their heart, that it would not so come to pass if the Divine Providence was in all and singular things; but they do not consider that the Divine Providence does not respect that which is fleeting and transitory, and which has an end with the life of man in the world, but that it respects that which remains to eternity, thus which has not an end. What has not an end, that is; but what has an end, that respectively is not.

10,776. Every considerate person may know, that eminence and opulence in the world are not real Divine blessings, although man, from his pleasurable principle, calls them so, for they pass away, and likewise seduce many and avert them from heaven; but that life in heaven and happiness there are real blessings, which are from the Divine; these things also the Lord teaches in Luke, "*Make to yourselves treasure in the heavens that faileth not, where the thief cometh not, nor the moth corrupteth; for where your treasure is, there also will your heart be,*" xii. 33, 34.

10,777. The reason why the evil succeed according to their arts, is, because it is from order that every one should act what he acts from reason, and also from freedom; wherefore unless it was left to man to act according to his reason from freedom, and thus also unless the arts succeeded which are thence derived, man could not in any wise be disposed to receive eternal life, for this is insinuated when man is in freedom and his reason is illustrated. For no one can be compelled to good, because nothing which is of compulsion inheres, for it is not his; that becomes his [the man's] which is done from freedom, for what is from the will is done from freedom, and the will is the man himself. Wherefore unless man be kept in the freedom also to do evil, good from the Lord cannot be provided for him.

10,778. To leave man from his freedom also to do evil, is called to permit.

10,779. To be led to things happy in the world, by arts, appears to man as if it was from his own proper prudence, nevertheless the Divine Providence continually accompanies by permitting and continually withdrawing from evil. But to be led to things happy in heaven, is known and perceived not to be of man's own proper prudence, because it is from the Lord, and is effected of His Divine Providence by disposing and continually leading to good.

10,780. That this is the case, man cannot comprehend from the lumen of nature, for from that lumen he does not know the laws of Divine Order.

10,781. It is to be noted, that there is providence and previdence [or foresight]; good is what is provided of the Lord, but evil is what is previded [or foreseen]; the one must be with the other, for what comes from man is nothing but evil, but what comes from the Lord is nothing but good.

CHAPTER XXXVIII.

1. AND he made the altar of burnt-offering of shittim-wood, five cubits the length thereof, and five cubits the breadth thereof, square, and three cubits the height thereof.

2. And he made its horns upon its four corners; from it were its horns; and he covered it over with brass.

3. And he made all the vessels of the altar, the pans, and shovels, and basins, and little flesh-hooks, and tongs, all its vessels he made of brass.

4. And he made for the altar a grate, the work of a net of brass, under its compass downwards even to its half.

5. And he fused four rings in the four extremities for the grate of brass, receptacles for the staves.

6. And he made staves of shittim-wood, and covered them over with brass.

7. And he brought in the staves into the rings on the ribs of the altar to carry it in them; a hollow table he made it.

8. And he made the laver of brass, and its base of brass for the views [or aspects] of those [women] who ministered, who ministered at the door of the tent of the congregation.

9. And he made the court at the corner of the south, southwards; the hangings of the court of fine linen woven together, a hundred in a cubit.

10. Their twenty pillars, and their twenty bases of brass, the hooks of the pillars and their fillets of silver.

11. And to the corner of the north a hundred in a cubit, their twenty pillars, and their twenty bases of brass, the hooks of the pillars and their fillets of silver.

12. And to the corner of the sea fifty hangings in a cubit, their ten pillars, and their ten bases, the hooks of the pillars and their fillets of silver.

13. And to the corner of the east, eastward, fifty in a cubit.

14. Fifteen hangings in a cubit at the shoulder, their three pillars, and their three bases.

15. And for the other shoulder on this side and on that side, at the gate of the court fifteen hangings in a cubit, their three pillars, and their three bases.

16. All the hangings of the court round about of fine linen woven together.

17. And their bases for the pillars of brass, the hooks of the pillars, and their fillets of silver, and their heads covered over with silver, and they were furnished with fillets of silver, all the pillars of the court.

18. And the covering of the gate of the court with the work of a worker with a needle, with blue, and purple, and scarlet double-dyed, and fine linen woven together, and twenty cubits the length, and the height in the breadth five cubits, over against the hangings of the court.

19. And their four pillars and their four bases of brass; their hooks of silver, and their heads and their fillets covered over with silver.

20. And all the pegs for the habitation and the court round about of brass.

21. These are the things numbered of the habitation, of the habitation of the testimony, which was numbered on the mouth of Moses, for the ministry of the Levites, by the hand of Ithamar the son of Aaron the priest.

22. And Bezaleel the son of Uri, the son of Hur, of the tribe of Judah, made all things which JEHOVAH commanded Moses.

23. And with him Aholiab the son of Ahisamach, of the tribe of Dan, an artificer and contriver, and worker with a needle in blue, and in purple, and in scarlet double-dyed, and in fine linen.

24. All the gold made for the work in all the work of the holy [place], and it was gold of shaking nine and twenty talents, and seven hundred and thirty shekels in the shekel of the holy [place].

25. And the silver of them that were numbered of the congregation was a hundred talents, and a thousand and seven hundred, and five and seventy shekels in the shekel of the holy [place].

26. A didrachma for a head the half of a shekel in the shekel of the holy place, for every one passing over the numbered from a son of twenty years and upwards, for six hundred thousand, and three thousand and five hundred and fifty.

27. And it came to pass, a hundred talents of silver were to fuse the bases of the holy [place], and the bases of the vail, a hundred bases for a hundred talents, a talent to a base.

28. And of the thousand and seven hundred and five and seventy he made hooks for the pillars and covered over their heads, and adorned them with fillets.

29. And the brass of shaking was seventy talents, and two thousand and four hundred shekels.

30. And he made with it bases of the door of the tent of the congregation, and the altar of brass, and the grate of brass which was for it, and all the vessels of the altar.

31. And the bases of the court round about, and the bases of the gate of the court, and all the pegs of the habitation, and all the pegs of the court round about.

THE CONTENTS.

10,782. INASMUCH as the subject treated of in this chapter is the altar of burnt-offering, and the court of the tent of the congregation, and the same things were in like manner described above in chap. xxvii. and there explained, therefore also these things are passed by without further explication as to the internal sense.

CONCERNING A SIXTH EARTH IN THE STARRY HEAVEN.

10,783. *I WAS again led to another earth, which was in the universe out of our solar world, and this also by changes of state continued nearly twelve hours; in company with me were several spirits and angels from our earth, with whom I discoursed in that way or in that progress; I was sometimes carried obliquely upwards, and sometimes obliquely downwards; continually towards the south; only in two places I saw spirits, and in one I discoursed with them.*

10,784. *In that way or progress it was given to observe how immense was the heaven of the Lord which is for the angels; for from what was not inhabited it was given to conclude that it was so immense, that if several myriads of earths were given, and in each as great a multitude of men as in our own, that still there would be room for them to eternity, and it would never be filled. This I could conclude from a comparison made with the extension of the heaven which is round our earth, and for it.*

10,785. *When the angelic spirits, who were from that earth, came into sight, they accosted us, asking who we were, and what we willed; we said that we were travellers, and that we had been conveyed thither, and that they need not be afraid of us; for they feared that we were of those who disturb them concerning God, concerning faith, and concerning things of a like nature, on account of whom they betook themselves into that quarter of their earth, shunning them by every possible method; they were asked by what things the disturbance was effected; they answered by an idea of three, and by an idea of the Divine without the Human in God, when yet they know and perceive that God is one, and that He is a man; it was then perceived that they who disturbed them, and whom they shunned, were from our earth; also from this circumstance, that from our earth there are those who so wander about in the other life, in consequence of the study and delight of travelling which they have contracted in the world, for in other earths it is not so customary to travel; it was next found that they were monks, who travelled in our world with a view of converting the Gentiles; wherefore we told them, that they do well to shun them, because their intention is not to teach, but to secure gain and dominion; and that by various things they first study to captivate minds, but afterwards to subject them to themselves as servants; moreover that they do well in not suffering their idea concerning the Lord to be disturbed by such.*

10,786. *They further said that they also confound them by this, that they say they ought to have faith, and to believe what is told them; and that the reply they make is, that they do not know what faith is, or what it is to believe, when they perceive in themselves that it is so; for they were of the Lord's celestial kingdom, where all from interior perception know the truths, which with us are called the* [truths] *of faith, for they are in illustration from the Lord, otherwise than those who are in the Lord's spiritual kingdom. That they were of such a quality, was also given to see from the flaming principle from which their ideas were. They who are of the Lord's celestial kingdom, when the discourse is concerning truths, say no more than so so, or no no, and in no case reason concerning them whether it be so, or be not so; these are they, concerning whom the Lord says,* "Your discourse shall be so so, no no, what is beyond is from evil;" *hence it is that those spirits said that they do not know what it is to have faith or to believe; they consider this as if any one should say to a companion, who with his own eyes sees houses or trees, that he ought to have faith or believe that they are houses and trees, when he sees clearly that it is so; such are they who are of the Lord's celestial kingdom, and such were these angelic spirits. We told them that there are few in our earth who have interior perception, by reason that in their youth they learn truths and do not do them; for man has two faculties, which are called understanding and will, and they who do not admit truths further than into the memory, and hence in some slight degree into the understanding, but not into the life, that is into the will, inasmuch as they cannot be in any illustration or in interior sight from the Lord, say that things are to be believed, or that man ought to have faith, and they also reason concerning things whether they be true or not, yea neither are they willing that they should be perceived by any interior sight or understanding; they say thus because truths with them are without light from heaven, and to those who see without light from heaven, falses may appear as truths, and truths as falses; hence so great a blindness has seized several there, that although man does not truths, or lives not according to them, still they say that he may be saved by faith alone.*

10,787. *We afterwards discoursed with them concerning the Lord, concerning love to Him, concerning love towards the neighbor, and concerning regeneration; that to love the Lord is to love the precepts which are from Him, which is, from love to live according to them; that love towards the neighbor is to will good and hence to do good to a fellow-citizen, to a man's country, to the church, to the Lord's kingdom, not for the sake of self to be seen or to merit, but from the affection of good. Concerning regeneration, that they who are regenerated of the Lord, and let-in truths instantly into the life, come into interior perception concerning them; but that they who receive truths first in the memory, and next in the understanding, and lastly in the will, are they who are in faith, for they act from faith, which in such case is called conscience. These things they said they perceived to be so, consequently also what faith is.*

10,788. *The continuation of the subject concerning this sixth earth in the starry heaven will be given at the close of the following chapter.*

EXODUS.

CHAPTER THE THIRTY-NINTH.

THE DOCTRINE OF CHARITY AND FAITH.

10,789. THERE are two things appertaining to men which ought to be in order, namely, the things which are of heaven and the things which are of the world. Those things which are of heaven are called ecclesiastical, those which are of the world, are called civil.

10,790. Order cannot be maintained in the world without governors, who are to observe all things which are done according to order, and which are done contrary to order; and who are to reward those who live according to order, and to punish those who live contrary to order.

10,791. If this be not effected, the human race must perish; for from an hereditary principle every one by birth wills to command others, and to possess the goods of others, whence come enmities, envyings, hatreds, revenges, deceits, cruelties, and several other evils; wherefore unless they be kept in bonds by the laws, and by rewards suited to their loves, which are honors and gains for those who do goods; and by punishments, contrary to their loves, which are the losses of honors, of possessions, and of life, for those who do evils, the human race would perish.

10,792. It is expedient therefore that there be governors, to keep associations of men in order; and that these governors be skilled in the knowledge of the law, full of wisdom and of the fear of God. It is expedient also that there should be order amongst the governors, lest any one, through lust or inadvertence, should allow evils against order, and thereby destroy it; and this may be best effected by an appointment of governors of different degrees, higher and lower, amongst whom there shall be subordination.

10,793. Governors in things ecclesiastic, or in the things of heaven appertaining to man, are called priests, and their office the priesthood. But governors in civil concerns, or such as relate to this world, are called magistrates, and their chief, where such a form of government prevails, is called king.

10,794. As to what concerns priests, they ought to teach men the way to heaven, and likewise to lead them; they must teach them according to the doctrine of their church, and they must lead them to live according to it. Priests, who teach truths, and thereby lead to good of life, and thus to the Lord, are the good shepherds of the sheep, but they who teach, and do not lead to good of life, and thus to the Lord, are evil shepherds; these latter are by the Lord called thieves and robbers, John chap. x. verse 7 to 16.

10,795. Priests ought not to claim to themselves any power over the souls of men, inasmuch as they do not know the state of the interiors of man; still less ought they to claim to themselves the power of opening and shutting heaven, since that power belongs to the Lord alone.

10,796. Priests ought to have dignity and honor on account of the sanctity of their office; but a wise priest gives honor unto the Lord, from whom all sanctity is derived, and not to himself; whereas an unwise priest attributes honor to himself and takes it from the Lord. They who attribute honor to themselves on account of the sanctity of their office, prefer honor and gain to the salvation of souls, which they ought to provide for; but they who give honor to the Lord, and not to themselves, prefer the salvation of souls to honor and gain.

10,797. No honor of any employment is in the person, but is adjoined to him according to the dignity of the thing which he administers, and what is adjoined is separate from the person, and also is separated with the employment. All personal honor is the honor of wisdom and of the fear of the Lord.

10,798. Priests ought to teach the people, and to lead by truths to good of life, but still they must not force any one, since no one can be forced to believe contrary to what he thinks in his heart to be true. He who believes otherwise than the priest, and makes no disturbance, ought to be left in peace, but he who makes disturbance must be separated, for this also is agreeable to the order, for the sake of which the priesthood is established.

10,799. As priests are appointed for the administration of those things which relate to the Divine law or worship, so kings and magistrates are appointed for the administration of those things which relate to civil law and judgment.

10,800. Forasmuch as the king alone cannot administer all things, therefore there are governors under him, to each of whom is given the province of administration, where that of the king cannot be extended; these governors taken collectively constitute the royalty, but the king himself is chief.

10,801. The royalty itself is not in the person, but is adjoined to the person; the king who believes that royalty is in his own person, and the governor who believes that the dignity of government is in his own person, is not wise.

10,802. Royalty consists in administering according to the laws of the kingdom, and in judging according to those laws from a principle of justice. The king who respects the laws as above him, consequently himself as below the law, is wise; but he who respects himself as above the laws, consequently the laws as beneath himself, is not wise.

10,803. The king who respects the laws as above himself, and thereby himself as beneath the laws, places royalty in the law, and the law has dominion over him, for he knows that the law is justice, and all justice as such is Divine. But he who respects the laws as beneath himself, and thus himself above them, places royalty in himself, and believes himself either to be the law, or the law which is justice to be from himself, hence he claims to himself what is Divine, to which nevertheless he ought to be in subjection.

10,804. The law, which is justice, ought to be enacted by persons in the realm skilled in law, who are at the same time full of wisdom and the fear of God; and the king and his subjects ought then to live according to it. The king, who lives according to the law which is justice, and therein sets an example to his subjects, is truly a king.

10,805. The king who has absolute power, and believes that his subjects are such slaves that he has a right to their lives and properties, if he exercises such a right, is not a king, but a tyrant.

10,806. The king ought to be obeyed according to the laws of the realm, nor in any wise to be injured by word or deed, for on this the public security depends.

CHAPTER XXXIX.

1. AND of the blue and purple, and scarlet double-dyed, they made garments of ministry to minister in the holy [place]; and they made garments of holiness which were for Aaron; as JEHOVAH commanded Moses.

2. And he made an ephod of gold, of blue, and purple, and scarlet double-dyed, and fine linen interwoven.

3. And they spread out plates of gold, and cut threads to make in the midst of the blue, and in the midst of the purple, and in the midst of the scarlet double-dyed, and in the midst of the fine linen, the work of the contriver.

4. Things for the shoulder they made for it connected together, on its two extremities it was connected.

5. And the girdle of its ephod which was upon it, it was from it according to its work, of gold, blue and purple, and scarlet double-dyed, and fine linen interwoven, as JEHOVAH commanded Moses.

6. And they made onyx stones encompassed with sockets of gold engraven with the engravings of a seal on the names of the sons of Israel.

7. And he set them on the shoulders of the ephod, stones of remembrance for the sons of Israel, as JEHOVAH commanded Moses.

8. And he made the breast-plate with the work of a contriver according to the work of the ephod, of gold, of blue, and of purple, and of scarlet double-dyed, and of fine linen interwoven.

9. It was square, they made the breast-plate two-fold, a span its length, and a span its breadth, two-fold.

10. And they filled in it four orders of stones; the order, a ruby, a topaz, and a carbuncle, the first order.

11. And the second order, a chrysoprase, a sapphire, and a diamond.

12. And the third order, a lasure, an agate, and an amethyst.

13. And the fourth order, a beryl, an onyx, and a jasper, encompassed with sockets of gold in their fillings.

14. And the stones were on the names of the twelve sons of Israel, on their names with the engravings of a seal, each on its name for the twelve tribes.

15. And they made on the breast-plate little border chains of cord-work of pure gold.

16. And they made two sockets of gold, and two rings of gold, and gave the two rings on the two extremities of the breast-plate.

17. And they gave the two cords of gold on the two rings on the extremities of the breast-plate.

18. And the two extremities of the two cords they gave on the two sockets, and gave them on the shoulders of the ephod over against its faces.

19. And they made two rings of gold, and set them on the two extremities of the breast-plate, on its edge which is on this side the ephod inwards.

20. And they made two rings of gold, and gave them on

the two shoulders of the ephod beneath, over against the faces thereof, opposite to the coupling above the girdle of the ephod.

21. And they tied the breast-plate from its rings to the rings of the ephod with a thread of blue, to be on the girdle of the ephod, lest the breast-plate should recede from being upon the ephod, as JEHOVAH commanded Moses.

22. And he made the robe of the ephod with the work of a weaver, the whole of blue.

23. And the mouth [or aperture] of the robe in the midst of it, as the mouth of a coat of mail, a brim to its mouth round about, lest it should be torn.

24. And they made on the borders of the robe pomegranates of blue, and purple, and scarlet double-dyed interwoven.

25. And they made bells of pure gold, and they gave the bells in the midst of the pomegranates on the borders of the robe round about in the midst of the pomegranates.

26. A bell and a pomegranate, a bell and a pomegranate on the borders of the robe round about to minister, as JEHOVAH commanded Moses.

27. And they made waistcoats of fine linen with the work of a weaver for Aaron and his sons.

28. And a mitre of fine linen, and an ornament of turbans of fine linen, and breeches of linen with fine linen interwoven.

29. And a belt with fine linen interwoven, and blue, and purple, and scarlet double-dyed, the work of one who works with a needle, as JEHOVAH commanded Moses.

30. And they made the plate of the crown of holiness of pure gold, and wrote upon it writing with the engraving of a seal, HOLINESS TO JEHOVAH.

31. And they gave upon it a thread of blue, to give upon the mitre above, as JEHOVAH commanded Moses.

32. And all the work of the habitation of the tent of the congregation was finished, and the sons of Israel did according to all things which JEHOVAH commanded Moses, so they did.

33. And they brought the habitation to Moses, the tent, and all its vessels, its little handles, its staves, its bars, and its pillars, and its bases.

34. And the covering of the skins of red rams, and the covering of the skins of badgers, and the vail of the covering.

35. The ark of the testimony, and its bars, and the propitiatory.

36. The table, all its vessels, and the bread of faces.

37. The pure candlestick, its lamps, the lamps of arrangement, and all its vessels, and the oil of the luminary.

38. And the altar of gold, and the oil of anointing, and the incense of spices, and the covering of the door of the tent.

39. The altar of brass, and the gate of brass, which was for it, its bars, and all its vessels, the laver and its base.
40. The hangings of the court, its pillars, and its bases, and the covering of the gate of the court, its cords, and its pegs, and all the vessels of service of the habitation for the tent of the congregation.
41. The garments of ministry to minister in the holy [place], the garments of holiness for Aaron the priest, and the garments of his sons to perform the office of the priesthood.
42. According to all things which JEHOVAH commanded Moses, so did the sons of Israel all service.
43. And Moses saw all the work, and behold they had made [or done] it as JEHOVAH commanded, so they did; and Moses blessed them.

THE CONTENTS.

10,807. INASMUCH as the things which are contained in this chapter, as to the internal sense, have been before explained, and what is said concerning the garments of Aaron and of his sons, in chapter xxviii. therefore also their further explication is needless.

CONTINUATION OF THE SUBJECT CONCERNING THE SIXTH EARTH IN THE STARRY HEAVEN.

10,808. *THESE spirits, with whom I now discoursed, were from the northern part of their earth. I was next conducted to others, who were from the western parts; these also were willing to explore who I was, and of what quality, saying immediately, that there appertained to me nothing but evil, thinking that I should thus be deterred from approaching nearer; it was perceived, that they so address all new comers; but it was given to answer, that I know well that it is so, and that in like manner there appertains to them nothing but evil, by reason that every one is born into evil, and therefore whatsoever comes from man, spirit, and angel, as from his own or the proprium, is nothing but evil, since all good which appertains to every one, is from the Lord: hence they perceived that I was in the truth, and I was admitted to speak with them; and then they showed me their idea concerning evil appertaining to man, and concerning good from the Lord, in what manner they are separated from each other. They set one near the other, almost as contiguous, but still separated, yet as it were bound in a manner ineffable, so that good led evil and bridled it, that it was not allowed it to act at pleasure, and that good thus bended evil to what it would, whilst evil knew nothing at all about it, thus they exhibited the dominion of good over evil, and at the same time the free state in which evil is led from good to good, thus to the Lord for respecting the idea of good, they have an idea of the Lord, inasmuch as it is from Him.*

10,809. *They then asked, how the Lord appears amongst angels from our earth. I said, that He appears in the sun as a man encompassed there with a solar fiery principle, from which the angels have all light in the heavens, and that the heat which proceeds thence, is Divine Good, and that the light which is thence is Divine Truth, each from the Divine Love, which is the fiery principle appearing about the Lord in that sun. But that that sun appears only to the angels in heaven, and not to the spirits who are beneath, since these latter are more remote from the reception of the good of love and of the truth of faith than the angels who are in the heavens. But as to what concerns the sun of the world, it appears to no one in the other life, yet it is presented in their idea as a black thing not visible, from its being opposite to the sun of heaven, which is the Lord. It was given them to inquire concerning the Lord, and concerning his appearance before the angels from our earth, inasmuch as it then pleased the Lord to exhibit Himself present with them, and to reduce into order those things which were in disturbance from the evil ones there, of whom they complained. That I might see these things, was also the cause of my being brought thither.*

10,810. *On this occasion there was seen an obscure cloud towards the east descending from a certain altitude, which in descending appeared by degrees lucid, and in a human form, and at length this form was in a flaming radiance, around which were little stars of the same color; thus the Lord exhibited Himself present with the spirits with whom I was discoursing. To the presence on this occasion were gathered together from all parts all the spirits who were there, and when they came, the good were separated from the evil, the good to the right and the evil to the left, and this instantly as of their own accord; and they who were to the right were arranged in order according to the quality of good, and they who were to the left according to the quality of evil, appertaining to them; they who were good were left to form a heavenly society amongst themselves, but the evil were cast into hells. I saw afterwards that that flaming radiance descended into the inferior parts of the earth there to a considerable depth, and on this occasion appeared at one time in a flaming principle verging to lucidity, at another time in lucidity verging to obscurity, and at another time in obscurity; and it was told me by the angels, that the appearance is according to the reception of truth from good, and of the false from evil, with those who inhabit the inferior parts of that earth, and not at all owing to that flaming radiance undergoing such varieties. They said also, that the inferior parts of that earth were inhabited both by the good and by the evil, but that they were well separated, to the intent that the evil might be governed by the good from the Lord; they added, that the good are by turns thence elevated into heaven by the Lord, and others succeed in their place, and so continually. In that descent the good were separated in like manner from the evil, and all things were reduced into order; for the evil by various arts and cunnings introduced themselves there into the abodes of the good, and infested them; and this was the cause of that visitation.*

10,811. *That cloud, which in descending appeared by degrees lucid, and in a human form, and afterwards as a flaming radiance, was an angelic society, in the midst of which was the Lord. Hence it was given to know what is meant by the Lord's words, where he speaks of the last judgment in the evangelists, "That He would come with the angels in the clouds of heaven with glory and virtue."*

10,812. *Afterwards there were seen monkish spirits, namely, such as had been travelling monks or missionaries in the world, spoken of above: and there was also seen a crowd, consisting of spirits of that earth, mostly evil, whom they had drawn over to their party and seduced. These were seen to the eastern quarter of that earth, from which they drove away the good, who appeared at the north side of the earth, spoken of above: that one crowd with their seducers were gathered together into one, to the amount of several thousands, and they were separated, and the evil amongst them were cast into hells. It was also given to discourse with one spirit, a monk, and to ask what he was doing there. He said, that he came to teach them concerning the Lord. What else? Concerning heaven and hell. What else? Concerning a belief in all things which he was about to say. What else? Concerning the power of remitting sins, and of opening and shutting heaven. He was then explored what he knew concerning the Lord, concerning the truths of faith, concerning the remission of sins, concerning the salvation of man, and concerning heaven and hell; and it was found that he knew scarce anything, and that he was in an obscure and in a false principle concerning all and singular things; and that he was possessed solely with the lust of gain and of dominion, which he contracted in the world, and thence brought along with him; wherefore he was told, that since from that lust he had travelled so far thither, and since he was of such a quality as to doctrine, he must needs take away heavenly light from the spirits of that earth, and introduce the darkness of hell, and thereby bring it to pass that hell, and not the Lord, would have dominion over them. Moreover he was cunning in the art of seducing, although stupid as to the things which were of heaven. In consequence of being of such a quality, he was next cast into hell. Thus the spirits of that earth were liberated from them.*

10,813. *Amongst other things, the spirits of that earth also said, that those strangers, who, as was said, were monkish spirits, were greatly desirous that they should live in society together, and not separate and solitary. For spirits and angels dwell and cohabit in like manner as in the world, inasmuch as every one's life in the world follows him after death; they who have dwelt in assembly together in the world, dwell also in assembly together in the other life; and they who have dwelt separated into houses and families, dwell also in like manner separated. These spirits in their earth, when they lived there, dwelt separated, houses and houses, families and families, and thus nations and nations, and hence they knew not what it was to dwell in society together. Wherefore when they were told that those strangers had such a desire, to the end that they might rule or have dominion over them, and that otherwise they could not subject them to themselves, and make them slaves, they replied, that they are altogether ignorant what it is to rule and to have dominion. That they fly at the very idea of rule or dominion, I observed from this circumstance, that one of them who accompanied us back, when I showed him the city in which I dwelt, at the first view of it fled away and was no more seen. It is to be noted, that spirits and angels, when it is well-pleasing to the Lord, can see those things which are in the world by* [or through] *the eyes of man, but this is not granted by the Lord to any other but him, to whom He gives to discourse with spirits and angels, and to be with them. By* [or through] *my eyes it was given them to see the things which are in the world, and as plainly as I myself; also to hear men discoursing with me.*

10,814. *It was then given to discourse with the angels, who were attendant on me, concerning dominions, that they are of two sorts, one of love towards the neighbor, and the other of self-love; and that the dominion of love towards the neighbor prevails amongst those who live separated into houses, families, and nations; but the dominion of the love of self amongst those who dwell together in society; amongst those who live separated into houses, families and nations, he has dominion who is the father of the nation, and under him the fathers of families, and under these the fathers of each house; he is called the father of the nation from whom the families are derived and from the families the houses; but all those have dominion from love like that of a father towards his children, who teaches them how they ought to live, is beneficent towards them, and as far as he is able, communicates to them from his own store; nor does it ever enter into his mind to subject them to himself as subjects, or as servants, but he loves that they should obey him as sons obey their fathers; and whereas this love increases in descending, as is a known thing, therefore the father of the nation acts from a more interior love than the father himself from whom the sons proximately spring. Such also is the dominion in the heavens, since such is the dominion of the Lord, for His dominion is grounded in Divine Love towards the universal human race. But the dominion of self-love, which is opposite to the dominion of love towards the neighbor, commenced when man alienated himself from the Lord, for so far as man does not love and worship the Lord, so far he loves and worships himself, and so far also he loves the world more than heaven. On this occasion, from a necessary regard to security, nations with families and houses consociated together in one, and entered into governments under various forms; for so far as that love increased, so far increased evils of every kind, as enmities, envyings, hatreds, revenges, deceits, cruelties exercised against all who opposed themselves; and also that love is of such a quality, that so far as the reins are granted, it rushes headlong until at length the person under its influence is willing to have dominion over all others in the universal world of the earths, and to possess all the goods of others; yea, neither is this sufficient, but he wills also to have dominion over the universal heaven, as may be manifest from modern Babylon. This now is the dominion of self-love, from which the dominion of love towards the neighbor differs as much as heaven from hell. But although the dominion of self-love is such in societies, there is nevertheless given a dominion of love towards the neighbor, in kingdoms also, with those who are wise by virtue of faith and love to God, for these love the neighbor. That these also dwell in the heavens distinguished into nations, families, and houses, although in societies together, but according to spiritual affinities, which are of the good of love and truth of faith, by the Divine Mercy of the Lord will be shown elsewhere.*

A continuation of the subject concerning this sixth earth in the starry heaven will be given at the close of the following chapter

EXODUS.

CHAPTER THE FORTIETH.

THE DOCTRINE OF CHARITY AND FAITH.

10,815. GOD is one, who is the Creator of the universe and the conservator of the universe; thus who is the God of heaven and the God of earth.

10,816. There are two [things or principles] which make the life of heaven with man, the truth of faith and the good of love; man has this life from God and nothing at all from man. Wherefore the primary [thing or principle] of the church is, to acknowledge God, to believe in God, and to love Him.

10,817. They who are born within the church, ought to acknowledge the Lord, His Divine and His Human, and to believe in Him, and to love Him; for from the Lord is all salvation. This the Lord teaches in John, "*He who believeth in the Son hath eternal life; but he who believeth not the Son shall not see life, but the wrath of God abideth with him,*" iii. 36. Again, "*This is the will of Him who sent Me, that every one who seeth the Son, and believeth in Him, may have eternal life; and I will raise him up in the last day,*" vi. 40. Again, "*Jesus said, I am the resurrection and the life, he who believes in Me, although he dies, shall live; but every one who lives and believes in Me, shall not die to eternity,*" xi. 25, 26.

10,818. Wherefore they within the church, who do not acknowledge the Lord and His Divine, cannot be conjoined with God, and thus cannot have any lot with the angels in heaven. For no one can be conjoined with God but from the Lord, and in the Lord.

That no one can be conjoined with God but from the Lord, the Lord teaches in John, "*No one hath seen God at any time, the Only-begotten Son, who is in the bosom of the Father, He hath brought Him forth to view,*" i. 20. Again, "*Ye have never heard the voice of the Father, nor seen His shape,*" v. 37. Again, "*No one knoweth the Father but the Son, and he to whom the Son shall be willing to reveal Him,*" xi. 27. And again, "*I am the way, the truth, and the life, no one cometh to the Father but by Me,*" xiv. 6.

That no one can be conjoined with God but in the Lord, the Lord teaches in John, "*As the branch cannot bear fruit of itself, except it abide in the vine, so neither can ye, except ye abide in Me; because without Me ye cannot do any thing,*" xv. 4, 5.

The reason why no one can be conjoined with God, except in the Lord, is, because the Father is in Him, and they are one, as also he teaches in John, "*He who hath seen Me hath seen Him who sent Me, if ye had known Me ye would have known My Father also, and henceforth ye have known Him; he who hath seen Me hath seen the Father. Philip, believest thou not that I am in the Father and the Father in Me? Believe Me that I am in the Father, and the Father in Me,*" xii. 45; chap. xiv. 8 to 12. And again, "*The Father and I are One; that ye may know and believe that I am in the Father and the Father in Me,*" x. 30, 38.

10,819. Inasmuch as the Father is in the Lord, and the Father and the Lord are one, and inasmuch as He ought to be believed in, and whoso believeth in Him hath eternal life, it is evident that the Lord is God. That the Lord is God, the Word teaches throughout, as in John, "*In the beginning was the Word, and the Word was with God, and God was the Word; all things were made by Him, and without Him was not any thing made which was made; and the Word was made flesh and dwelt amongst us, and we saw His glory, the glory as of the Only-begotten of the Father,*" i. 1, 3, 14. And in Isaiah, "*A boy is born to us, a son is given to us, on whose shoulder is the government, and His name shall be called God, Hero, the Father of Eternity, the Prince of Peace,*" ix. 5. And again, "*A virgin shall conceive and bring forth, and His name shall be called God with us,*" vii. 14; Matt. i. 23. And in Jeremiah, "*Behold the days shall come, when I will raise up to David a just branch, who shall reign a king and shall prosper, and this is His name, which they shall call Him, Jehovah our Justice,*" xxiii. 5, 6; chap. xxx. 15, 16.

10,820. All they who are of the church, and in light from heaven, see the Divine in the Lord, and this in His Human; but they who are not in light from heaven, see nothing but the Human in the Lord; when yet the Human and Divine in Him are so united, that they are one, as the Lord taught also elsewhere in John, "*Father, all Mine are Thine, and all Thine Mine,*" xvii. 10.

10,821. They who have an idea of three persons respecting the Divinity, cannot have an idea of one God; if with the mouth they say one, still they think three; but they who, in regard to the Divinity, have an idea of three in one person, can have an idea of one God, and profess one God, and also think one God.

10,822. An idea of three in one person is attained, when it is thought that the Father is in the Lord, and that the Holy Spirit proceeds from the Lord. The Trinity [*trinum*] in this case in the Lord is the Divine itself which is called Father, the Divine Human which is called Son, and the Divine Proceeding which is called the Holy Spirit.

10,823. Every man from his father has his esse of life, which is called his soul; the existere of life thence derived is what is called body; hence the body is the similitude of its soul, for the soul by it exercises the activities of its life at pleasure; hence it is that men are born into the similitude of their fathers, and that families are known asunder. From this consideration it is evident what was the quality of the body or of the Human of the Lord, namely, that it was as the Divine itself, which was the esse of His life, or the soul from the Father; wherefore He said, "*Whoso seeth Me seeth the Father*," John xiv. 9.

10,824. That the Divine and the Human of the Lord is one Person, is also agreeable to the faith received throughout the whole Christian world, which is to this effect, "*Although God and Christ is one Man, still He is not two but one Christ; yea, He is altogether one and a single person; because as body and soul are one man, so also God and man is one Christ;*" see the Athanasian creed.

10,825. That the Lord was conceived of Jehovah the Father, and was thus God from conception, is a known thing in the church; and also that He rose again with His whole body, for He left nothing in the sepulchre; of which He also afterwards confirmed His disciples, saying, "*See My hands and My feet, that it is I Myself; handle Me and see; for a spirit hath not flesh and bones, as ye see Me have*," Luke xxiv. 39. And although He was a man as to flesh and bones, still He entered in through the doors that were shut, and after that He manifested Himself, He became invisible, John xx. 19, 26; Luke xxiv. 31. The case is otherwise with every man, for man rises again only as to the spirit and not as to the body; wherefore when He said, *that He is not as a spirit*, He said that He is not as another man. Hence now it is evident, that the Human in the Lord is also Divine.

10,826. They who make the Human of the Lord like the human principle of another man, do not think of His conception from the Divine itself; nor of His resurrection with the whole body; nor of being seen when He was transformed, with His face shining as the sun; neither do they know and comprehend that the body of every one is a similitude or effigy of its soul; nor that the Lord is omnipresent even as to the Human; for hence comes the belief in His omnipresence in the sacred supper; omnipresence is Divine, Matt. xxviii. 20.

10,827. Inasmuch as in the Lord every thing is Divine, therefore He has all power in the heavens and in the earths; which also He Himself says in John, "*The Father hath given to the Son power over all flesh*," xvii. 2. And in Matthew, "*All things are delivered to Me by the Father*," xi. 27. And again, "*All power is given to Me in heaven and in earth*," xxviii. 18.

10,828. The Lord came into the world that He might save the human race, who would otherwise have perished in eternal death. And He saved them by this, that He subdued the hells, which infested every man coming into the world, and going out of the world; and at the same time by this, that He glorified His Human, for thereby He can keep the hells subdued to eternity. The subjugation of the hells, and the glorification of His Human at the same time, was effected by temptations admitted into His Human, and by continual victories on the occasion. His passion on the cross was the last temptation and full victory. That the Lord subdued the hells, He Himself teaches in John, "Jesus said, Now is My soul troubled, Father, snatch me from this hour; *but for this sake came I to this hour.* Father, glorify Thy name. There came forth a voice from heaven, I have both glorified and will again glorify it. Then said Jesus, *Now is the judgment of this world; now shall the prince of this world be cast out,*" xii. 27, 28, 31. Again, "*Have confidence, I have overcome the world,*" xvi. 33. And in Isaiah, '*Who is this that cometh from Edom, walking in the multitude of his strength, great to save. My own arm brought salvation to Me: therefore He became to them a Saviour,*" lxiii. 1 to 20; chap. lix. 16 to 21. That He glorified His Human, and that the passion of the cross was the last temptation and full victory by which He glorified it, He teaches also in John, "*After that Judas was gone out, Jesus said, Now is the Son of Man glorified, and God will glorify Him in Himself, and will immediately glorify Him,*" xiii. 31, 32. Again, "*Father, the hour is come, glorify Thy Son, that Thy Son also may glorify Thee; now glorify Me, O Thou Father, with the glory which I had with Thee before the world was,*" xvii. 1, 5. Again, "*Now is My soul troubled. Father, glorify Thy name: and there came forth a voice from heaven, I have both glorified and will glorify it again,*" xii. 27, 28. And in Luke, "*Ought not Christ to suffer these things and to enter into His glory,*" xxiv. 30. To glorify is to make Divine. Hence now it is manifest, that unless the Lord had come into the world, and been made a man, and in this manner liberated from hell all those who believe in Him and love Him, no mortal could have been saved; this is meant by what is said, that without the Lord there is no salvation.

10,829. To love the Lord is to live according to His precepts; that this is to love the Lord, He Himself teaches in John, "*If ye love Me keep My commandments; he who hath My precepts and doeth them, he it is who loveth Me. If any one loveth Me, he will keep My word; but he who loveth Me not, keepeth not My words,*" xiv. 15, 21, 23, 24. And that they are saved who receive the Lord and believe in Him, but not they who are in evils and in the falses thence derived, since these atter do not receive Him and believe in Him, is taught in John, '*As many as received Him, to them gave He power that they might be the sons of God, believing in His name; Who were born not of bloods, nor of the will of the flesh, nor of the will of man, but of God*," i. 12, 13. To be born of bloods, of the will of the flesh, and of the will of man, denotes to be in the evils of the loves of self and of the world, and in the falses thence derived; to be born of God is to be regenerated.

10,830. When the Lord fully glorified His Human, then He put off the Human from the mother, and put on the Human from the Father; wherefore then He was no longer the son of Mary, but of God, from whom He came forth.

10,831. That there is a threefold principle [*trinum*] in the Lord, namely, the Divine itself, the Divine Human, and the Divine proceeding, is an arcanum from heaven, and for those who shall be in the holy Jerusalem.

CHAPTER XL.

1. AND JEHOVAH spake to Moses, saying,

2. In the day of the first month, in the first of the month, thou shalt set up the habitation of the tent of the congregation.

3. And thou shalt set there the ark of the testimony, and shalt cover the vail over the ark.

4. And thou shalt bring in the table, and shalt arrange its arrangement; and thou shalt bring in the candlestick, and shalt make its lamps to ascend.

5. And thou shalt give the altar of gold for incense before the ark of the testimony, and thou shalt set the covering of the door for the habitation.

6. And thou shalt give the altar of burnt-offering before the door of the habitation of the tent of the congregation.

7. And thou shalt give the laver between the tent of the congregation, and between the altar, and thou shalt give waters there.

8. And thou shalt set the court round about, and shalt give a covering for the gate of the court.

9. And thou shalt take the oil of anointing, and shalt anoint the habitation, and all things which are in it, and shalt sanctify it, and all its vessels; and it shall be holy.

10. And thou shalt anoint the altar of burnt-offering, and all its vessels, and shalt sanctify the altar, and the altar shall be the holy of holies.

11. And thou shalt anoint the laver and its base, and shalt sanctify it.

12. And thou shalt make Aaron and his sons to approach to the door of the tent of the congregation, and thou shalt wash them with waters.

13. And thou shalt make Aaron to put on the garments of holiness, and thou shalt anoint him, and sanctify him, and he shall perform the office of the priesthood to Me.

14. And his sons thou shalt make to approach, and shalt make them to put on waistcoats.

15. And thou shalt anoint them as thou didst anoint their father, and they shall perform the office of the priesthood to Me, and their anointing shall be to be with them for the priesthood of an age to their generations.

16. And Moses did according to all things which JEHOVAH commanded him, so he did.

17. And it came to pass in the first month in the second year in the first of the month, that the habitation was set up.

18. And Moses set up the habitation, and gave its bases, and set its staves, and gave its bars, and set up its pillars.

19. And spread the tent over the habitation, and set the covering of the tent upon it above, as JEHOVAH commanded Moses.

20. And he took and gave the testimony into the ark, and set bars upon the ark, and gave the propitiatory upon the ark above.

21. And he introduced the ark into the habitation, and set the vail of the covering, and covered upon the ark of the testimony, as JEHOVAH commanded Moses.

22. And he gave the table into the tent of the congregation at the leg of the habitation towards the north from without the vail.

23. And he arranged upon it an arrangement of bread before JEHOVAH, as JEHOVAH commanded Moses.

24. And he set the candlestick in the tent of the congregation near the table of the leg of the habitation towards the south.

25. And he made the lamps to ascend before JEHOVAH, as JEHOVAH commanded Moses.

26. And he set the altar of gold in the tent of the congregation before the vail.

27. And he fumed upon it incense of spices, as JEHOVAH commanded Moses.

28. And he set the covering of the door for the habitation.

29. And he set the altar of burnt-offering at the door of the habitation of the tent of the congregation, and he made to ascend upon it the burnt-offering and the meat-offering, as JEHOVAH commanded Moses.

30. And he set the laver between the tent of the congregation and between the altar, and gave with it waters to wash.

31. And Moses and Aaron washed out of it, and his sons their hands and their feet.

32. In their entering-in to the tent of the congregation, and in their approaching to the altar, they washed, as JEHOVAH commanded Moses.

33. And he set up the court about the habitation and the altar, and gave the covering of the gate of the court: and Moses finished the work.

34. And a cloud covered the tent of the congregation, and the glory of JEHOVAH filled the habitation.

35. And Moses could not enter into the tent of the congregation, because the cloud tarried upon it, and the glory of JEHOVAH filled the habitation.

36. And when the cloud ascended from above the habitation the sons of Israel journeyed in all their journeyings.

37. And if the cloud did not ascend, they did not journey, even to the day that it ascended.

38. Because the cloud of JEHOVAH was upon the habitation in the day-time, and fire was by night in it, in the eyes of all the house of Israel, in all their journeyings.

THE CONTENTS.

10,832. THESE things are also passed by without further explication, because they are again the same with what have been before described and once explained, except those things which are mentioned at the end of this chapter, where it is said that after Moses had finished the work, a cloud covered the tent, and the glory of Jehovah filled the habitation; also that the cloud tarried on the tent in the day-time and fire in it by night; and that the sons of Israel journeyed as often as the cloud ascended. What these things signify, is also evident from what has been frequently before said and shown concerning the cloud, concerning the glory of Jehovah, concerning fire, and concerning journeyings.

CONTINUATION OF THE SUBJECT CONCERNING THE SIXTH EARTH IN THE STARRY HEAVEN.

10,833. *I AFTERWARDS asked those spirits concerning various things relating to the earth from which they were. First, concerning their Divine Worship; to which they replied, that nations with their families assemble every thirtieth day at one place, and hear preachings, and that the preacher on the occasion, from a pulpit elevated a little from the earth, teaches them Divine Truths which lead to good of life. It was inquired whence they know Divine Truths; they said, from revelation: concerning revelation they said further, that it is effected in the morning in a middle state between sleeping and waking, when they are in interior light not yet interrupted by the senses of the body and by worldly things, and that at such times they hear the angels of heaven discoursing concerning Divine Truths, and concerning a life according to them; and that when they are awake, an angel appears to them in a white garment at the bed-side, who then suddenly disappears from their eyes; and that hence they know that the things which they have heard are from heaven. Thus a Divine Vision is distinguished from a vision not Divine, for in a vision not Divine no angel appears. They added, that in such a manner revelations are made to their preachers, and occasionally also to others.*

10,834. *Concerning the sun of that earth, which is to us a star, they said, that it appears to the inhabitants of the size of a human head, of a flaming color; that their year is two hundred days; and that a day is equal to nine hours of our time, which they were able to conclude from the length of the days of our earth perceived in me; and further, that they have perpetual spring and summer, and hence that the fields are green, and that trees bear fruit continually. The reason of this is, because their year is so short, being equal only to the time of seventy-five days of our year, and where the years are so short, there the cold does not abide in winter, nor the heat in summer, whence the ground is in a continual spring.*

10,835. *To the inquiry concerning their houses, they replied, that they are low, of wood, with a plain roof, around which there is a battlement sloping downwards; and that in front dwell the husband and wife, in the next contiguous chamber the children, behind them the men-servants and maid-servants. Concerning their food, they said, that they feed on fruits and pulse, and that they drink milk with water, and that they have milk from cows, which are woolly like sheep.*

10,836. *Concerning their life, they said, that they walk altogether naked, and that nakedness is no shame to them; also that their conversations are with those who are within the families.*

10,837. *As to what concerns betrothings and marriages amongst the inhabitants in that earth, they related, that a daughter, when marriageable, is kept at home, nor is it allowed her to go abroad until the day on which she is to be married; and that then she is brought to a kind of connubial house, whither also several other young women, who are marriageable, are conducted, and are there placed beyond a bench elevated even to the middle part of their body; appearing thus naked only as to the breast and face; and that on this occasion the young men come thither, that they may choose for themselves some one for a wife; and when a young man sees one agreeable to himself, to whom his mind attracts him, he takes her by the hand, and if she then follows, he leads her into a house prepared, and she becomes his wife: for from the faces they there see whether they agree in minds, since the face of every one is there the index of the mind, being without pretence and deceit. That all things may be done decently and without lasciviousness, an old man sits behind the virgin girls, and at the side an old woman, who make their remarks. There are several such places to which the young women are led, and also stated times, that the young men may make their election; for if in one place they do not see a girl suitable to them, they go away to another; and if not at that time, they return at a future opportunity. They further said, that a husband has only one wife, and in no case more, because this is contrary to Divine Order.*

STEREOTYPED BY TOBITT AND GOLDER, 181 WILLIAM ST., N. Y.

www.ingramcontent.com/pod-product-compliance
Lightning Source LLC
LaVergne TN
LVHW021231110826
845150LV00002B/302

9781425562823